Levels 1 & 2

Paradigm PUBLISHING

Microsoft®

access

2007

BENCHMARK SERIES

Access

Nita Rutkosky
Pierce College at Puyallup
Puyallup, Washington

Denise Seguin
Fanshawe College
London, Ontario

Audrey Rutkosky Roggenkamp
Pierce College at Puyallup
Puyallup, Washington

Managing Editor	Sonja Brown
Production Editor	Donna Mears
Cover and Text Designer	Leslie Anderson
Copy Editor	Susan Capecchi
Desktop Production	John Valo, Desktop Solutions
Proofreader	Laura Nelson
Indexer	Nancy Fulton

Acknowledgments: The authors and editors wish to thank Pamela J. Silvers, Chairperson, Business Computer Technologies, Asheville-Buncombe Technical Community College, Asheville, North Carolina, for testing the instruction and exercises for accuracy and Janice Davidson, Office Administration, Lambton College, Sarnia, Ontario, for preparing annotated model answers.

Photo Credits: Introduction page 1 (clockwise from top), Lexmark International, Inc., courtesy of Dell Inc., all rights Hewlett-Packard Company, Logitech, Micron Technology, Inc.; Access Level 1 page 1, © Corbis; Access Level 2 page 1, © Corbis, page 3, © Getty Images; photos in Student Resources CD, courtesy of Kelly Rutkosky and Michael Rutkosky.

ISBN 978-0-76383-364-0 (Hardcover Text)
ISBN 978-0-76383-210-0 (Hardcover Text + CD)
ISBN 978-0-76382-989-6 (Softcover Text)
ISBN 978-0-76383-004-5 (Softcover Text + CD)

© 2008 by Paradigm Publishing, Inc.
875 Montreal Way
St. Paul, MN 55102
E-mail: educate@emcp.com
Web site: www.emcp.com

CONTENTS

Microsoft Access 2007 Level 2   1

Unit 1 Advanced Tables, Relationships, Queries, and Forms   5

Benchmark Microsoft Access 2007 is designed for students who want to learn how to use this feature-rich data management tool to track, report, and share information. No prior knowledge of database management systems is required. After successfully completing a course using this textbook, students will be able to

- Create database tables to organize business or personal records
- Modify and manage tables to ensure that data is accurate and up-to-date
- Perform queries to assist with decision-making
- Plan, research, create, revise, and publish database information to meet specific communication needs
- Given a workplace scenario requiring the reporting and analysis of data, assess the information requirements and then prepare the materials that achieve the goal efficiently and effectively

In addition to mastering Access skills, students will learn the essential features and functions of computer hardware, the Windows XP operating system, and Internet Explorer 7.0. Upon completing the text, they can expect to be proficient in using Access to organize, analyze, and present information.

Achieving Proficiency in Access 2007

Since its inception several Office versions ago, the Benchmark Series has served as a standard of excellence in software instruction. Elements of the book function individually and collectively to create an inviting, comprehensive learning environment that produces successful computer users. On this and following pages, take a visual tour of the structure and features that comprise the highly popular Benchmark model.

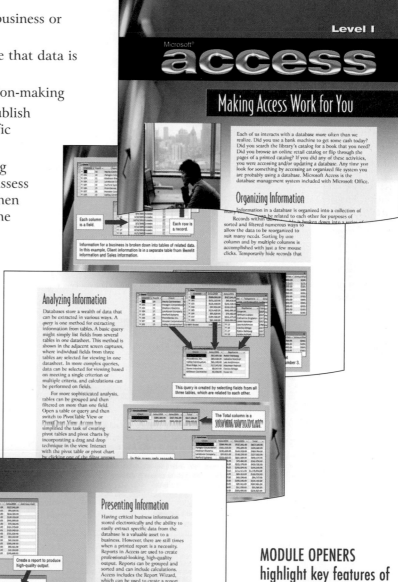

MODULE OPENERS highlight key features of Access 2007 within the context of organizing, analyzing, and presenting information.

UNIT OPENERS display the unit's four chapter titles. Each level has two units, which conclude with a comprehensive unit performance assessment that evaluates students' program skills, their ability to communicate database information in writing, and their Web research and navigation skills.

CHAPTER OPENERS present the Performance Objectives and highlight the practical relevance of the skills students will learn.

CD icon identifies a folder of data files to be copied to the student's storage medium.

SNAP icon alerts students to corresponding SNAP tutorial titles.

New! PROJECT APPROACH: Builds Skill Mastery within Realistic Context

 Project 1 Manage Data and Define Data Types

You will modify tables by adding and deleting fields, assign data types and default values to fields, validate field entries, insert a total row, and use the Input Mask Wizard and the Lookup Wizard. You will also move fields in a table and sort records in ascending and descending order.

Modifying a Table

Maintaining a table involves adding and/or deleting records as needed. It can also involve adding, moving, changing, or deleting fields in the table. Modify the structure of the table in Datasheet view or Design view. In Datasheet view, click the Table Tools Datasheet tab and then use options in the Fields & Columns group to insert or delete fields. To display a table in Design view, open the table, and then click the View button in the Views group in the Home tab. You can also change to Design view by clicking the View button arrow and then clicking *Design View* at the drop-down list or by clicking the Design View button located in the View area at the right side of the Status bar.

In Design view, *Field Name*, *Data Type*, and *Description* display at the top of the window and *Field Properties* displays toward the bottom of the window. In Design view, you can add fields, remove fields, and change the order of fields. When you switch to Design view, the Table Tools Design tab displays as shown in Figure 3.1. Use buttons in this tab to insert and delete rows and perform a variety of other tasks.

Figure 3.1 Table Tools Design Tab

HINT
Use options in the Data Type & Formatting group in the Table Tools Datasheet tab to set the data type.

Adding a Field

Situations change within a company, and a table must be flexible to accommodate changes that occur with new situations. Adding a field is a change that may need to be made to an existing table. For example, more information may be required to manage the data or an additional field may be needed for accounting purposes.

You can add a new field in Datasheet view or in Design view. One method for creating a new field is to simply type new records into a blank table or in the *Add New Field* column that displays at the right side of the last field in the table. Access sets a data type for each new field you type based on the type of data entered. For example, a column that contains dates is automatically assigned the Date/Time data type. You can also insert a new field by clicking the Table Tools Datasheet tab and then clicking the Insert button in the Fields & Columns group.

To add a row for a new field in Design view, position the insertion point on any text in the row that will be located immediately *below* the new field and then click the Insert Rows button in the Tools group in the Table Tools Design tab or

66   Chapter Three

Instruction and practice are organized into multipart projects that focus on related program features. A project overview identifies the tasks to accomplish and the key features to use in completing the work.

Following the project overview and between project parts, the text presents instruction on the features and skills necessary to accomplish the next tasks.

Typically, a file remains open throughout a project. Students build databases and save their work incrementally.

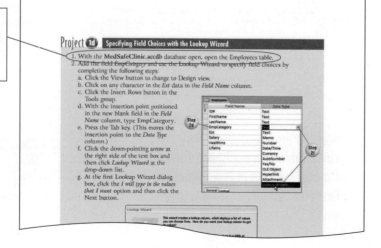

Project 1d Specifying Field Choices with the Lookup Wizard

1. With the **MedSafeClinic.accdb** database open, open the Employees table.
2. Add the field *EmpCategory* and use the Lookup Wizard to specify field choices by completing the following steps:
   a. Click the View button to change to Design view.
   b. Click on any character in the *Ext* data in the *Field Name* column.
   c. Click the Insert Rows button in the Tools group.
   d. With the insertion point positioned in the new blank field in the *Field Name* column, type EmpCategory.
   e. Press the Tab key. (This moves the insertion point to the *Data Type* column.)
   f. Click the down-pointing arrow at the right side of the text box and then click *Lookup Wizard* at the drop-down list.
   g. At the first Lookup Wizard dialog box, click the *I will type in the values that I want* option and then click the Next button.

Table 1.5 Commonly Used Input Mask Codes

Code	Description
0	Required digit
9	Optional digit
#	Digit, space, plus or minus symbol. If no data is typed at this position, Access leaves a blank space.
L	Required letter
?	Optional letter
A	Required letter or digit
a	Optional letter or digit
&	Required character or space
C	Optional character or space
!	The field is filled from left to right instead of right to left.
\	Access displays the character that immediately follows in the field.

Project 11 Creating Custom Input Masks

1. With the **RSRComputerServ.accdb** database open, create a custom input mask for the work order numbers by completing the following steps:
   a. Open the Work_Orders table in Design view.
   b. With *WO_No* the active field, click in the *Input Mask* property box and then type 00000;;_. This mask will require that a five-digit work order number is entered. The underscore character is used as the placeholder character.
   c. Save the table.
2. Create an input mask to require the two date fields to be entered as three characters for the month with the first letter uppercase followed by two digits for the day and four digits for the year by completing the following steps:
   a. Make *Call_Date* the active field.
   b. Click in the *Input Mask* property box and then type >L<LL\-00\-0000;0;_. This mask requires three letters for the month with the first letter converted to uppercase and the remaining two letters converted to lowercase. The \- symbols instruct Access to display the hyphen character after the month as data is entered. Two digits are required for the day followed h hyphen character and then four digits required for the year. The zero af semicolon instructs Access to store the display characters. Ending the m underscore character is again used as the placeholder character.

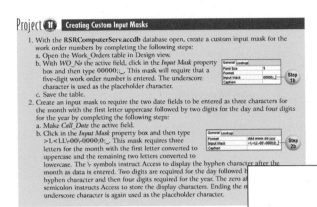

Each project exercise guides students step by step to the desired outcome. Screen captures illustrate what the screen should look like at key points.

   c. Make *Serv_Date* the active field, click in the *Input Mask* property box, and then type >L<LL\-00\-0000;0;_.
   d. Save the table.
3. Switch to Datasheet view.
4. Test the input masks using a new record by completing the following steps:
   a. Click the New Record button in the Records group of the Home tab.
   b. Type **6501**. Notice that as soon as you type the first character, the placeholders appear in the field.
   c. Press Tab or Enter to move to the next field in the datasheet. Since the mask contained five zeros indicating five required digits, Access displays a message box informing you the value entered is not appropriate for the input mask.
   d. Click OK at the Microsoft Office Access message box.

Text in magenta identifies material to type.

   e. Type **3** in the last position in the *WO_No* field and then press Tab or Enter to move to the next field.
   f. Type **1000** in the *Cust_ID* field and then press Tab or Enter.
   g. Type **10** in the *Tech_ID* field and then press Tab or Enter.
   h. Type **sep082009** in the *Call_Date* field and then press Tab or Enter. Notice that the placeholder characters appear as soon as you type the first letter. Notice also that you do not need to type the hyphen characters since Access moves automatically to the next position after the hyphen when you type the digits.
   i. Type **Replace keyboard** in the *Descr* field and then press Tab or Enter.
   j. Type **sep092009** in the *Serv_Date* field and then press Tab or Enter.
   k. Complete the remainder of the record as follows:
      Hours   .5
      Rate   25
      Parts   42.75
      Comments   Serial Number AWQ-982358
   l. Best Fit the *Serv_Date* field.
5. Close the Work_Orders table. Click Yes to save changes to the layout of the table.

At key phases of the project, students may be directed to print a table or a datasheet. Locked, watermarked model answers in PDF format on the Student Resources CD allow students to check their results. This option rewards careful effort and develops software mastery.

Other field properties that should be considered for data accuracy when designing database tables include the *Default Value*, *Validation Rule*, and *Validation Text* fields. Use the *Default Value* field to populate the field in new records with a field value that is used most often. For example, in a table where most employees have an address within the same city and state, you could use a default value to ensure consistent spelling and capitalization. The text appears automatically in the fields when new records are added to the table. The user can choose to either accept the default value by pressing Tab or Enter to move past the field, or type new data in the field.

CHAPTER REVIEW ACTIVITIES: A Hierarchy of Learning Assessments

CHAPTER summary

- Database designers plan the tables needed for a new database by analyzing sample data, input documents, and output requirements to generate the entire set of data elements needed.
- Once all data has been identified, the designer maps out the number of tables required.
- Each table holds data for a single topic only with data split out into the smallest unit that will be manipulated.
- Designers do not include fields for data that can be calculated.
- Designers also consider relationships that will be [n...] to be added to a table in order to join the tables.
- Data redundancy should be avoided, which means [...] repeated in another table.
- Fields are assigned one of 10 data types by selecti[...] the kind of data that will be accepted into the fiel[...]
- A diagram of a database portrays the database tab[...] types, and field sizes.
- Changing the field size property can be used to res[...] maximum length as one way to prevent longer ent[...] the field by accident.
- Add an entry to the *Caption* property to provide a [...] field in datasheet view.
- Change the *Required* property to *Yes* to force an ent[...] record is added to the table.
- Leaving a field blank when a new record is entered [...] in the field.
- A zero-length field is entered into a record by typi[...] symbols with no space between. This method is us[...] does not apply to the current record.
- You can disallow zero-length strings by changing t[...] property to *No*.
- The *Format* property controls the display of data a[...]
- A custom format can be created for a text field by [...] format codes in the *Format* property box.
- Predefined formats are available for Number, Auto[...] or you can create your own custom number forma[...] format codes in the *Format* property box.
- A custom numeric format can contain four section[...] values, one section for negative values, one sectio[...] section for null values.
- Access provides several format options for displayi[...] Date/Time field or you can create your own custo[...]

CHAPTER SUMMARY captures the purpose and execution of key features.

- Use an input mask to control the type and pattern of data entered into the field.
- Access provides the Input Mask Wizard for Text or Date/Time fields. Create an input mask for other fields or create a custom input mask for a Text or Date/Time field by typing the appropriate input mask codes in the *Input Mask* property box.
- A Memo field can be formatted using rich text formatting options in the Font group of the Home tab by changing the *Text Format* property to *Rich Text*.
- Change the *Append Only* property of a Memo field to maintain a history of changes made to the data stored in the field.
- A field with the data type set to *Attachment* can be used to store files associated with a record.
- Multiple files can be attached to a record with no single file exceeding 256 megabytes and the total of all files not exceeding two gigabytes.
- Double-click the paper clip in the Attachment field for a record to add, view, save, or remove a file attachment.

COMMANDS review

COMMANDS REVIEW summarizes visually the major features and alternative methods of access.

FEATURE	RIBBON TAB, GROUP	BUTTON	KEYBOARD SHORTCUT
Create table in Design view	Create, Table Design		
Minimize navigation pane		«	F11
Redisplay navigation pane		»	F11
Switch to Datasheet view from Design view	Table Tools Design, Views		
Switch to Design view from Datasheet view	Home, Views		

CONCEPTS check

Test Your Knowledge

Completion: In the space provided at the right, indicate the correct term, command, or number.

1. Use this data type for a field that will hold numeric data that is not a monetary value.

2. Use this data type to store alphanumeric text longer than 255 characters.

3. This data type is restricted to a field value used to test conditional logic that can be one of only two conditions.

4. The available properties that display for a field in the *Field Properties* section in Design view are dependent on this option.

5. This property is used to display a more descriptive title for the field in the datasheet.

6. To ensure a field is never left empty, set this property to *Yes*.

7. Typing two double quotation symbols with no space between assigns this field value.

8. This is the format code to convert all text in the field to uppercase.

9. This placeholder in a custom numeric format instructs Access to display a zero if the position is not used.

10. Type this entry in the *Format* property box of a Date/Time field to display dates beginning with the day of the week abbreviated, followed by the month as two digits, the day of the month as two digits, and the year as two digits with all sections separated with a hyphen character.

11. Type this entry in the *Input Mask* property box to require a three-digit identification number to be entered with the pound symbol (#) used as the placeholder.

12. Rich text formatting is enabled for a Memo field by changing this property option to *Rich Text*.

CONCEPTS CHECK questions assess knowledge recall.

13. For a Memo field with the *Append Only* property active, right-click in a record and click this option at the shortcut menu to display a dialog box with the history of the text changes made to the field.

14. Create a field with this data type to store a file with the record.

15. Add a file to the record by double-clicking this object in the record in Datasheet view.

SKILLS check
Demonstrate Your Proficiency

SKILLS CHECK exercises ask students to develop both standard and customized kinds of database elements without how-to directions.

Assessment

1 CREATE A NEW DATABASE
1. Create a new blank database named **BenchmarkGolf.accdb**.
2. Create the tables shown in Figure 1.6 to store membership records for the Benchmark Golf and Country Club including setting the primary key and assigning data types and field sizes.
3. Close any tables that have been left open.

Figure 1.6 Assessment 1

Members	
*Member_ID	Text
Fname	Text
Lname	Text
StreetAdd	Text
City	Text
State	Text
ZIP	Text
HPhone	Text
CPhone	Text
BirthDate	Date/Time
Category	Text
FamilyMem	Yes/No

Member_Types	
*Category	Text
Annual_Fee	Currency
Mth_Assmnt	Currency
Restrictions	Memo

	Birth Date	May 3, 1964	October 15, 1977
	Category	Gold	Silver
	Family Member?	Yes	No

Family_Members Table

Field	Record 1	Record 2
Supplementary ID	610	611
Main ID Number	100	100
First Name	Kayla	Roy
Last Name	Sampson	Sampson
Birth Date	July 18, 1992	March 16, 1994
Social Member?	No	No

Member_Types Table

Field	Record 1	Record 2	Record 3
Category	Gold	Silver	Bronze
Annual Fee	2725	1865	1480
Monthly Assessment	65	50	40
Restrictions	Unlimited weekdays and weekends; weekend ballot first	Unlimited weekdays; weekend ballot second	Unlimited weekdays; after 3 P.M.

2. Adjust all column widths to Best Fit and print each table in landscape orientation.
3. Close any tables that have been left open.
4. Close the **BenchmarkGolf.accdb** database.

CASE study
Apply Your Skills

The chapter CASE STUDY requires planning and executing multipart workplace projects.

Part 1

You started an internship today at Bestar Plumbing Service. Examine the customer invoice shown in Figure 1.7. This is a typical invoice for which the owner would like to start using an Access database. Design tables for the data using the invoice and the following additional information from the owner:

- Customer numbers are assigned using the first three letters of the customer's last name all uppercase and are followed by three digits after a hyphen character.
- Some invoices include parts with a labor charge. Individual parts are not itemized on the customer invoice. The service technician shows a single line on the invoice for all parts used.
- Bestar has two labor rates: $38.75 for a senior service technician and $25.00 for an apprentice technician.

Students strengthen their analytical and writing skills by using Microsoft Word to describe best uses of Access features or to explain the decisions they made in completing the Case Study.

Using Microsoft Word, create a document that diagrams the tables including table names, field names, data types, and field sizes. Use the asterisk to denote the primary key field in each table. Ask your instructor for the required format of the diagram in text boxes or tables in Word, or, if a handwritten diagram is acceptable. Save the Word document and name it **AccessL2_C1_CS_P1**. Save, print, and close **AccessL2_C1_CS_P1.docx**.

Figure 1.7 Invoice for Case Study, Part 1

Part 2

Using the table diagram created in Part 1, create a new database named **BestarService.accdb** and then create the tables.

Part 3

Consider the field properties learned in this chapter that can be used to ensure data integrity and consistency. Modify field properties in your tables that can be used to restrict data accepted into the ... accepted. Use the data ...

UNIT PERFORMANCE ASSESSMENT: Cross-Disciplinary, Comprehensive Evaluation

ASSESSING PROFICIENCY checks mastery of features.

WRITING ACTIVITIES involve applying program skills in a communication context.

JOB STUDY at the end of Unit 2 presents a capstone assessment requiring critical thinking and problem solving.

INTERNET RESEARCH project reinforces research and database management skills.

Student Courseware

Student Resources CD Each Benchmark Series textbook is packaged with a Student Resources CD containing the data files required for completing the projects and assessments. A CD icon and folder name displayed on the opening page of chapters reminds students to copy a folder of files from the CD to the desired storage medium before beginning the project exercises. Directions for copying folders are printed on the inside back cover. The Student Resources CD also contains the model answers in PDF format for the project exercises within chapters. Files are locked and watermarked, but students can compare their completed documents with the PDF files, either on screen or in hard copy (printed) format.

Internet Resource Center Additional learning tools and reference materials are available at the book-specific Web site at www.emcp.net/BenchmarkAccess07XP. Students can locate and use the same resources that are on the Student Resources CD along with study aids, Web links, and tips for working with computers effectively in academic and workplace settings.

SNAP Training and Assessment SNAP is a Web-based program that provides hands-on instruction, practice, and testing for learning Microsoft Office 2007 and Windows. SNAP course work simulates operations of Office 2007. The program is comprised of a Web-based learning management system, multimedia tutorials, performance skill items, a concept test bank, and online grade book and course planning tools. A CD-based set of tutorials teaching the basics of Office and Windows is also available for additional practice not requiring Internet access.

Class Connections Available for both WebCT and Blackboard e-learning platforms, Paradigm's Class Connection provides self-quizzes and study aids and facilitates communication among students and instructors via e-mail and e-discussion.

Instructor Resources

Curriculum Planner and Resources Instructor support for the Benchmark Series has been expanded to include a *Curriculum Planner and Resources* binder with CD. This all-in-one print resource includes planning resources such as Lesson Blueprints, teaching hints, and sample course syllabi; presentation resources such as PowerPoint presentations and handouts; and assessment resources including an overview of assessment venues, live program and PDF model answers for intrachapter projects, and live program and annotated PDF model answers for end-of-chapter and end-of-unit assessments. Contents of the *Curriculum Planner and Resources* binder are also available on the Instructor's CD and on the password-protected Instructor's section of the Internet Resource Center for this title at www.emcp.com.

Computerized Test Generator Instructors can use ExamView test generating software and the provided bank of multiple-choice items to create customized Web-based or print tests.

What is the Microsoft Business Certification Program?

The Microsoft Business Certification program enables candidates to show that they have something exceptional to offer—proven expertise in Microsoft Office programs. The two certification tracks allow candidates to choose how they want to exhibit their skills, either through validating skills within a specific Microsoft product or taking their knowledge to the next level and combining Microsoft programs to show that they can apply multiple skill sets to complete more complex office tasks. Recognized by businesses and schools around the world, over 3 million certifications have been obtained in over 100 different countries. The Microsoft Business Certification Program is the only Microsoft-approved certification program of its kind.

What is the Microsoft Certified Application Specialist Certification?

Microsoft®
CERTIFIED

Application Specialist

The Microsoft Certified Application Specialist Certification exams focus on validating specific skill sets within each of the Microsoft® Office system programs. Candidates can choose which exam(s) they want to take according to which skills they want to validate. The available Application Specialist exams include:

- Using Microsoft® Windows Vista™
- Using Microsoft® Office Word 2007
- Using Microsoft® Office Excel® 2007
- Using Microsoft® Office PowerPoint® 2007
- Using Microsoft® Office Access 2007
- Using Microsoft® Office Outlook 2007

What is the Microsoft Certified Application Professional Certification?

Microsoft®
CERTIFIED

Application Professional

The Microsoft Certified Application Professional Certification exams focus on a candidate's ability to use the 2007 Microsoft® Office system to accomplish industry-agnostic functions, for example, Budget Analysis and Forecasting, or Content Management and Collaboration. The available Application Professional exams currently include:

- Organizational Support
- Creating and Managing Presentations
- Content Management and Collaboration
- Budget Analysis and Forecasting

What do the Microsoft Business Certification Vendor of Approved Courseware logos represent?

Microsoft®
CERTIFIED

Application Specialist

Approved Courseware

Microsoft®
CERTIFIED

Application Professional

Approved Courseware

The logos validate that the courseware has been approved by the Microsoft® Business Certification Vendor program and that these courses cover objectives that will be included in the relevant exam. It also means that after utilizing this courseware, you may be prepared to pass the exams required to become a Microsoft Certified Application Specialist or Microsoft Certified Application Professional.

For more information:

To learn more about Microsoft Certified Application Specialist or Professional exams, visit www.microsoft.com/learning/msbc.

To learn about other Microsoft Certified Application Specialist or Professional approved courseware from Paradigm Publishing, visit www.emcp.com/microsoft-certified-courseware.

The availability of Microsoft Certified Application exams varies by Microsoft Office program, program version, and language. Visit www.microsoft.com/learning for exam availability.

Microsoft, the Office Logo, Outlook, and PowerPoint are either registered trademarks or trademarks of Microsoft Corporation in the United States and/or other countries. The Microsoft Certified Application Specialist and Microsoft Certified Application Professional Logos are used under license from Microsoft Corporation.

System Requirements

This text is designed for the student to complete projects and assessments on a computer running a standard installation of Microsoft Office 2007, Professional Edition, and the Microsoft Windows XP operating system with Service Pack 2 or later. To effectively run this suite and operating system, your computer should be outfitted with the following:

- 500 MHz processor or higher; 256 MB RAM or higher
- DVD drive
- 2 GB of available hard-disk space
- CD-ROM drive
- 800 by 600 minimum monitor resolution; 1024 by 768 recommended
  Note: Screen captures in this book were created using 1024 by 768 resolution; screens with higher resolution may look different.
- Computer mouse or compatible pointing device

About the Authors

Nita Rutkosky began teaching business education courses at Pierce College in Puyallup, Washington, in 1978. Since then she has taught a variety of software applications to students in postsecondary Information Technology certificate and degree programs. In addition to co-authoring texts in the *Benchmark Office 2007 Series*, she has co-authored *Signature Word 2007*, *Marquee Office 2007*, and *Using Computers in the Medical Office: Microsoft Word, Excel, and PowerPoint 2003*. Other textbooks she has written for Paradigm Publishing include books on previous versions of Microsoft Office along with WordPerfect, desktop publishing, keyboarding, and voice recognition.

Denise Seguin has been teaching at Fanshawe College in London, Ontario, since 1986. She has taught a variety of software applications to learners in postsecondary Information Technology diploma programs and in Continuing Education courses. In addition to co-authoring texts in the *Benchmark Office 2007 Series*, she has co-authored *Marquee Office 2007* and *Using Computers in the Medical Office*. Other textbooks she has written for Paradigm Publishing include previous editions of the *Marquee Series*, *Macromedia Flash MX: Design and Application*, and books on Microsoft Outlook 2007, 2003, 2002, and 2000.

Audrey Rutkosky Roggenkamp has been teaching courses in the Business Information Technology department at Pierce College in Puyallup including keyboarding, skill building, and Microsoft Office programs. In addition to titles in the *Benchmark Office 2007 Series*, she has co-authored *Using Computers in the Medical Office*, *Marquee Office 2007*, and *Signature Word 2007*.

Getting Started in Office 2007

In this textbook, you will learn to operate several computer application programs that combine to make an application "suite." This suite of programs is called Microsoft Office 2007. The programs you will learn to operate are the software, which includes instructions telling the computer what to do. Some of the application programs in the suite include a word processing program named Word, a spreadsheet program named Excel, a database program named Access, and a presentation program named PowerPoint.

Identifying Computer Hardware

The computer equipment you will use to operate the suite of programs is referred to as hardware. You will need access to a microcomputer system that should consist of the CPU, monitor, keyboard, printer, drives, and mouse. If you are not sure what equipment you will be operating, check with your instructor. The computer system shown in Figure G.1 consists of six components. Each component is discussed separately in the material that follows.

Figure G.1 Microcomputer System

CPU

CPU stands for Central Processing Unit and it is the intelligence of the computer. All the processing occurs in the CPU. Silicon chips, which contain miniaturized circuitry, are placed on boards that are plugged into slots within the CPU. Whenever an instruction is given to the computer, that instruction is processed through circuitry in the CPU.

Monitor

The monitor is a piece of equipment that looks like a television screen. It displays the information of a program and the text being input at the keyboard. The quality of display for monitors varies depending on the type of monitor and the level of resolution. Monitors can also vary in size—generally from 14-inch size up to 21-inch size or larger.

Keyboard

The keyboard is used to input information into the computer. Keyboards for microcomputers vary in the number and location of the keys. Microcomputers have the alphabetic and numeric keys in the same location as the keys on a typewriter. The symbol keys, however, may be placed in a variety of locations, depending on the manufacturer. In addition to letters, numbers, and symbols, most microcomputer keyboards contain function keys, arrow keys, and a numeric keypad. Figure G.2 shows an enhanced keyboard.

Figure G.2 Keyboard

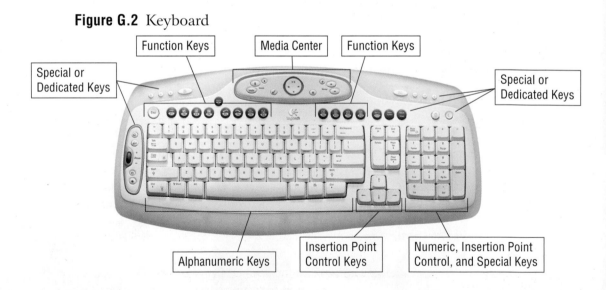

The 12 keys at the top of the keyboard, labeled with the letter F followed by a number, are called ***function keys***. Use these keys to perform functions within each of the suite programs. To the right of the regular keys is a group of ***special*** or ***dedicated keys***. These keys are labeled with specific functions that will be performed when you press the key. Below the special keys are arrow keys. Use these keys to move the insertion point in the document screen.

A keyboard generally includes three mode indicator lights. When you select certain modes, a light appears on the keyboard. For example, if you press the Caps Lock key, which disables the lowercase alphabet, a light appears next to Caps Lock. Similarly, pressing the Num Lock key will disable the special functions on the numeric keypad, which is located at the right side of the keyboard.

Disk Drives

Depending on the computer system you are using, Microsoft Office 2007 is installed on a hard drive or as part of a network system. Whether you are using Office on a hard drive or network system, you will need to have available a DVD or CD drive and a USB drive or other storage medium. You will insert the CD (compact disc) that accompanies this textbook in the DVD or CD drive and then copy folders from the CD to your storage medium. You will also save documents you complete at the computer to folders on your storage medium.

Printer

A document you create in Word is considered soft copy. If you want a hard copy of a document, you need to print it. To print documents you will need to access a printer, which will probably be either a laser printer or an ink-jet printer. A laser printer uses a laser beam combined with heat and pressure to print documents, while an ink-jet printer prints a document by spraying a fine mist of ink on the page.

Mouse

Many functions in the suite of programs are designed to operate more efficiently with a mouse. A mouse is an input device that sits on a flat surface next to the computer. You can operate a mouse with the left or the right hand. Moving the mouse on the flat surface causes a corresponding mouse pointer to move on the screen. Figure G.1 shows an illustration of a mouse.

Using the Mouse

The programs in the Microsoft Office suite can be operated using a keyboard or they can be operated with the keyboard and a mouse. The mouse may have two or three buttons on top, which are tapped to execute specific functions and commands. To use the mouse, rest it on a flat surface or a mouse pad. Put your hand over it with your palm resting on top of the mouse and your wrist resting on the table surface. As you move the mouse on the flat surface, a corresponding pointer moves on the screen.

When using the mouse, you should understand four terms—point, click, double-click, and drag. When operating the mouse, you may need to point to a specific command, button, or icon. Point means to position the mouse pointer on the desired item. With the mouse pointer positioned on the desired item, you may need to click a button on the mouse. Click means quickly tapping a button on the mouse once. To complete two steps at one time, such as choosing and then executing a function, double-click a mouse button. Double-click means to tap the left mouse button twice in quick succession. The term drag means to press and hold the left mouse button, move the mouse pointer to a specific location, and then release the button.

Using the Mouse Pointer

The mouse pointer will change appearance depending on the function being performed or where the pointer is positioned. The mouse pointer may appear as one of the following images:

- The mouse pointer appears as an I-beam (called the I-beam pointer) in the document screen and can be used to move the insertion point or select text.

- The mouse pointer appears as an arrow pointing up and to the left (called the arrow pointer) when it is moved to the Title bar, Quick Access toolbar, ribbon, or an option in a dialog box. For example, to open a new document with the mouse, position the I-beam pointer on the Office button located in the upper left corner of the screen until the pointer turns into an arrow pointer and then click the left mouse button. At the drop-down list that displays, make a selection by positioning the arrow pointer on the desired option and then clicking the left mouse button.

- The mouse pointer becomes a double-headed arrow (either pointing left and right, pointing up and down, or pointing diagonally) when performing certain functions such as changing the size of an object.

- In certain situations, such as moving an object or image, the mouse pointer becomes a four-headed arrow. The four-headed arrow means that you can move the object left, right, up, or down.

- When a request is being processed or when a program is being loaded, the mouse pointer may appear with an hourglass beside it. The hourglass image means "please wait." When the process is completed, the hourglass image is removed.

- The mouse pointer displays as a hand with a pointing index finger in certain functions such as Help and indicates that more information is available about the item.

Choosing Commands

Once a program is open, you can use several methods in the program to choose commands. A command is an instruction that tells the program to do something. You can choose a command using the mouse or the keyboard. When a program such as Word or PowerPoint is open, the ribbon contains buttons for completing tasks and contains tabs you click to display additional buttons. To choose a button on the Quick Access toolbar or in the ribbon, position the tip of the mouse arrow pointer on a button and then click the left mouse button.

The Office suite provides access keys you can press to use a command in a program. Press the Alt key on the keyboard to display KeyTips that identify the access key you need to press to execute a command. For example, press the Alt key in a Word document and KeyTips display as shown in Figure G.3. Continue pressing access keys until you execute the desired command. For example, if you want to begin spell checking a document, you would press the Alt key, press the R key on the keyboard to display the Review tab, and then press the letter S on the keyboard.

Figure G.3 Word KeyTips

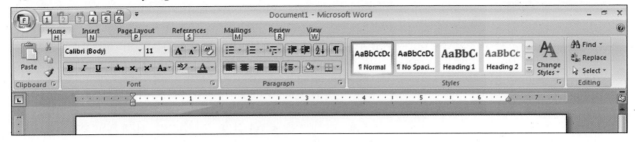

Choosing Commands from Drop-Down Lists

To choose a command from a drop-down list with the mouse, position the mouse pointer on the desired option and then click the left mouse button. To make a selection from a drop-down list with the keyboard, type the underlined letter in the desired option.

Some options at a drop-down list may be gray-shaded (dimmed), indicating that the option is currently unavailable. If an option at a drop-down list displays preceded by a check mark, that indicates that the option is currently active. If an option at a drop-down list displays followed by an ellipsis (…), a dialog box will display when that option is chosen.

Choosing Options from a Dialog Box

A dialog box contains options for applying formatting to a file or data within a file. Some dialog boxes display with tabs along the top providing additional options. For example, the Font dialog box shown in Figure G.4 contains two tabs—the Font tab and the Character Spacing tab. The tab that displays in the front is the

Figure G.4 Word Font Dialog Box

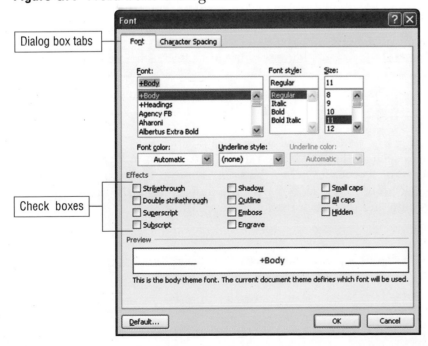

active tab. To make a tab active using the mouse, position the arrow pointer on the desired tab and then click the left mouse button. If you are using the keyboard, press Ctrl + Tab or press Alt + the underlined letter on the desired tab.

To choose options from a dialog box with the mouse, position the arrow pointer on the desired option and then click the left mouse button. If you are using the keyboard, press the Tab key to move the insertion point forward from option to option. Press Shift + Tab to move the insertion point backward from option to option. You can also hold down the Alt key and then press the underlined letter of the desired option. When an option is selected, it displays with a blue background or surrounded by a dashed box called a marquee. A dialog box contains one or more of the following elements: text boxes, list boxes, check boxes, option buttons, spin boxes, and command buttons.

Text Boxes

Some options in a dialog box require you to enter text. For example, the boxes below the *Find what* and *Replace with* options at the Excel Find and Replace dialog box shown in Figure G.5 are text boxes. In a text box, you type text or edit existing text. Edit text in a text box in the same manner as normal text. Use the Left and Right Arrow keys on the keyboard to move the insertion point without deleting text and use the Delete key or Backspace key to delete text.

Figure G.5 Excel Find and Replace Dialog Box

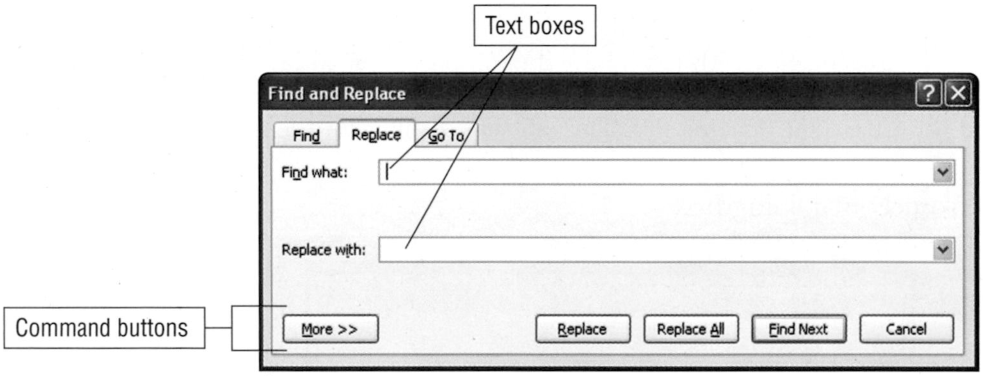

List Boxes

Some dialog boxes such as the Word Open dialog box shown in Figure G.6 may contain a list box. The list of files below the *Look in* option is contained in a list box. To make a selection from a list box with the mouse, move the arrow pointer to the desired option and then click the left mouse button.

Figure G.6 Word Open Dialog Box

Some list boxes may contain a scroll bar. This scroll bar will display at the right side of the list box (a vertical scroll bar) or at the bottom of the list box (a horizontal scroll bar). You can use a vertical scroll bar or a horizontal scroll bar to move through the list if the list is longer than the box. To move down through a list on a vertical scroll bar, position the arrow pointer on the down-pointing arrow and hold down the left mouse button. To scroll up through the list in a vertical scroll bar, position the arrow pointer on the up-pointing arrow and hold down the left mouse button. You can also move the arrow pointer above the scroll box and click the left mouse button to scroll up the list or move the arrow pointer below the scroll box and click the left mouse button to move down the list. To move through a list with a horizontal scroll bar, click the left-pointing arrow to scroll to the left of the list or click the right-pointing arrow to scroll to the right of the list.

To make a selection from a list using the keyboard, move the insertion point into the box by holding down the Alt key and pressing the underlined letter of the desired option. Press the Up and/or Down Arrow keys on the keyboard to move through the list.

In some dialog boxes where enough room is not available for a list box, lists of options are inserted in a drop-down list box. Options that contain a drop-down list box display with a down-pointing arrow. For example, the *Underline style* option at the Word Font dialog box shown in Figure G.4 contains a drop-down list. To display the list, click the down-pointing arrow to the right of the *Underline style* option box. If you are using the keyboard, press Alt + U.

Check Boxes

Some dialog boxes contain options preceded by a box. A check mark may or may not appear in the box. The Word Font dialog box shown in Figure G.4 displays a variety of check boxes within the *Effects* section. If a check mark appears in the box, the option is active (turned on). If the check box does not contain a check mark, the option is inactive (turned off). Any number of check boxes can be active. For example, in the Word Font dialog box, you can insert a check mark in any or all of the boxes in the *Effects* section and these options will be active.

To make a check box active or inactive with the mouse, position the tip of the arrow pointer in the check box and then click the left mouse button. If you are using the keyboard, press Alt + the underlined letter of the desired option.

Option Buttons

The Word Print dialog box shown in Figure G.7 contains options in the *Print range* section preceded by option buttons. Only one option button can be selected at any time. When an option button is selected, a green circle displays in the button. To select an option button with the mouse, position the tip of the arrow pointer inside the option button and then click the left mouse button. To make a selection with the keyboard, hold down the Alt key and then press the underlined letter of the desired option.

Figure G.7 Word Print Dialog Box

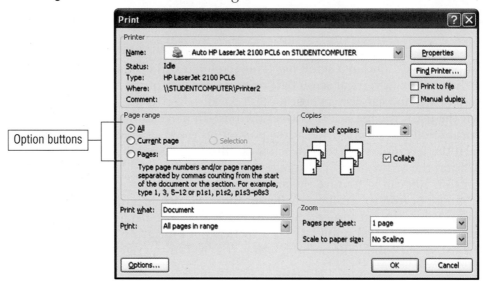

Option buttons

Spin Boxes

Some options in a dialog box contain measurements or numbers you can increase or decrease. These options are generally located in a spin box. For example, the Word Paragraph dialog box shown in Figure G.8 contains spin boxes located after the *Left*, *Right*, *Before*, and *After* options. To increase a number in a spin box, position the tip of the arrow pointer on the up-pointing arrow to the right of the desired option and then click the left mouse button. To decrease the number, click the down-pointing arrow. If you are using the keyboard, press Alt + the underlined letter of the desired option and then press the Up Arrow key to increase the number or the Down Arrow key to decrease the number.

Figure G.8 Word Paragraph Dialog Box

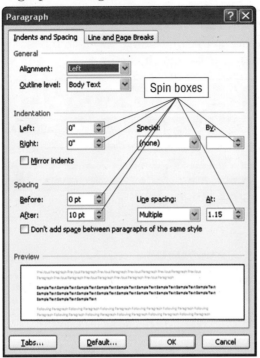

Command Buttons

In the Excel Find and Replace dialog box shown in Figure G.5, the boxes along the bottom of the dialog box are called command buttons. Use a command button to execute or cancel a command. Some command buttons display with an ellipsis (...). A command button that displays with an ellipsis will open another dialog box. To choose a command button with the mouse, position the arrow pointer on the desired button and then click the left mouse button. To choose a command button with the keyboard, press the Tab key until the desired command button contains the marquee and then press the Enter key.

Choosing Commands with Keyboard Shortcuts

Applications in the Office suite offer a variety of keyboard shortcuts you can use to executive specific commands. Keyboard shortcuts generally require two or more keys. For example, the keyboard shortcut to display the Open dialog box in an application is Ctrl + O. To use this keyboard shortcut, hold down the Ctrl key, type the letter O on the keyboard, and then release the Ctrl key. For a list of keyboard shortcuts, refer to the Help files.

Choosing Commands with Shortcut Menus

The software programs in the suite include menus that contain commands related to the item with which you are working. A shortcut menu appears in the file in the location where you are working. To display a shortcut menu, click the right mouse button or press Shift + F10. For example, if the insertion point is positioned in a paragraph of text in a Word document, clicking the right mouse button or pressing Shift + F10 will cause the shortcut menu shown in Figure G.9 to display in the document screen.

Figure G.9 Word Shortcut Menu

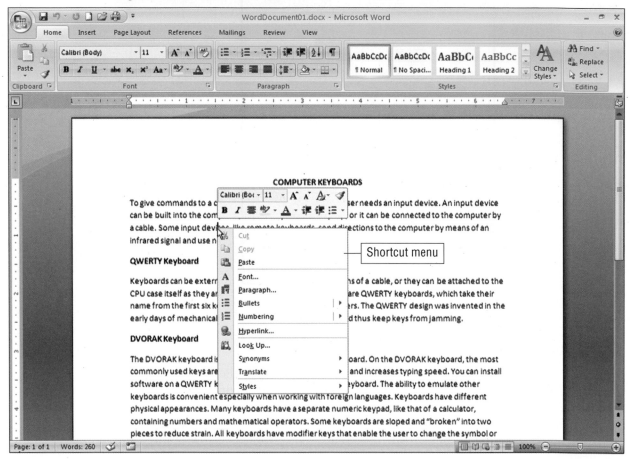

To select an option from a shortcut menu with the mouse, click the desired option. If you are using the keyboard, press the Up or Down Arrow key until the desired option is selected and then press the Enter key. To close a shortcut menu without choosing an option, click anywhere outside the shortcut menu or press the Esc key.

Working with Multiple Programs

As you learn the various programs in the Microsoft Office suite, you will notice how executing commands in each is very similar. For example, the steps to save, close, and print are virtually the same whether you are working in Word, Excel, or PowerPoint. This consistency between programs greatly enhances a user's ability to transfer knowledge learned in one program to another within the suite. Another appeal of Microsoft Office is the ability to have more than one program open at the same time. For example, you can open Word, create a document, and then open Excel, create a spreadsheet, and copy the spreadsheet into Word.

When you open a program, the name of the program displays in the Taskbar. If you open a file within the program, the file name follows the program name on the button on the Taskbar. If you open another program, the program name displays on a button positioned to the right of the first program button. Figure G.10 shows the Taskbar with Word, Excel, and PowerPoint open. To move from one program to another, click the button on the Taskbar representing the desired program file.

Figure G.10 Taskbar with Word, Excel, and PowerPoint Open

Completing Computer Projects

Some computer projects in this textbook require that you open an existing file. Project files are saved on the Student CD that accompanies this textbook. The files you need for each chapter are saved in individual folders. Before beginning a chapter, copy the necessary folder from the CD to your storage medium. After completing projects in a chapter, delete the chapter folder before copying the next chapter folder. (Check with your instructor before deleting a folder.)

The Student CD also contains model answers in PDF format for the project exercises within (but not at the end of) each chapter so you can check your work. To access the PDF files, you will need to have Adobe Acrobat Reader installed on your computer's hard drive. A free download of Adobe Reader is available at Adobe Systems' Web site at www.adobe.com.

Copying a Folder

As you begin working in a chapter, copy the chapter folder from the CD to your storage medium using the My Computer window by completing the following steps.

1. Insert the CD that accompanies this textbook in the CD drive.
2. Insert your storage medium in the appropriate drive.
3. At the Windows XP desktop, open the My Computer window by clicking the Start button and then clicking *My Computer* at the Start menu.
4. Double-click the CD drive in the contents pane (probably displays as *Office2007_Bench* or *Word2007, Excel 2007*, etc. followed by the drive letter).
5. Double-click the *StudentDataFiles* folder in the contents pane.
6. Double-click the desired folder name in the contents pane. (For example, if you are copying a folder for a Word Level 1 chapter, double-click the *Word2007L1* folder.)
7. Click once on the desired chapter subfolder name to select it.
8. Click the <u>Copy this folder</u> hyperlink in the *File and Folder Tasks* section of the task pane.
9. At the Copy Items dialog box, click the drive where your storage medium is located and then click the Copy button.
10. After the folder is copied to your storage medium, close the My Computer window by clicking the Close button (white X on red background) that displays in the upper right corner of the window.

Deleting a Folder

Before copying a chapter folder onto your storage medium, you may need to delete any previous chapter folders. Do this in the My Computer window by completing the following steps:

1. Insert your storage medium in the appropriate drive.
2. At the Windows XP desktop, open the My Computer window by clicking the Start button and then clicking *My Computer* at the Start menu.
3. Double-click the drive where you storage medium is located in the contents pane.
4. Click the chapter folder in the list box.
5. Click the <u>Delete this folder</u> hyperlink in the *File and Folder Tasks* section of the task pane.
6. At the message asking if you want to remove the folder and all its contents, click the Yes button.
7. If a message displays asking if you want to delete a read-only file, click the Yes to All button.
8. Close the My Computer window by clicking the Close button (white X on red background) that displays in the upper right corner of the window.

Viewing or Printing the Project Model Answers

If you want to access the PDF model answer files, first make sure that Adobe Acrobat Reader is installed on your hard drive. Double-click the folder, double-click the desired chapter subfolder name, and double-click the appropriate file name to open the file. You can view and/or print the file to compare it with your own completed exercise file.

Customizing the Quick Access Toolbar

The four applications in the Office 2007 suite—Word, Excel, PowerPoint, and Access—each contain a Quick Access toolbar that displays at the top of the screen. By default, this toolbar contains three buttons: Save, Undo, and Redo. Before beginning chapters in this textbook, customize the Quick Access toolbar by adding three additional buttons: New, Open, and Quick Print. To add these three buttons to the Word Quick Access toolbar, complete the following steps:

1. Open Word.
2. Click the Customize Quick Access Toolbar button that displays at the right side of the toolbar.
3. At the drop-down list, click *New*. (This adds the New button to the toolbar.)
4. Click the Customize Quick Access Toolbar button and then click *Open* at the drop-down list. (This adds the Open button to the toolbar.)
5. Click the Customize Quick Access Toolbar button and then click *Quick Print* at the drop-down list. (This adds the Quick Print button to the toolbar.)

Complete the same steps for Excel, Access, and PowerPoint. You will only need to add the buttons once to the Quick Access toolbar. These buttons will remain on the toolbar even when you exit and then reopen the application.

Using Windows XP

A computer requires an operating system to provide necessary instructions on a multitude of processes including loading programs, managing data, directing the flow of information to peripheral equipment, and displaying information. Windows XP Professional is an operating system that provides functions of this type (along with much more) in a graphical environment. Windows is referred to as a *graphical user interface* (GUI—pronounced *gooey*) that provides a visual display of information with features such as icons (pictures) and buttons. In this introduction, you will learn the basic features of Windows XP:

Tutorial WXP1
Exploring Windows XP
Tutorial WXP2
Working with Files and Folders
Tutorial WXP3
Customizing Windows
Tutorial WXP4
Using Applications

- Use desktop icons and the Taskbar to launch programs and open files or folders
- Organize and manage data, including copying, moving, creating, and deleting files and folders
- Customize the desktop by changing the theme, background, colors, and settings, and adding a screen saver
- Use the Help and Support Center features
- Customize monitor settings

Historically, Microsoft has produced two editions of Windows—one edition for individual users (on desktop and laptop computers) and another edition for servers (on computers that provide service over networks). Windows XP is an upgrade and a merging of these two Windows editions and is available in two versions. The Windows XP Home Edition is designed for home use and Windows XP Professional is designed for small office and workstation use. Whether you are using Windows XP Home Edition or Windows XP Professional, you will be able to complete the steps in the projects in this introduction.

Before using one of the software programs in the Microsoft Office suite, you will need to start the Windows XP operating system. To do this, turn on the computer. Depending on your computer equipment configuration, you may also need to turn on the monitor and printer. If you are using a computer that is part of a network system or if your computer is set up for multiple users, a screen will display showing the user accounts defined for your computer system. At this screen, click your user account name and, if necessary, type your password and then press the Enter key. The Windows XP operating system will start and, after a few moments, the desktop will display as shown in Figure W.1. (Your desktop may vary from what you see in Figure W.1.)

Figure W.1 Windows XP Desktop

icon

Recycle Bin

Taskbar

start   8:56 PM

Exploring the Desktop

When Windows XP is loaded, the main portion of the screen is called the *desktop*. Think of the desktop in Windows as the top of a desk in an office. A business person places necessary tools—such as pencils, pens, paper, files, calculator—on the desktop to perform functions. Like the tools that are located on a desk, the desktop contains tools for operating the computer. These tools are logically grouped and placed in dialog boxes or panels that you can display using icons on the desktop. The desktop contains a variety of features for using your computer and software programs installed on the computer. The features available on the desktop are represented by icons and buttons.

Using Icons

Icons are visual symbols that represent programs, files, or folders. Figure W.1 identifies the *Recycle Bin* icon located on the Windows XP desktop. The Windows XP desktop on your computer may contain additional icons. Programs that have been installed on your computer may be represented by an icon on the desktop. Also, icons may display on your desktop representing files or folders. Double-click an icon and the program, file, or folder it represents opens on the desktop.

Using the Taskbar

The bar that displays at the bottom of the desktop (see Figure W.1) is called the Taskbar. The Taskbar, shown in Figure W.2, contains the Start button, a section that displays task buttons representing open programs, and the notification area.

Figure W.2 Windows XP Taskbar

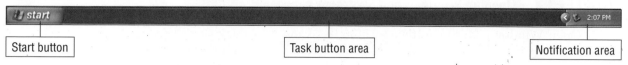

Start button   Task button area   Notification area

Click the Start button, located at the left side of the Taskbar, and the Start menu displays as shown in Figure W.3 (your Start menu may vary). You can also display the Start menu by pressing the Windows key on your keyboard or by pressing Ctrl + Esc. The left column of the Start menu contains *pinned programs*, which are programs that always appear in that particular location on the Start menu, and links to the most recently and frequently used programs. The right column contains links to folders, the Control Panel, online help, and the search feature.

Figure W.3 Start Menu

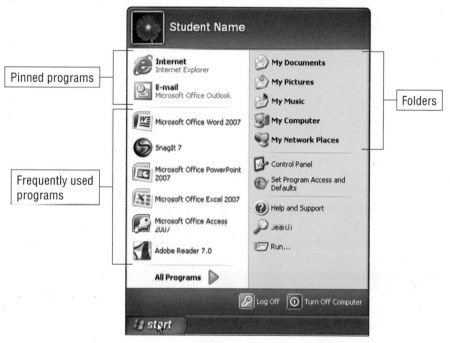

Pinned programs

Folders

Frequently used programs

To choose an option from the Start menu, drag the arrow pointer to the desired option (referred to as *pointing*) and then click the left mouse button. Pointing to options at the Start menu that are followed by a right-pointing arrow will cause a side menu to display with additional options. When a program is open, a task button representing the program appears on the Taskbar. If multiple programs are open, each program will appear as a task button on the Taskbar (a few specialized tools may not).

Project ① Opening Programs and Switching between Programs

1. Open Windows XP. (To do this, turn on the computer and, if necessary, turn on the monitor and/or printer. If you are using a computer that is part of a network system or if your computer is set up for multiple users, you may need to click your user account name and, if necessary, type your password and then press the Enter key. Check with your instructor to determine if you need to complete any additional steps.)

2. When the Windows XP desktop displays, open Microsoft Word by completing the following steps:
   a. Position the arrow pointer on the Start button on the Taskbar and then click the left mouse button.
   b. At the Start menu, point to *All Programs* (a side menu displays) and then point to *Microsoft Office* (another side menu displays).
   c. Drag the arrow pointer to *Microsoft Office Word 2007* in the side menu and then click the left mouse button.
   d. When the Microsoft Word program is open, notice that a task button representing Word displays on the Taskbar.

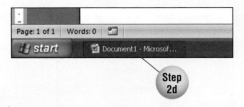

Step 2d

3. Open Microsoft Excel by completing the following steps:
   a. Position the arrow pointer on the Start button on the Taskbar and then click the left mouse button.
   b. At the Start menu, point to *All Programs* and then point to *Microsoft Office*.
   c. Drag the arrow pointer to *Microsoft Office Excel 2007* in the side menu and then click the left mouse button.
   d. When the Microsoft Excel program is open, notice that a task button representing Excel displays on the Taskbar to the right of the task button representing Word.

4. Switch to the Word program by clicking the task button on the Taskbar representing Word.

Step 4

Step 6

5. Switch to the Excel program by clicking the task button on the Taskbar representing Excel.
6. Exit Excel by clicking the Close button that displays in the upper right corner of the Excel window.
7. Exit Word by clicking the Close button that displays in the upper right corner of the Word window.

Exploring the Notification Area

The notification area is located at the right side of the Taskbar and contains the system clock along with small icons representing specialized programs that run in the background. Position the arrow pointer over the current time in the notification area of the Taskbar and today's date displays in a small yellow box above the time. Double-click the current time displayed on the Taskbar and the Date and Time Properties dialog box displays as shown in Figure W.4.

Figure W.4 Date and Time Properties Box

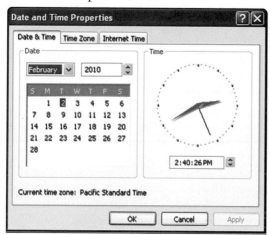

Change the date with options in the *Date* section of the dialog box. For example, to change the month, click the down-pointing arrow at the right side of the option box containing the current month and then click the desired month at the drop-down list. Change the year by clicking the up- or down-pointing arrow at the right side of the option box containing the current year until the desired year displays. To change the day, click the desired day in the monthly calendar that displays in the dialog box. To change the time, double-click either the hour, minute, or seconds and then type the appropriate time or use the up- and down-pointing arrows to adjust the time.

Some programs, when installed, will add an icon to the notification area of the Taskbar. Display the name of the icon by positioning the mouse pointer on the icon and, after approximately one second, the icon label displays in a small yellow box. Some icons may display information in the yellow box rather than the icon label. If more icons have been inserted in the notification area than can be viewed at one time, a left-pointing arrow button displays at the left side of the notification area. Click this left-pointing arrow button and the remaining icons display.

Setting Taskbar Properties

By default, the Taskbar is locked in its current position and size. You can change this default setting, along with other default settings, with options at the Taskbar and Start Menu Properties dialog box, shown in Figure W.5. To display this dialog box, position the arrow pointer on any empty spot on the Taskbar and then click the right mouse button. At the shortcut menu that displays, click *Properties*.

Figure W.5 Taskbar and Start Menu Properties Box

Each property is controlled by a check box. Property options containing a check mark are active. Click the option to remove the check mark and make the option inactive. If an option is inactive, clicking the option will insert a check mark in the check box and turn on the option (make it active).

Project ② **Changing Taskbar Properties**

1. Make sure Windows XP is open and the desktop displays.
2. Hide the Taskbar and remove the display of the clock by completing the following steps:
   a. Position the arrow pointer on any empty area on the Taskbar and then click the right mouse button.
   b. At the shortcut menu that displays, click *Properties*.
   c. At the Taskbar and Start Menu Properties dialog box, click *Auto-hide the taskbar*. (This inserts a check mark in the check box.)
   d. Click *Show the clock*. (This removes the check mark from the check box.)
   e. Click the Apply button.
   f. Click OK to close the dialog box.

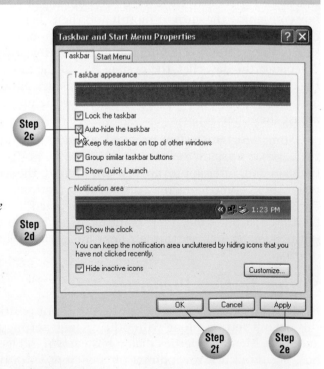

3. Display the Taskbar by positioning the mouse pointer at the bottom of the screen. When the Taskbar displays, notice that the time no longer displays at the right side of the Taskbar.

4. Return to the default settings for the Taskbar by completing the following steps:

   a. With the Taskbar displayed (if it does not display, position the mouse pointer at the bottom of the desktop), position the arrow pointer on any empty area on the Taskbar and then click the right mouse button.

   b. At the shortcut menu that displays, click *Properties*.

   c. At the Taskbar and Start Menu Properties dialog box, click *Auto-hide the taskbar*. (This removes the check mark from the check box.)

   d. Click *Show the clock*. (This inserts a check mark in the check box.)

   e. Click the Apply button.

   f. Click OK to close the dialog box.

Turning Off the Computer

When you are finished working with your computer, you can choose to shut down the computer completely, shut down and then restart the computer, put the computer on standby, or tell the computer to hibernate. Do not turn off your computer until your screen goes blank. Important data is stored in memory while Windows XP is running and this data needs to be written to the hard drive before turning off the computer.

To shut down your computer, click the Start button on the Taskbar and then click *Turn Off Computer* at the Start menu. At the Turn off computer window, shown in Figure W.6, click the *Stand By* option and the computer switches to a low power state causing some devices such as the monitor and hard drives to turn off. With these devices off, the computer uses less power. Stand By is particularly useful for saving battery power for portable computers. Tell the computer to "hibernate" by holding down the Shift key while clicking the *Stand By* option. In hibernate mode, the computer saves everything in memory, turns off the monitor and hard drive, and then turns off the computer. Click the *Turn Off* option if you want to shut down Windows XP and turn off all power to the computer. Click the *Restart* option if you want to restart the computer and restore the desktop exactly as you left it. You can generally restore your desktop from either standby or hibernate by pressing once on the computer's power button. Usually, bringing a computer out of hibernation takes a little longer than bringing a computer out of standby.

Figure W.6 Turn Off Computer Window

Managing Files and Folders

As you begin working with programs in Windows XP, you will create files in which data (information) is saved. A file might contain a Word document, an Excel workbook, or a PowerPoint presentation. As you begin creating files, consider creating folders into which those files will be stored. You can complete file management tasks such as creating a folder and copying and moving files and folders at the My Computer window. To display the My Computer window shown in Figure W.7, click the Start button on the Taskbar and then click My Computer. The various components of the My Computer window are identified in Figure W.7.

Figure W.7 My Computer Window

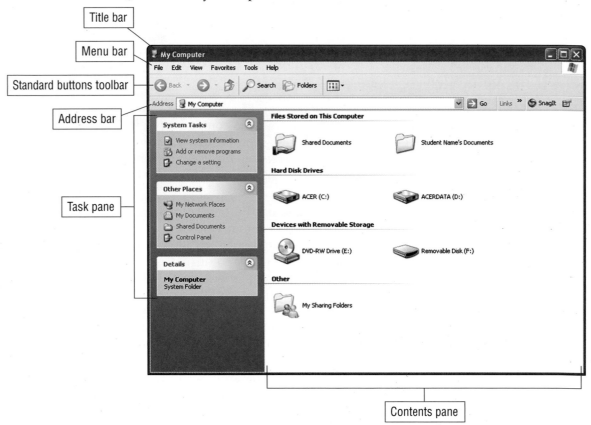

Copying, Moving, and Deleting Files/Folders

File and folder management activities might include copying and moving files or folders from one folder or drive to another, or deleting files or folders. The My Computer window offers a variety of methods for copying, moving, and deleting files/folders. You can use options in the task pane, drop-down menu options, or shortcut menu options. This section will provide you with the steps for copying, moving, and deleting files/folders using options in the task pane.

To copy a file/folder to another folder or drive, first display the file in the contents pane by identifying the location of the file. If the file is located in the My Documents folder, click the <u>My Documents</u> hyperlink in the *Other Places* section of the task pane. If the file is located on the hard drive, double-click the desired drive in the contents pane; if the file is located on a USB drive, DVD, or CD, double-click the desired drive letter. Next, click the folder or file name in the contents pane that you want to copy. This changes the options in the task pane to include management options such as renaming, moving, copying, and deleting folders or files. Click the Copy this folder (or Copy this file) hyperlink in the task pane and the Copy Items dialog box displays as shown in Figure W.8. At the Copy Items dialog box, click the desired folder or drive and then click the Copy button.

Figure W.8 Copy Items Dialog Box

To move adjacent files/folders, click the first file or folder, hold down the Shift key, and then click the last file or folder. This selects and highlights all files/folders from the first file/folder you clicked to the last file/folder you clicked. With the adjacent files/folders selected, click the Move the selected items hyperlink in the File and Folder Tools section of the task pane and then specify the desired location at the Move Items dialog box. To select nonadjacent files/folders, click the first file/folder to select it, hold down the Ctrl key, and then click any other files/folders you want to move or copy.

You can easily remove (delete) a file or folder from the My Computer window. To delete a file or folder, click the file or folder in the contents pane, and then click the Delete this folder (or Delete this file) hyperlink in the task pane. At the dialog box asking you to confirm the deletion, click Yes. A deleted file or folder is sent to the Recycle Bin. You will learn more about the Recycle Bin in the next section.

In Project 3, you will insert the CD that accompanies this book into the DVD or CD drive. When the CD is inserted, the drive may automatically activate and a dialog box may display on the screen telling you that the disk or device contains more than one type of content and asking what you want Windows to do. If this dialog box displays, click Cancel to remove the dialog box.

Project ③   Copying a File and Folder and Deleting a File

1. At the Windows XP desktop, insert the CD that accompanies this textbook into the appropriate drive. If a dialog box displays telling you that the disk or device contains more than one type of content and asking what you want Windows to do, click Cancel.
2. At the Windows XP desktop, open the My Computer window by clicking the Start button on the Taskbar and then clicking *My Computer* at the Start menu.
3. Copy a file from the CD that accompanies this textbook to the drive containing your storage medium by completing the following steps:
   a. Insert your storage medium in the appropriate drive.
   b. In the contents pane, double-click the drive containing the CD (probably displays as *Office2007_Bench* followed by a drive letter). (Make sure you double-click the mouse button because you want the contents of the CD to display in the contents pane.)
   c. Double-click the *StudentDataFiles* folder.
   d. Double-click the *WindowsXP* folder in the contents pane.
   e. Click **WordDocument01.docx** in the contents pane to select it.
   f. Click the <u>Copy this file</u> hyperlink located in the *File and Folder Tasks* section of the task pane.

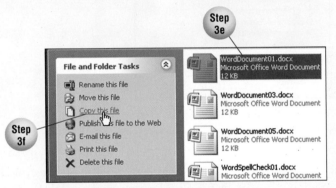

g. At the Copy Items dialog box, click in the list box the drive containing your storage medium.
h. Click the Copy button.

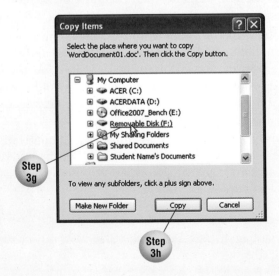

4. Delete **WordDocument01.docx** from your storage medium by completing the following steps:
   a. Click the <u>My Computer</u> hyperlink located in the *Other Places* section of the task pane.
   b. Double-click in the contents pane the drive containing your storage medium.
   c. Click ***WordDocument01.docx***.
   d. Click the <u>Delete this file</u> hyperlink in the *File and Folder Tasks* section of the task pane.

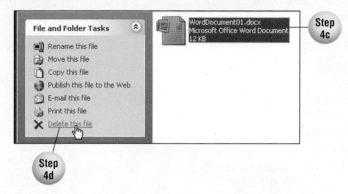

   e. At the message asking you to confirm the deletion, click Yes.
5. Copy the WindowsXP folder from the CD drive to the drive containing your storage medium by completing the following steps:
   a. Click the My Computer hyperlink in the *Other Places* section of the task pane.
   b. In the contents pane, double-click the drive containing the CD (probably displays as *Office2007_Bench* followed by a drive letter).
   c. Double-click the *StudentDataFiles* folder.
   d. Click the *WindowsXP* folder in the contents pane to select it.
   e. Click the <u>Copy this folder</u> hyperlink in the *File and Folder Tasks* section of the task pane.
   f. At the Copy Items dialog box, click the drive containing your storage medium.
   g. Click the Copy button.
6. Close the window by clicking the Close button (contains a white *X* on a red background) located in the upper right corner of the window. (You can also close the window by clicking File on the Menu bar and then clicking *Close* at the drop-down list.)

Selecting Files/Folders

You can move, copy, or delete more than one file or folder at the same time. Before moving, copying, or deleting files/folders, select the desired files or folders. Selecting files/folders is easier when you change the display in the contents pane to List or Details. To change the display, open the My Computer window and then click the Views button on the Standard Buttons toolbar. At the drop-down list that displays, click the *List* option or the *Details* option.

To move adjacent files/folders, click the first file or folder, hold down the Shift key, and click the last file or folder. This selects and highlights all files/folders from the first file/folder you clicked to the last file/folder you clicked. With the adjacent files/folders selected, click the <u>Move the selected items</u> hyperlink in the *File and Folder Tasks* section of the task pane and then specify the desired location at the Move Items dialog box. To select nonadjacent files/folders, click the first file/folder to select it, hold down the Ctrl key, and then click any other files/folders you want to move or copy.

Project ④   Copying and Deleting Files

1. At the Windows XP desktop, open the My Computer window by clicking the Start button and then clicking *My Computer* at the Start menu.
2. Copy files from the CD that accompanies this textbook to the drive containing your storage medium by completing the following steps:
   a. Make sure the CD that accompanies this textbook and your storage medium are inserted in the appropriate drives.
   b. Double-click the CD drive in the contents pane (probably displays as *Office2007_Bench* followed by the drive letter).
   c. Double-click the *StudentDataFiles* folder in the contents pane.
   d. Double-click the *WindowsXP* folder in the contents pane.
   e. Change the display to Details by clicking the Views button on the Standard Buttons toolbar and then clicking *Details* at the drop-down list.

   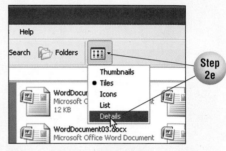

   f. Position the arrow pointer on **WordDocument01.docx** in the contents pane and then click the left mouse button.
   g. Hold down the Shift key, click **WordDocument05.docx**, and then release the Shift key. (This selects **WordDocument01.docx**, **WordDocument02.docx**, **WordDocument03.docx**, **WordDocument04.docx**, and **WordDocument05.docx**.)

   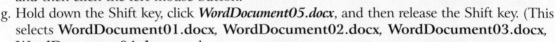

   h. Click the <u>Copy the selected items</u> hyperlink in the *File and Folder Tasks* section of the task pane.
   i. At the Copy Items dialog box, click the drive containing your storage medium and then click the Copy button.
3. Display the files and folder saved on your storage medium by completing the following steps:
   a. Click the <u>My Computer</u> hyperlink in the *Other Places* section of the task pane.
   b. Double-click the drive containing your storage medium.
4. Delete the files from your storage medium that you just copied by completing the following steps:
   a. Change the view by clicking the Views button on the Standard Buttons toolbar and then clicking *List* at the drop-down list.
   b. Click **WordDocument01.docx** in the contents pane.
   c. Hold down the Shift key, click **WordDocument05.docx**, and then release the Shift key. (This selects **WordDocument01.docx**, **WordDocument02.docx**, **WordDocument03.docx**, **WordDocument04.docx**, and **WordDocument05.docx**.)

   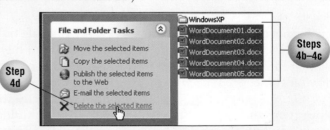

   d. Click the <u>Delete the selected items</u> hyperlink in the *File and Folder Tasks* section of the task pane.
   e. At the message asking you to confirm the deletion, click Yes.
5. Close the window by clicking the Close button (white *X* on red background) that displays in the upper right corner of the window.

Manipulating and Creating Folders

As you begin working with and creating a number of files, consider creating folders in which you can logically group the files. To create a folder, display the My Computer window and then display in the contents pane the drive where you want to create the folder. Click File on the Menu bar, point to *New*, and then click *Folder* at the side menu. This inserts a folder icon in the contents pane and names the folder *New Folder*. Type the desired name for the new folder and then press Enter.

Project 5 — Creating a New Folder

1. At the Windows XP desktop, open the My Computer window.
2. Create a new folder by completing the following steps:
   a. Double-click in the contents pane the drive that contains your storage medium.
   b. Double-click the *WindowsXP* folder in the contents pane. (This opens the folder.)
   c. Click File on the Menu bar, point to *New*, and then click *Folder*.
   d. Type **SpellCheckFiles** and then press Enter. (This changes the name from *New Folder* to *SpellCheckFiles*.)
3. Copy **WordSpellCheck01.docx**, **WordSpellCheck02.docx**, and **WordSpellCheck03.docx** into the SpellCheckFiles folder you just created by completing the following steps:
   a. Click the Views button on the Standard Buttons toolbar and then click *List* at the drop-down list.
   b. Click once on the file named **WordSpellCheck01.docx** located in the contents pane.
   c. Hold down the Shift key, click once on the file named ***WordSpellCheck03.docx***, and then release the Shift key. (This selects **WordSpellCheck01.docx**, **WordSpellCheck02.docx**, and **WordSpellCheck03.docx**.)
   d. Click the Copy the selected items hyperlink in the *File and Folder Tasks* section of the task pane.
   e. At the Copy Items dialog box, click in the list box the drive containing your storage medium.
   f. Click *WindowsXP* in the list box.
   g. Click *SpellCheckFiles* in the list box.
   h. Click the Copy button.
4. Display the files you just copied by double-clicking the *SpellCheckFiles* folder in the contents pane.

Step 2c

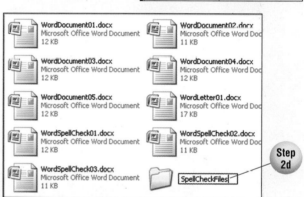

Step 2d

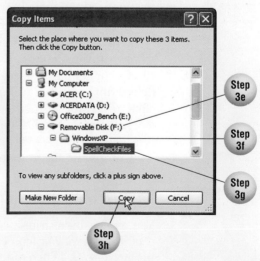

Step 3e

Step 3f

Step 3g

Step 3h

5. Delete the SpellCheckFiles folder and its contents by completing the following steps:

   a. Click the Up button on the Standard Buttons toolbar. (This displays the contents of the WindowsXP folder which is up one folder from the SpellCheckFiles folders.)

   b. Click the *SpellCheckFiles* folder in the contents pane to select it.

   c. Click the <u>Delete this folder</u> hyperlink in the *File and Folder Tasks* section of the task pane.

   d. At the message asking you to confirm the deletion, click Yes.

6. Close the window by clicking the Close button located in the upper right corner of the window.

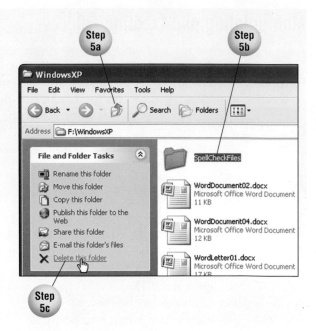

Using the Recycle Bin

Deleting the wrong file can be a disaster but Windows XP helps protect your work with the Recycle Bin. The Recycle Bin acts just like an office wastepaper basket; you can "throw away" (delete) unwanted files, but you can "reach in" to the Recycle Bin and take out (restore) a file if you threw it away by accident.

Deleting Files to the Recycle Bin

A file/folder or selected files/folders deleted from the hard drive are sent automatically to the Recycle Bin. Files/folders deleted from a disk are deleted permanently. (Recovery programs are available, however, that will help you recover deleted text. If you accidentally delete a file/folder from a disk, do not do anything more with the disk until you can run a recovery program.)

One method for deleting files is to display the My Computer window and then display in the contents pane the file(s) and/or folder(s) you want deleted. Click the file or folder or select multiple files or folders and then click the appropriate delete option in the task pane. At the message asking you to confirm the deletion, click Yes. Another method for deleting a file is to drag the file to the *Recycle Bin* icon on the desktop. Drag a file icon to the Recycle Bin until the *Recycle Bin* icon is selected (displays with a blue background) and then release the mouse button. This drops the file you are dragging into the Recycle Bin.

Recovering Files from the Recycle Bin

You can easily restore a deleted file from the Recycle Bin. To restore a file, double-click the *Recycle Bin* icon on the desktop. This opens the Recycle Bin window shown in Figure W.9. (The contents of the Recycle Bin will vary.) To restore a file, click

the file you want restored, and then click the <u>Restore this item</u> hyperlink in the
Recycle Bin Tasks section of the task pane. This removes the file from the Recycle
Bin and returns it to its original location. You can also restore a file by positioning
the arrow pointer on the file, clicking the right mouse button, and then clicking
Restore at the shortcut menu.

Figure W.9 Recycle Bin Window

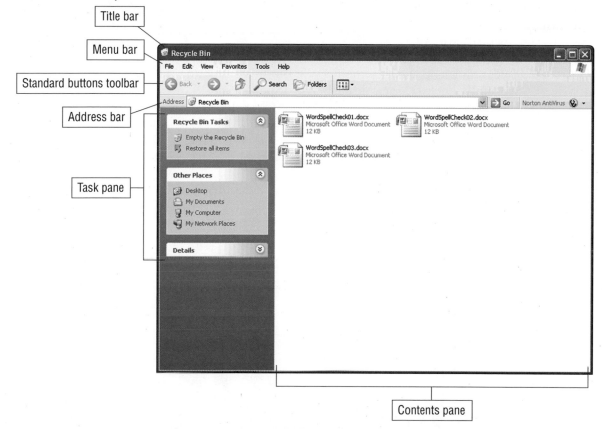

Title bar
Menu bar
Standard buttons toolbar
Address bar
Task pane
Contents pane

Project ⑥ Deleting Files to and Recovering Files from the Recycle Bin

*Before beginning this project, check with your instructor to determine if you can copy files to the
hard drive.*

1. At the Windows XP desktop, open the My Computer window.
2. Copy files from your storage medium to the My Documents folder on your hard drive by
   completing the following steps:
   a. Double-click in the contents pane the drive containing your storage medium.
   b. Double-click the *WindowsXP* folder in the contents pane.
   c. Click the Views button on the Standard Buttons toolbar and then click *List* at the drop-
      down list.
   d. Position the arrow pointer on **WordSpellCheck01.docx** and then click the left
      mouse button.
   e. Hold down the Shift key, click ***WordSpellCheck03.docx***, and then release the Shift key.

f. Click the Copy the selected items hyperlink in the *File and Folder Tasks* section of the task pane.

g. At the Copy Items dialog box, click *My Documents* in the list box.

h. Click the Copy button.

3. Click the <u>My Documents</u> hyperlink in the *Other Places* section of the task pane. (The files you copied, **WordSpellCheck01.docx** through **WordSpellCheck03.docx**, will display in the contents pane in alphabetical order.)

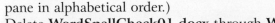

4. Delete **WordSpellCheck01.docx** through **WordSpellCheck03.docx** from the My Documents folder and send them to the Recycle Bin by completing the following steps:

a. Select **WordSpellCheck01.docx** through **WordSpellCheck03.docx** in the contents pane. (If these files are not visible, you will need to scroll down the list of files.)

b. Click the <u>Delete the selected items</u> hyperlink in the *File and Folder Tasks* section of the task pane.

c. At the message asking you to confirm the deletion to the Recycle Bin, click Yes.

5. Click the Close button to close the window.

6. At the desktop, display the contents of the Recycle Bin by double-clicking the *Recycle Bin* icon.

7. At the Recycle Bin window, restore **WordSpellCheck01.docx** through **WordSpellCheck03.docx** to the My Documents folder by completing the following steps:

a. Select **WordSpellCheck01.docx** through **WordSpellCheck03.docx** in the contents pane of the Recycle Bin window. (If these files are not visible, you will need to scroll down the list of files.)

b. With the files selected, click the <u>Restore the selected items</u> hyperlink in the *Recycle Bin Tasks* section of the task pane.

8. Close the Recycle Bin window by clicking the Close button located in the upper right corner of the window.

9. Display the My Computer window.

10. Click the <u>My Documents</u> hyperlink in the *Other Places* section of the task pane.

11. Delete the files you restored by completing the following steps:

a. Select **WordSpellCheck01.docx** through **WordSpellCheck03.docx** in the contents pane. (If these files are not visible, you will need to scroll down the list of files. These are the files you recovered from the Recycle Bin.)

b. Click the <u>Delete the selected items</u> hyperlink in the *File and Folder Tasks* section of the task pane.

c. At the message asking you to confirm the deletion, click Yes.

12. Close the window.

Emptying the Recycle Bin

Just like a wastepaper basket, the Recycle Bin can get full. To empty the Recycle Bin, position the arrow pointer on the *Recycle Bin* icon on the desktop and then click the right mouse button. At the shortcut menu that displays, click *Empty Recycle Bin*. At the message asking you to confirm the deletion, click Yes. You can also empty the Recycle Bin by double-clicking the *Recycle Bin* icon. At the Recycle Bin window, click the <u>Empty the Recycle Bin</u> hyperlink in the *Recycle Bin Tasks* section of the task pane. At the message asking you to confirm the deletion, click Yes. (You can also empty the Recycle Bin by clicking File on the Menu bar and then clicking *Empty Recycle Bin* at the drop-down menu.)

Emptying the Recycle Bin deletes all files/folders. You can delete a specific file/folder from the Recycle Bin (rather than all files/folders). To do this, double-click the *Recycle Bin* icon on the desktop. At the Recycle Bin window, select the file/folder or files/folders you want to delete. Click File on the Menu bar and then click *Delete* at the drop-down menu. (You can also right-click a selected file/folder and then click *Delete* at the shortcut menu.) At the message asking you to confirm the deletion, click Yes.

Project ⑦   Emptying the Recycle Bin

Before beginning this project, check with your instructor to determine if you can delete files/folders from the Recycle Bin.

1. At the Windows XP desktop, double-click the *Recycle Bin* icon.
2. At the Recycle Bin window, empty the contents of the Recycle Bin by completing the following steps:
   a. Click the <u>Empty the Recycle Bin</u> hyperlink in the *Recycle Bin Tasks* section of the task pane.

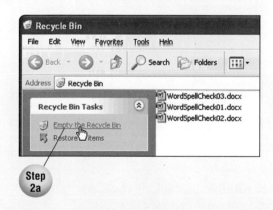

   b. At the message asking you to confirm the deletion, click Yes.
3. Close the Recycle Bin window by clicking the Close button located in the upper right corner of the window.

When you empty the Recycle Bin, the files cannot be recovered by the Recycle Bin or by Windows XP. If you have to recover a file, you will need to use a file recovery program such as Norton Utilities. These utilities are separate programs, but might be worth their cost if you ever need them.

Creating a Shortcut

If you use a file or program on a consistent basis, consider creating a shortcut to the file or program. A shortcut is a specialized icon that represents very small files that point the operating system to the actual item, whether it is a file, a folder, or an application. If you create a shortcut to a Word document, the shortcut icon is not the actual document but a path to the document. Double-click the shortcut icon and Windows XP opens the document in Word.

One method for creating a shortcut is to display the My Computer window and then display the drive or folder where the file is located. Right-click the desired file, point to *Send To*, and then click *Desktop (create shortcut)*. You can easily delete a shortcut icon from the desktop by dragging the shortcut icon to the Recycle Bin icon. This deletes the shortcut icon but does not delete the file to which the shortcut pointed.

Project ⑧   Creating a Shortcut

1. At the Windows XP desktop, display the My Computer window.
2. Double-click the drive containing your storage medium.
3. Double-click the *WindowsXP* folder in the contents pane.
4. Change the display of files to a list by clicking the Views button on the Standard Buttons toolbar and then clicking *List* at the drop-down list.
5. Create a shortcut to the file named **WordLetter01.docx** by right-clicking on **WordLetter01.docx**, pointing to *Send To*, and then clicking *Desktop (create shortcut)*.

Step 5

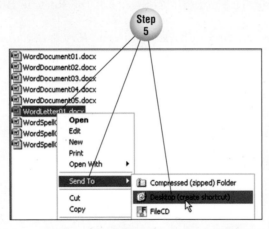

6. Close the My Computer window by clicking the Close button located in the upper right corner of the window.
7. Open Word and the file named **WordLetter01.docx** by double-clicking the *WordLetter01.docx* shortcut icon on the desktop.
8. After viewing the file in Word, exit Word by clicking the Close button that displays in the upper right corner of the window.

Step 7

9. Delete the *WordLetter01.docx* shortcut icon by completing the following steps:
   a. At the desktop, position the mouse pointer on the *WordLetter01.docx* shortcut icon.
   b. Hold down the left mouse button, drag the icon on top of the *Recycle Bin* icon, and then release the mouse button.

Customizing the Desktop

You can customize the Windows XP desktop to fit your particular needs and preferences. For example, you can choose a different theme, change the desktop background, add a screen saver, and apply a different appearance to windows, dialog boxes, and menus. To customize the desktop, position the arrow pointer on any empty location on the desktop and then click the right mouse button. At the shortcut menu that displays, click *Properties*. This displays the Display Properties dialog box with the Themes tab selected as shown in Figure W.10.

Figure W.10 Display Properties Dialog Box

Changing the Theme

A Windows XP theme specifies a variety of formatting such as fonts, sounds, icons, colors, mouse pointers, background, and screen saver. Windows XP contains two themes—Windows XP (the default) and Windows Classic (which appears like earlier versions of Windows). Other themes are available as downloads from the Microsoft Web site. Change the theme with the *Theme* option at the Display Properties dialog box with the Themes tab selected.

Changing the Desktop

With options at the Display Properties dialog box with the Desktop tab selected, as shown in Figure W.11, you can choose a different desktop background and customize the desktop. Click any option in the *Background* list box and preview the results in the preview screen. With the *Position* option, you can specify that the background image is centered, tiled, or stretched on the desktop. Use the *Color* option to change the background color and click the Browse button to choose a background image from another location or Web site.

Figure W.11 Display Properties Dialog Box with Desktop Tab Selected

Adding a Screen Saver

If your computer sits idle for periods of time, consider adding a screen saver. A screen saver is a pattern that changes constantly, thus eliminating the problem of an image staying on the screen too long. To add a screen saver, display the Display Properties dialog box and then click the Screen Saver tab. This displays the dialog box as shown in Figure W.12.

Figure W.12 Display Properties Dialog Box with Screen Saver Tab Selected

Click the down-pointing arrow at the right side of the *Screen saver* option box to display a list of installed screen savers. Click a screen saver and a preview displays in the monitor located toward the top of the dialog box. Click the Preview button and the dialog box is hidden and the screen saver displays on your monitor. Move the mouse or click a button on the mouse and the dialog box will reappear. Click the Power button in the *Monitor power* section and a dialog box displays with options for choosing a power scheme appropriate to the way you use your computer. The dialog box also includes options for specifying how long the computer can be left unused before the monitor and hard disk are turned off and the system goes to standby or hibernate mode.

Changing Colors

Click the Appearance tab at the Display Properties dialog box and the dialog box displays as shown in Figure W.13. At this dialog box, you can change the desktop scheme. Schemes are predefined collections of colors used in windows, menus, title bars, and system fonts. Windows XP loads with the Windows XP style color scheme. Choose a different scheme with the Windows and buttons option and choose a specific color with the Color scheme option.

Figure W.13 Display Properties Dialog Box with Appearance Tab Selected

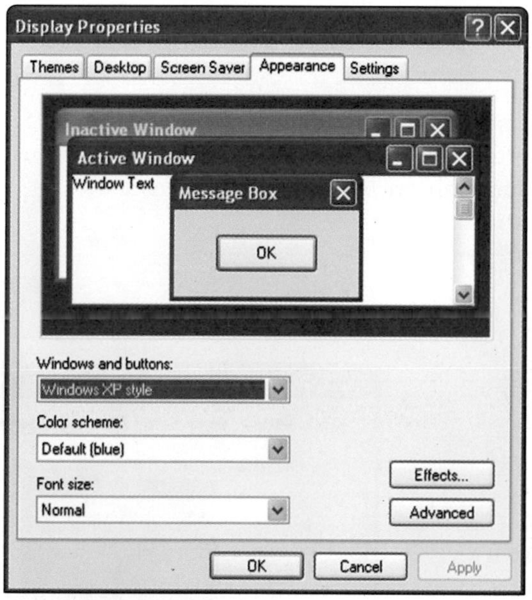

Changing Settings

Click the Settings tab at the Display Properties dialog box and the dialog box displays as shown in Figure W.14. At this dialog box, you can set color and screen resolution. The *Color quality* option determines how many colors your monitor displays. The more colors that are shown, the more realistic the images will appear. However, a lot of computer memory is required to show thousands of colors. Your exact choice is determined by the specific hardware you are using. The *Screen resolution* slide bar sets the screen's resolution. The higher the number, the more you can fit onto your screen. Again, your actual values depend on your particular hardware.

Figure W.14 Display Properties Dialog Box with Settings Tab Selected

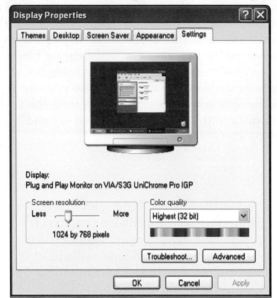

Project ⑨ Customizing the Desktop

Before beginning this project, check with your instructor to determine if you can customize the desktop.

1. At the Windows XP desktop, display the Display Properties dialog box by positioning the arrow pointer on an empty location on the desktop, clicking the right mouse button, and then clicking *Properties* at the shortcut menu.
2. At the Display Properties dialog box, change the desktop background by completing the following steps:
   a. Click the Desktop tab.
   b. If a background is selected in the *Background* list box (other than the *(None)* option), make a note of this background name.
   c. Click *Blue Lace 16* in the *Background* list box. (If this option is not available, choose another background.)
   d. Make sure *Tile* is selected in the *Position* list box.
   e. Click OK to close the dialog box.

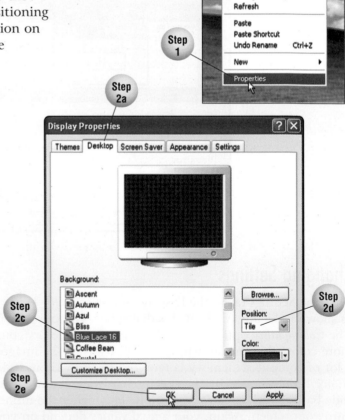

3. After viewing the desktop with the Blue Lace 16 background, remove the background image and change the background color by completing the following steps:

a. Display the Display Properties dialog box.

b. At the Display Properties dialog box, click the Desktop tab.

c. Click *(None)* in the *Background* list box.

d. Click the down-pointing arrow at the right side of the *Color* option and then click the dark red option at the color palette.

e. Click OK to close the Display Properties dialog box.

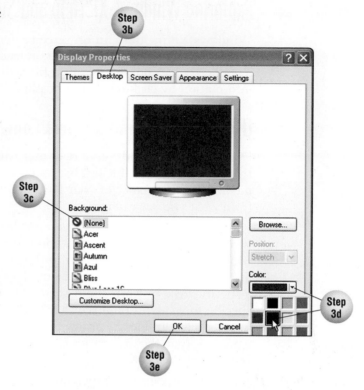

4. After viewing the desktop with the dark red background color, add a screen saver and change the wait time by completing the following steps:

a. Display the Display Properties dialog box.

b. At the Display Properties dialog box, click the Screen Saver tab. (If a screen saver is already selected in the *Screen saver* option box, make a note of this screen saver name.)

c. Click the down-pointing arrow at the right side of the *Screen saver* option box.

d. At the drop-down list that displays, click a screen saver that interests you. (A preview of the screen saver displays in the screen located toward the top of the dialog box.)

e. Click a few other screen savers to see how they will display on the monitor.

f. Click OK to close the Display Properties dialog box.

5. Return all settings back to the default by completing the following steps:

a. Display the Display Properties dialog box.

b. Click the Desktop tab.

c. If a background and color were selected when you began this project, click that background name in the *Background* list box and change the color back to the original color.

d. Click the Screen Saver tab.

e. At the Display Properties dialog box with the Screen Saver tab selected, click the down-pointing arrow at the right side of the *Screen saver* option box, and then click *(None)*. (If a screen saver was selected before completing this project, return to that screen saver.)

f. Click OK to close the Display Properties dialog box.

Exploring Windows XP Help and Support

Windows XP includes an on-screen reference guide providing information, explanations, and interactive help on learning Windows features. The on-screen reference guide contains complex files with hypertext used to access additional information by clicking a word or phrase.

Using the Help and Support Center Window

Display the Help and Support Center window shown in Figure W.15 by clicking the Start button on the Taskbar and then clicking *Help and Support* at the Start menu. The appearance of your Help and Support Center window may vary slightly from what you see in Figure W.15.

If you want to learn about a topic listed in the *Pick a Help topic* section of the window, click the desired topic and information about the topic displays in the window. Use the other options in the Help and Support Center window to get assistance or support from a remote computer or Windows XP newsgroups, pick a specific task, or learn about the additional help features. If you want help on a specific topic and do not see that topic listed in the *Pick a Help topic* section of the window, click inside the *Search* text box (generally located toward the top of the window), type the desired topic, and then press Enter or click the Start searching button (white arrow on a green background).

Figure W.15 Help and Support Center Window

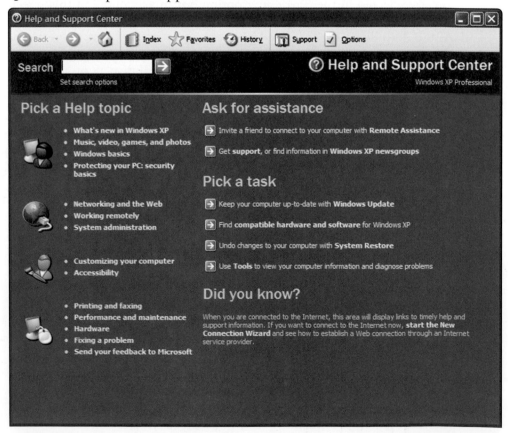

Project ⑩ Using the Help and Support Center

1. At the Windows XP desktop, use the Help and Support feature to learn about new Windows XP features by completing the following steps:
   a. Click the Start button on the Taskbar and then click *Help and Support* at the Start menu.
   b. At the Help and Support Center window, click the <u>What's new in Windows XP</u> hyperlink located in the *Pick a Help topic* section of the window.

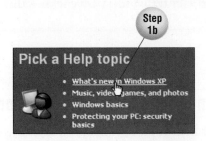

Step 1b

   c. Click the <u>What's new</u> hyperlink located in the *What's new in Windows XP* section of the window. (This displays a list of Help options at the right side of the window.)
   d. Click the <u>What's new in Windows XP</u> hyperlink located at the right side of the window below the subheading *Overviews, Articles, and Tutorials*.
   e. Read the information about Windows XP that displays at the right side of the window.
   f. Print the information by completing the following steps:
      1) Click the Print button located on the toolbar that displays above the information titled *What's new in Windows XP Professional*.

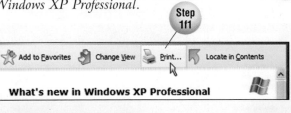

Step 1f1

Step 1d

      2) At the Print dialog box, make sure the correct printer is selected and then click the Print button.
2. Return to the opening Help and Support Center window by clicking the Home button located on the Help and Support Center toolbar.
3. Use the *Search* text box to search for information on deleting files by completing the following steps:
   a. Click in the *Search* text box located toward the top of the Help and Support Center window.
   b. Type **deleting files** and then press Enter.
   c. Click the <u>Delete a file or folder</u> hyperlink that displays in the *Search Results* section of the window (below the *Pick a task* subheading).

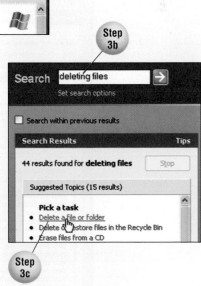

Step 3b

Step 3c

d. Read the information about deleting a file or folder that displays at the right side of the window and then print the information by clicking the Print button on the toolbar and then clicking the Print button at the Print dialog box.

e. Click the <u>Delete or restore files in the Recycle Bin</u> hyperlink that displays in the *Search Results* section of the window.

f. Read the information that displays at the right side of the window about deleting and restoring files in the Recycle Bin and then print the information.

4. Close the Help and Support Center window by clicking the Close button located in the upper right corner of the window.

Displaying an Index of Help and Support Topics

Display a list of help topics available by clicking the Index button on the Help and Support Center window toolbar. This displays an index of help topics at the left side of the window as shown in Figure W.16. Scroll through this list until the desired topic displays and then double-click the topic. Information about the selected topic displays at the right side of the window. If you are looking for a specific topic or keyword, click in the *Type in the keyword to find* text box, type the desired topic or keyword, and then press Enter.

Figure W.16 Help and Support Center Window with Index Displayed

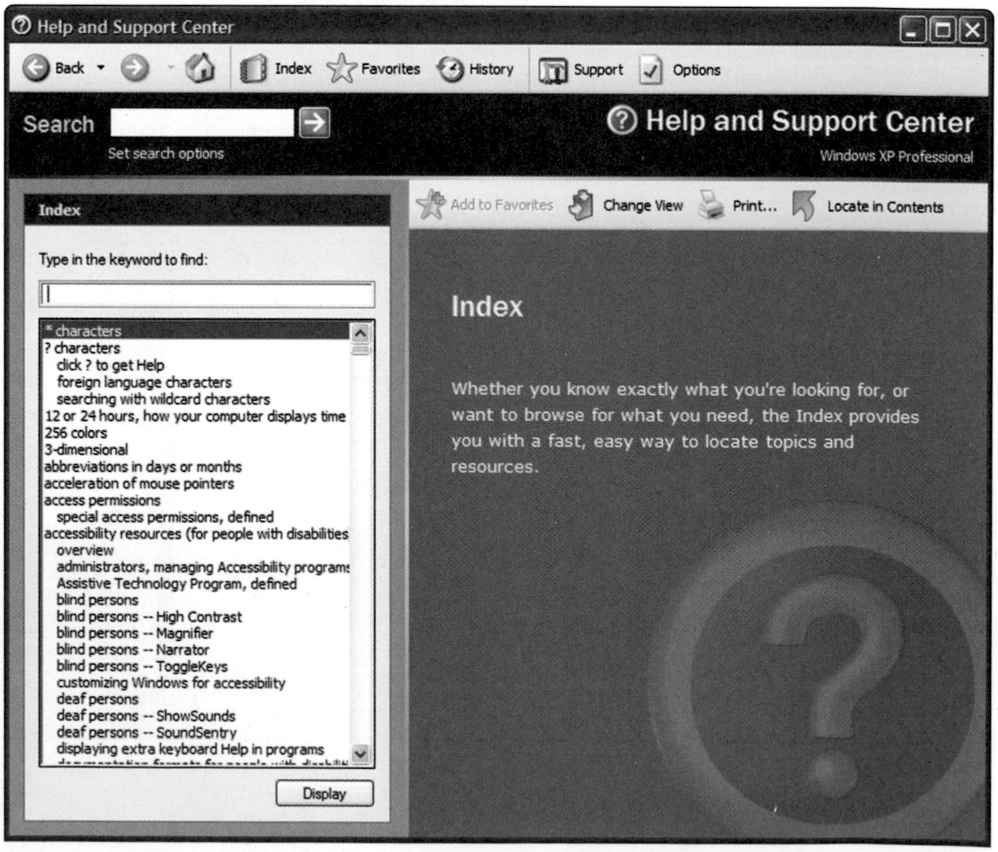

Project ⑪ Using the Index to Search for Information

1. At the Windows XP desktop, use the Index to display information on accessing programs by completing the following steps:
   a. Click the Start button on the Taskbar and then click *Help and Support* at the Start menu.
   b. Click the Index button on the Help and Support Center window toolbar.
   c. Scroll down the list of Index topics until *accessing programs* is visible and then double-click the subheading *overview* that displays below *accessing programs*.

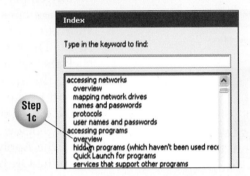

Step 1c

   d. Read the information that displays at the right side of the window and then print the information.
2. Find information on adding a shortcut to the desktop by completing the following steps:
   a. Select and delete the text *overview* that displays in the *Type in the keyword to find* text box and then type **shortcuts**.
   b. Double-click the subheading *for specific programs* that displays below the *shortcuts* heading.

Step 2a

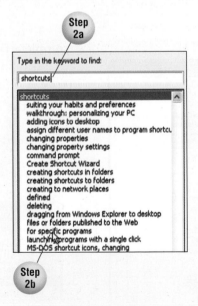

Step 2b

   c. Read the information that displays at the right side of the window and then print the information.
3. Close the Help and Support Center window by clicking the Close button located in the upper right corner of the window.

Customizing Settings

Before beginning computer projects in this textbook, you may need to customize the monitor settings and turn on the display of file extensions. Projects in the chapters in this textbook assume that the monitor display is set to 1024 by 768 pixels and that the display of file extensions is turned on. To change the monitor display to 1024 by 768, complete the following steps:

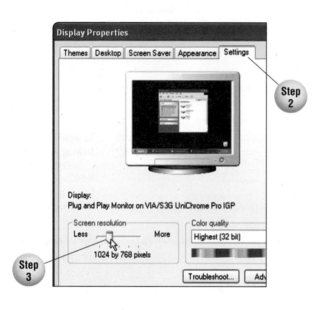

1. At the Windows XP desktop, right-click on any empty location on the desktop and then click *Properties* at the shortcut menu.
2. At the Display Properties dialog box, click the Settings tab.
3. Using the mouse, drag the slide bar button in the *Screen resolution* section to the left or right until *1024 by 768* displays below the slider bar.
4. Click the Apply button.
5. Click the OK button.

To turn on the display of file extensions, complete the following steps:

1. At the Windows XP desktop, click the Start button and then click *My Computer*.
2. At the My Computer window, click Tools on the Menu bar and then click *Folder Options* at the drop-down list.

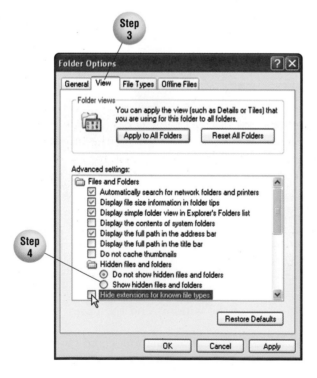

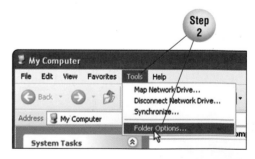

3. At the Folder Options dialog box, click the View tab.
4. Click the *Hide extentions for known file types* check box to remove the check mark.
5. Click the Apply button.
6. Click the OK button.

Browsing the Internet
Using Internet Explorer 7.0

Microsoft Internet Explorer 7.0 is a Web browser program with options and features for displaying sites as well as navigating and searching for information on the Internet. The *Internet* is a network of computers connected around the world. Users access the Internet for several purposes: to communicate using instant messaging and/or e-mail, to subscribe to newsgroups, to transfer files, to socialize with other users around the globe in "chat" rooms, and also to access virtually any kind of information imaginable.

Tutorial IE1
Browsing the Internet with Internet Explorer 7.0
Tutorial IE2
Gathering and Downloading Information and Files

Using the Internet, people can find a phenomenal amount of information for private or public use. To use the Internet, three things are generally required: an Internet Service Provider (ISP), a program to browse the Web (called a *Web browser*), and a *search engine*. In this section, you will learn how to:

- Navigate the Internet using URLs and hyperlinks
- Use search engines to locate information
- Download Web pages and images

Browsing the Internet

You will use the Microsoft Internet Explorer Web browser to locate information on the Internet. Uniform Resource Locators, referred to as URLs, are the method used to identify locations on the Internet. The steps for browsing the Internet vary but generally include: opening Internet Explorer, typing the URL for the desired site, navigating the various pages of the site, navigating to other sites using links, and then closing Internet Explorer.

To launch Internet Explorer 7.0, double-click the *Internet Explorer* icon on the Windows desktop. Figure IE.1 identifies the elements of the Internet Explorer, version 7.0, window. The Web page that displays in your Internet Explorer window may vary from what you see in Figure IE.1.

Figure IE.1 Internet Explorer Window

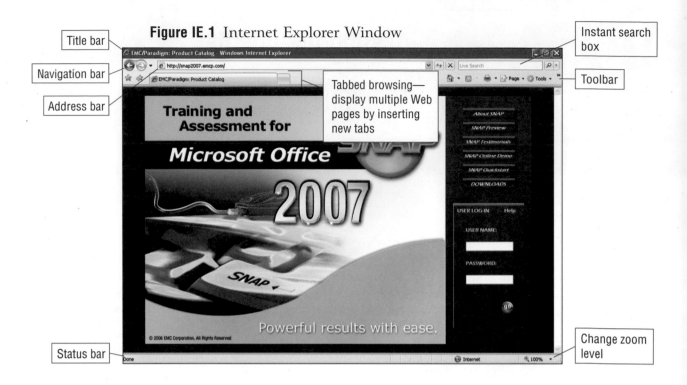

Title bar

Navigation bar

Address bar

Instant search box

Toolbar

Tabbed browsing—display multiple Web pages by inserting new tabs

Status bar

Change zoom level

If you know the URL for the desired Web site, click in the Address bar, type the URL, and then press Enter. The Web site's home page displays in a tab within the Internet Explorer window. URLs (Uniform Resource Locators) are the method used to identify locations on the Internet. The format of a URL is *http://server-name.path*. The first part of the URL, *http*, stands for HyperText Transfer Protocol, which is the protocol or language used to transfer data within the World Wide Web. The colon and slashes separate the protocol from the server name. The server name is the second component of the URL. For example, in the URL http://www.microsoft.com, the server name is *microsoft*. The last part of the URL specifies the domain to which the server belongs. For example, *.com* refers to "commercial" and establishes that the URL is a commercial company. Other examples of domains include *.edu* for "educational," *.gov* for "government," and *.mil* for "military."

Project ① Browsing the Internet Using URLs

1. Make sure you are connected to the Internet through an Internet Service Provider and that the Windows desktop displays. (Check with your instructor to determine if you need to complete steps for accessing the Internet such as typing a user name and password to log on.)
2. Launch Microsoft Internet Explorer by double-clicking the *Internet Explorer* icon located on the Windows desktop.
3. At the Internet Explorer window, explore the Web site for Yosemite National Park by completing the following steps:
   a. Click in the Address bar, type **www.nps.gov/yose**, and then press Enter.

Step 3a

b. Scroll down the home page for Yosemite National Park by clicking the down-pointing arrow on the vertical scroll bar located at the right side of the Internet Explorer window.

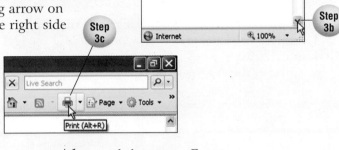

c. Print the home page by clicking the Print button located on the Internet Explorer toolbar.

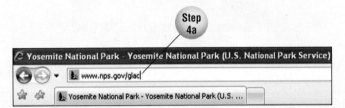

4. Explore the Web site for Glacier National Park by completing the following steps:

a. Click in the Address bar, type **www.nps.gov/glac**, and then press Enter.

Step 4a

	Yosemite National Park - Yosemite National Park (U.S. National Park Service)
⬅️ ➡️ ▾	🔒 www.nps.gov/glac
⭐ ✨	🔒 Yosemite National Park - Yosemite National Park (U.S. ...

b. Print the home page by clicking the Print button located on the Internet Explorer toolbar.

5. Close Internet Explorer by clicking the Close button (contains an X) located in the upper right corner of the Internet Explorer window.

Navigating Using Hyperlinks

Most Web pages contain "hyperlinks" that you click to connect to another page within the Web site or to another site on the Internet. Hyperlinks may display in a Web page as underlined text in a specific color or as images or icons. To use a hyperlink, position the mouse pointer on the desired hyperlink until the mouse pointer turns into a hand, and then click the left mouse button. Use hyperlinks to navigate within and between sites on the Internet. The navigation bar in the Internet Explorer window contains a Back button that, when clicked, takes you to the previous Web page viewed. If you click the Back button and then want to return to the previous page, click the Forward button. You can continue clicking the Back button to back your way out of several linked pages in reverse order since Internet Explorer maintains a history of the Web sites you visit.

Project ②   **Navigating Using Hyperlinks**

1. Make sure you are connected to the Internet and then double-click the *Internet Explorer* icon on the Windows desktop.
2. At the Internet Explorer window, display the White House Web page and navigate in the page by completing the following steps:

a. Click in the Address bar, type **whitehouse.gov**, and then press Enter.

b. At the White House home page, position the mouse pointer on a hyperlink that interests you until the pointer turns into a hand, and then click the left mouse button.

c. At the linked Web page, click the Back button. (This returns you to the White House home page.)

Step 2c

d. At the White House home page, click the Forward button to return to the previous Web page viewed.

e. Print the Web page by clicking the Print button on the Internet Explorer toolbar.

3. Display the Web site for Amazon.com and navigate in the site by completing the following steps:

a. Click in the Address bar, type **www.amazon.com**, and then press Enter.

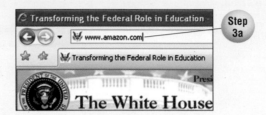

b. At the Amazon.com home page, click a hyperlink related to books.

c. When a book Web page displays, click the Print button on the Internet Explorer toolbar.

4. Close Internet Explorer by clicking the Close button (contains an X) located in the upper right corner of the Internet Explorer window.

Searching for Specific Sites

If you do not know the URL for a specific site or you want to find information on the Internet but do not know what site to visit, complete a search with a search engine. A search engine is a software program created to search quickly and easily for desired information. A variety of search engines are available on the Internet, each offering the opportunity to search for specific information. One method for searching for information is to click in the *Instant Search* box (displays the text *Live Search*) located at the right end of the navigation bar, type a keyword or phrase related to your search, and then click the Search button or press Enter. Another method for completing a search is to visit the Web site for a search engine and use options at the site.

Project **3**   **Searching for Information by Topic**

1. Start Internet Explorer.

2. At the Internet Explorer window, search for sites on bluegrass music by completing the following steps:

a. Click in the *Instant Search* box (may display with *Live Search*) located at the right end of the of the navigation bar.

b. Type **bluegrass music** and then press Enter.

c. When a list of sites displays in the Live Search tab, click a site that interests you.

d. When the page displays, click the Print button.

3. Use the Yahoo! search engine to find sites on bluegrass music by completing the following steps:
   a. Click in the Address bar, type **www.yahoo.com**, and then press Enter.
   b. At the Yahoo! Web site, with the insertion point positioned in the *Search* text box, type **bluegrass music** and then press Enter. (Notice that the sites displayed vary from sites displayed in the earlier search.)

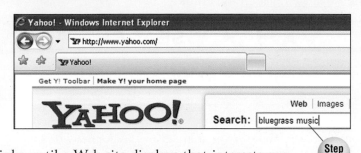

   c. Click hyperlinks until a Web site displays that interests you.
   d. Print the page.
4. Use the Google search engine to find sites on jazz music by completing the following steps:
   a. Click in the Address bar, type **www.google.com**, and then press Enter.
   b. At the Google Web site, with the insertion point positioned in the search text box, type **jazz music** and then press Enter.

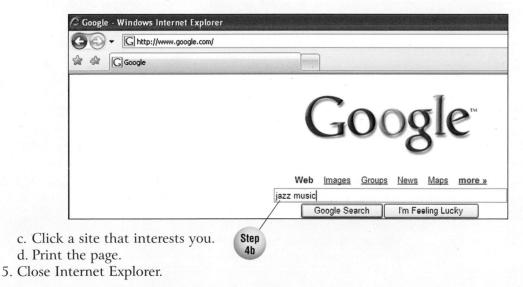

   c. Click a site that interests you.
   d. Print the page.
5. Close Internet Explorer.

Completing Advanced Searches for Specific Sites

The Internet contains an enormous amount of information. Depending on what you are searching for on the Internet and the search engine you use, some searches can result in several thousand "hits" (sites). Wading through a large number of sites can be very time-consuming and counterproductive. Narrowing a search to very specific criteria can greatly reduce the number of hits for a search. To narrow a search, use the advanced search options offered by the search engine.

Web Search

1. Start Internet Explorer.
2. Search for sites on skydiving in Oregon by completing the following steps:
   a. Click in the Address bar and then type **www.yahoo.com**.
   b. At the Yahoo! Web site, click the Web Search button next to the Search text box and then click the <u>Advanced Search</u> hyperlink.

c. At the Advanced Web Search page, click in the search text box next to *all of these words*.
d. Type **skydiving Oregon tandem static line**. (This limits the search to Web pages containing all of the words typed in the search text box.)

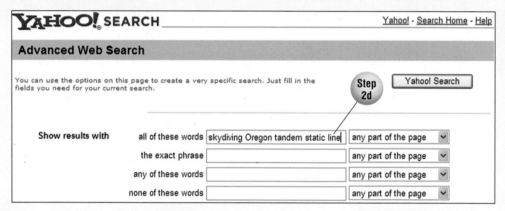

e. Choose any other options at the Advanced Web Search page that will narrow your search.
f. Click the Yahoo! Search button.
g. When the list of Web sites displays, click a hyperlink that interests you.
h. Print the page.
3. Close Internet Explorer.

Downloading Images, Text, and Web Pages from the Internet

The image(s) and/or text that display when you open a Web page as well as the Web page itself can be saved as a separate file. This separate file can be viewed, printed, or inserted in another file. The information you want to save in a separate file is downloaded from the Internet by Internet Explorer and saved in a folder of your choosing with the name you specify. Copyright laws protect much of the information on the Internet. Before using information downloaded from the Internet, check the site for restrictions. If you do use information, make sure you properly cite the source.

Project ⑤ Downloading Images and Web Pages

1. Start Internet Explorer.
2. Download a Web page and image from Banff National Park by completing the following steps:
   a. Search for sites on the Internet for Banff National Park.
   b. From the list of sites that displays, choose a site that contains information about Banff National Park and at least one image of the park.
   c. Save the Web page as a separate file by clicking the Page button on the Internet Explorer toolbar, and then clicking *Save As* at the drop-down list.
   d. At the Save Webpage dialog box, click the down-pointing arrow at the right side of the *Save in* option and then click the drive you are using as your storage medium at the drop-down list.
   e. Select the text in the *File name* text box, type **BanffWebPage**, and then press Enter.

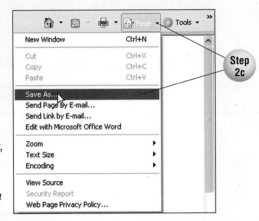

Step 2c

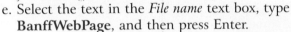

Step 2d

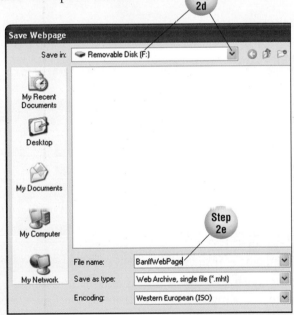

Step 2e

3. Save an image file by completing the following steps:
   a. Right-click an image that displays on the Web site. (The image that displays may vary from what you see below.)
   b. At the shortcut menu that displays, click *Save Picture As*.

Step 3b

c. At the Save Picture dialog box, change the *Save in* option to your storage medium.

d. Select the text in the *File name* text box, type **BanffImage**, and then press Enter.

4. Close Internet Explorer.

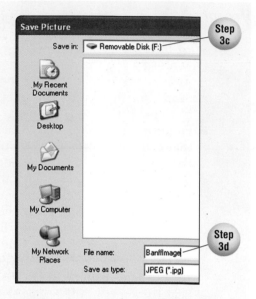

Step 3c

Step 3d

OPTIONAL

Project **Opening the Saved Web Page and Image in a Word Document**

1. Open Microsoft Word by clicking the Start button on the Taskbar, pointing to *All Programs*, pointing to *Microsoft Office*, and then clicking *Microsoft Office Word 2007*.

2. With Microsoft Word open, insert the image in a document by completing the following steps:

   a. Click the Insert tab and then click the Picture button in the Illustrations group.

   b. At the Insert Picture dialog box, change the *Look in* option to the location where you saved the Banff image and then double-click *BanffImage.jpg*.

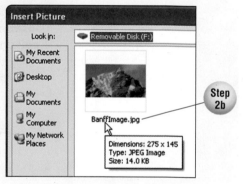

Step 2b

   c. When the image displays in the Word document, print the document by clicking the Print button on the Quick Access toolbar.

   d. Close the document by clicking the Office button and then clicking *Close* at the drop-down menu. At the message asking if you want to save the changes, click No.

3. Open the **BanffWebPage.mht** file by completing the following steps:

   a. Click the Office button and then click *Open* at the drop-down menu.

   b. At the Open dialog box, change the *Look in* option to the location where you saved the Banff Web page and then double-click *BanffWebPage.mht*.

Step 3b

   c. Print the Web page by clicking the Print button on the Quick Access toolbar.

   d. Close the **BanffWebPage.mht** file by clicking the Office button and then *Close*.

4. Close Word by clicking the Close button (contains an X) that displays in the upper right corner of the screen.

Microsoft® access

Making Access Work for You

Each of us interacts with a database more often than we realize. Did you use a bank machine to get some cash today? Did you search the library's catalog for a book that you need? Did you browse an online retail catalog or flip through the pages of a printed catalog? If you did any of these activities, you were accessing and/or updating a database. Any time you look for something by accessing an organized file system you are probably using a database. Microsoft Access is the database management system included with Microsoft Office.

Organizing Information

Information in a database is organized into a collection of *tables* that can be related to each other for purposes of exchanging data. Each table is broken down into a series of columns (called *fields*) and rows (called *records*). If you are familiar with a spreadsheet program such as Excel, you will be comfortable viewing a datasheet in Access. Much thought is put into the design of a database and its tables since all of the data a business collects in a database must

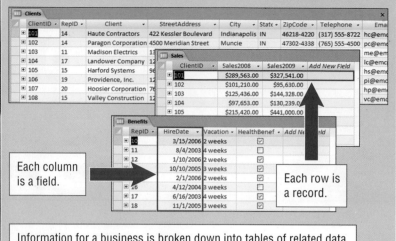

be organized into logical groups. Defining a *relationship* between two tables enables data from more than one table to be shared or exchanged for viewing, updating, or reporting purposes. Access allows for three kinds of relationships that can be created: one-to-one, one-to-many, and many-to-many.

Records within tables can be sorted and filtered numerous ways to allow the data to be reorganized to suit many needs. Sorting by one column and by multiple columns is accomplished with just a few mouse clicks. Temporarily hide records that

Each column is a field.

Each row is a record.

Information for a business is broken down into tables of related data. In this example, Client information is in a separate table from Benefit information and Sales information.

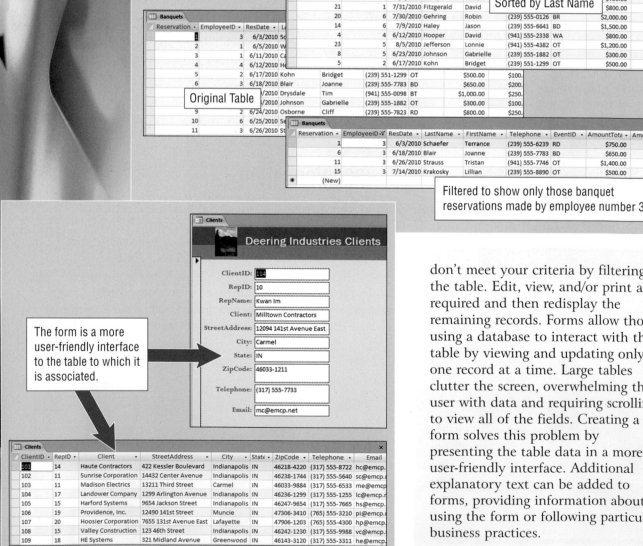

Sorted by Last Name

Original Table

Filtered to show only those banquet reservations made by employee number 3.

The form is a more user-friendly interface to the table to which it is associated.

don't meet your criteria by filtering the table. Edit, view, and/or print as required and then redisplay the remaining records. Forms allow those using a database to interact with the table by viewing and updating only one record at a time. Large tables clutter the screen, overwhelming the user with data and requiring scrolling to view all of the fields. Creating a form solves this problem by presenting the table data in a more user-friendly interface. Additional explanatory text can be added to forms, providing information about using the form or following particular business practices.

Analyzing Information

Databases store a wealth of data that can be extracted in various ways. A *query* is one method for extracting information from tables. A basic query might simply list fields from several tables in one datasheet. This method is shown in the adjacent screen captures, where individual fields from three tables are selected for viewing in one datasheet. In more complex queries, data can be selected for viewing based on meeting a single criterion or multiple criteria, and calculations can be performed on fields.

For more sophisticated analysis, tables can be grouped and then filtered on more than one field. Open a table or query and then switch to PivotTable View or PivotChart View. Access has simplified the task of creating pivot tables and pivot charts by incorporating a drag and drop technique in the view. Interact with the pivot table or pivot chart by clicking one of the filter arrows, selecting or deselecting the items you want to view, and then clicking OK. The data in the view is instantly updated to reflect the new settings.

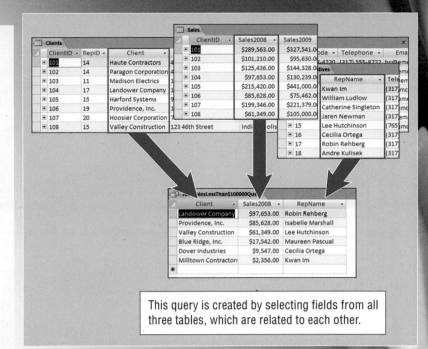

This query is created by selecting fields from all three tables, which are related to each other.

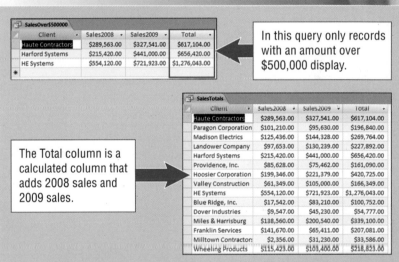

In this query only records with an amount over $500,000 display.

The Total column is a calculated column that adds 2008 sales and 2009 sales.

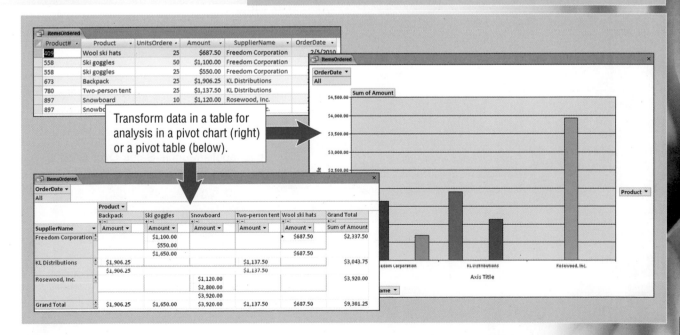

Transform data in a table for analysis in a pivot chart (right) or a pivot table (below).

Presenting Information

Having critical business information stored electronically and the ability to easily extract specific data from the database is a valuable asset to a business. However, there are still times when a printed report is a necessity. Reports in Access are used to create professional-looking, high-quality output. Reports can be grouped and sorted and can include calculations. Access includes the Report Wizard, which can be used to create a report such as the one shown at the left by choosing the table or query for the source data, specifying a group or sort order, and choosing from predefined styles and layouts. Once the report is generated, you can easily modify its design by moving, resizing, adding, or deleting objects, changing the layout or sort order, adding a calculation, applying gridlines, and so on.

Having a well designed database that is easy to update and maintain is a necessity for most businesses. Microsoft Access is a database management system that is easy to learn and use. In just a few pages, you will be exploring the world of databases and learning how to access the technology that drives business success.

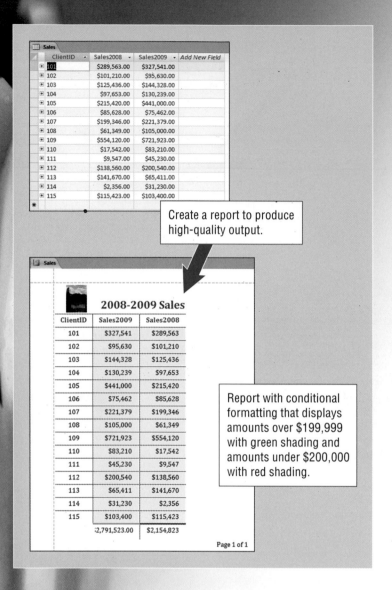

Create a report to produce high-quality output.

Report with conditional formatting that displays amounts over $199,999 with green shading and amounts under $200,000 with red shading.

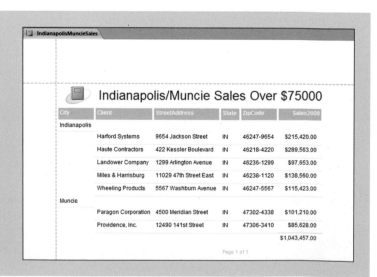

Report created from a query that displays Indianapolis and Muncie sales over $75,000.

Microsoft®

access

Unit 1: Creating Tables and Queries

- ➤ Creating Database Tables
- ➤ Creating Relationships between Tables
- ➤ Modifying and Managing Tables
- ➤ Performing Queries

Benchmark Microsoft® Access 2007 Level 1

Microsoft Certified Application Specialist Skills—Unit 1

Reference No.	Skill	Pages
1	**Structuring a Database**	
1.2	Define and print table relationships	
1.2.1	Create relationships	35-46
1.2.2	Modify relationships	40-50
1.2.3	Print table relationships	43, 46
1.3	Add, set, change, or remove primary keys	
1.3.1	Define and modify primary keys	37-40
2	**Creating and Formatting Database Elements**	
2.1	Create databases	
2.1.2	Create blank databases	8, 13-21
2.2	Create tables	
2.2.1	Create custom tables in Design view	13-21
2.3	Modify tables	
2.3.1	Modify table properties	66-70
2.3.5	Summarize table data by adding a Total row	70-72
2.4	Create fields and modify field properties	
2.4.1	Create commonly used fields	13-19
2.4.2	Modify field properties	70-76
3	**Entering and Modifying Data**	
3.1	Enter, edit, and delete records	26-28, 49-50
3.3	Find and replace data	84-86
4	**Creating and Modifying Queries**	
4.1	Create queries	99-105
4.1.1	Create queries based on single tables	99-105
4.1.2	Create queries based on more than one table	105-128
4.1.4	Create crosstab queries	121-123
4.2	Modify queries	
4.2.4	Create calculated fields in queries	116-118
4.2.6	Create sum, average, min/max, and count queries	118-121
5	**Presenting and Sharing Data**	
5.1	Sort data	
5.1.1	Sort data within tables	80-81
5.1.2	Sort data within queries	108-109
5.6	Print database objects	80-81
6	**Managing and Maintaining Databases**	
6.1	Perform routine database operations	
6.1.2	Back up databases	86-89
6.1.3	Compact and repair databases	87-89
6.2	Manage databases	
6.2.2	Configure database options	11-12

Note: The Level 1 and Level 2 texts each address approximately half of the Microsoft Certified Application Specialist skills. Complete coverage of the skills is offered in the combined Level 1 and Level 2 text titled *Benchmark Series Microsoft® Access 2007: Levels 1 and 2,* which has been approved as certified courseware and which displays the Microsoft Certified Application Specialist logo on the cover.

Creating Database Tables

PERFORMANCE OBJECTIVES

Upon successful completion of Chapter 1, you will be able to:

- **Open and close objects in a database**
- **Design a table**
- **Determine fields and assign data types in a table**
- **Enter data in a table**
- **Open, save, print, and close a table**
- **Add and delete records in a table**

access **Chapter 1**

Tutorial 1.1
Organizing Data in a Database Table

Managing information in a company is an integral part of operating a business. Information can come in a variety of forms, such as data about customers, including names, addresses, and telephone numbers; product data; purchasing and buying data; information on services performed for customers or clients; and much more. Most companies today manage data using a database management system software program. Microsoft Office Professional includes a database management system software program named *Access*. With Access, you can organize, store, maintain, retrieve, sort, and print all types of business data.

As an example of how Access might be used to manage data in an office, suppose a bookstore decides to send a mailer to all customers who have purchased a certain type of book in the past month (such as autobiographies). The bookstore uses Access and maintains data on customers, such as names, addresses, types of books purchased, and types of books ordered. With this data in Access, the manager of the bookstore can easily select those customers who have purchased or ordered autobiographies in the past month and send a mailer announcing a visit by an author who has written a recently-published autobiography. The bookstore could also use the information to determine what types of books have been ordered by customers in the past few months and use this information to determine what inventory to purchase.

Use the information in a database to perform a wide variety of functions. This chapter contains just a few ideas. With a properly designed and maintained database management system, a company can operate smoothly with logical, organized, and useful information. The Access program displays in the Start pop-up menu preceded by a picture of a key. The key symbolizes the importance of managing and maintaining data to a company's survival and success.

Note: Before beginning computer projects, copy to your storage medium the Access 2007L1C1 subfolder from the Access2007L1 folder on the CD that accompanies this textbook. Steps on how to copy a folder are presented on the inside of the back cover of this textbook. Do this every time you start a chapter's projects.

Project ① Explore an Access Database

You will open a database and open and close objects in the database including tables, queries, and forms.

Exploring a Database

A database is comprised of a series of objects such as tables, forms, reports, and queries that you use to enter, manage, view, and print data. Data in a database is organized into tables, which contain information for related items such as customers, employees, orders, and products. To view the various objects in a database, you will open a previously created database and then navigate in the database and open various objects.

To open a previously created database, click the Start button on the Taskbar, point to *All Programs*, point to *Microsoft Office*, and then click *Microsoft Office Access 2007*. (These steps may vary depending on your operating system and/or system configuration.) This displays the *Getting Started with Microsoft Office Access* screen shown in Figure 1.1. This screen is divided into three sections. Use the *Template Categories* section at the left to preview and download database templates. Start a new database by clicking the Blank Database button in the *New Blank Database* section and open an existing database by clicking a database name in the *Open Recent Database* section.

Opening and Closing a Database

HINT

Only one database can be open at a time.

Office button

To open a database, click the file name located in the *Open Recent Database* section of the *Getting Started with Microsoft Office Access* screen or click the Office button and then click *Open* at the drop-down list. At the Open dialog box, navigate to the desired folder and then double-click the desired database name in the list box. When you open a database, the Access screen displays as shown in Figure 1.2. Refer to Table 1.1 for a description of the Access screen elements. To close a database, click the Office button and then click *Close Database* at the drop-down list. To exit Access, click the Close button that displays in the upper right corner of the screen, or click the Office button and then click the Exit Access button that displays in the lower right corner of the drop-down list.

Figure 1.1 Getting Started with Microsoft Office Access Screen

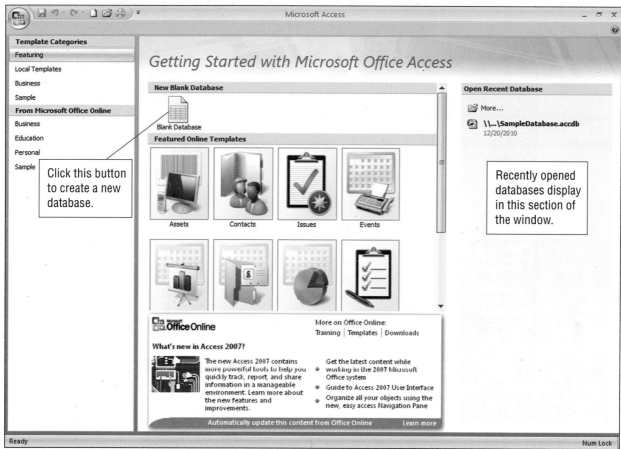

Table 1.1 Access Screen Elements

Feature	Description
Office button	Displays as a Microsoft Office logo and, when clicked, displays a list of options along with the most recently opened databases
Quick Access toolbar	Contains buttons for commonly-used commands
Title bar	Displays database name followed by program name
Tabs	Contains commands and features organized into groups
Ribbon	Area containing the tabs and commands divided into groups
Message bar	Displays security alerts if the database you open contains potentially unsafe content
Navigation pane	Displays names of objects within database grouped by categories
Work area	Area in screen where opened objects display
Status bar	Displays number of pages and words, View buttons, and the Zoom slider bar

Figure 1.2 Access Screen

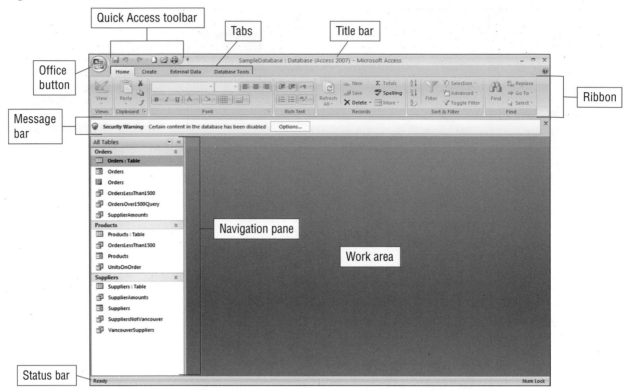

Security features in Access 2007 cause a message bar to display a security alert message below the ribbon. This message displays when you open an Access 2007 database outside of a trusted location (a list of drives and folder names stored in the Trust Center dialog box). If you know that the database is virus-free, click the Options button in the Message bar. At the Microsoft Office Security Options dialog box that displays, click the *Enable this content* option and then click OK. The Message bar closes when you identify the database as a trusted source.

The Navigation pane at the left side of the Access screen displays the objects that are contained in the database. Some common objects found in a database include tables, forms, reports, and queries. Refer to Table 1.2 for a description of these four types of objects.

Table 1.2 Database Objects

Object	Description
Table	Organizes data in fields (columns) and rows (records). A database must contain at least one table. The table is the base upon which other objects are created.
Query	Used to display data from a table or related tables that meets a conditional statement and/or to perform calculations. For example, display only those records in which the city is Vancouver.
Form	Allows fields and records to be presented in a different layout than the datasheet. Used to facilitate data entry and maintenance.
Report	Prints data from tables or queries.

Opening and Closing Objects

Database objects display in the Navigation pane. Control what displays in the pane by clicking the Menu bar at the top of the Navigation pane and then clicking the desired option at the drop-down list. For example, to display a list of all saved objects in the database, click the *Object Type* option at the drop-down list. This view displays the objects grouped by type—Tables, Queries, Forms, and Reports. To open an object, double-click the object in the Navigation pane. The object opens in the work area and a tab displays with the object name at the left side of the object.

To view more of an object, consider closing the Navigation pane by clicking the Shutter Bar Open/Close button located in the upper right corner of the pane. Click the button again to open the Navigation pane.

You can open more than one object in the work area. Each object opens with a visible tab. You can navigate to objects by clicking the object tab. To close an object, click the Close button that displays at the right side of the work area.

HINT

Hide the Navigation pane by clicking the button in the upper right corner of the pane (called the Shutter Bar Open/Close Button) or by pressing F11.

Close Object

Project ① Opening and Closing a Database and Objects

1. Open Access by clicking the Start button on the Taskbar, pointing to *All Programs*, pointing to *Microsoft Office*, and then clicking *Microsoft Office Access 2007*. (These steps may vary.)
2. At the Getting Started with Microsoft Office Access screen, click the Office button and then click *Open* at the drop-down list.
3. At the Open dialog box, navigate to the Access2007L1C1 folder on your storage medium and then double-click the database *SampleDatabase.accdb*.
4. Click the Options button in the Message bar.
5. At the Microsoft Office Security Options dialog box, click *Enable this content* and then click OK.
6. Click the Navigation pane Menu bar and then click *Object Type* at the drop-down list. (This option displays the objects grouped by type—Tables, Queries, Forms, and Reports.)
7. Double-click *Suppliers* in the *Tables* section of the Navigation pane. This opens the Suppliers table in the work area as shown in Figure 1.3. The fields in the table display in the top row of the table and some of the field names are not completely visible.
8. Close the Suppliers table by clicking the Close button in the upper right corner of the work area.
9. Double-click *OrdersLessThan1500* in the *Queries* section of the Navigation pane. A query displays data that meets a conditional statement and this query displays orders that meet the criterion of being less than $1,500.

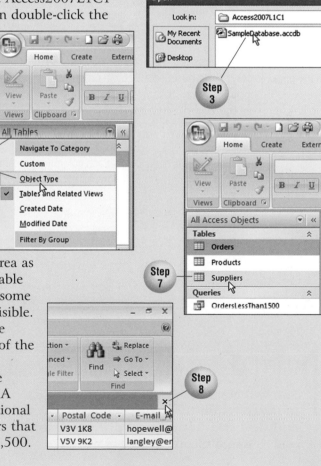

10. Close the query by clicking the Close button in the upper right corner of the work area.
11. Double-click the *SuppliersNotVancouver* query in the Navigation pane and notice that the query displays information about suppliers that are not located in Vancouver.
12. Click the Close button in the work area.
13. Double-click *Orders* in the *Forms* section of the Navigation pane. This displays an order form. A form is used to view and edit data in a table one record at a time.
14. Click the Close button in the work area.
15. Double-click *Orders* in the *Reports* section of the Navigation pane. This displays a report with information about orders and order amounts.
16. Close the Navigation pane by clicking the Shutter Bar Open/Close Button located in the upper right corner of the pane.
17. After viewing the report, click the button again to open the Navigation pane.
18. Click the Close button in the work area.
19. Close the database by clicking the Office button and then clicking *Close Database* at the drop-down list.
20. Exit Access by clicking the Close button (contains an X) that displays in the upper right corner of the screen.

Figure 1.3 Open Suppliers Table

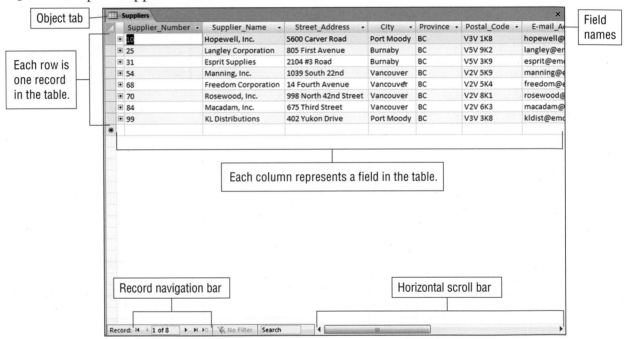

Object tab

Each row is one record in the table.

Field names

Each column represents a field in the table.

Record navigation bar

Horizontal scroll bar

Supplier_Number	Supplier_Name	Street_Address	City	Province	Postal_Code	E-mail_A
10	Hopewell, Inc.	5600 Carver Road	Port Moody	BC	V3V 1K8	hopewell@
25	Langley Corporation	805 First Avenue	Burnaby	BC	V5V 9K2	langley@er
31	Esprit Supplies	2104 #3 Road	Burnaby	BC	V5V 3K9	esprit@em
54	Manning, Inc.	1039 South 22nd	Vancouver	BC	V2V 5K9	manning@e
68	Freedom Corporation	14 Fourth Avenue	Vancouver	BC	V2V 5K4	freedom@e
70	Rosewood, Inc.	998 North 42nd Street	Vancouver	BC	V2V 8K1	rosewood@
84	Macadam, Inc.	675 Third Street	Vancouver	BC	V2V 6K3	macadam@
99	KL Distributions	402 Yukon Drive	Port Moody	BC	V3V 3K8	kldist@em

Project ② Create and Maintain Tables

You will create tables for a Premium database by determining the field names and data types and then entering records in the tables. You will change the page layout and field widths and then print the tables; you will also maintain tables by adding and deleting records.

Organizing Data in a Table

Data is not very useful to a company if it is not organized in a logical manner. Organizing data in a manageable and logical manner allows the data to be found and used for a variety of purposes. As mentioned earlier, the information in a database is organized into tables. A table contains information for related items such as customers, suppliers, inventory, or human resources broken down into individual units of information. Creating a new table generally involves determining fields, assigning a data type to each field, modifying properties, designating the primary key, and naming the table. This process is referred to as defining the table structure.

Determining Fields

Microsoft Access is a database management system software program that allows you to design, create, input, maintain, manipulate, sort, and print data. Access is considered a relational database in which you organize data in related tables. In this chapter, you will be creating tables as part of a database, and learn how to relate tables in Chapter 2.

The first step in creating a table is to determine the fields. A field is one piece of information about a person, a place, or an item. For example, one field could be a customer's name, another field could be a customer's address, and another a customer number. All fields for one unit, such as a customer, are considered a record. For example, in Project 2a, a record is all of the information pertaining to one employee of Premium Health Services. A collection of records becomes a table.

When designing a table, determine fields for information to be included on the basis of how you plan to use the data. When organizing fields, be sure to consider not only current needs for the data but also any future needs. For example, a company may need to keep track of customer names, addresses, and telephone numbers for current mailing lists. In the future, the company may want to promote a new product to customers who purchase a specific type of product. For this situation, a field that identifies product type must be included in the database. When organizing fields, consider all potential needs for the data but also try to keep the fields logical and manageable.

After deciding what data you want included in a table, you need to determine field names. Consider the following guidelines when naming fields in a table:

- Each field must contain a unique name.
- The name should describe the contents of the field.
- A field name can contain up to 64 characters.
- A field name can contain letters, numbers, spaces, and symbols except the period (.), comma (,), exclamation point (!), square brackets ([]), and grave accent (`).
- A field name cannot begin with a space.

In Project 2a, you will create a table containing information on employees of a medical corporation. The fields in this table and the names you will give to each field are shown in Figure 1.4.

Figure 1.4 Field Information and Names for Project 2a

Employee Information	Field Name
ID number	*Emp#*
Last name	*LastName*
First name	*FirstName*
Middle initial	*MI*
Street address	*StreetAddress*
City	*City*
State	*State*
ZIP code	*ZipCode*
Department code	*DeptCode*
Date of hire	*HireDate*
Supplemental health insurance	*Yes/No*

Assigning a Data Type to Fields

HINT
Assign a data type for each field that determines the values that can be entered for the field.

Part of the process of designing a table includes specifying or assigning a data type to each field. The data type specifies the type of data you can enter in a field. Assigning a data type to fields helps maintain and manage the data and helps identify for anyone entering information in the field what type of data is expected. The data types you will use in fields in this chapter include *Text*, *Date/Time*, and *Yes/No*.

Assign the Text data type to a field where text will be entered such as names, addresses, and numbers that do not require calculations, such as telephone numbers, Social Security numbers, and ZIP codes. You can store up to 255 characters in the text data field with 255 as the default. Assign the Date/Time data type to a field where a date and/or time will be entered. You will assign the data types and field sizes shown in Figure 1.5 when you create a table in Project 2a.

Figure 1.5 Data Types for Project 2a

Field Name	Data Type
Emp#	Text (Field Size = 5)
LastName	Text (Field Size = 30)
FirstName	Text (Field Size = 30)
MI	Text (Field Size = 2)
StreetAddress	Text (Field Size = 30)
City	Text (Field Size = 20)
State	Text (Field Size = 2)
ZipCode	Text (Field Size = 5)
DeptCode	Text (Field Size = 2)
HireDate	Date/Time
SuppIns	Yes/No

Data entered for some fields in Project 2a, such as *ZipCode,* will be numbers. These numbers, however, are not values and will not be used in calculations. This is why they are assigned the data type of Text (rather than Number or Currency).

When assigning a field size, consider the data that will be entered in the field, and then shorten or lengthen (up to the maximum number) the number to accommodate any possible entries. For the *FirstName* field or the *LastName* field, for example, shortening the number to 30 would be appropriate, ensuring that all names would fit in the field. The two-letter state abbreviation will be used in the *State* field, so the number of characters is changed to 2.

Creating a Table

When you create a new blank database, the database opens and a blank table displays in the work area in Datasheet view. Datasheet view is used primarily for entering data. To specify fields and identify data types for your table, you need to change to Design view. To do this, click the View button that displays in the Views group in the Home tab or the Table Tools Datasheet tab. Before switching to Design view, you must save the table. At the Save As dialog box, type a name for the table and then press Enter or click OK and the table displays in Design view as shown in Figure 1.6.

Create a Table
1. Click Create tab.
2. Click Table button.
3. Click View button.
4. Type name for table.
5. Press Enter or click OK.
6. Type field names, specify types, and include descriptions.

Figure 1.6 Table in Design View

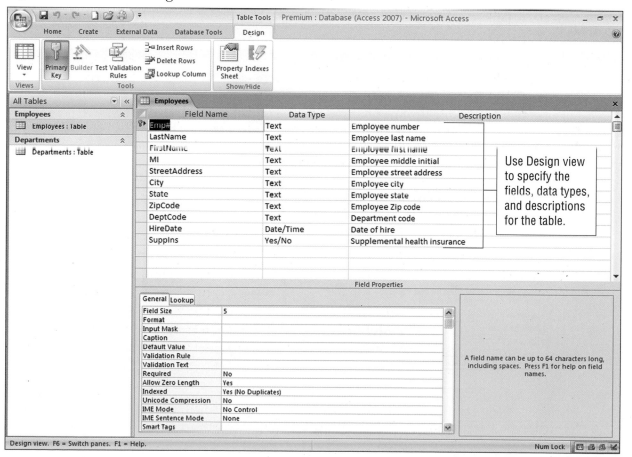

Save

By default, Access provides the *ID* field as the first field in the record and assigns the AutoNumber data type to the field. You can use the *ID* field or type your own field name. Accept the *ID* field name or type a new name and then press the Tab key. This moves the insertion point to the *Data Type* column. In this column, accept the data type or click the down-pointing arrow at the right side of the data type text and then click the desired data type at the drop-down list. Press the Tab key to move the insertion point to the *Description* column and then type a description for the field that specifies what should be entered in the field. Continue typing field names, assigning a data type to each field, and typing a description of all fields. When the table design is complete, save the table by clicking the Save button on the Quick Access toolbar or by clicking the Office button and then clicking *Save* at the drop-down list. Click the View button in the Views group in the Table Tools Design tab to switch to Datasheet view and enter records or click the Close button in the work area to close the table.

At the Table window shown in Figure 1.6, field names are entered, data types are assigned, and descriptions are typed. When assigning a data type, Access displays information in the bottom portion of the window in a section with the General tab selected. Information in this section can be changed to customize a data type for a field. For example, you can specify that only a maximum of two characters can be entered in the *MI* field.

A database can contain more than one table. Tables containing related data are saved in the same database. In Project 2a, you will create a table named Employees that is part of the database named Premium. In Project 2b, you will create another table as part of the Premium database that includes payroll information.

Project 2a Creating an Employee Table

1. Open Access by clicking the Start button on the Taskbar, pointing to *All Programs*, pointing to *Microsoft Office*, and then clicking *Microsoft Office Access 2007*. (These steps may vary.)
2. At the Getting Started with Microsoft Office Access screen, click the Blank Database button in the *New Blank Database* section.
3. Click the folder icon located at the right side of the *File Name* text box in the *Blank Database* section.

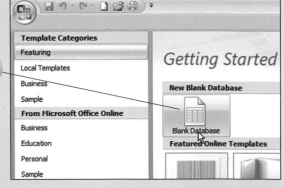

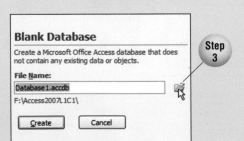

4. At the File New Database dialog box, navigate to the drive where your storage medium is located, type **Premium** in the *File name* text box, and then press Enter.

5. At the Getting Started with Microsoft Office Access screen, click the Create button located below the *File Name* text box in the *Blank Database* section.
6. At the Database window, change to Design view by clicking the View button in the Views group in the Home tab.

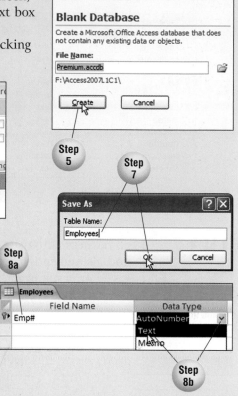

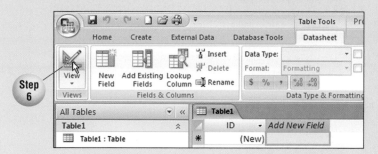

7. At the Save As dialog box, type **Employees** in the *Table Name* text box and then click OK.
8. In the table, type the fields shown in Figure 1.7 by completing the following steps:
   a. Type **Emp#** in the *Field Name* text box and then press the Tab key.
   b. Change the *Data Type* to *Text* by clicking the down-pointing arrow located in the *Data Type* box and then clicking *Text* at the drop-down list.
   c. Change the field size from the default of 255 to 5. To do this, select *255* that displays after *Field Size* in the *Field Properties* section of the window and then type 5.

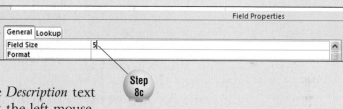

   d. Position the I-beam pointer in the *Description* text box (for the *Emp#*) and then click the left mouse button. Type **Employee number** in the *Description* text box and then press Tab.
   e. Type **LastName** in the *Field Name* text box and then press Tab.
   f. Change the field size to 30 and then click in the *Description* text box for the *LastName* field. Type **Employee last name** and then press Tab.
   g. Type **FirstName** in the *Field Name* text box and then press Tab.
   h. Change the field size to 30 and then click in the *Description* text box for the *FirstName* field. Type **Employee first name** and then press Tab.
   i. Continue typing the field names, data types, and descriptions as shown in Figure 1.7. Identify the following sizes: *MI = 2, StreetAddress = 30, City = 20, State = 2, ZipCode = 5,* and *DeptCode = 2.* (Refer to Figure 1.5.) To change the data type for the *HireDate* field, click the down-pointing arrow after *Text* and then click *Date/Time* at the drop-down list. To change the data type for the *SuppIns* field, click the down-pointing arrow after *Text* and then click *Yes/No* at the drop-down list.
9. When all of the fields are entered, save the table by clicking the Save button on the Quick Access toolbar.
10. Close the Employees table by clicking the Close button located at the upper right corner of the datasheet.

Figure 1.7 Project 2a

Field Name	Data Type	Description
🔑 Emp#	Text	Employee number
LastName	Text	Employee last name
FirstName	Text	Employee first name
MI	Text	Employee middle initial
StreetAddress	Text	Employee street address
City	Text	Employee city
State	Text	Employee state
ZipCode	Text	Employee Zip code
DeptCode	Text	Department code
HireDate	Date/Time	Date of hire
SuppIns	Yes/No	Supplemental health insurance

Employees

HINT

The active database is saved automatically on a periodic basis and also when you make another record active, close the table, or close the database.

✕ E**x**it Access

Access automatically saves an open (or active) database on a periodic basis and also when the database is closed. If you are working with a database that is saved on a removable storage medium, never remove the storage medium while the database is open because Access saves the database periodically. If the storage medium is not available when Access tries to save it, problems will be encountered and you run the risk of damaging the database. Exit (close) Access by clicking the Close button located in the upper right corner of the Access Title bar (contains an *X*) or by clicking the Office button and then clicking the Exit Access button located in the bottom right corner of the drop-down list.

The Employees table contains a *DeptCode* field. This field will contain a two-letter code identifying the department within the company. In Project 2b, you will create a table named Departments containing only two fields—the department code and the department name. Establishing a department code decreases the amount of data entered in the Employees table. For example, in an employee record, you type a two-letter code identifying the employee department rather than typing the entire department name. Imagine the time this saves when entering hundreds of employee records. This is an example of the power of a relational database.

Project 2b Creating a Department Table

1. At the Premium : Database window, create a new table in Design view. To do this, click the Create tab and then click the Table button in the Tables group.
2. At the Table1 window, click the View button in the Views group.
3. At the Save As dialog box, type **Departments** and then press Enter.
4. Type the fields shown in Figure 1.8 by completing the following steps:
   a. Type **DeptCode** in the *Field Name* text box and then press Tab.
   b. Click the down-pointing arrow after *AutoNumber* and then click *Text*.
   c. Change the field size to 2 and then click in the *Description* text box for the *DeptCode* field.
   d. Type **Department code** in the *Description* text box and then press the Tab key.

e. Type **Department** in the *Field Name* text box and then press Tab.

f. Change the field size to 30 and then click in the *Description* text box for the *Department* field.

g. Type **Department name** in the *Description* text box.

5. When all of the fields are entered, click the Save button on the Quick Access toolbar.

6. Close the Departments table by clicking the Close button located in the upper right corner of the table.

Figure 1.8 Project 2b

Field Name	Data Type	Description
DeptCode	Text	Department code
Department	Text	Department name

Departments ×

Entering Data in a Table

Enter data in a table in a database in Datasheet view. A table datasheet displays the contents of a table in rows and columns in the same manner as a Word table or Excel worksheet. Each row in a datasheet represents one record. In the Employees table of the Premium database, one record will contain the information for one employee.

When you type data for the first field in the record, another row of cells is automatically inserted below the first row. Type the data for the first record, pressing Tab to move the insertion point to the next field or pressing Shift + Tab to move the insertion point to the previous field. The description you typed for each field when creating the table displays at the left side of the Access Status bar.

If you assigned the Yes/No data type to a field, a square displays in the field. You can leave this square empty or insert a check mark. If the field is asking a yes/no question, an empty box signifies "No" and a box with a check mark signifies "Yes." If the field is asking for a true/false answer, an empty box signifies "False" and a box with a check mark signifies "True." This field can also have an on/off response. An empty box signifies "Off" and a box with a check mark signifies "On." To insert a check mark in the box, tab to the field and then press the spacebar.

As you enter data in fields, the description you typed for each field displays at the left side of the Status bar. The descriptions help identify to the person entering data in the table what data is expected.

QUICK STEPS

Enter Data in a Table
1. Open database.
2. Double-click table name.
3. Make sure table displays in Datasheet view.
4. Type data in fields.

Project **2c** **Entering Data in the Employees and the Departments Tables**

1. At the Premium : Database window, double-click *Employees : Table* in the Navigation pane.
2. At the Employees window, type the following data for five records in the specified fields. (Press Tab to move the insertion point to the next field or press Shift + Tab to move the insertion point to the previous field. When typing data, not all of the data may be visible. You will adjust column widths in a later project. For the *SuppIns* field, press the spacebar to insert a check mark indicating "Yes" and leave the check box blank indicating "No.")

Emp#	=	21043
LastName	=	Brown
FirstName	=	Leland
MI	=	C.
StreetAddress	=	112 Kansas Avenue
City	=	Missoula
State	=	MT
ZipCode	=	84311
DeptCode	=	PA
HireDate	=	11/5/2007
SuppIns	=	*Yes (Insert a check mark)*

Emp#	=	19034
LastName	=	Guenther
FirstName	=	Julia
MI	=	A.
StreetAddress	=	215 Bridge West
City	=	Lolo
State	=	MT
ZipCode	=	86308
DeptCode	=	MS
HireDate	=	2/15/2005
SuppIns	=	*No (Leave blank)*

Emp#	=	27845
LastName	=	Oaklee
FirstName	=	Thomas
MI	=	E.
StreetAddress	=	2310 Keating Road
City	=	Missoula
State	=	MT
ZipCode	=	84325
DeptCode	=	HR
HireDate	=	6/8/2009
SuppIns	=	*No (Leave blank)*

| *Emp#* | = | 08921 |
| *LastName* | = | Avery |

Step 1

```
FirstName      =   Michael
MI             =   W.
StreetAddress  =   23155 Neadham Avenue
City           =   Florence
State          =   MT
ZipCode        =   85901
DeptCode       =   PA
HireDate       =   11/5/2006
SuppIns        =   Yes (Insert a check mark)

Emp#           =   30091
LastName       =   Latora
FirstName      =   Gina
MI             =   M.
StreetAddress  =   13221 138th Street
City           =   Missoula
State          =   MT
ZipCode        =   84302
DeptCode       =   HR
HireDate       =   9/16/2010
SuppIns        =   No (Leave blank)
```

3. After typing the data, save the table by clicking the Save button on the Quick Access toolbar.
4. Close the Employees table by clicking the Close button located in the upper right corner of the work area.
5. At the Premium : Database window, double-click *Departments : Table* in the Navigation pane.
6. At the Departments window, type the following data for four departments in the specified fields (press Tab to move the insertion point to the next field or press Shift + Tab to move the insertion point to the previous field):

Step
5

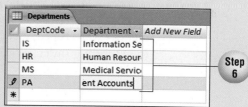

Step
6

```
DeptCode         =   IS
DepartmentName   =   Information Services

DeptCode         =   HR
DepartmentName   =   Human Resources

DeptCode         =   MS
DepartmentName   =   Medical Services

DeptCode         =   PA
DepartmentName   =   Patient Accounts
```

7. After typing the data, save the table by clicking the Save button on the Quick Access toolbar.
8. Close the Departments table by clicking the Close button located in the upper right corner of the table in the work area.

Printing a Table

Print a Table
1. Open database.
2. Open table.
3. Click Quick Print button.

Quick Print

Customize Quick
Access Toolbar

Various methods are available for printing data in a table. One method for printing is to open the table and then click the Quick Print button on the Quick Access toolbar. If the Quick Print button is not visible on the Quick Access toolbar, click the Customize Quick Access Toolbar button that displays at the right side of the toolbar and then click *Quick Print* at the drop-down list.

When you click the Quick Print button, the information is sent directly to the printer without any formatting changes. In some fields created in the Employees table, this means that you would not be able to see all printed text in a field if all of the text did not fit in the field. For example, when typing the data in Project 2c, did you notice that the *StreetAddress* data was longer than the field column could accommodate? You can change the table layout to ensure that all data is visible. You will first print the Employees and Departments tables with the default settings, learn about changing the layout, and then print the tables again.

Project 2d Printing the Employees and Departments Tables with the Default Settings

1. Open the Employees table.
2. Click the Quick Print button on the Quick Access toolbar. (The table will print on two pages.)
3. Close the Employees table.
4. Open the Departments table.
5. Click the Quick Print button on the Quick Access toolbar.
6. Close the Departments table.

Look at the printing of the Employees table and notice how the order of records displays differently in the printing (and in the table) than the order in which the records were typed. Access automatically sorted the records by employee number in ascending order. Access automatically sorted the records in the Departments table alphabetically by department name. You will learn more about sorting later in this chapter.

Previewing a Table

Preview a Table
1. Click Office button.
2. Point to *Print*.
3. Click *Print Preview*.

Before printing a table, you may want to display the table in Print Preview to determine how the table will print on the page. To display a table in Print Preview, click the Office button, point to *Print*, and then click *Print Preview*. This displays the table as it will appear when printed as well as the Print Preview tab as shown in Figure 1.9.

Figure 1.9 Print Preview

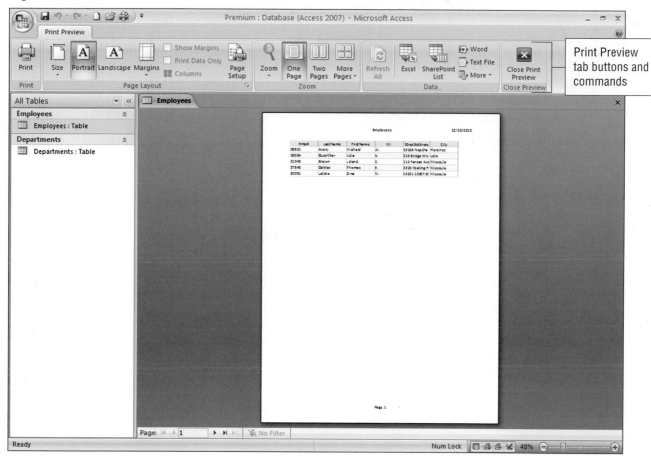

Changing Page Layout

The Employees table printed on two pages in portrait orientation with default margins. You can change page orientation and page margins with options in the Page Layout group in Print Preview. By default, Access prints a table in standard page size that is 8.5 inches wide and 11 inches tall. Click the Size button in the Page Layout group and a drop-down list displays with options for changing the page size to legal size, executive size, envelope size, and so on.

Access prints a page in Portrait orientation by default. At this orientation, the page is 8.5 inches wide and 11 inches tall. You can change this orientation to landscape, which makes the page 11 inches wide and 8.5 inches tall. The orientation buttons are located in the Page Layout group. Access uses default top, bottom, left, and right margins of 1 inch. Change these default margins by clicking the Margins button in the Page Layout group and then clicking one of the predesigned margin options.

You can also change page layout with options at the Page Setup dialog box shown in Figure 1.10. To display this dialog box, click the Page Setup button in the Page Layout group. You can also display the dialog box by clicking the Page Layout group dialog box launcher.

Display Page Setup Dialog Box
1. Click Office button, *Print, Print Preview.*
2. Click Page Setup button.
OR
1. Click Office button, *Print, Print Preview.*
2. Click Page Layout group dialog box launcher.

Size

Margins

Page Setup

Figure 1.10 Page Setup Dialog Box with Print Options Tab Selected

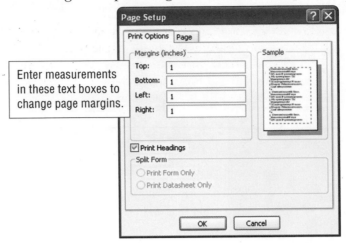

Enter measurements in these text boxes to change page margins.

At the Page Setup dialog box with the Print Options tab selected, notice that the default margins are 1 inch. Change these defaults by typing a different number in the desired margin text box. By default, the table name prints at the top center of the page. For example, when you printed the Employees table, *Employees* printed at the top of the page along with the current date (printed at the right side of the page). *Page 1* also printed at the bottom of the page. If you do not want the name of the table and the date as well as the page number printed, remove the check mark from the *Print Headings* option at the Page Setup dialog box with the Print Options tab selected.

Change the table orientation at the Page Setup dialog box with the Page tab selected as shown in Figure 1.11. To change to landscape orientation, click *Landscape*. You can also change the paper size with options in the *Paper* section of the dialog box and specify the printer with options in the *Printer for (table name)* section of the dialog box.

Figure 1.11 Page Setup Dialog Box with Page Tab Selected

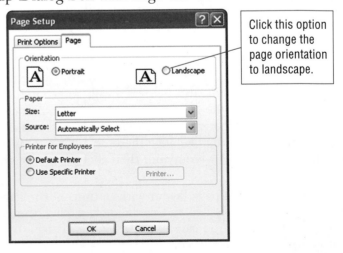

Click this option to change the page orientation to landscape.

Changing Field Width

In the printing of the Employees table, not all of the data is visible in the *StreetAddress* field. You can remedy this situation by changing the width of the fields. Automatically adjust one field (column) in a table to accommodate the longest entry in the field by positioning the arrow pointer on the column boundary at the right side of the column until it turns into a double-headed arrow pointing left and right with a line between and then double-clicking the left mouse button. Automatically adjust adjacent columns by selecting the columns first and then double-clicking on a column boundary.

Project 2e Changing Page Layout and Printing the Employees Table

1. Open the Employees table.
2. Display the table in Print Preview by clicking the Office button, pointing to *Print*, and then clicking *Print Preview*.
3. Change the page orientation by clicking the Landscape button in the Page Layout group in the Print Preview tab.
4. Change margins by completing the following steps:
   a. Click the Page Setup button in the Page Layout group in the Print Preview tab.
   b. At the Page Setup dialog box with the Print Options tab selected, select *1* in the *Top* text box and then type **2**.
   c. Select *1* in the *Left* text box and then type **0.5**.
   d. Select *1* in the *Right* text box and then type **0.5**.
   e. Click OK to close the dialog box.
5. Click the Close Print Preview button.
6. Automatically adjust columns in the table to accommodate the longest entry by completing the following steps:
   a. Position the arrow pointer on the *Emp#* field name (the arrow pointer turns into a down-pointing black arrow).
   b. Hold down the left mouse button, drag the arrow pointer to the *ZipCode* field name, and then release the mouse button.

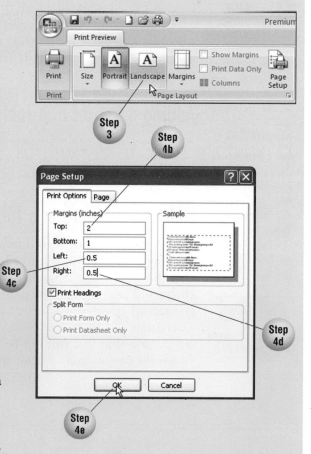

c. Position the arrow pointer on one of the column boundaries until it turns into a double-headed arrow pointing left and right with a line between and then double-click the left mouse button.

d. Click in any entry in the *ZipCode* column.

e. Drag the scroll box on the horizontal scroll bar to the right so the remaining fields (*DeptCode*, *HireDate*, and *SuppIns*) are visible.

f. Position the arrow pointer on the *DepCode* field name until the pointer turns into a down-pointing black arrow.

g. Hold down the left mouse button and then drag to the *SuppIns* field.

h. Double-click a column boundary between two of the selected columns.

i. Drag the scroll box to the left on the horizontal scroll bar so the *Emp#* field name displays.

j. Click in any entry in the *Emp#* field.

7. Send the table to the printer by clicking the Quick Print button on the Quick Access toolbar.

	Step 6c

Emp#	LastName	FirstName
08921	Avery	Michael
19034	Guenther	Julia
21043	Brown	Leland
27845	Oaklee	Thomas
30091	Latora	Gina
*		

QUICK STEPS

Add a Record to a Table
1. Open table in Datasheet view.
2. Click New button in Records group.
OR
1. Open table in Datasheet view.
2. Press Ctrl + Shift + +.

Delete a Record from a Table
1. Open table in Datasheet view.
2. Click Delete button arrow in Records group.
3. Click *Delete Record* at drop-down list.
4. Click Yes.

Maintaining a Table

Once a table is created, more than likely it will require maintenance. For example, newly hired employees will need to be added to the Employees table. A system may be established for deleting an employee record when an employee leaves the company. The type of maintenance required on a table is related to the type of data stored in the table.

Adding a Record to a Table

Add a new record to an existing table by clicking the New button in the Records group in the Home tab or with the keyboard shortcut Ctrl + Shift + +. Type the data in the appropriate fields in the new record.

Deleting a Record in a Table

To delete an existing record in a table, select the row containing the record by clicking in the record selector bar. The record selector bar is the light blue area that displays at the left side of a record. When the mouse pointer is positioned in the record selector bar, the pointer turns into a black, right-pointing arrow. With the record selected, click the Delete button arrow in the Records group in the Home tab and then click *Delete Record* at the drop-down list. A message displays telling you that you will not be able to undo the delete operation and asking if you want to continue. At this message, click Yes.

Project **2f**   Adding and Deleting Records in the Employees Table

1. With the Employees table open, add two new records to the table by completing the
   following steps:
   a. With the Home tab selected, click the New button in the Records group.

Step 1a

   b. Type the following data in the specified fields:
Emp#	=	30020
LastName	=	Pang
FirstName	=	Eric
MI	=	R.
StreetAddress	=	15512 Country Drive
City	=	Lolo
State	=	MT
ZipCode	=	86308
DeptCode	=	IS
HireDate	=	8/15/2009
SuppIns	=	*Yes (Insert a check mark)*
   c. Click the New button in the Records group (or just press the Tab key).
   d. Type the following data in the specified fields:
Emp#	=	30023
LastName	=	Zajac
FirstName	=	Elizabeth
MI	=	A.
StreetAddress	=	423 Corrin Avenue
City	=	Missoula
State	=	MT
ZipCode	=	84325
DeptCode	=	HR
HireDate	=	8/15/2007
SuppIns	=	*Yes (Insert a check mark)*

2. Delete a record in the table by completing the following steps:
   a. Select the row containing the record for Julia Guenther by clicking in the record selector
      bar that displays at the left side of the record. (When the mouse pointer is positioned in
      the record selector bar it turns into a black, right-pointing arrow.)

b. Click the Delete button arrow in the Records group and then click *Delete Record* at the drop-down list.

c. At the message telling you that you will not be able to undo the delete operation and asking if you want to continue, click Yes.
3. Click the Save button again on the Quick Access toolbar to save the Employees table.
4. Print the Employees table by completing the following steps:
   a. Click the Office button, point to *Print*, and then click *Print Preview*.
   b. In Print Preview, click the Landscape button in the Page Layout group.
   c. Click the Margins button in the Page Layout group and then click *Normal* at the drop-down list.
   d. Click the Print button at the left side of the Print Preview tab.
   e. Click OK at the Print dialog box.
5. Click the Close Print Preview button.
6. Save and then close the Employees table.
7. Close the **Premium.accdb** database.

CHAPTER summary

- Microsoft Access is a database management system software program that will organize, store, maintain, retrieve, sort, and print all types of business data.

- Open a database by double-clicking the file name in the *Open Recent Database* section of the Getting Started with Microsoft Office Access screen. You can also open a database by double-clicking the desired database at the Open dialog box. Display this dialog box by clicking the Open button on the Quick Access toolbar or clicking the Microsoft Office button and then clicking *Open* at the drop-down list.

- Organize data in Access in related tables in a database.

- The first step in organizing data for a table is determining fields. A field is one piece of information about a person, place, or item. All fields for one unit, such as an employee or customer, are considered a record.

- A field name should be unique and describe the contents of the field. It can contain up to 64 characters including letters, numbers, spaces, and some symbols.

- Part of the process of designing a table is assigning a data type to each field, which helps maintain and manage data and helps identify what type of data is expected for the field.

- When assigning a data type, you can assign a specific field size to a field.

- Access automatically saves a database on a periodic basis and also when the database is closed.

- Enter data in a table in Datasheet view. Type data in a field, pressing the Tab key to move to the next field or pressing Shift + Tab to move to the previous field.

- Print a table by opening the table and then clicking the Quick Print button on the Quick Access toolbar.

- Change margins in a table with the Margins button in the Page Layout group in the Print Preview tab or with options at the Page Setup dialog box with the Print Options tab selected.

- Change the paper size with the Size button in the Page Layout group in the Print Preview tab or with the *Size* option at the Page Setup dialog box with the Page tab selected.

- Click the Landscape button in the Page Layout group in the Print Preview tab to change the page orientation or with options in the *Orientation* section of the Page Layout dialog box with the Page tab selected.

- Adjust field widths in a table in the same manner as column widths in an Excel worksheet. Double-click a column boundary to automatically adjust the width to accommodate the longest entry.

- Maintaining a table can include adding and/or deleting records.

COMMANDS review

FEATURE	RIBBON TAB, GROUP	BUTTON	QUICK ACCESS TOOLBAR	OFFICE BUTTON DROP-DOWN LIST	KEYBOARD SHORTCUT
Open dialog box			📂	Open	Ctrl + O
Close database				Close Database	
Design view	Home, Views	✏️ OR 📐			
Datasheet view	Home, Views	▦ OR ▤			
Save database			💾	Save	Ctrl + S
Save As dialog box				Save As	
Print table			🖨️		
Print Preview				Print, Print Preview	
Portrait orientation	Print Preview, Page Layout	A			
Landscape orientation	Print Preview, Page Layout	A			
Page Setup dialog box	Print Preview, Page Layout	▣			
Margins	Print Preview, Page Layout	▢			
Add record	Home, Records	New			Ctrl + Shift + +
Delete record	Home, Records	✕ Delete ▾			

CONCEPTS check

Test Your Knowledge

Completion: For each description, indicate the correct term, symbol, or number.

1. This toolbar contains buttons for commonly used commands. — *Quick Access toolbar*

2. This displays the names of objects within a database grouped by categories. — *Navigation Pane*

3. All fields for one unit, such as an employee or customer, are considered to be this.

Record

4. In a field assigned the Yes/No data type, a check mark in the box in the field asking a yes/no question signifies this.

Yes

5. This view is used in a table to define field names and assign data types.

Design

6. Use this view to enter data in fields.

Data Sheet

7. Change to landscape orientation by clicking the Landscape button in this group in the Print Preview tab.

Page Layout

8. Add a new record to a table in this view.

Data Sheet

9. The Delete button is located in this group in the Home tab.

Records

10. Click this to select the row.

Record Selector Bar

SKILLS check
Demonstrate Your Proficiency

Assessment

1 CREATE AN ORDERS TABLE IN A HEALTHPLUS DATABASE

1. Use Access to create a database for a store that sells vitamins and other health aids. The table you create will keep track of what vitamins are ordered for the store. (This table assumes that the database includes at least two other tables— one table containing information on suppliers and the other containing information on products. You will learn more about how tables are related in Chapter 2.) Use the name of the store, HealthPlus, as the database name, and name the table *Orders*. Create the following fields in the Orders table and assign the data type shown (you determine the Description):

Field Name		Data Type
OrderNumber	=	Text (field size = 3)
ProductCode	=	Text (field size = 2)
SupplierNumber	=	Text (field size = 2)
DateOfOrder	=	Date/Time
AmountOfOrder	=	Currency

2. Save the table.
3. Change to Datasheet view and then enter the following data:

OrderNumber	=	214
ProductCode	=	MT
SupplierNumber	=	10
DateOfOrder	=	4/5/2010
AmountOfOrder	=	$875.50

OrderNumber	=	223
ProductCode	=	PA
SupplierNumber	=	27
DateOfOrder	=	4/6/2010
AmountOfOrder	=	$1,005.45

OrderNumber	=	241
ProductCode	=	GS
SupplierNumber	=	10
DateOfOrder	=	4/8/2010
AmountOfOrder	=	$441.95

OrderNumber	=	259
ProductCode	=	AV
SupplierNumber	=	18
DateOfOrder	=	4/8/2010
AmountOfOrder	=	$772.00

4. Automatically adjust the width of fields.
5. Save, print, and then close the Orders table.

Assessment

2 ADD RECORDS TO THE ORDERS TABLE

1. With the **HealthPlus.accdb** database open, open the Orders table and then add the following records (remember to do this in Datasheet view):

OrderNumber	=	262
ProductCode	=	BC
SupplierNumber	=	27
DateOfOrder	=	4/9/2010
AmountOfOrder	=	$258.65

OrderNumber	=	265
ProductCode	=	VC
SupplierNumber	=	18
DateOfOrder	=	4/13/2010
AmountOfOrder	=	$1,103.45

2. Delete the record for order number 241.
3. Print the table with a top margin of 2 inches.
4. Close the Orders table.

Assessment

3 CREATE A SUPPLIERS TABLE

1. With the **HealthPlus.accdb** database open, create a new table named Suppliers with the following fields and assign the data type shown (you determine the Description):

Field Name		**Data Type**
SupplierNumber	=	Text (field size = 2)
SupplierName	=	Text (field size = 20)
StreetAddress	=	Text (field size = 30)
City	=	Text (field size = 20)
State	=	Text (field size = 2)
ZipCode	=	Text (field size = 10)

2. After creating and saving the table with the fields shown above, enter the following data in the table (remember to do this in Datasheet view):

SupplierNumber	=	10
SupplierName	=	VitaHealth, Inc.
StreetAddress	=	12110 South 23rd
City	=	San Diego
State	=	CA
ZipCode	=	97432-1567

SupplierNumber	=	18
SupplierName	=	Mainstream Supplies
StreetAddress	=	312 Evergreen Building
City	=	Seattle
State	=	WA
ZipCode	=	98220-2791

SupplierNumber	=	21
SupplierName	=	LaVerde Products
StreetAddress	=	121 Vista Road
City	=	Phoenix
State	=	AZ
ZipCode	=	86355-6014

SupplierNumber	=	27
SupplierName	=	Redding Corporation
StreetAddress	=	554 Ninth Street
City	=	Portland
State	=	OR
ZipCode	=	97466-3359

3. Automatically adjust the width of fields.
4. Save the Suppliers table.
5. Change the page orientation to landscape and then print the table.
6. Close the Suppliers table.
7. Close the **HealthPlus.accdb** database.

CASE study
Apply Your Skills

Part 1

You are the manager of Miles Music, a small music store that specializes in CDs, DVDs, and Laserdiscs. Recently, the small store has increased its volume of merchandise, requiring better organization and easier retrieval of information. You decide to create a database named *MilesMusic* that contains two tables. Name one table *Inventory* and include fields that identify the category of music, the name of the CD or DVD, the name of the performer or band, and the media type (such as CD or DVD). Create a second table named *Category* that includes a short abbreviation for a category (such as R for Rap, A for Alternative, and C for Country). When entering records in the Inventory table, enter the category abbreviation you established in the Category table (rather than the entire category name). Enter at least eight records in the Inventory table and identify at least five categories of music. Print the Inventory and Category tables.

Part 2

As part of the maintenance of the database, you need to delete and add records as items are sold or orders are received. Delete two records from the Inventory table and then add three additional records. Print the Inventory table and then close the **MilesMusic.accdb** database.

Part 3

In Microsoft Word, create a document that describes the tables you created in the **MilesMusic.accdb** database. In the document, specify the fields in each table, the data types assigned to each field, and the field size (if appropriate). Apply any formatting to the document to enhance the visual appeal and then save the document and name it **Access_C1_CS_P3**. Print and then close **Access_C1_CS_P3.docx**.

Creating Relationships between Tables

PERFORMANCE OBJECTIVES

Upon successful completion of Chapter 2, you will be able to:

- Create a database table with a primary key and a foreign key
- Create a one-to-many relationship between tables
- Create a one-to-one relationship between tables
- Display related records in a subdatasheet

Tutorial 2.1
Working with Tables and
Relationships

Access is a relational database program that allows you to create tables that have a relation or connection to each other within the same database. In Chapter 1, you created a table containing information on employees and another containing department information. With Access, you can connect these tables through a common field that appears in both tables.

In this chapter you will learn how to identify a primary key field in a table that is unique to that table. In Access, data can be divided into logical groupings in tables for easier manipulation and management. Duplicate information is generally minimized in tables in the same database. A link or relationship, however, should connect the tables. In this chapter, you will define primary keys and define relationships between tables.

Note: Before beginning computer projects, copy the Access2007L1C2 subfolder from the Access2007L1 folder on the CD that accompanies this textbook to your storage medium and make Access2007L1C2 the active folder.

Project **1** Establish Relationships between Tables

You will specify primary keys in tables, establish one-to-many and one-to-one relationships between tables, specify referential integrity, and print the relationships. You will also edit and delete a relationship and display records in a datasheet.

Creating Related Tables

Generally, a database management system fits into one of two categories—either a file management system (also sometimes referred to as a *flat file database*) or a relational database management system. In a file management system, data is stored without indexing and sequential processing. This type of system lacks flexibility in manipulating data and requires the same data to be stored in more than one place.

In a relational database management system, like Access, relationships are defined between sets of data allowing greater flexibility in manipulating data and eliminating data redundancy (entering the same data in more than one place). In projects in this chapter, you will define relationships between tables in the insurance company database. Because these tables will be related, information on a client does not need to be repeated in a table on claims filed. If you used a file management system to maintain insurance records, you would need to repeat the client information for each claim filed.

Determining Relationships

Taking time to plan a database is extremely important. Creating a database with related tables takes even more consideration. You need to determine how to break down the required data and what tables to create to eliminate redundancies. One idea to help you determine the necessary tables in a database is to think of the word "about." For example, an insurance company database will probably need a table "about" clients, another "about" the type of coverage, another "about" claims, and so on. A table should be about only one subject, such as a client, customer, department, or supplier.

Figure 2.1 SouthwestInsurance.accdb Tables

Clients table	**Insurance table**
ClientNumber	LicenseNumber
Client	ClientNumber
StreetAddress	InsuranceCode
City	UninsuredMotorist
State	
ZipCode	

Claims table	**Coverage table**
ClaimNumber	InsuranceCode
ClientNumber	TypeOfInsurance
LicenseNumber	
DateOfClaim	
AmountOfClaim	

Along with deciding on the necessary tables for a database, you also need to determine the relationship between tables. The ability to relate, or "join," tables is part of what makes Access a relational database system. Figure 2.1 illustrates the tables and fields that either are or will become part of the SouthwestInsurance.accdb database. Notice how each table is about only one subject—clients, type of insurance, claims, or coverage.

Some fields such as *ClientNumber*, *LicenseNumber*, and *InsuranceCode* appear in more than one table. These fields are used to create a relationship between tables. For example, in Project 1b you will create a relationship between the Clients table and the Insurance table with the *ClientNumber* field.

Creating relationships between tables tells Access how to bring the information in the database back together again. With relationships defined, you can bring information together to create queries, forms, and reports. (You will learn about these features in future chapters.)

HINT

Access uses a primary key to associate data from multiple tables.

Creating a Primary Field

Before creating a relationship between tables, you need to define the primary key in a table. In a table, at least one field must be unique so that one record can be distinguished from another. A field (or several fields) with a unique value is considered a ***primary key***. When a primary key is defined, Access will not allow duplicate values in the primary field. For example, the *ClientNumber* field in the Clients table must contain a unique number (you would not assign the same client number to two different clients). If you define this as the primary key field, Access will not allow you to type the same client number in two different records.

In a field specified as a primary key, Access expects a value in each record in the table. This is referred to as ***entity integrity***. If a value is not entered in a field, Access actually enters a null value. A null value cannot be given to a primary key field. Access will not let you close a database containing a primary field with a null value.

To define a field as a primary key, open the table and then change to Design view. Position the insertion point somewhere in the row containing the field you want to identify as the primary key and then click the Primary Key button in the Tools group. An image of a key is inserted at the beginning of the row identified as the primary key field. To define more than one field as a primary key, select the rows containing the fields you want as primary keys and then click the Primary Key button in the Tools group.

Specify a Primary Key
1. Open table in Design view.
2. Click desired field.
3. Click Primary Key button.
4. Click Save button.

HINT

You must enter a value in the primary key field in every record.

Primary Key

Creating a Foreign Key

A primary key field in one table may be a foreign key in another. For example, if you define the *ClientNumber* field in the Clients table as the primary key, the *ClientNumber* field in the Insurance table will then be considered a ***foreign key***. The primary key field and the foreign key field form a relationship between the two tables. In the Clients table, each entry in the *ClientNumber* field will be unique (it is the primary key), but the same client number may appear more than once in the *ClientNumber* field in the Insurance table (such as a situation where a client has insurance on more than one vehicle). Each table in Figure 2.1 contains a unique field that will be defined as the primary key. Figure 2.2 identifies the primary keys and also foreign keys.

Figure 2.2 Primary and Foreign Keys

Clients table
ClientNumber *(primary key)*
Client
StreetAddress
City
State
ZipCode

Insurance table
LicenseNumber *(primary key)*
ClientNumber *(foreign key)*
InsuranceCode *(foreign key)*
UninsuredMotorist

Claims table
ClaimNumber *(primary key)*
ClientNumber *(foreign key)*
LicenseNumber *(foreign key)*
DateOfClaim
AmountOfClaim

Coverage table
InsuranceCode *(primary key)*
TypeOfInsurance

In Project 1a, you will create another table for the SouthwestInsurance.accdb database, enter data, and then define primary keys for the tables. In the section following Project 1a, you will learn how to create relationships between the tables.

Project 1a   Creating a Table and Defining Primary Keys

1. Display the Open dialog box and make the Access2007L1C2 folder on your storage medium the active folder.
2. Open the **SouthwestInsurance.accdb** database.
3. At the SouthwestInsurance : Database window, create a new table by completing the following steps:
   a. Click the Create tab.
   b. Click the Table button in the Tables group.
   c. At the Table window, click the View button in the Views group in the Table Tools Datasheet tab.
   d. At the Save As dialog box, type Insurance in the *Table Name* text box and then press Enter or click OK.
   e. Type the fields, assign the data types, and type the descriptions as shown below (for assistance, refer to Chapter 1, Project 1a):

Field Name	Data Type	Description
LicenseNumber	Text (Field Size = 7)	Vehicle license number
ClientNumber	Text (Field Size = 4)	Client number
InsuranceCode	Text (Field Size = 1)	Insurance code
UninsuredMotorist	Yes/No	Uninsured motorist coverage

4. Click the Save button on the Quick Access toolbar.
5. Notice the key that displays at the left side of the *LicenseNumber* field identifying the field as a primary key.
6. Close the Insurance table by clicking the Close button located in the upper right corner of the window.

7. Define primary keys for the other tables in the database by completing the following steps:
   a. At the SouthwestInsurance : Database window, double-click *Claims* in the Navigation pane.
   b. With the Claims table open, click the View button to switch to Design view.
   c. Click anywhere in the text *ClaimNumber* and then click the Primary Key button in the Tools group.

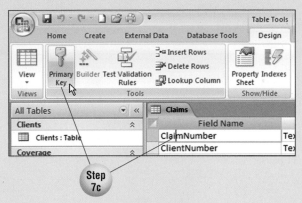

Step 7c

   d. Click the Save button on the Quick Access toolbar.
   e. Close the Claims table.
   f. At the SouthwestInsurance : Database window, double-click *Clients* in the Navigation pane.
   g. With the Clients table open, click the View button to switch to Design view.
   h. Click anywhere in the text *ClientNumber* and then click the Primary Key button in the Tools group.

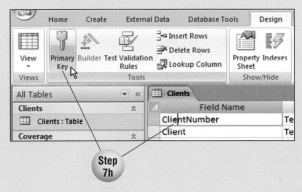

Step 7h

   i. Click the Save button on the Quick Access toolbar.
   j. Close the Clients table.
   k. At the SouthwestInsurance : Database window, double-click *Coverage* in the Navigation pane.
   l. With the Coverage table open, click the View button to switch to Design view.
   m. Click anywhere in the text *InsuranceCode* and then click the Primary Key button in the Tools group.

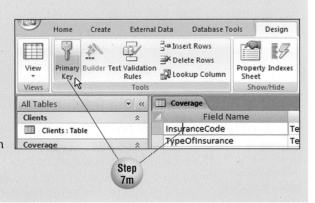

Step 7m

n. Click the Save button on the Quick Access toolbar.

o. Close the Coverage table.

8. Open the Insurance table and then type the following data in the specified fields. (If the *Uninsured Motorist* field is Yes, insert a check mark in the field by pressing the spacebar. If the field is No, leave the check box blank.)

LicenseNumber	=	341 VIT
ClientNumber	=	3120
InsuranceCode	=	F
UninsuredMotorist	=	Yes

LicenseNumber	=	776 ERU
ClientNumber	=	9383
InsuranceCode	=	F
UninsuredMotorist	=	No

LicenseNumber	=	984 CWS
ClientNumber	=	7335
InsuranceCode	=	L
UninsuredMotorist	=	Yes

LicenseNumber	=	877 BNN
ClientNumber	=	4300
InsuranceCode	=	L
UninsuredMotorist	=	Yes

LicenseNumber	=	310 YTV
ClientNumber	=	3120
InsuranceCode	=	F
UninsuredMotorist	=	Yes

Insurance

LicenseNum ▾	ClientNumb ▾	InsuranceCo ▾	UninsuredM ▾	Add New Field
341 VIT	3120	F	☑	
776 ERU	9383	F	☐	
984 CWS	7335	L	☑	
877 BNN	4300	L	☑	
310 YTV	3120	F	☑	
*			☐	

Step 8

9. Save and then close the Insurance table.

HINT

Defining a relationship between tables is one of the most powerful features of a relational database management system.

Establishing a Relationship between Tables

In Access, one table can be related to another, which is generally referred to as performing a *join*. When tables with a common field are joined, data can be extracted from both tables as if they were one large table. Another reason for relating tables is to ensure the integrity of the data. For example, in Project 1b, you will create a relationship between the Clients table and the Claims table. The relationship that is established will ensure that a client cannot be entered in the Claims table without first being entered in the Clients table. This ensures that a claim is not processed on a person who is not a client of the insurance company. This type of relationship is called a one-to-many relationship, which means that one record in the Clients table will match zero, one, or many records in the Claims table.

In a one-to-many relationship, the table containing the "one" is referred to as the *primary table* and the table containing the "many" is referred to as the *related table*. Access follows a set of rules known as *referential integrity*, which enforces consistency between related tables. These rules are enforced when data is updated in related tables. The referential integrity rules ensure that a record added to a related table has a matching record in the primary table.

HINT
Use the Table Analyzer Wizard to analyze your tables and restructure them to better conform to relational theory. Start the wizard by clicking the Database Tools tab and then clicking the Analyze Table button.

Creating a One-to-Many Relationship

A relationship is specified between existing tables in a database. To create a one-to-many relationship, open the database containing the tables to be related. Click the Database Tools tab and then click the Relationships button in the Show/Hide group. This displays the Show Table dialog box, as shown in Figure 2.3. At the Show Table dialog box, each table that will be related must be added to the Relationships window. To do this, click the first table name to be included and then click Add. Continue in this manner until all necessary table names have been added to the Relationships window and then click the Close button.

Figure 2.3 Show Table Dialog Box

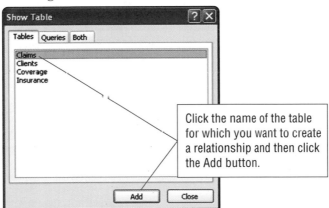

Click the name of the table for which you want to create a relationship and then click the Add button.

At the Relationships window, such as the one shown in Figure 2.4, use the mouse to drag the common field from the primary table (the "one") to the related table (the "many"). This causes the Edit Relationships dialog box to display as shown in Figure 2.5. At the Edit Relationships dialog box, check to make sure the correct field name displays in the *Table/Query* and *Related Table/Query* list boxes and the relationship type at the bottom of the dialog box displays as *One-To-Many*.

Figure 2.4 Relationships Window

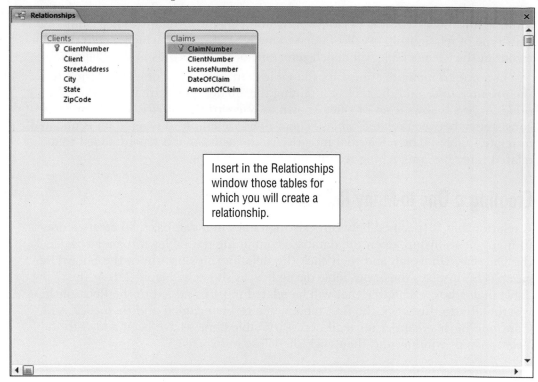

Insert in the Relationships window those tables for which you will create a relationship.

Figure 2.5 Edit Relationships Dialog Box

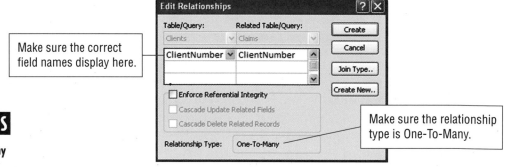

Make sure the correct field names display here.

Make sure the relationship type is One-To-Many.

QUICK STEPS

Create a One-to-Many Relationship
1. Click Database Tools tab.
2. Click Relationships button.
3. At Show Table dialog box, add tables to be related.
4. At Relationships window, drag "one" field from primary table to "many" field in related table.
5. At Edit Relationships dialog box, enforce referential integrity.
6. Click Create button.
7. Click Save button.

Specify the relationship options by choosing *Enforce Referential Integrity*, as well as *Cascade Update Related Fields* and/or *Cascade Delete Related Records*. Click the Create button. This causes the Edit Relationships dialog box to close and the Relationships window to display showing the relationship between the tables.

In Figure 2.6, the Clients table displays with a black line attached along with the number *1* (signifying the "one" side of the relationship). The black line is connected to the Claims table along with the infinity symbol ∞ (signifying the "many" side of the relationship). The black line, called the ***join line***, is thick at both ends if the enforce referential integrity option has been chosen. If this option is not chosen, the line is thin at both ends. Click the Save button on the Quick Access toolbar to save the relationship. Close the Relationships window by clicking the Close button located in the upper right corner of the window.

Figure 2.6 One-to-Many Relationship

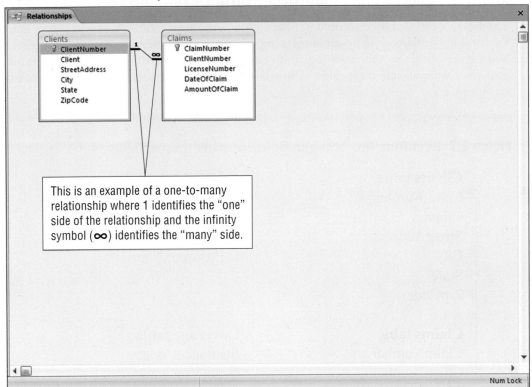

This is an example of a one-to-many relationship where 1 identifies the "one" side of the relationship and the infinity symbol (∞) identifies the "many" side.

Specifying Referential Integrity

Choose *Enforce Referential Integrity* at the Edit Relationships dialog box to ensure that the relationships between records in related tables are valid. Referential integrity can be set if the field from the primary table is a primary key and the related fields have the same data type. When referential integrity is established, a value for the primary key must first be entered in the primary table before it can be entered in the related table.

If you select only *Enforce Referential Integrity* and the related table contains a record, you will not be able to change a primary key value in the primary table. You will not be able to delete a record in the primary table if its key value equals a foreign key value in the related table. If you choose *Cascade Update Related Fields*, you will be able to change a primary key value in the primary table and Access will automatically update the matching value in the related table. Choose *Cascade Delete Related Records* and you will be able to delete a record in the primary table and Access will delete any related records in the related table.

Printing Relationships

You can print a report displaying the relationships between tables. To do this, display the Relationships window and then click the Relationship Report button in the Tools group. This displays the Relationships report in Print Preview. Click the Print button in the Print group in the Print Preview tab. After printing the relationships report, click the Close button that displays at the right side of the Relationships window.

HINT
Referential integrity ensures that a record exists in the "one" table before the record can be entered in the "many" table.

QUICK STEPS

Print Database Relationships
1. Click Database Tools tab.
2. Click Relationships button.
3. Click Relationships Report button.
4. Click Print button.
5. Click OK at Print dialog box.
6. Click Close button.

 Relationship Report

Print

Relating Tables in the SouthwestInsurance Database

The SouthwestInsurance.accdb database contains the four tables shown in Figure 2.1. Each table contains data about something—clients, insurance, claims, and coverage. You can relate these tables so that data can be extracted from more than one table as if they were all one large table. The relationships between the tables are identified in Figure 2.7.

Figure 2.7 Relationships between SouthwestInsurance Tables

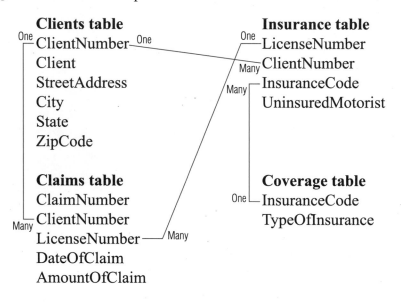

Relate the tables shown in Figure 2.7 so you can extract information from more than one table. For example, you can design a report about claims that contains information on claims as well as information on the clients submitting the claims.

Project 1b   Creating a One-to-Many Relationship between the Client and Claims Tables

1. With the **SouthwestInsurance.accdb** database open, click the Database Tools tab and then click the Relationships button in the Show/Hide group.

2. At the Show Table dialog box, add the Clients and Claims tables to the Relationships window by completing the following steps:
   a. Click *Clients* in the list box and then click Add.
   b. Click *Claims* in the list box and then click Add.
3. Click the Close button to close the Show Table dialog box.
4. At the Relationships window, drag the *ClientNumber* field from the Clients table to the Claims table by completing the following steps:
   a. Position the arrow pointer on the *ClientNumber* field that displays in the Clients table.
   b. Hold down the left mouse button, drag the arrow pointer (with a field icon attached) to the *ClientNumber* field in the *Claims* table, and then release the mouse button. (This causes the Edit Relationships dialog box to display.)

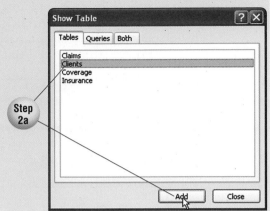

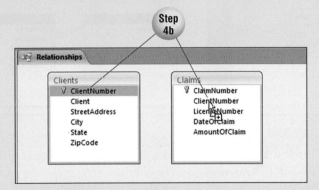

5. At the Edit Relationships dialog box, make sure *ClientNumber* displays in the *Table/Query* and *Related Table/Query* list boxes and the relationship type at the bottom of the dialog box displays as *One-To-Many*.
6. Enforce the referential integrity of the relationship by completing the following steps:
   a. Click *Enforce Referential Integrity*. (This makes the other two options available.)
   b. Click *Cascade Update Related Fields*.
   c. Click *Cascade Delete Related Records*.
7. Click the Create button. (This causes the Edit Relationships dialog box to close and the Relationships window to display showing a thick black line connecting Clients to Claims. At the Clients side, a *1* will appear and an infinity symbol ∞ will display at the Claims side of the thick black line.)

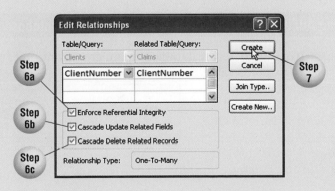

8. Click the Save button on the Quick Access toolbar to save the relationship.
9. Print the relationships by completing the following steps:
   a. At the Relationships window, click the Relationship Report button in the Tools group. (This displays the Relationships report in Print Preview.)
   b. Click the Print button in the Print group.

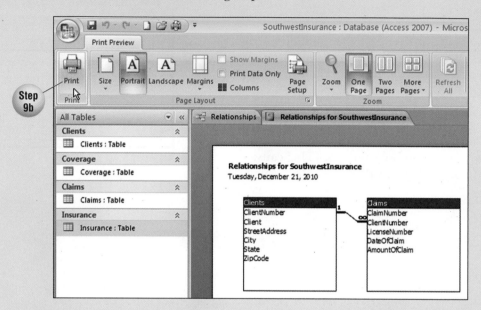

c. Click OK at the Print dialog box.
d. Click the Close button that displays at the right side of the Relationships window.
e. At the message asking if you want to save changes to the design of the report, click No.
10. Close the Relationships window by clicking the Close button that displays at the right side of the Relationships window.

Once a relationship has been established between tables, clicking the Relationships button causes the Relationships window to display (rather than the Show Table dialog box). To create additional relationships, click the Database Tools tab, click the Relationships button in the Show/Hide group, and then click the Show Table button in the Relationships group. This displays the Show Table dialog box where you can specify the tables you need for creating another relationship.

Project 1c Creating Additional One-to-Many Relationships in a Database

1. With the **SouthwestInsurance.accdb** database open, create another one-to-many relationship between the Clients table and the Insurance table. Begin by clicking the Database Tools tab.
2. Click the Relationships button in the Show/Hide group.
3. At the Relationships window, click the Show Table button in the Relationships group.

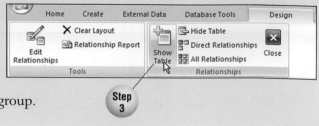

4. At the Show Table dialog box, click *Insurance* in the list box, and then click the Add button. (You do not need to add the Clients table because it was added in Project 1b.)
5. Click the Close button to close the Show Table dialog box.
6. At the Relationships window, drag the *ClientNumber* field from the Clients table to the Insurance table by completing the following steps:
   a. Position the arrow pointer on the *ClientNumber* field that displays in the Clients table.
   b. Hold down the left mouse button, drag the arrow pointer (with a field icon attached) to the *ClientNumber* field in the Insurance table, and then release the mouse button. (This causes the Edit Relationships dialog box to display.)

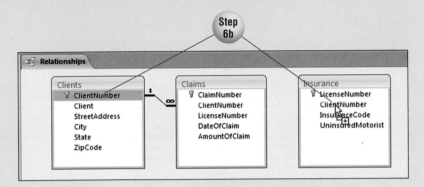

7. At the Edit Relationships dialog box, make sure *ClientNumber* displays in the *Table/Query* and *Related Table/Query* list boxes and the relationship type at the bottom of the dialog box displays as *One-To-Many*.
8. Enforce the referential integrity of the relationship by completing the following steps:
   a. Click *Enforce Referential Integrity*. (This makes the other two options available.)
   b. Click *Cascade Update Related Fields*.
   c. Click *Cascade Delete Related Records*.
9. Click the Create button. (This causes the Edit Relationships dialog box to close and the Relationships window to display showing a thick black line connecting Clients to Insurance. At the Clients side, a *1* will appear and an infinity symbol ∞ will display at the Insurance side of the thick black line.)

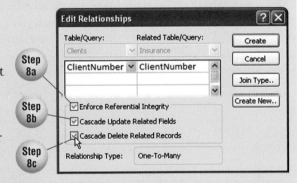

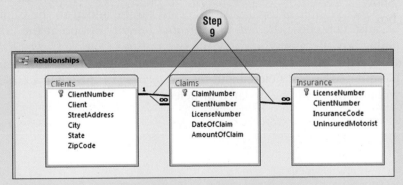

10. Click the Save button on the Quick Access toolbar to save the relationship.

11. With the Relationships window still open, create the following one-to-many relationships by completing steps similar to those in Steps 3 through 10:

   a. Create a relationship between *LicenseNumber* in the Insurance table and the Claims table. (*LicenseNumber* in the Insurance table is the "one" and *LicenseNumber* in the Claims table is the "many.") At the Edit Relationships dialog box, be sure to choose *Enforce Referential Integrity*, *Cascade Update Related Fields*, and *Cascade Delete Related Records*.

   b. Add the Coverage table to the Relationships window and then create a relationship between *InsuranceCode* in the Coverage table and the Insurance table. (*InsuranceCode* in the Coverage table is the "one" and *InsuranceCode* in the Insurance table is the "many." At the Edit Relationships dialog box, be sure to choose *Enforce Referential Integrity*, *Cascade Update Related Fields*, and *Cascade Delete Related Records*.

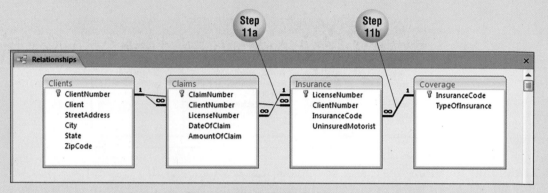

12. Click the Save button on the Quick Access toolbar.
13. Print the relationships by completing the following steps:

   a. At the Relationships window, click the Relationship Report button in the Tools group. (This displays the Relationships report in Print Preview.)

   b. Click the Print button in the Print group and then click OK at the Print dialog box.

   c. Click the Close button that displays at the right side of the Relationships window.

   d. At the message asking if you want to save changes to the design of the report, click No.

14. Close the Relationships window by clicking the Close button that displays at the right side of the Relationships window.

In the relationship established in Project 1b, a record must first be added to the Clients table before a related record can be added to the Claims table. This is because you chose the *Enforce Referential Integrity* option at the Edit Relationships dialog box. Because you chose the two options *Cascade Update Related Fields* and *Cascade Delete Related Records*, records in the Clients table (the primary table) can be updated and/or deleted and related records in the Claims table (related table) will automatically be updated or deleted.

1. With the **SouthwestInsurance.accdb** database open, open the Clients table.
2. Change two client numbers in the Clients database (Access will automatically change it in the Claims table) by completing the following steps:
   a. Make sure the Clients window displays in Datasheet view.
   b. Click once in the *ClientNumber* field for Paul Vuong containing the number *4300*.
   c. Change the number from *4300* to *4308*.
   d. Click once in the *ClientNumber* field for Vernon Cook containing the number *7335*.
   e. Change the number from *7335* to *7325*.
   f. Click the Save button on the Quick Access toolbar.
   g. Close the Clients table.
   h. Open the Claims table. (Notice that the client numbers for Vernon Cook and Paul Vuong automatically changed.)
   i. Close the Claims table.

3. Open the Clients table, make sure the table displays in Datasheet view, and then add the following records at the end of the table:

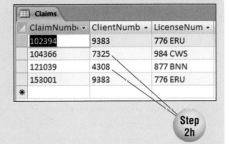

ClientNumber	= 5508
Client	= **Martina Bentley**
StreetAddress	= **6503 Taylor Street**
City	= **Scottsdale**
State	= **AZ**
ZipCode	= **85889**

ClientNumber	= 2511
Client	= **Keith Hammond**
StreetAddress	= **21332 Janski Road**
City	= **Glendale**
State	= **AZ**
ZipCode	= **85310**

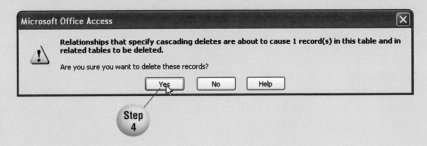

4. With the Clients table still open, delete the record for Elaine Hueneka. At the message telling you that relationships that specify cascading deletes are about to cause records in this table and related tables to be deleted, click Yes.

5. Save, print, and then close the Clients table.
6. Open the Insurance table, make sure the table displays in Datasheet view, and then add the following records at the end of the table:

LicenseNumber	=	422 RTW
ClientNumber	=	5508
InsuranceCode	=	L
UninsuredMotorist	=	Yes

LicenseNumber	=	130 YWR
ClientNumber	=	5508
InsuranceCode	=	F
UninsuredMotorist	=	No

LicenseNumber	=	795 GRT
ClientNumber	=	2511
InsuranceCode	=	L
UninsuredMotorist	=	Yes

Step 6

	LicenseNum ▾	ClientNumb ▾	InsuranceCo ▾	UninsuredM ▾	A
⊞	310 YTV	3120	F	☑	
⊞	341 VIT	3120	F	☑	
⊞	877 BNN	4308	L	☑	
⊞	984 CWS	7325	L	☑	
⊞	422 RTW	5508	L	☑	
⊞	130 YWR	5508	F	☐	
⊞	795 GRT	2511	L	☑	
*				☐	

Insurance

7. Save, print, and then close the Insurance table.
8. Open the Claims table, make sure the table displays in Datasheet view, and then add the following record:

ClaimNumber	=	130057
ClientNumber	=	2511
LicenseNumber	=	795 GRT
DateOfClaim	=	3/4/2010
AmountOfClaim	=	$186.40

Claims

ClaimNumb ▾	ClientNumb ▾	LicenseNum ▾	DateOfClaim ▾	AmountOfCl ▾	A
104366	7325	984 CWS	1/18/2010	$834.95	
121039	4308	877 BNN	2/3/2010	$5,230.00	
130057	2511	795 GRT	3/4/2010	$186.40	
*					

Step 8

9. Save and then print the Claims table.
10. With the Claims table still open, try to enter a record for a client who has not been entered in the Clients table by completing the following steps (Access will not allow this because of the one-to-many relationship that was established in Project 1b):
    a. Add the following record to the Claims table:

ClaimNumber	=	201221
ClientNumber	=	5824
LicenseNumber	=	640 TRS
DateOfClaim	=	3/11/2010
AmountOfClaim	=	$895.25

    b. Click the Close button to close the Claims table. This causes a message to display telling you that the record cannot be added or changed because a related record is required in the Clients table. At this message, click OK.
    c. A message displays warning you that Access cannot save the table, that closing the object will cause the changes to be made, and asking if you want to close the database object. At this warning, click Yes.

Editing and Deleting a Relationship

You can make changes to a relationship that has been established between tables. The relationship can also be deleted. To edit a relationship, open the database containing the tables with the relationship, click the Database Tools tab, and then click the Relationships button in the Show/Hide group. This displays the Relationships window with the related tables displayed in boxes. Click the Edit Relationships button located in the Tools group to display the Edit Relationships dialog box such as the one shown in Figure 2.5, where you can change the current relationship. You can also display the Edit Relationships dialog box by positioning the arrow pointer on the thin portion of one of the black lines that connects the related tables and then clicking the *right* mouse button. This causes a shortcut menu to display. At this shortcut menu, click the left mouse button on Edit Relationship.

To delete a relationship between tables, display the related tables in the Relationships window. Position the arrow pointer on the thin portion of the black line connecting the related tables and then click the *right* mouse button. At the shortcut menu that displays, click the left mouse button on Delete. At the message asking if you are sure you want to permanently delete the selected relationship from your database, click Yes.

Creating a One-to-One Relationship

You can create a one-to-one relationship between tables in which each record in the first table matches only one record in the second table and one record in the second table matches only one record in the first table. A one-to-one relationship is not as common as a one-to-many relationship since the type of information used to create the relationship can be stored in one table. A one-to-one relationship can be helpful in a situation where you divide a table with many fields into two tables.

Edit a Relationship
1. Click Database Tools tab.
2. Click Relationships button.
3. Click Edit Relationships button.
4. At Edit Relationships dialog box, make desired changes.
5. Click OK.

Delete a Relationship
1. Click Database Tools tab.
2. Click Relationships button.
3. Right-click on black line connecting related tables.
4. Click Delete.
5. Click Yes.

HINT

The Relationships window displays any relationship you have defined between tables.

Edit Relationships

Project 1e Creating Tables and Defining a One-to-One Relationship

1. With the **SouthwestInsurance.accdb** database open, create a new table by completing the following steps:
   a. Click the Create tab.
   b. Click the Table button in the Tables group.
   c. At the Table window, click the View button in the Views group in the Table Tools Datasheet tab.
   d. At the Save As dialog box, type Assignments in the *Table Name* text box and then press Enter or click OK.
   e. Type the fields, assign the data types, and type the descriptions as shown below (for assistance, refer to Chapter 1, Project 1a):

Field Name	Data Type	Description
ClientNumber	Text (Field Size = 4)	Client number
AgentNumber	Text (Field Size = 3)	Agent number

2. Make sure a key displays at the left side of the *ClientNumber* field and then click the Save button on the Quick Access toolbar.

3. Click the View button to change to Datasheet view and then type the following in the specified fields:

ClientNumber	2511	*ClientNumber*	2768
AgentNumber	210	*AgentNumber*	142
ClientNumber	3120	*ClientNumber*	3976
AgentNumber	173	*AgentNumber*	210
ClientNumber	4308	*ClientNumber*	5231
AgentNumber	245	*AgentNumber*	173
ClientNumber	5508	*ClientNumber*	7325
AgentNumber	245	*AgentNumber*	142

4. Save, print, and then close the Assignments table.
5. At the SouthwestInsurance : Database window, create a new table by completing the following steps:
   a. Click the Create tab.
   b. Click the Table button in the Tables group.
   c. At the Table window, click the View button in the Views group in the Table Tools Datasheet tab.
   d. At the Save As dialog box, type **Agents** in the *Table Name* text box and then press Enter or click OK.
   e. Type the fields, assign the data types, and type the descriptions as shown below (for assistance, refer to Chapter 1, Project 2a):

Field Name	Data Type	Description
AgentNumber	Text (Field Size = 3)	Agent number
FirstName	Text (Field Size = 20)	Agent first name
LastName	Text (Field Size = 20)	Agent last name
Telephone	Text (Field Size = 12)	Agent phone number
Email	Text (Field Size = 30)	Agent e-mail address

6. Make sure a key displays at the left side of the *AgentNumber* field and then click the Save button on the Quick Access toolbar.
7. Click the View button to change to Datasheet view and then type the following in the specified fields:

AgentNumber	142	*AgentNumber*	173
FirstName	James	*FirstName*	Tamara
LastName	Moriyama	*LastName*	Sadler
Telephone	602-555-2676	*Telephone*	602-555-2698
Email	jmoriyama@emcp.net	*Email*	tsadler@emcp.net
AgentNumber	210	*AgentNumber*	245
FirstName	Phillip	*FirstName*	Dayton
LastName	Cowans	*LastName*	Hubbard
Telephone	602-555-2683	*Telephone*	602-555-2644
Email	pcowans@emcp.net	*Email*	dhubbard@emcp.net

8. Automatically adjust the width of columns.

9. Save, print, and then close the Agents table.
10. Create a one-to-one relationship between the Assignments table and the Clients table by completing the following steps:
    a. Click the Database Tools tab.
    b. Click the Relationships button in the Show/Hide group.
    c. At the Relationships window, click the Show Table button in the Relationships group.
    d. At the Show Table dialog box, click *Assignments* in the list box, and then click the Add button.
    e. Click the Close button to close the Show Table dialog box.
    f. At the Relationships window, drag the *ClientNumber* field from the Assignments table to the *ClientNumber* field in the Clients table.

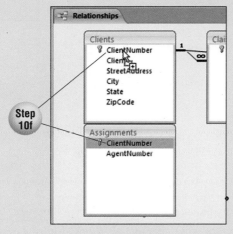

g. At the Edit Relationships dialog box, make sure *ClientNumber* displays in the *Table/Query* and *Related Table/Query* list boxes and the relationship type at the bottom of the dialog box displays as *One-To-One*.
h. Enforce the referential integrity of the relationship by completing the following steps:
    1) Click *Enforce Referential Integrity*. (This makes the other two options available.)
    2) Click *Cascade Update Related Fields*.
    3) Click *Cascade Delete Related Records*.

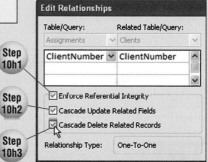

i. Click the Create button. (This causes the Edit Relationships dialog box to close and the Relationships window to display showing a thick black line connecting the *ClientNumber* field in the Assignments and Clients tables.
j. Click the Save button on the Quick Access toolbar to save the relationship.
11. Create a one-to-many relationship between the Assignments table and the Agents table by completing the following steps:
    a. With the Relationships window open, click the Show Table button in the Relationships group.
    b. At the Show Table dialog box, click *Agents* in the list box and then click the Add button.
    c. Click the Close button to close the Show Table dialog box.

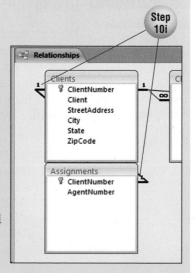

d. At the Relationships window, drag the *AgentNumber* field from the Agents table to the *AgentNumber* field in the Assignments table.

e. At the Edit Relationships dialog box, make sure *AgentNumber* displays in the *Table/Query* and *Related Table/Query* list boxes and the relationship type at the bottom of the dialog box displays as *One-To-Many*.

f. Enforce the referential integrity of the relationship by completing the following steps:
1) Click *Enforce Referential Integrity*. (This makes the other two options available.)
2) Click *Cascade Update Related Fields*.
3) Click *Cascade Delete Related Records*.

g. Click the Create button.

h. Click the Save button on the Quick Access toolbar to save the relationship.

12. Print the relationships by completing the following steps:
a. At the Relationships window, click the Relationship Report button in the Tools group. (This displays the Relationships report in Print Preview.)
b. Click the Print button in the Print group.
c. Click OK at the Print dialog box.
d. Click the Close button that displays at the right side of the Relationships window.
e. At the message asking if you want to save changes to the design of the report, click No.

13. Close the Relationships window by clicking the Close button that displays at the right side of the Relationships window.

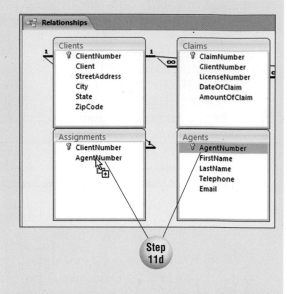

Step 11d

QUICK STEPS

Display Subdatasheet
1. Open table in Datasheet view.
2. Click expand indicator at left of desired record.
3. At Insert Subdatasheet dialog box, click desired table.
4. Click OK.

Displaying Related Records in a Subdatasheet

When a relationship is established between tables, you can view and edit fields in related tables with a subdatasheet. Figure 2.8 displays the Clients table with the subdatasheet displayed for the client Keith Hammond. The subdatasheet displays the fields in the Insurance table related to Keith Hammond. Use this subdatasheet to view information and also to edit information in the Clients table as well as the Insurance table. Changes made to fields in a subdatasheet affect the table and any related table.

Access automatically inserts plus symbols (referred to as *expand indicators*) before each record in a table that is joined to another table by a one-to-many relationship. Click the expand indicator and, if the table is related to only one other table, a subdatasheet containing fields from the related table displays below the record as shown in Figure 2.8. To remove the subdatasheet, click the minus sign (referred to as the *collapse indicator*) preceding the record. (The plus symbol turns into the minus symbol when a subdatasheet displays.)

Figure 2.8 Table with Subdatasheet Displayed

Subdatasheet

ClientNumb ▾	Client ▾	StreetAddress ▾	City ▾	State ▾	ZipCode ▾
⊟ 2511	Keith Hammon	21332 Janski Road	Glendale	AZ	85310

	ClaimNumbe ▾	LicenseNum ▾	DateOfClain ▾	AmountOfCl ▾	Add New Field
	130057	795 GRT	3/4/2010	$186.40	

⊞ 2768	Marcus LeVign	15676 North 32nd	Phoenix	AZ	86231
⊞ 3120	Spenser Winte	12304 132nd Street	Glendale	AZ	85310
⊞ 3976	Joely Lindhal	8809 South 142nd Stre	Scottsdale	AZ	85230
⊞ 4308	Paul Vuong	3451 South Varner	Glendale	AZ	85901
⊞ 5231	Helena Myersc	9032 45th Street East	Phoenix	AZ	86203
⊞ 5508	Martina Bentle	6503 Taylor Street	Scottsdale	AZ	85889
⊞ 7325	Vernon Cook	1230 South Mesa	Phoenix	AZ	86201

If a table has more than one relationship defined, clicking the expand indicator will display the Insert Subdatasheet dialog box shown in Figure 2.9. At this dialog box, click the desired table in the Tables list box and then click OK. You can also display the Insert Subdatasheet dialog box by clicking the More button in the Records group in the Home tab, pointing to *Subdatasheet*, and then clicking *Subdatasheet*.

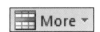

You can display subdatasheets for all records by clicking the More button, pointing to *Subdatasheet*, and then clicking *Expand All*. Remove all subdatasheets by clicking the More button, pointing to *Subdatasheet*, and then clicking *Collapse All*.

Figure 2.9 Insert Subdatasheet Dialog Box

Insert Subdatasheet

Tables | Queries | Both

Agents
Assignments
Claims
Clients
Coverage
Insurance

Click the desired table in this list box for which you want to display a subdatasheet.

Link Child Fields:
Link Master Fields:

OK | Cancel

If a table is related to two or more tables, specify the desired subdatasheet at the Subdatasheet dialog box. If you decide to display a different subdatasheet, remove the subdatasheet first before selecting the next subdatasheet. Do this by clicking the More button, pointing to *Subdatasheet*, and then clicking *Remove*.

1. With the **SouthwestInsurance.accdb** database open, open the Clients table.
2. Display a subdatasheet by completing the following steps:
    a. Click the expand indicator (plus symbol) that displays at the left side of the first row (the row for Keith Hammond).
    b. At the Insert Subdatasheet dialog box, click *Claims* in the list box and then click OK.

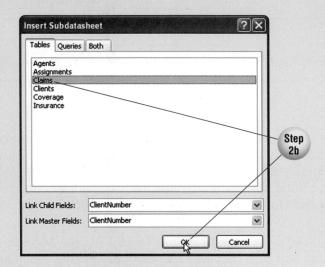

3. Remove the subdatasheet by clicking the collapse indicator (minus sign) that displays at the left side of the record for Keith Hammond.
4. Display subdatasheets for all of the records by clicking the More button in the Records group, pointing to *Subdatasheet*, and then clicking *Expand All*.

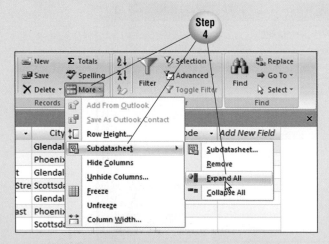

5. Remove the display of all subdatasheets by clicking the More button, pointing to *Subdatasheet*, and then clicking *Collapse All*.
6. Remove the connection between Clients and Claims by clicking the More button, pointing to *Subdatasheet*, and then clicking *Remove*.

7. Suppose that the client, Vernon Cook, has moved to a new address and purchased insurance for a new car. Display the Insurance subdatasheet and make changes to fields in the Clients table and the Insurance table by completing the following steps:

a. Click the expand indicator (plus symbol) that displays at the left side of the *Vernon Cook* record.

b. At the Insert Subdatasheet dialog box, click *Insurance* in the list box and then click OK.

c. Change his street address from *1230 South Mesa* to *22135 Cactus Drive*.

d. Change his ZIP code from *86201* to *85344*.

e. Add the following information in the second row in the Insurance subdatasheet:

    LicenseNumber   =   **430 DWT**
    InsuranceCode   =   **F**
    UninsuredMotorist =   *Yes*

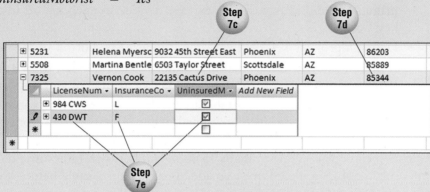

f. Click the Save button on the Quick Access toolbar.

g. Close the Clients table.

8. Open the Clients table, print it, and then close it.

9. Open the Insurance table, print it, and then close it.

10. Close the **SouthwestInsurance.accdb** database.

CHAPTER summary

- Access is a relational database software program in which you can create tables that have a relation or connection to one another.

- When planning a table, take time to determine how to break down the required data and what relationships will need to be defined to eliminate data redundancies.

- In a table at least one field must be unique so that one record can be distinguished from another. A field with a unique value is considered a primary key.

- In a field defined as a primary key, duplicate values are not allowed in the primary field and Access also expects a value in each record in the primary key field.

- Define a primary key field with the Primary Key button in the Tools group.

- A primary key field included in another table is referred to as a foreign key. Unlike a primary key field, a foreign key field can contain duplicate data.

- In Access, you can relate a table to another by performing a join. When tables that have a common field are joined, you can extract data from both tables as if they were one large table.

- You can create a one-to-many relationship between tables in a database. In this relationship, a record must be added to the "one" table before it can be added to the "many" table.

- You can create a one-to-one relationship between tables in which each record in the first table matches only one record in the second table and one record in the second table matches only one record in the first table.

- You can edit or delete a relationship between tables.

- To print a relationship, display the Relationships window, click the Relationship Report button in the Tools group, and then click the Print button in the Print Preview tab.

- When a relationship is established between tables, you can view and edit fields in related tables with a subdatasheet.

- To display a subdatasheet for a record, click the expand indicator (plus symbol) that displays at the left side of the record. To display subdatasheets for all records, click the More button in the Reports group in the Home tab, point to *Subdatasheet*, and then click *Expand All*.

- Display the Insert Subdatasheet dialog box by clicking the More button in the Reports group in the Home tab, pointing to *Subdatasheet*, and then clicking *Subdatasheet*.

- Turn off the display of a subdatasheet by clicking the collapse indicator (minus symbol) at the beginning of a record. To turn off the display of subdatasheets for all records, click the More button, point to *Subdatasheet*, and then click *Collapse All*.

COMMANDS review

FEATURE	RIBBON TAB, GROUP	BUTTON, OPTION
Primary key	Table Tools Design, Tools	
Relationships window	Database Tools, Show/Hide	
Edit Relationships window	Relationship Tools Design, Tools	
Show Table dialog box	Relationship Tools Design, Relationships	
Relationship report window	Relationship Tools Design, Tools	Relationship Report
Insert Subdatasheet dialog box	Home, Records	More ▾ , Subdatasheet, Subdatasheet

CONCEPTS check

Test Your Knowledge

Completion: For each description, indicate the correct term, symbol, or character.

1. A primary key field must contain unique data while this type of key field can contain duplicate data.

2. In Access, one table can be related to another, which is generally referred to as performing this. _____

3. In a one-to-many relationship, the table containing the "one" is referred to as this. _____

4. In a one-to-many relationship, the table containing the "many" is referred to as this. _____

5. In a one-to-many relationship, Access follows a set of rules that enforces consistency between related tables and is referred to as this. _____

6. In related tables, this symbol displays near the black line next to the related table. _____

7. The black line that connects related tables is referred to as this. _____

8. Establish this type of relationship between tables in which each record in the first table matches only one record in the second table and one record in the second table matches only one record in the first table.

_____

9. The plus symbol that displays at the beginning of a record in a related table with a subdatasheet displayed is referred to as this.

_____

10. The minus symbol that displays at the beginning of a record in a related table with a subdatasheet displayed is referred to as this.

_____

11. Display subdatasheets for all records by clicking the More button, pointing to *Subdatasheet*, and then clicking this option.

_____

SKILLS check
Demonstrate Your Proficiency

Assessment

1   CREATE AUTHORS, BOOKS, AND CATEGORIES TABLES IN A MYBOOKS DATABASE

1. Use Access to create a database for keeping track of books. Name the database *MyBooks*. Create a table named *Authors* that includes the following fields (you determine the data type, field size, and description):

   Field Name
   AuthorNumber (primary key)
   FirstName
   LastName
   MiddleInitial

2. After creating the table with the fields shown above and defining the primary key, save the table. Switch to Datasheet view and then enter the following data in the table:

AuthorNumber	=	1
FirstName	=	**Branson**
LastName	=	**Walters**
MiddleInitial	=	**A.**

AuthorNumber	=	2
FirstName	=	**Christiana**
LastName	=	**Copeland**
MiddleInitial	=	**M.**

AuthorNumber	=	3
FirstName	=	**Shirley**
LastName	=	**Romero**
MiddleInitial	=	**E.**

```
AuthorNumber   =   4
FirstName      =   Jeffrey
LastName       =   Fiedler
MiddleInitial  =   R.
```

3. Automatically adjust the width of columns.
4. Save, print, and then close the Authors table.
5. With the **MyBooks.accdb** database open, create another table named *Books* with the following fields (you determine the data type, field size, and description):
   Field Name
   ISBN (primary key)
   AuthorNumber
   Title
   CategoryCode
   Price
6. After creating the table with the fields shown above and defining the primary key, save the table. Switch to Datasheet view and then enter the following data in the table:

```
ISBN           =   12-6543-9008-7
AuthorNumber   =   4
Title          =   Today's Telecommunications
CategoryCode   =   B
Price          =   $34.95

ISBN           =   09-5225-5466-6
AuthorNumber   =   2
Title          =   Marketing in the Global Economy
CategoryCode   =   M
Price          =   $42.50

ISBN           =   23-9822-7645-0
AuthorNumber   =   1
Title          =   International Business Strategies
CategoryCode   =   B
Price          =   $45.00

ISBN           =   08-4351-4890-3
AuthorNumber   =   3
Title          =   Technological Advances
CategoryCode   =   B
Price          =   $36.95
```

7. Automatically adjust the width of columns (to accommodate the longest entry).
8. Save, print, and then close the Books table.
9. Create another table named *Categories* with the following fields (you determine the data type, field size, and description):
   Field Name
   CategoryCode (primary key)
   Category

10. After creating the table with the fields shown above and defining the primary key, save the table. Switch to Datasheet view and then enter the following data in the table:

CategoryCode = B
Category = Business

CategoryCode = M
Category = Marketing

11. Save, print, and then close the Categories table.

Assessment

2 CREATE RELATIONSHIPS BETWEEN TABLES

1. With the **MyBooks.accdb** database open, create the following relationships:
   a. Create a one-to-many relationship with the *AuthorNumber* field in the Authors table the "one" and the *AuthorNumber* field in the Books table the "many." (At the Edit Relationships dialog box, choose *Enforce Referential Integrity*, *Cascade Update Related Fields*, and *Cascade Delete Related Records*.)
   b. Create a one-to-many relationship with the *CategoryCode* field in the Categories table the "one" and the *CategoryCode* field in the Books table the "many." (At the Edit Relationships dialog box, choose *Enforce Referential Integrity*, *Cascade Update Related Fields*, and *Cascade Delete Related Records*.)
2. Print the relationships.
3. After creating, saving, and printing the relationships, add the following record to the Authors table:
   AuthorNumber = 5
   FirstName = Glenna
   LastName = Zener-Young
   MiddleInitial = A.
4. Adjust the column width for the *LastName* field.
5. Save, print, and then close the Authors table.
6. Add the following records to the Books table:

   ISBNNumber = 23-8931-0084-7
   AuthorNumber = 2
   Title = Practical Marketing Strategies
   Category = M
   Price = $28.50

   ISBNNumber = 87-4009-7134-6
   AuthorNumber = 5
   Title = Selling More
   Category = M
   Price = $40.25

7. Save, print, and then close the Books table.
8. Close the **MyBooks.accdb** database.

CASE study

Apply Your Skills

You are the owner of White Gloves Cleaning, a small housekeeping and cleaning service for residences and businesses. Since your business is continuing to grow, you decide to manage your records electronically instead of on paper. Create a database named **WhiteGloves** that contains three tables. Create a table named *Clients* that includes fields for a client number; name; address; city, state, ZIP code, contact person, location number, and rate number. Create another table named *Locations* that includes a location number field and a location field. Create a third table named *Rates* that includes a rate number field and a rates field.

In the Locations table, create the following:

Location number	Location
1	Residence
2	Business
3	Construction Site

In the Rates table, create the following:

Rate number	Rate
1	$15.00
2	$25.00
3	$40.00

Assign primary keys in each table and then create a one-to-many relationship with the *Location number* field in the Locations table the "one" and the *Location number* field in the Clients the "many." Create another one-to-many relationship with the *Rate number* field in the Rates table the "one" and the *Rate number* field in the Clients table the "many." Save and then print the relationships.

Enter six records in the Clients table. Specify that the location number for two records is 1 (residence) and the rate is 1 ($15.00). Specify that the location number for two records is 2 (business) and the rate is 2 ($25.00). Specify that the location number for two records is 3 (construction site) and the rate is 3 ($40.00). Save and print each table (print the Clients table in landscape orientation) and then close the **WhiteGloves.accdb** database.

Your business is growing and you have been hired to provide cleaning services to one additional business and one additional construction company. Add the appropriate information in the fields in the Clients table. One of your clients has cancelled services with your company so delete a client of your choosing from the Clients table. Print the Clients table. You have raised your hourly rates for cleaning a residence to $20.00. Make this change to the Rates table. Print the Rates table.

Part 3

In Microsoft Word, create a document that describes the tables, fields, and relationships you created in the WhiteGloves database. In the document, specify the fields in each table, the data types assigned to each field, the field size (if appropriate), and describe the one-to-many relationships you created. Apply formatting to the document to enhance the visual appeal and then save the document and name it **Access_C2_CS_P3**. Print and then close **Access_C2_CS_P3.docx**.

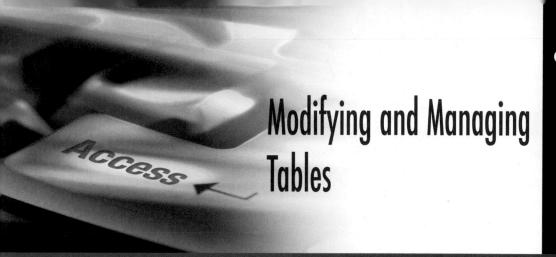

Modifying and Managing Tables

PERFORMANCE OBJECTIVES

Upon successful completion of Chapter 3, you will be able to:

- Modify a table by adding, deleting, or moving fields
- Assign a default value and validate a field entry
- Insert a Total row
- Use the Input Mask Wizard and the Lookup Wizard
- Complete a spelling check on data in a table
- Find specific records in a table
- Find specific data in a table and replace with other data
- Backup a database
- Compact and repair a database
- Use the Help feature

Tutorial 3.1
Managing a Database Table
Tutorial 3.2
Backing Up and Compacting Databases

An Access database requires maintenance to keep the database up to date. Maintenance might include modifying the table by inserting or deleting fields, defining values and validating field entries, inserting a Total row, using wizards to identify data type, and sorting data in tables. In this chapter, you will learn how to modify tables as well as how to use the spelling checker to find misspelled words in a table and how to use the find and replace feature to find specific records in a table or find specific data in a table and replace with other data. As you continue working with a database, consider compacting and repairing the database to optimize performance and back up the database to protect your data from accidental loss or hardware failure. Microsoft Office contains an on-screen reference manual containing information on features and commands for each program within the suite. In this chapter, you will learn to use the Help feature to display information about Access.

Note: Before beginning computer projects, copy the Access2007L1C3 subfolder from the Access2007L1 folder on the CD that accompanies this textbook to your storage medium and make Access2007L1C3 the active folder.

Project 1 Manage Data and Define Data Types

You will modify tables by adding and deleting fields, assign data types and default values to fields, validate field entries, insert a total row, and use the Input Mask Wizard and the Lookup Wizard. You will also move fields in a table and sort records in ascending and descending order.

Modifying a Table

Maintaining a table involves adding and/or deleting records as needed. It can also involve adding, moving, changing, or deleting fields in the table. Modify the structure of the table in Datasheet view or Design view. In Datasheet view, click the Table Tools Datasheet tab and then use options in the Fields & Columns group to insert or delete fields. To display a table in Design view, open the table, and then click the View button in the Views group in the Home tab. You can also change to Design view by clicking the View button arrow and then clicking *Design View* at the drop-down list or by clicking the Design View button located in the View area at the right side of the Status bar.

In Design view, *Field Name*, *Data Type*, and *Description* display at the top of the window and *Field Properties* displays toward the bottom of the window. In Design view, you can add fields, remove fields, and change the order of fields. When you switch to Design view, the Table Tools Design tab displays as shown in Figure 3.1. Use buttons in this tab to insert and delete rows and perform a variety of other tasks.

Figure 3.1 Table Tools Design Tab

HINT

Use options in the Data Type & Formatting group in the Table Tools Datasheet tab to set the data type.

Adding a Field

Situations change within a company, and a table must be flexible to accommodate changes that occur with new situations. Adding a field is a change that may need to be made to an existing table. For example, more information may be required to manage the data or an additional field may be needed for accounting purposes.

You can add a new field in Datasheet view or in Design view. One method for creating a new field is to simply type new records into a blank table or in the *Add New Field* column that displays at the right side of the last field in the table. Access sets a data type for each new field you type based on the type of data entered. For example, a column that contains dates is automatically assigned the Date/Time data type. You can also insert a new field by clicking the Table Tools Datasheet tab and then clicking the Insert button in the Fields & Columns group.

To add a row for a new field in Design view, position the insertion point on any text in the row that will be located immediately *below* the new field and then click the Insert Rows button in the Tools group in the Table Tools Design tab or position the insertion point on any text in the row that will be immediately *below* the new field, click the *right* mouse button, and then click *Insert Rows*. If you insert a row for a new field and then change your mind, immediately click the Undo button on the Quick Access toolbar.

Deleting a Field

Delete a field in a table and all data entered in that field is also deleted. When a field is deleted, it cannot be undone with the Undo button. Delete a field only if you are sure you really want it and the data associated with it completely removed from the table.

To delete a field in Datasheet view, click in any entry in the field you want to delete, click the Table Tools Datasheet tab, and then click the Delete button in the Fields & Columns group. To delete a field in Design view, click in the record selector bar at the left side of the row you want to delete and then click the Delete Rows button in the Tools group. At the message asking if you want to permanently delete the field and all of the data in the field, click Yes.

Assigning Data Type

In Chapter 1, you created tables and assigned data types of *Text*, *Date/Time*, or *Yes/No*. Access includes these data types as well as additional types as described in Table 3.1. Assign a data type with the *Data Type* column in Design view.

Table 3.1 Data Types

Data type	Description
Text	Alphanumeric data up to 255 characters in length, such as a name, address, or value such as a telephone number or Social Security number that it used as an identifier and not for calculating.
Memo	Alphanumeric data up to 64,000 characters in length.
Number	Positive or negative values that can be used in calculations. Do *not* use for value that will calculate monetary amounts (see Currency).
Date/Time	Use this type to ensure dates and times are entered and sorted properly.
Currency	Values that involve money. Access will not round off during calculations.
AutoNumber	Access automatically numbers each record sequentially (incrementing by 1) when you begin typing a new record.
Yes/No	Data in the field will be either Yes or No, True or False, or On or Off.
OLE Object	Used to embed or link objects created in other Office applications.
Hyperlink	Field that will store a hyperlink such as a URL.
Attachment	Use this data type to add file attachments to a record such as a Word document or an Excel workbook.
Lookup Wizard	Use the Lookup Wizard to enter data in the field from another existing table or display a list of values in a drop-down list from which the user chooses.

QUICK STEPS

Add a Field to a Table
1. Open table in Design view.
2. Click in row that will follow the new field.
3. Click Insert Rows button.

Delete a Field from a Table
1. Open table in Design view.
2. Click in row to be deleted.
3. Click Delete Rows button.
4. Click Yes.

Insert Rows

Undo

Delete Rows

1. In Access, display the Open dialog box with the drive active containing your storage medium and Access2007L1C3 the active folder.
2. Open the **MedSafeClinic.accdb** database.
3. At the MedSafeClinic : Database window, double-click the *Products* table to open it.
4. Insert a new field by completing the following steps:
   a. Click in the empty field below the *Add New Field* column heading.
   b. Type **50** and then press the Down Arrow key on your keyboard.
   c. Type **50** and then press the Down Arrow key.
   d. Type **125** and then press the Down Arrow key.
   e. Type **100** and then press the Down Arrow key.
   f. Type **150** and then press the Down Arrow key.
   g. Type **100** and then press the Down Arrow key.

UnitsInStock ▾	Field1 ▾	Add New Field
63	50	
38	50	
144	125	
57	100	
122	150	
78	100	

Steps 4b–4g

5. Click the View button to switch to Design view and notice that Access automatically selected the Number data type for the new field you created. Modify the field by completing the following steps:
   a. Select *Field1* that displays in the *Field Name* column and then type **ReorderLevel**.
   b. Click in the *Description* text box for the *ReorderLevel* field and then type **Reorder level number.**

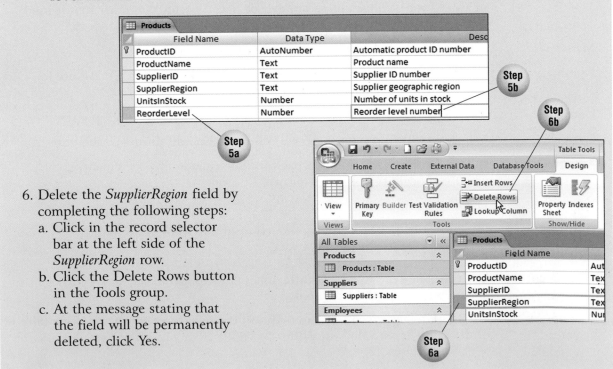

Field Name	Data Type	Desc
ProductID	AutoNumber	Automatic product ID number
ProductName	Text	Product name
SupplierID	Text	Supplier ID number
SupplierRegion	Text	Supplier geographic region
UnitsInStock	Number	Number of units in stock
ReorderLevel	Number	Reorder level number

Step 5a

Step 5b

Step 6b

6. Delete the *SupplierRegion* field by completing the following steps:
   a. Click in the record selector bar at the left side of the *SupplierRegion* row.
   b. Click the Delete Rows button in the Tools group.
   c. At the message stating that the field will be permanently deleted, click Yes.

Step 6a

7. Insert a new field by completing the
   following steps:
   a. Click on any character in the
      ReorderLevel field name.
   b. Click the Insert Rows button in the
      Tools group.
   c. With the insertion point positioned in
      the new blank field in the *Field Name*
      column, type **UnitsOnOrder**.
   d. Press the Tab key.
   e. Click the down-pointing arrow at the
      right side of the Text box and then click
      Number at the drop-down list.
   f. Press the Tab key and then type
      Number of units on order.
8. Insert a new field by completing the following steps:
   a. Click on any character in the *ReorderLevel* field name.
   b. Click the Insert Rows button in the Tools group.
   c. With the insertion point positioned in the new blank field in the *Field Name* column,
      type **UnitPrice**.
   d. Press the Tab key.
   e. Click the down-pointing arrow at the right side of the Text box and then click *Currency*
      at the drop-down list.
   f. Press the Tab key and then type **Unit price.**
9. Click the Save button on the Quick Access toolbar to save the modified table.
10. Click the View button to switch to Datasheet view and then enter the following
    information in the specified fields:

UnitsOnOrder	UnitPrice
0	12.50
50	24.00
0	5.70
100	9.90
150	4.50
100	10.00

11. Click the Save button on the Quick Access toolbar.
12. Display the table in Print Preview, change the orientation to landscape, and then print the
    table.
13. Close Print Preview and close the Products table.
14. Define a one-to-many relationship between the Suppliers and the Products tables by
    completing the following steps:
    a. Click the Database Tools tab and then click the Relationships button in the Show/Hide
       group.
    b. At the Show Table dialog box, click *Suppliers* in the list box and then click Add.
    c. Click *Products* in the list box and then click Add.
    d. Click the Close button to close the Show Table dialog box.
    e. At the Relationships window, drag the *SupplierID* field from the Suppliers table to the
       SupplierID field in the Products table.
    f. At the Edit Relationships dialog box, click *Enforce Referential Integrity*, click *Cascade
       Update Related Fields*, and then click *Cascade Delete Related Records.*
    g. Click the Create button.

15. Click the Save button on the Quick Access toolbar to save the relationship.
16. Print the relationships by completing the following steps:
    a. At the Relationships window, click the Relationship Report button in the Tools group. (This displays the Relationships report in Print Preview.)
    b. Click the Print button in the Print group.
    c. Click OK at the Print dialog box.
    d. Click the Close button that displays at the right side of the Relationships window.
    e. At the message asking if you want to save changes to the design of the report, click No.
17. Close the Relationships window by clicking the Close button that displays at the right side of the Relationships window.

Assigning a Default Value

In Design view, the available field properties that display in the lower half of the work area vary depending on the data type of the active field. You can use a field property to control how the field displays or how the field interacts with data. For example, you have been using the *Field Size* option in the Field Properties section to limit the numbers of characters allowed when entering data in the field. If most records are likely to contain the same field value, use the *Default Value* property to insert the most common field entry. In Project 1b, you will insert a health insurance field with a Yes/No data type. Since most employees sign up for health insurance benefits, you will set the default value for the field as *Yes*. If you add a new field that contains a default value to an existing table, the existing records will not reflect the default value, only new records entered in the table.

Validating Field Entries

QUICK STEPS

Insert a Total Row
1. Open table in Datasheet view.
2. Click Totals button.
3. Click in Total row.
4. Click down-pointing arrow that appears.
5. Click desired function at drop-down list.

HINT

The Total row option provides a number of aggregate functions which are functions that calculate values across a range of data.

Use the *Validation Rule* property to enter a statement containing a conditional test that is checked each time data is entered into a field. When data is entered that fails to satisfy the conditional test, Access does not accept the entry and displays an error message. By entering a conditional statement in the *Validation Rule* property that checks each entry against the acceptable range, you can reduce errors. Enter in the *Validation Text* property the content of the error message that you want to display.

Inserting a Total Row

A new feature in Access 2007 is the ability to add a total row to a datasheet and then choose from a list of functions to add or to find the average, maximum, minimum, count, standard deviations, or variance result in a numeric column. To insert a total row, click the Totals button in the Records group in the Home tab. Access adds a row to the bottom of the datasheet with the label *Total* at the left. Click in the Total row, click the down-pointing arrow that appears, and then click the desired function at the drop-down list.

Project 1b Assigning a Default Value, Validating an Entry, and Inserting Total Row

1. With the **MedSafeClinic.accdb** database open, open the Employees table.
2. Insert a new field by completing the following steps:
   a. Click the View button to switch to Design view.
   b. Click in the empty field immediately below the *Salary* field in the *Field Name* column and then type **HealthIns**.
   c. Press the Tab key.
   d. Click the down-pointing arrow at the right side of the Text box and then click *Yes/No* at the drop-down list.
   e. Select the current entry in the *Default Value* field property box and then type Yes.

   Step 2e

   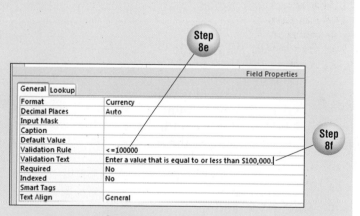

   f. Click in the field in the *Description* column for the *HealthIns* field and then type **Employee signed up for health insurance benefits**.
3. Click the Save button on the Quick Access toolbar.
4. Click the View button to switch to Datasheet view. (Notice that the *HealthIns* check box for existing records does not contain a check mark [the default value] but the check box in the new record contains a check mark.)
5. Enter the following new records:

ID#	265		*ID#*	199
FirstName	Randy		*FirstName*	Kristen
LastName	Lewandowski		*LastName*	Ridgway
Ext	3217		*Ext*	2122
Salary	29000		*Salary*	33550
HealthIns	(Press Tab to accept default)		*HealthIns*	(Press Tab to accept default)

6. Click in each of the existing *HealthIns* check boxes to insert a check mark except the check box for *Chris Weaver*.
7. Save the Employees table.
8. Insert a new field by completing the following steps:
   a. Click the View button to switch to Design view.
   b. Click in the empty field immediately below the *HealthIns* field in the *Field Name* column and then type **LifeIns**.
   c. Press the Tab key.
   d. Click the down-pointing arrow at the right side of the Text box and then click *Currency* at the drop-down list.
   e. Click in the *Validation Rule* property box, type <=100000, and then press Enter.
   f. With the insertion point positioned in the *Validation Text* property box, type **Enter a value that is equal to or less than $100,000**.

   Step 8e

   Step 8f

g. Click in the box in the *Description* column for the *LifeIns* field and then type **Optional life insurance amount.**

9. Click the Save button on the Quick Access toolbar. Since the validation rule was created *after* data was entered into the table, Access displays a warning message indicating that some data may not be valid. At this message, click No.

10. Click the View button to switch to Datasheet view.

11. Click in the first empty field in the *LifeIns* column, type **200000**, and then press the Down Arrow key.

12. Access inserts the error message telling you to enter an amount that is equal to or less than $100,000. At this error message, click OK.

13. Edit the amount in the field so it displays as 100000 and then press the Down Arrow key.

14. Type the following entries in the remaining fields in the *LifeIns* column:

> 25000
> 0
> 50000
> 50000
> 0
> 100000
> 50000
> 25000

15. Save the Employees table.

16. Insert a Total row and insert a function by completing the following steps:

a. In Datasheet view, click the Totals button in the Records group in the Home tab.

b. Click in the blank field in the *Salary* column in the Total row.

c. Click the down-pointing arrow at the left side of the field and then click *Average* at the drop-down list.

d. Click in any other field.

e. Save and then print the Employees table.

f. Click in the field containing the salary average amount.

g. Click the down-pointing arrow at the left side of the field and then click *Sum* at the drop-down list.

h. Click in any other field.

17. Save, print, and then close the Employees table.

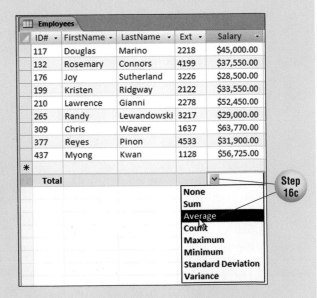

Using the Input Mask Wizard

For some fields, you may want to control the data entered in the field. For example, in a *ZipCode* field, you may want the nine-digit ZIP code entered (rather than the five-digit ZIP code); or you may want the three-digit area code included in a telephone number. Use the *Input Mask* field property to set a pattern for how data is entered in a field. An input mask ensures that data in records conforms to a standard format. Access includes an Input Mask Wizard that guides you through creating an input mask.

Use the Input Mask Wizard when assigning a data type to a field. After specifying the *Field Size* in the *Field Properties* section in Design view, click in the Input Mask box. Run the Input Mask Wizard by clicking the Build button (button containing three black dots) that appears to the right of the Input Mask box. This displays the first Input Mask Wizard dialog box as shown in Figure 3.2. In the Input Mask list box, choose which input mask you want your data to look like and then click the Next button. At the second Input Mask Wizard dialog box as shown in Figure 3.3, specify the appearance of the input mask and the desired placeholder character and then click the Next button. At the third Input Mask Wizard dialog box, specify whether you want the data stored with or without the symbol in the mask and then click the Next button. At the fourth dialog box, click the Finish button.

QUICK STEPS

Use Input Mask
1. Open table in Design view.
2. Type text in *Field Name* column.
3. Press Tab key.
4. Click Save button.
5. Click in Input Mask box.
6. Click Build button.
7. At first Input Mask Wizard, click desired option.
8. Click Next.
9. At second Input Mask Wizard dialog box, make any desired changes.
10. Click Next.
11. At third Input Mask dialog box, make any desired changes.
12. Click Next.
13. Click Finish.

HINT

An input mask is a set of characters that control what you can and cannot enter in a field.

Build

Figure 3.2 First Input Mask Wizard Dialog Box

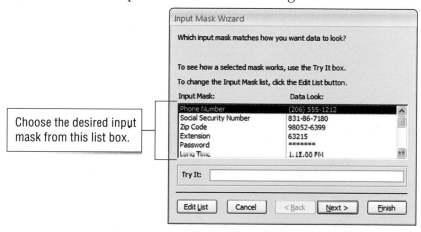

Choose the desired input mask from this list box.

Figure 3.3 Second Input Mask Wizard Dialog Box

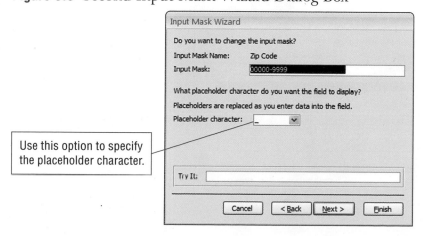

Use this option to specify the placeholder character.

1. With the **MedSafeClinic.accdb** database open, open the Suppliers table.
2. Create a new *ZipCode* field with an Input Mask by completing the following steps:
    a. Click the View button in the Views group.
    b. Click anywhere in the text *Email* that displays in the *Field Name* column.
    c. Click the Insert Rows button in the Tools group.
    d. With the insertion point positioned in the new blank field in the *Field Name* column, type **ZipCode**.
    e. Press the Tab key. (This moves the insertion point to the *Data Type* column.)
    f. Select *255* that displays in the *Field Size* text box in the *Field Properties* section of the window and then type **10**.
    g. Click the Save button to save the table. (You must save the table before using the Input Mask Wizard.)
    h. Click in the *Input Mask* box in the *Field Properties* section of the window.
    i. Click the Build button (button containing three black dots) that displays to the right of the *Input Mask* box.

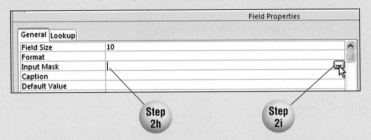

    j. At the first Input Mask Wizard dialog box, click *Zip Code* in the *Input Mask* list box and then click the Next button.

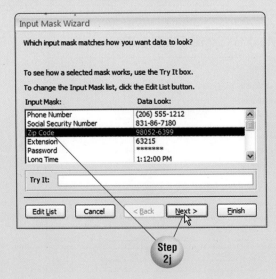

k. At the second Input Mask Wizard dialog box, click the Next button.
l. At the third Input Mask Wizard dialog box, click the *With the symbols in the mask, like this* option.

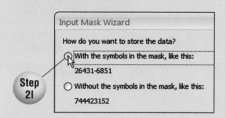

Step 2l

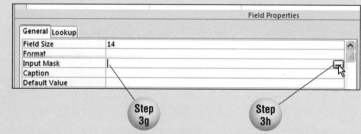

Step 2k

m. Click the Next button.
n. At the fourth Input Mask Wizard dialog box, click the Finish button.
o. Click in the *Description* column in the *ZipCode* row and then type **Supplier nine-digit Zip code**.

3. Create a new *Telephone* field with an Input Mask by completing the following steps:
   a. Click anywhere in the text *Email* that displays in the *Field Name* column.
   b. Click the Insert Rows button in the Tools group.
   c. With the insertion point positioned in the new blank field in the *Field Name* column, type **Telephone**.
   d. Press the Tab key. (This moves the insertion point to the *Data Type* column.)
   e. Select *255* that displays in the *Field Size* text box in the *Field Properties* section of the window and then type **14**.
   f. Click the Save button to save the table. (You must save the table before using the Input Mask Wizard.)
   g. Click in the Input Mask box in the *Field Properties* section of the window.
   h. Click the Build button (button containing three black dots) that displays to the right of the Input Mask box.

Step 3g

Step 3h

   i. At the first Input Mask Wizard dialog box, make sure *Phone Number* is selected in the *Input Mask* list box and then click the Next button.

Step 3i

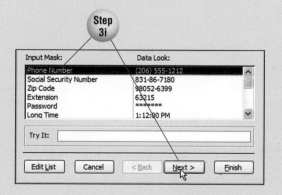

j. At the second Input Mask Wizard dialog box, click the down-pointing arrow at the right side of the *Placeholder character* box and then click # at the drop-down list.

k. Click the Next button.

l. At the third Input Mask Wizard dialog box, click the *With the symbols in the mask, like this* option.

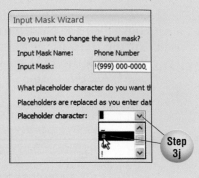

Step 3j

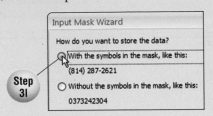

Step 3l

m. Click the Next button.

n. At the fourth Input Mask Wizard dialog box, click the Finish button.

o. Click in the *Description* column in the *Telephone* row and then type **Supplier telephone number**.

p. Click the Save button on the Quick Access toolbar.

4. Add ZIP codes for the records in the Suppliers table by completing the following steps:
   a. Click the View button to switch to Datasheet view.
   b. Click in the field containing *LA* (immediately left of the new blank field below *ZipCode*) and then press the Tab key.
   c. Type **303239089** and then press the Down Arrow key. (This moves the insertion point to the next blank field in the *ZipCode* column. The Input Mask automatically inserts a hyphen between 30323 and 9089.)

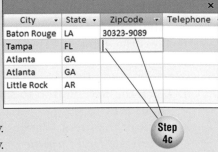

Step 4c

   d. Type **303542487** and then press the Down Arrow key.
   e. Type **303573652** and then press the Down Arrow key.
   f. Type **303654311** and then press the Down Arrow key.
   g. Type **303253499**.

5. Add telephone numbers for the records in the Suppliers table by completing the following steps:
   a. Click in the field containing the ZIP code *30323-9089* and then press the Tab key.
   b. Type **2255557454** and then press the Down Arrow key. (The Input Mask automatically inserts the parentheses, spaces, and hyphens in the telephone numbers.)
   c. Type **8135553495** and then press the Down Arrow key.
   d. Type **4045557732** and then press the Down Arrow key.
   e. Type **4045550926** and then press the Down Arrow key.
   f. Type **5015554509**.

6. Save, print, and then close the Suppliers table.

Using the Lookup Wizard

Like the Input Mask Wizard, you can use the Lookup Wizard to control the data entered in a field. Use the Lookup Wizard to confine the data entered into a field to a specific list of items. For example, in Project 1d you will use the Lookup Wizard to restrict the new *EmpCategory* field to one of three choices—*Salaried, Hourly,* and *Temporary*. When the user clicks in the field in the datasheet, a down-pointing arrow displays. The user clicks this down-pointing arrow to display a drop-down list of available entries and then clicks the desired item.

Use the Lookup Wizard when assigning a data type to a field. Click in the *Data Type* text box and then click the down-pointing arrow that displays at the right side of the box. At the drop-down list that displays, click *Lookup Wizard*. This displays the first Lookup Wizard dialog box as shown in Figure 3.4. At this dialog box, indicate that you want to enter the field choices by clicking the *I will type in the values that I want* option, and then click the Next button. At the second Lookup Wizard dialog box shown in Figure 3.5, click in the blank text box below *Col1* and then type the first choice. Press the Tab key and then type the second choice. Continue in this manner until all desired choices are entered and then click the Next button. At the third Lookup Wizard dialog box, make sure the proper name displays in the *What label would you like for your lookup column?* text box and then click the Finish button.

QUICK STEPS

Use Lookup Wizard
1. Open table in Design view.
2. Type text in *Field Name* column.
3. Press Tab key.
4. Click down-pointing arrow.
5. Click *Lookup Wizard*.
6. At first Lookup Wizard dialog box, make desired changes.
7. Click Next.
8. At second Lookup Wizard dialog box, click in blank text box.
9. Type desired text.
10. Press Tab key.
11. Continue typing text and pressing Tab until all desired text is entered.
12. Click Next.
13. Click Finish.

HINT
You can activate the Lookup Wizard by clicking the Lookup Column button in the Table Tools Datasheet tab.

Figure 3.4 First Lookup Wizard Dialog Box

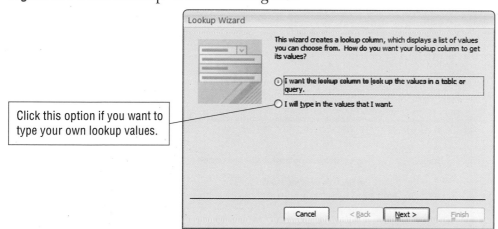

Click this option if you want to type your own lookup values.

Figure 3.5 Second Lookup Wizard Dialog Box

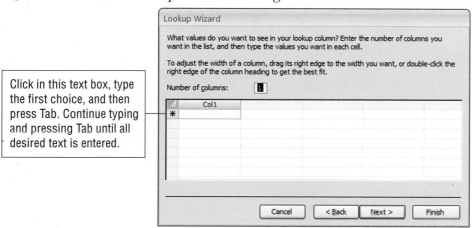

Click in this text box, type the first choice, and then press Tab. Continue typing and pressing Tab until all desired text is entered.

1. With the **MedSafeClinic.accdb** database open, open the Employees table.
2. Add the field *EmpCategory* and use the Lookup Wizard to specify field choices by completing the following steps:
   a. Click the View button to change to Design view.
   b. Click on any character in the *Ext* data in the *Field Name* column.
   c. Click the Insert Rows button in the Tools group.
   d. With the insertion point positioned in the new blank field in the *Field Name* column, type **EmpCategory**.
   e. Press the Tab key. (This moves the insertion point to the *Data Type* column.)
   f. Click the down-pointing arrow at the right side of the text box and then click *Lookup Wizard* at the drop-down list.
   g. At the first Lookup Wizard dialog box, click the *I will type in the values that I want* option and then click the Next button.

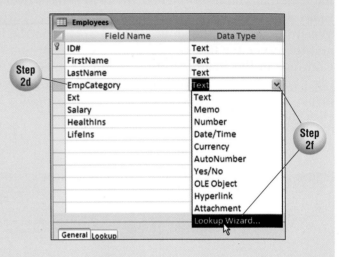

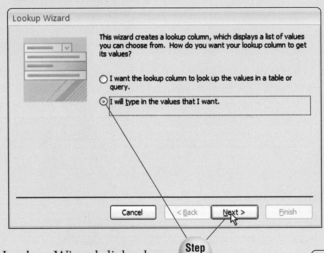

   h. At the second Lookup Wizard dialog box, click in the blank text box below *Col1*, type **Salaried**, and then press the Tab key.
   i. Type **Hourly** and then press the Tab key.
   j. Type **Temporary**.
   k. Click the Next button.
   l. At the third Lookup Wizard dialog box, click the Finish button.
   m. Press the Tab key and then type **Employee category** in the *Description* column.
3. Click the Save button on the Quick Access toolbar.

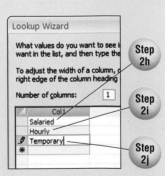

4. Insert information in the *EmpCategory* for the records by completing the following steps:
   a. Click the View button to switch to Datasheet view.
   b. Click in the first blank field below the new *EmpCategory* field.
   c. Click the down-pointing arrow at the right side of the field and then click *Hourly* at the drop-down list.
   d. Click in the next blank field in the *EmpCategory*, click the down-pointing arrow, and then click *Salaried* at the drop-down list.
   e. Continue entering information in the *EmpCategory* by completing similar steps. Choose the following in the specified record:

Step 4c

	ID#	FirstName	LastName	EmpCategor	Ext
	117	Douglas	Marino		2218
	132	Rosemary	Connors	Salaried	4199
	176	Joy	Sutherland	Hourly	3226
	199	Kristen	Ridgway	Temporary	2122
	210	Lawrence	Gianni		2278
	265	Randy	Lewandowski		3217

Third record	Hourly
Fourth record	Salaried
Fifth record	Temporary
Sixth record	Hourly
Seventh record	Salaried
Eighth record	Temporary
Ninth record	Hourly

5. Save and then print the Employees table in landscape orientation.

Moving a Field

You can move a field in a table to a different location. To do this, open the table and then change to Design view. Click in the record selector bar at the left side of the row you want to move. With the row selected, position the arrow pointer in the record selector bar at the left side of the selected row until the pointer turns into the normal arrow pointer (white arrow pointing up and to the left). Hold down the left mouse button, drag the arrow pointer with the gray square attached until a thick black line displays in the desired position, and then release the mouse button.

QUICK STEPS

Move a Field
1. Open table in Design view.
2. Select row to be moved.
3. Drag selected row to new position.

Project 1e Moving Fields in Tables

1. With the Employees table open, click the View button to switch to Design view.
2. Move the *EmpCategory* field immediately below the *Ext* field by completing the following steps:
   a. Click in the record selector bar at the left side of the *EmpCategory* field to select the row.
   b. Position the arrow pointer in the record selector bar of the selected row until it turns into the normal arrow pointer (white arrow pointing up and to the left).
   c. Hold down the left mouse button, drag the arrow pointer with the gray square attached until a thick black line displays below the *Ext* field, and then release the mouse button.

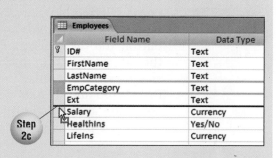

Step 2c

Field Name	Data Type
ID#	Text
FirstName	Text
LastName	Text
EmpCategory	Text
Ext	Text
Salary	Currency
HealthIns	Yes/No
LifeIns	Currency

3. Click the Save button on the Quick Access toolbar.
4. Click the View button to switch to Datasheet view.
5. Print the table in landscape orientation.
6. Close the Employees table.
7. Open the Products table and then move the *ReorderLevel* field by completing the following steps:
   a. Click the View button to switch to Design view.
   b. Select the row containing the *ReorderLevel* field.
   c. Position the arrow pointer on the blue button at the left side of the selected row until the pointer turns into the normal arrow pointer (white arrow pointing up and to the left).
   d. Hold down the left mouse button, drag the arrow pointer below the *UnitsOnOrder* field, and then release the mouse button.

Products	
Field Name	Data Type
ProductID	AutoNumber
ProductName	Text
SupplierID	Text
UnitsInStock	Number
UnitsOnOrder	Number
UnitPrice	Currency
ReorderLevel	Number

Step 7d

8. Click the Save button on the Quick Access.
9. Click the View button to switch to Datasheet view.
10. Print the Products table in landscape orientation.
11. Close the Products table.

Sort Records
1. Open table in Datasheet view.
2. Click in field in desired column.
3. Click Ascending button or Descending button.

Print Selected Records
1. Open table and select records.
2. Click Office button, *Print*.
3. Click *Selected Record(s)*.
4. Click OK.

Ascending

Descending

Sorting Records

The Sort & Filter group in the Home tab contains two buttons you can use to sort data in records. Click the Ascending button to sort from lowest to highest on the field where the insertion point is located or click the Descending button to sort from highest to lowest.

Printing Specific Records

If you click the Quick Print button on the Quick Access toolbar, all of the records in the selected or open table are printed. If you want to print specific records in a table, select the records and then display the Print dialog box by clicking the Office button and then clicking *Print* at the drop-down list. At the Print dialog box, click the *Selected Records* option in the *Print Range* section and then click OK. To select specific records, display the table in Datasheet view, click the record selector of the first record and then drag to select the desired records. The record selector is the light blue square that displays at the left side of the record. When you position the mouse pointer on the record selector, the pointer turns into a right-pointing black arrow.

1. With the **MedSafeClinic.accdb** database open, open the Employees table.
2. With the table in Datasheet view, sort records in ascending alphabetical order by completing the following steps:
   a. Click any last name in the table.
   b. Click the Ascending button in the Sort & Filter group in the Home tab.

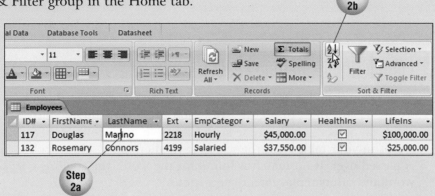

Step 2b

Step 2a

   c. Print the Employees table in landscape orientation.
3. Sort records in descending order (highest to lowest) by employee ID number by completing the following steps:
   a. Click on any number in the *ID#* field.
   b. Click the Descending button in the Sort & Filter group.

Step 3a

Step 3b

   c. Print the Employees table in landscape orientation.
4. Sort and print selected records of the salaried employees by completing the following steps:
   a. Click any entry in the *EmpCategory* field.
   b. Remove the Totals row by clicking the Totals button in the Records group in the Home tab.
   c. Click the Ascending button in the Sort & Filter group.
   d. Position the mouse pointer on the record selector of the first salaried employee, hold down the mouse button, and then drag to select the three records of salaried employees.
   e. Click the Office button and then click *Print* at the drop-down list.
   f. At the Print dialog box, click the *Selected Record(s)* option in the *Print Range* section.
   g. Click OK.
5. Click the Save button on the Quick Access toolbar.
6. Close the Employees table and then close the **MedSafeClinic.accdb** database.

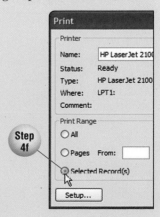

Step 4f

You will complete a spelling check on data in tables and find data and replace it with other data in tables. You will also back up a database and compact and repair a database.

HINT

You can also begin spell checking with the keyboard shortcut F7.

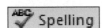

Completing a Spelling Check

The spelling checker feature in Access finds misspelled words and offers replacement words. It also finds duplicate words and irregular capitalizations. When you spell check an object in a database such as a table, the spelling checker compares the words in your table with the words in its dictionary. If a match is found, the word is passed over. If no match is found for the word, the spelling checker selects the word and offers replacement suggestions.

To complete a spelling check, open the desired table in Datasheet view and then click the Spelling button in the Records group in the Home tab. If the spelling checker does not find a match for a word in your table, the Spelling dialog box displays with replacement options. Figure 3.6 displays the Spelling dialog box with the word *Montain* selected and possible replacements displayed in the *Suggestions* list box. At the Spelling dialog box, you can choose to ignore the word (for example, if the spelling checker has selected a proper name), change to one of the replacement options, or add the word to the dictionary or AutoCorrect feature. You can also complete a spelling check on other objects in a database such as a query, form, or report. (You will learn about these objects in future chapters.)

Figure 3.6 Spelling Dialog Box

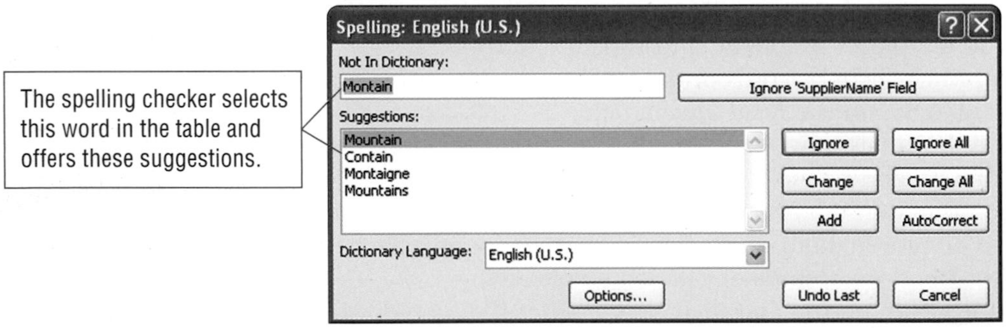

The spelling checker selects this word in the table and offers these suggestions.

Project 2a   Checking Spelling in a Table

1. Open the **MedSafeClinic.accdb** database.
2. Open the Suppliers table.
3. In Datasheet view, add the following record at the end of the table. (Type the misspelled words as shown below. You will correct the spelling in a later step.)

SupplierID	=	6
SupplierName	=	Blue Montain Supplies
Address	=	9550 Unaversity Avenue
City	=	Little Rock
State	=	AR
ZipCode	=	322093412
Telephone	=	5015554400
Email	=	bluem@emcp.net

Step 3

	SupplierID	SupplierName	Address	City	State	ZipCode	Telephone
⊞	1	Robicheaux Suppliers	3200 Linden Drive	Baton Rouge	LA	30323-9089	(225) 555-745
⊞	2	Quality Medical Supplies	211 South Fourth Avenue	Tampa	FL	30354-2487	(813) 555-349
⊞	3	Peachtree Medical Supplies	764 Harmon Way	Atlanta	GA	30357-3652	(404) 555-773
⊞	4	Lafferty Company	12031 Ruston Way	Atlanta	GA	30365-4311	(404) 555-092
⊞	5	National Products	2192 Second Street	Little Rock	AR	30325-3499	(501) 555-450
⊞	6	Blue Montain Supplies	9550 Unaversity Avenue	Little Rock	AR	72209-3412	(501) 555-440

4. Save the Suppliers table.
5. Click in the first entry in the *SupplierID* column.
6. Click the Spelling button in the Records group in the Home tab.
7. The spelling checker selects the name *Robicheaux*. This is a proper name, so click the Ignore button to tell the spelling checker to leave the name as written.
8. The spelling checker selects *Montain*. The proper spelling (*Mountain*) is selected in the *Suggestions* list box, so click the Change button.
9. The spelling checker selects *Unaversity*. The proper spelling (*University*) is selected in the *Suggestions* list box, so click the Change button.
10. At the message telling you that the spelling check is complete, click the OK button.

Step 7

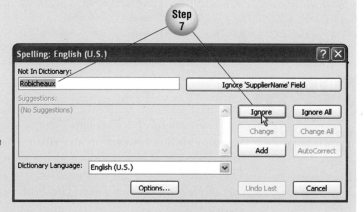

Step 8

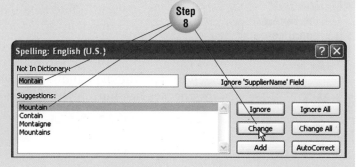

QUICK STEPS

Find Data
1. Open table in Datasheet view.
2. Click Find button.
3. Type data in *Find What* text box.
4. Click Find Next button.
5. Continue clicking Find Next button until entire table is searched.

Finding and Replacing Data

If you need to find a specific entry in a field in a table, consider using options at the Find and Replace dialog box with the Find tab selected as shown in Figure 3.7. Display this dialog box by clicking the Find button in the Find group in the Home tab. At the Find and Replace dialog box, enter the data for which you are searching in the *Find What* text box. By default, Access will look in the specific column where the insertion point is positioned. Click the Find Next button to find the next occurrence of the data or click the Cancel button to remove the Find and Replace dialog box.

HINT

Press Ctrl + F to display the Find and Replace dialog box with the Find tab selected.

Find

Figure 3.7 Find and Replace Dialog Box with Find Tab Selected

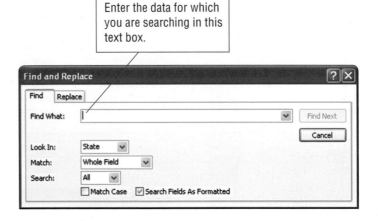

Enter the data for which you are searching in this text box.

QUICK STEPS

Find and Replace Data
1. Open table in Datasheet view.
2. Click Replace button.
3. Type find data in *Find What* text box.
4. Type replace data in *Replace With* text box.
5. Click Find Next button.
6. Click Replace button or Find Next button.

The *Look In* option defaults to the column where the insertion point is positioned. You can choose to look in the entire table by clicking the down-pointing arrow at the right side of the option and then clicking the table name at the drop-down list. The *Match* option has a default setting of *Whole Field*. You can change this to *Any Part of Field* or *Start of Field*. The *Search* option has a default setting of *All*, which means that Access will search all data in a specific column. This can be changed to *Up* or *Down*. If you want to find data that contains specific uppercase and lowercase letters, insert a check mark in the *Match Case* check box. By default, Access will search fields as they are formatted.

You can use the Find and Replace dialog box with the Replace tab selected to search for specific data and replace with other data. Display this dialog box by clicking the Replace button in the Find group in the Home tab.

HINT

Press Ctrl + H to display the Find and Replace dialog box with the Replace tab selected.

 Replace

1. With the Suppliers table open, find any records containing the two-letter state abbreviation *GA* by completing the following steps:
   a. Click in the first entry in the *State* column.
   b. Click the Find button in the Find group in the Home tab.

c. At the Find and Replace dialog box with the Find tab selected, type **GA** in the *Find What* text box.
   d. Click the Find Next button. (Access finds and selects the first occurrence of *GA*. If the Find and Replace dialog box covers the data, drag the dialog box to a different location on the screen.)

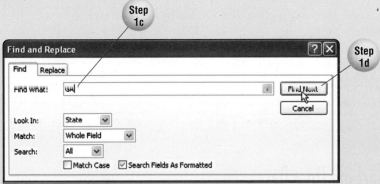

e. Continue clicking the Find Next button until a message displays telling you that Access has finished searching the records. At this message, click OK.
   f. Click the Cancel button to close the Find and Replace dialog box.
2. Suppose Quality Medical Supplies has changed its telephone number. Complete the following steps to find the current telephone number and replace it with the new telephone number:
   a. Click in the first entry in the *Telephone* column.
   b. Click the Replace button in the Find group.

c. At the Find and Replace dialog box with the Replace tab selected, type (813) 555-3495 in the *Find What* text box.
d. Press the Tab key. (This moves the insertion point to the *Replace With* text box.)
e. Type (813) 555-9800 in the *Replace With* text box.
f. Click the Find Next button.
g. When Access selects the telephone number *(813) 555-3495*, click the Replace button.

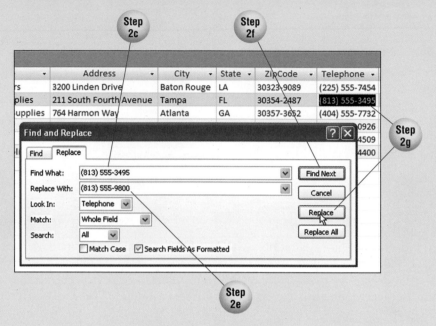

h. Click the Cancel button to close the Find and Replace dialog box.
3. Save the Suppliers table.
4. Display the table in Print Preview, change the page orientation to landscape, change the margins to *Normal*, and then print the table.
5. Close the Suppliers table.

QUICK STEPS Backing Up a Database

Back Up Database
1. Open database.
2. Click Office button, Manage, Back Up Database.
3. Navigate to desired folder or drive.
4. Type file name.
5. Click Save button.

Back up a database on a consistent basis to protect the data in the database from accidental loss or from any hardware failure. To back up a database, click the Office button, point to *Manage*, and then click *Back Up Database*. At the Save As dialog box, navigate to the desired folder or drive, type a name for the database, and then press Enter or click the Save button.

Compacting and Repairing a Database

To optimize performance of your database, compact and repair the database on a consistent basis. As you work with a database, data in the database can become fragmented causing the amount of space the database takes on the storage medium or in the folder to be larger than necessary.

To compact and repair a database, open the database, click the Office button, point to *Manage*, and then click *Compact and Repair Database*. As the database is compacting and repairing, a message displays on the Status bar indicating the progress of the procedure. When the procedure is completed, close the database.

You can tell Access to compact and repair a database each time you close the database. To do this, click the Office button and then click the Access Options button located in the lower right corner of the drop-down list. At the Access Options dialog box, click *Current Database* in the left panel. This displays the Access Options dialog box as shown in Figure 3.8. Click the *Compact on Close* option to insert a check mark and then click OK to close the window.

QUICK STEPS

Compact and Repair Database
1. Open database.
2. Click Office button, Manage, Compact and Repair Database.

HINT

Before compacting and repairing a database in a multi-user environment, make sure that no other user has the database open.

Figure 3.8 Access Options Dialog Box with *Current Database* Selected

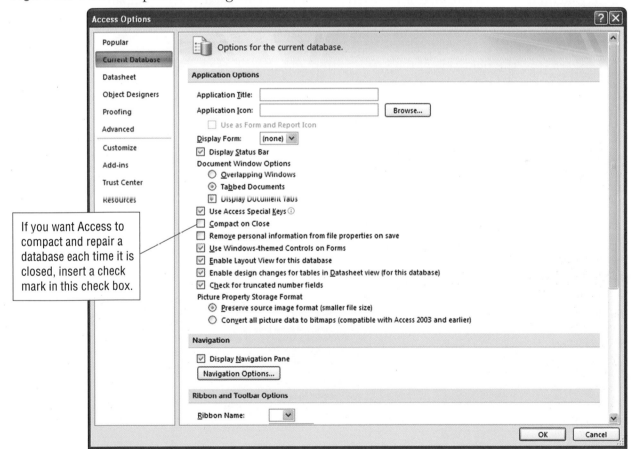

If you want Access to compact and repair a database each time it is closed, insert a check mark in this check box.

1. With the **MedSafeClinic,accdb** database open, create a backup of the database by completing the following steps:
   a. Click the Office button, point to *Manage*, and then click *Back Up Database*.
   b. At the Save As dialog box, type MSCBackup10-01-2010 in the *File name* text box. (This file name assumes that the date is October 1, 2010. You do not have to use the date in the file name but it does help when using the backup feature to archive databases.)
   c. Click the Save button.

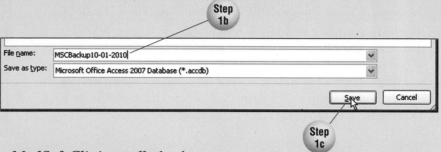

2. Close the **MedSafeClinic.accdb** database.
3. Determine the current size of the **MedSafeClinic.accdb** database (to compare to the size after compacting and repairing) by completing the following steps:
   a. Click the Open button on the Quick Access toolbar.
   b. At the Open dialog box, click the down-pointing arrow at the right side of the Views button and then click *Details* at the drop-down list.
   c. Display the drive (or folder) where your **MedSafeClinic.accdb** database is located and then check the size of the database.
   d. Close the Open dialog box.
4. Compact and repair the **MedSafeClinic.accdb** database by completing the following steps:
   a. Open the **MedSafeClinic.accdb** database.
   b. Click the Office button, point to *Manage*, and then click *Compact and Repair Database*.

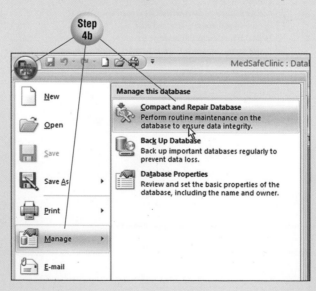

c. When the compact and repair procedure is completed, close the **MedSafeClinic.accdb** database.

5. Determine the size of the compacted and repaired **MedSafeClinic.accdb** database by completing the following steps:

a. Click the Open button on the Quick Access toolbar.

b. At the Open dialog box, make sure the details display in the list box and then look at the size of the **MedSafeClinic.accdb** database and compare this size to the previous size. (Notice that the size of the compacted and repaired **MedSafeClinic.accdb** database is approximately the same size as the **MSCBackup10-01-2010.accdb** database. The backup database was automatically compacted and repaired when saved.)

c. Return the display to a list by clicking the down-pointing arrow at the right side of the Views button and then clicking *List* at the drop-down list.

6. Close the Open dialog box.

Project ③ Use Access Help

You will use the Access Help feature to display information on creating an input mask and performing diagnostic tests.

Using Help

The Access Help feature is an on-screen reference manual containing information about all Access features and commands. The Access Help feature is similar to the Windows Help and the Help features in Word, PowerPoint, and Excel. Get help by clicking the Microsoft Office Access Help button located in the upper right corner of the screen (the button containing a question mark) or by pressing F1. This displays the Access Help window shown in Figure 3.9.

Use Help Feature
1. Click Microsoft Office Access Help button.
2. Type topic, feature, or question.
3. Press Enter.
4. Click desired topic.

HINT
Press F1 to display the Access Help window.

Help

Figure 3.9 Access Help Window

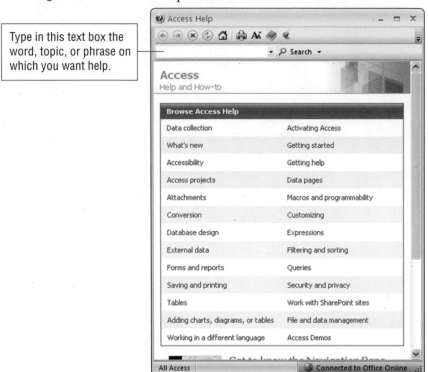

Type in this text box the word, topic, or phrase on which you want help.

Project ③ Getting Help

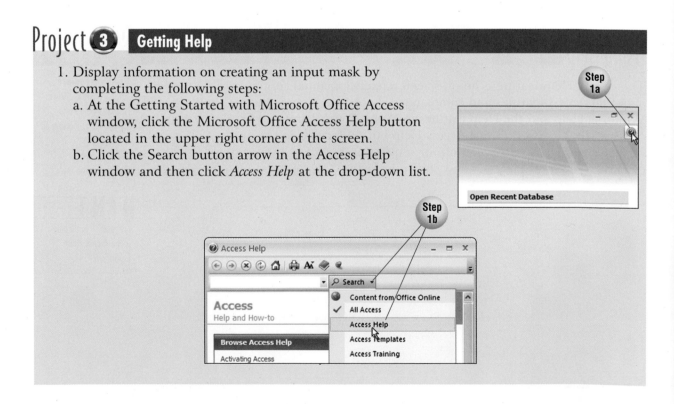

1. Display information on creating an input mask by completing the following steps:
   a. At the Getting Started with Microsoft Office Access window, click the Microsoft Office Access Help button located in the upper right corner of the screen.
   b. Click the Search button arrow in the Access Help window and then click *Access Help* at the drop-down list.

Step 1a

Open Recent Database

Step 1b

c. Click in the *Search* text box.

d. Type **input mask** and then press the Enter key.

e. Click the *Create an input mask to enter field or control values in a specific format* option that displays in the Help window.

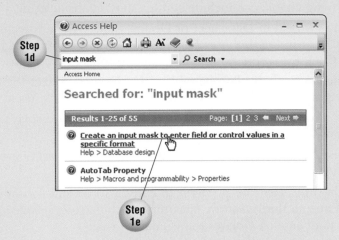

f. Read the information on creating an input mask.

2. Find information on performing diagnostic tests by completing the following steps:

a. Select the text *input mask* that displays in the *Search* text box.

b. Type **diagnostic test** and then press Enter.

c. Click the *Diagnose and repair crashing Office programs by using Office Diagnostics* option.

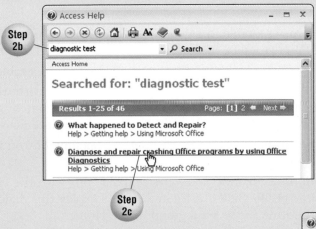

d. Read the information on using Office diagnostics.

e. Print the information by clicking the Print button on the toolbar located towards the top of the Help window.

f. At the Print dialog box, click the Print button.

3. Close the Help window by clicking the Close button located in the upper right corner of the window.

CHAPTER summary

- Modifying a table can include adding, moving, or deleting a field.

- Add a new field in Datasheet or Design view. Type new records in a blank database or in the *Add New Field* column or add a row for a new field in Design view. Click the Insert Rows button in the Tools group to insert a new field.

- To delete a field, display the table in Design view, select the record you want deleted, and then click the Delete Rows button. Click Yes at the message.

- Select a row by clicking the record selector bar that displays at the left side of the row.

- Use the *Default Value* property in the *Field Properties* section to insert the most common field entry.

- Use the *Validation Rule* property to enter a statement containing a conditional test. Enter in the *Validation Text* property the error message you want to display if the data entered violates the validation rule.

- Click the Totals button in the Records group in the Home tab and Access inserts a row at the bottom of the datasheet with the label *Total* at the left. Click the down-pointing arrow in the Total row and then click the desired function at the drop-down list.

- Use the Input Mask Wizard to set a pattern for how data is entered in a field.

- Use the Lookup Wizard to confine data entered in a field to a specific list of items.

- Sort records in a table in ascending order with the Ascending button in the Sort & Filter group or in descending order with the Descending button.

- Use the spelling checker to find misspelled words in a table.

- The spelling checker compares the words in a table with words in its dictionary. If a match is found, the word is passed over. If no match is found, the spelling checker will select the word and offer possible replacements.

- Begin the spelling checker by clicking the Spelling button in the Records group in the Home tab.

- Use options at the Find and Replace dialog box with the Find tab selected to search for specific field entries in a table. Display this dialog box by clicking the Find button in the Find group in the Home tab.

- Use options at the Find and Replace dialog box with the Replace tab selected to search for specific data and replace with other data. Display this dialog box by clicking the Replace button in the Find group in the Home tab.

- Back up a database on a consistent basis to protect the data in the database from accidental loss or from any hardware failure. To back up a database, click the Office button, point to *Manage*, and then click *Back Up Database*.

- Compact and repair a database to optimize the performance of the database. Compact and repair a database by clicking the Office button, pointing to *Manage*, and then clicking *Compact and Repair Database*.

- Display the Access Help window by clicking the Microsoft Office Access Help button located in the upper right corner of the screen.

COMMANDS review

FEATURE	RIBBON TAB, GROUP	BUTTON, OPTION	KEYBOARD SHORTCUT
Add field	Table Tools Design, Tools	Insert Rows	
Delete field	Table Tools Design, Tools	Delete Rows	
Sort records ascending	Home, Sort & Filter	A↓Z	
Sort records descending	Home, Sort & Filter	Z↓A	
Spelling checker	Home, Records	Spelling	F7
Find and Replace dialog box with Find tab selected	Home, Find		Ctrl + F
Find and Replace dialog box with Replace tab selected	Home, Find	Replace	Ctrl + H
Back up database		, Manage, Back Up Database	
Compare and repair database		, Manage, Compact and Repair Database	
Access Help window		?	F1

CONCEPTS check

Test Your Knowledge

Completion: For each description, indicate the correct term, symbol, or character.

1. Select a row by clicking this bar that displays at the left side of the row.

   Record Selector Bar

2. If most records are likely to contain the same field value, use this property to insert the most common field entry.

   Default Value

3. Use this property to enter a statement containing a conditional test that is checked each time data is entered into a field.

   Validation Rule

4. Use this wizard to set a pattern for how data is entered in a field.

   Input Mask

5. Use this wizard to confine data entered in a field to a specific list of items.

   Lookup

6. The Ascending and Descending sort buttons are located in this group in the Home tab.

   Sort & Filter

7. The Spelling button is located in this group in the Home tab.

   Records

8. This is the keyboard shortcut to begin spell checking.

   F7

9. Use options at the Find and Replace dialog box with this tab selected to search for specific data and replace with other data.

   Home

10. To back up a database, click the Office button, point to this option, and then click *Back Up Database*.

    manage

11. Perform this action on a database to optimize the performance of the database.

    Compact & Repair

12. This is the keyboard shortcut to display the Access Help window.

    F1

SKILLS check

Demonstrate Your Proficiency

Assessment

1 CREATE TABLES AND RELATIONSHIPS BETWEEN TABLES IN A LAFFERTYCOMPANY DATABASE

1. Create a database named *LaffertyCompany* that contains two tables. Create the first table and name it *MarketingEmployees* and include the following fields (make sure the *EmpID* is identified as the primary key):

Field Name	Data Type
EmpID	Text (field size = 4)
FirstName	Text (field size = 20)
MiddleName	Text (field size = 20)
LastName	Text (field size = 30)
Status	Text (field size = 20; assign a default value of *Full-time*)
HireDate	Date/Time (use the Input Mask to control the date so it is entered as a short date)
Vacation	Text (field size = 10; use the Lookup Wizard to confine the field entry to one of three entries: *0 weeks*, *2 weeks*, or *3 weeks*

2. Type the following data or choose a field entry in the specified fields:

EmpID	1002		*EmpID*	3192
FirstName	Samantha		*FirstName*	Ralph
MiddleName	Lee		*MiddleName*	Edward
LastName	Murray		*LastName*	Sorrell
Status	Full-time		*Status*	Full-time
HireDate	06/15/2005		*HireDate*	11/04/2006
Vacation	3 weeks		*Vacation*	3 weeks
EmpID	1799		*EmpID*	2217
FirstName	Brandon		*FirstName*	Leland
MiddleName	Michael		*MiddleName*	John
LastName	Perrault		*LastName*	Nitsche
Status	Full-time		*Status*	Part-time
HireDate	03/12/2007		*HireDate*	09/05/2008
Vacation	2 weeks		*Vacation*	0 weeks
EmpID	1340		*EmpID*	1877
FirstName	Jack		*FirstName*	Immanuel
MiddleName	Ryan		*MiddleName*	Nolan
LastName	McCleary		*LastName*	Shandra
Status	Full-time		*Title*	Part-time
HireDate	07/01/2007		*HireDate*	08/01/2009
Vacation	2 weeks		*Vacation*	0 weeks

3. Complete a spelling check on the table. (Assume proper names are spelled correctly.)
4. Adjust the column widths.
5. Save the MarketingEmployees table.
6. Change the orientation to landscape and then print the table.
7. Close the MarketingEmployees table.
8. Create the second table and name it *Expenses* and include the following fields (make sure the *Item#* field is identified as the primary key):

Field Name	Data Type
Item#	AutoNumber
EmpID	Text (field size = 4)
Expense	Text (field size = 30)
Amount	Currency (Type a condition in the *Validation Rule* property that states the entry must be $500 or less. Type an error message in the *Validation Text* property box.)
DateSubmitted	Date/Time (Use the Input Mask to control the date so it is entered as a short date.)

9. Type the following data or choose a field entry in the specified fields (Access automatically inserts a number in the *Item#* field):

EmpID	3192	*EmpID*	1799
Expense	**Brochures**	*Expense*	**Marketing Conference**
Amount	$245.79	*Amount*	$500.00
DateSubmitted	02/01/2010	*DateSubmitted*	02/08/2010
EmpID	3192	*EmpID*	1340
Expense	**Business Cards**	*Expense*	**Marketing Conference**
Amount	$150.00	*Amount*	$500.00
DateSubmitted	02/10/2010	*DateSubmitted*	02/10/2010
EmpID	1799	*EmpID*	1340
Expense	**Supplies**	*Expense*	**Reference Material**
Amount	$487.25	*Amount*	$85.75
DateSubmitted	02/14/2010	*DateSubmitted*	02/15/2010

10. Complete a spelling check on the table.
11. Adjust the column widths.
12. Save, print, and then close the Expenses table.
13. Create a one-to-many relationship where *EmpID* in the MarketingEmployees table is the "one" and *EmpID* in the Expenses table is the "many."
14. Print the relationship and then close the relationships report window and the relationships window.

Assessment

2 MODIFY A TABLE AND FIND AND REPLACE DATA IN A TABLE

1. With the **LaffertyCompany.accdb** database open, open the MarketingEmployees table and then make the following changes:
   a. Delete the *MiddleName* field.
   b. Insert a *Title* field between *LastName* and *Status*. (You determine the data type and description.)
   c. Move the *Status* field below the *HireDate* field.
   d. In Datasheet view, add the data to the *Title* field as specified below:

EmpID	Title
1002	Manager
3192	Assistant Manager
1799	Manager
2217	Assistant
1340	Assistant
1877	Assistant

2. Save the MarketingEmployees table.
3. Find all occurrences of *Manager* and replace with *Director*. **Hint: Position the insertion point in the first entry in the Title *column and then display the Find and Replace dialog box. At the dialog box, change the* Match *option to* Any Part of Field.**
4. Find all occurrences of *Assistant* and replace with *Associate*.
5. Save and then print the table in landscape orientation with *Normal* margins.
6. Close the MarketingEmployees table.
7. Open the Expenses table, insert a Total row in the table, and then calculate the sum of the expenses.
8. Save, print, and then close the Expenses table.
9. Close the **LaffertyCompany.accdb** database.

CASE study
Apply Your Skills

Part 1

You work for Sunrise Enterprises and your supervisor has asked you to create a database with information about clients and sales representatives. Create a database named *Sunrise* that contains two tables. Create a table named *Representatives* that includes fields for representative ID number, representative name, representative telephone number (use the Input Mask Wizard), insurance plan (use the Lookup Wizard and include four options: *Platinum*, *Premium*, *Standard*, and *None*) and yearly bonus (type a condition in the *Validation Rule* property that states the entry must be between $2,000 and $10,000 and type an error message in the *Validation Text* property box). Make sure the representative ID number is the primary key in the table. In Datasheet view, enter seven records in the table. Insert a total row and then sum the bonus amounts. Save, print, and then close the table.

Create a second table in the **Sunrise.accdb** database named *Clients* that includes fields for company ID number, representative ID number (the same field you created in the Representative table) company name, address, city, state, ZIP code (use the Input Mask Wizard and specify a nine digit ZIP code), telephone number (use the Input Wizard), and type of business (specify that *Wholesaler* is the default value). Make sure that the company ID number is identified as the primary key. In Datasheet view, enter at least five companies. Make sure you use representative ID numbers in the Clients table that match numbers in the Representative table. Identify that one of the clients is a "*Retailer*" rather than a "*Wholesaler*." Save, print, and then close the table.

Part 2

Create a one-to-many relationship with the representative ID number in the Representatives table as the "one" and the representative ID number in the Clients table as the "many." Save and then print the relationship.

Part 3

Open the Representatives table and then reverse the order of the yearly bonus and the insurance plan fields. Save, print, and then close the table. Open the Clients table and then reverse the order of the telephone number and type of business fields. Save, print, and then close the table.

Part 4

In Microsoft Word, create a document that describes three situations where you would use the Lookup Wizard, three situations where you would assign a default value to a field, and three situations where you would write a conditional statement for a field. Apply any formatting to the document to enhance the visual appeal and then save the document and name it **Access_C3_CS_P4**. Print and then close **Access_C3_CS_P4.docx**.

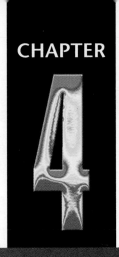

CHAPTER 4

Performing Queries

PERFORMANCE OBJECTIVES

Upon successful completion of Chapter 4, you will be able to:

access Chapter 4

- Design a query to extract specific data from a table
- Use the Simple Query Wizard to extract specific data from a table
- Modify a query

- Design queries with Or and And criteria
- Create a calculated field
- Use aggregate functions in queries
- Create crosstab, duplicate, and unmatched queries

Tutorial 4.1
Extracting Specific Data
Tutorial 4.2
Performing Advanced Queries
and Filtering Records

One of the primary uses of a database is to extract specific information from the database. A company might need to know such information as: How much inventory is currently on hand? What products have been ordered? What accounts are past due? What customers live in a particular city? You can extract this type of information from a table by completing a query. You will learn how to perform a variety of queries on information in tables in this chapter.

Note: Before beginning computer projects, copy the Access2007L1C4 subfolder from the Access2007L1 folder on the CD that accompanies this textbook to your storage medium and make Access2007L1C4 the active folder.

Project 1 Design Queries

You will design and run a number of queries including queries with fields from one table and queries with fields from more than one table. You will also use the Simple Query Wizard to design queries.

Performing Queries

Being able to extract (pull out) specific data from a table is one of the most important functions of a database. Extracting data in Access is referred to as performing a query. The word *query* means to ask a question. Access provides several methods for performing a query. You can design your own query, use a simple query wizard, or use complex query wizards. In this chapter, you will learn to design your own query; use the Simple Query Wizard; use aggregate functions in a query; and use the Crosstab, Find Duplicates, and Unmatched Query Wizards.

Designing a Query

Designing a query consists of identifying the table from which you are gathering data, the field or fields from which the data will be drawn, and the criteria for selecting the data. To design a query and perform the query, open a database, click the Create tab, and then click the Query Design button in the Other group. This displays a query window in the work area and also displays the Show Table dialog box as shown in Figure 4.1.

Figure 4.1 Query Window with Show Table Dialog Box

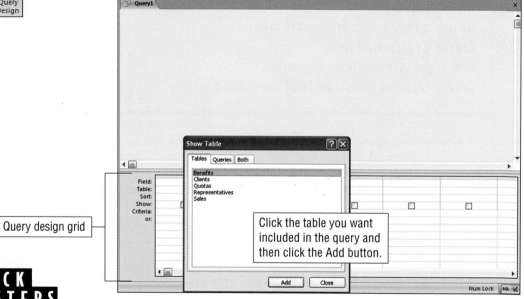

Query design grid

Click the table you want included in the query and then click the Add button.

Click the table in the Show Table list box that you want included in the query and then click the Add button or double-click the desired table. Add any other tables required for the query. When all tables have been added, click the Close button. In the query window, click the down-pointing arrow at the right of the first *Field* text box in the query design grid and then click the desired field from the drop-down list. Figure 4.2 displays a sample query window.

Figure 4.2 Query Window

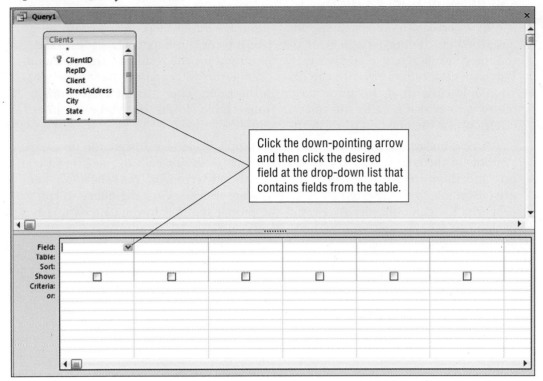

Click the down-pointing arrow and then click the desired field at the drop-down list that contains fields from the table.

To establish a criterion, click inside the *Criteria* text box in the column containing the desired field name in the query design grid and then type the criterion. With the fields and criteria established, click the Run button in the Results group in the Query Tools Design tab. Access searches the specified tables for records that match the criteria and then displays those records in the query results datasheet. If you plan to use the query in the future, save the query and name it. If you do not need the query again, close the query results datasheet without saving it.

You can click the down-pointing arrow at the right side of a *Field* text box and then click the desired field at the drop-down list. You can also double-click a field in a table and it is inserted in the first available *Field* text box in the query design grid. As an example, suppose you wanted to find out how many purchase orders were issued on a specific date. To do this, you would double-click *PurchaseOrderID* in the table (this inserts *PurchaseOrderID* in the first *Field* text box in the query design grid) and then double-click *OrderDate* in the table (this inserts *OrderDate* in the second *Field* text box in the query design grid). In this example, both fields are needed so the purchase order ID is displayed along with the specific order date. After inserting fields, you would then insert the criterion. The criterion for this example would be something like *#1/15/2010#*. After you insert the criterion, click the Run button in the Results group and the results of the query display in the query results datasheet.

A third method for inserting a field in the query design grid is to drag a field from the table to the desired field in the query design grid. To do this, position the mouse pointer on the desired field in the table, hold down the left mouse button, drag to the desired *Field* text box in the query design grid, and then release the mouse button.

HINT

Insert fields in the *Field* text boxes in the query design grid in the order in which you want the fields to display in the query results datasheet.

Run

QUICK
STEPS

Establish Query Criterion

1. At query window, click in desired *Criteria* text box in query design grid.
2. Type criterion and then press Enter.
3. Click Run button.

Establishing Query Criteria

A query does not require that specific criteria are established. In the example described on the previous page, if the criterion for the date was not included, the query would "return" (*return* is the term used for the results of the query) all Purchase Order numbers with the dates. While this information may be helpful, you could easily find this information in the table. The value of performing a query is to extract specific information from a table. To do this, you must insert a criterion like the one described in the example.

Access makes writing a criterion fairly simple because it inserts the necessary symbols in the criterion. If you type a city such as *Indianapolis* in the *Criteria* text box and then press Enter, Access changes the criterion to *"Indianapolis"*. The quotation marks are inserted by Access and are necessary for the query to run properly. You can either let Access put the proper symbols in the *Criteria* text box, or you can type the criterion with the symbols. Table 4.1 shows some criteria examples including what is typed and what is returned.

Table 4.1 Criteria Examples

Typing this criteria	*Returns this*
"Smith"	Field value matching *Smith*
"Smith" or "Larson"	Field value matching either *Smith* or *Larson*
Not "Smith"	Field value that is not *Smith* (the opposite of "Smith")
"S*"	Field value that begins with *S* and ends in anything
"*s"	Field value that begins with anything and ends in *s*
"[A-D]*"	Field value that begins with *A* through *D* and ends in anything
#01/01/2010#	Field value matching the date 01/01/2010
<#04/01/2010#	Field value less than (before) 04/01/2010
>#04/01/2010#	Field value greater than (after) 04/01/2010
Between #01/01/2010 And #03/31/2010	Any date between 01/01/2010 and 03/31/2010

HINT

Access inserts quotation marks around text criteria and the pound symbol around date criteria.

In Table 4.1, notice the quotation marks surrounding field values (such as "Smith"). If you do not type the quotation marks when typing the criterion, Access will automatically insert them. The same is true for the pound symbol (#). If you do not type the pound symbol around a date, Access will automatically insert the symbols. Access automatically inserts the correct symbol when you press the Enter key after typing the query criteria.

In the criteria examples, the asterisk was used as a wild card indicating any character. This is consistent with many other software applications where the asterisk is used as a wildcard character. Two of the criteria examples in Table 4.1 use the less than and greater than symbols. You can use these symbols for fields containing numbers, values, dates, amounts, and so forth. In the next several projects, you will be designing queries to extract specific information from different tables in databases.

Project 1a — Performing Queries on Tables

1. Display the Open dialog box with Access2007L1C4 on your storage medium the active folder.
2. Open the **Deering.accdb** database.
3. Create the following relationships:
   a. Create a one-to-one relationship where the *ClientID* field in the Clients table is the "one" and the *ClientID* field in the Sales table is the "one."
   b. Create a one-to-one relationship where the *RepID* field in the Representatives table is the "one" and the *RepID* field in the Benefits table is the "one."
   c. Create a one-to-many relationship where the *RepID* field in the Representatives table is the "one" and the *RepID* field in the Clients table is the "many."
   d. Create a one-to-many relationship where the *QuotaID* field in the Quotas table is the "one" and the *QuotaID* field in the Representatives table is the "many."
4. Save, print, and then close the relationships report and relationships window.
5. Extract records of those clients located in Indianapolis by completing the following steps:
   a. Click the Create tab.
   b. Click the Query Design button in the Other group.

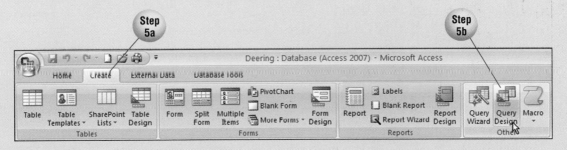

c. At the Show Table dialog box with the Tables tab selected (see Figure 4.1), click *Clients* in the list box, click the Add button, and then click the Close button.
d. Insert fields from the table to *Field* text boxes in the query design grid by completing the following steps:
   1) Click the down-pointing arrow located at the right of the first *Field* text box in the query design grid and then click *Client* in the drop-down list.

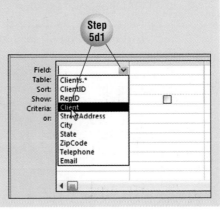

2) Click inside the next *Field* text box (to the right of *Client*) in the query design grid, click the down-pointing arrow, and then click *StreetAddress* in the drop-down list.
3) Click inside the next *Field* box (to the right of *StreetAddress*), click the down-pointing arrow, and then click *City* in the drop-down list.
4) Click inside the next *Field* box (to the right of *City*), click the down-pointing arrow, and then click *State* in the drop-down list.
5) Click inside the next *Field* box (to the right of *State*), click the down-pointing arrow, and then select *ZipCode* in the drop-down list.

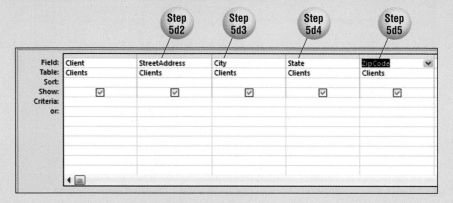

e. Insert the criterion text telling Access to display only those suppliers located in Indianapolis by completing the following steps:
1) Click in the *Criteria* text box in the *City* column in the query design grid. (This positions the insertion point inside the text box.)
2) Type **Indianapolis** and then press Enter. (This changes the criterion to "Indianapolis").

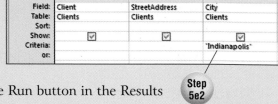

f. Return the results of the query by clicking the Run button in the Results group. (This displays the results in the query results datasheet.)
g. Save the results of the query by completing the following steps:
1) Click the Save button on the Quick Access toolbar.
2) At the Save As dialog box, type **IndianapolisQuery** and then press Enter or click OK.

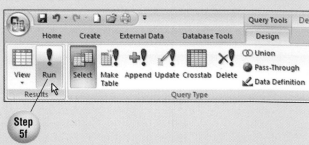

h. Print the query results datasheet by clicking the Quick Print button on the Quick Access toolbar.
i. Close IndianapolisQuery.

6. Extract those records with quota identification numbers higher than 2 by completing the following steps:
a. Click the Create tab and then click the Query Design button in the Other group.
b. Double-click *Representatives* in the Show Table list box and then click the Close button.
c. In the query window, double-click *RepName* (this inserts the field in the first *Field* text box in the query design grid).
d. Double-click *QuotaID* (this inserts the field in the second *Field* text box in the query design grid).

e. Insert the query criterion by completing the following steps:
   1) Click in the *Criteria* text box in the *QuotaID* column in the query design grid.
   2) Type >2 and then press Enter. (Access will automatically insert quotation marks around 2 since the data type for the field is set at *Text* [rather than *Number*].)

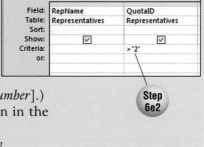

Step 6e2

f. Return the results of the query by clicking the Run button in the Results group.

g. Save the query and name it *QuotaIDGreaterThanTwoQuery*.

h. Print and then close the query.

7. Extract those 2009 sales greater than $99,999 by completing the following steps:
  a. Click the Create tab and then click the Query Design button.
  b. Double-click *Sales* in the Show Table dialog box and then click the Close button.
  c. At the query window, double-click *ClientID* (this inserts the field in the first *Field* text box in the query design grid).
  d. Insert the *Sales2009* field in the second *Field* text box.
  e. Insert the query criterion by completing the following steps:
   1) Click in the *Criteria* text box in the *Sales2009* column in the query design grid.
   2) Type >99999 and then press Enter. (Access will not insert quotation marks around *99999* since the field is identified as *Currency*.)

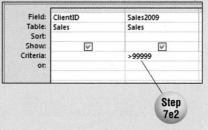

Step 7e2

f. Return the results of the query by clicking the Run button in the Results group.

g. Save the query and name it *2009SalesOver$99999Query*.

h. Print and then close the query.

8. Extract records of those representatives with a telephone number that begins with the 765 area code by completing the following steps:
  a. Click the Create tab and then click the Query Design button.
  b. Double-click *Representatives* in the Show Table dialog box and then click the Close button.
  c. Insert the *RepName* field in the first *Field* text box.
  d. Insert the *Telephone* field in the second *Field* text box.
  e. Insert the query criterion by completing the following steps:
   1) Click in the *Criteria* text box in the *Telephone* column.
   2) Type *765* and then press Enter.

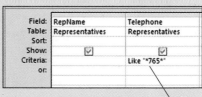

f. Return the results of the query by clicking the Run button in the Results group.

Step 8e2

g. Save the query and name it *RepsWith765AreaCodeQuery*.

h. Print and then close the query.

In Project 1a, you performed several queries on specific tables. A query can also be performed on fields from more than one table. In Project 1b, you will be performing queries on related tables. As mentioned earlier, one method for inserting fields in the query design grid is to drag the field from the table to the desired *Field* text box.

1. With the **Deering.accdb** database open, extract information on representatives hired between March of 2006 and November of 2006 and include the representative's name by completing the following steps:

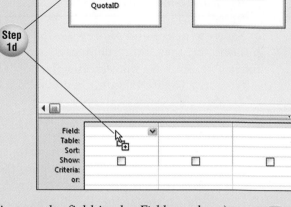

   a. Click the Create tab and then click the Query Design button.

   b. Double-click *Representatives* in the Show Table dialog box.

   c. Double-click *Benefits* in the Show Table dialog box list box and then click the Close button.

   d. At the query window, position the mouse pointer on the *RepName* field in the Representatives table, hold down the left mouse button, drag to the first *Field* text box in the query design grid, and then release the mouse button. (This inserts the field in the *Field* text box.)

   e. Drag the *HireDate* field from the Benefits table to the second *Field* text box.

   f. Insert the query criterion by completing the following steps:

      1) Click in the *Criteria* text box in the *HireDate* column.

      2) Type **Between 3/1/2006 And 11/30/2006** and then press Enter. (Make sure you type zeros and not capital *O*s.)

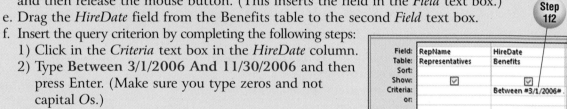

   g. Return the results of the query by clicking the Run button in the Results group.

   h. Save the query and name it *MarToNov2006HiresQuery*.

   i. Print and then close the query.

2. Extract records of those representatives who were hired in 2004 by completing the following steps:

   a. Click the Create tab and then click the Query Design button.

   b. Double-click *Representatives* in the Show Table dialog box.

   c. Double-click *Benefits* in the Show Table dialog box and then click the Close button.

   d. At the query window, drag the *RepID* field from the Representatives table to the first *Field* text box in the query design grid.

   e. Drag the *RepName* field from the Representatives table to the second *Field* text box.

   f. Drag the *HireDate* field from the Benefits table to the third *Field* text box.

   g. Insert the query criterion by completing the following steps:

      1) Click in the *Criteria* text box in the *HireDate* column.

      2) Type ***2004** and then press Enter.

   h. Return the results of the query by clicking the Run button in the Results group.

   i. Save the query and name it *RepsHiredIn2004Query*.

   j. Print and then close the query.

3. Suppose you need to determine 2008 and 2009 sales for a company but you can only remember that the company name begins with *Blue*. Create a query that finds the company and identifies the sales by completing the following steps:

a. Click the Create tab and then click the Query Design button.

b. Double-click *Clients* in the Show Table dialog box.

c. Double-click *Sales* in the Show Table dialog box and then click the Close button.

d. At the query window, insert the *ClientID* field in the Clients table in the first *Field* text box in the query design grid.

e. Insert the *Client* field in the Clients table in the second *Field* text box.

f. Insert the *Sales2008* field from the Sales table in the third *Field* text box.

g. Insert the *Sales2009* field from the Sales table in the fourth *Field* text box.

h. Insert the query criterion by completing the following steps:

1) Click in the *Criteria* text box in the *Client* column.

2) Type **Blue*** and then press Enter.

Field:	ClientID	Client	Sales2008	Sales2009
Table:	Clients	Clients	Sales	Sales
Sort:				
Show:	☑	☑	☑	☑
Criteria:		Like "Blue*"		
or:				

Step 3h2

i. Return the results of the query by clicking the Run button in the Results group.

j. Save the query and name it *BlueRidgeSalesQuery*.

k. Print and then close the query.

4. Close the **Deering.accdb** database.

5. Display the Open dialog box with Access2007L1C4 on your storage medium the active folder.

6. Open the **OutdoorOptions.accdb** database.

7. Extract information on products ordered between February 15 and February 28, 2010, and include the supplier's name by completing the following steps:

a. Click the Create tab and then click the Query Design button.

b. Double-click *Products* in the Show Table dialog box.

c. Double-click *Orders* in the Show Table dialog box and then click the Close button.

d. At the query window, insert the *Product#* field from the Products table in the first *Field* text box.

e. Insert the *Product* field from the Products table in the second *Field* text box.

f. Insert the *OrderDate* field from the Orders table in the third *Field* list box.

g. Insert the query criterion by completing the following steps:

1) Click in the *Criteria* text box in the *OrderDate* column.

2) Type **Between 2/15/2010 And 2/28/2010** and then press Enter. (Make sure you type zeros and not capital *O*s.)

Field:	Product#	Product	OrderDate
Table:	Products	Products	Orders
Sort:			
Show:	☑	☑	☑
Criteria:			Between #2/15/2010#
or:			

Step 7g2

h. Return the results of the query by clicking the Run button in the Results group.

i. Save the query and name it *Feb15-28OrdersQuery*.

j. Print and then close the query.

QUICK STEPS

Sort Fields in Query
1. At query window, click in *Sort* text box in query design grid.
2. Click down arrow in *Sort* text box.
3. Click *Ascending* or *Descending*.

Sorting Fields in a Query

When designing a query, you can specify the sort order of a field or fields. Click inside one of the columns in the *Sort* text box and a down-pointing arrow displays at the right of the field. Click this down-pointing arrow and a drop-down list displays with the choices *Ascending, Descending,* and *(not sorted)*. Click Ascending to sort from lowest to highest or click Descending to sort from highest to lowest.

Project 1c   Performing a Query on Related Tables and Sorting in Ascending Order

1. With the **OutdoorOptions.accdb** database open, extract information on orders less than $1,500 by completing the following steps:
   a. Click the Create tab and then click the Query Design button.
   b. Double-click *Products* in the Show Table dialog box.
   c. Double-click *Orders* in the Show Table dialog box and then click the Close button.
   d. At the query window, insert the *Product#* field from the Products table in the first *Field* text box.
   e. Insert the *Supplier#* field from the Products table in the second *Field* text box.
   f. Insert the *UnitsOrdered* field from the Orders table in the third *Field* text box.
   g. Insert the *Amount* field from the Orders table in the fourth *Field* text box.
   h. Insert the query criterion by completing the following steps:
      1) Click in the *Criteria* text box in the *Amount* column.
      2) Type **<1500** and then press Enter. (Make sure you type zeros and not capital Os.)

Field:	Product#	Supplier#	UnitsOrdered	Amount
Table:	Products	Products	Orders	Orders
Sort:				
Show:	☑	☑	☑	☑
Criteria:				<1500
or:				

Step 1h2

   i. Sort the *Amount* field values from lowest to highest by completing the following steps:
      1) Click in the *Sort* text box in the *Amount* column. (This causes a down-pointing arrow to display at the right side of the text box.)
      2) Click the down-pointing arrow at the right side of the *Sort* text box and then click *Ascending*.
   j. Return the results of the query by clicking the Run button in the Results group.
   k. Save the query and name it *OrdersLessThan$1500Query*.
   l. Print and then close the query.
2. Close the **OutdoorOptions.accdb** database.
3. Open the **Deering.accdb** database.

Step 1i1

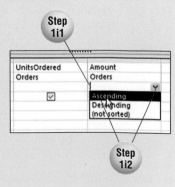

UnitsOrdered	Amount
Orders	Orders
☑	Ascending
	Descending
	(not sorted)

Step 1i2

4. Extract information on sales below $100,000 for 2008 by completing the following steps:
   a. Click the Create tab and then click the Query Design button.
   b. Double-click *Clients* in the Show Table dialog box.
   c. Double-click *Sales* in the list Show Table dialog box.
   d. Double-click *Representatives* in the Show Table dialog box and then click the Close button.
   e. At the query window, insert the *Client* field from the Clients table in the first *Field* text box.
   f. Insert the *Sales2008* field from the Sales table in the second *Field* text box.
   g. Insert the *RepName* field from the Representatives table in the third *Field* text box.
   h. Insert the query criterion by completing the following steps:
      1) Click in the *Criteria* text box in the *Sales2008* column.
      2) Type **<100000** and then press Enter. (Make sure you type zeros and not capital *O*s.)
   i. Sort the *Sales2008* field values from highest to lowest by completing the following steps:
      1) Click in the *Sort* text box in the *Sales2008* column. (This causes a down-pointing arrow to display at the right side of the text box.)
      2) Click the down-pointing arrow at the right side of the *Sort* text box and then click *Descending*.
   j. Return the results of the query by clicking the Run button in the Results group.
   k. Save the query and name it *2008SalesLessThan$100000Query*.
   l. Print and then close the query.

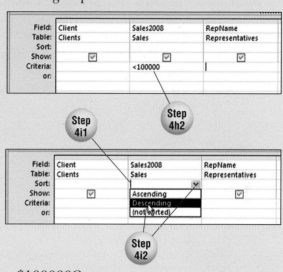

Modifying a Query

You can modify a saved query. For example, suppose after designing the query that displays the 2008 sales that are less than $100,000, you decide that you want to find sales for 2009 that are less than $100,000. Rather than designing a new query, open the existing query, make any needed changes, and then run the query.

To modify an existing query, double-click the query in the Navigation pane (this displays the query in Datasheet view). Click the View button to display the query in Design view. Make the desired changes and then click the Run button in the Results group. Click the Save button on the Quick Access toolbar to save the query with the same name. If you want to save the query with a new name, click the Office button and then click Save As. At the Save As dialog box, type a name for the query and then press Enter.

If your database contains a number of queries, you can group and display them in the Navigation pane. To do this, click the down-pointing arrow in the Navigation pane Menu bar and then click *Object Type* at the drop-down list. This displays objects grouped in categories such as *Tables* and *Queries*.

QUICK STEPS

Modify a Query
1. Double-click query in Navigation pane.
2. Click View button.
3. Make desired changes to query.
4. Click Run button.
5. Click Save button.

HINT
Save time designing a query by modifying an existing query.

Project 1d Modifying Queries

1. With the **Deering.accdb** database open, find the sales less than $100,000 for 2009 by completing the following steps:

   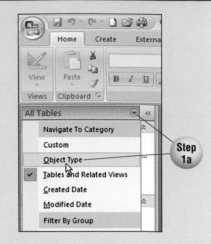

   Step 1a

   a. Change the display of objects in the Navigation pane by clicking the down-pointing arrow in the Navigation pane Menu bar and then clicking *Object Type* at the drop-down list.

   b. Double-click the *2008SalesLessThan$100000Query* in the *Queries* section of the Navigation pane.

   c. Click the View button in the Views group to switch to Design view.

   d. Click in the *Field* text box containing the text *Sales2008*.

   e. Click the down-pointing arrow that displays at the right side of the *Field* text box and then click *Sales2009* at the drop-down list.

   Step 1e

   f. Click the Run button in the Results group.

2. Save the query with a new name by completing the following steps:

   a. Click the Office button and then click Save As.

   b. At the Save As dialog box, type **2009SalesLessThan$100000Query** and then press Enter.

   Step 2b

   c. Print and then close the query.

3. Modify an existing query and find employees with three weeks of vacation by completing the following steps:

   a. Double-click the *MarToNov2006HiresQuery*.

   b. Click the View button in the Views group to switch to Design view.

   c. Click in the *Field* text box containing the text *HireDate*.

   d. Click the down-pointing arrow that displays at the right side of the *Field* text box and then click *Vacation* at the drop-down list.

   e. Select the current text in the *Criteria* text box in the *Vacation* column, type **3 weeks**, and then press Enter.

   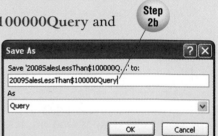

   f. Click the Run button in the Results group.

   Step 3e

4. Save the query with a new name by completing the following steps:

   a. Click the Office button and then click Save As.

   b. At the Save As dialog box, type **RepsWith3WeekVacationsQuery** and then press Enter.

   c. Print and then close the query.

Designing Queries with *Or* and *And* Criteria

The query design grid contains an *Or* row you can use to design a query that instructs Access to display records that match either of the two criteria. For example, to display a list of employees with three weeks of vacation *or* four weeks of vacation, you would type **3 weeks** in the *Criteria* text box for the *Vacation* field and then type **4 weeks** in the field immediately below *3 weeks* in the *Or* row. Other examples include finding clients that live in *Muncie* or *Lafayette* or finding representatives with a quota of *1* or *2*.

You can also select records by entering criteria statements into more than one *Criteria* field. Multiple criteria all entered in the same row becomes an *And* statement where each criterion must be met for Access to select the record. For example, you could search for clients in the Indianapolis area with sales greater than $100,000.

HINT
You can design a query that combines *And* and *Or* statements.

Project 1e — Designing Queries with *Or* and *And* Criteria

1. With the **Deering.accdb** database open, modify an existing query and find employees with three weeks or four weeks of vacation by completing the following steps:
   a. Double-click the *RepsWith3WeekVacationsQuery*.
   b. Click the View button in the Views group to switch to Design view.
   c. Click in the empty field below "*3 weeks*" in the *Or* row, type **4 weeks**, and then press Enter.

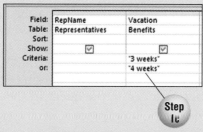

Step 1c

   d. Click the Run button in the Results group.
2. Save the query with a new name by completing the following steps:
   a. Click the Office button and then click Save As.
   b. At the Save As dialog box, type **RepsWith3Or4WeekVacationsQuery** and then press Enter.
   c. Print and then close the query.
3. Design a query that finds records of clients in the Indianapolis area with sales over $100,000 for 2008 and 2009 by completing the following steps:
   a. Click the Create tab and then click the Query Design button.
   b. Double-click *Clients* in the Show Table dialog box.
   c. Double-click *Sales* in the Show Table dialog box and then click the Close button.
   d. At the query window, insert the *Client* field from the Clients table in the first *Field* text box.
   e. Insert the *City* field from the Clients table in the second *Field* text box.
   f. Insert the *Sales2008* field from the Sales table in the third *Field* text box.
   g. Insert the *Sales2009* field from the Sales table in the fourth *Field* text box.

h. Insert the query criteria by completing the following steps:
   1) Click in the *Criteria* text box in the *City* column.
   2) Type **Indianapolis** and then press Enter.
   3) With the insertion point positioned in the *Criteria* text box in the *Sales2008* column, type >100000 and then press Enter.
   4) With the insertion point positioned in the *Criteria* text box in the *Sales2009* column, type >100000 and then press Enter.

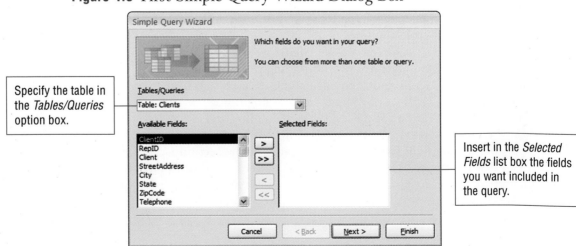

Field:	Client	City	Sales2008	Sales2009
Table:	Clients	Clients	Sales	Sales
Sort:				
Show:	☑	☑	☑	☑
Criteria:		"Indianapolis"	>100000	>100000
or:				

Step 3h2 Step 3h3 Step 3h4

i. Click the Run button in the Results group.
j. Save the query and name it **IndianapolisSalesOver$100000**.
k. Print and then close the query.

Performing a Query with the Simple Query Wizard

The Simple Query Wizard provided by Access guides you through the steps for preparing a query. To use this wizard, open the database, click the Create tab, and then click the Query Wizard button in the Other group. At the New Query dialog box, make sure *Simple Query Wizard* is selected in the list box and then click the OK button. At the first Simple Query Wizard dialog box, shown in Figure 4.3, specify the table(s) in the *Tables/Queries* option box. After specifying the table, insert the fields you want included in the query in the *Selected Fields* list box, and then click the Next button.

Figure 4.3 First Simple Query Wizard Dialog Box

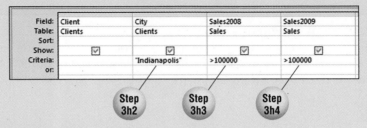

Specify the table in the *Tables/Queries* option box.

Insert in the *Selected Fields* list box the fields you want included in the query.

At the second Simple Query Wizard dialog box, specify whether you want a detail or summary query, and then click the Next button. At the third (and last) Simple Query Wizard dialog box, shown in Figure 4.4, type a name for the completed query or accept the name provided by the wizard. At this dialog box, you can also specify that you want to open the query to view the information or modify the query design. If you want to extract specific information, be sure to choose the *Modify the query design* option. After making any necessary changes, click the Finish button.

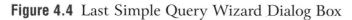

Create a Query with Simple Query Wizard
1. Click Create tab.
2. Click Query Wizard button.
3. Make sure *Simple Query Wizard* is selected in list box and then click OK.
4. Follow query steps.

Figure 4.4 Last Simple Query Wizard Dialog Box

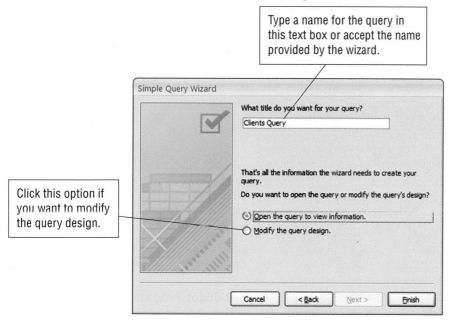

Type a name for the query in this text box or accept the name provided by the wizard.

Click this option if you want to modify the query design.

If you do not modify the query design in the last Simple Query Wizard dialog box, the query displays all records for the fields identified in the first Simple Query Wizard dialog box. In Project 1f you will perform a query without modifying the design, and in Project 1g you will modify the query design.

Project 1f   Performing a Query with the Simple Query Wizard

1. With the **Deering.accdb** database open, click the Create tab and then click the Query Wizard button in the Other group.
2. At the New Query dialog box, make sure *Simple Query Wizard* is selected in the list box and then click OK.
3. At the first Simple Query Wizard dialog box, click the down-pointing arrow at the right of the *Tables/Queries* option box and then click *Table: Clients*. (You will need to scroll up the list to display this table.)

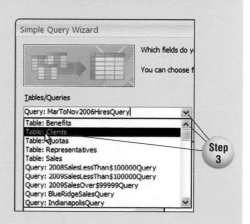

4. With *ClientID* selected in the *Available Fields* list box, click the button containing the greater than symbol. (This inserts the *ClientID* field in the *Selected Fields* list box.)

5. Click *Client* in the *Available Fields* list box and then click the button containing the greater than symbol.

6. Click the down-pointing arrow at the right of the *Tables/Queries* option box and then click *Table: Sales*.

7. Click *Sales2008* in the *Available Fields* list box and then click the button containing the greater than symbol.

8. With *Sales2009* selected in the *Available Fields* list box, click the button containing the greater than symbol.

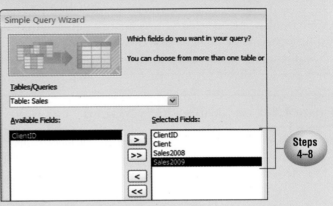

Steps 4–8

9. Click the Next button.

10. At the second Simple Query Wizard dialog box, click the Next button.

11. At the last Simple Query Wizard dialog box, click the Finish button.

12. When the results of the query display, print the results.

13. Close the Clients Query window.

14. Close the **Deering.accdb** database.

15. Open the **OutdoorOptions.accdb** database.

16. Click the Create tab and then click the Query Wizard button.

17. At the New Query dialog box, make sure *Simple Query Wizard* is selected in the list box and then click OK.

18. At the first Simple Query Wizard dialog box, click the down-pointing arrow at the right side of the *Tables/Queries* option box and then click *Table: Suppliers*.

19. With *Supplier#* selected in the *Available Fields* list box, click the button containing the greater than symbol. (This inserts the *Supplier#* field in the *Selected Fields* list box.)

20. With *SupplierName* selected in the *Available Fields* list box, click the button containing the greater than symbol.

21. Click the down-pointing arrow at the right of the *Tables/Queries* option box and then click *Table: Orders*.

22. Click *Product#* in the *Available Fields* list box and then click the button containing the greater than symbol.

23. Click *Amount* in the *Available Fields* list box and then click the button containing the greater than symbol.

Steps 19–23

24. Click the Next button.

25. At the second Simple Query Wizard dialog box, click the Next button.

26. At the last Simple Query Wizard dialog box, click the Finish button.

27. When the results of the query display, print the results.

28. Close the query window.

To extract specific information when using the Simple Query Wizard, tell the wizard that you want to modify the query design. This displays the query window with the query design grid where you can insert query criteria.

Project ⓛⓖ Performing and Modifying a Query with the Simple Query Wizard

1. With the **OutdoorOptions.accdb** database open, click the Create tab and then click the Query Wizard button.
2. At the New Query dialog box, make sure *Simply Query Wizard* is selected and then click OK.
3. At the first Simple Query Wizard dialog box, click the down-pointing arrow at the right side of the *Tables/Queries* option box and then click *Table: Suppliers*.
4. Insert the following fields in the *Selected Fields* list box:
   - SupplierName
   - StreetAddress
   - City
   - Province
   - PostalCode
5. Click the Next button.
6. At the second Simple Query Wizard dialog box, select the current text in the *What title do you want for your query?* text box and then type **SuppliersNotVancouver**.
7. Click the *Modify the query design* option and then click the Finish button.
8. At the query window, complete the following steps:
   a. Click in the *Criteria* text box in the City column in the query design grid.
   b. Type **Not Vancouver** and then press Enter.
9. Specify that the fields are to be sorted in ascending order by postal code by completing the following steps:
   a. Click in the *Sort* text box in the PostalCode column. (You may need to scroll to see this column.)
   b. Click the down-pointing arrow that displays at the right side of the text box and then click *Ascending*.

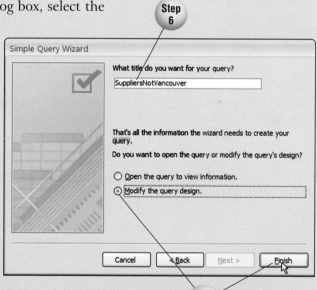

Step 3 — Simple Query Wizard — Which fields do you want in your query? You can choose from more than one table or query. Tables/Queries: Table: Suppliers. Available Fields: Supplier#, Email. Selected Fields (**Step 4**): SupplierName, StreetAddress, City, Province, PostalCode.

Step 6 / **Step 7** — Simple Query Wizard — What title do you want for your query? SuppliersNotVancouver. That's all the information the wizard needs to create your query. Do you want to open the query or modify the query's design? ○ Open the query to view information. ◉ Modify the query design. [Cancel] [< Back] [Next >] [Finish]

Field:	[SupplierName]	[StreetAddress]	[City]	[Province]	[PostalCode]
Table:	Suppliers	Suppliers	Suppliers	Suppliers	Suppliers
Sort:					⌄
Show:	☑	☑	☑	☑	Ascending
Criteria:			Not "Vancouver"		Descending
or:					(not sorted)

Step 8b   **Step 9b**

10. Click the Run button in the Results group. (This displays suppliers that are not located in Vancouver and displays the records sorted by PostalCode in ascending order.)
11. Save, print, and then close the query.
12. Close the **OutdoorOptions.accdb** database.
13. Open the **Deering.accdb** database.
14. Click the Create tab and then click the Query Wizard button.
15. At the New Query dialog box, make sure *Simply Query Wizard* is selected and then click OK.
16. At the first Simple Query Wizard dialog box, click the down-pointing arrow at the right of the *Tables/Queries* option box and then click *Table: Clients.* (You will need to scroll up the list to display this table.)
17. Insert the following fields in the *Selected Fields* list box:

> Client
> StreetAddress
> City
> State
> ZipCode

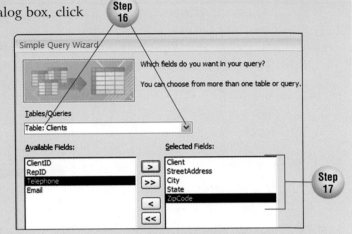

18. Click the Next button.
19. At the second Simple Query Wizard dialog box, select the current text in the *What title do you want for your query?* text box and then type **IndianapolisClients**.
20. Click the *Modify the query design* option and then click the Finish button.
21. At the query window, complete the following steps:
    a. Click in the *Criteria* text box in the *City* column.
    b. Type **Indianapolis** and then press Enter.
22. Click the Run button in the Results group. (This displays clients located in Indianapolis.)
23. Save, print, and then close the query.

Creating a Calculated Field

In Chapter 3, you learned how to insert a total row in a datasheet and then choose from a list of functions. You can also calculate values using a calculated control that uses a mathematical equation to determine the contents that display in the control object. In a query, you can insert a calculated field that performs mathematical equations by inserting a calculated field in the *Fields* text box. To insert a calculated field, click in the desired *Field* text box, type the desired field name followed by a colon, and then type the equation. For example, to add 2008 sales amounts with 2009 sales, you would type **Total:[Sales2008]+[Sales2009]** in the *Field* text box.

Project 1h   Creating a Calculated Field in a Query

1. With the **Deering.accdb** database open, click the Create tab and then click the Query Wizard button in the Other group.
2. With *Simple Query Wizard* selected in the New Query dialog box, click OK.

3. At the first Simple Query Wizard dialog box, click the down-pointing arrow at the right of the *Tables/Queries* option box, and then click *Table: Clients*. (You will need to scroll up the list to display this table.)

4. Insert the *Client* field in the *Selected Fields* list box.

5. Click the down-pointing arrow at the right of the *Tables/Queries* option box, click *Table: Sales*, and then insert the following fields in the *Selected Fields* list box:
   Sales2008
   Sales2009

6. Click the Next button.

7. At the second Simple Query Wizard dialog box, click the Next button.

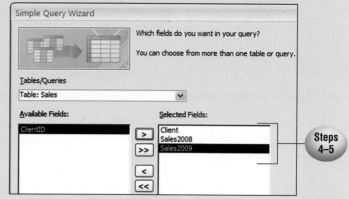

Steps 4–5

8. At the last Simple Query Wizard dialog box, select the current text in the *What title do you want for your query?* text box and then type **SalesTotals**.

9. Click the *Modify the query design* option and then click the Finish button.

10. At the query window, insert a calculated field that calculates the total sales for 2008 and 2009 for each client by completing the following steps:
    a. Click in the fourth *Field* text box.
    b. Type **Total:[Sales2008]+[Sales2009]** and then press Enter.

Field:	Client	Sales2008	Sales2009	Total: [Sales2008]+[Sa
Table:	Clients	Sales	Sales	
Sort:				
Show:	☑	☑	☑	☑
Criteria:				
or:				

Step 10b

11. Click the Run button in the Results group. (All records will display with the total of the 2008 and 2009 sales.)

12. Save, print, and then close the query.

13. Close the **Deering.accdb** database.

14. Open the **OutdoorOptions.accdb** database.

15. Click the Create tab and then click the Query Wizard button in the Other group.

16. With the *Simple Query Wizard* option selected in the New Query dialog box, click OK.

17. At the first Simple Query Wizard dialog box, select *Table: Suppliers* in the *Tables/Queries* option box.

18. Insert the *SupplierName* field in the *Selected Fields* list box.

19. Click the down-pointing arrow at the right of the *Tables/Queries* option box, click *Table: Orders*, and then insert the following fields in the *Selected Fields* list box:
    Order#
    UnitsOrdered
    Amount

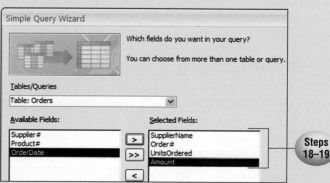

Steps 18–19

20. Click the Next button.

21. At the second Simple Query Wizard dialog box, click the Next button.
22. At the last Simple Query Wizard dialog box, select the current text in the *What title do you want for your query?* text box and then type **UnitPrices**.
23. Click the *Modify the query design* option and then click the Finish button.
24. At the query window, insert a calculated field that calculates the unit price by completing the following steps:
    a. Click in the fifth *Field* text box in the query design grid.
    b. Type **UnitPrice: [Amount]*[UnitsOrdered]** and then press Enter.

Field:	SupplierName	Order#	UnitsOrdered	Amount	UnitPrice: [Amount]*[U
Table:	Suppliers	Orders	Orders	Orders	
Sort:					
Show:	☑	☑	☑	☑	☑
Criteria:					
or:					

Step 24b

25. Click the Run button in the Results group. (All records will display with the unit price calculated for each order.)
26. Save, print, and then close the query.
27. Close the **OutdoorOptions.accdb** database.

Project 2 Create Aggregate Functions, Crosstab, Find Duplicates, and Find Unmatched Queries

You will create an aggregate functions query that determines the total, average, minimum, and maximum order amounts and determine total and average order amounts grouped by supplier. You will also use the Crosstab, Find Duplicates, and Find Unmatched query wizards to design queries.

QUICK STEPS

Design Query with Aggregate Function
1. At query window, click the Totals button.
2. Click the down-pointing arrow in *Group By* list box.
3. Click desired aggregate function.

Σ
Totals

Designing Queries with Aggregate Functions

You can include an aggregate function such as Sum, Avg, Min, Max, or Count in a query to calculate statistics from numeric field values of all the records in the table. When an aggregate function is used, Access displays one row in the query results datasheet with the formula result for the function used. For example, in a table with a numeric field containing the annual salary amounts, you could use the Sum function to calculate the total of all salary amount values.

To display the aggregate function list, click the Totals button in the Show/Hide group. Access adds a Total row to the design grid with a drop-down list from which you select the desired function. Access also inserts the words *Group By* in the list box. Click the down-pointing arrow and then click the desired aggregate function from the drop-down list. In Project 2a, you will create a query in Design view and use aggregate functions to find the total of all sales, the average sales amount, the maximum and the minimum sales, and the total number of sales. The completed query will display as shown in Figure 4.5. Access automatically chooses the column heading names.

Figure 4.5 Query Results for Project 2a

Access automatically determined the column heading names.

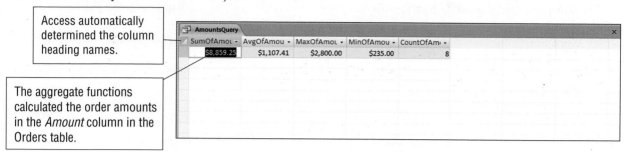

The aggregate functions calculated the order amounts in the *Amount* column in the Orders table.

Project 2a Using Aggregate Functions in a Query

1. Open the **OutdoorOptions.accdb** database.
2. Determine the total, average, minimum, and maximum order amounts as well as the total number of orders. To begin, click the Create tab and then click the Query Design button in the Other group.
3. At the Show Table dialog box, make sure *Orders* is selected in the list box, click the Add button, and then click the Close button.
4. Drag the *Amount* field to the first, second, third, fourth, and fifth *Field* text boxes.

Step 4

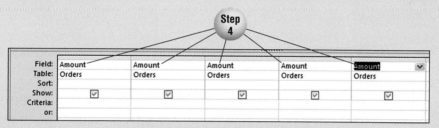

5. Click the Totals button in the Show/Hide group. (This adds a *Total* row to the design grid between *Table* and *Sort* with the default option of *Group By*.)
6. Specify a Sum function for the first *Group By* list box by completing the following steps:
   a. Click in the first *Group By* list box in the *Total* row.
   b. Click the down-pointing arrow that displays at the right side of the list box.
   c. Click *Sum* at the drop-down list.

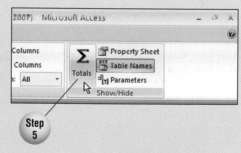

Step 5

Step 6a Step 6b

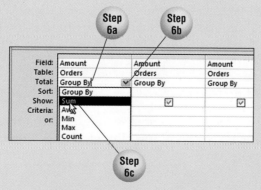

Step 6c

7. Complete steps similar to those in Step 6 to insert *Avg* in the second *Group By* list box in the *Total* row.
8. Complete steps similar to those in Step 6 to insert *Max* in the third *Group By* list box in the *Total* row.
9. Complete steps similar to those in Step 6 to insert *Min* in the fourth *Group By* list box in the *Total* row.
10. Complete steps similar to those in Step 6 to insert *Count* in the fifth *Group By* list box in the *Total* row.

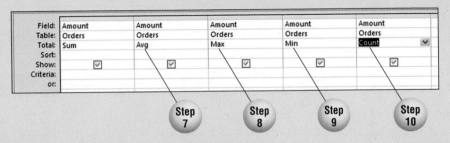

11. Click the Run button in the Results group. (Notice the headings that Access chooses for the columns.)
12. Save the query and name it *AmountsQuery*.
13. Automatically adjust the widths of the columns.
14. Print and then close the query.

Using the *Group By* option in the Total drop-down list you can add a field to the query upon which you want Access to group records for statistical calculations. For example, to calculate the total of all orders for a specific supplier, add the *Supplier#* field to the design grid with the Total set to *Group By*. In Project 2b, you will create a query in Design view and use aggregate functions to find the total of all order amounts and the average order amounts grouped by the supplier number.

Project ➋ᵇ Using Aggregate Functions and Grouping Records

1. With the **OutdoorOptions.accdb** database open, determine the total and average order amounts for each supplier. To begin, click the Create tab and then click the Query Design button.
2. At the Show Table dialog box, make sure *Orders* is selected in the list box and then click the Add button.
3. Click *Suppliers* in the list box, click the Add button, and then click the Close button.
4. Insert the *Amount* field from the Orders table list box to the first *Field* text box.
5. Insert the *Amount* field from the Orders table list box to the second *Field* text box.
6. Insert the *Supplier#* field from the Orders table list box to the third *Field* text box.
7. Insert the *SupplierName* field from the Suppliers table to the fourth *Field* text box.

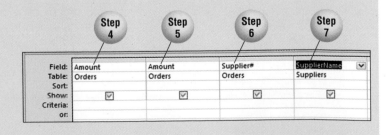

8. Click the Totals button in the Show/Hide group.
9. Click in the first *Group By* list box in the *Total* row, click the down-pointing arrow, and then click *Sum* at the drop-down list.
10. Click in the second *Group By* list box in the *Total* row, click the down-pointing arrow, and then click *Avg* at the drop-down list.
11. Make sure *Group By* displays in the third and fourth *Group By* list boxes.

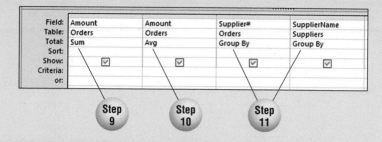

12. Click the Run button in the Results group.
13. Save the query and name it *SupplierAmountsQuery*.
14. Print and then close the query.

Creating a Crosstab Query

A crosstab query calculates aggregate functions such as Sum and Avg in which field values are grouped by two fields. A wizard is included that guides you through the steps to create the query. The first field selected causes one row to display in the query results datasheet for each group. The second field selected displays one column in the query results datasheet for each group. A third field is specified which is the numeric field to be summarized. The intersection of each row and column holds a value which is the result of the specified aggregate function for the designated row and column group.

Create a crosstab query from fields in one table. If you want to include fields from more than one table, you must first create a query containing the desired fields, and then create the crosstab query. For example, in Project 2c, you will create a new query that contains fields from each of the three tables in the OutdoorOptions.accdb database. Using this query, you will use the Crosstab Query Wizard to create a query that summarizes the order amounts by supplier name and by product ordered. Figure 4.6 displays the results of that crosstab query. The first column displays the supplier names, the second column displays the total of amounts for each supplier, and the remaining columns display the amounts by suppliers for specific items.

QUICK STEPS

Create a Crosstab Query
1. Click Create tab.
2. Click Query Wizard button.
3. Double-click *Crosstab Query Wizard*.
4. Complete wizard steps.

Figure 4.6 Crosstab Query Results for Project 2c

In this query, the order amounts are grouped by supplier name and by individual product.

OrdersBySupplierByProduct

SupplierNan ▾	Total Of Am ▾	Backpack ▾	Ski goggles ▾	Snowboard ▾	Two-person ▾	Wool ski hat ▾
Freedom Corp	$1,787.50		$1,100.00			$687.50
KL Distribution	$3,043.75	$1,906.25			$1,137.50	
Rosewood, Inc	$2,800.00			$2,800.00		

Project 2c   Creating a Crosstab Query

1. With the **OutdoorOptions.accdb** database open, create a query containing fields from the three tables by completing the following steps:
   a. Click the Create tab and then click the Query Design button.
   b. At the Show Table dialog box with *Orders* selected in the list box, click the Add button.
   c. Double-click *Products* in the Show Table dialog box.
   d. Double-click *Suppliers* in the list box and then click the Close button.
   e. Insert the following fields to the specified *Field* text boxes:
      1) From the Orders table, insert the *Product#* field to the first *Field* text box.
      2) From the Products table, insert the *Product* field to the second *Field* text box.
      3) From the Orders table, insert the *UnitsOrdered* field to the third *Field* text box.
      4) From the Orders table, insert the *Amount* field to the fourth *Field* text box.
      5) From the Suppliers table, insert the *SupplierName* field to the fifth *Field* text box.
      6) From the Orders table, insert the *OrderDate* field to the sixth *Field* text box.

Step 1e

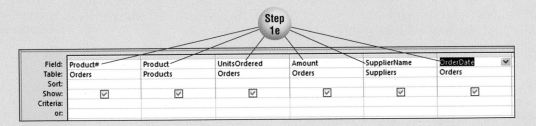

Field:	Product#	Product	UnitsOrdered	Amount	SupplierName	OrderDate	⌄
Table:	Orders	Products	Orders	Orders	Suppliers	Orders	
Sort:							
Show:	☑	☑	☑	☑	☑	☑	
Criteria:							
or:							

   f. Click the Run button to run the query.
   g. Save the query and name it *ItemsOrdered*.
   h. Close the query.
2. Create a crosstab query that summarizes the orders by supplier name and by product ordered by completing the following steps:
   a. Click the Create tab and then click the Query Wizard button.
   b. At the New Query dialog box, double-click *Crosstab Query Wizard* in the list box.

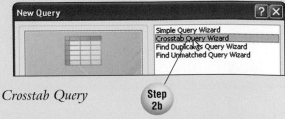

New Query

Simple Query Wizard
Crosstab Query Wizard
Find Duplicates Query Wizard
Find Unmatched Query Wizard

Step 2b

c. At the first Crosstab Query Wizard dialog box, click the *Queries* option in the *View* section and then click *Query: ItemsOrdered* in the list box.

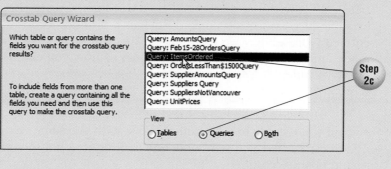

d. Click the Next button.
e. At the second Crosstab Query Wizard dialog box, click *SupplierName* in the *Available Fields* list box and then click the button containing the greater than (>) symbol. (This inserts *SupplierName* in the *Selected Fields* list box and specifies that you want *SupplierName* for the row headings.)
f. Click the Next button.
g. At the third Crosstab Query Wizard dialog box, click *Product* in the list box. (This specifies that you want *Product* for the column headings.)
h. Click the Next button.
i. At the fourth Crosstab Query Wizard dialog box, click *Amount* in the *Fields* list box and click *Sum* in the *Functions* list box.

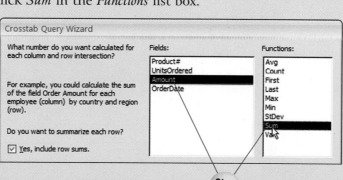

j. Click the Next button.
k. At the fifth Crosstab Query Wizard dialog box, select the current text in the *What do you want to name your query?* text box and then type **OrdersBySupplierByProduct**.
l. Click the Finish button.

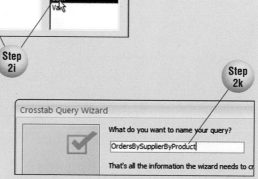

3. Change the orientation to landscape and then print the query.
4. Close the OrdersBySupplierByProduct query.

Creating a Find Duplicates Query

**Create a Find
Duplicates Query**
1. Click Create tab.
2. Click Query Wizard
   button.
3. Double-click *Find
   Duplicates Query
   Wizard.*
4. Complete wizard steps.

Use the find duplicates query to search a specified table or query for duplicate field values within a designated field or fields. Create this type of query, for example, if you suspect a record, such as a product record has inadvertently been entered twice under two different product numbers. A find duplicates query has many applications. A few other examples of how you can use a find duplicates query include:

- Find the records in an Orders table with the same customer number so that you can identify your loyal customers.

- Find the records in a Customers table with the same last name and mailing address so that you send only one mailing to a household to save on printing and postage costs.

- Find the records in an EmployeeExpenses table with the same employee number so that you can see which employee is submitting the most claims.

Access provides the Find Duplicates Query Wizard that builds the select query based on the selections made in a series of dialog boxes. To use this wizard, open the desired table, click the Create tab, and then click the Query Wizard button. At the New Query dialog box, double-click *Find Duplicates Query Wizard* in the list box, and then complete the steps provided by the wizard.

In Project 2d, you will assume that you have been asked to update the address for a supplier in the OutdoorOptions.accdb database. Instead of updating the address, you create a new record. You will then use the Find Duplicates Query wizard to find duplicate field values in the Suppliers table.

Project 2d Creating a Find Duplicates Query

1. With the **OutdoorOptions.accdb** database open, double-click the *Suppliers: Table* option located in the *Suppliers* section of the Navigation pane.
2. Add the following record to the table:
Supplier#	29
SupplierName	**Langley Corporation**
StreetAddress	**805 First Avenue**
City	**Burnaby**
Province	**BC**
PostalCode	**V5V 9K2**
Email	**lc@emcp.net**
3. Close the Suppliers table.
4. Use the Find Duplicates Query wizard to find any duplicate supplier names by completing the following steps:
   a. Click the Create tab and then click the Query Wizard button.
   b. At the New Query dialog box, double-click *Find Duplicates Query Wizard*.
   c. At the first wizard dialog box, click *Table: Suppliers* in the list box.
   d. Click the Next button.

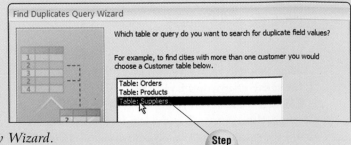

Step 4c

e. At the second wizard dialog box, click *SupplierName* in the *Available fields* list box and then click the button containing the greater than (>) symbol. (This moves the *SupplierName* field to the *Duplicate-value fields* list box.)

f. Click the Next button.

g. At the third wizard dialog box, click the button containing the two greater than (>>) symbols. (This moves all the fields to the *Additional query fields* list box. You are doing this because if you find a duplicate supplier name, you want to view all the fields to determine which record is accurate.)

h. Click the Next button.

i. At the fourth (and last) wizard dialog box, type **DuplicateSuppliers** in the *What do you want to name your query?* text box.

j. Click the Finish button.

k. Change the orientation to landscape and then print the DuplicateSuppliers query.

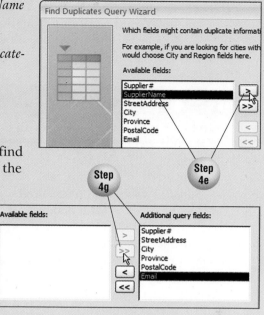

Step 4g   Step 4e

5. As you look at the query results, you realize that an inaccurate record was entered for Langley so you decide to delete one of the records. To do this, complete the following steps:

a. With the DuplicateSuppliers query open, click in the record selector bar next to the first record (the one with a Supplier# of *29*). (This selects the entire row.)

b. Click the Home tab and then click the Delete button in the Records group.

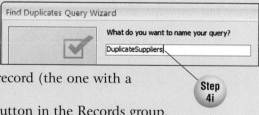

Step 4i

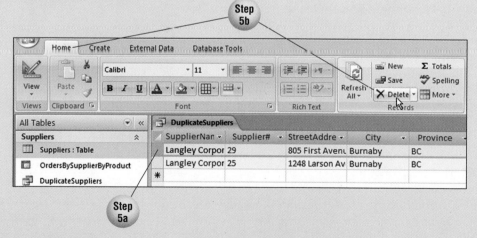

Step 5b

Step 5a

c. At the message asking you to confirm, click the Yes button.

d. Close the DuplicateSuppliers query.

6. Change the street address for Langley Corporation by completing the following steps:

a. Double-click the *Suppliers: Table* option located in the *Suppliers* section of the Navigation pane.

b. With the Suppliers table open in Datasheet view, change the address for Langley Corporation from *1248 Larson Avenue* to *805 First Avenue*. Leave the other fields as displayed.

c. Close the *Suppliers* table.

In Project 2d, you used the Find Duplicates Query Wizard to find records containing the same field. In Project 2e, you will use the Find Duplicates Query Wizard to find information on the suppliers you order from the most. You could use this information to negotiate for better prices or to ask for discounts.

Project 2e Finding Duplicate Orders

1. With the **OutdoorOptions.accdb** database open, create a query with the following fields (in the order shown) from the specified tables:

Order#	Orders table
Supplier#	Orders table
SupplierName	Suppliers table
Product#	Orders table
UnitsOrdered	Orders table
Amount	Orders table
OrderDate	Orders table

2. Run the query.
3. Save the query with the name *SupplierOrders* and then close the query.
4. Use the Find Duplicates Query Wizard to find the suppliers you order from the most by completing the following steps:

   a. Click the Create tab and then click the Query Wizard tab.
   b. At the New Query dialog box, double-click *Find Duplicates Query Wizard*.
   c. At the first wizard dialog box, click *Queries* in the *View* section, and then click *Query: SupplierOrders*. (You may need to scroll down the list to display this query.)
   d. Click the Next button.
   e. At the second wizard dialog box, click *Supplier#* in the *Available fields* list box and then click the button containing the greater than (>) symbol.
   f. Click the Next button.
   g. At the third wizard dialog box, click the button containing the two greater than (>>) symbols. (This moves all the fields to the *Additional query fields* list box.)
   h. Click the Next button.
   i. At the fourth (and last) wizard dialog box, type **DuplicateSupplierOrders** in the *What do you want to name your query?* text box.
   j. Click the Finish button.
   k. Change the orientation to landscape and then print the DuplicateSupplierOrders query.

5. Close the query.

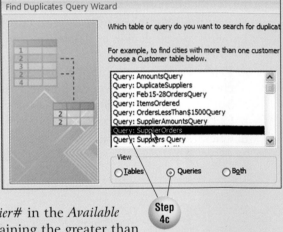

Step 4c

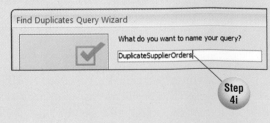

Step 4i

Creating an Unmatched Query

Create a find unmatched query to compare two tables and produce a list of the records in one table that have no matching record in the other related table. This type of query is useful to produce lists such as customers who have never placed an order or an invoice with no payment record. Access provides the Find Unmatched Query Wizard that builds the select query by guiding you through a series of dialog boxes.

In Project 2f, you will use the Find Unmatched Query Wizard to find all products that have no units on order. This information is helpful because it indicates which products are not selling and might need to be discontinued or returned. To use the Find Unmatched Query Wizard, click the Create tab and then click the Query Wizard button in the Other group. At the New Query dialog box, double-click *Find Unmatched Query Wizard* in the list box and then follow the wizard steps.

QUICK STEPS

Create an Unmatched Query
1. Click Create tab.
2. Click Query Wizard button.
3. Double-click *Find Unmatched Query Wizard*.
4. Complete wizard steps.

Project 2f   Creating a Find Unmatched Query

1. With the **OutdoorOptions.accdb** database open, use the Find Unmatched Query Wizard to find all products that do not have any units on order by completing the following steps:
   a. Click the Create tab and then click the Query Wizard button.
   b. At the New Query dialog box, double-click *Find Unmatched Query Wizard*.
   c. At the first wizard dialog box, click *Table: Products* in the list box. (This is the table containing the fields you want to see in the query results.)
   d. Click the Next button.
   e. At the second wizard dialog box, make sure *Table: Orders* is selected in the list box. (This is the table containing the related records.)
   f. Click the Next button.
   g. At the third wizard dialog box, make sure *Product#* is selected in the *Fields in 'Products'* list box and in the *Fields in 'Orders'* list box.

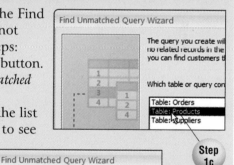

Step 1c

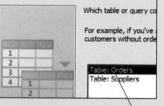

Step 1e

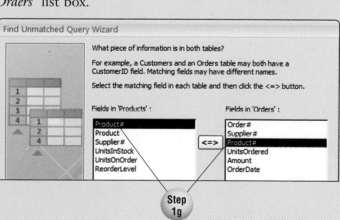

Step 1g

   h. Click the Next button.

i. At the fourth wizard dialog box, click the button containing the two greater than symbols (>>) to move all fields from the *Available fields* list box to the *Selected fields* list box.

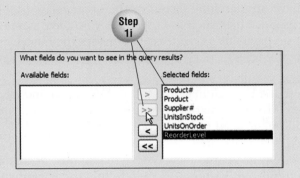

j. Click the Next button.
k. At the fifth wizard dialog box, click the Finish button. (Let the wizard determine the query name: *Products Without Matching Orders*.)
2. Print and then close the Products Without Matching Orders query.
3. Close the **OutdoorOptions.accdb** database.

CHAPTER summary

- Being able to extract specific information is one of the most important functions of a database. Data can be extracted from an Access database by performing a query, which can be accomplished by designing a query or using a query wizard.

- Designing a query consists of identifying the table, the field or fields from which the data will be drawn, and the criteria for selecting the data.

- During the designing of a query, write the criterion (or criteria) for extracting the specific data. Access inserts any necessary symbols in the criterion when the Enter key is pressed.

- In a criterion, quotation marks surround field values and pound symbols (#) surround dates. Use the asterisk (*) as a wildcard symbol.

- You can perform a query on fields within one table or on fields from related tables.

- When designing a query, you can specify the sort order of a field or fields.

- You can modify an existing query. To do this, double-click the query in the Navigation pane, click the View button to display the query in Design view, make the desired changes, and then click the Run button.

- Enter criterion in the *Or* row in the query design grid to instruct Access to display records that match either of the two criteria.

- Multiple criteria entered in the *Criteria* row in the query design grid become an *And* statement where each criterion must be met for Access to select the record.

- The Simple Query Wizard guides you through the steps for preparing a query. You can modify a query you create with the wizard.

- You can insert a calculated field in a *Field* text box when designing a query.

- Include an aggregate function such as Sum, Avg, Min, Max, or Count to calculate statistics from numeric field values. Click the Totals button in the Show/Hide group to display the aggregate function list.

- Use the *Group By* option in the Total drop-down list to add a field to a query upon which you want Access to group records for statistical calculations.

- Create a crosstab query to calculate aggregate functions such as Sum and Avg in which fields are grouped by two fields. Create a crosstab query from fields in one table. If you want to include fields from more than one table, create a query first, and then create the crosstab query.

- Use the find duplicates query to search a specified table or query for duplicate field values within a designated field or fields.

- Create a find unmatched query to compare two tables and produce a list of the records in one table that have no matching record in the other related table.

COMMANDS review

FEATURE	RIBBON TAB, GROUP	BUTTON, OPTION
Query design window	Create, Other	
Run query	Query Tools Design, Results	!
New Query dialog box	Create, Other	
Simple Query Wizard	Create, Other	, Simple Query Wizard
Add Total row to query design	Query Tools Design, Show/Hide	Σ
Crosstab Query Wizard	Create, Other	, Crosstab Query Wizard
Find Duplicates Query Wizard	Create, Other	, Find Duplicates Query Wizard
Find Unmatched Query Wizard	Create, Other	, Find Unmatched Query Wizard

CONCEPTS check

Test Your Knowledge

Completion: For each description, indicate the correct term, symbol, or command.

1. The Query Design button is located in the Other group in this tab.
   Create

2. Click the Query Design button and the query window displays with this dialog box open.
   Show table

3. To establish a criterion for the query, click in this text box in the column containing the desired field name and then type the criterion.
   Criteria

4. This is the term used for the results of the query.
   Return

5. This is the symbol Access automatically inserts around a date when writing a criterion for the query.
   #

6. Use this symbol to indicate a wildcard character when writing a query criterion.
   *

7. This is the criterion you would type to return field values greater than $500.
   > 500

8. This is the criterion you would type to return field values that begin with the letter *L*.

L*

9. This is the criterion you would type to return field values that are not in Oregon.

not "oregon"

10. You can sort a field in a query in ascending order or this order.

Descending

11. Enter a criterion in this row in the query design grid to instruct Access to display records that match either of the two criteria.

or

12. This wizard guides you through the steps for preparing a query.

Simple Query Wizard

13. This type of query calculates aggregate functions in which field values are grouped by two fields.

Crosstab Query

14. Use this type of query to compare two tables and produce a list of the records in one table that have no matching record in the other related table.

find duplicates Query or unmatched.

SKILLS check
Demonstrate Your Proficiency

Assessment

1 DESIGN QUERIES IN A LEGALSERVICES DATABASE

1. Display the Open dialog box with Access2007L1C4 on your storage medium the active folder.
2. Design a query that extracts records from the Billing table with the following specifications:
   a. Include the fields *Billing#*, *ClientID*, and *Category* in the query.
   b. Extract those records with the *SE* category.
   c. Save the query and name it *SECategoryBillingQuery*.
   d. Print and then close the query.
3. Design a query that extracts records from the Billing table with the following specifications:
   a. Include the fields *Billing#*, *ClientID*, and *Date*.
   b. Extract those records in the *Date* field with dates between 6/8/2010 and 6/10/2010.
   c. Save the query and name it *June8-10BillingQuery*.
   d. Print and then close the query.

4. Design a query that extracts records from the Clients table with the following specifications:
   a. Include the fields *FirstName*, *LastName*, and *City*.
   b. Extract those records with any city other than Kent in the *City* field.
   c. Save the query and name it *ClientsNotInKentQuery*.
   d. Print and then close the query.
5. Design a query that extracts information from two tables with the following specifications:
   a. Include the fields *Billing#*, *ClientID*, *Date*, and *Rate#* from the Billing table.
   b. Include the field *Rate* from the Rates table.
   c. Extract those records with a rate number greater than 2.
   d. Save the query and name it *RateGreaterThan2Query*.
   e. Print and then close the query.
6. Design a query that extracts information from three tables with the following specifications:
   a. Include the field *Attorney* from the Attorneys table.
   b. Include the fields *FirstName* and *LastName* from the Clients table.
   c. Include the fields *AttorneyID*, *Date,* and *Hours* from the Billing table.
   d. Extract those records with an *AttorneyID* of 12.
   e. Save the query and name it *Attorney12Query*.
   f. Print and then close the query.
7. Design a query that extracts records from four tables with the following specifications:
   a. Add the Attorneys, Billing, Rates, and Clients tables to the query window.
   b. Insert the *Attorney* field from the Attorneys table to the first *Field* text box.
   c. Insert the *AttorneyID* field from the Billing table to the second *Field* text box.
   d. Insert the *Rate#* field from the Billing table to the third *Field* text box.
   e. Insert the *Rate* field from the Rates table to the fourth *Field* text box.
   f. Insert the *FirstName* field from the Clients table to the fifth *Field* text box.
   g. Insert the *LastName* field from the Clients table to the sixth *Field* text box.
   h. Extract those records with an *AttorneyID* of 17 and a *Rate#* of 4.
   i. Run the query.
   j. Save the query and name it *Attorney17Rate4*.
   k. Print and then close the query.

Assessment

2   USE THE SIMPLE QUERY WIZARD AND DESIGN QUERIES

1. With **LegalServices.accdb** database open, use the Simple Query Wizard to extract specific information from three tables with the following specifications:
   a. At the first Simple Query Wizard dialog box, include the following fields:
      From Attorneys table: *AttorneyID* and *Attorney*
      From Categories table: *CategoryName*
      From Billing table: *Hours*
   b. At the second Simple Query Wizard dialog box, click Next.
   c. At the third Simple Query Wizard dialog box, click the *Modify the query design* option, and then click the Finish button.
   d. At the query window, insert *14* in the *Criteria* text box in the *AttorneyID* column.
   e. Run the query.

f. Save the query with the default name.

g. Print and then close the query.

2. Create a query in Design view with the Billing table with the following specifications:

   a. Insert the *Hours* field from the Billing table to the first, second, third, and fourth *Field* text boxes.

   b. Click the Totals button in the Show/Hide group.

   c. Insert *Sum* in the first *Group By* list box in the *Total* row.

   d. Insert *Min* in the second *Group By* list box in the *Total* row.

   e. Insert *Max* in the third *Group By* list box in the *Total* row.

   f. Insert *Count* in the fourth *Group By* list box in the *Total* row.

   g. Run the query.

   h. Save the query and name it *HoursAmountQuery*.

   i. Automatically adjust the widths of the columns.

   j. Print and then close the query.

3. Create a query in Design view with the following specifications:

   a. Add the Attorneys table and the Billing table to the query window.

   b. Insert the *Attorney* field from the Attorneys table to the first *Field* text box.

   c. Insert the *AttorneyID* field from the Billing table to the second *Field* text box.

   d. Insert the *Hours* field from the Billing table to the third *Field* text box.

   e. Click the Totals button in the Show/Hide group.

   f. Insert *Sum* in the third *Group By* list box in the *Hours* column (in the *Total* row).

   g. Run the query.

   h. Save the query and name it *AttorneyHours*.

   i. Print and then close the query.

4. Create a query in Design view with the following specifications:

   a. Add the Attorneys, Clients, Categories, and Billing tables to the query window.

   b. Insert the *Attorney* field from the Attorneys table to the first *Field* text box.

   c. Insert the *ClientID* field from the Clients table to the second *Field* text box.

   d. Insert the *CategoryName* field from the Categories table to the third *Field* text box.

   e. Insert the *Hours* field from the Billing table to the fourth *Field* text box.

   f. Run the query.

   g. Save the query and name it *AttorneyClientHours*.

   h. Print and then close the query.

Assessment

3 CREATE A CROSSTAB QUERY AND USE THE FIND DUPLICATES AND FIND UNMATCHED QUERY WIZARDS

1. With the **LegalServices.accdb** database open, create a crosstab query that summarizes the hours by attorney by category with the following specifications:

   a. At the first Crosstab Query Wizard dialog box, click the *Queries* option in the *View* section, and then click *Query: AttorneyClientHours* in the list box.

   b. At the second Crosstab Query Wizard dialog box, click *Attorney* in the *Available Fields* list box and then click the button containing the greater than (>) symbol.

   c. At the third Crosstab Query Wizard dialog box, click *CategoryName* in the list box.

   d. At the fourth Crosstab Query Wizard dialog box, click *Hours* in the *Fields* list box and click *Sum* in the *Functions* list box.

e. At the fifth Crosstab Query Wizard dialog box, type **HoursByAttorneyByCategory** in the *What do you want to name your query?* text box.

f. Print the query in landscape orientation and then close the query.

2. Use the Find Duplicates Query Wizard to find those clients with the same last name with the following specifications:

   a. At the first wizard dialog box, click *Table: Clients* in the list box.

   b. At the second wizard dialog box, click *LastName* in the *Available fields* list box and then click the button containing the greater than (>) symbol.

   c. At the third wizard dialog box, click the button containing the two greater than (>>) symbols.

   d. At the fourth wizard dialog box, name the query *DuplicateLastNames*.

   e. Print the query in landscape orientation and then close the query.

3. Use the Find Unmatched Query Wizard to find all clients who do not have any billing hours with the following specifications:

   a. At the first wizard dialog box, click *Table: Clients* in the list box.

   b. At the second wizard dialog box, click *Table: Billing* in the list box.

   c. At the third wizard dialog box, make sure *ClientID* is selected in the *Fields in 'Products'* list box and in the *Fields in 'Orders'* list box.

   d. At the fourth wizard dialog box, click the button containing the two greater than symbols (>>) to move all fields from the *Available fields* list box to the *Selected fields* list box.

   e. At the fifth wizard dialog box, click the Finish button. (Let the wizard determine the query name: *Clients Without Matching Billing*.)

4. Print the query in landscape orientation and then close the Clients Without Matching Billing query.

5. Close the **LegalServices.accdb** database.

Assessment

4 DESIGN AND HIDE FIELDS IN A QUERY

1. You can use the check boxes in the query design grid *Show* row to show or hide fields in the query. Experiment with these check boxes and then open the **LegalServices.accdb** database and design the following query:

   a. At the Show Table dialog box, add the Billing table, the Clients table, and the Rates table.

   b. At the query window, insert the following fields to *Field* text boxes:

   Clients table:
   > *FirstName*
   > *LastName*

   Billing table:
   > *Hours*

   Rates table:
   > *Rate*

   c. Insert in the fifth *Field* text box the calculated field *Total:*[Hours]*[Rate].

   d. Hide the *Hours* and the *Rate* fields.

   e. Run the query.

   f. Save the query and name it *ClientBillingQuery*.

   g. Print and then close the query.

2. Close the **LegalServices.accdb** database.

CASE study

Apply Your Skills

You work for the Skyline Restaurant in Fort Myers, Florida. Your supervisor is reviewing the restaurant operations and has asked for a number of query reports. Before running queries, you realize that the tables in the restaurant database, **Skyline.accdb**, are not related. Open the **Skyline.accdb** database and then create the following relationships:

Field Name	"One" Table	"Many" Table
EmployeeID	Employees	Banquets
Item#	Inventory	Orders
SupplierID	Suppliers	Orders
EventID	Events	Banquets

Save and then print the relationships.

As part of the review of the restaurant records, your supervisor has asked you for the following information. Create a separate query for each bulleted item listed below and save, name, and print the queries (you determine the name).

- Suppliers in Fort Myers (include supplier identification number, supplier name, and telephone number)
- Suppliers that are not located in Fort Myers (include supplier identification number, supplier name, and telephone number)
- Employees hired in 2007 (include employee identification number, first and last names, and hire date)
- Wedding receptions booked in the banquet room (include the reservation identification number; reservation date; and last name, first name, and telephone number of the person making the reservation)
- Banquet reservations booked between 6/15/2010 and 6/30/2010 (include reservation identification number; reservation date; and last name, first name, and telephone number of the person making the reservation)
- Banquet reservations that have not been confirmed (include reservation identification number and first name, last name, and telephone number)
- Names of employees that are signed up for health insurance (include employee first and last names)
- Items ordered from supplier number 4 (include the item number, item, supplier name, and supplier telephone number)
- Banquet room reserved by someone whose last name begins with "Wie" (include the first and last names of the employee who booked the reservation and the first and last names and telephone number of the person making the reservation)
- A query that inserts a calculated field that calculates the total of the number of units ordered by the unit price (information located in the Orders table) for all orders for supplier number 2

Part 3

Design at least three additional queries that require fields from at least two tables. Run the queries and then save and print the queries. In Microsoft Word, write the query information and include specific information about each query and format the document to enhance the visual appeal. Save the document and name it **Access_C4_CS_P3**. Print and then close **Access_C4_CS_P3.docx**.

Creating Tables and Queries

ASSESSING proficiency

In this unit, you have learned to design, create, and modify tables and to create one-to-many relationships and one-to-one relationships between tables. You also learned how to perform queries on data in tables.

Note: The Student Resources CD does not include an Access Level 1, Unit 1 subfolder of files because no data files are required for the Unit 1 assessments. You will create all of the files yourself. Before beginning the assessments, create a folder called Access2007L1U1 for the new files.

Assessment 1 Create Tables in a Cornerstone Catering Database

1. Use Access to create tables for Cornerstone Catering. Name the database **Cornerstone**. Create a table named *Employees* that includes the following fields (you determine the field name, data type, field size, and description):

    Employee# (primary key)
    FirstName
    LastName
    CellPhone (Consider using the Input Mask Wizard for this field.)

2. After creating the table, switch to Datasheet view and then enter the following data in the appropriate fields:

    Employee#: 10
    FirstName: Erin
    LastName: Jergens
    CellPhone: (505) 555-3193

    Employee#: 14
    FirstName: Mikio
    LastName: Ogami
    CellPhone: (505) 555-1087

    Employee#: 19
    FirstName: Martin
    LastName: Vaughn
    CellPhone: (505) 555-4461

    Employee#: 21
    FirstName: Isabelle
    LastName: Baptista
    CellPhone: (505) 555-4425

    Employee#: 24
    FirstName: Shawn
    LastName: Kettering
    CellPhone: (505) 555-3885

    Employee#: 26
    FirstName: Madison
    LastName: Harris
    CellPhone: (505) 555-2256

3. Automatically adjust the column widths.
4. Save, print, and then close the Employees table.

5. Create a table named *Plans* that includes the following fields:
   PlanCode (primary key)
   Plan

6. After creating the table, switch to Datasheet view and then enter the following data in the appropriate fields:

   PlanCode: A   *PlanCode:* B
   Plan: Sandwich Buffet   *Plan:* Cold Luncheon Buffet

   PlanCode: C   *PlanCode:* D
   Plan: Hot Luncheon Buffet   *Plan:* Combination Dinner

7. Automatically adjust the column widths.
8. Save, print, and then close the Plans table.
9. Create a table named *Prices* that includes the following fields:
   PriceCode (primary key)
   PricePerPerson (identify this data type as Currency)

10. After creating the table, switch to Datasheet view and then enter the following data in the appropriate fields:

    PriceCode: 1   *PriceCode:* 2
    PricePerPerson: $11.50   *PricePerPerson:* $12.75

    PriceCode: 3   *PriceCode:* 4
    PricePerPerson: $14.50   *PricePerPerson:* $16.00

    PriceCode: 5
    PricePerPerson: $18.50

11. Automatically adjust the column widths.
12. Save, print, and then close the Prices table.
13. Create a table named *Clients* that includes the following fields:
    Client# (primary key)
    ClientName
    StreetAddress
    City
    State
    ZipCode
    Telephone (Consider using the Input Mask Wizard for this field.)

14. After creating the table, switch to Datasheet view and then enter the following data in the appropriate fields:

    Client#: 104   *Client#:* 155
    ClientName: Sarco Corporation   *ClientName:* Creative Concepts
    StreetAddress: 340 Cordova Road   *StreetAddress:* 1026 Market Street
    City: Santa Fe   *City:* Los Alamos
    State: NM   *State:* NM
    ZipCode: 87510   *ZipCode:* 87547
    Telephone: (505) 555-3880   *Telephone:* (505) 555-1200

Client#: 218
ClientName: **Allenmore Systems**
StreetAddress: **7866 Second Street**
City: **Espanola**
State: **NM**
ZipCode: 87535
Telephone: (505) 555-3455

Client#: 286
ClientName: **Sol Enterprises**
StreetAddress: **120 Cerrillos Road**
City: **Santa Fe**
State: **NM**
ZipCode: 87560
Telephone: (505) 555-7700

15. Automatically adjust the column widths and change the orientation to landscape.
16. Save, print, and then close the Clients table.
17. Create a table named *Events* that includes the following fields:
    Event# (primary key; identify this data type as AutoNumber)
    Client#
    Employee#
    DateOfEvent (identify this data type as Date/Time)
    PlanCode
    PriceCode
    NumberOfPeople (identify this data type as Number)
18. After creating the table, switch to Datasheet view and then enter the following data in the appropriate fields:

Event#: (AutoNumber)
Client#: 218
Employee#: 14
DateOfEvent: 7/1/2010
PlanCode: B
PriceCode: 3
NumberOfPeople: 250

Event#: (AutoNumber)
Client#: 104
Employee#: 19
DateOfEvent: 7/2/2010
PlanCode: D
PriceCode: 5
NumberOfPeople: 120

Event#: (AutoNumber)
Client#: 155
Employee#: 24
DateOfEvent: 7/8/2010
PlanCode: A
PriceCode: 1
NumberOfPeople: 300

Event#: (AutoNumber)
Client#: 286
Employee#: 10
DateOfEvent: 7/9/2010
PlanCode: C
PriceCode: 4
NumberOfPeople: 75

Event#: (AutoNumber)
Client#: 218
Employee#: 14
DateOfEvent: 7/10/2010
PlanCode: C
PriceCode: 4
NumberOfPeople: 50

Event#: (AutoNumber)
Client#: 104
Employee#: 10
DateOfEvent: 7/12/2010
PlanCode: B
PriceCode: 3
NumberOfPeople: 30

19. Automatically adjust the column widths and change the orientation to landscape.
20. Save, print, and then close the Events table.

Assessment 2 Create Relationships between Tables

1. With the **Cornerstone.accdb** database open, create the following one-to-many relationships:
   a. *Client#* in the Clients table is the "one" and *Client#* in the Events table is the "many."
   b. *Employee#* in the Employees table is the "one" and *Employee#* in the Events table is the "many."
   c. *PlanCode* in the Plans table is the "one" and *PlanCode* in the Events table is the "many."
   d. *PriceCode* in the Prices table is the "one" and *PriceCode* in the Events table is the "many."
2. Save and then print the relationships.

Assessment 3 Modify Tables

1. With the **Cornerstone.accdb** database open, open the Plans table in Datasheet view and then add the following record at the end of the table:
   PlanCode: **E**
   Plan: **Hawaiian Luau Buffet**
2. Save, print, and then close the Plans table.
3. Open the Events table in Datasheet view and then add the following record at the end of the table:
   Event#: (AutoNumber)
   Client#: 104
   Employee#: 21
   Date: 7/16/2010
   PlanCode: E
   PriceCode: 5
   NumberOfPeople: 125
4. Save, print (in landscape orientation), and then close the Events table.

Assessment 4 Design Queries

1. With the **Cornerstone.accdb** database open, create a query to extract records from the Events table with the following specifications:
   a. Include the fields *Client#*, *DateOfEvent*, and *PlanCode*.
   b. Extract those records with a PlanCode of C.
   c. Save the query and name it *PlanCodeC*.
   d. Print and then close the query.
2. Extract records from the Clients table with the following specifications:
   a. Include the fields *ClientName*, *City*, and *Telephone*.
   b. Extract those records with a city of Santa Fe.
   c. Save the query and name it *SantaFeClients*.
   d. Print and then close the query.
3. Extract information from two tables with the following specifications:
   a. From the Clients table, include the fields *ClientName* and *Telephone*.
   b. From the Events table, include the fields *DateOfEvent*, *PlanCode*, and *NumberOfPeople*.
   c. Extract those records with a date between July 10 and July 25, 2010.
   d. Save the query and name it *July10-25Events*.
   e. Print and then close the query.

Assessment 5 Design a Query with a Calculated Field Entry

1. With the **Cornerstone.accdb** database open, create a query in Design view with the Events table and the Prices table and insert the following fields to the specified locations:
   a. Insert *Event#* from the Events table to the first *Field* text box.
   b. Insert *DateOfEvent* from the Events table to the second *Field* text box.
   c. Insert *NumberOfPeople* from the Events table to the third *Field* text box.
   d. Insert *PricePerPerson* from the Prices table to the fourth *Field* text box.
2. Insert the following calculated field entry in the fifth *Field* text box: *Amount: [NumberOfPeople]*[PricePerPerson]*.
3. Run the query.
4. Save the query and name it *EventAmounts*.
5. Print and then close the query.

Assessment 6 Design a Query with Aggregate Functions

1. With the **Cornerstone.accdb** database open, create a query in Design view using the EventAmounts query with the following specifications:
   a. At the Cornerstone : Database window, click the Create tab and then click the Query Design button.
   b. At the Show Tables dialog box, click the Queries tab.
   c. Double-click *EventAmounts* in the list box and then click the Close button.
   d. Insert the *Amount* field to the first, second, third, and fourth *Field* text boxes.
   e. Click the Totals button in the Show/Hide group.
   f. Insert *Sum* in the first *Group By* list box in the *Total* row.
   g. Insert *Avg* in the second *Group By* list box in the *Total* row.
   h. Insert *Min* in the third *Group By* list box in the *Total* row.
   i. Insert *Max* in the fourth *Group By* list box in the *Total* row.
2. Run the query.
3. Automatically adjust the column widths.
4. Save the query and name it *AmountTotals*.
5. Print and then close the query.

Assessment 7 Design a Query Using Fields from Tables and a Query

1. With the **Cornerstone.accdb** database open, create a query in Design view using the Employees table, the Clients table, the Events table, and the EventAmounts query with the following specifications:
   a. At the Cornerstone : Database window, click the Create tab and then click the Query Design tab.
   b. At the Show Tables dialog box, double-click *Employees*.
   c. Double-click *Clients*.
   d. Double-click *Events*.
   e. Click the Queries tab, double-click *EventAmounts* in the list box, and then click the Close button.
   f. Insert the *LastName* field from the Employees table to the first *Field* text box.
   g. Insert the *ClientName* field from the Clients table to the second *Field* text box.
   h. Insert the *Amount* field from the EventAmounts query to the third *Field* text box.

i. Insert the *DateOfEvent* field from the Events table to the fourth *Field* text box.
2. Run the query.
3. Save the query and name it *EmployeeEvents*.
4. Close the query.
5. Using the Crosstab Query Wizard, create a query that summarizes the total amount of events by employee by client using the following specifications:
   a. At the first Crosstab Query Wizard dialog box, click the *Queries* option in the *View* section, and then click *Query: EmployeeEvents* in the list box.
   b. At the second Crosstab Query Wizard dialog box, click *Last Name* in the *Available Fields* list box and then click the button containing the greater than (>) symbol.
   c. At the third Crosstab Query Wizard dialog box, make sure *ClientName* is selected in the list box.
   d. At the fourth Crosstab Query Wizard dialog box, make sure *Amount* is selected in the *Fields* list box, and then click *Sum* in the *Functions* list box.
   e. At the fifth Crosstab Query Wizard dialog box, type **AmountsByEmployeeByClient** in the *What do you want to name your query?* text box.
6. Automatically adjust the column widths and change the orientation to landscape.
7. Print and then close the AmountsByEmployeeByClient query.

Assessment 8 Use the Find Duplicates Query Wizard

1. With the **Cornerstone.accdb** database open, use the Find Duplicates Query Wizard to find employees who are responsible for at least two events with the following specifications:
   a. At the first wizard dialog box, double-click *Table: Events* in the list box.
   b. At the second wizard dialog box, click *Employee#* in the *Available fields* list box and then click the button containing the greater than (>) symbol.
   c. At the third wizard dialog box, move the *DateOfEvent* field and the *NumberOfPeople* field from the *Available fields* list box to the *Additional query fields* list box.
   d. At the fourth wizard dialog box, name the query *DuplicateEvents*.
2. Print and then close the DuplicateEvents query.

Assessment 9 Use the Find Unmatched Query Wizard

1. With the **Cornerstone.accdb** database open, use the Find Unmatched Query Wizard to find any employees who do not have an upcoming event scheduled with the following specifications:
   a. At the first wizard dialog box, click *Table: Employees* in the list box.
   b. At the second wizard dialog box, click *Table: Events* in the list box.
   c. At the third wizard dialog box, make sure *Employee#* is selected in the *Fields in 'Employees'* list box and in the *Fields in 'Events'* list box.
   d. At the fourth wizard dialog box, click the button containing the two greater than symbols (>>) to move all fields from the *Available fields* list box to the *Selected fields* list box.
   e. At the fifth wizard dialog box, click the Finish button. (Let the wizard determine the query name: *Employees Without Matching Events*.)
2. Print and then close the *Employees Without Matching Events* query.

WRITING activities

no

The following activity gives you the opportunity to practice your writing skills along with demonstrating an understanding of some of the important Access features you have mastered in this unit. Use correct grammar, appropriate word choices, and clear sentence constructions.

Create a Payroll Table and Word Report

The manager of Cornerstone Catering has asked you to add information to the **Cornerstone.accdb** database on employee payroll. You need to create another table that will contain information on payroll. The manager wants the table to include the following (you determine the appropriate field name, data type, field size, and description):

Employee Number: 10
Status: **Full-time**
Monthly Salary: $2,850

Employee Number: 14
Status: **Part-time**
Monthly Salary: $1,500

Employee Number: 19
Status: **Part-time**
Monthly Salary: $1,400

Employee Number: 21
Status: **Full-time**
Monthly Salary: $2,500

Employee Number: 24
Status: **Part-time**
Monthly Salary: $1,250

Employee Number: 26
Status: **Part-time**
Monthly Salary: $1,000

Print and then close the payroll table. Open Word and then write a report to the manager detailing how you created the table. Include a title for the report, steps on how the table was created, and any other pertinent information. Save the completed report and name it **Access_U01_Act01**. Print and then close **Access_U01_Act01.docx**.

INTERNET research

no

Vehicle Search

In this activity you will search the Internet for information on different vehicles before doing actual test drives. Learning about a major product, such as a vehicle, can increase your chances of finding a good buy, can potentially guide you away from a poor purchase, and can help speed up the process of narrowing the search to the type of vehicle that will meet your needs. Before you begin, list the top five criteria you would look for in a vehicle. For example, it must be a four-door vehicle, needs to be four-wheel drive, etc.

Using key search words, find at least two Web sites that list vehicle reviews. Use the search engines provided within the different review sites to find vehicles that fulfill the criteria you listed to meet your particular needs. Create a database in Access and create a table in that database that will contain the results from your vehicle search. Design the table keeping in mind what type of data you need to record for each vehicle that meets your requirements. Include at least the make, model, year, price, description, and special problems in the table. Also, include the ability to rate the vehicle as poor, fair, good, or excellent. You will decide on the rating of each vehicle depending on your findings.

Level 1

Microsoft® access

Unit 2:   Creating Forms and Reports

➤ Creating Forms

➤ Creating Reports and Mailing Labels

➤ Modifying, Filtering, and Viewing Data

➤ Importing and Exporting Data

Benchmark Microsoft® Access 2007 Level 1

Microsoft Certified Application Specialist Skills—Unit 2

Reference No.	Skill	Pages
2	**Creating and Formatting Database Elements**	
2.5	Create forms	
2.5.3	Create multiple item forms	168-169
2.5.4	Create split forms	166-167
2.5.6	Create PivotTable forms	229-231
2.5.7	Create forms using Layout view	154-166
2.5.8	Create simple forms	147-152
2.6	Create reports	
2.6.1	Create reports as a simple report	183-185
2.6.2	Create reports using the Report Wizard	198-203
2.6.6	Set the print layout	185-186
2.6.7	Create labels using the Label Wizard	203-206
2.7	Modify the design of reports and forms	
2.7.7	Apply AutoFormats to forms and reports	164-166, 194, 196-198
3	**Entering and Modifying Data**	
3.2	Navigate among records	149-150
3.5	Import data	
3.5.1	Import data from a specific source	260-261
3.5.2	Link to external data sources	262-263

Note: The Level 1 and Level 2 texts each address approximately half of the Microsoft Certified Application Specialist skills. Complete coverage of the skills is offered in the combined Level 1 and Level 2 text titled *Benchmark Series Microsoft® Access 2007: Levels 1 and 2,* which has been approved as certified courseware and which displays the Microsoft Certified Application Specialist logo on the cover.

Creating Forms

PERFORMANCE OBJECTIVES

Upon successful completion of Chapter 5, you will be able to:

- Create a form using the Form button
- Change views in a form
- Print and navigate in a form
- Add records to and delete records from a form
- Customize a form with options at the Form Layout Tools Format tab
- Create a form using the Simple Form button
- Create a form using the Multiple Items button
- Create a form using the Form Wizard

Tutorial 5.1
Creating Forms
Tutorial 5.2
Customizing Forms and Using the Form Wizard

In this chapter, you will learn to create forms from database tables, improving the data display and making data entry easier. Access offers several methods for presenting data on the screen for easier data entry. You will create a form using the Form, Split Form, and Multiple Items buttons as well as the Form Wizard. You will also learn how to customize control objects in a form.

Note: Before beginning computer projects, copy to your storage medium the Access2007L1C5 subfolder from the Access2007L1 folder on the CD that accompanies this textbook and make Access2007L1C5 the active folder.

Project 1 Create Forms with the Form Button

You will use the Form button to create forms with fields in the Clients, Representatives, and Sales tables. You will also add, delete, and print records and use buttons in the Form Layout Tools Format tab to apply formatting to control objects in the forms.

Creating a Form

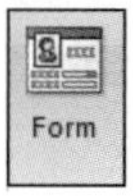

Access offers a variety of options for presenting data in a more easily read and attractive format. When entering data in a table in Datasheet view, multiple records display at the same time. If a record contains several fields, you may not be able to view all fields within a record at the same time. If you create a form, generally all fields for a record are visible on the screen. Several methods are available for creating a form. In this section, you will learn how to create a form using the Form, Split Form, and Multiple Items buttons as well as the Form Wizard.

Creating a Form with the Form Button

You can view, add, or edit data in a table in Datasheet view. You can also perform these functions on data inserted in a form. A form is an object you can use to enter and edit data in a table or query and is a user-friendly interface for viewing, adding, editing, and deleting records. A form is also useful in helping prevent incorrect data from being entered and it can be used to control access to specific data.

You can use a variety of methods to create a form. The simplest method to create a form is to click the Create tab and then click the Form button in the Forms groups. Figure 5.1 displays the form you will create in Project 1a with the Clients table in the Deering.accdb database. Access creates the form using all fields in the table in a vertical layout and displays the form in Layout view with the Form Layout Tools Format tab active.

Figure 5.1 Form Created from Data in the Clients Table

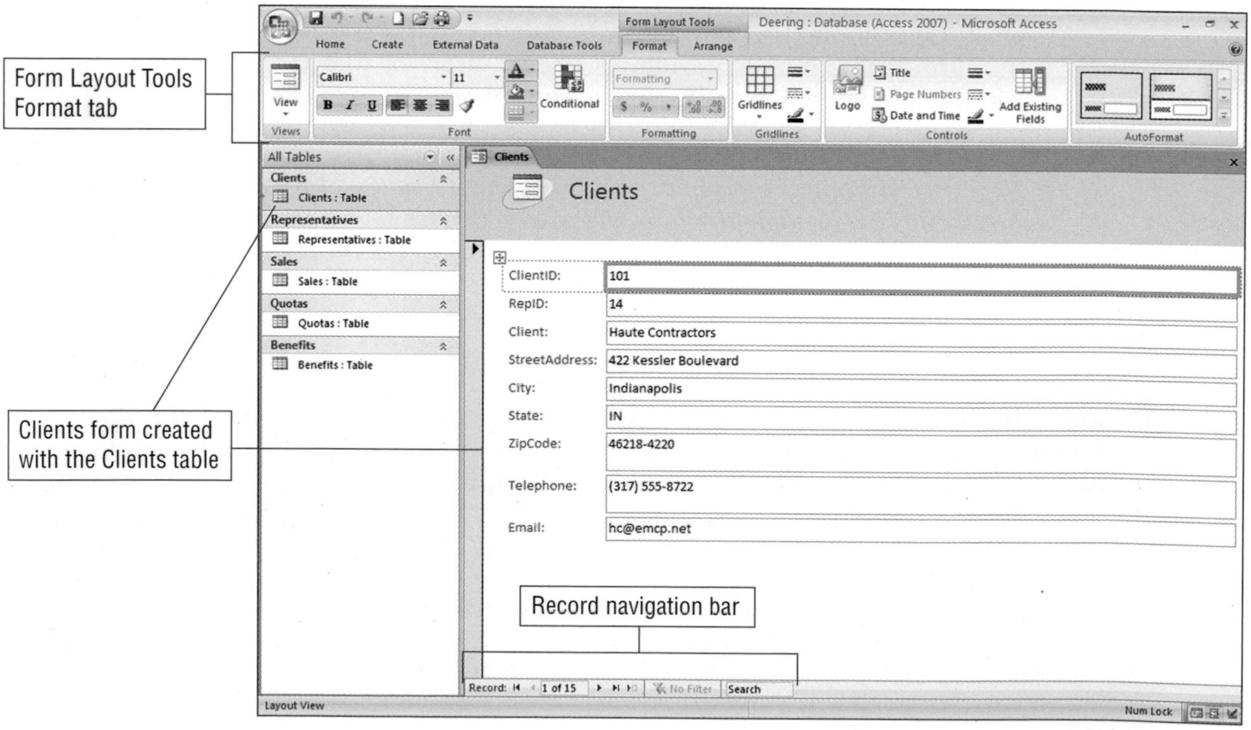

Form Layout Tools Format tab

Clients form created with the Clients table

Record navigation bar

Changing Views

When you click the Form button to create a form, the form displays in Layout view. This is one of three views you can use when working with forms. Use the Form view to enter and manage records. Use the Layout view to view the data as well as modify the appearance and contents of the form and use the Design view to view the structure of the form and modify the form. Change views with the View button in the Views group in the Form Layout Tools Format tab or with buttons in the view area located at the right side of the Status bar.

View

Printing a Form

Print all records in the form by clicking the Quick Print button on the Quick Access toolbar or by displaying the Print dialog box with *All* selected in the *Print Range* section and then clicking OK. If you want to print a specific record, display the desired record and then display the Print dialog box. At the Print dialog box, click the *Selected Record(s)* option and then click OK. You can also print a range of records by clicking the *Pages* option in the *Print Range* section of the Print dialog box and then entering the beginning record number in the *From* text box and the ending record number in the *To* text box.

Print Specific Record
1. Display form.
2. Click Office button, Print.
3. Click *Selected Record(s)*.
4. Click OK.

Navigating in a Form

When a form displays in either Form view or Layout view, navigation buttons display along the bottom of the form in the Record navigation bar as identified in Figure 5.1. Using these navigation buttons, you can display the first record in the form, the previous record, the next record, the last record, and a new record.

Along with the Record navigation bar, you can display records in a form using the keyboard. Press the Page Down key to move forward a single record or press the Page Up key to move back a single record. Press Ctrl + Home to display the first record or Press Ctrl + End to display the last record.

First record   Previous record

Next record   Last record

Project 1a   Creating a Form with the Clients Table

1. Display the Open dialog box with Access2007L1C5 on your storage medium the active folder.
2. Open the **Deering.accdb** database.
3. Create a form with the Clients table by completing the following steps:
   a. Click the Clients table in the Navigation pane.
   b. Click the Create tab.
   c. Click the Form button in the Forms group.

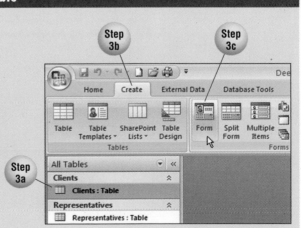

4. Switch to the Form view by clicking the View button in the Views group in the Form Layout Tools Format tab.

Step 4

5. Navigate in the form by completing the following steps:
   a. Click the Next record button in the Record navigation bar to display the next record.
   b. Click the Last record button in the Record navigation bar to display the last record.
   c. Click the First record button in the Record navigation bar to display the first record.

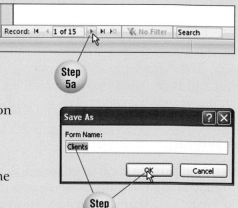

Step 5a

6. Save the form by completing the following steps:
   a. Click the Save button on the Quick Access toolbar.
   b. At the Save As dialog box, with *Clients* inserted in the *Form Name* text box, click OK.

Step 6b

7. Change orientation and print the current record in the form by completing the following steps:
   a. Display Print Preview, change the orientation to landscape, and then close Print Preview.
   b. Click the Office button and then click *Print* at the drop-down menu.
   c. At the Print dialog box, click the *Select Record(s)* option in the *Print Range* section and then click OK.

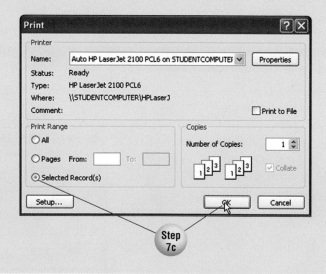

Step 7c

Adding and Deleting Records

Add a new record to the form by clicking the New (blank) record button (contains a right arrow followed by a yellow asterisk) that displays in the Record navigation bar along the bottom of the form. You can also add a new record to a form by clicking the Home tab and then clicking the New button in the Records group. To delete a record, display the record, click the Home tab, click the Delete button arrow in the Records group, and then click *Delete Record* at the drop-down list. At the message telling you that the record will be deleted permanently, click Yes.

Sorting Records

You can sort data in a form by clicking in the field containing data on which you want to sort and then clicking the Ascending button or Descending button in the Sort & Filter group in the Home tab. Click the Ascending button to sort text in alphabetic order from A to Z or numbers from lowest to highest or click the Descending button to sort text in alphabetic order from Z to A or numbers from highest to lowest.

New record

Project 1b Adding and Deleting Records in a Form

1. With the Clients form open and the first record displayed, add a new record by completing the following steps:
   a. Click the New (blank) record button located in the Record navigation bar.
   b. At the new blank record, type the following information in the specified fields (move to the next field by pressing Tab or Enter; move to the previous field by pressing Shift + Tab):

ClientID	=	116
RepID	=	14
Client	=	Gen-Erin Productions
StreetAddress	=	1099 15th Street
City	=	Muncie
State	=	IN
ZipCode	=	473067963
Telephone	=	7655553120
Email	=	gep@emcp.net

2. Print the current record in the form by completing the following steps:
   a. Click the Office button and then click *Print* at the drop-down menu.
   b. At the Print dialog box, click the *Select Record(s)* option in the *Print Range* section and then click OK.

Record: ◄ ◄ 1 of 15 ► ►| ►⊞ No Filter Search

Step 1a

Clients

Clients

ClientID: 116
RepID: 14
Client: Gen-Erin Productions
StreetAddress: 1099 15th Street
City: Muncie
State: IN
ZipCode: 47306-7963
Telephone: (765) 555-3120
Email: gep@emcp.net|

Step 1b

3. Delete the second record (ClientID 102) by completing the following steps:
   a. Click the First record button in the Record navigation bar.
   b. Click the Next record button in the Record navigation bar.
   c. With Record 2 active, click the Home tab.
   d. Click the Delete button arrow and then click *Delete Record* at the drop-down list.

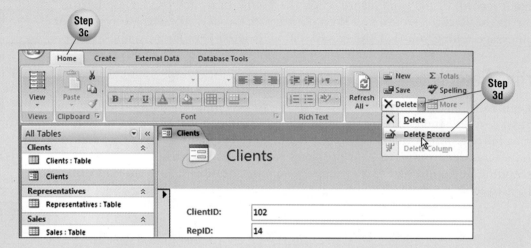

   e. At the message telling you that you will not be able to undo the delete operation, click Yes.
4. Click the New (blank) record button in the Record navigation bar and then type the following information in the specified fields.

ClientID	=	102
RepID	=	11
Client	=	**Sunrise Corporation**
StreetAddress	=	**14432 Center Avenue**
City	=	**Indianapolis**
State	=	**IN**
ZipCode	=	462381744
Telephone	=	3175555640
Email	=	**sc@emcp.net**

5. Sort the records in the form by completing the following steps:
   a. Click in the field containing the data *Sunrise Corporation* and then click the Ascending button in the Sort & Filter group in the Home tab.
   b. Click in the field containing the data *Indianapolis* and then click the Descending button in the Sort & Filter group.
   c. Click in the field containing the data *47306-4839* and then click the Ascending button in the Sort & Filter group.
   d. Click in the field containing the data *114* and then click the Ascending button in the Sort & Filter group.
6. Click the Save button on the Quick Access toolbar.
7. Close the Clients form by clicking the Close button located in the upper right corner of the forms window.

Creating a Form with a Related Table

When you created the form with the Clients table, only the Clients table fields displayed in the form. If you create a form with a table that has a one-to-many relationship established, Access adds a datasheet to the form that is based on the related table. For example, in Project 1c, you will create a one-to-many relationship between the Clients table and the Representatives table and then create a form with the Representatives table. Since it is related to the Clients table by a one-to-many relationship, Access inserts a datasheet at the bottom of the form containing all of the records in the Clients table. Figure 5.2 displays the form you will create in Project 1c. Notice the datasheet that displays at the bottom of the form.

If you have created only a single one-to-many relationship, the datasheet for the related table displays in the form. If you have created more than one relationship in a table, Access will not display any datasheets when you create a form with the table.

Figure 5.2 Representatives Form with Clients Datasheet

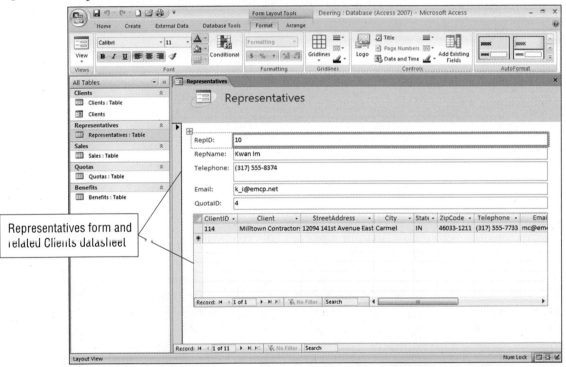

Representatives form and related Clients datasheet

Project 1c   Creating a Form with a Related Table

1. With the **Deering.accdb** database open, create a one-to-many relationship where the *RepID* field in the Representatives table is the "one" and the *RepID* field in the Clients table is the "many." Save and then close the relationships window.
2. Create a form with the Representatives table by completing the following steps:
   a. Click the Representatives table in the Navigation pane.
   b. Click the Create tab.
   c. Click the Form button in the Forms group.

3. Insert a new record in the Clients table for representative 12 (Catherine Singleton) by completing the following steps:

   a. Click twice on the Next record button in the Record navigation bar at the bottom of the form window (not the Record navigation bar in the Clients datasheet) to display the record for Catherine Singleton.

   b. Click in the cell immediately below *113* in the *ClientID* field in the Clients datasheet.

   c. Type the following information in the specified fields:

ClientID	=	117
Client	=	**Dan-Built Construction**
StreetAddress	=	**903 James Street**
City	=	**Carmel**
State	=	**IN**
ZipCode	=	**46033-9050**
Telephone	=	**(317) 555-1122**
Email	=	**dc@emcp.net**

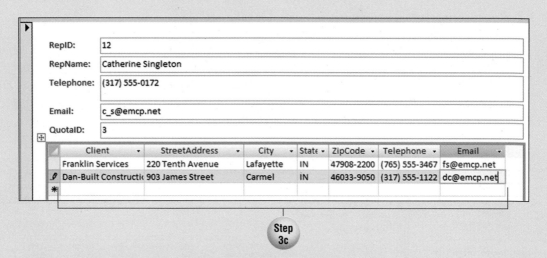

Step 3c

4. Click the Save button on the Quick Access toolbar and at the Save As dialog box with *Representatives* in the *Form Name* text box, click OK.

5. Print the current record in the form by completing the following steps:

   a. Click the Office button and then click *Print* at the drop-down menu.

   b. At the Print dialog box, click the *Select Record(s)* option in the *Print Range* section and then click OK.

6. Close the Representatives form.

Customizing a Form

A form is comprised of a series of control objects, which are objects that display titles or descriptions, accept data, or perform actions. You can customize control objects with buttons in the Form Layout Tools Format tab. This tab is active when you display a form in Layout view and contains buttons for changing the font, alignment, and formatting of text; applying gridlines; and inserting controls such as a logo, title, and the date and time.

To customize an individual control object, click the object to select it. A selected control object displays with an orange border. To apply formatting to multiple objects, hold down the Shift key while clicking each object. To select all objects in a column, click the first object, position the mouse pointer at the top of the selected object until the pointer turns into a black, down-pointing arrow, and then click the left mouse button.

Changing the Font

With buttons in the Font group, you can change the font, font style, font size, and font color. You can also change the alignment of text in a field and apply fill to fields. The Font group also contains a Format Painter button to copy formatting and apply it to other data.

Project 1d   Applying Font Formatting to a Form

1. With the **Deering.accdb** database open, open the Clients form by completing the following steps:
   a. Click the Navigation pane Menu bar.
   b. Click *Object Type* at the drop-down list. (This option displays the objects grouped by type—Tables, Queries, Forms, and Reports. The **Deering.accdb** database only contains tables and forms, so you will see only those two types in the Navigation pane.)
   c. Double-click *Clients* in the *Forms* section of the Navigation pane.
2. Click the Layout View button located at the right side of the Status bar. (The form must display in Layout view to display the Form Layout Tools Format tab.)
3. Change the font and alignment formatting of form elements by completing the following steps:
   a. Click the *ClientID* control object.
   b. Hold down the Shift key.
   c. Click each of the field names through *Email.*
   d. With the nine control objects selected, click the Font button arrow in the Font group and then click *Candara* at the drop-down list.
   e. Click the Bold button and then click the Italic button in the Font group.
   f. Click the Align Text Right button in the Font group.
   g. Click the Font Color button arrow and then click *Maroon 5* at the drop-down color palette. (See image at the right.)
4. Change the font and width of control objects by completing the following steps:
   a. Click the control object containing the text *101.*
   b. Position the mouse pointer at the top of the selected object until the mouse pointer displays as a black, down-pointing arrow and then click the left mouse button.

c. With the nine control objects selected, position the mouse pointer on the right edge of any of the selected control objects until the pointer changes to a left- and right-pointing arrow, drag the right border left to the approximate width shown in the image below, and then release the mouse button.

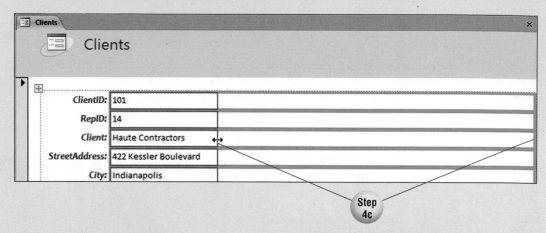

d. Click the Font Color button arrow and then click *Dark Blue* at the drop-down color palette (second color from the *right* in the bottom row of the *Standard Colors* section).

e. Click the Fill/Back Color button arrow and then click *Maroon 1* at the drop-down color palette.

f. Click outside the selected control objects to deselect them.

5. Click the Save button on the Quick Access toolbar.

6. Click the Next record button in the Record navigation bar to display the next record. Continue navigating through the records to view the records with the font formatting applied.

7. Click the First record button in the Record navigation bar.

Applying Conditional Formatting

Click the Conditional button in the Font group in the Form Layout Tools Format tab and the Conditional Formatting dialog box displays as shown in Figure 5.3. In the *Default Formatting* section, specify the type of formatting you want applied to the control object if the condition (or conditions) is not met. A preview box displays in the *Default Formatting* section showing you how the control object will display if the condition is not met. Use options in the *Condition 1* section of the dialog box to specify a criterion and choose the formatting you want applied to data in a control object that meet the criterion. For example, in Project 1e you will specify that you want any *Indianapolis* entries in the *City* field to display in red.

Click the down-pointing arrow at the right side of the second option box in a condition section and a drop-down list displays with the options *between, not between, equal to, not equal to, greater than, less than, greater than or equal to,* and *less than or equal to*. Use these options when creating conditional formatting.

Figure 5.3 Conditional Formatting Dialog Box

Use options in this dialog box to apply conditions to text in a form.

Click the Add button to insert up to two additional conditions.

Project 1e Applying Conditional Formatting

1. With the **Deering.accdb** database open, the Clients form open, and the first record displayed, click the control object containing the word *Indianapolis*.
2. Click the Conditional button in the Font group in the Form Layout Tools Format tab.
3. At the Conditional Formatting dialog box, click the down-pointing arrow in the second list box in the *Condition 1* section (the list box containing the word *between*) and then click *equal to* at the drop-down list.
4. Click in the text box immediately right of the option box containing *equal to* and then type **Indianapolis**.
5. Click the Fill/Back Color button in the *Condition 1* section (this inserts light maroon fill in the preview cell).
6. Click the Font/Fore Color button arrow in the *Condition 1* section and then click the red color at the drop-down color palette (second color from the left in the bottom row).
7. Click OK to close the dialog box.
8. Navigate through the records and notice that *Indianapolis* in the *City* field displays in red while the other cities display in the dark blue color your chose in the previous project.
9. Save the Clients form.
10. Click the First record button in the Record navigation bar and then print the record.
11. Close the Clients form.

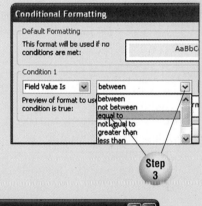

Step 3

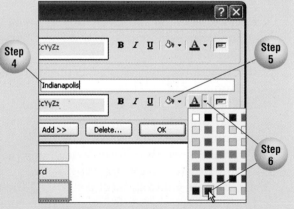

Step 4

Step 5

Step 6

Adding Additional Conditions

<table>
<tr><td>

HINT

You can apply up to three conditions on a field.

</td></tr>
</table>

In Project 1e you created one condition for the *City* field—if the field is equal to *Indianapolis* then the font color changes to red. At the Conditional Formatting dialog box, you can create up to three conditions. Click the Add button in the dialog box to insert additional conditions. For example, in Project 1f you will create two conditions specifying that if an amount is greater than $99,999 then the font color changes to green and if an amount is less than $100,000 then the font color changes to red.

Formatting Numbers and Applying Gridlines

Use options in the Formatting group of the Form Layout Tools Format tab to apply Currency, Percentage, or Comma formatting to numbers and choose a number style from the Format option drop-down list. With options in the Gridlines group, you can apply gridlines to control objects and then change the width, style, and color of the lines. To apply gridlines, you must select at least one control object to make active the buttons in the Gridline group. By default, Access applies formatting to all control objects in the form.

Project 1f — Formatting Numbers and Applying Gridlines and Conditional Formatting

1. With the **Deering.accdb** database open, create a form with the Sales table by completing the following steps:
   a. Click the Sales table in the Navigation pane.
   b. Click the Create tab.
   c. Click the Form button in the Forms group.
2. Decrease the number of decimals in the *Sales2008* and *Sales2009* fields by completing the following steps:
   a. Make sure the form displays in Layout view.
   b. Click in the control object containing the number *$289,563.00*.
   c. Click twice on the Decrease Decimals button in the Formatting group in the Form Layout Tools Format tab.
   d. Click in the control object containing the number *$327,541.00*.
   e. Click twice on the Decrease Decimals button in the Formatting group in the Form Layout Tools Form tab.
3. Change the width of form control objects by completing the following steps:
   a. Click the control object containing the text *101*.
   b. Hold down the Shift key and then click each of the two remaining control objects containing money amounts.

c. With the three control objects selected, position the mouse pointer on the right edge of any of the selected control objects until the pointer changes to a left- and right-pointing arrow, drag the right border left to the approximate width shown in the image below, and then release the mouse button.

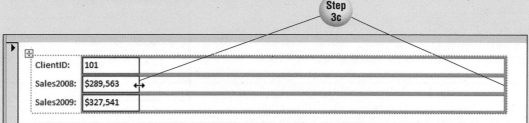

d. Click the Font Color button arrow and then click *Dark Blue* at the drop-down color palette (second color from the *right* in the bottom row of the *Standard Colors* section).

e. Click the Fill/Back Color button arrow and then click *Maroon 1* at the drop-down color palette.

f. Click outside the selected control objects to deselect them.

4. Format the three field name control objects by completing the following steps:

a. Select the *ClientID*, *Sales2008*, and *Sales2009* control objects.

b. Click the Font Color button arrow and then click *Maroon 5* at the drop-down color palette.

c. Click the Bold button and the Italic button in the Font group.

d. Click the Align Text Right button in the Font group.

e. Click outside the selected control objects to deselect them.

5. Apply and format gridlines by completing the following steps:

a. Click the *ClientID* control object.

b. Click the Gridlines button in the Gridlines group and then click *Horizontal* at the drop-down list.

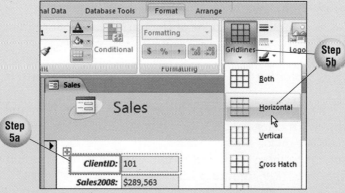

c. Click the Width button in the Gridlines group and then click the *Hairline* option (top option in the drop-down list).

d. Click the Style button in the Gridlines group and then click the *Dashes* option (third option from the top of the drop-down list).

e. Click the Color button arrow in the Gridlines group and then click *Dark Blue* at the drop-down color gallery.

f. After looking at the gridlines, you decide to change them by clicking the Gridlines button and then clicking *Cross Hatch* at the drop-down list.

6. Scroll through the records and notice the formatting you applied to the control objects.

7. Click the Save button on the Quick Access toolbar and at the Save As dialog box with *Sales* in the *Form Name* text box, click OK.

8. Apply conditional formatting by completing the following steps:
   a. Click the First record button in the Record navigation bar.
   b. Click the control object containing the amount *$289,563*.
   c. Click the Conditional button in the Font group in the Form Layout Tools Format tab.
   d. At the Conditional Formatting dialog box, click the down-pointing arrow in the second list box in the *Condition 1* section (the list box containing the word *between*) and then click *greater than* at the drop-down list.

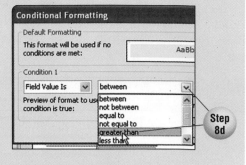

Step 8d

   e. Click in the text box immediately right of the option box containing *greater than* and then type **99999**.
   f. Click the Bold button
   g. Click the Fill/Back Color button in the *Condition 1* section (this inserts light maroon fill in the preview cell).
   h. Click the Font/Fore Color button arrow in the *Condition 1* section and then click the green color at the drop-down color palette (sixth color from the left in the bottom row).
   i. Click the Add button. (This inserts a *Condition 2* section toward the bottom of the dialog box.)

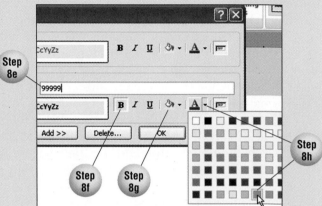

Step 8e

Step 8f

Step 8g

Step 8h

   j. Click the down-pointing arrow in the second list box in the *Condition 2* section and then click *less than* at the drop-down list.
   k. Click in the text box immediately right of the option box containing *less than* and then type **100000**.
   l. Click the Bold button.
   m. Click the Fill/Back Color button in the *Condition 2* section (this inserts light maroon fill in the preview cell).
   n. Click the Font/Fore Color button arrow in the *Condition 2* section and then click the red color at the drop-down color palette (second color from the left in the bottom row).
   o. Click OK to close the dialog box.
9. Complete steps similar to those in Step 8 to apply the same conditional formatting to the field containing the *Sales2009* amount *$327,541*.
10. Scroll through the records and notice the conditional formatting applied to amounts in the *Sales2008* and *Sales2009* fields.
11. Click the First record button and then print the current record.
12. Save and then close the *Sales* form.

Formatting Controls

With options in the Controls group in the Form Layout Tools Format tab, you can insert a logo, form title, page numbers, and date and time. You can also apply lines to control objects and then change the line thickness, type, and color.

Click the Add Existing Fields button in the Controls group and the Field List window opens and displays at the right side of the screen. This window displays the fields available in the current view, fields available in related tables, and fields available in other tables. Figure 5.4 presents the Field List window you display in Project 1g. You can add fields to the form by double-clicking a field or by dragging the field from the Field List window into the form.

Figure 5.4 Field List Window

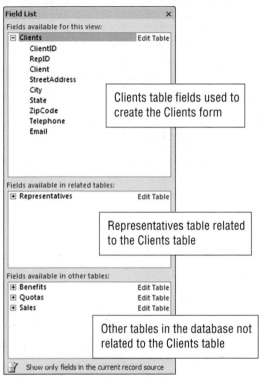

In the *Fields available for this view* section, Access displays all fields in any tables used to create the form. So far, you have been creating a form with all fields in one table. In the *Fields available in related tables*, Access displays tables that are related to the table(s) used to create the form. To display the fields in the related table, click the plus symbol that displays before the table name in the Field List window and the list expands to display all field names. To add a field to the form, double-click the desired field in the Field List window. This inserts the field below the existing fields in the form.

You can also drag a field from the Field List window into the form. To do this, position the mouse pointer on the desired field in the Field List window, hold down the left mouse button, drag into the form window, and then release the mouse button. A horizontal gold bar displays as you drag the field in the existing fields in the form. When the gold bar is positioned in the desired location, release the mouse button. You can insert multiple fields in a form from the Field List window. To do this, hold down the Ctrl key while clicking the desired fields and then drag the fields into the form.

If you try to drag a field from a table in the *Fields available in other tables* section, the Specify Relationship dialog box will display. To move a field from the Field List window to the form, the field must be located in a table that is related to the table(s) used to create the form.

Changing Field Order

When you drag a field from the Field List window into the form window, a horizontal gold bar displays as you drag in the existing fields in the form. Position the gold bar at the location where you want the field inserted and then release the mouse button. You can also change the order of existing fields by clicking the field control object and then dragging the field to the desired position.

Sizing a Control Object

You can change the size of a selected control object. To do this, select the object and then position the mouse pointer on the object border until the mouse pointer displays as a double-headed arrow pointing in the desired direction. Drag in or out to decrease or increase the size of the object.

Moving a Control Object in the Form Header

A form contains a form header that is the top portion of the form containing the logo container control object and the form title. You can move control objects in a form header to different locations within the header. To move a control object in a header, click the object to select it and then drag it with the mouse to the desired position.

Project 1g Formatting Controls in a Form

1. With the **Deering.accdb** database open, right-click the Clients form in the Navigation pane and then click *Layout View* at the shortcut menu. (Make sure you right-click the Clients form and not the Clients table.)
2. Insert a logo image by completing the following steps:
   a. Click the logo container control object that displays in the upper left corner of the form (in the form header).
   b. Click the Logo button in the Controls group in the Form Layout Tools Format tab.

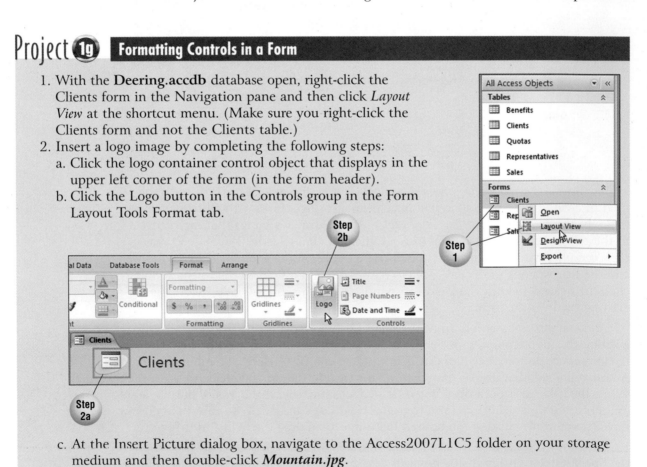

   c. At the Insert Picture dialog box, navigate to the Access2007L1C5 folder on your storage medium and then double-click *Mountain.jpg*.

3. Increase the size of the logo control object by completing the following steps:
   a. With the logo control object selected, position the mouse pointer on the bottom right corner of the object until the mouse pointer displays as a diagonally-pointing two-headed arrow.
   b. Drag down and to the right until the logo control object is approximately the size shown at the right and then release the mouse button.

Step 3b

4. Change the form title and format the title by completing the following steps:
   a. Click the Title button in the Controls group.
   b. With *Clients* selected, type **Deering Industries Clients**.

Step 4a

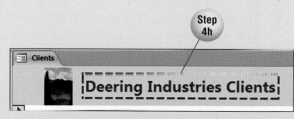

   c. Click the Font Color button arrow in the Font group and then click the *Maroon 5* color at the drop-down color palette.

Step 4b

   d. Click the Bold button in the Font group.
   e. Click the Line Thickness button in the Controls group and then click the *2 pt* option (third option from the top).
   f. Click the Line Type button in the Controls group and then click the *Dashes* option (third option from the top).
   g. Click the Line Color button arrow and then click *Dark Blue* at the color palette.
   h. Drag the title control object so it is centered vertically in the form header.

Step 4h

5. Insert and format the date and time by completing the following steps:
   a. Click the Date and Time button in the Controls group.
   b. At the Date and Time dialog box, click the bottom option in the *Include Date* section.
   c. Click the middle option in the *Include Time* section.
   d. Click OK to close the dialog box.
   e. Click the date control object, hold down the Shift key, and then click the time control object.
   f. Click the Font color button in the Font group. (This applies the *Maroon 5* color you choose in Step 4c.)
   g. Click the Bold button in the Font group.
   h. Click outside the control objects to deselect them.

Step 5b

Step 5c

Step 5d

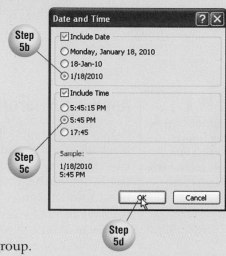

6. Insert an additional field into the Clients form from the Representatives table by completing the following steps:
   a. Click the Add Existing Fields button in the Controls group.

b. Click the plus symbol that displays immediately left of the Representatives table name located in the *Fields available in related tables* section of the Field List window. (If this section does not display, click the <u>Show all tables</u> hyperlink that displays at the bottom of the Field List window.)

c. Position the mouse pointer on the *RepName* field, hold down the left mouse button, drag into the form until the gold horizontal bar displays immediately below the *RepID* field in the form, and then release the mouse button. (This inserts the field with a down-pointing arrow at the right side. Access inserts the field as a Lookup field.)

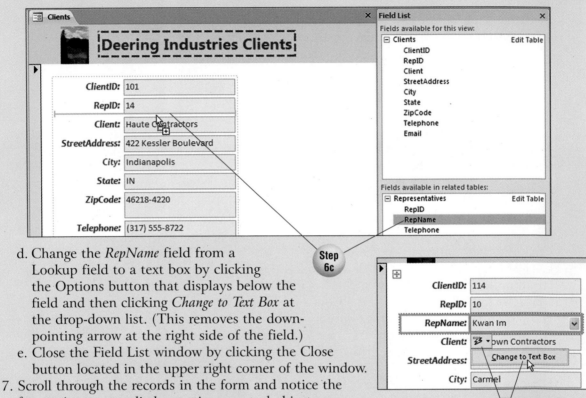

d. Change the *RepName* field from a Lookup field to a text box by clicking the Options button that displays below the field and then clicking *Change to Text Box* at the drop-down list. (This removes the down-pointing arrow at the right side of the field.)

e. Close the Field List window by clicking the Close button located in the upper right corner of the window.

7. Scroll through the records in the form and notice the formatting you applied to various control objects.

8. Click the First record button in the Record navigation bar.

9. Save the form and then print the current record.

10. Close the Clients form.

Applying AutoFormats

HINT

Autoformats have the same names as themes in Word, Excel, and PowerPoint and apply similar formatting.

Access includes autoformats you can apply to a form. These autoformats are available in the AutoFormat group of the Form Layout Tools Format tab. Generally, two autoformats display—the Access 2003 and the Access 2007 autoformats. Click the More button at the right side of the autoformats to display a drop-down list of additional choices. Hover the mouse pointer over an autoformat and the name displays in the ScreenTip. The names of the autoformats align with the theme names in Word, Excel, and PowerPoint. To maintain a consistent appearance in company documents, you can apply the same autoformat to a form that matches the theme you apply to a Word document, Excel spreadsheet, or PowerPoint presentation.

1. With the **Deering.accdb** database open, *right-click* the Representatives form and then click *Layout View* at the shortcut menu. (Make sure you right-click the Representatives form and not the Representatives table.)

2. Apply an autoformat by clicking the More button located at the right side of the AutoFormat group and then clicking the *Urban* autoformat at the drop-down list.

3. After looking at the formatting, you decide that you want to change the autoformat. To do this, click the More button at the right side of the AutoFormat group and then click *Equity* at the drop-down list.

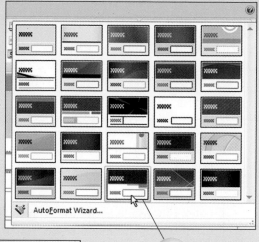

Step 2

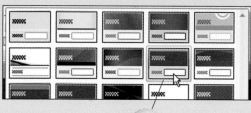

Step 3

4. Apply conditional formatting to the numbers in the *QuotaID* field by completing the following steps:

   a. Click the First record button in the Record navigation bar.
   b. Click the *QuotaID* control object containing the number *4*.
   c. Click the Conditional button in the Font group in the Form Layout Tools Format tab.
   d. At the Conditional Formatting dialog box, click the down-pointing arrow in the second list box in the *Condition 1* section (the list box containing the word *between*) and then click *equal to* at the drop-down list.
   e. Click in the text box immediately right of the option box containing *equal to* and then type *2*.
   f. Click the Font/Fore Color button arrow in the *Condition 1* section and then click the purple color at the drop-down color palette (last color in the bottom row).

Step 4d   Step 4e   Step 4f

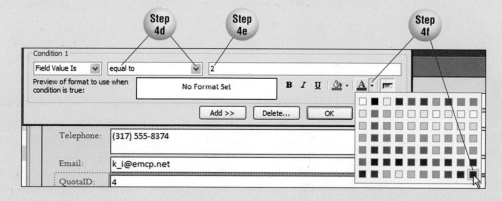

   g. Click the Add button. (This inserts a *Condition 2* section toward the bottom of the dialog box.)

h. Click the down-pointing arrow in the second list box in the *Condition 2* section and then click *equal to* at the drop-down list.

i. Click in the text box immediately right of the option box containing *equal to* and then type 3.

j. Click the Font/Fore Color button arrow in the *Condition 2* section and then click the green color at the drop-down color palette (sixth color from the left in the bottom row).

k. Click the Add button. (This inserts a *Condition 3* section toward the bottom of the dialog box.)

l. Click the down-pointing arrow in the second list box in the *Condition 3* section and then click *equal to* at the drop-down list.

m. Click in the text box immediately right of the option box containing *equal to* and then type 4.

n. Click the Font/Fore Color button arrow in the *Condition 3* section and then click the red color at the drop-down color palette (second color from the left in the bottom row).

o. Click OK to close the dialog box.

5. Scroll through the records and notice the coloring of the quote ID number.

6. Save the Representatives form.

7. Click the First record button in the Record navigation bar and then print the record.

8. Close the Representatives form.

9. Open the Clients form by right-clicking the Clients form name in the Navigation pane and then clicking *Layout View* at the shortcut menu.

10. Apply the Equity format by clicking the More button located at the right side of the AutoFormat group and then clicking *Equity* option at the drop-down list. (Position the date and time on the orange background.)

11. Make the first record active and then print the current record.

12. Save and then close the Clients form.

13. Open the Sales form in Layout view, apply the Equity autoformat, and then save the form.

14. Print the first record in the form and then close the form.

15. Close the **Deering.accdb** database.

Project 2 Create Forms with the Split Form and Multiple Items Buttons and the Form Wizard

You will create a form with the Split Form button, the Multiple Form button, and the Form Wizard.

Creating a Split Form

Create a Split Form
1. Click desired table.
2. Click Create tab.
3. Click Split Form button.

Split Form

You can create a form with the Split Form button in the Forms group in the Create tab. When you use this button to create a form, Access splits the screen in the work area and provides two views for the form. The top half of the work area displays the form in Layout view and the bottom half of the work area displays the form in Datasheet view. The two views are connected and are synchronous, which means that displaying or modifying a specific field in the Form view portion will cause the same action to occur in the field in the Datasheet view portion. Figure 5.5 displays the split form you will create for Project 2a.

Figure 5.5 Split Form

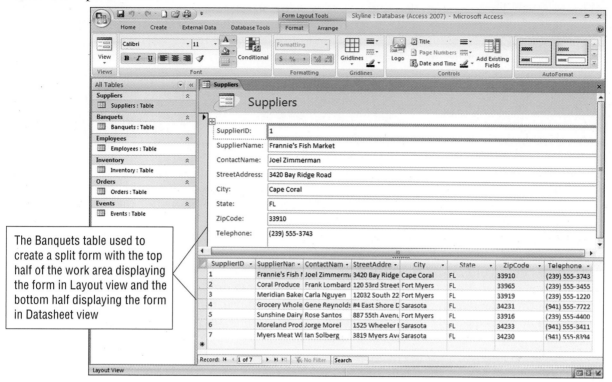

The Banquets table used to create a split form with the top half of the work area displaying the form in Layout view and the bottom half displaying the form in Datasheet view

Project 2a Creating a Split Form

1. Display the Open dialog box with Access2007L1C5 on your storage medium the active folder.
2. Open the **Skyline.accdb** database.
3. Create a split form with the Suppliers table by completing the following steps:
   a. Click the Suppliers table in the Navigation pane.
   b. Click the Create tab.
   c. Click the Split Form button in the Forms group.
   d. Click several times on the Next record button in the Record navigation bar. (Notice that as you scroll through records, the current record in Form view in the top portion of the window is the same record selected in Datasheet view in the lower portion of the window.)
4. Apply an autoformat by completing the following steps:
   a. Make sure the form displays in Layout view.
   b. Click the More button located at the right side of the AutoFormat group.
   c. Click the *Flow* autoformat at the drop-down list.

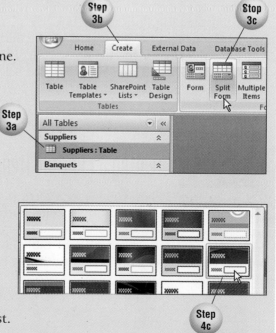

5. Insert a logo image by completing the following steps:
   a. Click the logo container control object that displays in the upper left corner of the form.
   b. Click the Logo button in the Controls group in the Form Layout Tools Format tab.
   c. At the Insert Picture dialog box, navigate to the Access2007L1C5 folder on your storage medium and then double-click *Cityscape.jpg*.
6. Increase the size of the logo so it displays as shown in the image at the right.
7. Change the form title and format the title by completing the following steps:
   a. Click the Title button in the Controls group.
   b. With *Suppliers* selected, type **Skyline Suppliers**.
   c. Click the Font Color button arrow in the Font group and then click the *White* color at the drop-down color palette (first color from the left in the first row of the *Standard Colors* section).
   d. Click the Bold button in the Font group.
   e. Click the Font Size button arrow and then click *24* at the drop-down list.
8. Insert a new record in the Suppliers form by completing the following steps:
   a. Click the Form View button located in the lower right corner of the Status bar.
   b. Click the New (blank) record button in the Record navigation bar.
   c. Click in the *SupplierID* field in the Form view portion of the window and then type the following information in the specified fields:

Supplier10	=	8
SupplierName	=	**Jackson Produce**
ContactName	=	**Marshall Jackson**
StreetAddress	=	**5790 Cypress Avenue**
City	=	**Fort Myers**
State	=	**FL**
ZipCode	=	**33917**
Telephone	=	**2395555002**

9. Click the Save button on the Quick Access toolbar and save the form with the name *Suppliers*.
10. Print the current form by completing the following steps:
    a. Display the Print dialog box.
    b. At the Print dialog box, click the Setup button.
    c. At the Page Setup dialog box, click Print Form Only and then click OK.
    d. At the Print dialog box, click the Selected Record(s) option and then click OK.
11. Close the *Suppliers* form.

Step 6

Suppliers

Suppliers

SupplierID: 1

QUICK STEPS

Create a Multiple Item Form
1. Click desired table.
2. Click Create tab.
3. Click Multiple Items button.

Multiple Items

Creating a Multiple Item Form

When you create a form with the Form button, a single record displays. You can use the Multiple Items button in the Forms group in the Create tab to create a form that displays multiple records. The advantage to creating a multiple item form over displaying the table in Datasheet view is that you can customize the form using options in the Form Layout Tools Format tab.

Project 2b   **Creating a Multiple Item Form**

1. With the **Skyline.accdb** database open, create a multiple item form by completing the following steps:
   a. Click the Orders table in the Navigation pane.
   b. Click the Create tab.
   c. Click the Multiple Items button in the Forms group.
2. Apply the Flow autoformat to the form.
3. Insert the **Cityscape.jpg** image as the logo.
4. Insert the title *Skyline Orders* and turn on bold.
5. Insert the date and time in the form header. Change the font color of the date and time to white, turn on bold, and then drag the date and time so they are right-aligned with the SupplierID heading.
6. Save the form with the name *Orders*.
7. Print the first record in the form by completing the following steps:
   a. Display the Print dialog box.
   b. Click the *Pages* option in the *Print Range* section.
   c. Type 1 in the *From* text box, press the Tab key, and then type 1 in the *To* text box.
   d. Click OK.
   e. At the message that displays, click OK.
8. Close the Orders form.

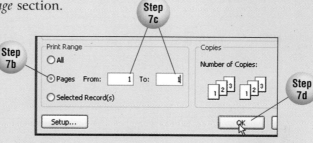

Creating a Form Using the Form Wizard

Access offers a Form Wizard that will guide you through the creation of a form. To create a form using the Form Wizard, click the Create tab, click the More Forms button in the Forms group, and then click *Form Wizard* at the drop-down list. At the first Form Wizard dialog box, shown in Figure 5.6, specify the table and then the fields you want included in the form. To select the table, click the down-pointing arrow at the right side of the *Tables/Queries* option box and then click the desired table. Select the desired field in the *Available Fields* list box and then click the button containing the greater than symbol (>). This inserts the field in the *Selected Fields* list box. Continue in this manner until you have inserted all desired fields in the *Selected Fields* list box. If you want to insert all fields into the *Selected Fields* list box at one time, click the button containing the two greater than symbols (>>). After specifying fields, click the Next button.

QUICK STEPS

Create a Form Using Form Wizard
1. Click Create tab.
2. Click More Forms button.
3. Click *Form Wizard* at drop-down list.
4. Choose desired options at each of the Form Wizard dialog boxes.

HINT
Using the Form Wizard, you can be more selective about what fields you insert in a form.

Figure 5.6 First Form Wizard Dialog Box

Click this down-pointing arrow and then click the desired table at the drop-down list.

Add a field to the *Selected Fields* list box by clicking the desired field in the *Available Fields* list box and then clicking the button with the > symbol.

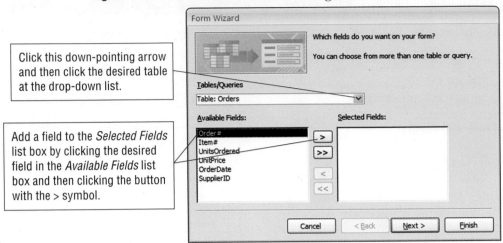

At the second Form Wizard dialog box, shown in Figure 5.7, specify the layout for the records. You can choose from *Columnar, Tabular, Datasheet,* and *Justified* (with *Columnar* the default). After choosing the layout, click the Next button.

Figure 5.7 Second Form Wizard Dialog Box

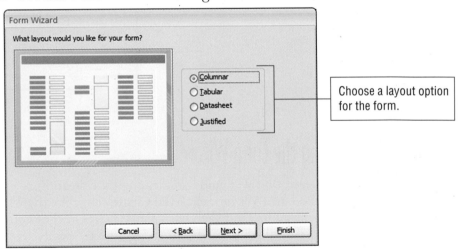

Choose a layout option for the form.

At the third Form Wizard dialog box, shown in Figure 5.8, choose an autoformat style. These are the same autoformats that are available in the AutoFormat group in the Form Layout Tools Format tab. Click a format style and the results of the style display in the preview box. After selecting the desired format style, click the Next button.

Figure 5.8 Third Form Wizard Dialog Box

Click the desired format from options in the list box and then preview the format in the preview box at the left side of the dialog box.

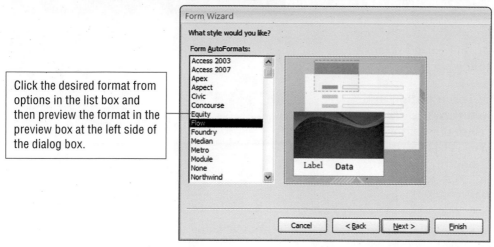

At the final Form Wizard dialog box, shown in Figure 5.9, the Form Wizard offers a title for the form and also provides the option *Open the form to view or enter information*. Make any necessary changes in this dialog box and then click the Finish button.

Figure 5.9 Fourth Form Wizard Dialog Box

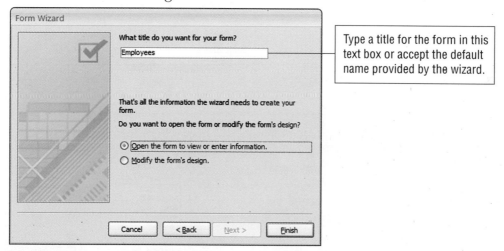

Type a title for the form in this text box or accept the default name provided by the wizard.

1. With the **Skyline.accdb** database open, create a form with the Form Wizard by completing the following steps:
   a. Click the Create tab.
   b. Click the More Forms button in the Forms group and then click *Form Wizard* at the drop-down list.
   c. At the first Form Wizard dialog box, click the down-pointing arrow at the right side of the *Tables/Queries* option box and then click *Table: Employees* at the drop-down list.
   d. Specify that you want all fields included in the form by clicking the button containing the two greater than symbols (>>).
   e. Click the Next button.

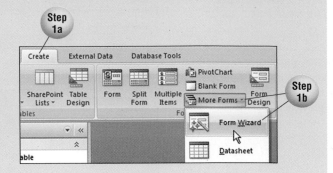

Step 1a

Step 1b

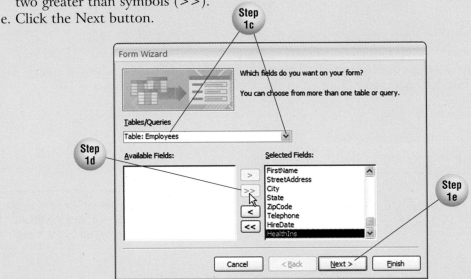

Step 1c

Step 1d

Step 1e

f. At the second Form Wizard dialog box, click the Next button. (This leaves the layout at the default of *Columnar*.)
g. At the third Form Wizard dialog box, make sure the Flow autoformat is selected in the list box and then click the Next button.
h. At the fourth Form Wizard dialog box, leave the options at the default, and then click the Finish button.

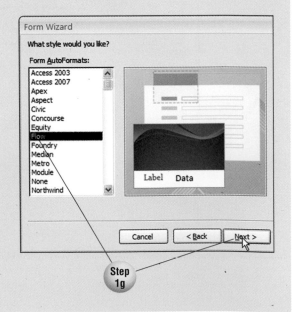

Step 1g

2. When the first record displays, click the New (blank) record button and then add the following records:

EmployeeID	=	11
LastName	=	Thompson
FirstName	=	Carol
StreetAddress	=	6554 Willow Drive, Apt. B
City	=	Fort Myers
State	=	FL
ZipCode	=	33915
Telephone	=	2395553719
HireDate	=	12/1/2007
HealthIns	=	*(Click in the check box to insert a check mark.)*

EmployeeID	=	12
LastName	=	Hahn
FirstName	=	Eric
StreetAddress	=	331 South 152nd Street
City	=	Cape Coral
State	=	FL
ZipCode	=	33906
Telephone	=	2395558107
HireDate	=	12/1/2007
HealthIns	=	*(Leave blank.)*

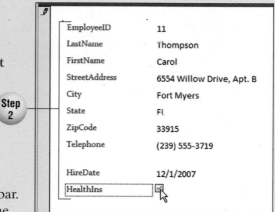

Step 2

3. Click the Save button on the Quick Access toolbar.
4. Print the record for Eric Hahn and then print the record for Carol Thompson.
5. Close the Employees form.

Creating a Form with Fields from Related Tables

In Project 2c you used the Form Wizard to create a form with all of the fields in one table. If tables are related, you can create a form using fields from related tables. At the first Form Wizard dialog box (see Figure 5.6), choose fields from the selected table and then choose fields from a related table. To change to the related table, click the down-pointing arrow at the right of the *Tables/Queries* option box and then click the name of the desired table.

Project **2d** | **Creating a Form with Related Tables**

1. With the **Skyline.accdb** database open, create the following relationships:

Field Name	"One" Table	"Many" Table
EmployeeID	Employees	Banquets
EventID	Events	Banquets

2. Create a form with fields from related tables by completing the following steps:
   a. Click the Create tab.
   b. Click the More Forms button in the Forms group and then click *Form Wizard* at the drop-down list.
   c. At the first Form Wizard dialog box, click the down-pointing arrow at the right of the *Tables/Queries* option box and then click *Table: Banquets*.
   d. Click *ResDate* in the *Available Fields* list box and then click the button containing the greater than symbol (>). (This inserts *ResDate* in the *Selected Fields* list box.)
   e. Click *AmountTotal* in the *Available Fields* list box and then click the button containing the greater than symbol.
   f. Click *AmountPaid* in the *Available Fields* list box and then click the button containing the greater than symbol.
   g. Click the down-pointing arrow at the right side of the *Tables/Queries* option box and then click *Table: Events* at the drop-down list.
   h. Click *Event* in the *Available Fields* list box and then click the button containing the greater than symbol.
   i. Click the down-pointing arrow at the right side of the *Tables/Queries* option box and then click *Table: Employees* at the drop-down list.
   j. Click *LastName* in the *Available Fields* list box and then click the button containing the greater than symbol.
   k. Click the Next button.
   l. At the second Form Wizard dialog box, click the Next button.
   m. At the third Form Wizard dialog box, click the Next button.
   n. At the fourth Form Wizard dialog box, make sure *Flow* is selected in the list box and then click the Next button.
   o. At the fifth Form Wizard dialog box, select the text in the *What title do you want for your form?* text box, type **Upcoming Banquets**, and then click the Finish button.

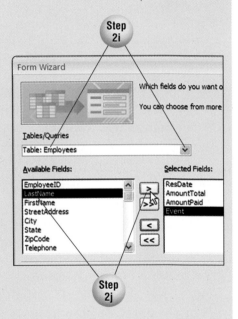

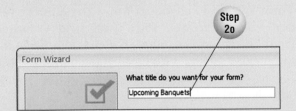

3. When the first record displays, print the record.
4. Save and then close the form.
5. Close the **Skyline.accdb** database.

CHAPTER summary

- A form generally improves the ease with which data is entered into a table. Some methods for creating a form include using the Form, Split Form, or Multiple Items buttons or the Form Wizard.

- A form is an object you can use to enter and edit data in a table or query and to help prevent incorrect data from being entered in a database.

- The simplest method for creating a form is to click a table in the Navigation pane, click the Create button, and then click the Form button in the Forms group.

- When you create a form, it displays in Layout view. Use this view to display data as well as modify the appearance and contents of the form. Other form views include Form view and Design view. Use Form view to enter and manage records and use Design view to view the structure of the form and modify the form.

- Print a form with options at the Print dialog box or by clicking the Quick Print button. To print an individual record, display the Print dialog box, click the *Select Record(s)* option, and then click OK.

- Navigate in a form with buttons in the Record navigation bar.

- Add a new record to a form by clicking the New Record button in the Record navigation bar or by clicking the Home tab and then clicking the New button in the Records group.

- Delete a record from a form by displaying the record, clicking the Home tab, clicking the Delete button arrow, and then clicking *Delete Record* at the drop-down list.

- If you create a form with a table that has a one-to-many relationship established, Access adds a datasheet at the bottom of the form.

- A form is comprised of a series of control objects and you can customize these control objects with buttons in the Form Layout Tools Format tab, which is active when you display a form in Layout view.

- Use options in the Font group in the Form Layout Tools Format tab to change the font, font style, font size, and font color. Use the Conditional button to apply specific formatting to data that matches a specific criterion.

- Format numbers and apply and customize gridlines with buttons in the Formatting group in the Form Layout Tools Format tab.

- With options in the Controls group in the Form Layout Tools Format tab, you can insert a logo, form title, page numbers, and date and time; apply lines to control objects; and customize the lines.

- Click the Add Existing Fields button in the Controls group to display the Field List window. Add fields to the form by double-clicking on or dragging the field from the window.

- Change the order of fields in a form by dragging the field to the desired position.

- Change the size of a selected control object by dragging a border of the object with the mouse.

- Move a selected control object by dragging the object with the mouse.

- Apply an autoformat to a form by clicking one of the two autoformats that display in the Form Layout Tools Form tab or by clicking the More button at the right side of the autoformats and then clicking the desired autoformat at the drop-down list.
- Create a split form by clicking the Split Form button in the Forms group in the Create tab. Access displays the form in Form view in the top portion of the work area and the form in Datasheet view in the bottom of the work area. The two views are connected and are synchronous.
- Create a form with the Multiple Items button and the form displays multiple records.
- The Form Wizard walks you through the steps for creating a form and lets you specify the fields you want included in the form, a layout for the records, the desired formatting, and a name for the form.
- You can create a form with the Form Wizard that contains fields from tables connected by a one-to-many relationship.

COMMANDS review

FEATURE	RIBBON TAB, GROUP	BUTTON, OPTION
Form	Create, Forms	
Conditional Formatting dialog box	Form Layout Tools Format, Font	
Field List window	Form Layout Tools Format, Controls	
Split Form	Create, Forms	
Multiple Items form	Create, Forms	
Form Wizard	Create, Forms	More Forms , Form Wizard

CONCEPTS check

Test Your Knowledge

Completion: In the space provided at the right, indicate the correct term, symbol, or command.

1. The simplest method to create a form is to click this tab and then click the Form button. _____

2. When you click the Form button to create a form, the form displays in this view. _____

3. To print the current record in a form, click this option at the Print dialog box and then click OK. _____

4. Navigate in a form using buttons in this bar. _____

5. Click this button to add a new record to a form. _____

6. The Form Layout Tools Format tab is active when a form displays in this view. _____

7. The Conditional button is located in this group in the Form Layout Tools Format tab. _____

8. Click the Add Existing Fields button in the Controls group in the Form Layout Tools Format tab and this window displays. _____

9. The top portion of the form containing the logo container control object and the form title is referred to as this. _____

10. When you create a form with the Split Form button, the form displays in this view in the top half of the work area. _____

11. Click this button in the Forms group in the Create tab to create a form that displays multiple records. _____

12. Click this button in the Forms group in the Create tab to display a drop-down list containing the option *Form Wizard*. _____

SKILLS check
Demonstrate Your Proficiency

1 CREATE AND CUSTOMIZE A SALES FORM

1. Display the Open dialog box with Access2007L1C5 on your storage medium the active folder.
2. Open the **OutdoorOptions.accdb** database.
3. Use the Form button in the Forms group in the Create tab to create a form with the Suppliers table.
4. Switch to Form view and then add the following records to the Suppliers form:

Supplier#	=	12
SupplierName	=	Seaside Suppliers
StreetAddress	=	4120 Shoreline Drive
City	=	Vancouver
Province	=	BC
PostalCode	=	V2V 8K4
Email	=	ss@emcp.net

Supplier#	=	34
SupplierName	=	Carson Company
StreetAddress	=	120 Plaza Center
City	=	Vancouver
Province	=	BC
PostalCode	=	V2V 1K6
Email	=	cc@emcp.net

5. Delete the record containing information on Manning, Inc.
6. Switch to Layout view and then apply the Civic autoformat to the form.
7. Select the seven field names (from *Supplier#* through *Email*) and then change the font color to Aqua Blue 5, alignment to Align Text Right, and turn on bold.
8. Click in the *City* field entry and then apply conditional formatting that changes the font color to red and turns on bold for any *City* field that contains the name *Calgary*.
9. Insert the image named **River.jpg** in the logo container control object.
10. Change the name of the form title to *Company Suppliers*. Change the font color of the title to Aqua Blue 5 and turn on bold.
11. Insert the date and time in the form header. Change the font color of the date and time to Aqua Blue 5 and turn on bold.
12. Save the form with the name *Suppliers*.
13. Print the first record in the form in landscape orientation and then close the Suppliers form.

Assessment

2 CREATE AND CUSTOMIZE AN ORDERS FORM AND A PRODUCTS FORM

1. With the **OutdoorOptions.accdb** database open, create a form with the Orders table using the Form button in the Create tab.
2. Make the following changes to the form:
   a. Display the Field List window and then, if necessary, click the <u>Show all tables</u> hyperlink (located toward the bottom of the window). Expand the Suppliers table in the *Fields available in related tables* section and then drag the field named *SupplierName* into the form and position it between *Supplier#* and *Product#*.
   b. Apply the Civic autoformat to the form.
   c. Apply horizontal gridlines to the form.
   d. Select the seven field names (from *Order#* through *OrderDate*) and then change the font color to Aqua Blue 5, the alignment to Align Text Right, and turn on bold.
   e. Apply conditional formatting that changes the font color to green for any *Amount* field entry that contains an amount greater than $999 and changes the font color to blue for any amount less than $1000. (Do not use the dollar sign when specifying the conditions.)
   f. Insert the image named **River.jpg** in the logo container control object.
3. Save the form with the name *Orders*.
4. Print the first record in the form and then close the Orders form.
5. Create a form with the Products table using the Split Form button in the Create tab with the following specifications:
   a. Apply the Civic autoformat to the form.
   b. Apply horizontal gridlines to the form.
   c. Select the six field names (from *Product#* through *ReorderLevel*) and then change the font color to Aqua Blue 5, the alignment to Align Text Right, and turn on bold.
   d. Change to Form view, create a new record, and then enter the following information in the specified fields:

Product#	=	303
Product	=	**Ski helmet**
Supplier#	=	68
UnitsInStock	=	12
UnitsOnOrder	=	0
ReorderLevel	=	10

6. Save the form with the name *Products*.
7. Print the current record (the record you just typed). (Hint: Display the Print dialog box, click the Setup button, and then click the *Print Form Only* option. Click *Selected Record(s)* at the Print dialog box.)
8. Close the Products form.

Assessment

3 CREATE A FORM USING THE FORM WIZARD

1. With the **OutdoorOptions.accdb** database open, create a form from two related database tables using the Form Wizard with the following specifications:
   a. At the first Form Wizard dialog box, insert the following fields in the *Selected Fields* list box:

   From the Products table:
   - *Product#*
   - *Product*
   - *UnitsOnOrder*

   From the Suppliers table:
   - *Supplier#*
   - *SupplierName*
   - *StreetAddress*
   - *City*
   - *Province*
   - *PostalCode*

   b. Do not make any changes at the second Form Wizard dialog box.
   c. Do not make any changes at the third Form Wizard dialog box.
   d. Do not make any changes at the fourth Form Wizard dialog box.
   e. At the fifth Form Wizard dialog box, select the text in the *What title do you want for your form?* text box, type the name **Units On Order**, and then click the Finish button.
   f. Switch to the Layout view and then apply the Civic autoformat.

2. Print only the first record.
3. Close the Units On Order form.
4. Create a form with the Suppliers table using the Form Wizard with the following specifications:
   a. At the first Form Wizard dialog box, insert all of the Suppliers table fields in the *Selected fields* list box.
   b. At the second Form Wizard dialog box, specify that you want the layout of the form to be *Tabular*.
   c. At the third Form Wizard dialog box, make sure *Civic* is selected.
   d. At the fourth Form Wizard dialog box, select the text in the *What title do you want for your form?* text box, type the name **Company Suppliers**, and then click the Finish button.

5. Print the form.
6. Close the Company Suppliers form and then close the **OutdoorOptions.accdb** database.

CASE study

Apply Your Skills

Part 1

You are the office manager at the Lewis Vision Care Center and your center is switching over to Access to manage files. You have already created four basic tables and now need to create relationships and enter data. Open the **LewisCenter.accdb** database and then create the following relationships between tables:

Field Name	"One" Table	"Many" Table
Patient#	Patients	Billing
ServiceID	Services	Billing
Doctor#	Doctors	Billing

Save and then print the relationships.

Part 2

Before entering data in the tables, create a form for each table and apply the same autoformat to each form. Apply any additional formatting to enhance the visual appeal of each form. Using the forms, insert the information on the next page in the correct fields in the specified forms. After entering the information in the forms, print the first record of each form.

Part 3

Apply the following conditions to fields in forms:

- In the Patients form, apply the condition that the city *Tulsa* displays in red and the city *Broken Arrow* displays in blue in the *City* field.
- In the Billing form, apply the condition that amounts in the *Fee* field over $99 display in green.

Print the first record of the form. Close the Patients form and then close the **LewisCenter.accdb** database.

Part 4

Your center has a procedures manual that describes processes and procedures in the center. Open Word and then create a document for the procedures manual that describes the formatting and conditions you applied to the forms in the **LewisCenter.accdb** database. Save the completed document and name it **Access_C5_CS_P4**. Print and then close **Access_C5_CS_P4.docx**.

Patients form

Patient number 030
Rhonda J. Mahler
130 East 41st Street
Tulsa, OK 74155
(918) 555-3107

Patient number 076
Patrick S. Robbins
3281 Aspen Avenue
Tulsa, OK 74108
(918) 555-9672

Patient number 092
Oren L. Vargas
21320 Tenth Street
Broken Arrow, OK 74012
(918) 555-1188

Patient number 085
Michael A. Dempsey
506 Houston Street
Tulsa, OK 74142
(918) 555-5541

Patient number 074
Wendy L. Holloway
23849 22nd Street
Broken Arrow, OK 74009
(918) 555-8842

Patient number 023
Maggie M. Winters
4422 South 121st
Tulsa, OK 74142
(918) 555-8833

Doctors form

Doctor number 1
Carolyn Joswick
(918) 555-4772

Doctor number 2
Gerald Ingram
(918) 555-9890

Doctor number 3
Kay Feather
(918) 555-7762

Doctor number 4
Sean Granger
(918) 555-1039

Doctor number 5
Jerome Deltoro
(918) 555-8021

Services form

Co = Consultation

V = Vision Screening

G = Glaucoma Testing

C = Cataract Testing

S = Surgery

E = Emergency

Billing form

Patient number 076
Doctor number 2
Date of visit = 04/01/2010
Service ID = C
Fee = $85

Patient number 076
Doctor number 3
Date of visit = 04/01/2010
Service ID = V
Fee = $150

Patient number 085
Doctor number 1
Date of visit = 04/01/2010
Service ID = Co
Fee = $0

Patient number 074
Doctor number 3
Date of visit = 4/1/2010
Service ID = V
Fee = $150

Patient number 023
Doctor number 5
Date of visit = 04/01/2010
Service ID = S
Fee = $750

Patient number 092
Doctor number 1
Date of visit = 04/01/2010
Service ID = G
Fee = $85

CHAPTER

6

Creating Reports and Mailing Labels

PERFORMANCE OBJECTIVES

Upon successful completion of Chapter 6, you will be able to:

- Create a report using the Report button
- Display a report in Print Preview
- Create a report with a query
- Format and customize a report
- Group and sort records in a report
- Create a report using the Report Wizard
- Create mailing labels using the Label Wizard

Tutorial 6.1
Working with Reports and
Creating Mailing Labels

In this chapter, you will learn how to prepare reports from data in a table using the Report button in the Reports group in the Create tab and with the Report Wizard. You will also learn how to format and customize a report with options in the Report Layout Tools Format tab and create mailing labels using the Label Wizard.

Note: Before beginning computer projects, copy to your storage medium the Access2007L1C6 subfolder from the Access2007L1 folder on the CD that accompanies this textbook and make Access2007L1C6 the active folder.

Project 1 Create and Customize Reports Using Tables and Queries

You will create reports with the Report button using tables and queries. You will change the report views; select, move, and resize control objects; sort records; customize reports; apply conditional formatting; and group and sort fields in a report.

Creating a Report

The primary purpose for inserting data in a form is to improve the display of the data and to make data entry easier. You can also insert data in a report. The purpose for this is to control what data appears on the page when printed. Reports generally answer specific questions (queries). For example, a report could answer the question

QUICK
STEPS

Create a Report
1. Click Create tab.
2. Click desired table or query in Navigation pane.
3. Click Report button.

HINT

Create a report to control what data appears on the page when printed.

What customers have submitted claims? or *What products do we currently have on order?* You can use the Report button in the Reports group in the Create tab to create a report based on a table or query. You can also use the Report Wizard that walks you through the process of creating a report.

Creating a Report with the Report Button

To create a report with the Report button, click the desired table or query in the Navigation pane, click the Create tab, and then click the Report button in the Reports group. This displays the report in columnar style in Layout view with the Report Layout Tools Format tab active as shown in Figure 6.1. Access creates the report using all of the fields in the table.

Figure 6.1 Report Created with Sales Table

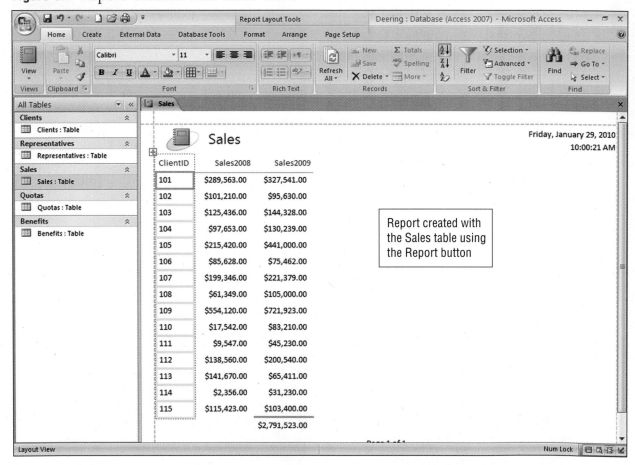

Project 1a Creating a Report with the Report Button

1. Display the Open dialog box with Access2007L1C6 on your storage medium the active folder.
2. Open the **Deering.accdb** database.
3. Create a report by completing the following steps:
   a. Click the Sales table in the Navigation pane.
   b. Click the Create tab.
   c. Click the Report button in the Reports group.

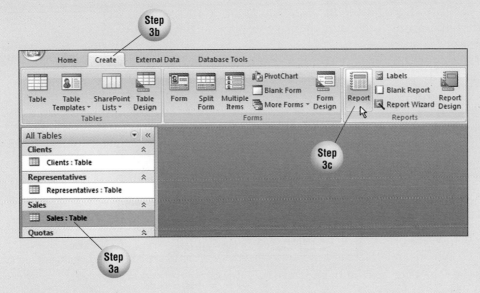

4. Print the report by clicking the Quick Print button on the Quick Access toolbar.
5. Save the report by clicking the Save button on the Quick Access toolbar, making sure *Sales* displays in the *Report Name* text box in the Save As dialog box, and then clicking OK.

Displaying a Report in Print Preview

When you create a report, the report displays in the work area in Layout view. This is one of four views available including Report view, Print Preview, and Design view. Use Print Preview to display the report as it will appear when printed. To change to Print Preview, click the Print Preview button in the view area located at the right side of the Status bar. You can also click the View button arrow in the Views group in either the Home tab or the Report Layout Tools Format tab and then click *Print Preview* at the drop-down list.

At the Print Preview tab, send the report to the printer by clicking the Print button. Use options in the Page Layout group to specify the size, orientation, and margins of the printed report. Click the Size button and a drop-down list of size choices displays. By default, a report prints in portrait orientation. Click the Landscape button if you want the report printed in landscape orientation. Change margins with the Margins button in the Page Layout group and click the Page Setup button to display a dialog box with page layout options. If you want to print only the report data and not the column headings or report title, click the *Print Data Only* check box to insert a check mark. Use options in the Zoom group to display specific

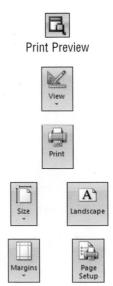

locations in the report. The Print Preview tab also contains options for exporting a report to Word or to a text format. You will learn more about exporting data in Chapter 8.

Project 1b Displaying a Report in Print Preview

1. With the Sales report open, click the Print Preview button in the view area at the right side of the Status bar.
2. Click the Two Pages button in the Zoom group. (Since this report contains only one page, the page displays at the left side of the work area.)
3. Click the Zoom button arrow in the Zoom group and then click *50%* at the drop-down list.

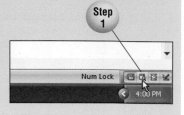

Step 1

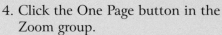

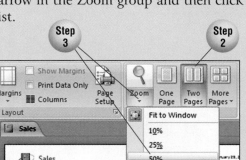

Step 3

Step 2

4. Click the One Page button in the Zoom group.
5. Click the Landscape button in the Page Layout group.
6. Click the Margins button in the Page Layout group and then click the *Wide* option at the drop-down list.
7. Print the report by clicking the Print button in the Print Preview tab and then clicking OK at the Print dialog box.
8. Close Print Preview by clicking the Close Print Preview button located at the right side of the Print Preview tab.
9. Close the Sales report.
10. Create a report with the Clients table by completing the following steps:
    a. Click the Clients table in the Navigation pane.
    b. Click the Create tab.
    c. Click the Report button in the Reports group.
11. Click the Print Preview button in the view area at the right side of the Status bar.
12. Click the Two Pages button in the Zoom group.
13. Change the setup of the report by completing the following steps:
    a. Click the Page Setup button in the Page Layout group.

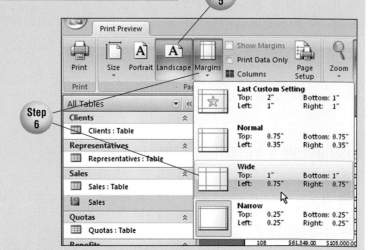

Step 5

Step 6

b. At the Page Setup dialog box with the Print Options tab selected, change the *Top*, *Bottom*, *Left*, and *Right* measurements to 1.

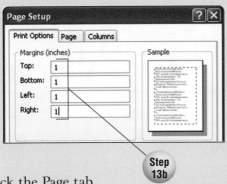

Step 13c

Step 13d

Step 13b

c. Click the Page tab.

d. At the Page Setup dialog box with the Page tab selected, click the *Landscape* option.

e. Click OK to close the dialog box.

Step 13e

14. After looking at the report, you decide to return to portrait orientation by clicking the Portrait button in the Page Layout group.

15. Print the report by clicking the Print button in the Print Preview tab and then clicking OK at the Print dialog box.

16. Close Print Preview by clicking the Close Print Preview button.

17. Save the report with the name *Clients*.

18. Close the Clients report.

Creating a Report with a Query

Since one of the purposes of a report is to answer specific questions, design and run a query and then create a report based on that query. Create a report from a query in the same manner as creating a report from a table.

Project 1c Creating a Report with a Query

1. With the **Deering.accdb** database open, create the following one-to-many relationships:

Field Name	"One" Table	"Many" Table
RepID	Representatives	Clients
RepID	Benefits	Clients
QuotaID	Quotas	Representatives

2. Create a one-to-one relationship between the *ClientID* field in the Clients table and the Sales table.

3. Save and then close the relationships window.

4. Design a query that extracts records from two tables with the following specifications:
   a. Add the Clients and Sales tables to the query window.
   b. Insert the *Client* field from the Clients table to the first *Field* text box.
   c. Insert the *StreetAddress* field from the Clients table to the second *Field* text box.

d. Insert the *City* field from the Clients table to the third *Field* text box.
e. Insert the *State* field from the Clients table to the fourth *Field* text box.
f. Insert the *ZipCode* field from the Clients table to the fifth *Field* text box.
g. Insert the *Sales2008* field from the Sales table to the sixth *Field* text box.
h. Insert the criterion *Indianapolis Or Muncie* in the *Criteria* text box in the *City* column.
i. Insert the criterion *>75000* in the *Criteria* text box in the *Sales2008* column.

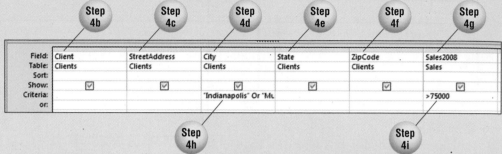

j. Run the query.
k. Save the query and name it *IndianapolisMuncieSalesOver$75000*.
l. Close the query.
5. Create a report with the query by completing the following steps:
   a. Click the IndianapolisMuncieSalesOver$75000 query in the Navigation pane.
   b. Click the Create tab.
   c. Click the Report button in the Reports group.
   d. Click the View button arrow in the Views group at the left side of the Report Layout Tools Format tab and then click *Print Preview* at the drop-down list.
   e. Click the Landscape button in the Page Layout group.
   f. Click the Margins button in the Page Layout group and then click the *Wide* option at the drop-down list.
   g. Close Print Preview by clicking the Close Print Preview button.
6. Save the report and name it *IndianapolisMuncieSales*.
7. Print and then close the report.

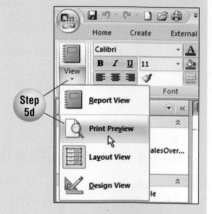

Selecting Control Objects

To apply formatting to specific control objects in a report, click the object to select it. If you click a data field in the report, Access selects all data in the column except the column heading. To select all control objects in a report, press Ctrl + A. You can also select multiple objects in a report by holding down the Shift key as you click each object.

Sizing and Moving a Control Object

Change the size of a selected control object by positioning the mouse pointer on the object border until the mouse pointer displays as a double-headed arrow and then drag in or out to decrease or increase the size of the object. A report, like a form, contains a report header that is the top portion of the report containing the logo container control object, the report title, and the current date and time. You can move a control object in a report header by clicking the object to select it and then dragging with the mouse to the desired location.

Changing the Width and Order of a Column

You can change the width of columns in a report. To do this, click in any data field in the column, position the mouse pointer on the right border of the column until the mouse pointer displays as a two-headed arrow pointing left and right, hold down the left mouse button, drag in or out to decrease or increase the width of the column, and then release the mouse button.

You can change the order of columns in a report. To do this, click the desired column heading, position the mouse pointer in the column heading until the pointer displays with a four-headed arrow attached, and then drag the column left or right to the desired position. As you drag the column, a vertical orange bar displays indicating the location at which the column will be placed when you release the mouse button.

Sorting Records

You can sort data in a report by clicking in the field containing data on which you want to sort and then clicking the Ascending button or Descending button in the Sort & Filter group in the Home tab. Click the Ascending button to sort text in alphabetic order from A to Z or numbers from lowest to highest, or click the Descending button to sort text in alphabetic order from Z to A or numbers from highest to lowest.

Sort Records
1. Click in field containing data.
2. Click Ascending or click Descending button.

Ascending

Descending

Project **1d** **Sizing, Moving, and Sorting Control Objects**

1. With the **Deering.accdb** database open, open the Sales report by right-clicking the Sales report in the Navigation pane and then clicking *Layout View* at the shortcut menu.
2. Close the Navigation pane by clicking the Shutter Bar Open/Close Button located in the upper right corner of the pane.

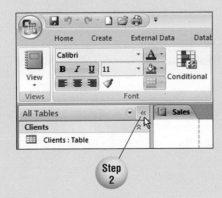

Step 2

3. Move the date control object by completing the following steps:
   a. Click the current date that displays in the upper right corner of the report.
   b. Position the mouse pointer inside the selected object (mouse displays with a four-headed arrow attached), drag to the left to the approximate location shown in the image below, and then release the mouse button.
4. Complete steps similar to those in Step 3 to move the time control object so it is right-aligned with the date (see image below).

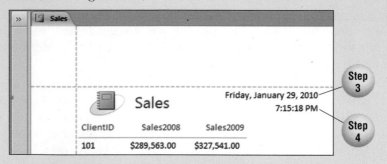

5. Change the width of the *ClientID* column by completing the following steps:
   a. Click the *ClientID* column heading.
   b. Position the mouse pointer on the right border of the *ClientID* column until the mouse pointer displays as a double-headed arrow pointing left and right.
   c. Hold down the left mouse button, drag to the right the approximate distance shown in the image at the right, and then release the mouse button.

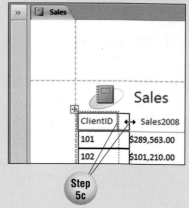

6. Reverse the order of the *Sales2008* and *Sales2009* columns by completing the following steps:
   a. Click the *Sales2009* column heading.
   b. Position the mouse pointer inside the *Sales2009* column heading until the pointer displays with a four-headed arrow attached.
   c. Hold down the left mouse button, drag to the left until the vertical orange bar displays between *ClientID* and *Sales2008*, and then release the mouse button.

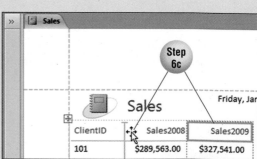

7. Sort the records in the report by completing the following steps:
   a. Click in the field containing the amount *$289,563.00* (located below the *Sales2008* column heading).
   b. Click the Home tab.
   c. Click the Ascending button in the Sort & Filter group.

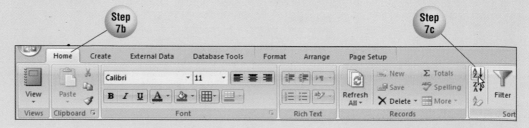

d. Click in the field containing the amount $31,230.00 (located below the *Sales2009* column heading) and then click the Descending button in the Sort & Filter group.

8. Save the Sales report.

Customizing a Report

A report, like a form, is comprised of a series of control objects, which are objects that display titles or descriptions, accept data, or perform actions. You can customize control objects with buttons in the Report Layout Tools Format tab.

HINT
Customize the formatting of control objects with options at the Report Layout Tools Format tab.

Changing the Font

Use options in the Font group to change the font, font style, font size, and font color of the selected control object in the report. You can also change the alignment of text and apply fill to fields in the report.

Applying Conditional Formatting

Click the Conditional button in the Font group in the Report Layout Tools Format tab and the Conditional Formatting dialog box displays. This is the same dialog box that displays when you click the Conditional button in the Font group in the Form Layout Tools Format tab. With the options at this dialog box, specify the formatting you want applied to control objects that meet a specific criterion (condition).

Totaling Numbers

You can use the Totals button in the Grouping & Totals group in the Report Layout Tools Format tab to perform functions such as finding the sum, average, maximum, or minimum of the numbers in a column. To use the Totals button, click the column heading of the column containing data you want to total, click the Totals button in the Grouping & Totals group, and then click the desired function at the drop-down list.

Formatting Numbers and Applying Gridlines

The Report Layout Tools Format tab contains numbering and gridline options similar to those in the Form Layout Tools Format tab. Use options in the Formatting group to apply Currency, Percent, or Comma Number formatting to numbers and choose a number style from the Format option drop-down list. Use options in the Gridlines group to apply and customize gridlines to control objects.

Formatting Controls

Use options in the Controls group in the Report Layout Tools Format tab to insert a logo, title, or date and time. The group also contains buttons for applying lines to control objects and then changing the line thickness, type, and color. Click the

Add Existing Fields button in the Controls group and the Field List window displays. This window displays the fields available in the current view, fields available in related tables, and fields available in other tables.

Project 1e Applying Fonts and Conditional Formatting to a Report

1. With the Sales report open, change the font for all control objects in the report by completing the following steps:
   a. Press Ctrl + A to select all control objects in the report (an orange border displays around objects).
   b. Click the Font button arrow in the Font group in the Report Layout Tools Format tab and then click *Cambria* at the drop-down list. (You will need to scroll down the list to display *Cambria*.)
2. Change the font style and alignment of the column headings by completing the following steps:
   a. Click *ClientID* to select the control object (orange border surrounds the object).
   b. Hold down the Shift key, click *Sales2009*, and then click *Sales2008*.
   c. Click the Center button in the Font group.
   d. Click the Bold button in the Font group.

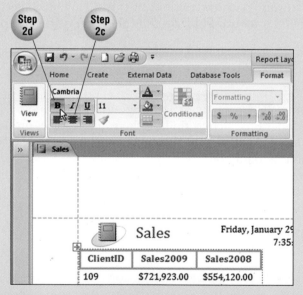

3. Change the alignment of data in the *ClientID* column by clicking *109* (below the *ClientID* column heading) and then clicking the Center button in the Font group.
4. Format amounts and apply conditional formatting to the amounts in the report by completing the following steps:
   a. Click the control object containing the amount *$721,923.00*. (This selects all of the amounts in the column.)
   b. Hold down the Shift key and then click the control object containing the amount *$554,120.00*.

c. Click twice on the Decrease Decimals button in the Formatting group in the Report Layout Tools Format tab.

d. Click the Conditional button in the Font group.

e. At the Conditional Formatting dialog box, click the down-pointing arrow in the second list box in the *Condition 1* section and then click *greater than* at the drop-down list.

f. Click in the text box immediately right of the option box containing *greater than* and then type **199999**.

g. Click the Fill/Back Color button arrow and then click the seventh color option from the left in the third row (light green).

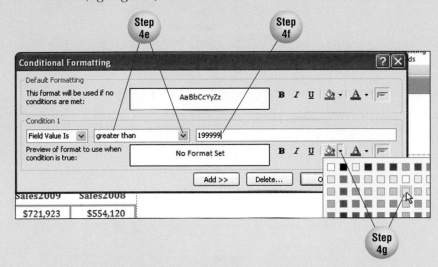

h. Click the Add button. (This inserts a *Condition 2* section toward the bottom of the dialog box.)

i. Click the down-pointing arrow in the second list box in the *Condition 2* section and then click *less than* at the drop-down list.

j. Click in the text box immediately right of the option containing *less than* and then type **200000**.

k. Click the Fill/Back Color button arrow and then click the sixth color from the left in the second row (light red).

l. Click OK to close the dialog box.

5. Apply and format gridlines by completing the following steps:

a. Click the *ClientID* column heading, hold down the Shift key, click *Sales2009*, and then click *Sales2008*.

b. Click the Gridlines button in the Gridlines group in the Report Layout Tools Format tab and then click *Cross Hatch* at the drop-down list.

c. Click the Color button arrow in the Gridlines group and then click the purple color at the drop-down list (last color in the bottom row in the *Standard Colors* section).

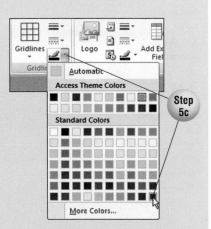

d. Click in the control object containing the number *109*, hold down the Shift key, click the amount *$721,923*, and then click the amount *$554,120*.

e. Click the Gridlines button in the Gridlines group and then click *Cross Hatch* at the drop-down list.

f. Click the Color button. (This applies the purple color to the line.)

6. Sum the totals in the *Sales2008* column by completing the following steps:
   a. Click in the *Sales2008* column heading.
   b. Click the Totals button and then click *Sum* at the drop-down list.

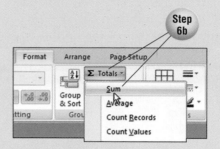

7. Insert a logo image by completing the following steps:
   a. Click the logo container content control object.
   b. Click the Logo button in the Controls group.
   c. At the Insert Picture dialog box, navigate to the Access2007L1C6 folder on your storage medium and then double-click ***Mountain.jpg***.
8. Insert a title by completing the following steps:
   a. Click the Title button in the Controls group.
   b. Type **2008-2009 Sales**.
   c. Click the Bold button in the Font group.
   d. If the title overlaps the date and time, select the date and time control objects and then move them to the right.
9. Save, print, and then close the Sales report.
10. Display the Navigation pane by clicking the Shutter Bar Open/Close Button.

QUICK STEPS

Apply AutoFormat
1. Click Report Layout Tools Format tab.
2. Click AutoFormat button.
3. Click desired autoformat at drop-down list.

Applying AutoFormats

Click the AutoFormat button in the Report Layout Tools Format tab to display a list of autoformats. These are the same autoformats available in the Form Layout Tools Format tab. The names of the autoformats align with the theme names in Word, Excel, and PowerPoint. Apply an autoformat by clicking the AutoFormat button and then clicking the desired autoformat at the drop-down list.

Changing Page Setup

The Print Preview tab contains options for changing page setup options such as margins, orientation, and size. Many of these options are also available in the Report Layout Tools Page Setup tab. Display this tab by opening a report in Layout view and then clicking the Page Setup tab in the Report Layout Tools tab.

HINT

Autoformats apply formatting similar to themes in Word, Excel, and PowerPoint.

AutoFormat

Grouping and Sorting Records

A report presents database information in a printed form and generally displays data that answers a specific question. To make the data in a report easy to understand you can divide the data into groups. For example, you can divide data in a report by region, sales, dates, or any other division that helps identify the data to the reader. Access contains a powerful group and sort feature you can use in a report. In this section you will complete basic group and sort functions. For more detailed information on grouping and sorting, please refer to the Access help files.

Click the Group & Sort button in the Grouping & Totals group in the Report Layout Tools Format tab and the Group, Sort, and Total pane displays at the bottom of the work area as shown in Figure 6.2. Click the Add a group button in the Group, Sort, and Total pane and Access adds a new grouping level row to the pane along with a list of available fields. Click the field on which you want to group data in the report and Access adds the grouping level in the report. With options in the grouping level row, you can change the group, specify the sort order, and expand the row to display additional options.

Figure 6.2 Group, Sort, and Total Pane

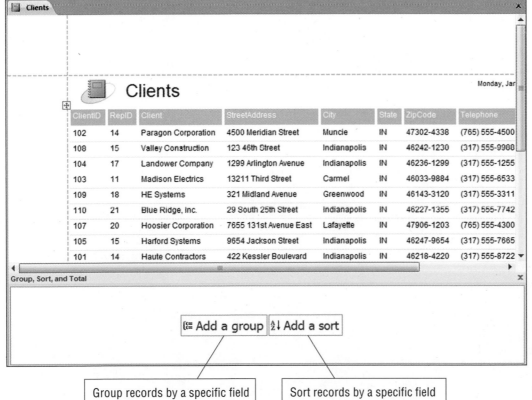

ClientID	RepID	Client	StreetAddress	City	State	ZipCode	Telephone
102	14	Paragon Corporation	4500 Meridian Street	Muncie	IN	47302-4338	(765) 555-4500
108	15	Valley Construction	123 46th Street	Indianapolis	IN	46242-1230	(317) 555-9908
104	17	Landower Company	1299 Arlington Avenue	Indianapolis	IN	46236-1299	(317) 555-1255
103	11	Madison Electrics	13211 Third Street	Carmel	IN	46033-9884	(317) 555-6533
109	18	HE Systems	321 Midland Avenue	Greenwood	IN	46143-3120	(317) 555-3311
110	21	Blue Ridge, Inc.	29 South 25th Street	Indianapolis	IN	46227-1355	(317) 555-7742
107	20	Hoosier Corporation	7655 131st Avenue East	Lafayette	IN	47906-1203	(765) 555-4300
105	15	Harford Systems	9654 Jackson Street	Indianapolis	IN	46247-9654	(317) 555-7665
101	14	Haute Contractors	422 Kessler Boulevard	Indianapolis	IN	46218-4220	(317) 555-8722

Group records by a specific field by clicking this button and then clicking the desired field.

Sort records by a specific field by clicking this button and then clicking the desired field.

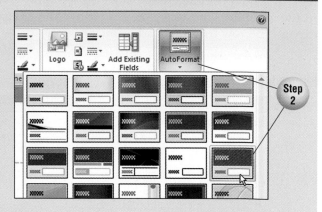

When you specify a grouping level, Access automatically sorts that level in ascending order (from A to Z or from lowest to highest). You can then sort additional data within the report by clicking the Add a sort button in the Group, Sort, and Total pane. This inserts a sorting row in the pane below the grouping level row along with a list of available fields. At this list, click the field on which you want to sort. For example, in Project 1f you will specify that a report is grouped by city (which will display in ascending order) and then specify that the client names display in alphabetical order within the city.

To delete a grouping or sorting level in the Group, Sort, and Total pane, click the Delete button that displays at the right side of the level row. After specifying the grouping and sorting levels, close the Group, Sort, and Total pane by clicking the close button located in the upper right corner of the pane.

Project 1f Applying an AutoFormat and Grouping and Sorting Data

1. With the **Deering.accdb** database open, open the Clients report in Layout view.
2. Click the AutoFormat button in the AutoFormat group in the Report Layout Tools Format tab and then click *Northwind* at the drop-down list.
3. Click each of the column headings individually and then decrease the size of each column so the right border of the column is just right of the longest entry in each column.
4. Change the orientation to landscape by completing the following steps:
   a. Click the Report Layout Tools Page Setup tab.
   b. Click the Landscape button in the Page Setup group.
5. Group the report by RepID and then sort by clients by completing the following steps:
   a. Click the Report Layout Tools Format tab.
   b. Click the Group & Sort button in the Grouping & Tools group.
   c. Click the Add a group button in the Group, Sort, and Total pane.
   d. Click the *RepID* field in the list box.
   e. Scroll through the report and notice that the records are grouped by the *RepID* field. Also, notice that the client names within each RepID group are not in alphabetic order.
   f. Click the Add a sort button in the Group, Sort, and Total pane.
   g. Click the *Client* field in the list box.
   h. Scroll through the report and notice that client names are now alphabetized within RepID groups.

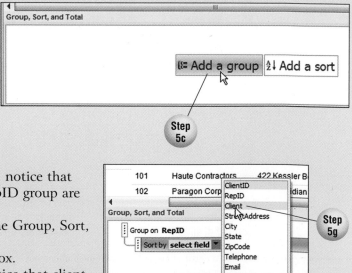

    i. Close the Group, Sort, and Total pane by clicking the Close button located in the upper right corner of the pane.

6. Save, print, and then close the Clients report.
7. Open the IndianapolisMuncieSales report in Layout view.
8. Click the AutoFormat button in the AutoFormat group in the Report Layout Tools Format tab and then click *Northwind* at the drop-down list.
9. Click each of the column headings individually and then decrease the size of each column so the right border of the column is near the longest entry in each column.
10. Group the report by city and then sort by clients by completing the following steps:
    a. Click the Group & Sort button in the Grouping & Tools group in the Report Layout Tools Format tab.
    b. Click the Add a group button in the Group, Sort, and Total pane.
    c. Click the *City* field in the list box.
    d. Click the Add a sort button in the Group, Sort, and Total pane and then click the *Client* field in the list box.
    e. Close the Group, Sort, and Total pane by clicking the Close button located in the upper right corner of the pane.
11. Save, print, and then close the IndianapolisMuncieSales report.
12. Close the **Deering.accdb** database.
13. Display the Open dialog box with Access2007L1C6 on your storage medium the active folder.
14. Open the **LegalServices.accdb** database.
15. Design a query that extracts records from three tables with the following specifications:
    a. Add the Billing, Clients, and Rates tables to the query window.
    b. Insert the *LastName* field from the Clients table to the first *Field* text box.
    c. Insert the *Date* field from the Billings table to the second *Field* text box.
    d. Insert the *Hours* field from the Billings table to the third *Field* text box.
    e. Insert the *Rate* field from the Rates table to the fourth *Field* text box.
    f. Click in the fifth *Field* text box, type **Total: [Hours]*[Rate]**, and then press Enter.

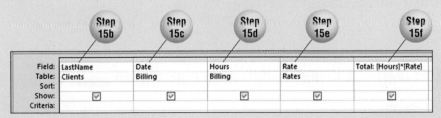

    g. Run the query.
    h. Save the query and name it *ClientBilling*.
    i. Close the query.
16. Create a report with the query by completing the following steps:
    a. Click the ClientBilling query in the Navigation pane.
    b. Click the Create tab.
    c. Click the Report button in the Reports group.
17. Click the AutoFormat button in the Report Layout Tools Format tab and then click *Median* at the drop-down list.

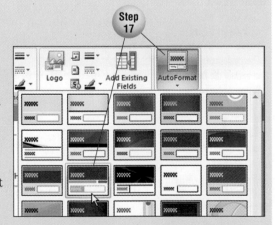

18. Click each of the column headings individually and then decrease the size of each column so the right border of the column is near the longest entry.

19. Click in the first field below the *Total* column (the field containing the data *262.5*) and then click the Apply Currency Format button in the Formatting group. If necessary, increase the column width to display all amounts.

20. Group the report by last name by completing the following steps:
    a. Click the Group & Sort button in the Grouping & Tools group.
    b. Click the Add a group button in the Group, Sort, and Total pane.
    c. Click the *LastName* field in the list box.
    d. Click the Add a sort button in the Group, Sort, and Total pane.
    e. Click the *Date* field in the list box.
    f. Close the Group, Sort, and Total pane by clicking the Close button located in the upper right corner of the pane.

21. Save the report and name it *ClientBillingReport*.

22. Print and then close the report.

23. Close the **LegalServices.accdb** database.

Project 2 Use Wizards to Create Reports and Labels

You will create reports using the Report Wizard and prepare mailing labels using the Label Wizard.

QUICK STEPS

Create a Report Using Report Wizard
1. Click Create tab.
2. Click Report Wizard button.
3. Choose desired options at each of the Report Wizard dialog boxes.

Creating a Report Using the Report Wizard

Access offers a Report Wizard that will guide you through the steps for creating a report. To create a report using the wizard, click the Create tab and then click the Report Wizard button in the Reports group. At the first wizard dialog box, shown in Figure 6.3, choose the desired table with options from the *Tables/Queries* option box. Specify the fields you want included in the report by inserting them in the *Selected Fields* list box and then clicking the Next button.

HINT
Use the Report Wizard to select specific fields and specify how data is grouped and sorted.

Report Wizard

Figure 6.3 First Report Wizard Dialog Box

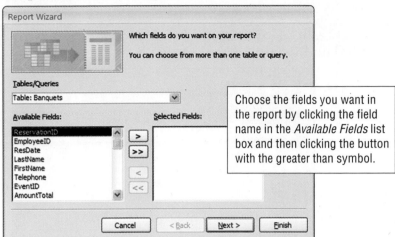

Choose the fields you want in the report by clicking the field name in the *Available Fields* list box and then clicking the button with the greater than symbol.

At the second Report Wizard dialog box, shown in Figure 6.4, you can specify the grouping level of data in the report. To group data by a specific field, click the field in the list box at the left side of the dialog box and then click the button containing the greater than symbol. Use the button containing the left-pointing arrow to remove an option as a grouping level. Use the up-pointing and down-pointing arrows to change the priority of the field.

Figure 6.4 Second Report Wizard Dialog Box

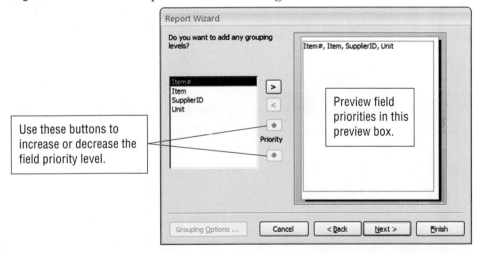

Use these buttons to increase or decrease the field priority level.

Preview field priorities in this preview box.

Specify a sort order with options at the third Report Wizard dialog box shown in Figure 6.5. To specify a sort order, click the down-pointing arrow at the right of the option box preceded by a number 1 and then click the field name. The default sort is done in ascending order. You can change this to descending by clicking the button that displays at the right side of the text box. After identifying the sort order, click the Next button.

Figure 6.5 Third Report Wizard Dialog Box

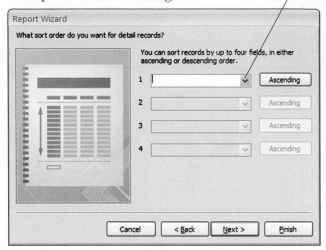

Specify a sort order by clicking this down-pointing arrow and then clicking the desired field name.

Use options at the fourth Report Wizard dialog box as shown in Figure 6.6 to specify the layout and orientation of the report. The *Layout* option has a default setting of *Stepped*. You can change this to *Block* or *Outline*. By default the report will print in *Portrait* orientation. You can change this to *Landscape* in the *Orientation* section of the dialog box. Access will adjust field widths in the report so all fields fit on one page. If you do not want Access to make the adjustment, remove the check mark from the *Adjust the field width so all fields fit on a page* option.

Figure 6.6 Fourth Report Wizard Dialog Box

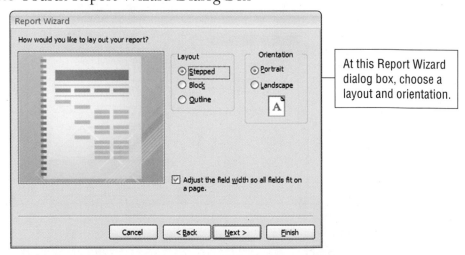

At this Report Wizard dialog box, choose a layout and orientation.

Choose an autoformat for the report at the fifth Report Wizard dialog box. By default, Access selects the autoformat that was previously applied to a report. Click the desired autoformat and then click the Next button. At the final Report Wizard dialog box, type a name for the report and then click the Finish button.

1. Display the Open dialog box with Access2007L1C6 on your storage medium the active folder.
2. Open the **Skyline.accdb** database.
3. Create a report using the Report Wizard by completing the following steps:
   a. Click the Create tab.
   b. Click the Report Wizard button in the Reports group.
   c. At the first Report Wizard dialog box, click the down-pointing arrow at the right side of the *Tables/Queries* option box and then click *Table: Inventory* at the drop-down list.
   d. Click the button containing the two greater than symbols to insert all Inventory fields in the *Selected Fields* list box.
   e. Click the Next button.

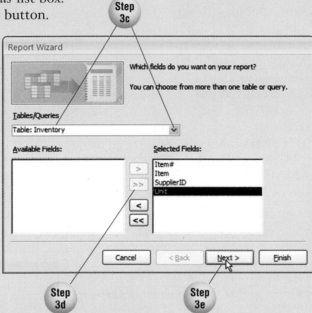

f. At the second Report Wizard dialog box, click the *SupplierID* field in the list box at the left side of the dialog box and then click the button containing the greater than symbol. (This tells Access that you want data in the report grouped by the supplier identification number.)

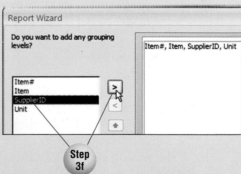

g. Click the Next button.
h. At the third Report Wizard dialog box, click the Next button. (You want to use the sorting defaults.)
i. At the fourth Report Wizard dialog box, click the *Block* option in the *Layout* section and then click the Next button.
j. At the fifth Report Wizard dialog box, click *Concourse* in the style list box and then click the Next button.
k. At the sixth Report Wizard dialog box, make sure *Inventory* displays in the *What title do you want for your report?* text box and then click the Finish button.
4. Change to Layout view. (If the *Field List* option box displays, close it.)
5. Decrease the column width for the *Item* and *Unit* columns so the right border of the column is just right of the longest entry.
6. Save, print, and then close the Inventory report.

If you create a report with fields from only one table, you will choose options from six Report Wizard dialog boxes. If you create a report with fields from more than one table, you will choose options from seven Report Wizard dialog boxes. After choosing the tables and fields at the first dialog box, the second dialog box that displays asks how you want to view the data. For example, if you specify fields from a Suppliers table and fields from an Orders table, the second Report Wizard dialog box will ask you if you want to view data "by Suppliers" or "by Orders."

Project 2b Creating a Report with Fields from Multiple Tables

1. With the **Skyline.accdb** database open, create the following one-to-many relationships:

Field Name	"One" Table	"Many" Table
SupplierID	Suppliers	Orders
EmployeeID	Employees	Banquets
EventID	Events	Banquets

2. Save and then close the relationships window.
3. Create a report with the Report Wizard by completing the following steps:

   a. Click the Create tab.
   b. Click the Report Wizard button in the Reports group.
   c. At the first Report Wizard dialog box, click the down-pointing arrow at the right side of the *Tables/Queries* option box and then click *Table: Events* at the drop-down list.

   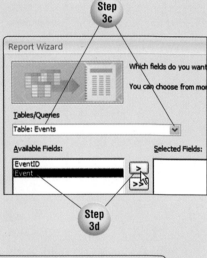

   Step 3c

   d. Click the *Event* field in the *Available Fields* list box and then click the button containing the greater than (>) symbol.
   e. Click the down-pointing arrow at the right side of the *Tables/Queries* option box and then click *Table: Banquets* at the drop-down list.

   Step 3d

   f. Insert the following fields in the *Selected Fields* list box:

   > *ResDate*
   > *LastName*
   > *FirstName*
   > *Telephone*
   > *AmountTotal*
   > *AmountPaid*

   g. After inserting the fields, click the Next button.
   h. At the second Report Wizard dialog box, make sure *by Events* is selected and then click the Next button.
   i. At the third Report Wizard dialog box, click the Next button. (The report preview shows that the report will be grouped by event.)

   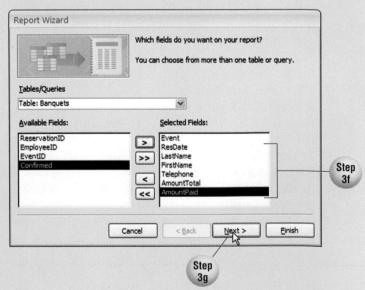

   Step 3f

   Step 3g

j. At the fourth Report Wizard dialog box, click the Next button. (You want to use the sorting defaults.)

k. At the fifth Report Wizard dialog box, click the *Block* option in the *Layout* section, click *Landscape* in the *Orientation* section, and then click the Next button.

l. At the sixth Report Wizard dialog box, make sure *Concourse* is selected in the style list box and then click the Next button.

m. At the seventh Report Wizard dialog box, select the current name in the *What title do you want for your report?* text box, type **BanquetEvents**, and then click the Finish button.

4. Change to Layout view.

5. Increase and/or decrease the size of each column to display the longest entry in each column.

6. Save, print, and then close the BanquetEvents report.

7. Close the **Skyline.accdb** database.

Preparing Mailing Labels

Access includes a mailing label wizard that walks you through the steps for creating mailing labels with fields in a table. To create mailing labels, click the Create tab and then click the Labels button in the Reports group. At the first Label Wizard dialog box shown in Figure 6.7, specify the label size, units of measure, and the label type, and then click the Next button.

Figure 6.7 First Label Wizard Dialog Box

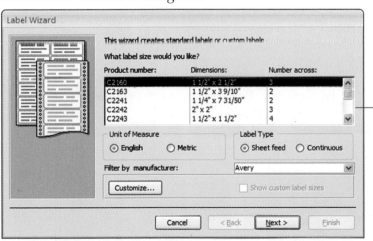

At the second Label Wizard dialog box shown in Figure 6.8, specify the font name, size, weight, and color, and then click the Next button.

Figure 6.8 Second Label Wizard Dialog Box

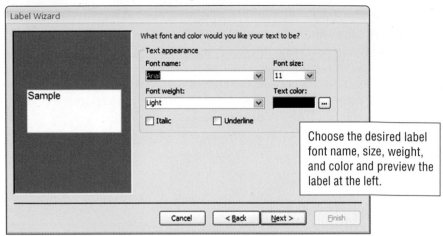

Choose the desired label font name, size, weight, and color and preview the label at the left.

Specify the fields you want included in the mailing labels at the third Label Wizard dialog box shown in Figure 6.9. To do this, click the field in the *Available fields* list box, and then click the button containing the greater than symbol (>). This moves the field to the *Prototype label* box. Insert the fields in the *Prototype label* box as you want the text to display on the label. After inserting the fields in the *Prototype label* box, click the Next button.

Figure 6.9 Third Label Wizard Dialog Box

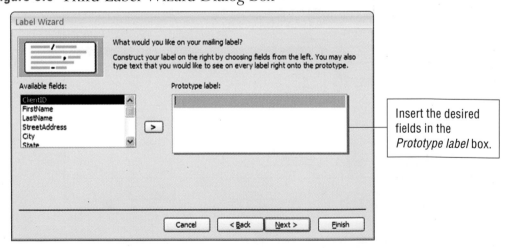

Insert the desired fields in the *Prototype label* box.

At the fourth Label Wizard dialog box, shown in Figure 6.10, you can specify a field from the database by which the labels are sorted. If you want the labels sorted (for example, by last name, postal code, etc.), insert the field by which you want the fields sorted in the *Sort by* list box and then click the Next button.

Figure 6.10 Fourth Label Wizard Dialog Box

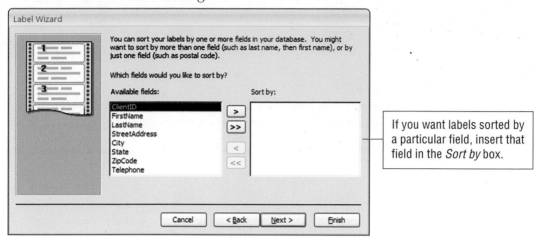

If you want labels sorted by a particular field, insert that field in the *Sort by* box.

At the last Label Wizard dialog box, type a name for the label file, and then click the Finish button. After a few moments, the labels display on the screen in Print Preview. Print the labels and/or close Print Preview.

Project ②c Preparing Mailing Labels

1. Open the **LegalServices.accdb** database.
2. Click the Clients table in the Navigation pane.
3. Click the Create tab and then click the Labels button in the Reports group.
4. At the first Label Wizard dialog box, make sure *English* is selected in the *Unit of Measure* section, *Avery* is selected in the *Filter by manufacturer* list box, *Sheet feed* is selected in the *Label Type* section, *C2160* is selected in the *Product number* list box, and then click the Next button.

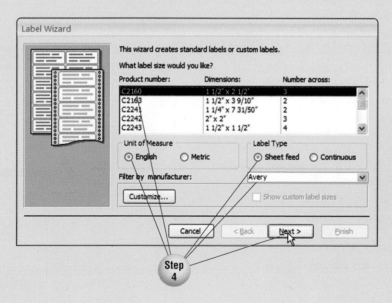

5. At the second Label Wizard dialog box, if necessary, change the font size to 11, and then click the Next button.

6. At the third Label Wizard dialog box, complete the following steps to insert the fields in the *Prototype label* box:

    a. Click *FirstName* in the *Available fields* list box and then click the button containing the greater than symbol (>).

    b. Press the spacebar, make sure *LastName* is selected in the *Available fields* list box, and then click the button containing the greater than symbol (>).

    c. Press the Enter key (this moves the insertion point down to the next line in the *Prototype label* box).

    d. With *StreetAddress* selected in the *Available fields* list box, click the button containing the greater than symbol (>).

    e. Press the Enter key.

    f. With *City* selected in the *Available fields* list box, click the button containing the greater than symbol (>).

    g. Type a comma (,) and then press the spacebar.

    h. With *State* selected in the *Available fields* list box, click the button containing the greater than symbol (>).

    i. Press the spacebar.

    j. With *ZipCode* selected in the *Available fields* list box, click the button containing the greater than symbol (>).

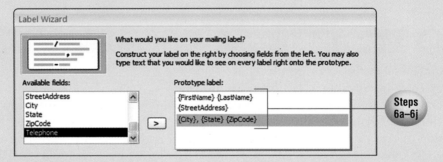

    k. Click the Next button.

7. At the fourth Label Wizard dialog box, sort by ZIP code. To do this, click *ZipCode* in the *Available fields* list box and then click the button containing the greater than symbol (>).

8. Click the Next button.

9. At the last Label Wizard dialog box, click the Finish button. (The Label Wizard automatically names the label report *Labels Clients*.)

10. Print the labels by clicking the Quick Print button on the Quick Access toolbar.

11. Close the labels report and then close the **LegalServices.accdb** database.

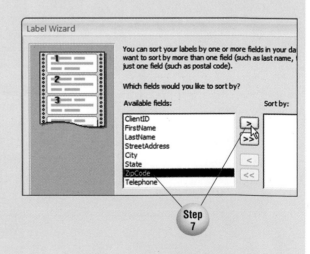

CHAPTER summary

- You can create a report with data in a table or query to control how data appears on the page when printed.
- Create a report with the Report button in the Reports group in the Create tab.
- Four views are available for viewing a report — Report view, Print Preview, Layout view, and Design view.
- Use options in the Print Preview tab to specify how a report prints.
- In Layout view, you can select a report control object and then size or move the object. You can also change column width by clicking a column heading and then dragging the border to the desired width.
- Sort data in a record using the Ascending or Descending buttons in the Sort & Filter group in the Home tab.
- Customize a report with options in the Report Layout Tools Format tab.
- Apply font formatting to a report with options in the Font group in the Report Layout Tools Format tab.
- Apply conditional formatting to a report with options at the Conditional Formatting dialog box. Display this dialog box by clicking the Conditional button in the Font group in the Report Layout Tools Format tab.
- Use the Totals button in the Grouping & Totals group in the Report Layout Tools Format tab to perform functions such as finding the sum, average, maximum, or minimum of the numbers in a column.
- Apply formatting to numbers with options in the Formatting group in the Report Layout Tools Format tab and apply gridline formatting with options in the Gridlines group.
- Use options in the Controls group in the Report Layout Tools Format tab to insert a logo, title, or the date and time. Click the Add Existing Fields button in the Controls group to display the Field List window.
- Click the AutoFormat button in the Report Layout Tools Format tab to display a list of autoformats.
- Use options in the Report Layout Tools Page Setup tab to change the page setup for a report.
- To make data in a report easier to understand, divide the data into groups using the Group, Sort, and Total pane. Display this pane by clicking the Group & Sort button in the Grouping & Totals group in the Report Layout Tools Format tab.
- Use the Report Wizard to guide you through the steps for creating a report. Begin the wizard by clicking the Create tab and then clicking the Report Wizard button in the Reports group.
- Create mailing labels with data in a table using the Label Wizard. Begin the wizard by clicking the Create tab and then clicking the Labels button in the Reports group.

COMMANDS review

FEATURE	RIBBON TAB, GROUP	BUTTON, OPTION
Report	Create, Reports	
Conditional Formatting dialog box	Report Layout Tools Format, Font	
Field List window	Report Layout Tools Format, Controls	
Group, Sort, and Total pane	Report Layout Tools Format, Grouping & Totals	
Report Wizard	Create, Reports	Report Wizard
Labels Wizard	Create, Reports	Labels

CONCEPTS check

Test Your Knowledge

Completion: In the space provided at the right, indicate the correct term, symbol, or command.

1. Create a report with the Report button in the Create tab and the report displays in the work area in this view. _____

2. Layout view is one of four views available in a report including Report view, Design view, and this. _____

3. Press these keys to select all control objects in a report in Layout view. _____

4. The Ascending button is located in this group in the Home tab. _____

5. Click the Conditional button in the Font group in the Report Layout Tools Format tab and this dialog box displays. _____

6. Click this button in the Grouping & Totals group in the Report Layout Tools Format tab to perform functions such as finding the sum, average, maximum, or minimum of the numbers in a column. _____

7. Click the Add Existing Fields button in the Controls group in the Report Layout Tools Format tab and this displays. _____

8. The Group & Sort button is located in this group in the Report Layout Tools Format tab.

_____

9. Click the Group & Sort button and this pane displays.

_____

10. Use this to guide you through the steps for creating a report.

_____

SKILLS check
Demonstrate Your Proficiency

Assessment

1 CREATE AND FORMAT REPORTS IN THE HILLTOP DATABASE

1. Open the **Hilltop.accdb** database.
2. Create a report with the Inventory table.
3. With the report in Layout view, apply the following formatting:
   a. Center the data below each of the following column headings: *Equipment#*, *AvailableHours*, *ServiceHours*, and *RepairHours*.
   b. Select all of the control objects and then change the font to Constantia.
   c. Select the date control object and then move the object so the right side aligns with the right side of the *RepairHours* column.
   d. Select the time control object and then move the object so the right side aligns with the right side of the date.
   e. Select the money amounts below the *PurchasePrice* column heading and then decrease the decimal so the money amounts display without a decimal point.
   f. Click in the $473,260.00 amount and then decrease the decimal so the amount displays without a decimal.
   g. Apply horizontal gridlines to the column headings and the data below each column heading (except the amount *$473,260*).
   h. Change the title of the report to *Inventory Report*.
4. Save the report and name it *Inventory Report*.
5. Print and then close Inventory Report.
6. Create a query in Design view with the following specifications:
   a. Add the Customers, Equipment, Invoices, and Rates tables to the query window.
   b. Insert the *Customer* field from the Customers table in the first *Field* text box.
   c. Insert the *Equipment* field from the Equipment table in the second *Field* text box.
   d. Insert the *Hours* field from the Invoices table in the third *Field* text box.
   e. Insert the *Rate* field from the Rates table in the fourth *Field* text box.
   f. Click in the fifth *Field* text box, type **Total: [Hours]*[Rate]**, and then press Enter.
   g. Run the query.
   h. Save the query and name it *CustomerRentals* and then close the query.
7. Create a report with the CustomerRentals query using the Report button.

8. With the report in Layout view, apply the following formatting:
   a. Decrease the width of columns so the right border of each column displays near the right side of the longest entry.
   b. Select the money amounts and then decrease the decimal so the amounts display with no decimal point.
   c. Click in the 8305 amount (located at the bottom of the Total column), click the Apply Currency Format button, and then decrease the decimal so the amount displays without a decimal point.
   d. Display the Group, Sort, and Total pane, group the records by *Customer*, sort by *Equipment*, and then close the pane.
   e. Apply the Apex autoformat.
   f. Select the date control object and the time control object, change the font color to black, and then drag the objects to the left so the right border of the objects aligns with the right side of the *Total* column.
   g. Select the five column headings and then change the font color to white and turn on bold.
   h. Change the title to *Rentals*.
   i. Make sure the margins are set to *Narrow*.
   j. Display the report in Print Preview and make sure the data will print on one page, and then change to Layout view.
9. Save the report and name it *Rental Report*.
10. Print and then close Rental Report.

Assessment

2 CREATE REPORTS USING THE REPORT WIZARD

1. With the **Hilltop.accdb** database open, create a report using the Report Wizard with the following specifications:
   a. At the first Report Wizard dialog box, insert the following fields in the *Selected Fields* list box:
      From the Equipment table:
         Equipment
      From the Inventory table:
         Purchase Date
         Purchase Price
         Available Hours
   b. Do not make any changes at the second Report Wizard dialog box.
   c. Do not make any changes at the third Report Wizard dialog box.
   d. At the fourth Report Wizard dialog box, choose the *Columnar* option.
   e. At the fifth Report Wizard dialog box, make sure the Apex autoformat is selected.
   f. At the last Report Wizard dialog box, click the Finish button. (This accepts the default report name of *Equipment*.)
2. Print and then close the report.
3. Create a report using the Report Wizard with the following specifications:
   a. At the first Report Wizard dialog box, insert the following fields in the *Selected Fields* list box:
      From the Customers table:
         Customer

From the Invoices table:
    BillingDate
    Hours
From the Equipment table:
    Equipment
From the Rates table:
    Rate

  b. Do not make any changes at the second Report Wizard dialog box.
  c. Do not make any changes at the third Report Wizard dialog box.
  d. Do not make any changes at the fourth Report Wizard dialog box.
  e. At the fifth Report Wizard dialog box, choose the *Block* option.
  f. At the sixth Report Wizard dialog box, make sure the Apex autoformat is selected.
  g. At the last Report Wizard dialog box, name the report *Rentals*.

4. Increase or decrease column widths to display column data.
5. Print and then close the report.

Assessment

3   CREATE MAILING LABELS

1. With the **Hilltop.accdb** database open, click the Customers table in the Navigation pane.
2. Use the Label Wizard to create mailing labels (you determine the label type) with the customer names and addresses and sorted by customer names. Name the mailing label report *Customer Mailing Labels*.
3. Print the mailing labels.
4. Close the mailing labels.

Assessment

4   ADD A FIELD TO A REPORT

1. In Chapter 5, you added a field list to an existing form using the Field List window. Experiment with adding a field to an existing report and then complete the following:
  a. Open the report named Rental Report (created in Assessment 1) in Layout view.
  b. Display the Field List window and display all tables.
  c. Drag the *BillingDate* field from the Invoices table so the field is positioned between the *Equipment* column and the *Hours* column.
  d. At the message indicating that Access will modify the RecordSource property and asking if you want to continue, click Yes.
2. Decrease the widths of the columns to ensure that all columns will fit on one page.
3. Save, print, and then close the report.
4. Close the **Hilltop.accdb** database.

CASE study

Apply Your Skills

As the office manager at Millstone Legal Services, you need to enter records for three new clients in the **MillstoneLegal.accdb** database. Using the following information, enter the data in the appropriate tables:

Client number 42 Martin Costanzo 1002 Thomas Drive Casper, WY 82602 (307) 555-5001 Mr. Costanzo saw Douglas Sheehan regarding divorce proceedings on 3/14/2010 with a fee of $150.	Client number 43 Susan Nordyke 23193 Ridge Circle East Mills, WY 82644 (307) 555-2719 Ms. Nordyke saw Loretta Ryder regarding support enforcement on 3/14/2010 with a fee of $75.	Client number 44 Monica Sommers 1105 Riddell Avenue Casper, WY 82609 (307) 555-1188 Ms. Sommers saw Anita Leland regarding a guardianship on 3/15/2010 for a fee of $150.

Part 2

Create the following queries, reports, and labels:

- Create a report with the Clients table. Apply formatting to enhance the visual appeal of the report.
- Create a query that displays the client ID, first name, and last name; attorney last name; date of visit; and fee. Name the query *ClientBilling*.
- Create a report with the ClientBilling query. Group the records in the report by attorney last name (the second *LastName* field in the drop-down list) and sort alphabetically in ascending order by client last name (the first *LastName* field in the drop-down list). Apply formatting to enhance the visual appeal of the report.
- Create a telephone directory by creating a report that includes client last names, first names, and telephone numbers. Sort the records in the report alphabetically by last name and in ascending order.
- Edit the ClientBilling query so it includes a criterion that displays only visits between 3/01/2010 and 3/05/2010. Save the query with Save As and name it *ClientBilling01-05*.
- Create a report with the ClientBilling01-05 query. Apply formatting to enhance the visual appeal of the report.
- Create mailing labels for the clients.

Part 3

Apply the following conditions to fields in reports:

- In the Clients report, apply the condition that the city *Casper* displays in red and the city *Mills* displays in blue in the *City* field.
- In the ClientBilling report, apply the condition that amounts over $99 display in green and amounts less than $100 display in blue.

Your center has a procedures manual that describes processes and procedures in the center. Open Word and then create a document for the procedures manual that describes the process for creating a report using the Report button, the Report Wizard, and the process for preparing mailing labels using the Label Wizard. Save the completed document and name it **Access_C6_CS_P4**. Print and then close **Access_C6_CS_P4.docx**.

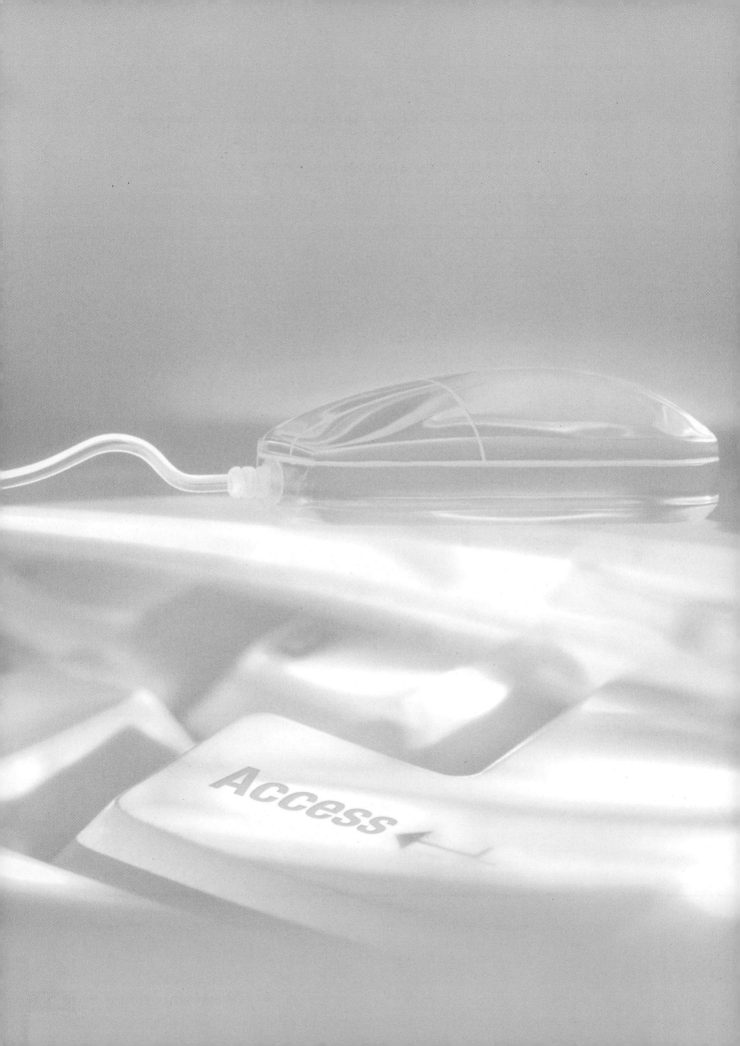

Modifying, Filtering, and Viewing Data

PERFORMANCE OBJECTIVES

Upon successful completion of Chapter 7, you will be able to:

- Filter data by selection and by form
- Remove a filter
- Summarize and analyze data in PivotTable view
- Summarize and analyze data in a PivotTable form
- Summarize and analyze data in PivotChart view
- View and customize document properties
- View object dependencies

access Chapter 7

SNAP

Tutorial 7.1
Modifying and Viewing Data

You can filter data in a database object to view specific records without having to change the design of the object. In this chapter, you will learn how to filter data, filter by selection, and filter by form. You will also learn how to summarize and analyze data in an object in PivotTable and PivotChart view and view document properties and object dependencies.

Note: Before beginning computer projects, copy to your storage medium the Access2007L1C7 subfolder from the Access2007L1 folder on the CD that accompanies this textbook and make Access2007L1C7 the active folder.

Project **1** Filter Records

You will filter records in a table, query, and report in the Skyline database using the Filter button, Selection button, Toggle Filter button, and shortcut menu. You will also remove filters and filter by form.

Filtering Data

You can place a set of restrictions, called a *filter*, on records in a table, query, form, or report to isolate temporarily specific records. A filter, like a query, lets you view specific records without having to change the design of the table, query, form, or report. Access provides a number of buttons and options for filtering data. You can filter data using the Filter button in the Sort & Filter group in the Home tab, right-click specific data in a record and then specify a filter, and use the Selection and Advanced buttons in the Sort & Filter group.

Filtering Using the Filter Button

Filter Records
1. Open desired object.
2. Click in entry of desired field column to filter.
3. Click Filter button.
4. Select desired sorting option at drop-down list.

You can use the Filter button in the Sort & Filter group in the Home tab to filter records in an object (table, query, form or report). To use this button, open the desired object, click in any entry in the field column on which you want to filter and then click the Filter button. This displays a drop-down list with sorting options and a listing of all of the field entries. Figure 7.1 displays the drop-down list that displays when you click in the *City* field and then click the Filter button. To sort on a specific criterion, click the *(Select All)* check box to move all check marks from the list of field entries. Click the item in the list box on which you want to sort and then click OK.

Figure 7.1 City Field Drop-down List

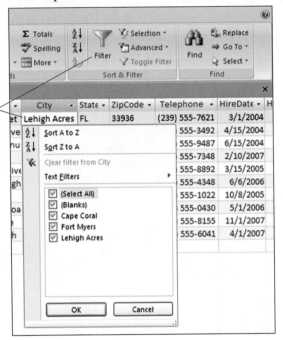

To filter on the *City* field, click in any entry in the field column and then click the Filter button. This displays a drop-down list with sorting options and a listing of all field entries.

Filters available depend on the type of data selected in a column.

When you open a table, query, or form, the Record navigation bar contains the dimmed words *No Filter* preceded by a filter icon with a delete symbol (an X). If you filter records in one of these objects, *Filtered* displays in place of *No Filter*, the delete symbol is removed, and the text and filter icon display with an orange background. In a report, the word *Filtered* displays at the right side of the Status bar if you apply a filter to records.

Removing a Filter

When you filter data, the underlying data in the object is not deleted. You can switch back and forth between the data and the filtered data by clicking the Toggle Filter button in the Sort & Filter group in the Home tab. If you click the Toggle Filter button and turn off the filter, all of the data in a table, query, or form displays and the message *Filtered* in the Record navigation bar changes to *Unfiltered*.

Clicking the Toggle Filter button may redisplay all data in an object but it does not remove the filter. To remove the filter, click in the field column containing the filter and then click the Filter button in the Sort & Filter group in the Home tab. At the drop-down list that displays, click the *Clear filter from xxx* (where *xxx* is the name of the field). You can remove all filters from an object by clicking the Advanced button in the Sort & Filter group and then clicking the *Clear All Filters* option.

Project 1a — Filtering Records in a Table, Form, and Report

1. Display the Open dialog box with Access2007L1C7 on your storage medium the active folder.
2. Open the **Skyline.accdb** database.
3. Filter records in the Employees table by completing the following steps:
   a. Open the Employees table.
   b. Click in any entry in the *City* field.
   c. Click the Filter button in the Sort & Filter group in the Home tab. (This displays a drop-down list in the *City* field.)
   d. Click the *(Select All)* check box in the filter drop-down list box. (This removes all check marks from the list options.)
   e. Click the *Fort Myers* check box in the list box. (This inserts a check mark in the check box.)

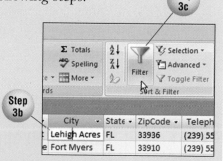

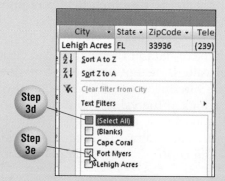

   f. Click OK. (Access displays only those records with a city field of *Fort Myers* and also displays *Filtered* and the filter icon with an orange background in the Record navigation bar.)
   g. Click the Quick Print button on the Quick Access toolbar.
4. Toggle the display of filtered data by clicking the Toggle Filter button in the Sort & Filter group in the Home tab. (This redisplays all data in the table.)

5. Remove the filter by completing the following steps:
   a. Click in any entry in the *City* field.
   b. Click the Filter button in the Sort & Filter group.
   c. Click the *Clear filter from City* option at the drop-down list. (Notice that the message on the Record navigation bar changes to *No Filter* and dims the words.)
6. Save and then close the Employees table.
7. Create a form by completing the following steps:
   a. Click the Orders table in the Navigation pane.
   b. Click the Create tab and then click the Form button in the Forms group.
   c. Click the Form View button in the view area at the right side of the Status bar.
   d. Save the form and name it Orders.
8. Filter the records and display only those records with a supplier identification number of 2 by completing the following steps:
   a. Click in the *SupplierID* field containing the text *2*.
   b. Click the Filter button in the Sort & Filter group.
   c. At the filter drop-down list, click *(Select All)* to remove all of the check marks from the list options.
   d. Click the *2* option to insert a check mark.
   e. Click OK.
   f. Navigate through the records and notice that only the records with a supplier identification number of 2 display.
   g. Close the Orders form.

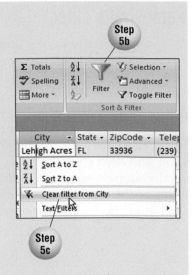

Step 5b

Step 5c

Hover the mouse over a column heading to display a tip showing the filter criterion.

Filtering on Specific Values

When you filter on a specific field, you can display a list of unique values for that field. If you click the Filter button for a field containing text, the drop-down list for the specific field will contain a *Text Filters* option. Click this option and a values list displays next to the drop-down list. The options in the values list will vary depending on the type of data in the field. If you click the Filter button for a field containing number values, the option in the drop-down list displays as *Number Filters* and if you are filtering dates, the option at the drop-down list displays as *Date Filters*. Use options in the values list to refine further a filter for a specific field. For example, you can use the values list to display money amounts within a specific range or order dates between certain dates. You can use the values list to find fields that are "equal to" or "not equal to" text in the current field.

Project 1b   Filtering Records in a Query and a Report

1. With the **Skyline.accdb** database open, create the following one-to-many relationships:

Field Name	"One" Table	"Many" Table
EmployeeID	Employees	Banquets
Item#	Inventory	Orders
SupplierID	Suppliers	Orders
EventID	Events	Banquets

2. Create a query in Design view with the following specifications:
   a. Add the Banquets and Events tables to the query window.
   b. Insert the *ResDate* field from the Banquets table to the first *Field* text box.
   c. Insert the *LastName* field from the Banquets table to the second *Field* text box.
   d. Insert the *FirstName* field from the Banquets table to the third *Field* text box.
   e. Insert the *Telephone* field from the Banquets table to the fourth *Field* text box.
   f. Insert the *Event* field from the Events table to the fifth *Field* text box.
   g. Insert the *EmployeeID* field from the Banquets table to the sixth *Field* text box.
   h. Run the query.
   i. Save the query and name it *BanquetReservations*.

3. Filter records of reservations before July 15, 2010, in the query by completing the following steps:
   a. With the BanquetReservations query open, make sure the first entry is selected in the *ResDate* field.
   b. Click the Filter button in the Sort & Filter group in the Home tab.
   c. Point to the *Date Filters* option in the drop-down list box.
   d. Click *Before* in the values list.

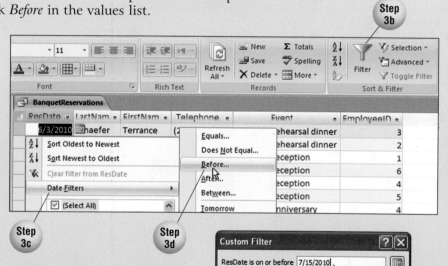

   e. At the Custom Filter dialog box, type 7/15/2010 and then click OK.
   f. Print the filtered query by clicking the Quick Print button on the Quick Access toolbar.

4. Remove the filter by clicking the filter icon that displays at the right side of the *ResDate* column heading and then clicking *Clear filter from ResDate* at the drop-down list.

5. Save and then close the BanquetReservations query.

6. Create a report by completing the following steps:
   a. Click the BanquetReservations query in the Navigation pane.
   b. Click the Create tab and then click the Report button in the Reports group.
   c. With the report in Layout view, decrease the column widths so the right column border displays near the longest entry in each column.
   d. Click the Report View button in the view area at the right side of the Status bar.
   e. Save the report and name it *BanquetReport*.
7. Filter the records and display all records of events except *Other* events by completing the following steps:
   a. Click in the first entry in the *Event* field.
   b. Click the Filter button in the Sort & Filter group.
   c. Point to the *Text Filters* option in the drop-down list box and then click *Does Not Equal* at the values list.

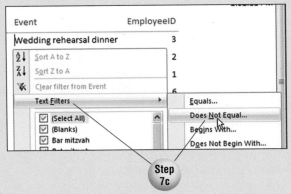

Step 7c

   d. At the Custom Filter dialog box, type **Other** and then click OK.
8. Further refine the filter by completing the following steps:
   a. Click in the first entry in the *EmployeeID* field.
   b. Click the Filter button.
   c. At the filter drop-down list, click the *(Select All)* check box to remove all of the check marks from the list options.
   d. Click the *3* check box to insert a check mark.
   e. Click OK.
9. Click the Quick Print button on the Quick Access toolbar.
10. Save and then close the BanquetReport report.

Filtering by Selection

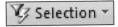

If you click in a field in an object and then click the Selection button in the Sort & Filter group in the Home tab, a drop-down list displays below the button with options for filtering on the data in the field. For example, if you click in a field containing the city name *Fort Myers*, clicking the Selection button will cause a drop-down list to display as shown in Figure 7.2. Click one of the options at the drop-down list to filter records. You can select specific text in a field entry and then filter based on the specific text. For example, in Project 1c you will select the word *peppers* in the entry *Green peppers* and then filter records containing the word *peppers*.

Figure 7.2 Selection Button Drop-down List

> To filter by selection, click in a field containing the text on which to filter and then click the Selection button. This displays a drop-down list of filtering options.

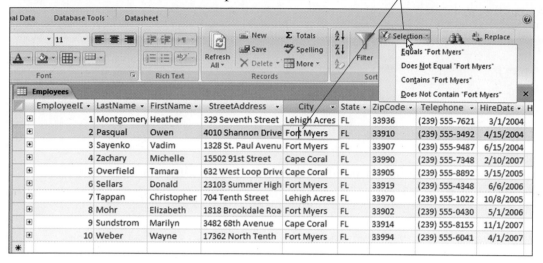

Filtering by Shortcut Menu

If you right-click on a field entry, a shortcut menu displays with options to sort the text, display a values list, or filter on a specific value. For example, if you right-click the field entry *Schaefer* in the *LastName* field, a shortcut menu displays as shown in Figure 7.3. Click a sort option to sort text in the field in ascending or descending order, point to the *Text Filters* option to display a values list, or click one of the values filters located toward the bottom of the menu. You can also select specific text within a field entry and then right-click the selection to display the shortcut menu.

Figure 7.3 Filtering Shortcut Menu

> Right-click a field entry and a shortcut menu displays with sorting and filtering options.

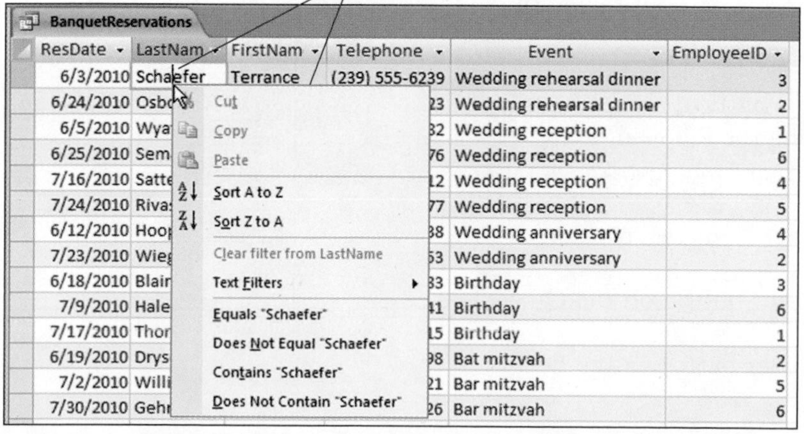

1. Open the Inventory table.
2. Filter only those records with a supplier number of 6 by completing the following steps:
   a. Click in the first entry containing *6* in the *SupplierID* field.
   b. Click the Selection button and then click *Equals "6"* at the drop-down list.
   c. Click the Quick Print button on the Quick Access toolbar.
   d. Click the Toggle Filter button in the Sort & Filter group.

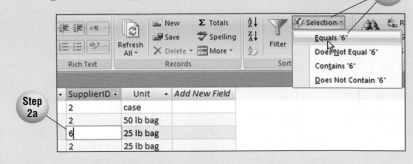

Step 2b

Step 2a

3. Filter any records in the *Item* field containing the word "pepper" by completing the following steps:
   a. Click in the entry in the *Item* field containing the entry *Green peppers*.
   b. Using the mouse, select the word *peppers*.
   c. Click the Selection button and then click *Contains "peppers"* at the drop-down list.

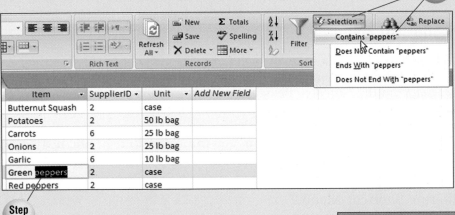

Step 3c

Step 3b

   d. Click the Quick Print button on the Quick Access toolbar.
4. Close the Inventory table without saving the changes.
5. Open the BanquetReservations query.
6. Filter records in the *Event* field except *Wedding reception* by completing the following steps:
   a. Right-click in the first *Wedding reception* entry in the *Event* field.
   b. Click *Does Not Equal "Wedding reception"* at the shortcut menu.
   c. Click the Quick Print button on the Quick Access toolbar.
   d. Click the Toggle Filter button in the Sort & Filter group.

Step 6a

Step 6b

7. Filter any records in the *Event* field containing the word *mitzvah* by completing the following steps:
    a. Click in the entry in the *Event* field containing the entry *Bar mitzvah*.
    b. Using the mouse, select the word *mitzvah*.
    c. Right-click on the selected word and then click *Contains "mitzvah"* at the shortcut menu.
    d. Click the Quick Print button on the Quick Access toolbar.
8. Close the BanquetReservations query without saving the changes.

Using Filter By Form

One of the options from the Advanced button drop-down list is *Filter By Form*. Click this option and a blank record displays in a Filter by Form window in the work area. In the Filter by Form window, the *Look for* and *Or* tabs display toward the bottom of the form. The *Look for* tab is active by default and tells Access to look for whatever data you insert in a field. Click in the empty field below the desired column and a down-pointing arrow displays at the right side of the field. Click the down-pointing arrow and then click the item on which you want to filter. Click the Toggle Filter button to display the desired records. Add an additional value to a filter by clicking the *Or* tab at the bottom of the form.

QUICK STEPS

Use Filter By Form
1. Click Advanced button.
2. Click *Filter By Form* at drop-down list.
3. Click in empty field below desired column to filter.
4. Click down-pointing arrow.
5. Click on item to filter.

Project 1d Using Filter By Form to Display Specific Records

1. With the **Skyline.accdb** database open, open the Banquets table.
2. Filter records for a specific employee identification number by completing the following steps:
    a. Click the Advanced button in the Sort & Filter group in the Home tab and then click *Filter By Form* at the drop-down list.
    b. At the Filter by Form window, click in the blank record below the *EmployeeID* field.
    c. Click the down-pointing arrow at the right side of the field and then click *3* at the drop-down list.
    d. Click the Toggle Filter button in the Sort & Filter group.
3. Print the filtered table by completing the following steps:
    a. Click the Office button, point to *Print*, and then click *Print Preview* at the side menu.
    b. Click the Landscape button in the Page Layout group.
    c. Click the Print button and then click OK at the Print dialog box.
    d. Click the Close Print Preview button.
4. Close the Banquets table without saving the changes.
5. Open the Inventory table.
6. Filter records for supplier numbers 2 or 7 by completing the following steps:
    a. Click the Advanced button in the Sort & Filter group in the Home tab and then click *Filter By Form* at the drop-down list.

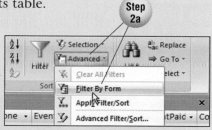

Step 2a

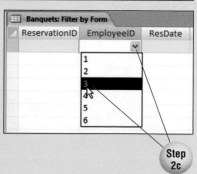

Step 2c

b. At the Filter by Form window, click in the blank record below the *SupplierID* field.

c. Click the down-pointing arrow at the right side of the field and then click *2* at the drop-down list.

d. Click the *Or* tab located toward the bottom of the form.

e. If necessary, click in the blank record below the *SupplierID* field.

f. Click the down-pointing arrow at the right side of the field and then click *7* at the drop-down list.

g. Click the Toggle Filter button in the Sort & Filter group.

h. Click the Quick Print button on the Quick Print toolbar.

i. Click the Toggle Filter button to redisplay all records in the table.

j. Click the Advanced button and then click *Clear All Filters* from the drop-down list.

7. Close the Inventory table without saving the changes.

8. Close the **Skyline.accdb** database.

Project ❷ Summarize and Analyze Data in PivotTable and PivotChart Views

You will view and analyze data in the OutdoorOptions database in PivotTable view and create a PivotTable form. You will also save an object as a different object and with a new name and view and analyze data in PivotChart view.

QUICK STEPS

Display PivotTable View
1. Open table or query.
2. Click PivotTable View button in view area at right side of Status bar.
OR
1. Open table or query.
2. Click View button arrow.
3. Click PivotTable View at drop-down list.

PivotTable View

Summarizing Data by Changing Views

Access provides additional views in a table and query that you can use to summarize data. Change to the PivotTable view to create a PivotTable, which is an interactive table that organizes and summarizes data. Use the PivotChart view to create a PivotChart that summarizes data in a graph.

Summarizing Data Using PivotTable View

A PivotTable is an interactive table that organizes and summarizes data based on the fields you designate for row headings, column headings, and source record filtering. In PivotTable view, you can easily add aggregate functions to the table such as sum, avg, and count. A PivotTable provides more options for viewing data than a Crosstab query because you can easily change the results by filtering data by an item in a row, a column, or for all source records. This interactivity allows you to analyze the data for numerous scenarios.

To create a PivotTable, open a table or query in Datasheet view and then click the PivotTable View button in the view area at the right side of the Status bar. You can also display a table or query in PivotTable view by clicking the View button arrow in the Views group in the Home tab and then clicking *PivotTable View* at the drop-down list. This displays the datasheet in PivotTable layout with four sections along with a *PivotTable Field List* box as shown in Figure 7.4. Dimmed text in each section describes the types of fields you should drag and drop.

Figure 7.4 PivotTable Layout

Drag the desired item from this list box and drop it in the appropriate location.

Dimmed text in each section describes the types of fields that should be dragged and dropped.

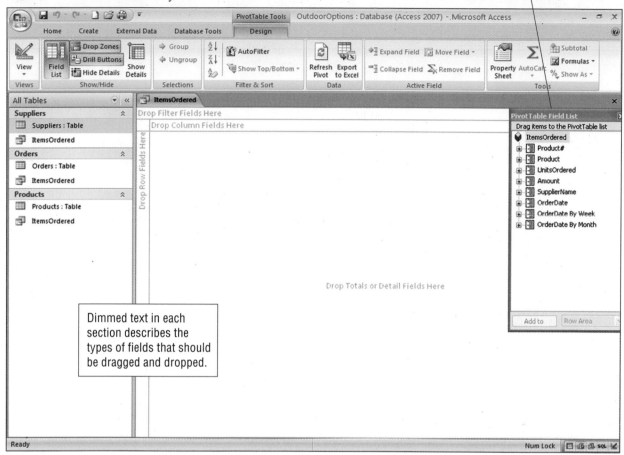

Drag the fields from the *PivotTable Field List* box to the desired locations in the PivotTable layout. The dimmed text in the PivotTable layout identifies the field you should drop in the location. In Project 2a, you will drag the *SupplierName* field to the Row field section, the *Product* field to the Column field section, the *Amount* field to the Totals or Details field section, and the *OrderDate* to the Filter section. The PivotTable will then display as shown in Figure 7.5.

Figure 7.5 PivotTable for Project 2a

ItemsOrdered						
OrderDate ▾						
All						

	Product ▾					
	Backpack	Ski goggles	Snowboard	Two-person tent	Wool ski hats	Grand Total
SupplierName ▾	Amount ▾	Amount ▾	Amount ▾	Amount ▾	Amount ▾	No Totals
Freedom Corporation		$1,100.00			$687.50	
KL Distributions	$1,906.25			▶ $1,137.50		
Rosewood, Inc.			$2,800.00			
Grand Total						

1. Display the Open dialog box with Access2007L1C7 on your storage medium the active folder.
2. Open the **OutdoorOptions.accdb** database.
3. Create a new query in Design view with the following specifications:
   a. Add the Orders, Products, and Suppliers tables to the design grid.
   b. Add the following fields from the specified tables:

Product#	=	Orders table
Product	=	Products table
UnitsOrdered	=	Orders table
Amount	=	Orders table
SupplierName	=	Suppliers table
OrderDate	=	Orders table

Step 3b

Field:	Product#	Product	UnitsOrdered	Amount	SupplierName	OrderDate
Table:	Orders	Products	Orders	Orders	Suppliers	Orders
Sort:						
Show:	☑	☑	☑	☑	☑	☑
Criteria:						
or:						

   c. Run the query.
   d. Save the query and name it *ItemsOrdered*.
4. Click the PivotTable View button in the view area at the right side of the Status bar.
5. At the PivotTable layout, drag and drop the *SupplierName* field to the Row field section by completing the following steps:
   a. Position the mouse pointer on the *SupplierName* field in the *PivotTable Field List* box.
   b. Hold down the left mouse button, drag to the dimmed text *Drop Row Fields Here* located at the left side of the query window, and then release the mouse button.

Step 5b

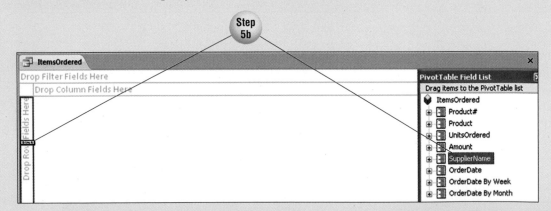

6. Complete steps similar to those in Step 5 to drag and drop the following fields:
   a. Drag the *Product* field from the *PivotTable Field List* box and drop it on the dimmed text *Drop Column Fields Here*.
   b. Drag the *Amount* field from the *PivotTable Field List* box and drop it on the dimmed text *Drop Totals or Detail Fields Here*.
   c. Drag the *OrderDate* field from the *PivotTable Field List* box and drop it on the dimmed text *Drop Filter Fields Here*.

7. Remove the *PivotTable Field List* box from the screen by clicking the Field List button in the Show/Hide group in the PivotTable Tools Design tab. (Your PivotTable should look like the one shown in Figure 7.5.)
8. Click the Quick Print button on the Quick Access toolbar to print the query in PivotTable view.
9. Click the View button arrow in the Views group in the Home tab and then click *Datasheet View* at the drop-down list.
10. Save and then close the query.

When you create a PivotTable in a query or table, it becomes a part of and is saved with the table or query. The next time you open the table or query, display the PivotTable by clicking the PivotTable View button in the view area on the Status bar or by clicking the View button arrow in the Views group in the Home tab and then clicking *PivotTable View* at the drop-down list. If you make changes to data in fields that are part of the table or query (and PivotTable), the data is automatically updated in the table or query.

The power of a PivotTable is the ability to analyze data for numerous scenarios. For example, in the PivotTable you created in Project 2a, you can display orders for a specific date or isolate a specific supplier. Use the plus and minus symbols that display in a row or column heading to show (plus symbol) or hide (minus symbol) data. Use the down-pointing arrow (called the ***filter arrow***) that displays in a field to display specific data in the field. You can also use buttons in the PivotTable Tools Design tab to perform actions such as filtering data and performing calculations on data.

Project 2b Analyzing Data in PivotTable View

1. With the **OutdoorOptions.accdb** database open, open the Orders table.
2. Add the following records to the table:

        Order#   =   (AutoNumber)
        Supplier#   =   68
        Product#   =   558
        UnitsOrdered   =   25
        Amount   = $550
        OrderDate   =   2/26/2010

        Order#   =   (AutoNumber)
        Supplier#   =   70
        Product#   =   897
        UnitsOrdered   =   10
        Amount   = $1,120
        OrderDate   =   2/26/2010

3. Close the Orders table.
4. Double-click the ItemsOrdered query in the *Orders* list box.

5. With the query open, click the View button arrow in the Views group in the Home tab and then click *PivotTable View* at the drop-down list. (Notice the PivotTable reflects the two new order records you inserted in the Orders table.)

6. Display only items ordered on February 26 by completing the following steps:

a. Click the filter arrow (down-pointing arrow) at the right of the *OrderDate* field (located in the upper left corner of the query window).

b. At the drop-down list that displays, click the *(All)* check box to remove the check mark before each date.

c. Click the check box to the left of *2/26/2010*.

d. Click the OK button.

e. Click the Quick Print button on the Quick Access toolbar.

f. Redisplay all items by clicking the filter arrow at the right of the *OrderDate* field, clicking the check box to the left of *(All)*, and then clicking OK.

7. Display only those order amounts for Freedom Corporation by completing the following steps:

a. Click the filter arrow at the right of the *SupplierName* field.

b. At the drop-down list, click the *(All)* check box to remove the check mark before each supplier name.

c. Click the check box to the left of *Freedom Corporation*.

d. Click the OK button.

e. Click the Quick Print button on the Quick Access toolbar.

f. Redisplay all supplier names by clicking the filter arrow at the right of the *SupplierName* field, clicking the check box to the left of *(All)*, and then clicking OK.

8. Display subtotals and totals of order amounts by completing the following steps:

a. Position the mouse pointer on any *Amount* column heading until the pointer displays with a four-headed arrow attached and then click the left mouse button. (This displays all the *Amount* column headings and amounts with a light blue background.)

b. Click the AutoCalc button in the Tools group in the PivotTable Tools Design tab and then click *Sum* at the drop-down list. (This inserts subtotals and totals in the PivotTable.)

9. Save, print, and then close the PivotTable.

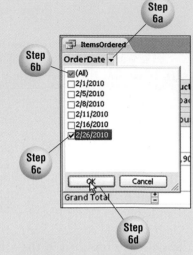

Step 6a

Step 6b

Step 6c

Step 6d

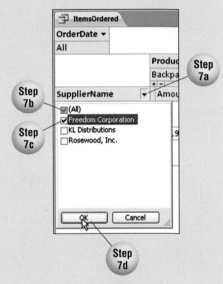

Step 7a

Step 7b

Step 7c

Step 7d

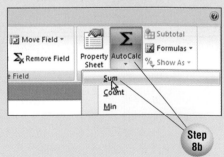

Step 8b

Summarizing and Analyzing Data in a PivotTable Form

When you create a PivotTable in a query or table, the PivotTable settings are saved and become part of the table or query. When you open a table or query in which you have created a PivotTable and then switch to PivotTable view, the table or query displays with the PivotTable settings you created. If you want to view different fields or perform other functions in PivotTable view, you have to edit the last settings. For example, if you created a PivotTable in an Employees query that summed the salary field by department by year of hire, and then wanted to sum by month, you would have to edit the previous PivotTable. If you want to view data by year and month or other date, consider creating a PivotTable form. A PivotTable form is a separate object from the query or table, so you could create one showing the sum by year and another showing the sum by month.

To create a PivotTable form, click the desired object in the Navigation pane and then click the Create tab. Click the More Forms button in the Forms group and then click *PivotTable* at the drop-down list. This displays the object in PivotTable layout. Click the Field List button in the Show/Hide group to display the *PivotTable Field List* box. (You may need to click the button twice to display the list box.)

Field
List

Saving Objects

If you want to create an object that is similar to another object in the database, use the *Save As* option from the Office button drop-down list. For example, if you want to save a query as a form, open the query, click the Office button, and then click *Save As*. At the Save As dialog box, type a name for the new object, click the down-pointing arrow at the right side of the *As* list box, click the desired object type, and then click OK. If you want to save an open object with a new name, click the Office button, and then click *Save As*. At the Save As dialog box, type a new name for the object, leave the *As* list box as the default, and then click OK.

Project **2c** **Creating a PivotTable Form**

1. With the **OutdoorOptions.accdb** database open, save the ItemsOrdered query as a form by completing the following steps:
   a. Click the ItemsOrdered query in the Navigation pane.
   b. Click the Office button and then click *Save As* at the drop-down list.
   c. At the Save As dialog box, type **ItemsOrdered** in the *Save 'ItemsOrdered' to* text box.
   d. Click the down-pointing arrow at the right side of the *As* list box and then click *Form* at the drop-down list.
   e. Click OK.
   f. Close the ItemsOrdered form.

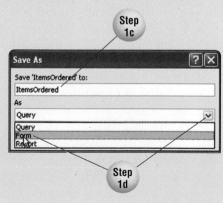

2. Create a PivotTable form by completing the following steps:
   a. Click the ItemsOrdered form in the Navigation pane.
   b. Click the Create tab.
   c. Click the More Forms button in the Forms group and then click *PivotTable* at the drop-down list.

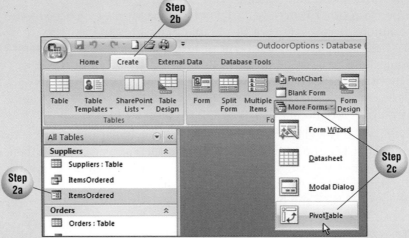

   d. At the PivotTable form, click twice on the Field List button in the Show/Hide group in the PivotTable Tools Design tab.
   e. Drag the *SupplierName* field in the *PivotTable Field List* box and drop it on the dimmed text *Drop Row Fields Here*.
   f. Drag the *Product* field from the *PivotTable Field List* box and drop it on the dimmed text *Drop Column Fields Here*.
   g. Drag the *Amount* field from the *PivotTable Field List* box and drop it on the dimmed text *Drop Totals or Detail Fields Here*.
   h. Drag the *OrderDate* field from the *PivotTable Field List* box and drop it on the dimmed text *Drop Filter Fields Here*.
   i. Close the PivotTable Field List box.
3. Display subtotals and totals of order amounts by completing the following steps:
   a. Position the mouse pointer on any *Amount* column heading until the pointer displays with a four-headed arrow attached and then click the left mouse button. (This displays all the *Amount* column headings and amounts with a light blue background.)
   b. Click the AutoCalc button in the Tools group in the PivotTable Tools Design tab and then click *Sum* at the drop-down list. (This inserts subtotals and totals in the PivotTable.)
4. Display only the order amounts for Freedom Corporation by completing the following steps:
   a. Click the filter arrow at the right of the *SupplierName* field.
   b. At the drop-down list, click the *(All)* check box to remove the check mark before each supplier name.
   c. Click the check box to the left of *Freedom Corporation*.
   d. Click the OK button.
5. Save the PivotTable form by completing the following steps:
   a. Click the Save button on the Quick Access toolbar.
   b. At the Save As dialog box, type **FreedomOrders** and then click OK.

6. Display only the order amounts for KL Distributions by completing the following steps:
   a. Click the filter arrow at the right of the *SupplierName* field.
   b. At the drop-down list, click the *Freedom Corporation* check box to remove the check mark.
   c. Click the check box to the left of *KL Distributions*.
   d. Click the OK button.

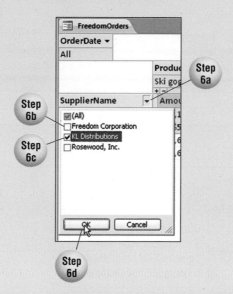

7. Save and print the PivotTable form by completing the following steps:
   a. Click the Office button and then click *Save As* at the drop-down list.
   b. At the Save As dialog box, type **KLOrders** and then click OK.
   c. Click the Quick Print button on the Quick Access toolbar.
8. Complete steps similar to those in Steps 6 and 7 to save and print a PivotTable form that displays order amounts for Rosewood, Inc. and name the form *RosewoodOrders*.
9. Close the RosewoodOrders PivotTable form.

Summarizing Data Using PivotChart View

A PivotChart performs the same function as a PivotTable with the exception that Access displays the source data in a graph instead of a table or query. You create a chart by dragging fields from the *Chart Field List* box to the Filter, Data, Category, and Series sections of the chart. As with a PivotTable, you can easily alter the PivotChart using the filter arrows.

To create a PivotChart, open a table or query in Datasheet view, click the PivotChart View button in the view area at the right side of the Status bar or click the View button arrow in the Views group in the Home tab, and then click PivotChart View at the drop-down list. This changes the datasheet to PivotChart layout, which contains four sections, and displays the *Chart Field List* box. Dimmed text in each section describes the types of fields that you should drag and drop. Figure 7.6 displays the PivotChart layout you will be using in Project 2d.

Display PivotChart View
1. Open table or query.
2. Click PivotChart View button in view area at right side of Status bar.
OR
1. Open table or query.
2. Click View button arrow.
3. Click PivotChart View at drop-down list.

PivotChart View

Figure 7.6 PivotChart Layout

Drag the desired item from this list box and drop it in the appropriate location.

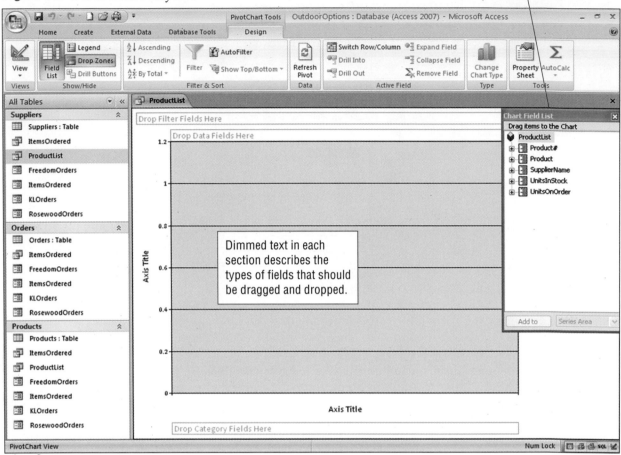

Dimmed text in each section describes the types of fields that should be dragged and dropped.

HINT

A PivotTable is linked dynamically to a PivotChart. Changes made to the filter settings in PivotChart view are also updated in PivotTable view.

Drag the fields from the *Chart Field List* box to the desired locations in the PivotChart layout. The dimmed text in the PivotChart layout identifies the field you should drop in the location. In Project 2d, you will drag the *SupplierName* field to the Row field section, the *Product* field to the Column field section, the *Amount* field to the Totals or Details field section, and the *OrderDate* to the Filter section. The PivotChart will then display as shown in Figure 7.7. When you create a PivotChart, Access automatically creates a PivotTable. View a PivotTable based on a PivotChart by changing to PivotTable view.

Figure 7.7 PivotChart for Project 2d

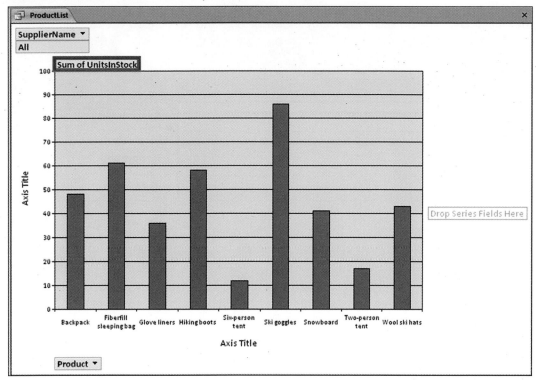

Project 2d Summarizing Data Using PivotChart View

1. With the **OutdoorOptions.accdb** database open, create a new query in Design view with the following specifications:
   a. Add the Products and Suppliers tables to the design grid.
   b. Add the following fields from the specified tables:

Product#	=	Products table
Product	=	Products table
SupplierName	=	Suppliers table
UnitsInStock	=	Products table
UnitsOnOrder	=	Products table

   c. Run the query.
   d. Save the query and name it *ProductList*.
2. Click the View button arrow in the Views group in the Home tab and then click *PivotChart View* at the drop-down list.

3. At the PivotChart layout, drag and drop the following fields:
   a. Drag the *SupplierName* field from the *Chart Field List* box and drop it on the dimmed text *Drop Filter Fields Here*.

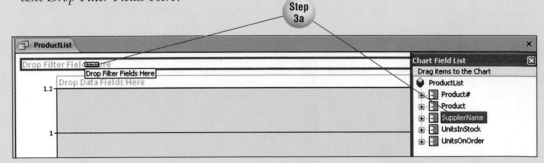

   b. Drag the *Product* field from the *Chart Field List* box and drop it on the dimmed text *Drop Category Fields Here*.
   c. Drag the *UnitsInStock* field from the *Chart Field List* box and drop it on the dimmed text *Drop Data Fields Here*.
4. Remove the *Chart Field List* box from the screen by clicking the Field List button in the Show/Hide group. (Your PivotChart should look like the PivotChart shown in Figure 7.7.)
5. Click the Quick Print button on the Quick Access toolbar to print the query in PivotChart view.
6. Display specific items on order by completing the following steps:
   a. Click the filter arrow at the right of the *Product* field (located in the lower left corner of the query window).
   b. At the pop-up list that displays, click the *(All)* check box to remove the check mark before each date.
   c. Click the check box to the left of *Ski goggles*.
   d. Click the check box to the left of *Snowboard*.
   e. Click the check box to the left of *Wool ski hats*.
   f. Click the OK button.

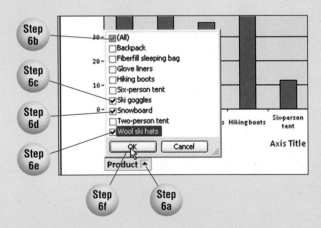

   g. Click the Quick Print button on the Quick Access toolbar.
   h. Redisplay all items by clicking the filter arrow at the right of the *Product* field, clicking the check box to the left of *(All)*, and then clicking OK.

7. Display only those products ordered from KL Distributions by completing the following steps:
   a. Click the filter arrow at the right of the *SupplierName* field.
   b. At the drop-down list, click the *(All)* check box to remove the check mark before each supplier name.
   c. Click the check box to the left of *KL Distributions*.
   d. Click the OK button.
   e. Click the Quick Print button in the Quick Access toolbar.
   f. Redisplay all supplier names by clicking the filter arrow at the right of the *SupplierName* field, clicking the check box to the left of *(All)*, and then clicking OK.

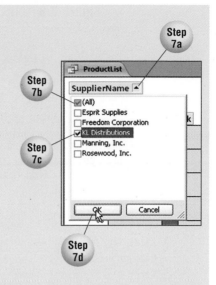

Step 7a

Step 7b

Step 7c

Step 7d

8. Click the View button arrow in the Views group and then click *PivotTable View* at the drop-down list. (This displays the chart in PivotTable view.)
9. Click the Quick Print button in the Quick Access toolbar.
10. Click the View button arrow in the Views group and then click *Datasheet View* at the drop-down list. (This returns the query to the Datasheet view.)
11. Save and then close the query.
12. Close the **OutdoorOptions.accdb** database.

P roject ❸ View Document Properties and Object Dependencies

You will view and customize document properties for the OutdoorOptions database and view object dependencies in the Hilltop database.

Viewing and Customizing Document Properties

The Properties dialog box contains **metadata**, which is data that describes other data. Data in the Properties dialog box describes details about the database such as title, author name, and subject, and contains options you can use to further describe or identify the database. You can display properties for the current database or display properties for a database at the Open dialog box.

Viewing Properties at the Open Dialog Box

View properties for a database at the Open dialog box by clicking the Tools button located in the lower left corner of the Open dialog box and then clicking *Properties* at the drop-down list. This displays the Properties dialog box similar to what you see in Figure 7.8. The Properties dialog box with the General tab selected displays information about the document type, size, and location.

View Properties at Open Dialog Box
1. Display Open dialog box.
2. Click desired database.
3. Click Tools button.
4. Click *Properties* at drop-down list.

Figure 7.8 OutdoorOptions.accdb Properties Dialog Box

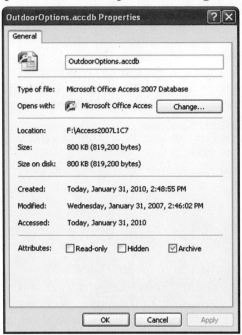

Click the **OutdoorOptions.accdb** database in the Open dialog box list box, click the Tools button, and then click *Properties*, and this dialog box displays.

If you display the properties for a database saved on the hard drive, the Properties dialog box will display the Summary tab along with the General tab. The Summary tab contains fields where you can enter the title, subject, category, keywords, and comments about the database. Move the insertion point to a field by clicking in the field or by pressing the Tab key until the insertion point is positioned in the desired field.

Project 3a Viewing Database Properties

1. At the *Getting Started with Microsoft Office Access* window, click the Open button on the Quick Access toolbar.
2. At the Open dialog box, make sure the Access2007L1C7 folder on your storage medium is active and then click **OutdoorOptions.accdb** in the list box.
3. Click the Tools button located in the lower left corner of the dialog box and then click *Properties* at the drop-down list.
4. At the Properties dialog box, read the information that displays in the dialog box with the General tab selected and then click the Cancel button.
5. Click **Skyline.accdb** in the list box, click the Tools button, and then click *Properties*.
6. Read the information that displays and then click the Cancel button.
7. Close the Open dialog box.

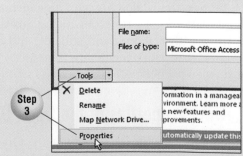

Viewing and Customizing Properties for the Current Database

View Properties of Current Database
1. Open desired database.
2. Click Office button, point to *Manage*, click *Database Properties*.

To view properties for the currently open database, click the Office button, point to *Manage*, and then click *Database Properties*. This displays the Properties dialog box similar to what you see in Figure 7.9. The Properties dialog box for an open database contains additional tabs with information on the database. The General tab contains the same options as the Properties dialog box that displays when you click the Tools button in the Open dialog box and then click *Properties*. Click the Summary tab and fields display such as title, subject, author, category, keywords, and comments. Some fields may contain data and others may be blank. You can insert, edit, or delete text in the fields. Move the insertion point to a field by clicking in the field or by pressing the Tab key until the insertion point is positioned in the desired field.

Click the Statistics tab and information displays such as dates for when the database was created, modified, accessed, and printed. You can view the objects in the database by clicking the Contents tab. The *Document contents* section displays the objects in the database including tables, queries, form, reports, macros, and modules.

Figure 7.9 Current Database Properties Dialog Box

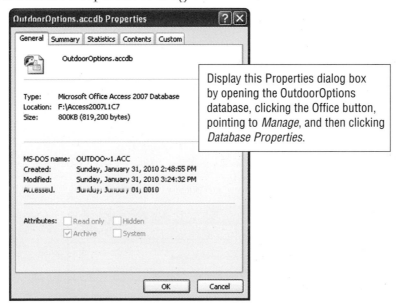

Display this Properties dialog box by opening the OutdoorOptions database, clicking the Office button, pointing to *Manage*, and then clicking *Database Properties*.

Use options at the Properties dialog box with the Custom tab selected to add custom properties to the database. For example, you can add a property that displays the date the database was completed, information on the department in which the database was created, and much more. The list box below the *Name* option box displays the predesigned properties provided by Access. You can choose a predesigned property or create your own.

To choose a predesigned property, select the desired property in the list box, specify what type of property it is (value, date, number, yes/no), and then type a value. For example, to specify the department in which the database was created, you would click *Department* in the list box, make sure the *Type* displays as *Text*, click in the *Value* text box, and then type the name of the department.

Project 3b Customizing Database Properties for the Current Database

1. Open the **OutdoorOptions.accdb** database.
2. Display database properties by clicking the Office button, pointing to *Manage*, and then clicking *Database Properties*.

Step
2

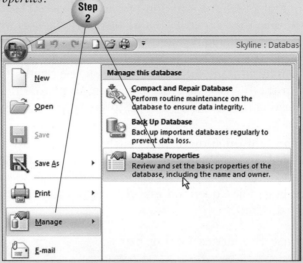

3. At the Properties dialog box, make sure the General tab is selected and then read the information that displays in the dialog box.
4. Click the Summary tab and then type the following text in the specified text boxes:

    Title = **OutdoorOptions database**
    Subject = **Outdoor equipment and supplies**
    Author = *(type your first and last names)*
    Category = **Retail store**
    Keywords = **retail, equipment, products, suppliers**
    Comments = **This database contains information on Outdoor Options suppliers,**
    products, and orders.

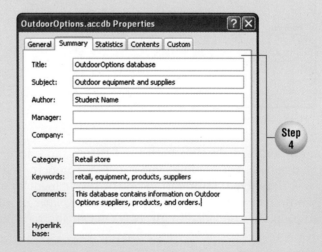

Step
4

5. Click the Statistics tab and read the information that displays in the dialog box.
6. Click the Contents tab and notice that the *Document contents* section of the dialog box displays the objects in the database.

7. Click the Custom tab and then create custom properties by completing the following steps:
   a. Click the *Date completed* option in the *Name* list box.
   b. Click the down-pointing arrow at the right of the *Type* option box and then click *Date* at the drop-down list.
   c. Click in the *Value* text box and then type the current date in this format: ##/##/####.
   d. Click the Add button.

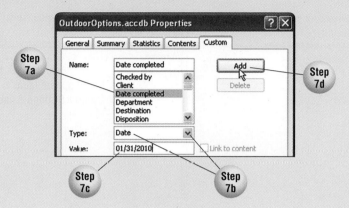

   e. With the insertion point positioned in the *Name* text box, type **Course**.
   f. Click the down-pointing arrow at the right of the *Type* option box and then click *Text* at the drop-down list.
   g. Click in the *Value* text box, type your current course number, and then press Enter.
   h. Click OK to close the dialog box.

Viewing Object Dependencies

The structure of a database is comprised of table, query, form, and report objects. Tables are related to other tables by creating relationships. Queries, forms, and reports draw the source data from records in the tables to which they have been associated and forms and reports can include subforms and subreports which further expand the associations between objects. A database with a large number of interdependent objects is more complex to work with. Viewing a list of the objects within a database and viewing the dependencies between objects can be beneficial to ensure an object is not deleted or otherwise modified causing an unforeseen effect on another object.

Display the structure of a database, including tables, queries, forms, and reports as well as relationships, at the Object Dependencies task pane. Display this task pane by opening the database, clicking the Database Tools tab, and then clicking the Object Dependencies button in the Show/Hide group. The Object Dependencies task pane in Figure 7.10 displays the objects for the Hilltop database.

QUICK STEPS

View Object Dependencies
1. Open desired database.
2. Click Database Tools tab.
3. Click Object Dependencies button.

Figure 7.10 Object Dependencies Task Pane

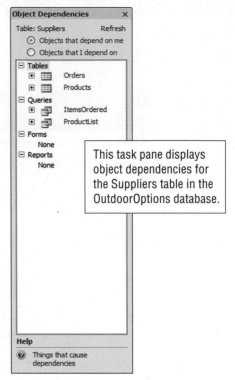

This task pane displays object dependencies for the Suppliers table in the OutdoorOptions database.

By default, *Objects that depend on me* is selected in the Object Dependencies task pane and the list box displays the names of objects for which the Employee Dates and Salaries table is the source. Next to each object in the task pane list is an expand button (plus symbol). Clicking the expand button will show objects dependent at the next level. For example, if a query is based upon the Employee Dates and Salaries table and the query is used to generate a report, clicking the expand button next to the query name would show the report name.

Clicking an object name in the Object Dependencies task pane opens the object in Design view so that you can remove the dependency by deleting bound fields, controls, or otherwise changing the source from which the data is obtained. Relationships between tables are deleted by opening the Relationships window (as you learned in Chapter 2).

Project 3c   Viewing Object Dependencies

1. With the **OutdoorOptions.accdb** database open, display the structure of the database by completing the following steps:

    a. Click the Suppliers table in the Navigation pane.

    b. Click the Database Tools tab and then click Object Dependencies in the Show/Hide group. (This displays the Object Dependencies task pane. By default, *Objects that depend on me* is selected and the task pane lists the names of objects for which the Suppliers table is the source.)

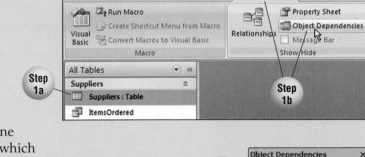

    c. Click the expand button (plus symbol) to the left of *Orders* in the Tables section. (This displays all objects that are dependent on the Orders table.)

    d. Click the *Objects that I depend on* option located toward the top of the Object Dependencies task pane.

    e. Click the Products table in the Navigation pane.

    f. Click the Refresh hyperlink located in the upper right corner of the Object Dependencies task pane.

    g. Click the *Objects that depend on me* option located toward the top of the Object Dependencies task pane. Notice the objects that are dependent on the Products table.

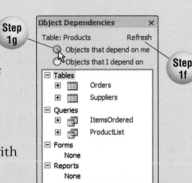

    h. Close the Object Dependencies task pane.

2. Delete the relationship between the Orders table and the Products table by completing the following steps:

    a. Click the Relationships button in the Show/Hide group with the Database Tools tab selected.

    b. Right-click the black join line between the Orders and Products tables.

    c. At the shortcut menu that displays, click *Delete*.

    d. At the message asking if you are sure you want to permanently delete the relationship, click Yes.

    e. Close the Relationships window.

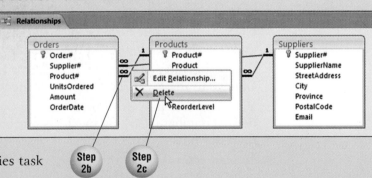

3. Display the Object Dependencies task pane for the Invoices table by completing the following steps:

    a. Click the Orders table in the Navigation pane.

    b. Click the Database Tools tab and then click Object Dependencies in the Show/Hide group. (Notice that the Products table is not listed in the Tables section of the Object Dependencies task pane.)

4. Close the Object Dependencies task pane.

5. Close the **OutdoorOptions.accdb** database.

CHAPTER summary

- A set of restrictions, called a filter, can be set on records in a table or form. A filter lets you select specific field values.
- You can filter records with the Filter button in the Sort & Filter group in the Home tab.
- Click the Toggle Filter button in the Sort & Filter group to switch back and forth between data and filtered data.
- Remove a filter by clicking the Filter button in the Sort & Filter group and then clicking the *Clear filter from xxx* (where *xxx* is the name of the field).
- Another method for removing a filter is to click the Advanced button in the Sort & Filter group and then click *Clear All Filters*.
- Display a list of filter values by clicking the Filter button and then pointing to *Text Filters* (if the data is text), *Number Filters* (if the data is numbers), or *Date Filters* (if the data is a date).
- Filter by selection by clicking the Selection button in the Sort & Filter group.
- Right-click a field entry to display a shortcut menu with filtering options.
- Filter by form by clicking the Advanced button in the Sort & Filter group and then clicking *Filter By Form* at the drop-down list. This displays a blank record with the two tabs *Look for* and *Or*.
- A PivotTable is an interactive table that organizes and summarizes data. Create a PivotTable for an object to analyze data for numerous scenarios. Change to the PivotTable view to create a PivotTable.
- A PivotTable you create in a query or table is saved with the object. You can also create a PivotTable form that is saved as a separate object from the table or query.
- You can save an open object as a different object with the *As* option at the Save As dialog box. Display this dialog box by clicking the Office button and then clicking *Save As* at the drop-down list.
- Create a PivotTable form by clicking the More Forms button in the Forms group in the Create tab and then clicking *PivotTable* at the drop-down list.
- Create a PivotChart to analyze data in a chart rather than a table or query. Change to the PivotChart view to create a PivotChart.
- View database properties by displaying the Open dialog box, clicking the desired database, clicking the Tools button, and then clicking *Properties* at the drop-down list.
- To view properties for the currently open database, click the Office button, point to *Manage*, and then click *Database Properties*.
- Customize database properties with options at the Properties dialog box with the Custom tab selected.
- Display the structure of a database and the relationship between objects at the Object Dependencies task pane. Display this task pane by clicking the Database Tools tab and then clicking the Object Dependencies button in the Show/Hide group.

COMMANDS review

FEATURE	RIBBON TAB, GROUP	BUTTON, OPTION
Filter	Home, Sort & Filter	▽
Toggle filter	Home, Sort & Filter	▽ Toggle Filter
Remove filter	Home, Sort & Filter	▽ , Clear filter from *xxx*, OR
		Advanced ▾ , Clear All Filters
Filter by selection	Home, Sort & Filter	Selection ▾
Filter by form	Home, Sort & Filter	Advanced ▾ , Filter By Form
PivotTable view	Home, Views	, PivotTable View
PivotTable form	Create, Forms	More Forms ▾ , PivotTable
PivotChart	Home, Views	, PivotChart View
Object Dependencies task pane	Database Tools, Show/Hide	Object Dependencies

CONCEPTS check

Test Your Knowledge

Completion: In the space provided at the right, indicate the correct term, symbol, or command.

1. The Filter button is located in this group in the Home tab. _____

2. If you filter data, you can switch between the data and the filtered data by clicking this button. _____

3. Remove filtering from an object with the Filter button or by clicking this button and then clicking *Clear All Filters*. _____

4. In the Filter By Form window, these two tabs display toward the bottom of the form. _____

5. Display a table or query in this view to summarize data based on the fields you designate for row headings, column headings, and source record filtering. _____

6. To create a PivotTable form, click this button in the Forms group and then click *PivotTable* at the drop-down list. _____

7. Click this button in the Show/Hide group in the PivotTable Tools Design tab to display the *PivotTable Field List* box. _____

8. Use this view to display data in a graph. _____

9. View properties for a database at the Open dialog box by clicking this button located in the lower left corner of the dialog box and then clicking *Properties*. _____

10. Display the structure of a database at this task pane. _____

SKILLS check

Demonstrate Your Proficiency

Assessment

1 FILTER RECORDS IN TABLES

1. Display the Open dialog box with Access2007L1C7 on your storage medium the active folder.
2. Open the **LegalServices.accdb** database.
3. Open the Clients table and then filter the records to display the following records:
   a. Display only those records of clients who live in Renton. When the records of clients in Renton display, print the results and then remove the filter.
   b. Display only those records of clients with the Postal Code of 98033. When the records of clients with the ZIP code 98033 display, print the results in landscape orientation and then remove the filter. (Hint: Change to landscape orientation in Print Preview.)
4. Close the Clients table without saving the changes.
5. Open the Billing table and then filter records by selection to display the following records:
   a. Display only those records with a Category of CC. Print the CC records and then remove the filter.
   b. Display only those records with an Attorney ID of 12. Print the records and then remove the filter.
   c. Display only those records between the dates 6/1/2010 and 6/10/2010. Print the records and then remove the filter.
6. Close the Billing table without saving the changes.
7. Open the Clients table and then use Filter By Form to display clients in Auburn or Renton. (Be sure to use the Or tab at the very bottom of the table.) Print the table in landscape orientation and then remove the filter.
8. Close the Clients table without saving the changes.
9. Open the Billing table and then use Filter By Form to display categories G or P. Print the table and then remove the filter.
10. Close the Billing table without saving the changes.
11. Close the **LegalServices.accdb** database.

Assessment

2 VIEW AND ANALYZE DATA IN PIVOTTABLE AND PIVOTCHART VIEW

1. Open the **Hilltop.accdb** database.
2. Create a query in Design view with the following specifications:
   a. Add the Invoices, Customers, Equipment, and Rates tables to the design grid.
   b. Add the following fields from the specified tables:

BillingDate	=	Invoices table
Customer	=	Customers table
Equipment	=	Equipment table
Hours	=	Invoices table
Rate	=	Rates table

    c. Click in the sixth *Field* text and then insert a calculation to total the rental hour amounts by typing **Total: [Hours]*[Rate]**. (Press the Tab key to move to the next field.)

    d. Run the query.

    e. Save the query and name it *RentalTotals*.

3. Display the query in PivotTable view.

4. At the PivotTable layout, drag and drop the fields as follows:

    a. Drag the *Equipment* field to the *Drop Row Fields Here* section.

    b. Drag the *Customer* field to the *Drop Column Fields Here* section.

    c. Drag the *Total* field to the *Drop Totals or Detail Fields Here* section.

    d. Drag the *BillingDate* field to the *Drop Filter Fields Here* section.

5. Remove the *PivotTable Field List* box from the screen.

6. Click the Quick Print button on the Quick Access toolbar to print the query in PivotTable view. (If the total amounts in the Cascade Enterprises and Country Electrical columns print as number symbols instead of amounts, increase the size of the Total column by dragging to the right the border at the right side of the Total heading below Cascade Enterprises.)

7. In the *BillingDate* field, display only equipment rentals for May 1, 2010.

8. Print the PivotTable and then redisplay all rental dates.

9. In the *Equipment* field, display records only for the Hydraulic Pump and Pressure Sprayer.

10. Print the PivotTable and then redisplay all equipment.

11. Switch to Datasheet view, save the query, and then close the query.

12. Create a query in Design view with the following specifications:

    a. Add the Equipment, Customers, and Invoices tables to the design grid.

    b. Add the following fields from the specified tables:

        Equipment = Equipment table

        Customer = Customers table

        Hours = Invoices table

    c. Run the query.

    d. Save the query and name it *CustomerHours*.

13. Click the View button arrow in the Views group in the Home tab and then click *PivotChart View* at the drop-down list.

14. At the PivotChart layout, drag and drop the following fields:

    a. Drag the *Equipment* field to the *Drop Filter Fields Here* section.

    b. Drag the *Customer* field to the *Drop Category Fields Here* section.

    c. Drag the *Hours* field to the *Drop Data Fields Here* section.

15. Remove the *Chart Field List* box from the screen.

16. Click the Quick Print button on the Quick Access toolbar to print the query in PivotChart view.

17. In the *Equipment* field, display only records for Backhoe, print the PivotChart, and then redisplay all equipment.

18. In the *Customer* field, display only the customers Allied Builders and Cascade Enterprises, print the PivotChart, and then redisplay all customers.

19. Save the PivotChart, switch to Datasheet view, and then close the query.

20. Create a PivotTable form with the RentalTotals query and drag and drop the following fields in the PivotTable layout:

    a. Drag the *Equipment* field to the *Drop Row Fields Here* section.

    b. Drag the *Customer* field to the *Drop Column Fields Here* section.

    c. Drag the *Total* field to the *Drop Totals or Detail Fields Here* section.

    d. Drag the *BillingDate* field to the *Drop Filter Fields Here* section.

21. Save the PivotTable form and name it *CustomerRentals*.
22. Display only those records for Able Construction. Save the PivotTable form with Save As and name it *AbleConstruction*. Print the form.
23. Display only those records for Cascade Enterprises. Save the PivotTable form with Save As and name it *CascadeEnterprises*. Print and then close the form.

Assessment

3 DELETE AND RENAME OBJECTS

1. With the **Hilltop.accdb** database open, experiment with the options in the shortcut menu that displays when you right-click an object and then complete the following:
   a. Delete the AbleConstruction form.
   b. Rename the CascadeEnterprises form to *CascadeHours*.
   c. Rename the RentalTotals query to *RentalHoursTotals*.
2. Close the **Hilltop.accdb** database.

CASE study
Apply Your Skills

Part
1

As the office manager at the Summit View Medical Services, you are responsible for maintaining clinic records. Open the **SummitView.accdb** database and then insert the following additional services into the appropriate table:

- Edit the *Doctor visit* entry in the Services table so it displays as *Clinic visit*.
- Add the entry *X-ray* with a service identification of *X*.
- Add the entry *Cholesterol screening* with a service identification of *CS*.

Add the following new patient information in the database in the appropriate tables or forms:

Patient number 118
Brian M. Gould
2887 Nelson Street
Helena, MT 59604
(406) 555-3121
Mr. Gould saw Dr. Wallace for a clinic visit on 4/5/2010, which has a fee of $75.

Patient number 119
Ellen L. Augustine
12990 148th Street
East Helena, MT 59635
(406) 555-0722
Ms. Augustine saw Dr. Kennedy for cholesterol screening on 4/5/2010, which has a fee of $90.

Patient number 120
Jeff J. Masura
3218 Eldridge Avenue
Helena, MT 59624
(406) 555-6212
Mr. Masura saw Dr. Rowe for an x-ray on 4/5/2010, which has a fee of $75.

Add the following information to the Billing form:

- Patient 109 came for cholesterol screening with Dr. Kennedy on 4/5/2010 with a $90 fee.
- Patient 106 came for immunizations with Dr. Pena on 4/5/2010 with a $100 fee.
- Patient 114 came for an x-ray with Dr. Kennedy on 4/5/2010 with a $75 fee.

Part 2

Create the following filters, queries, PivotTable, and PivotChart:

- Open the Billing table and then filter and print the records for the date 04/01/2010. Clear the filter and then filter and then print the records with a doctor number of 18. Save and then close the table.
- Create a report that displays the patient's first name, last name, street address, city, state, and ZIP code. Apply formatting to enhance the visual appeal of the report. Filter and print the records of those patients living in Helena and then filter and print the records of those patients living in East Helena. Close the report.
- Design a query that includes the doctor number, doctor last name, patient number, date of visit, and fee. Save the query with the name *DoctorBillingFees* and then print the query.
- Create a PivotTable with the DoctorBillingFees query with the following specifications: Drop the *DateOfVisit* field in the Filter Fields section, the *Patient#* field in the Column Fields section, the *LastName* field in the Row Fields, and the *Fee* field in the Totals or Detail Fields. Save and then print the PivotTable.
- Filter records in the PivotTable for Dr. Kennedy and Dr. Pena. Print the filtered PivotTable.
- Remove the filter and then filter records for the dates 4/1/2010 and 4/2/2010. Print the filtered table. Save and then close the query.

Part 3

Using the PivotTable layout you designed in the DoctorBillingFees query in Part 2, create a PivotTable form in the same layout. Save the PivotTable form and name it *BillingFees* and then print the PivotTable form. Decide on two different filters you can apply to the data in the PivotTable form. Complete each filter and save the filtered PivotTable form with a new name and print the form.

Part 4

Your clinic has a procedures manual that describes processes and procedures in the center. Open Word and then create a document for the procedures manual that describes the process for creating the PivotTable form you created in Part 3. Save the completed document and name it **Access_C7_CS_P4**. Print and then close **Access_C7_CS_P4.docx**.

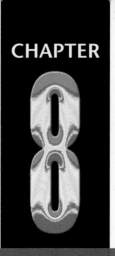
Importing and Exporting Data

PERFORMANCE OBJECTIVES

Upon successful completion of Chapter 8, you will be able to:

- Export Access data to Excel
- Export Access data to Word
- Merge Access data with a Word document
- Import data to a new table
- Link data to a new table
- Use the Office Clipboard
- Save a database in an earlier version of Access

Tutorial 8.1
Exporting Data
Tutorial 8.2
Importing Data and Viewing
Object Dependencies

Microsoft Office 2007 is a suite of programs that allows easy data exchange between programs. In this chapter you will learn how to export data from Access to Excel and Word, merge Access data with a Word document, import and link data to a new table, and copy and paste data between programs. You will also learn how to copy and paste data between applications and save a database in an earlier version of Access.

Note: Before beginning computer projects, copy to your storage medium the Access2007L1C8 subfolder from the Access2007L1 folder on the CD that accompanies this textbook and make Access2007L1C8 the active folder.

Project **1** **Export Data to Excel and Export and Merge Data to Word**

You will export a table and query to Excel and export a table and report to Word. You will also merge data in an Access table and query with a Word document.

Exporting Data

One of the advantages of a suite like Microsoft Office is the ability to exchange data between one program and another. Access, like other programs in the suite, offers a feature to export data from Access into Excel and/or Word. The Export group in the External Data tab contains buttons for exporting a table, query, form, or report to other programs such as Excel and Word.

Exporting Data to Excel

Use the Excel button in the Export group in the External Data tab to export data in a table, query, or form to an Excel worksheet. Click the object containing data you want to export to Excel, click the External Data tab, click the Excel button in the Export group and the first Export - Excel Spreadsheet wizard dialog box displays as shown in Figure 8.1.

> Click the Browse button and then navigate to the desired folder and file.

Figure 8.1 Export - Excel Spreadsheet Dialog Box

> Insert a check mark in this check box to export all object formatting and layout.

> Insert a check mark in this check box to open the file in the destination program.

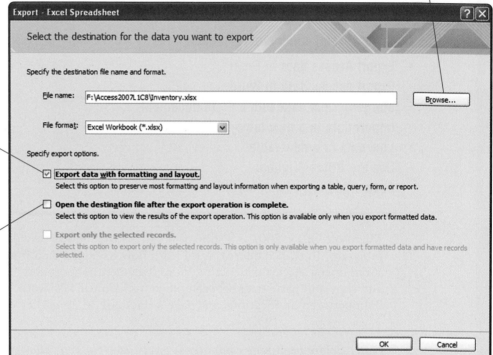

At the first wizard dialog box, Access uses the name of the object as the Excel workbook name. You can change this by selecting the current name and then typing a new name and you can specify the file format with the *File format* option. Click the *Export data with formatting and layout* check box to insert a check mark. This exports all data formatting to the Excel workbook. If you want Excel to open with the exported data, click the *Open the destination file after the export operation is complete* option to insert a check mark. When you have made all desired changes, click the OK button. This opens Excel with the data in a workbook. Make any desired changes to the workbook and then save, print, and close the workbook. Exit Excel and Access displays with a second wizard dialog box asking if you want to save the export steps. At this dialog box, insert a check mark in the *Save export steps* if you want to save the export steps, or leave the option blank and then click the Close button.

Project 1a Exporting a Table and Query to Excel

1. Display the Open dialog box with Access2007L1C8 on your storage medium the active folder.
2. Open the **Hilltop.accdb** database.
3. Save the Inventory table as an Excel worksheet by completing the following steps:
   a. Click the Inventory table in the Navigation pane.
   b. Click the External Data tab and then click the Excel button in the Export group.

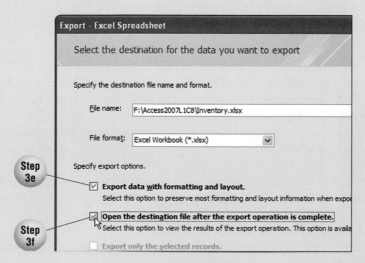

Step 3b

Step 3a

   c. At the Export - Excel Spreadsheet dialog box, click the Browse button.
   d. At the File Save dialog box, navigate to the Access2007L1C8 folder on your storage medium and then click the Save button.
   e. Click the *Export data with formatting and layout* option to insert a check mark in the check box.
   f. Click the *Open the destination file after the export operation is complete* option to insert a check mark in the check box.

Step 3e

Step 3f

   g. Click OK.

h. When the data displays on the screen in Excel as a worksheet, select cells A2 through A11 and then click the Center button in the Alignment group in the Home tab.

i. Select cells D2 through F11 and then click the Center button.

j. Click the Save button on the Quick Access toolbar.

k. Click the Quick Print button on the Quick Access toolbar.

l. Close the worksheet and then exit Excel.

4. In Access, click the Close button to close the second wizard dialog box.

5. Design a query that extracts records from three tables with the following specifications:

a. Add the Invoices, Customers, and Rates tables to the query window.

b. Insert the *BillingDate* field from the Invoices table to the first *Field* text box.

c. Insert the *Customer* field from the Customers table to the second *Field* text box.

d. Insert the *Hours* field from the Invoices table to the third *Field* text box.

e. Insert the *Rate* field from the Rates table to the fourth *Field* text box.

f. Click in the fifth *Field* text box, type **Total: [Hours]*[Rate]** and then press Enter.

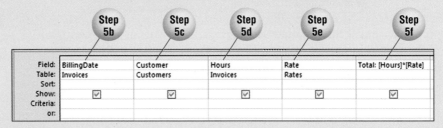

g. Run the query.

h. Save the query and name it *CustomerInvoices*.

i. Close the query.

6. Export the CustomerInvoices query to Excel by completing the following steps:

a. Click the CustomerInvoices query in the Navigation pane.

b. Click the External Data tab and then click the Excel button in the Export group.

c. At the Export - Excel Spreadsheet dialog box, click the *Export data with formatting and layout* option to insert a check mark in the check box.

d. Click the *Open the destination file after the export operation is complete* option to insert a check mark in the check box.

e. Click OK.

f. When the data displays on the screen in Excel as a worksheet, select cells A2 through A20 and then click the Center button in the Alignment group in the Home tab.

g. Select cells C2 through C20 and then click the Center button.

h. Click the Save button on the Quick Access toolbar.

i. Click the Quick Print button on the Quick Access toolbar.

j. Close the worksheet and then exit Excel.

7. In Access, click the Close button to close the second wizard dialog box.

Exporting Data to Word

Export data from Access to Word in the same manner as exporting to Excel. To export data to Word, select the desired object in the Navigation pane, click the External Data tab, and then click the Word button in the Export group. At the Export - RTF File dialog box, make desired changes and then click OK. Word automatically opens and the data displays in a Word document that is saved automatically with the same name as the database object. The difference is that the file extension .rtf is added to the name. An RTF file is saved in "rich-text format," which preserves formatting such as fonts and styles. You can export a document saved with the .rtf extension in Word and other Windows word processing or desktop publishing programs.

QUICK STEPS

Export Data to Word
1. Click the desired table, query, form, or report.
2. Click External Data tab.
3. Click Word button in Export group.
4. Make desired changes at Export - RTF File dialog box.
5. Click OK.

HINT

Data exported from Access to Word is saved with the .rtf file extension.

Project 1b   Exporting a Table and Report to Word

1. Click the Invoices table in the Navigation pane.
2. Click the External Data tab and then click the Word button in the Export group.

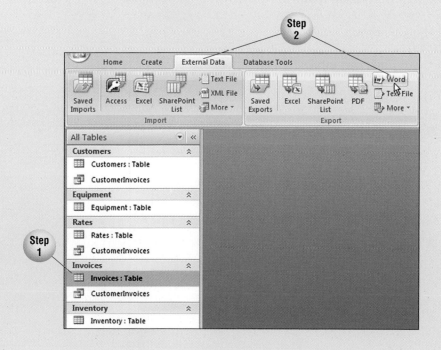

3. At the Export - RTF File wizard dialog box, click the Browse button.
4. At the File Save dialog box, navigate to the Access2007L1C8 folder on your storage medium and then click the Save button.
5. At the Export - RTF File wizard dialog box, click the *Open the destination file after the export operation is complete* check box.

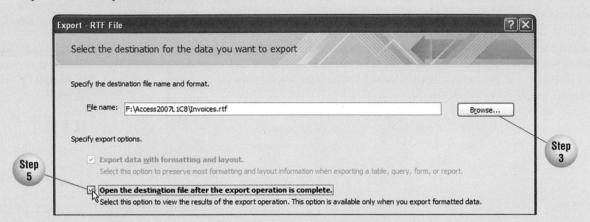

6. Click OK.
7. With the **Invoices.rtf** file open in Word, click the Quick Print button on the Quick Access toolbar.
8. Close the **Invoices.rtf** file and then exit Word.
9. Click the Close button to close the wizard dialog box.
10. Create a report with the Report Wizard by completing the following steps:
   a. Click the Create tab and then click the Report Wizard button in the Reports group.
   b. At the first Report Wizard dialog box, insert the following fields in the *Selected Fields* list box:

   From the Customers table:
       Customer
   From the Equipment table:
       Equipment
   From the Invoices table:
       BillingDate
       Hours

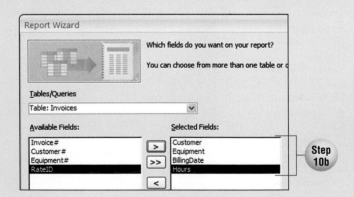

c. After inserting the fields, click the Next button.

d. At the second Report Wizard dialog box, make sure *by Customers* is selected in the list box in the upper left corner and then click the Next button.

e. At the third Report Wizard dialog box, click the Next button.

f. At the fourth Report Wizard dialog box, click the Next button.

g. At the fifth Report Wizard dialog box, click *Block* in the *Layout* section and then click the Next button.

h. At the sixth Report Wizard dialog box, click *Solstice* in the list box and then click the Next button.

i. At the seventh Report Wizard dialog box, select the current name in the *File name* text box, type **CustomerReport**, and then click the Finish button.

j. When the report displays in Print Preview, click the Layout View button located in the view area at the right side of the Status bar.

k. Click the *Customer* column heading and then increase the width of the column so all of the customer names display in the fields.

l. Click the Quick Print button on the Quick Access toolbar.

m. Save and then close the CustomerReport report.

11. Export the CustomerReport report to Word by completing the following steps:

a. Click the CustomerReport report in the Navigation pane.

b. Click the External Data tab and then click the Word button in the Export group.

c. At the Export - RTF File wizard dialog box, click the *Open the destination file after export operation is complete* option to insert a check mark in the check box and then click OK.

d. When the data displays on the screen in Word, click the Quick Print button on the Quick Access toolbar.

e. Save and then close the CustomerReport document.

f. Exit Word.

12. In Access, click the Close button to close the second wizard dialog box.

Merging Access Data with a Word Document

You can merge data from an Access table with a Word document. When merging data, the data in the Access table is considered the data source and the Word document is considered the main document. When the merge is completed, the merged documents display in Word. To merge data, click the desired table in the Navigation pane and then click the External Data tab. Click the More button in the Export group and then click the *Merge it with Microsoft Office Word* option at the drop-down list. When merging Access data, you can either type the text in the main document or merge Access data with an existing Word document.

Merge Data with Word

1. Click the desired table or query.
2. Click External Data tab.
3. Click More button, Merge it with Microsoft Office Word.
4. Make desired choices at each wizard dialog box.

1. Click the Customers table in the Navigation pane.
2. Click the External Data tab.
3. Click the More button in the Export group and then click the *Merge it with Microsoft Office Word* option at the drop-down list.

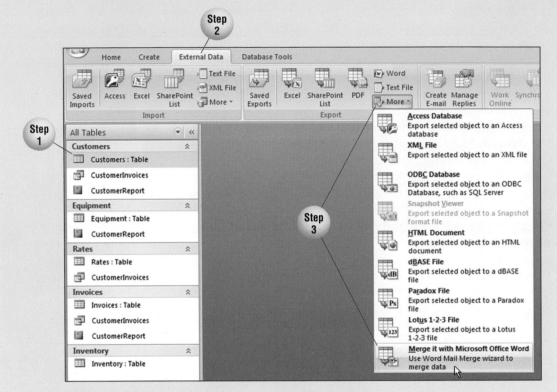

4. At the Microsoft Word Mail Merge Wizard dialog box, make sure *Link your data to an existing Microsoft Word document* is selected and then click OK.
5. At the Select Microsoft Word Document dialog box, make the Access2007L1C8 folder on your storage medium the active folder and then double-click the document named *HilltopLetter.docx*.
6. Click the Maximize button located at the right side of the HilltopLetter.docx title bar and then close the Mail Merge task pane.
7. Press the down arrow key six times (not the Enter key) and then type the current date.
8. Press the down arrow key five times and then insert fields for merging from the Customers table by completing the following steps:

   a. Click the Insert Merge Field button arrow located in the Write & Insert Fields group and then click *Customer1* in the drop-down list. (This inserts the *«Customer1»* field in the document. The drop-down list contains a *Customer* and a *Customer1* option. The first *Customer* option is actually the *Customer#* field. Word dropped the # symbol from the field name and added the *1* to the second *Customer* field to differentiate the two fields.)

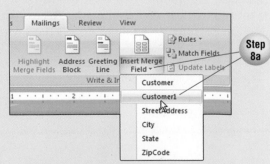

b. Press Enter, click the Insert Merge Field button arrow, and then click *StreetAddress* in the drop-down list.

c. Press Enter, click the Insert Merge Field button arrow, and then click *City* in the drop-down list.

d. Type a comma (,) and then press the spacebar.

e. Click the Insert Merge Field button arrow and then click *State* in the drop-down list.

f. Press the spacebar, click the Insert Merge Field button arrow, and then click *ZipCode* in the drop-down list.

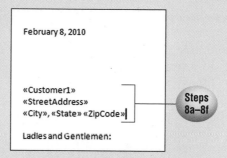

g. Replace the letters *XX* that display toward the bottom of the letter with your initials.

h. Click the Finish & Merge button in the Finish group and then click *Edit Individual Documents* in the drop-down list.

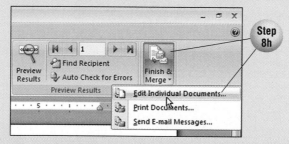

i. At the Merge to New Document dialog box, make sure *All* is selected and then click OK.

j. When the merge is completed, save the new document and name it **AccessL1_C8_P1a** in the Access2007L1C8 folder on your storage medium.

9. Print just the first two pages (two letters) of **AccessL1_C8_P1a.docx**.

10. Close **AccessL1_C8_P1a.docx** and then close **HilltopLetter.docx** without saving the changes.

11. Exit Word.

Merging Query Data with a Word Document

You can perform a query in a database and then use the query to merge with a Word document. In Project 1d you merged a table with an existing Word document. You can also merge a table or query and then type the Word document. You will create a query in Project 1e and then merge data in the query with a new document in Word.

1. Perform a query with the Query Wizard and modify the query by completing the following steps:
   a. Click the Create tab and then click the Query Wizard button in the Other group.
   b. At the New Query dialog box, make sure Simple Query Wizard is selected and then click OK.
   c. At the first Simple Query Wizard dialog box, click the down-pointing arrow at the right of the *Tables/Queries* option box and then click *Table: Customers*.
   d. Click the button containing the two greater than symbols (>>) to insert all of the fields in the *Selected Fields* list box.
   e. Click the Next button.
   f. At the second Simple Query Wizard dialog box, make the following changes:
      1) Select the current name in the *What title do you want for your query?* text box and then type DenverCustomersQuery.
      2) Click the *Modify the query design* option.
      3) Click the Finish button.
   g. At the query window, click in the *Criteria* text box in the *City* column, type **Denver**, and then press Enter.

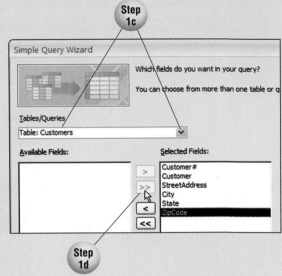

Step 1c

Step 1d

Field:	[Customer#]	[Customer]	[StreetAddress]	[City]	[State]	[ZipCode]
Table:	Customers	Customers	Customers	Customers	Customers	Customers
Sort:						
Show:	☑	☑	☑	☑	☑	☑
Criteria:				"Denver"		
or:						

Step 1g

h. Click the Run button in the Results group. (Those customers located in Denver will display.)
i. Save and then close the DenverCustomersQuery query.
2. Click the DenverCustomersQuery query in the Navigation pane.
3. Click the External Data tab, click the More button in the Export group, and then click the *Merge it with Microsoft Office Word* option at the drop-down list.
4. At the Microsoft Word Mail Merge Wizard dialog box, click the *Create a new document and then link the data to it.* option and then click OK.
5. Click the Maximize button located at the right side of the Document1 title bar and then close the Mail Merge task pane.
6. Complete the following steps to type text and insert fields in the blank Word document:
   a. Click the Home tab and then click the No Spacing style in the Styles group.
   b. Press Enter six times.

Step 4

Microsoft Word Mail Merge Wizard

This wizard links your data to a Microsoft Word document, so that you can print form letters or address envelopes.

What do you want the wizard to do?

○ Link your data to an existing Microsoft Word document.

⦿ Create a new document and then link the data to it.

OK Cancel

c. Type the current date.
d. Press Enter five times.
e. Click the Mailings tab.
f. Insert the following fields at the left margin in the order shown below (start by clicking the Insert Merge Field button arrow in the Write & Insert Fields group):

«Customer1»
«StreetAddress»
«City», «State» «ZipCode»

g. Press Enter twice and then type the salutation **Ladies and Gentlemen:**.
h. Press Enter twice and then type the following paragraphs of text:

> **To provide quality service to our customers, we have opened a new branch office in downtown Denver. The branch office hours are 7:30 a.m. to 7:00 p.m. Monday through Friday, 8:00 a.m. to 5:00 p.m. Saturday, and 9:00 a.m. to 3:30 p.m. Sunday.**
>
> **Our new branch is located at 7500 Alameda Avenue. Stop by during the next two weeks and receive a 10% discount on your next equipment rental.**

i. Press Enter twice and then type the following complimentary close (at the left margin):

> **Sincerely,**

> **Lou Galloway**
> **Manager**

> **XX:AccessL1_C8_P1b.docx**

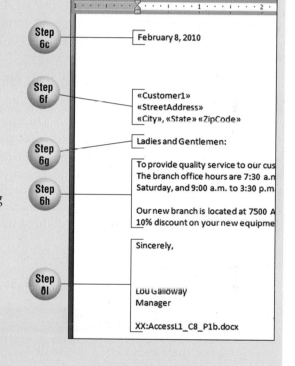

Step 6c — February 8, 2010

Step 6f — «Customer1» «StreetAddress» «City», «State» «ZipCode»

Step 6g — Ladies and Gentlemen:

Step 6h — To provide quality service to our cus... The branch office hours are 7:30 a.m... Saturday, and 9:00 a.m. to 3:30 p.m... Our new branch is located at 7500 A... 10% discount on your new equipme...

Step 6l — Sincerely, Lou Galloway Manager XX:AccessL1_C8_P1b.docx

j. Click the Finish & Merge button in the Finish group and then click *Edit Individual Documents* in the drop-down menu.
k. At the Merge to New Document dialog box, make sure *All* is selected, and then click OK.
l. When the merge is complete, save the new document as **AccessL1_C8_P1b** in the Access2007L1C8 folder on your storage medium.
7. Print the first two pages (two letters) of **AccessL1_C8_P1b.docx**.
8. Close **AccessL1_C8_P1b.docx**.
9. Save the main document as **AccessHilltopLetter** in the Access2007L1C8 folder on your storage medium and then close the document.
10. Exit Word.
11. Close the **Hilltop.accdb** database.

Project 2 Import and Link Excel Worksheets with an Access Table

You will import an Excel worksheet into an Access table. You will also link an Excel worksheet into an Access table and then add a new record to the Access table.

QUICK STEPS

Import Data to a New Table
1. Click External Data tab.
2. Click desired application in Import group.
3. Click Browse button.
4. Double-click desired file name.
5. Make desired choices at each wizard dialog box.

Importing and Linking Data to a New Table

In this chapter, you learned how to export Access data to Excel and Word. You can also import data from other programs into an Access table. For example, you can import data from an Excel worksheet and create a new table in a database using data from the worksheet. Data in the original program is not connected to the data imported into an Access table. If you make changes to the data in the original program, those changes are not reflected in the Access table. If you want the imported data connected to the original program, link the data.

Importing Data to a New Table

HINT
Store data in Access and use Excel to analyze data.

HINT
You can import and link data between Access databases.

To import data, click the External Data tab and then determine where you would like to retrieve data with options in the Import group. At the Import dialog box that displays, click Browse and then double-click the desired file name. This activates the Import Wizard and displays the first wizard dialog box. The appearance of the dialog box varies depending on the file selected. Complete the steps of the Import Wizard specifying information such as the range of data, whether or not the first row contains column headings, whether you want to store the data in a new table or store it in an existing table, the primary key, and the name of the table.

Project 2a Importing an Excel Worksheet into an Access Table

1. Display the Open dialog box with Access2007L1C8 on your storage medium the active folder.
2. Open the **SouthwestInsurance.accdb** database.
3. Import an Excel worksheet into a new table in the **SouthwestInsurance.accdb** database by completing the following steps:
   a. Click the External Data tab and then click the Excel button in the Import group.
   b. At the Get External Data - Excel Spreadsheet dialog box, click Browse and then make the Access2007L1C8 folder on your storage medium the active folder.
   c. Double-click *ExcelC08_01.xlsx* in the list box.
   d. Click OK at the Get External Data - Excel Spreadsheet dialog box.

e. At the first Import Spreadsheet Wizard dialog box, click the Next button.

f. At the second Import Spreadsheet Wizard dialog box, make sure the *First Row Contains Column Headings* option contains a check mark and then click the Next button.

g. At the third Import Spreadsheet Wizard dialog box, click the Next button.

h. At the fourth Import Spreadsheet Wizard dialog box, click the *Choose my own primary key* option (this inserts *Policy#* in the text box located to the right of the option) and then click the Next button.

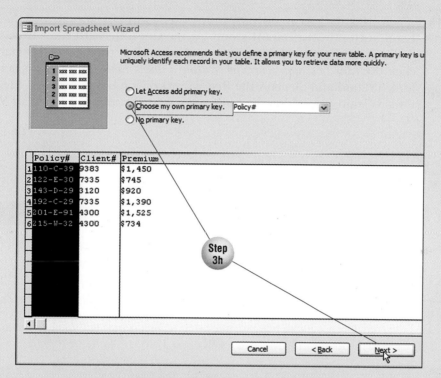

i. At the fifth Import Spreadsheet Wizard dialog box, type **Policies** in the *Import to Table* text box and then click the Finish button.

j. At the Get External Data - Excel Spreadsheet dialog box, click the Close button.

4. Open the new Policies table in Datasheet view.

5. Print and then close the Policies table.

QUICK
STEPS

Linking Data to an Excel Worksheet

Link Data to Excel Worksheet
1. Click External Data tab.
2. Click Excel button in Import group.
3. Click Browse button.
4. Double-click desired file name.
5. Click *Link to a data source by creating a linked table*.
6. Make desired choices at each wizard dialog box.

Imported data is not connected to the source program. If you know that you will use your data only in Access, import it. However, if you want to update data in a program other than Access, link the data. Changes made to linked data in the source program file are reflected in the destination program file. For example, you can link an Excel worksheet with an Access table and when you make changes in the Excel worksheet, the changes are reflected in the Access table.

To link data to a new table, click the External Data tab and then click the Excel button in the Import group. At the Get External Data - Excel Spreadsheet dialog box, click the Browse button, double-click the desired file name, and then click the *Link to a data source by creating a linked table* option. This activates the Link Wizard and displays the first wizard dialog box. Complete the steps of the Link Wizard, specifying the same basic information as the Import Wizard.

Excel

Project 2b Linking an Excel Worksheet with an Access Table

1. With the **SouthwestInsurance.accdb** database open, click the External Data tab and then click the Excel button in the Import group.
2. At the Get External Data - Excel Spreadsheet dialog box, click the Browse button, navigate to the Access2007L1C8 folder on your storage medium, and then double-click **ExcelC08_01.xlsx**.
3. At the Get External Data - Excel Spreadsheet dialog box, click the *Link to the data source by creating a linked table* option and then click OK.

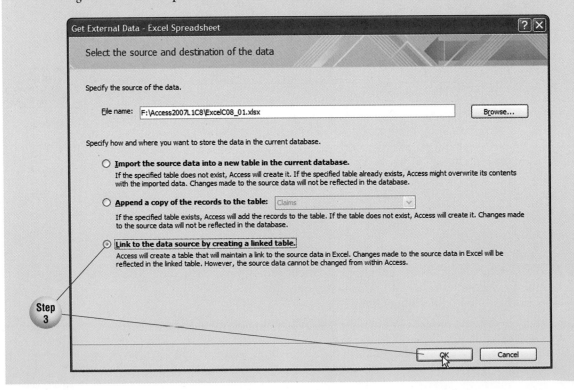

4. At the first Link Spreadsheet Wizard dialog box, make sure *Show Worksheets* and *Sheet 1* are selected in the list box and then click the Next button.

5. At the second Link Spreadsheet Wizard dialog box, make sure the *First Row Contains Column Headings* option contains a check mark and then click the Next button.

6. At the third Link Spreadsheet Wizard dialog box, type **LinkedPolicies** in the *Linked Table Name* text box and then click the Finish button.

7. At the message stating the linking is finished, click OK.

8. Open the new LinkedPolicies table in Datasheet view.

9. Close the LinkedPolicies table.

10. Open Excel, open the **ExcelC08_01.xlsx** workbook and then make the following changes:

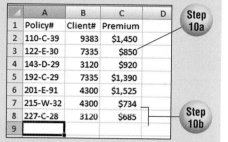

Step 10a

a. Change the amount *$745* in cell C3 to *$850*.

b. Add the following information in the specified cells:
   A8 = **227-C-28**
   B8 = **3120**
   C8 = **$685**

Step 10b

11. Save, print, and then close **ExcelC08_01.xlsx**.

12. Exit Excel.

13. With Access the active program and the **SouthwestInsurance.accdb** database open, open the LinkedPolicies table. Notice the changes you made in Excel are reflected in the table.

14. Close the LinkedPolicies table and then close the **SouthwestInsurance.accdb** database.

Project 3 Collect Data in Word and Paste in an Access Table

You will open a Word document containing Hilltop customer names and addresses and then copy the data and paste it into an Access table.

Using the Office Clipboard

Use the Office Clipboard to collect and paste multiple items. You can collect up to 24 different items in Access or other programs in the Office suite and then paste the items in various locations. To copy and paste multiple items, display the Clipboard task pane shown in Figure 8.2 by clicking the Clipboard group dialog box launcher.

Display Clipboard Task Pane
Click Clipboard group dialog box launcher.

Select data or an object you want to copy and then click the Copy button in the Clipboard group in the Home tab. Continue selecting text or items and clicking the Copy button. To insert an item from the Clipboard task pane to a field in an Access table, make the desired field active and then click the button in the task pane representing the item. If the copied item is text, the first 50 characters display. When all desired items are inserted, click the Clear All button to remove any remaining items from the Clipboard task pane.

You can copy data from one object to another in an Access database or from a file in another program to an Access database. In Project 3a, you will copy data from a Word document and paste it into a table. You can also collect data from other programs such as PowerPoint and Excel.

Figure 8.2 Office Clipboard Task Pane

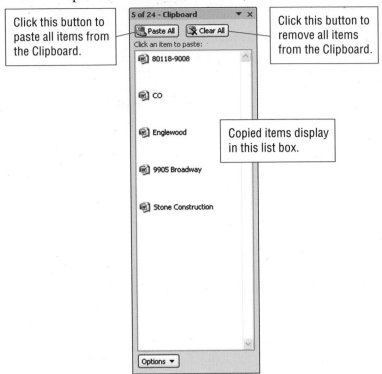

Click this button to paste all items from the Clipboard.

Click this button to remove all items from the Clipboard.

Copied items display in this list box.

Project 3a — Collecting Data in Word and Pasting it in an Access Table

1. Open the **Hilltop.accdb** database.
2. Open the Customers table.
3. Copy data from Word and paste it into the Customers table by completing the following steps:
   a. Open Word, make the Access2007L1C8 folder active, and then open **HilltopCustomers.docx**.
   b. Make sure the Home tab is active.
   c. Click the Clipboard group dialog box launcher to display the Clipboard task pane.
   d. Select the first company name, *Stone Construction*, and then click the Copy button in the Clipboard group.
   e. Select the street address, *9905 Broadway*, and then click the Copy button.

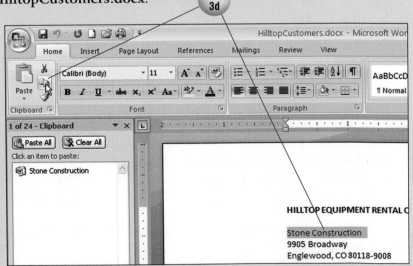

f. Select the city, *Englewood*, and then click the Copy button.

g. Select the state, *CO* (select only the two letters and not the space after the letters), and then click the Copy button.

h. Select the ZIP code, *80118-9008*, and then click the Copy button.

i. Click the button on the Taskbar representing Access. (Make sure the Customer table is open and displays in Datasheet view.)

j. Click in the first empty cell in the *Customer#* field and then type *178*.

k. Display the Clipboard task pane by clicking the Clipboard group dialog box launcher.

l. Close the Navigation pane by clicking the Shutter Bar Open/Close Button.

m. Click in the first empty cell in the *Customer* field and then click *Stone Construction* in the Clipboard task pane.

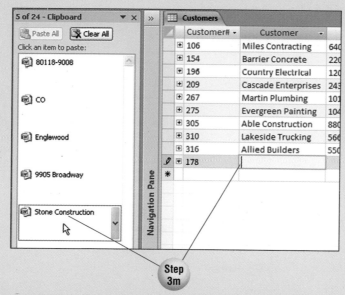

Step 3m

n. Click in the *StreetAddress* field and then click *9905 Broadway* in the Clipboard task pane.

o. Click in the *City* field and then click *Englewood* in the Clipboard task pane.

p. Click in the *State* field and then click *CO* in the Clipboard task pane.

q. Click in the *ZipCode* field, make sure the insertion point is positioned at the left side of the field, and then click *80118-9008* in the Clipboard task pane.

r. Click the Clear All button in the Clipboard task pane. (This removes all entries from the Clipboard.)

Step 3r

4. Complete steps similar to those in 3c through 3q to copy the information for Laughlin Products and paste it into the Customers table. (The Customer# is 225.)

5. Click the Clear All button in the Clipboard task pane.

6. Close the Clipboard task pane by clicking the Close button (contains an *X*) located in the upper right corner of the task pane.

7. Save, print, and then close the Customers table.

8. Open the Navigation pane by clicking the Shutter Bar Open/Close Button.

9. Make Word the active program, close **HilltopCustomers.docx** without saving changes, and then exit Word.

Saving a Database in a Previous Version Format

If you need to share an Access 2007 database with someone who is using an earlier version of Access, you will need to save the database in a different format. An Access 2007 database is saved with the .accdb file extension. Earlier versions of Access such as versions 2003, 2002, or 2000 save a database with the .mdb file extension. To save an Access 2007 database in an earlier version, open the database, click the Office button, point to *Save As*, and then click the desired version at the side menu shown in Figure 8.3.

Figure 8.3 Save As Side Menu

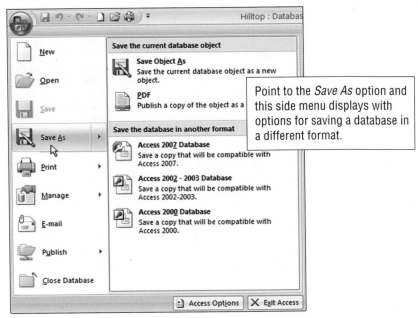

Point to the *Save As* option and this side menu displays with options for saving a database in a different format.

If you want to create a database in an earlier version, change the *Default file format* at the Access Options dialog box with the *Popular* option selected. To display this dialog box, click the Office button and then click the Access Options button located toward the bottom right side of the drop-down list. At the Access Options dialog box with *Popular* selected, click the down-pointing arrow at the right side of the *Default file format* option and then click *Access 2000* or *Access 2002 - 2003* at the drop-down list. This default format change remains in effect even if you exit and then open Access.

Project 3b   Saving a Database in a Previous Version

1. With the **Hilltop.accdb** database open, save the database in a previous version of Access by completing the following steps:

   a. Click the Office button, point to *Save As*, and then click *Access 2002 - 2003 Database* at the side menu.

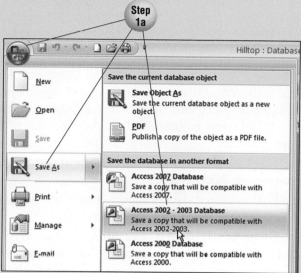

Step 1a

   b. At the Save As dialog box, type **Hilltop2003Format**.

   c. Notice that the *Save as type* option displays as *Microsoft Access Database (2002-2003) (*.mdb)*.

   d. Click the Save button.

2. Notice the Title bar displays the database file name *Hilltop2003Format : Database (Access 2002 - 2003 file format)*.

3. Close **Hilltop2003Format.mdb**.

CHAPTER summary

- Use the Excel button in the Export group in the External Data tab to export data in a table, query, or form to an Excel worksheet.
- Use the Word button in the Export group in the External Data tab to export data in a table, query, form, or report to a Word document. Access exports the data to an RTF (rich-text format) file.
- You can merge Access data with a Word document. The Access data is the data source and the Word document is the main document. To merge data, click the desired table or query and then click the External Data tab. Click the More button in the Export group and then click *Merge it with Microsoft Office Word* at the drop-down list.
- Use the Excel button in the Import group in the External Data tab to import Excel data to an Access table.
- You can link imported data. Changes made to the data in the source program file are reflected in the destination source file.
- If you want to link imported data, click the *Link to the data source by creating a linked table* option at the Get External Data dialog box.
- Use the Clipboard task pane to collect up to 24 different items in Access or other programs and paste them in various locations.
- Display the Clipboard task pane by clicking the Clipboard group dialog box launcher.
- Save an Access database in an earlier version of Access by clicking the Office button, pointing to *Save As*, and then clicking *Access 2002 - 2003 Database* or *Access 2000 Database* at the side menu.

COMMANDS review

FEATURE	RIBBON TAB, GROUP	BUTTON, OPTION
Export object to Excel	External Data, Export	
Export object to Word	External Data, Export	Word
Merge Access data with Word	External Data, Export	More ▾ , Merge it with Microsoft Office Word
Import Excel data	External Data, Import	
Clipboard task pane	Home, Clipboard	
Save as 2002 - 2003 database		, Save As, Access 2002 - 2003 Database
Save as 2000 Database		, Save As, Access 2000 Database

CONCEPTS check

Test Your Knowledge

Completion: In the space provided at the right, indicate the correct term, symbol, or command.

1. Click this tab to display the Export group.
   _____

2. Click this button in the Export group to display the Export - Excel Spreadsheet wizard dialog box.
   _____

3. At the first Export - Excel Spreadsheet wizard dialog box, click this option if you want Excel to open with the exported data.
   _____

4. When you export Access data to Word, the document is saved with this file format.
   _____

5. When merging data, the data in the Access table is considered this.
   _____

6. To merge data, click the More button in the Export group and then click this option.
   _____

7. If you want imported data connected to the original program, do this to the data.
   _____

8. Use this task pane to collect and paste multiple items.
   _____

9. To save a database in the 2003 format, click the Office button, point to *Save As*, and then click this option at the side menu.
   _____

10. To create a database in an earlier version, change the *Default file format* option at this dialog box with the *Popular* option selected.
    _____

SKILLS check

Demonstrate Your Proficiency

Assessment

1 EXPORT A FORM TO EXCEL AND A REPORT TO WORD

1. Display the Open dialog box with Access2007L1C8 on your storage medium the active folder.
2. Open the **LegalServices.accdb** database.
3. Create a form named *Billing* using the Form Wizard with the following fields:
   From the Billing table:
   > *Billing#*
   > *ClientID*
   > *Date*
   > *Hours*

   From the Rates table:
   > *Rate*
4. When the form displays, close it.
5. Create an Excel worksheet with the Billing form.
6. Make the following changes to the Excel Billing worksheet:
   a. Select columns A through E and then autofit the column widths.
   b. Select cells A2 through B28 and then click the Center button in the Alignment group in the Home tab.
   c. Save the Billing worksheet.
   d. Print and then close the Billing worksheet.
   e. Exit Excel.
7. In Access, close the Export Wizard.
8. Create a report named *ClientBilling* using the Report Wizard with the following fields:
   From the Clients table:
   > *FirstName*
   > *LastName*

   From the Billing table:
   > *Date*
   > *Hours*

   From the Rates table:
   > *Rate*
9. Apply the Foundry autoformat to the report.
10. When the report displays, change to Layout view and then decrease the size of the columns so the right border of the column displays just right of the longest entry in the column.
11. Save and then close the report.
12. Create a Word document with the ClientBilling report and save it to the Access2007L1C8 folder on your storage medium with the default name. In the Word document, make the following changes:
    a. Press Ctrl + A to select the entire document, change the font color to black, and then deselect the text.
    b. Insert a space between *Client* and *Billing* in the title.
    c. Position the insertion point immediately right of the word *Billing*, press the spacebar, and then type **of Legal Services**.

13. Save and then print **ClientBilling.rtf**.
14. Close the document and then exit Word.
15. In Access, close the wizard dialog box.

Assessment

2 MERGE TABLE AND QUERY DATA WITH A WORD DOCUMENT

1. With the **LegalServices.accdb** database open, merge data in the Clients table to a new Word document using the *Merge it with Microsoft Office Word* option.
2. Maximize the Word document, close the Mail Merge task pane, and then compose a letter with the following elements:
   a. Click the Home tab and then click the No Spacing style in the Styles group.
   b. Press Enter six times, type the current date, and then press Enter five times.
   c. Click the Mailings tab and then insert the proper field names for the recipient's name and address. *Hint: Use the Insert Merge Field button in the Write & Insert Fields group.*
   d. Insert a proper salutation.
   e. Compose a letter to clients that includes the following information:

   > The last time you visited our offices, you may have noticed how crowded we were. To alleviate the overcrowding, we are leasing new offices in the Meridian Building and will be moving in at the beginning of next month.

   > Stop by and see our new offices at our open house planned for the second Friday of next month. Drop by any time between 2:00 and 5:30 p.m. We look forward to seeing you.

   f. Include an appropriate complimentary close for the letter. Use the name and title *Marjorie Shaw, Senior Partner* for the signature and add your reference initials and the document name (**AccessL1_C8_A2a.docx**).
3. Merge to a new document and then save the document with the name **AccessL1_C8_A2a**.
4. Print only the first two letters in the document and then close **AccessL1_C8_A2a.docx**.
5. Save the main document and name it **AccessL1_C8_A2_MD1**, close the document, and then exit Word.
6. At the LegalServices database, extract the records from the Clients table of those clients located in Kent and then name the query *KentQuery*.
7. Merge the KentQuery to a new Word document using the *Merge it with Microsoft Office Word* option.
8. Maximize the Word document, close the Mail Merge task pane, and then compose a letter with the following elements:
   a. Click the Home tab and then click the No Spacing style in the Styles group.
   b. Press Enter six times, type the current date, and then press Enter five times.
   c. Click the Mailings tab and then insert the proper field names for the inside address.
   d. Insert a proper salutation.

e. Compose a letter to clients that includes the following information:
> The City of Kent Municipal Court has moved from 1024 Meeker Street to a new building located at 3201 James Avenue. All court hearings after the end of this month will be held at the new address. If you need directions to the new building, please call our office.

f. Include an appropriate complimentary close for the letter. Use the name *Thomas Zeiger* and the title *Attorney* in the complimentary close and add your reference initials and the document name (**AccessL1_C8_A2b.docx**).

9. Merge the letter to a new document and then save the document with the name **AccessL1_C8_A2b**.
10. Print only the first two letters in the document and then close **AccessL1_C8_A2b.docx**.
11. Save the main document and name it **AccessL1_C8_A2_MD2**, close the document, and then exit Word.

Assessment

3 IMPORT AND LINK AN EXCEL WORKBOOK

1. At the **LegalServices.accdb** database, import and link **ExcelC8_02.xlsx** into a new table named *Cases*.
2. Open the Cases table in Datasheet view.
3. Print and then close the Cases table.
4. Open Excel, open the **ExcelC08_02.xlsx** workbook and then add the following data in the specified cell:

A8	=	57-D
B8	=	130
C8	=	$1,100
A9	=	42-A
B9	=	144
C9	=	$3,250
A10	=	29-C
B10	=	125
C10	=	$900

5. Save, print, and then close **ExcelC08_02.xlsx**.
6. Exit Excel.
7. In Access, open the Cases table in Datasheet view. (Notice the changes you made in Excel are reflected in the table.)
8. Print and then close the Cases table.

CASE study

Apply Your Skills

As the office manager at Woodland Dermatology Center, you are responsible for managing the center database. In preparation for an upcoming meeting, open the **Woodland.accdb** database and prepare the following with data in the database:

- Create a query that displays the patient number, first name, and last name; doctor last name; date of visit; and fee. Name the query *PatientBilling*.
- Export the PatientBilling query to an Excel worksheet. Apply formatting to enhance the appearance of the worksheet and then print the worksheet.
- Create mailing labels for the patients.
- Export the patient labels to a Word (.rtf) document and then print the document.
- Import and link the **WoodlandPayroll.xlsx** Excel worksheet to a new table named *WeeklyPayroll*. Print the WeeklyPayroll table.

You have been given some updated information about the weekly payroll and need to make the following changes to the **WoodlandPayroll.xlsx** worksheet: Change the hours for Irene Vaughn to *30*, change the wage for Monica Saunders to *$10.50*, and change the hours for Dale Jorgensen to *20*. After making the changes, open, print, and then close the WeeklyPayroll table.

The center is expanding and will be offering cosmetic dermatology services at the beginning of next month to residents in the Altoona area. Design a query that extracts records of patients living in the city of Altoona and then merge the query with Word. At the Word document, write a letter describing the new services which include microdermabrasion, chemical peels, laser resurfacing, sclerotherapy, and photorejuvenation as well as an offer for a free facial and consultation. Insert the appropriate fields in the document and then complete the merge. Save the merged document and name it **Access_C8_CS_P2**. Print the first two letters of the document and then close the document. Close the main document without saving it and then exit Word.

You need to save objects in the Woodland database in a format that can be read by employees that do not have Access available. You have researched the various file formats available and have determined that the PDF format is the most universal. Use the Access Help feature to learn how to save a database object in PDF format. (You may need to download an add-in to save an object in PDF format.) Save the Patients table in PDF format and then print the PDF file. Save the Doctors table in PDF format and then print the PDF file.

Since you are responsible for updating the clinic procedures manual, you decide to create a Word document that describes the steps for saving an object in PDF format. Save the completed document and name it **Access_C8_CS_P4**. Print and then close **Access_C8_CS_P4.docx**.

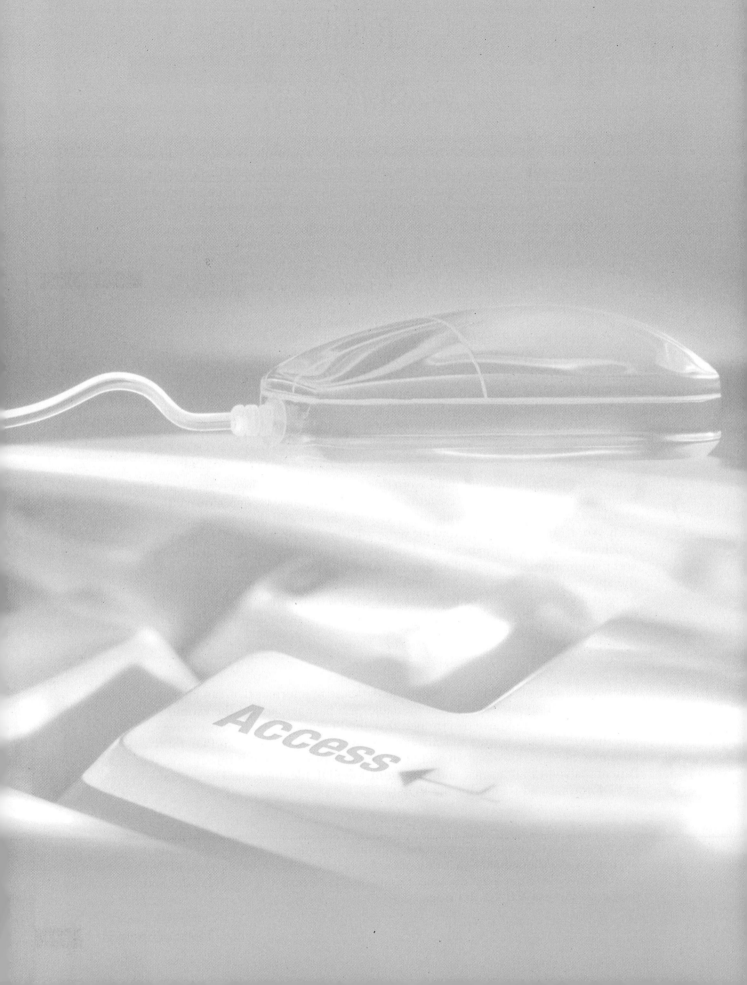

Creating Forms and Reports

In this unit, you have learned to create forms, reports, and mailing labels; filter data; and summarize and analyze data in PivotTable and PivotChart view as well as create a PivotTable form. You also learned how to modify document properties; view object dependencies; and export, import, and link data between programs.

Note: Before beginning unit assessments, copy to your storage medium the Access2007L1U2 subfolder from the Access2007L1 folder on the CD that accompanies this textbook and then make Access2007L1U2 the active folder.

Assessment 1 Create Tables in a Clinic Database

1. Use Access to create a database for clients of a mental health clinic. Name the database **LancasterClinic**. Create a table named *Clients* that includes the following fields (you determine the field name, data type, field size, and description):
    ClientNumber (primary key)
    ClientName
    StreetAddress
    City
    State
    ZipCode
    Telephone
    DateOfBirth
    DiagnosisID
2. After creating the table, switch to Datasheet view and then enter the following data in the appropriate fields:

ClientNumber: 1831	*ClientNumber:* 3219
George Charoni	Marian Wilke
3980 Broad Street	12032 South 39th
Philadelphia, PA 19149	Jenkintown, PA 19209
(215) 555-3482	(215) 555-9083
DateOfBirth: 4/12/1958	*DateOfBirth:* 10/23/1981
DiagnosisID: SC	*DiagnosisID:* OCD
ClientNumber: 2874	*ClientNumber:* 5831
Arthur Shroeder	Roshawn Collins
3618 Fourth Avenue	12110 52nd Court East

Philadelphia, PA 19176   Cheltenham, PA 19210
(215) 555-8311   (215) 555-4779
DateOfBirth: 3/23/1958   *DateOfBirth:* 11/3/1965
DiagnosisID: OCD   *DiagnosisID:* SC

ClientNumber: 4419   *ClientNumber:* 1103
Lorena Hearron   Raymond Mandato
3112 96th Street East   631 Garden Boulevard
Philadelphia, PA 19132   Jenkintown, PA 19209
(215) 555-3281   (215) 555-0957
DateOfBirth: 7/2/1984   *DateOfBirth:* 9/20/1979
DiagnosisID: AD   *DiagnosisID:* MDD

3. Save, print, and then close the Clients table.
4. Create a table named *Diagnoses* that includes the following fields:
   DiagnosisID (primary key)
   Diagnosis
5. After creating the table, switch to Datasheet view and then enter the following data in the appropriate fields:

   DiagnosisID   =   AD
   Diagnosis   =   Adjustment Disorder

   DiagnosisID   =   MDD
   Diagnosis   =   Manic-Depressive Disorder

   DiagnosisID   =   OCD
   Diagnosis   =   Obsessive-Compulsive Disorder

   DiagnosisID   =   SC
   Diagnosis   =   Schizophrenia

6. Save, print, and then close the Diagnoses table.
7. Create a table named *Fees* that includes the following fields (you determine the field name, data type, field size, and description):
   FeeCode (primary key)
   HourlyFee
8. After creating the table, switch to Datasheet view and then enter the following data in the appropriate fields:

   FeeCode   =   A
   HourlyFee   = $75.00

   FeeCode   =   B
   HourlyFee   = $80.00

   FeeCode   =   C
   HourlyFee   = $85.00

   FeeCode   =   D
   HourlyFee   = $90.00

FeeCode	=	E
HourlyFee	=	$95.00

FeeCode	=	F
HourlyFee	=	$100.00

FeeCode	=	G
HourlyFee	=	$105.00

FeeCode	=	H
HourlyFee	=	$110.00

9. Save, print, and then close the Fees table.

10. Create a table named *Employees* that includes the following fields (you determine the field name, data type, field size, and description):

    ProviderNumber (primary key)
    ProviderName
    Title
    Extension

11. After creating the table, switch to Datasheet view and then enter the following data in the appropriate fields:

ProviderNumber: 29	*ProviderNumber:* 15
ProviderName: James Schouten	*ProviderName:* Lynn Yee
Title: Psychologist	*Title:* Child Psychologist
Extension: 399	*Extension:* 102
ProviderNumber: 33	*ProviderNumber:* 18
ProviderName: Janice Grisham	*ProviderName:* Craig Chilton
Title: Psychiatrist	*Title:* Psychologist
Extension: 11	*Extension:* 20

12. Save, print, and then close the Employees table.

13. Create a table named *Billing* that includes the following fields (you determine the field name, data type, field size, and description):

    BillingNumber (primary key; identify the data type as *AutoNumber*)
    ClientNumber
    DateOfService (apply the Date/Time data type)
    Insurer
    ProviderNumber
    Hours
    FeeCode

14. After creating the table, switch to Datasheet view and then enter the following data in the appropriate fields:

ClientNumber: 4419	*ClientNumber:* 1831
DateOfService: 3/1/2010	*DateOfService:* 3/1/2010
Insurer: Health Plus	*Insurer:* Self
ProviderNumber: 15	*ProviderNumber:* 33
Hours: 2	*Hours:* 1
FeeCode: B	FeeCode: H

ClientNumber: 3219
DateOfService: 3/2/2010
Insurer: Health Plus
ProviderNumber: 15
Hours: 1
FeeCode: D

ClientNumber: 5831
DateOfService: 3/2/2010
Insurer: Penn-State Health
ProviderNumber: 18
Hours: 2
FeeCode: C

ClientNumber: 4419
DateOfService: 3/3/2010
Insurer: Health Plus
ProviderNumber: 15
Hours: 1
FeeCode: A

ClientNumber: 1103
DateOfService: 3/3/2010
Insurer: Penn-State Health
ProviderNumber: 18
Hours: 0.5
FeeCode: A

ClientNumber: 1831
DateOfService: 3/4/2010
Insurer: Self
ProviderNumber: 33
Hours: 1
FeeCode: H

ClientNumber: 5831
DateOfService: 3/4/2010
Insurer: Penn-State Health
ProviderNumber: 18
Hours: 0.5
FeeCode: C

15. Save, print, and then close the Billing table.

Assessment 2 Relate Tables and Create Forms in a Clinic Database

1. With the **LancasterClinic.accdb** database open, create the following one-to-many relationships:
   a. *ClientNumber* in the Clients table is the "one" and *ClientNumber* in the Billing table is the "many."
   b. *DiagnosisID* in the Diagnoses table is the "one" and *DiagnosisID* in the Clients table is the "many."
   c. *ProviderNumber* in the Employees table is the "one" and *ProviderNumber* in the Billing table is the "many."
   d. *FeeCode* in the Fees table is the "one" and *FeeCode* in the Billing table is the "many."
2. Create a form with the data in the Clients table.
3. After creating the form, add the following record to the Clients form:
   ClientNumber: 1179
   Timothy Fierro
   1133 Tenth Southwest
   Philadelphia, PA 19178
   (215) 555-5594
   DateOfBirth: 12/7/1987
   DiagnosisID: AD
4. Save the form as Clients, print the form, and then close the form.
5. Add the following records to the Billing table:
   ClientNumber: 1179
   DateOfService: 3/8/2010
   Insurer: Health Plus
   ProviderNumber: 15
   Hours: 0.5
   FeeCode: C

   ClientNumber: 1831
   DateOfService: 3/8/2010
   Insurer: Self
   ProviderNumber: 33
   Hours: 1
   FeeCode: H
6. Save and then print the Billing table.
7. Close the Billing table.

Assessment 3 Create Forms Using the Form Wizard

1. With the **LancasterClinic.accdb** database open, create a form with fields from related tables using the Form Wizard with the following specifications:
   a. At the first Form Wizard dialog box, insert the following fields in the Selected Fields list box:

   From the Clients table:
   ClientNumber
   DateOfBirth
   DiagnosisID
   From the Billing table:
   Insurer
   ProviderNumber
   b. Do not make any changes at the second Form Wizard dialog box.
   c. Do not make any changes at the third Form Wizard dialog box.
   d. You determine the format style at the fourth Form Wizard dialog box.
   e. At the fifth Form Wizard dialog box, type the name **ProviderInformation** in the *Form* text box.
2. When the first record displays, print the first record.
3. Close the form.

Assessment 4 Create Labels with the Label Wizard

1. With the **LancasterClinic.accdb** database open, use the Label Wizard to create mailing labels with the client names and addresses and sorted by ZIP code. Name the mailing label file **ClientMailingLabels**.
2. Print the mailing labels.
3. Close the mailing labels file.

Assessment 5 Filter Records in Tables

1. With the **LancasterClinic.accdb** database open, open the Billing table and then filter the records to display the following records:
   a. Display only those records with the Health Plus Insurer. Print the results and then remove the filter.
   b. Display only those records with the 4419 client number. Print the results and then remove the filter.
2. Filter records by selection to display the following records:
   a. Display only those records with a C fee code. Print the results and then remove the filter.
   b. Display only those records between the dates of 3/1/2010 and 3/3/2010. Print the results and then remove the filter.
3. Close the Billing table without saving the changes.
4. Open the Clients table and then use Filter By Form to display clients in Jenkintown or Cheltenham. Print the results and then remove the filter.
5. Close the Clients table without saving the changes.

Assessment 6 View and Analyze Data in PivotTable View

1. With the **LancasterClinic.accdb** database open, create a query in Design view with the following specifications:
   a. Add the Billing, Employees, and Clients tables to the design grid.
   b. Add the following fields from the specified tables:

DateOfService	=	Billing table	
ProviderNumber	=	Employees table	
ClientNumber	=	Clients table	
Hours	=	Billing table	

    c. Run the query.

    d. Save the query and name it *ProviderHours*.

2. Display the query in PivotTable view.

3. At the PivotTable layout, drag and drop the fields as follows:

    a. Drag the *ProviderNumber* field to the *Drop Row Fields Here* section.

    b. Drag the *ClientNumber* field to the *Drop Column Fields Here* section.

    c. Drag the *Hours* field to the *Drop Totals or Detail Fields Here* section.

    d. Drag the *DateOfService* field to the *Drop Filter Fields Here* section.

4. Remove the *PivotTable Field List* box from the screen.

5. Click the Quick Print button to print the query in PivotTable view.

6. In the *ProviderNumber* field, display only the hours for provider number 15.

7. Print the PivotTable and then redisplay all providers.

8. In the *DateOfService* field, display only hours for March 2, 2010.

9. Print the PivotTable and then redisplay all rental dates.

10. Switch to Datasheet view, save the query, and then close the query.

Assessment 7 Export a Table to Excel

1. With the **LancasterClinic.accdb** database open, export the Billing table to an Excel workbook.

2. Apply formatting to the cells in the Excel workbook to enhance the appearance of the data.

3. Change the page orientation to landscape.

4. Save, print, and then close the workbook.

5. Exit Excel.

Assessment 8 Merge Records to Create Letters in Word

1. With the **LancasterClinic.accdb** database open, merge data in the Clients table to a blank Word document. *Hint: Use the* **Merge** it with **Microsoft Office Word** *option from the More button in the Export group in the External Data tab.* You determine the fields to use in the inside address and an appropriate salutation. Type March 10, 2010 as the date of the letter and type the following text in the body of the document:

    The building of a new wing for the Lancaster Clinic will begin April 1, 2010. We are excited about this new addition to our clinic. With the new facilities, we will be able to offer additional community and group services along with enhanced child-play therapy treatment.

    During the construction, the main entrance will be moved to the north end of the building. Please use this entrance until the construction of the wing is completed. We apologize in advance for any inconvenience this causes you.

    Include an appropriate complimentary close for the letter. Use the name and title *Marianne Lambert, Clinic Director* for the signature and add your reference initials and the document name (**AccessL1_U2_A8.docx**).

2. Merge to a new document and then save the document with the name **AccessL1_U2_A8**.
3. Print the first two letters of the document and then close **AccessL1_U2_A8.docx**.
4. Save the main document as **ConstructionLetter** and then close **ConstructionLetter.docx**.
5. Exit Word.

Assessment 9 Import and Link Excel Data to an Access Table

1. With the **LancasterClinic.accdb** database open, import and link **ExcelU02_01.xlsx** into a new table named *StaffHours*.
2. Open the StaffHours table in Datasheet view.
3. Print and then close the StaffHours table.
4. Open **ExcelU02_01.xlsx** in Excel.
5. Insert a formula in cell D2 that multiplies B2 with C2 and then copy the formula down to cells D3 through D7.
6. Save and then close **ExcelU02_01.xlsx**.
7. Exit Excel.
8. In Access with the **LancasterClinic.accdb** database open, open the StaffHours table.
9. Print and then close the StaffHours table.

WRITING activities

The following activities give you the opportunity to practice your writing skills along with demonstrating an understanding of some of the important Access features you have mastered in this unit. Use correct grammar, appropriate word choices, and clear sentence constructions.

Activity 1 Add a Table to the Clinic Database

The director at Lancaster Clinic has asked you to add information to the **LancasterClinic.accdb** database on insurance companies contracted by the clinic. You need to create a table that will contain information on insurance companies. The director wants the table to include the insurance company name, address, city, state, and ZIP code along with a telephone number and the name of a representative. You determine the field names, data types, field sizes, and description for the table and then include the following information (in the appropriate fields):

Health Plus
4102 22nd Street
Philadelphia, PA 19166
(212) 555-0990
Representative: Byron Tolleson

Penn-State Health
5933 Lehigh Avenue
Philadelphia, PA 19148
(212) 555-3477
Representative: Tracey Pavone

Quality Medical
51 Cecil B. Moore Avenue
Philadelphia, PA 19168
(212) 555-4600
Representative: Lee Stafford

Delaware Health
4418 Front Street
Philadelphia, PA 19132
(212) 555-6770
Representative: Melanie Chon

Save, print, and then close the insurance company table. Open Word and then write a report to the clinic director detailing how you created the table. Include a title for the report, steps on how you created the table, and any other pertinent information. Save the completed report and name it **AccessL1_U2_Act1**. Print and then close **AccessL1_U2_Act1.docx**.

Activity 2 Merge Records to Create Letters to Insurance Companies

Merge data in the insurance company database to a blank Word document. You determine the fields to use in the inside address and an appropriate salutation. Compose a letter to the insurance companies informing them that Lancaster Clinic is providing mental health counseling services to people with health insurance through their company. You are sending an informational brochure about Lancaster Clinic and are requesting information from the insurance companies on services and service limitations. Include an appropriate complimentary close for the letter. Use the name and title *Marianne Lambert, Clinic Director* for the signature and add your reference initials. When the merge is completed, name the document containing the merged letters **AccessL1_U2_Act2**. Print the first two letters in the merged document and then close **AccessL1_U2_Act2.docx**. Close the main document without saving it and then exit Word. Close the **LancasterClinic.accdb** database.

Health Information Search

In this activity, you will search the Internet for information on a health concern or disease that interests you. You will be looking for specific organizations, interest groups, or individuals who are somehow connected to the topic you have chosen. Your topic may be an organization that raises money to support research, it may be a support group that posts information or answers questions, or you may find information about clinics or doctors who specialize in your topic. Try to find at least ten different groups that support the health concern you are researching.

Create a database in Access and create a table that includes information from your search. Design the table so that you can store the name, address, phone number, and Web address of the organizations you find. You will also want to identify the connection the group has to your topic (supports research, interest group, treats patients, etc.). Create a report to summarize your findings. In Microsoft Word, create a letter that you can use to write for further information about the organization. Use the names and addresses in your database to merge with the letter. Select and then print the first two letters that result from the merge. Finally, write a paragraph describing information you learned about the health concern that you previously did not know.

City Improvement Projects

In this activity, you are working with the city council in your area to keep the public informed of the progress being made on improvement projects throughout the city. These projects are paid for through tax dollars voted on by the public, and the city council feels that an informed public leads to a good voter turnout when it is time to make more improvements.

Your job is to create a database and a table in the database that will store the following information for each project: a project ID number, a description of the project, the budgeted dollar amount to be spent, the amount spent so far, the amount of time allocated to the project, and the amount of time spent so far. Enter five city improvement projects into the table (sample data created by you). Create a query based on the table that calculates the percent of budgeted dollars spent so far and the percent of budgeted time spent so far. Print the table and the query.

INDEX

Microsoft® access

Making Access Work for You!

A well designed database provides solid footing for a business to grow and prosper.

A house or an office tower is built upon a good foundation to provide lifelong support and to provide a stable base upon which the rest of the rooms and floors are built. Using this analogy, consider that databases form the foundation that supports a business and provides the stable base upon which a business can grow. Without secure, timely access to its data, a business will quickly deteriorate. Learning how to best use the more advanced features in Microsoft Access will help you build databases that can support a business well into the future.

Use Field Properties such as *Field Size*, *Input Mask*, and *Allow Zero Length* to place restrictions on the number of characters and the type of characters that are allowed to be entered into a field. The *Required* property in this example caused the Microsoft Office Access message box to appear indicating the field cannot be left empty.

General	Lookup	
Field Size	10	
Format		
Input Mask	00000\-0000;;#	
Caption	ZIP Code	
Default Value		
Validation Rule		
Validation Text		
Required	Yes	
Allow Zero Length	No	
Indexed	No	
Unicode Compression	Yes	
IME Mode	No Control	
IME Sentence Mode	None	
Smart Tags		

City	State	ZIP Code	Home Phone	Cell Phone	Birth Date	Category
Apache Junction	AZ	85220-4956	602-555-1587	602-555-3496	May 03 1964	Gold
Mesa	AZ	85207-6501	480-555-1385	480-555-1699	Oct 15 1977	Silver
Mesa	AZ					

Microsoft Office Access

⚠ You must enter a value in the 'Members.ZIP' field.

[OK]   [Help]

Organizing Information

Each field in a table has a set of characteristics or attributes called ***properties*** that control how the field looks and behaves in the table, form, query, or report. Learning about best practices in table design and how to use various properties to control and validate data input saves time and reduces errors. For example, you can create custom input masks that restrict data entered into a field to alphabetic characters, numbers, or a combination thereof. Each character can be a required entry or an optional entry. Properties such as formats, input masks, and limited lookup lists help to make sure employees follow established business policies.

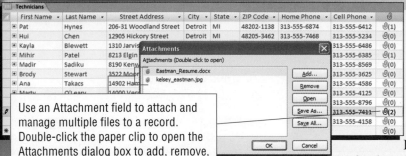

Use an Attachment field to attach and manage multiple files to a record. Double-click the paper clip to open the Attachments dialog box to add, remove, open, or export an attached file.

Use the new Attachment data type to create a field in which you can attach and manage multiple files to be stored with a record such as a picture, a resume, a specifications document, or any external file that you want to bring into the database.

Lookup lists can be used to select multiple values from a drop-down list to be stored in a field or to choose the field value from a list of records in another table. Sorting and finding records can be made more efficient by creating *indexes,* which speed up processing so that records are displayed faster. Consider creating an index for a field that is the frequent target of a sort or find operation. Indexes can be based on a single field or on multiple fields.

Create custom forms by adding a field that calculates a value based on other field values within the form. Save time for end users by creating a form with multiple pages and subforms that displays related information in one screen. The users of the database will appreciate not having to open more than one object to view or update information to the tables. Add graphics to forms such as a logo, a picture, clip art, or draw lines for that finishing touch that improves the form's appearance.

Microsoft Access includes a variety of tools with which you can manage and secure data in a database. Set startup options and protect objects to prevent users from unintentionally making changes to the design of tables, forms, queries, or reports. Assign a password to a database to prevent the database from being opened by unauthorized personnel.

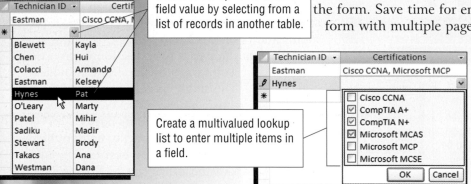

Create a lookup list to enter a field value by selecting from a list of records in another table.

Create a multivalued lookup list to enter multiple items in a field.

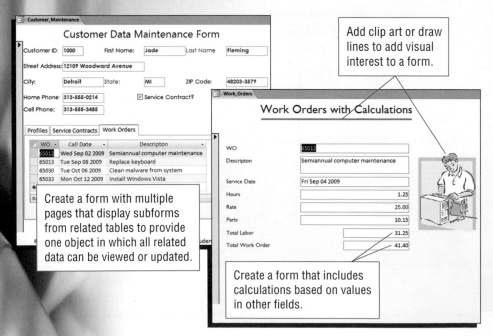

Add clip art or draw lines to add visual interest to a form.

Create a form with multiple pages that display subforms from related tables to provide one object in which all related data can be viewed or updated.

Create a form that includes calculations based on values in other fields.

Analyzing Information

Extracting records from tables using select queries allows you to view information from multiple tables in a single datasheet or analyze information based on multiple criteria. Design and create a parameter query to select records by a field with criteria you will enter when the query is run. Add calculations to a query and nest one query inside another to perform complex calculations or reuse a query object.

Action queries add new meaning to the term *multitasking.* Envision a query that finds and displays records that meet your criteria and then changes data in those selected records, all in one operation. This is exactly what occurs in four types of action queries in Microsoft Access: delete, append, make-table, and update. Not only will using an action query save time and effort but you can rest assured that *only the selected records* have been changed, thereby reducing the potential for errors. Imagine the task of having to change all records in a table due to a price increase. In mere seconds, you can create an update query and the price increase is instantly applied.

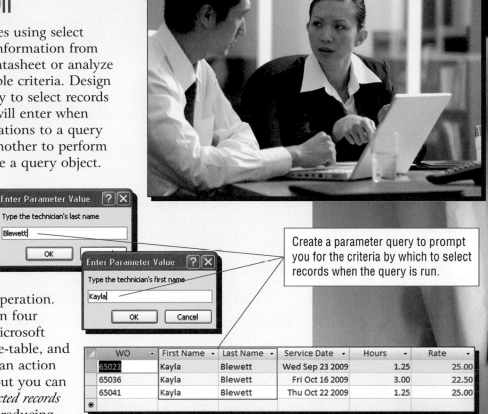

Create a parameter query to prompt you for the criteria by which to select records when the query is run.

Suppose you need Excel's analysis tools to help with a business decision. With just a few mouse clicks, you can export data from Microsoft Access tables and queries for analysis in Excel. Integration between Microsoft Access and Microsoft Excel is seamless so you can focus on what you need to do rather than how to do it. You can also export a report as a rich text format file (rtf) that can be opened and edited in Microsoft Word.

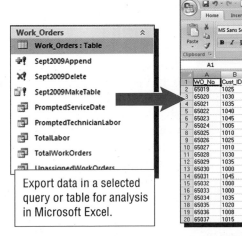

Export data in a selected query or table for analysis in Microsoft Excel.

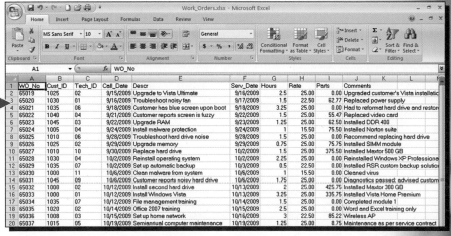

Linking two tables within Access or linking an Excel worksheet to an Access table is one more way in which you can save time and reduce errors. Changes made to data in either linked Access table or changes made in a linked Excel worksheet are updated automatically.

Presenting Information

Embed a subreport within a report to provide information from more than one source in the same printout. Include calculations such as totals and averages in the report and spruce up its appearance by drawing lines or adding pictures such as a company logo. Producing output in an easy-to-read-and-understand format involves techniques similar to those used with forms. Professional-looking reports that meet the needs of a variety of stakeholders are just a few mouse clicks away.

Embed a subreport to print data from more than one object.

RSR Computer Service Work Orders

Add clip art and draw lines to add visual interest.

WO	CustID	First Name	Last Name	Call Date	Descripton
65019	1025	Lana	Bodzek	Tue Sep 15 2009	Upgrade to Vista Ultimate

Service Date	Total Labor	Parts	Total Work Order
Wed Sep 16 2009	$62.50	$0.00	$62.50

WO	CustID	First Name	Last Name	Call Date	Descripton
65020	1030	Adrian	Pierson	Wed Sep 16 2009	Troubleshoot noisy fan

Service Date	Total Labor	Parts	Total Work Order
Thu Sep 17 2009	$33.75	$62.77	$96.52

WO	CustID	First Name	Last Name	Call Date	Descripton
65021	1035	Josleyn	Woodside	Fri Sep 18 2009	Customer has blue screen upon boot

Service Date	Total Labor	Parts	Total Work Order
Fri Sep 18 2009	$81.25	$0.00	$81.25

Group and sort data in reports and include subtotals in each group and a grand total at the end of the report. Add a chart to a report to visually portray numerical data. Publish an Access report in PDF or XPS format to distribute the report to users who do not have Microsoft Access.

Work Orders by Month

Serv_Date by Month	WO	Cust_ID	Description of Call	Service Date	Total Labor	Parts	Total Work Order
September 2009							
	65019	1025	Upgrade to Vista Ultimate	16-Sep-09	$62.50	$0.00	$62.50
	65020	1030	Troubleshoot noisy fan	17-Sep-09	$33.75	$62.77	$96.52
	65021	1035	Customer has blue screen upon boot	18-Sep-09	$81.25	$0.00	$81.25
	65022	1040	Customer reports screen is fuzzy	22-Sep-09	$37.50	$55.47	$92.97
	65023	1045	Upgrade RAM	23-Sep-09	$31.25	$62.50	$93.75
	65024	1005	Install malware protection	24-Sep-09	$15.50	$75.50	$91.00
	65025	1010	Troubleshoot hard drive noise	28-Sep-09	$37.50	$0.00	$37.50
	65026	1025	Upgra		$18.75	$75.75	$94.50
						Month Total:	649.99
October 2009							
	65027	1010	Replace hard drive	02-Oct-09	$37.50	$375.50	$413.00
	65028	1030	Reinstall operating system	02-Oct-09	$56.25	$0.00	$56.25
	65029	1035	Set up automatic backup	03-Oct-09	$11.25	$0.00	$11.25
	65031	1045	Customer reports noisy hard drive	06-Oct-09	$43.75	$0.00	$43.75

Add subtotals to grouped selections within a report.

Learning the more advanced features of Microsoft Access will help you to manage data efficiently. You will be able to use tools that will protect the business investment thereby building a solid foundation for your career as well.

Microsoft®

access

Unit 1: Advanced Tables, Relationships, Queries, and Forms

- ➤ Designing the Structure of Tables
- ➤ Designing and Building Relationships and Lookup Fields
- ➤ Advanced Query Techniques
- ➤ Creating and Using Custom Forms

Benchmark Microsoft® Access 2007 Level 2

Microsoft Certified Application Specialist Skills—Unit 1

Reference No.	Skill	Pages
1	**Structuring a Database**	
1.1	Define data needs and types	
1.1.1	Define table fields	8-9
1.1.2	Define appropriate table field data types for fields in each table	10-12, 25-27, 57-59
1.1.3	Define tables in databases	8-13, 62-63
1.2	Define and print table relationships	
1.2.1	Create relationships	39-43, 48-49
1.2.2	Modify relationships	43-47
1.3	Add, set, change, or remove primary keys	
1.3.2	Define and modify multifield primary keys	51-52
2	**Creating and Formatting Database Elements**	
2.3	Modify tables	
2.3.1	Modify table properties	13-15
2.4	Create fields and modify field properties	
2.4.1	Create commonly used fields	25-27
2.4.2	Modify field properties	16-24, 25-27
2.4.3	Create and modify multivalued fields	57-59
2.4.4	Create and modify attachment fields	28-30
2.5	Create forms	
2.5.1	Create forms using Design view	106-109
2.5.2	Create datasheet forms	135-137
2.5.5	Create subforms	119-124
2.7	Modify the design of reports and forms	
2.7.1	Add controls	107-111
2.7.2	Bind controls to fields	109-113
2.7.3	Define the tab order of controls	116-117
2.7.4	Format controls	113-116, 125-134
2.7.5	Arrange controls	127-134
3	**Entering and Modifying Data**	
3.3	Find and replace data	137-140
3.4	Attach documents to and detach from records	28-30
4	**Creating and Modifying Queries**	
4.1	Create queries	
4.1.2	Create queries based on more than one table	79-81
4.1.3	Create action queries	91-97
4.1.5	Create subqueries	85-88
4.1.6	Save filters as queries	74-75
4.2	Modify queries	
4.2.1	Add tables to and remove tables from queries	82-85
4.2.2	Add criteria to queries	76-78
4.2.3	Create joins	79-81
4.2.5	Add aliases to query fields	89-91
5	**Presenting and Sharing Data**	
5.1	Sort data	
5.1.4	Sort data within forms	137-140
5.2	Filter data	
5.2.1	Filter data within tables	74-75

Note: The Level 1 and Level 2 texts each address approximately half of the Microsoft Certified Application Specialist skills. Complete coverage of the skills is offered in the combined Level 1 and Level 2 text titled *Benchmark Series Microsoft® Access 2007: Levels 1 and 2,* which has been approved as certified courseware and which displays the Microsoft Certified Application Specialist logo on the cover.

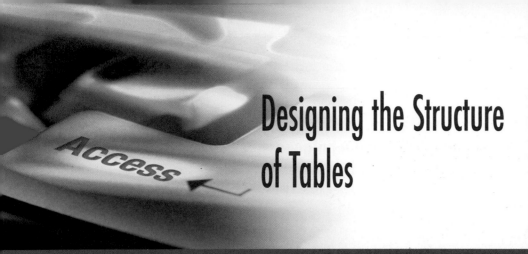

CHAPTER 1

Designing the Structure of Tables

Upon successful completion of Chapter 1, you will be able to:

- Design the structure of tables to optimize efficiency and accuracy of data
- Select the appropriate field data type based on analysis of source data
- Add captions to fields for descriptive purposes
- Disallow blank field values
- Allow or disallow zero-length strings in a field
- Create a custom format for text, number, and date fields
- Create a custom input mask
- Define rich text formatting for a memo field
- Store history of changes to a memo field
- Define and use an attachment field with multiple attachments

access Chapter 1

Tutorial 1.1
Modifying Advanced Tables

Tables in Access are the first objects created in a new database since a query, form, or report relies on a table for the data source. Creating a new database involves planning the number of tables needed and the fields that will be included in each table. In this chapter you will learn the basic steps to plan a new database by analyzing existing data. In addition to organizing the data structure, you will also learn to select appropriate data types and use field properties to control, restrict, or otherwise validate data.

In this chapter, prior knowledge of the steps to create a new table in Design view, including changing the data type and field size and assigning the primary key, as well as the meaning of the terms *field*, *record*, *table*, and *database* is assumed.

Note: Before beginning computer projects, copy to your storage medium the Access2007L2C1 subfolder from the Access2007L2 folder on the CD that accompanies this textbook. Steps on how to copy a folder are presented on the inside of the back cover of this textbook. Do this every time you start a chapter's projects.

Project 1 Create Tables by Analyzing Sample Data and Applying Database Design Techniques

You will analyze sample data to decide how to structure a new database to track computer service work orders using best practices for table design and then create the tables.

Designing Tables and Fields for a New Database

Most of the databases you will work with in the workplace will have already been created by database designers. An introduction to the process involved in creating a new database will be of benefit to you so that you will better understand the reasons why objects are organized and related. Creating a new database from scratch involves careful advance planning. Database designers spend considerable time analyzing existing data and asking questions of users and managers. Designers will want to know how data will be used to help identify the required forms, queries, and reports to be generated from the data. Often, designers work backwards by modeling a report required from the database to see data that is required to populate the report. A data dictionary (a list of fields and attributes of each field) is then compiled from which the designer can next map out the number of required tables.

In Project 1, you will be analyzing a sample work order for RSR Computer Services. RSR started out as a small computer service company. The owners used Excel worksheets to enter information from service records and then produce revenue reports. The company's success has led to a need to move to a relational database to track customer information. The owners want to be able to generate queries and reports from the service records to assist with decision making. Examine the data in a typical work order shown in Figure 1.1. The work order form that the technicians have been filling out at the customer site will be used as the input source document for the database.

Figure 1.1 Sample Work Order for RSR Computer Services

RSR Computer Services
WORK ORDER

Contact Date: 9/2/2009
Work Order Number: 65012

Customer Name and Address:
Jade Fleming
12109 Woodward Avenue
Detroit, MI 48203-3579

Telephone: 313-555-0214
Cell: 313-555-3485

Service Contract? No

Description of service request:
Semiannual desktop computer cleaning and maintenance

Technician assigned: Kelsey Eastman
Date of service: 9/4/2009

Hours:	1.25
Rate:	25.00
Total Labor:	31.25
Parts:	10.15
Total Due:	41.40

Comments:
"H" key is sticking; cleaning did not resolve. Customer is considering buying new keyboard.

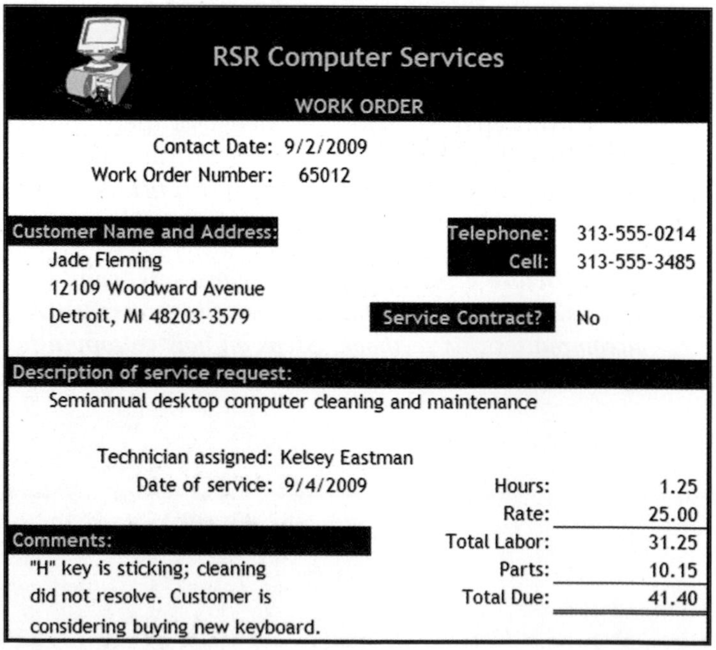

Designers analyze all input documents and output requirements to capture the entire set of data elements that need to be created. Once all data has been identified, the designer maps out the number of tables required to hold the data. During the process in which the designer is mapping the tables and fields to be associated with each table, the designer incorporates the following techniques:

- Each table is considered an *entity* and should describe a single person, place, object, event, or other subject. Each table should store facts that are related to the entity's subject only.

- Data should be segmented until it is in its smallest unit that you will want to manipulate. For example, in the work order shown in Figure 1.1, the customer's name and address would be split into separate fields for first name, last name, street address, city, state, and ZIP code. This approach provides maximum flexibility for generating other objects and allows the designer to sort or filter by any individual data element.

- Do not include fields that can be calculated by using data in other fields. For example, the total labor and total due amounts in the work order can be calculated using other numeric data elements.

- Identify fields that can be used to apply Boolean logic to answer questions from the data. Boolean expressions are sometimes referred to as conditional expressions and generate a true or false answer. Queries and reports can be designed to extract information based on the results of a conditional expression. For example, the technician enters on the work order whether the customer has a service contract or not. A field that stores a Yes or No (true or false) condition for the service contract data element allows the business to generate reports of customers that have subscribed to a service contract (true condition) and those that have not subscribed (false condition).

- Identify a field in each table that will hold data that uniquely identifies each record. This field becomes the primary key.

- Determine each table that will relate to another table and the field you will use to join the two when you create relationships. Identifying relationships at this stage helps you determine if you need to add a field to a related table to allow you to join the table.

- Relational databases are built upon the concept that data redundancy should be avoided. Data redundancy means data in one table is repeated in another table. Repeating fields in multiple tables wastes storage space, promotes inefficiency, inconsistency, and increases the likelihood that errors will be made when adding, updating, and deleting field values.

The design process may seem time-consuming; however, the time expended to produce a well-designed database saves time later. A database that is poorly designed will likely have logic errors or structure errors that require redefining of data or objects after live data has been entered.

Diagramming a Database

Designers often create a visual representation of the database's structure in a diagram similar to the one shown in Figure 1.2. Each table is represented in a box with the table name at the top of the box. Within each box, the fields that will be stored in the table are listed with the field names that will be used when the tables are created. The primary key field is denoted with an asterisk. Tables that will be joined have lines drawn connecting them together. You will design and build the relationships for this database in Chapter 2.

Figure 1.2 Diagram of Table Structure for RSR Computer Service Database

Customers
*Cust_ID
Fname
Lname
StreetAdd
City
State
ZIP
HPhone
CPhone
Serv_Cont

Service_Contracts
*Cust_ID
SC_No
Start_Date
End_Date
Fee_Pd

Work_Orders
*WO_No
Cust_ID
Tech_ID
Call_Date
Descr
Serv_Date
Hours
Rate
Parts
Comments

Technicians
*Tech_ID
SSN
Fname
Lname
StreetAdd
City
State
ZIP
HPhone
CPhone

Notice that many of the field names in the diagram are abbreviated. Although a field name can contain up to 64 characters, field names that are short enough to be understood are easier to manage and type into expressions. You will learn about the *Caption* property later in this chapter that is used to enter a more descriptive heading for viewing data. Also notice that none of the field names contain spaces. Spaces are allowed in field names; however, most database designers use underscore characters (_) or hyphens (-) as separators in field names.

Assigning Data Types

Each field is assigned a data type by the designer based on the type of entries that the designer wants to allow into the field and the operations that will need to be used to manipulate the data. Selecting the appropriate data type is important since restrictions will be placed on a field based upon the field's data type. For example, in a field designated with the Number data type, only numbers, a period to represent a decimal point, and a plus or minus sign can be entered into the field in a datasheet or form. Table 1.1 reviews the 10 available data types.

Table 1.1 Data Types

Data Type	Description
Text	Alphanumeric data up to 255 characters such as a name or address. Text fields can also store values such as a customer number, telephone number, or social security number that is used as an identifier and not for calculating.
Memo	Alphanumeric data longer than 255 characters with up to 65,535 characters displayed in the field. Use a Memo field to store longer passages of text in a record. You can add rich text formatting in a Memo field such as bold, italics, or font color.
Number	Positive or negative values that can be used in calculations. Do not use for monetary values (see Currency).
Date/Time	Accepts only valid dates and times into the field. Use to ensure dates and times are entered and sorted properly.
Currency	Holds monetary values. Access does not round off during calculations.
AutoNumber	Field value is automatically assigned by Access by sequentially incrementing the field value by 1 when a new record is added.
Yes/No	Entry in the field is restricted to conditional logic of Yes or No, True or False, On or Off.
OLE Object	Stores an embedded or linked object created in other Microsoft Office applications.
Hyperlink	Links to a URL.
Attachment	Attach a file to the record such as a picture, Word document, or Excel worksheet.

Using the Field Size Property to Restrict Field Length

By default, text fields are set to a width of 255 in the *Field Size* property. Access uses only the amount of space needed for the data that is entered even when the field size allows for more characters. Consider changing the *Field Size* property to restrict the length of data that is allowed into the field. For example, if RSR Computer Services has developed a 4-character numbering system for customer numbers, setting the field size for the *Cust_ID* field to *4* will ensure that no one enters a customer number longer than 4 characters by accident since Access will disallow all characters typed after the fourth character.

Figure 1.3 shows the table structure diagram for the RSR Computer Services database expanded to include each field's data type and field size property. You will use this diagram in Project 1a to create the tables.

Figure 1.3 Expanded Table Structure Diagram with Data Types and Field Sizes for Project 1a

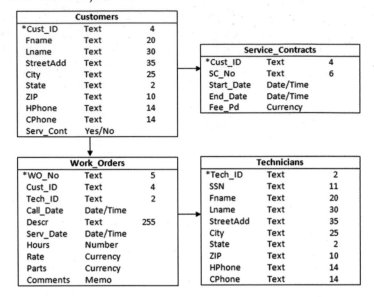

Project 1a Creating Tables in Design View

1. Start Access.
2. At the *Getting Started with Microsoft Office Access* screen, complete the following steps to create a new database to store the work orders for RSR Computer Services:
   a. Click *Blank Database* in the *New Blank Database* section of the center pane.
   b. Select the existing text in the *File Name* text box in the *Blank Database* section of the right pane and then type **RSRComputerServ**.
   c. Click the Browse button (displays as a folder icon) at the right of the *File Name* text box. At the File New Database dialog box, navigate to the Access2007L2C1 folder on your storage medium and then click OK.
   d. Click the Create button in the *Blank Database* section of the right pane.
3. Close the Table1 blank table datasheet that displays.
4. Click the Create tab and then click the Table Design button in the Tables group. Create the fields shown in the Customers table in Figure 1.3.
5. Assign the primary key to the *Cust_ID* field.
6. Save the table and name it **Customers**.

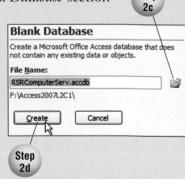

Step 2c

Step 2d

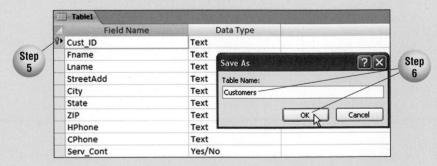

Step 5

Step 6

7. Close the table.
8. Create the Service_Contracts, Work_Orders, and Technicians tables shown in Figure 1.3 by completing steps similar to those in Steps 4–7. Assign the primary key in each table using the field denoted with an asterisk in Figure 1.3.
9. Make sure all tables are closed.

Restricting Data Entry and Data Display Using Field Properties

The properties that are available for a field depend on the field's data type. For example, a Yes/No field has 7 properties while a Text field has 14 and a Number field has 12. Use the options available in the *Field Properties* section in Design view to place restrictions on data accepted into the field and to ensure data is entered and displayed consistently. Field properties should be defined for the fields before other objects such as forms or reports are created. The properties carry over to the other objects and taking the time to define the properties when the table is created reduces the number of times you have to make changes if you decide to modify properties later on.

You have already used the *Field Size* property in Project 1a to restrict the length of entries allowed in fields. In this section you will learn to apply other field properties to fields to further control data entry and display.

Adding Captions

The *Caption* property allows you to enter a more descriptive title for the field if the field name has been truncated or abbreviated. You can also use a caption to display spaces between words in a field name rather than underscore or hyphen characters. In the absence of an entry in the *Caption* property, Access displays the field name in datasheets, queries, forms, and reports.

Requiring Data in a Field

A field that you want to make sure is never left empty when a new record is added can be controlled using the *Required* field property. By default, the *Required* property is set to No. Change this value to Yes to make sure data is typed into the field when a new record is added. For example, you can force all new records to have a ZIP code entry. You do not need to set this property for a field that is defined as a primary key, since a primary key field cannot be left empty.

Disallowing Zero-Length Strings in a Field

A zero-length field can be used to indicate a value is not going to be entered into the field because the field does not apply to the current record. When you are entering a new record and leave a field blank, Access records a null value in the field. For example, if you are adding a new record for a customer and you do not know the customer's cell phone number, you can leave the field empty with the intention of updating the field at a later time. This is an example of leaving the field blank with a null value. Alternatively, if you know the customer does not own a cell phone, you can enter a zero-length string in the field to indicate no field value applies to this record.

QUICK STEPS

Add a Caption
1. Open table in Design view.
2. Activate desired field.
3. Click in *Caption* property box.
4. Type descriptive text.
5. Save table.

Require Data in Field
1. Open table in Design view.
2. Activate desired field.
3. Click in *Required* property box.
4. Click down-pointing arrow.
5. Click *Yes.*
6. Save table.

Disallow Zero-Length String in Field
1. Open table in Design view.
2. Activate desired field.
3. Click in *Allow Zero Length* property box.
4. Click down-pointing arrow.
5. Click *No.*
6. Save table.

To enter a zero-length string, type two double quotation symbols with no space between (""). When viewing the field in a datasheet, query, form, or report, you cannot distinguish between a field with a null value and a field with a zero-length string because both display as blanks; however, you can create a control in a form or report that returns a user-defined message in the blank fields that distinguishes one from the other. For example, you could display the word *Unknown* in a field with a null value and *Not applicable* in a field with a zero-length string. In some cases, you will want to see in a form or report which records will not have a value in the field as opposed to those records that are incomplete.

By default, Text, Memo, and Hyperlink data fields can have zero-length strings entered into the field. Change *Allow Zero Length* to *No* to disallow zero-length strings.

Project 1b — Modifying Field Properties to Add Captions and Disallow Blank Values in a Field

1. With the **RSRComputerServ.accdb** database open, add captions to the fields in the Customers table by completing the following steps:

a. Right-click *Customers : Table* in the navigation pane and then click *Design View* at the shortcut menu.

b. With *Cust_ID* the active field, click in the *Caption* property box in the *Field Properties* section and then type **Customer ID**.

c. Click in the *Fname* field row to activate the field, click in the *Caption* property box in the *Field Properties* section, and then type **First Name**.

d. Add captions to the following fields by completing a step similar to Step 1c.

Lname	**Last Name**
StreetAdd	**Street Address**
HPhone	**Home Phone**
CPhone	**Cell Phone**
Serv_Cont	**Service Contract?**

e. Click the Save button on the Quick Access toolbar.

f. Click the View button (do not click the down-pointing arrow on the button) to switch to Datasheet view and then select all columns in the datasheet. If necessary, click the Shutter Bar Open/Close button « to minimize the navigation pane.

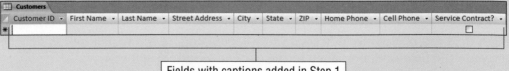

Fields with captions added in Step 1

g. Click the More button in the Records group in the Home tab, click *Column Width* at the drop-down list, and then click the Best Fit button at the Column Width dialog box. Best Fit adjusts the width to the length of the longest entry.

h. Click in the *Customer ID* field in the first row of the datasheet to deselect the columns.

2. Switch to Design View and click the Shutter Bar Open/Close button 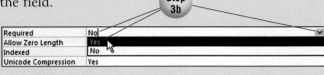 to redisplay the navigation pane if you minimized the pane in Step 1f.

3. You want to ensure that no record is entered without an entry in the *ZIP* field. You decide to disallow blank values in the field, including zero-length strings.

  a. Click in the *ZIP* field row to activate the field.

  b. Click in the *Required* property box in the *Field Properties* section (currently displays *No*), click the down-pointing arrow that appears, and then click *Yes* at the drop-down list.

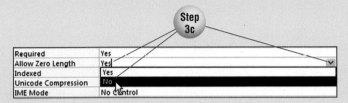

Step 3b

  c. Click in the *Allow Zero Length* property box (currently displays *Yes*), click the down-pointing arrow that appears, and then click *No* at the drop-down list.

Step 3c

  d. Save the changes to the table design.

4. Test the restrictions on the *ZIP* field using a new record by completing the following steps:

  a. Switch to Datasheet view.

  b. Add the following data in the fields indicated.

Customer ID	1000
First Name	Jade
Last Name	Fleming
Street Address	12109 Woodward Avenue
City	Detroit
State	MI

  c. At the *ZIP* field, press Enter or Tab to move past the field, leaving the field blank.

  d. Type 313-555-0214 in the *Home Phone* field.

  e. Type 313-555-3485 in the *Cell Phone* field.

  f. Press the spacebar in the *Service Contract?* field to insert a check mark in the check box.

  g. Press Enter. Access displays an error message since the record cannot be written to disk without an entry in the *ZIP* field.

  h. Click OK at the Microsoft Office Access message box.

  i. Click in the *ZIP* field, type 48203-3579, and then press Enter four times to move to the *Customer ID* field in the second row of the datasheet.

5. Close the Customers table.

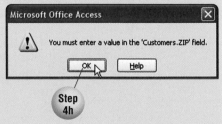

Step 4h

Format Text Field
1. Open table in Design view.
2. Activate desired field.
3. Click in *Format* property box.
4. Type desired format codes.
5. Save table.

Creating a Custom Format for a Text Field

The *Format* property controls how data is displayed in the field in the datasheet, query, form, or report. The available formats that you can use are dependent on the field's data type. Some data types have predefined formats available which can be selected from a drop-down list in the *Format* property box. No predefined formats exist for Text or Memo fields. If no predefined format exists or if the predefined format options do not meet your needs, you can create your own custom format. Table 1.2 displays commonly used format codes for text or memo fields. The *Format* property does NOT control how data is entered into the field. Formatting a field controls the display of accepted field values. See the section on input masks to learn how to control how data is entered.

Table 1.2 Format Codes for Text or Memo Fields

Code	Description	Format *Property Example*
@	Use as a placeholder, one symbol for each character position. Unused positions in a field value are replaced with blank spaces to the left of the text entered into the field.	@@@@ Field value is 123. Access displays one blank space followed by 123, left-aligned in the field.
!	Access fills the placeholder positions with characters from left to right instead of the default right to left sequence.	!@@@@ Field value entered is 123. Access displays 123 left-aligned in the field with one blank space after 3.
>	All text is converted to uppercase.	> Field value is mi. Access displays MI in the field.
<	All text is converted to lowercase.	< Field value is Jones@EMCP.NET. Access displays jones@emcp.net in the field.
[color]	Text is displayed in the font color specified. Available colors are: black, blue, cyan, green, magenta, red, yellow, and white.	[red]@@@@@-@@@@ Field value entered is 482033579. Access displays 48203-3579.

Project 1c — Formatting Text Fields Using a Custom Format

1. With the **RSRComputerServ.accdb** database open, format the *State* field to ensure all text is displayed uppercase by completing the following steps:
   a. Right-click *Customers : Table* in the navigation pane and then click *Design View* at the shortcut menu.
   b. Click in the *State* field row to activate the field.
   c. Click in the *Format* property box and then type >.
   d. Save the table.

   Step 1c:
General	Lookup	
Field Size		2
Format		>
Input Mask		

2. Format the *ZIP* field to fill the field with characters from left to right, display the text in red, and provide for the five-plus-four–character U.S. ZIP code separated by a hyphen by completing the following steps:
   a. Click in the *ZIP* field row to activate the field.
   b. Click in the *Format* property box and then type ![red]@@@@@-@@@@.
   c. Save the table.

   Step 2b:
General	Lookup	
Field Size		10
Format		![red]@@@@@-@@@@
Input Mask		

3. Test the custom formats in the *State* and *ZIP* fields using a new record by completing the following steps:
   a. Switch to Datasheet view and then Best Fit the *ZIP* field.
   b. Add the following data in a new record. Type the text for the *State* field as indicated in lowercase text. Notice when you move to the next field, Access automatically converts the lowercase text to uppercase. As you type the ZIP text, notice the text is displayed in red. Since no field values are entered for the last four characters of the ZIP field, Access displays blank spaces in these positions.

Customer ID	1005
First Name	Cayla
Last Name	Fahri
Street Address	12793 Riverdale Avenue
City	Detroit
State	mi
ZIP	48223
Home Phone	313-555-6845
Cell Phone	313-555-4187
Service Contract?	Press spacebar for *Yes*

4. Look at the data in the *ZIP* field for the first record. This data was entered before you formatted the *ZIP* field. Since a hyphen was typed when the data was entered and the field is now formatted to automatically add the hyphen, two hyphen characters appear in the existing record. Edit the field value for record 1 in the *ZIP* field to remove the extra hyphen.

   Step 4:
Customer ID	First Name	Last Name	Street Address	City	State	ZIP
1000	Jade	Fleming	12109 Woodward /	Detroit	MI	48203-3579
1005	Cayla	Fahri	12793 Riverdale Av	Detroit	MI	48223-

5. Adjust all column widths to Best Fit.
6. Display the datasheet in Print Preview. Change the orientation to landscape. Set the margins to a top margin of 1-inch and the bottom, left, and right margins of 0.25 inch. Print the datasheet and then close Print Preview.
7. Close the Customers table. Click Yes when prompted to save changes to the table layout.

Format Number Field
1. Open table in Design view.
2. Activate desired field.
3. Click in *Format* property box.
4. Type desired format codes or select from predefined list.
5. Save table.

Creating a Custom Format for a Numeric Field

Access provides predefined formats for the Number, AutoNumber, and Currency fields that include options for fixed decimal places, commas in the thousands, the currency symbol, percentages and exponential notation. Table 1.3 displays commonly used format codes that you can use to create a custom format. Use the placeholders shown in Table 1.3 in combination with other characters such as a dollar symbol, comma, and period to create the desired custom numeric format.

Numeric formats can specify up to four different formats for displaying positive values, negative values, zero values, and null values. Examine the following custom format code:

#,###.00;-#,###.00[Red];0.00;"Unknown"

Each of the four sections is separated with a semicolon (;). The first section *#,###.00* defines the format for positive values that includes the comma in thousands and two decimal places with zeros used if no decimal value is entered. The second section *-#,###.00[Red]* defines negative values with the same placeholders as positive but starts the field with a minus symbol and displays the numbers in red. The third section *0.00* instructs Access to show 0.00 in the field if a zero is entered. Finally, a field value that is left blank would display the text "Unknown" in the field.

Table 1.3 Format Codes for Numeric Fields

Code	Description	Format *Property Example*
#	Used as a placeholder to display a number.	#.## Field value entered is 123.45. Access displays 123.45 in the field. Note that the number of placeholder positions does not restrict the data entered into the field.
0	Used as a placeholder to display a number. Access displays a zero in place of a position for which no value is entered.	000.00 Field value entered is 55.4. Access displays 055.40 in the field.
%	Multiplies the value times 100 and adds a percent symbol.	#.0% Field value entered is .1242. Access displays 12.4% in the field.

Project 1d Formatting Numeric Fields Using a Custom Format and a Predefined Format

1. With the **RSRComputerServ.accdb** database open, format the *Rate* field with a custom format by completing the following steps:
   a. Open the Work_Orders table in Design view.
   b. Make the *Rate* field active.
   c. Click in the *Format* property box, delete the current entry, and then type #.00[blue];-#.00[red];0.00;"Not Available".

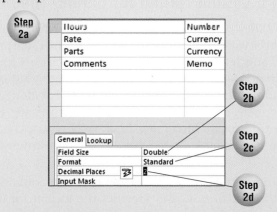

Step 1b

Hours	Number
Rate	Currency
Parts	Currency
Comments	Memo

Field Properties

General | Lookup

Format	#.00[blue];-#.00[red];0.00;"Not Available"
Decimal Places	Auto

Step 1c

   d. Save the table.
2. Format the *Hours* field using a predefined format and change the field size by completing the following steps:
   a. Make the *Hours* field active.
   b. Click in the *Field Size* property box, click the down-pointing arrow that appears, and then click *Double*. The default setting for a Number field is *Long Integer*, which stores whole numbers only, meaning a decimal value entered into the field is rounded. Changing the field size property to *Double* allows you to store decimal values.
   c. Click in the *Format* property box, click the down-pointing arrow that appears, and then click *Standard* at the drop-down list.
   d. Click in the *Decimal Places* property box, click the down-pointing arrow that appears and then click *2* at the pop-up list.

Step 2a

Hours	Number
Rate	Currency
Parts	Currency
Comments	Memo

General | Lookup

Field Size	Double
Format	Standard
Decimal Places	2
Input Mask	

Step 2b

Step 2c

Step 2d

   e. Save the table.
3. Switch to Datasheet view.

4. Test the custom format and the predefined format using a new record by completing the following step:

    a. Add the following data in a new record.

WO_No	**65012**
Cust_ID	**1000**
Tech_ID	**11**
Call_Date	**09-02-2009**
Descr	**Semiannual desktop computer cleaning and maintenance**
Serv_Date	**09-04-2009**
Hours	**1.25**
Rate	**25**
Parts	**10.15**
Comments	**"H" key is sticking; cleaning did not resolve. Customer is considering buying a new keyboard.**

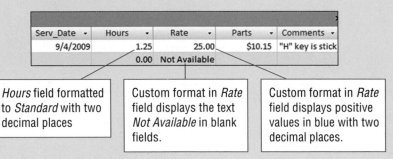

Hours field formatted to *Standard* with two decimal places

Custom format in *Rate* field displays the text *Not Available* in blank fields.

Custom format in *Rate* field displays positive values in blue with two decimal places.

5. Close the Work_Orders table.

QUICK STEPS

Format Date Field
1. Open table in Design view.
2. Activate desired field.
3. Click in *Format* property box.
4. Type desired format codes or select from predefined list.
5. Save table.

Creating a Custom Format for a Date/Time Field

Access provides predefined formats for fields with a data type of Date/Time that provide for a variety of combinations of month, day, and year display options for dates, and hours and minutes display options for time. If the predefined formats do not meet your needs, you can create your own custom format using a combination of the codes described in Table 1.4 along with the desired symbols such as hyphens or slashes between parts of the date. If you do not specify a format option for a Date/Time field, Access displays the date in the format m/dd/yyyy. For example, in Project 1d, the date entered into the *Call_Date* field displayed as 9/02/2009.

A custom format for a Date/Time field can contain two sections separated by a semicolon. The first section specifies the format for displaying dates. To add a format for displaying times, type a semicolon and then add the format codes to specify the time.

Table 1.4 Format Codes for Date/Time Fields

Code	Description
d or dd	Displays the day of the month as one digit (d) or two digits (dd)
ddd or dddd	Spells out the day of the week abbreviated (ddd) or in full (dddd)
m or mm	Displays the month as one digit (m) or two digits (mm)
mmm or mmmm	Spells out the month abbreviated (mmm) or in full (mmmm)
yy or yyyy	Displays the year as the last two digits (yy) or all four digits (yyyy)
h or hh	Displays the hour as one digit (h) or two digits (hh)
n or nn	Displays the minutes as one digit (n) or two digits (nn)
s or ss	Displays the seconds as one digit (s) or two digits (ss)
AM/PM	Displays 12-hour clock values followed by AM or PM

Project 1e Formatting a Date Field Using a Custom Date Format

1. With the **RSRComputerServ.accdb** database open, format the *Call_Date* field with a custom format by completing the following steps:
   a. Open the Work_Orders table in Design view.
   b. Make *Call_Date* the active field.
   c. Click in the *Format* property box and then type **ddd mmm dd yyyy**. This format will display dates beginning with the day of the week in abbreviated form, followed by the month in abbreviated form, the day of the month as two digits, and then the year as four digits. A space separates each section of the date.

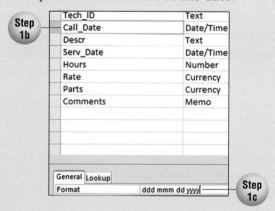

   d. Save the table.
2. Switch to Datasheet view.

3. Adjust the column width of the *Call_Date* field to Best Fit.

Step
3

Work_Orders				
WO_No ▾	Cust_ID ▾	Tech_ID ▾	Call_Date ▾	Descr
65012	1000	11	Wed Sep 02 2009	Semiannual

Custom format for *Call_Date*
field created in Step 1c

4. Switch to Design view.
5. Format the *Serv_Date* field using the same custom format as the one entered for *Call_Date* by completing steps similar to those in Steps 1b–1d.
6. Switch to Datasheet view and view the custom date format in both date fields.
7. Close the Work_Orders table.

QUICK STEPS

Create Custom Input Mask
1. Open table in Design view.
2. Activate desired field.
3. Click in *Input Mask* property box.
4. Type input mask codes.
5. Save table.

Restricting Data Entry Using Input Masks

An input mask is used when you want to control the type of data and the pattern in which the data is entered into a field. Using input masks ensures data is entered consistently in all records. For example, to force all telephone numbers to have the area code entered, you can create an input mask that requires ten numbers. Access includes the Input Mask Wizard that can be used to create an input mask for a text or date field. Commonly used masks are available within the wizard for telephone numbers, social security numbers, ZIP codes, dates, and times. To create your own input mask without the wizard, use the codes described in Table 1.5.

An input mask can contain up to three sections separated by semicolons. The first section contains the input mask codes for the data entry in the field. The second section instructs Access to store the display characters used in the field (such as hyphens or brackets) or not store the characters. A zero indicates that Access should store the characters. Leaving the second section blank means the display characters will not be stored. The third section specifies the placeholder character to display in the field.

An example of an input mask to store a four-digit customer identification number with a pound symbol (#) as the placeholder would be: 0000;;#. The first section *0000* is the four required digits for the customer identification. Since the mask contains no display characters, the second section is blank. The pound symbol after the second semicolon is the placeholder character.

In addition to the symbols in Table 1.5, you can include the format code > to force characters to be uppercase or < to force characters to be lowercase, as well as decimal points, hyphens, slashes, or other punctuation symbols between parts of the mask.

HINT

If you create a custom input mask for a date field that also contains a custom format, make sure the two properties do not conflict to avoid confusion. For example, a format code that displays the dates with the year first followed by the month and then the day would be confusing if the input mask required the date entered as month first followed by day and then year.

Table 1.5 Commonly Used Input Mask Codes

Code	Description
0	Required digit
9	Optional digit
#	Digit, space, plus or minus symbol. If no data is typed at this position, Access leaves a blank space.
L	Required letter
?	Optional letter
A	Required letter or digit
a	Optional letter or digit
&	Required character or space
C	Optional character or space
!	The field is filled from left to right instead of right to left.
\	Access displays the character that immediately follows in the field.

Project 1f Creating Custom Input Masks

1. With the **RSRComputerServ.accdb** database open, create a custom input mask for the work order numbers by completing the following steps:
   a. Open the Work_Orders table in Design view.
   b. With *WO_No* the active field, click in the *Input Mask* property box and then type 00000;;_. This mask will require that a five-digit work order number is entered. The underscore character is used as the placeholder character.

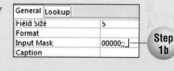
Step 1b

   c. Save the table.

2. Create an input mask to require the two date fields to be entered as three characters for the month with the first letter uppercase followed by two digits for the day and four digits for the year by completing the following steps:
   a. Make *Call_Date* the active field.
   b. Click in the *Input Mask* property box and then type >L<LL\-00\-0000;0;_. This mask requires three letters for the month with the first letter converted to uppercase and the remaining two letters converted to lowercase. The \- symbols instruct Access to display the hyphen character after the month as data is entered. Two digits are required for the day followed by another hyphen character and then four digits required for the year. The zero after the first semicolon instructs Access to store the display characters. Ending the mask, the underscore character is again used as the placeholder character.

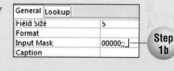

Step 2b

  c. Make *Serv_Date* the active field, click in the *Input Mask* property box, and then type **>L<LL\-00\-0000;0;_**.

  d. Save the table.

3. Switch to Datasheet view.

4. Test the input masks using a new record by completing the following steps:

  a. Click the New button in the Records group of the Home tab.

  b. Type **6501**. Notice that as soon as you type the first character, the placeholders appear in the field.

  c. Press Tab or Enter to move to the next field in the datasheet. Since the mask contained five zeros indicating five required digits, Access displays a message box informing you the value entered is not appropriate for the input mask.

  d. Click OK at the Microsoft Office Access message box.

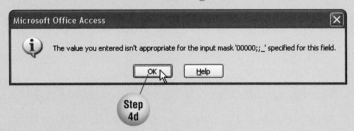

Step
4d

  e. Type **3** in the last position in the *WO_No* field and then press Tab or Enter to move to the next field.

  f. Type **1000** in the *Cust_ID* field and then press Tab or Enter.

  g. Type **10** in the *Tech_ID* field and then press Tab or Enter.

  h. Type **sep082009** in the *Call_Date* field and then press Tab or Enter. Notice that the placeholder characters appear as soon as you type the first letter. Notice also that you do not need to type the hyphen characters since Access moves automatically to the next position after the hyphen when you type the digits.

  i. Type **Replace keyboard** in the *Descr* field and then press Tab or Enter.

  j. Type **sep092009** in the *Serv_Date* field and then press Tab or Enter.

  k. Complete the remainder of the record as follows.

      Hours   .5
      Rate   25
      Parts   42.75
      Comments   **Serial Number AWQ-982358**

  l. Best Fit the *Serv_Date* field.

5. Close the Work_Orders table. Click Yes to save changes to the layout of the table.

      Other field properties that should be considered for data accuracy when designing database tables include the *Default Value*, *Validation Rule*, and *Validation Text* fields. Use the *Default Value* field to populate the field in new records with a field value that is used most often. For example, in a table where most employees have an address within the same city and state, you could use a default value to ensure consistent spelling and capitalization. The text appears automatically in the fields when new records are added to the table. The user can choose to either accept the default value by pressing Tab or Enter to move past the field, or type new data in the field.

Use the *Validation Rule* and *Validation Text* properties to enter conditional statements that are checked against new data entered into the field. Invalid entries that do not meet the conditional statement test are rejected. For example, a validation rule on a field used to store labor rates could check that a minimum labor rate value is entered in all records.

Project ② Work with Memo and Attachment Fields

You will edit properties for a Memo field, apply rich text formatting to text, and attach files to records using an Attachment field.

Working with Memo Fields

By default, Access formats a field that has been defined using Memo as the data type to plain text. In Access 2007, the ability to apply rich text formatting was added to Memo fields. For example, you can change the font, apply bold or italic formatting, or add font color to text in a Memo field. To add rich text formatting capability, change the *Text Format* property to *Rich Text*.

The *Append Only* property for a Memo field is set to *No* by default. Change the property to *Yes* to allow new data only into the field. You may need to scroll down the General tab in the *Field Properties* section to locate the *Append Only* property. When this property is set to *Yes*, Access maintains a history of additions to the field which can be viewed in the datasheet. Changing the *Append Only* property to *No* causes Access to delete any existing history.

QUICK STEPS

Enable Rich Text Formatting in Memo Field
1. Open table in Design view.
2. Select desired field defined as Memo.
3. Click in *Text Format* property box.
4. Click down-pointing arrow that appears.
5. Click *Rich Text*.
6. Click Yes.
7. Save table.

Set Memo Field as Append Only
1. Open table in Design view.
2. Select desired field defined as Memo.
3. If necessary, scroll down General tab.
4. Click in *Append Only* property box.
5. Click down-pointing arrow that appears.
6. Click *Yes*.
7. Save table.

Enabling Rich Text Formatting and Maintaining a History of Changes in a Memo Field

1. With the **RSRComputerServ.accdb** database open, enable rich text formatting and turn on tracking of history in a field defined as a Memo field by completing the following steps:
   a. Open the Work_Orders table in Design view.
   b. Make *Comments* the active field.
   c. Click in the *Text Format* property box, click the down-pointing arrow that appears, and then click *Rich Text* at the drop-down list.

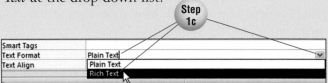

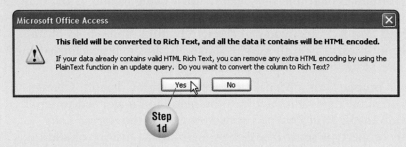

   d. At the Microsoft Office Access message box indicating that the field will be converted to Rich Text, click Yes.

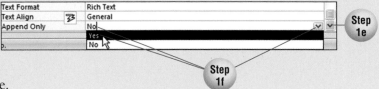

   e. If necessary, scroll down the General tab in the *Field Properties* section until you can see the *Append Only* property box.
   f. Click in the *Append Only* property box, click the down-pointing arrow that appears, and then click *Yes* at the drop-down list.

   g. Save the table.
2. Switch to Datasheet view.
3. Minimize the navigation pane and then adjust all column widths *except* the *Descr* and *Comments* fields to Best Fit.
4. Change the column width of the *Comments* field to 25.
5. Select the serial number text (AWQ-982358) in the second record in the *Comments* field and then apply bold and red font color using the buttons in the Font group of the Home tab. Click at the end of the serial number to deselect the text.

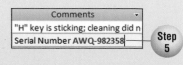

6. Click in the *Comments* field in the first record. Press the End key to move the insertion point to the end of the existing text. Press the spacebar once, type **Microsoft wireless keyboard.**, and then press Enter to save the changes and move to the next row.
7. Right-click the *Comments* field in the first record and then click *Show column history* at the shortcut menu.

8. Click OK after reading the text in the History for Comments dialog box.

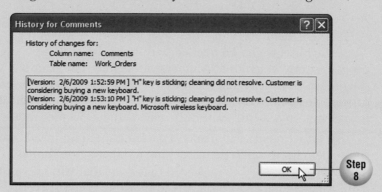

9. Click in the *Comments* field in the first record. Press the End key to move the insertion point to the end of the current text. Press the spacebar once, type **See work order 65013 for replacement keyboard request.**, and then press Enter.

10. Right-click the *Comments* field in the first record and then click *Show column history* at the shortcut menu.

11. Click OK after reading the text in the History for Comments dialog box.

When *Append Only* is *Yes*, Access keeps a history of additions to the field.

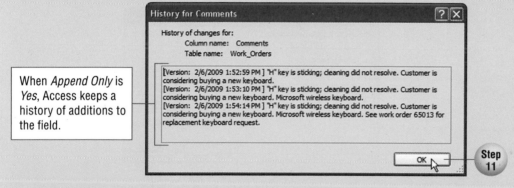

12. Display the datasheet in Print Preview. Change the orientation to landscape. Set the margins to a top margin of 1-inch and bottom, left, and right margins of 0.25-inch. Print the datasheet and then close Print Preview.

13. Close the Work_Orders table. Click Yes when prompted to save changes to the layout of the table.

Creating an Attachment Field and Attaching Files to Records

A new data type available in Access 2007 is an Attachment field. Using an Attachment field you can store several files in a single field attached to a record. The attachments can be opened within Access and are viewed and edited in the program from which the document originated. For example, you can attach a Word document to a field in a record. Opening the attached file in the Access table causes Microsoft Word to start with the document opened for editing. A file that is attached to a record cannot be larger than 256 megabytes.

An attachment field displays with a paper clip in Datasheet view. Double-click the paper clip to open the Attachments dialog box shown in Figure 1.4 in which you manage attached files. A field that is created with a data type set to Attachment cannot be changed. You can attach multiple files to a record provided the total size of all files attached does not exceed two gigabytes.

Create Attachment Field
1. Open table in Design view.
2. Click in first blank field row.
3. Type desired field name.
4. Click in *Data Type* column.
5. Click down-pointing arrow.
6. Click *Attachment*.
7. Save table.

Attach Files to Record
1. Open table in Datasheet view.
2. Double-click paper clip in desired record.
3. Click Add button.
4. Navigate to drive and/or folder location.
5. Double-click file name.
6. Click OK.

View Attached File
1. Open table in Datasheet view.
2. Double-click paper clip in desired record.
3. Double-click file name.
4. View file contents.
5. Exit source program.
6. Click OK.

Figure 1.4 Attachments Dialog Box

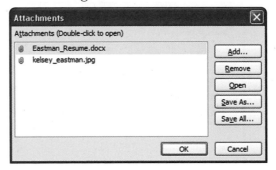

Project 2b — Creating an Attachment Field, Attaching Files to a Record, and Viewing the Contents of Attached Files

1. With the **RSRComputerServ.accdb** database open, create a new field in which you will store file attachments by completing the following steps:
   a. Open the Technicians table in Design view.
   b. Click in the blank row below *CPhone*, type **Attachments**, and then press Tab or Enter.
   c. Click the down-pointing arrow in the *Data Type* column and then click *Attachment* at the drop-down list.
   d. Save the table.
2. Switch to Datasheet view.

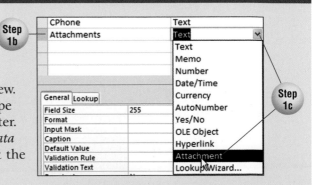

Step 1b

Step 1c

3. Add the following data in the first row of the datasheet.

Tech_ID	10
SSN	000-43-5789
Fname	Kelsey
Lname	Eastman
StreetAdd	550 Montclair Street
City	Detroit
State	MI
ZIP	48214-3274
HPhone	313-555-6315
CPhone	"" (Recall that double quotation marks indicate a zero-length field.)

4. Attach two files to the record for Kelsey Eastman by completing the following steps:

a. Double-click the paper clip in the first row of the datasheet. Attachment fields display a paper clip in each record in a column with a paper clip in the field name row. The number in brackets next to the paper clip indicates the number of files attached to the record.

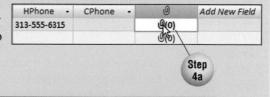

Step 4a

b. At the Attachments dialog box, click the Add button.

c. At the Choose File dialog box, navigate to the Access2007L2C1 folder on your storage medium.

d. Click the file named **Eastman_Resume.docx**.

e. Hold down the Ctrl key and click the file named **kelsey_eastman.jpg**.

f. Click the Open button.

g. Click OK. Access closes the Attachments dialog box and displays *(2)* next to the paper clip in the first record.

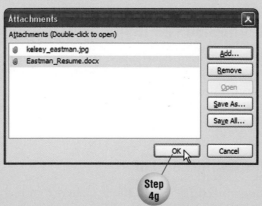

Step 4g

5. Open the attached files by completing the following steps:

a. Double-click the paper clip in the first row of the datasheet to open the Attachments dialog box.

b. Double-click **Eastman_Resume.docx** in the *Attachments* list box to open the Word document.

c. Read the resume in Microsoft Word and then exit Word.

d. Double-click *kelsey_eastman.jpg* in the *Attachments* list box to open the picture file.

e. View the picture and then exit the picture viewer program.

f. Click OK to close the Attachments dialog box.

6. Adjust all column widths to Best Fit.

7. Display the datasheet in Print Preview. Change the orientation to landscape, print the datasheet, and then close Print Preview.

8. Close the Technicians table. Click Yes when prompted to save changes to the table layout.

9. Close the **RSRComputerServ.accdb** database.

Editing an Attached File

If you open a file attachment and make changes to the file, click the Save button in the source program to save changes. The changes are saved to a temporary folder on your computer's hard drive. To save the changes permanently, exit the Source program and then click OK at the Attachments dialog box in Access. Access displays the Save Attachment dialog box shown in Figure 1.5. Click Yes to update the changes in the database.

Figure 1.5 Save Attachment Dialog Box

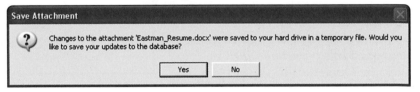

Saving an Attached File to Another Location

You can export a file that is attached to a record to make a copy of the document in another storage location by selecting the file and then clicking the Save As button in the Attachments dialog box. At the Save Attachment dialog box, navigate to the drive and/or folder in which you want to save the duplicate copy of the file, click the Save button, and then click OK to close the Attachments dialog box.

Removing an Attached File

If you no longer need to store a file attached to a record in the database, open the Attachments dialog box in the record containing the file attachment, click the file name for the file you want to delete, and then click the Remove button.

CHAPTER summary

- Database designers plan the tables needed for a new database by analyzing sample data, input documents, and output requirements to generate the entire set of data elements needed.

- Once all data has been identified, the designer maps out the number of tables required.

- Each table holds data for a single topic only with data split out into the smallest unit that will be manipulated.

- Designers do not include fields for data that can be calculated.

- Designers also consider relationships that will be needed in case a field needs to be added to a table in order to join the tables.

- Data redundancy should be avoided, which means a field should not be repeated in another table.

- Fields are assigned one of 10 data types by selecting a data type appropriate for the kind of data that will be accepted into the field.

- A diagram of a database portrays the database tables with field names, data types, and field sizes.

- Changing the field size property can be used to restrict entries in the field to a maximum length as one way to prevent longer entries that might be added to the field by accident.

- Add an entry to the *Caption* property to provide a more descriptive title for the field in datasheet view.

- Change the *Required* property to *Yes* to force an entry into the field when a new record is added to the table.

- Leaving a field blank when a new record is entered results in a null value stored in the field.

- A zero-length field is entered into a record by typing two double quotation symbols with no space between. This method is used to indicate a field value does not apply to the current record.

- You can disallow zero-length strings by changing the *Allow Zero Length* property to *No*.

- The *Format* property controls the display of data accepted into a field.

- A custom format can be created for a text field by typing the appropriate format codes in the *Format* property box.

- Predefined formats are available for Number, AutoNumber, and Currency fields or you can create your own custom number format by typing the appropriate format codes in the *Format* property box.

- A custom numeric format can contain four sections; one section for positive values, one section for negative values, one section for zero values, and the last section for null values.

- Access provides several format options for displaying dates and times in a Date/Time field or you can create your own custom date and/or time format.

- Use an input mask to control the type and pattern of data entered into the field.
- Access provides the Input Mask Wizard for Text or Date/Time fields. Create an input mask for other fields or create a custom input mask for a Text or Date/Time field by typing the appropriate input mask codes in the *Input Mask* property box.
- A Memo field can be formatted using rich text formatting options in the Font group of the Home tab by changing the *Text Format* property to *Rich Text*.
- Change the *Append Only* property of a Memo field to maintain a history of changes made to the data stored in the field.
- A field with the data type set to *Attachment* can be used to store files associated with a record.
- Multiple files can be attached to a record with no single file exceeding 256 megabytes and the total of all files not exceeding two gigabytes.
- Double-click the paper clip in the Attachment field for a record to add, view, save, or remove a file attachment.

COMMANDS review

FEATURE	RIBBON TAB, GROUP	BUTTON	KEYBOARD SHORTCUT
Create table in Design view	Create, Table Design		
Minimize navigation pane		«	F11
Redisplay navigation pane		»	F11
Switch to Datasheet view from Design view	Table Tools Design, Views		
Switch to Design view from Datasheet view	Home, Views		

CONCEPTS check

Test Your Knowledge

Completion: In the space provided at the right, indicate the correct term, command, or number.

1. Use this data type for a field that will hold numeric data that is not a monetary value. _____

2. Use this data type to store alphanumeric text longer than 255 characters. _____

3. This data type is restricted to a field value used to test conditional logic that can be one of only two conditions. _____

4. The available properties that display for a field in the *Field Properties* section in Design view are dependent on this option. _____

5. This property is used to display a more descriptive title for the field in the datasheet. _____

6. To ensure a field is never left empty, set this property to *Yes*. _____

7. Typing two double quotation symbols with no space between assigns this field value. _____

8. This is the format code to convert all text in the field to uppercase. _____

9. This placeholder in a custom numeric format instructs Access to display a zero if the position is not used. _____

10. Type this entry in the *Format* property box of a Date/Time field to display dates beginning with the day of the week abbreviated, followed by the month as two digits, the day of the month as two digits, and the year as two digits with all sections separated with a hyphen character. _____

11. Type this entry in the *Input Mask* property box to require a three-digit identification number to be entered with the pound symbol (#) used as the placeholder. _____

12. Rich text formatting is enabled for a Memo field by changing this property option to *Rich Text*. _____

13. For a Memo field with the *Append Only* property active, right-click in a record and click this option at the shortcut menu to display a dialog box with the history of the text changes made to the field.

_____

14. Create a field with this data type to store a file with the record.

_____

15. Add a file to the record by double-clicking this object in the record in Datasheet view.

_____

SKILLS check
Demonstrate Your Proficiency

Assessment

1 CREATE A NEW DATABASE

1. Create a new blank database named **BenchmarkGolf.accdb**.
2. Create the tables shown in Figure 1.6 to store membership records for the Benchmark Golf and Country Club including setting the primary key and assigning data types and field sizes.
3. Close any tables that have been left open.

Figure 1.6 Assessment 1

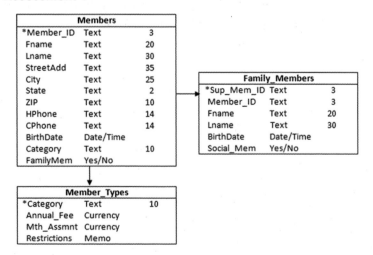

Members		
*Member_ID	Text	3
Fname	Text	20
Lname	Text	30
StreetAdd	Text	35
City	Text	25
State	Text	2
ZIP	Text	10
HPhone	Text	14
CPhone	Text	14
BirthDate	Date/Time	
Category	Text	10
FamilyMem	Yes/No	

Family_Members		
*Sup_Mem_ID	Text	3
Member_ID	Text	3
Fname	Text	20
Lname	Text	30
BirthDate	Date/Time	
Social_Mem	Yes/No	

Member_Types		
*Category	Text	10
Annual_Fee	Currency	
Mth_Assmnt	Currency	
Restrictions	Memo	

Assessment

2 ADD CAPTIONS AND DISALLOW BLANK VALUES

1. With the **BenchmarkGolf.accdb** database open, create captions for the fields as follows:

Members Table

Field Name	Caption
Member_ID	ID Number
Fname	First Name
Lname	Last Name
StreetAdd	Street Address
ZIP	ZIP Code
HPhone	Home Phone
CPhone	Cell Phone
BirthDate	Birth Date
FamilyMem	Family Member?

Family_Members Table

Field Name	Caption
Sup_Mem_ID	Supplementary ID
Member_ID	Main ID Number
Fname	First Name
Lname	Last Name
BirthDate	Birth Date
Social_Mem	Social Member?

Member_Types Table

Field Name	Caption
Annual_Fee	Annual Fee
Mth_Assmnt	Monthly Assessment

2. Make the *ZIP* field a required field and disallow zero-length strings.
3. Close any tables that have been left open.

Assessment

3 CREATE CUSTOM FORMATS AND INPUT MASKS

1. With the **BenchmarkGolf.accdb** database open, create the following custom formats:
   a. Display the state text in uppercase characters.
   b. Display all birth dates with the month abbreviated followed by the day of the month as two digits and the year as four digits with one space separating each section.
   c. Display the monthly assessment number in green with two decimal values that will show zeros if no number is entered.
2. Create the following custom input masks:
   a. In the *Member_ID* field in the Members table and the *Sup_Mem_ID* field in the Family_Members table, require all three digits and display the underscore character as the placeholder.
   b. Require all ZIP codes in the pattern five required digits followed by a hyphen and then four required digits. Display the pound symbol (#) as the placeholder.
   c. Require all telephone numbers to include the area code and be entered with hyphens between each section of the number. Display the pound symbol as the placeholder.
   d. Create an input mask for both birth date fields that will match the custom format pattern created in Step 1b except include hyphens between each section. Store the display characters in the field and display the underscore character as the placeholder. For example, the custom format should display the date as *May 03 1964* in the datasheet. The input mask needs to match this pattern for data entry purposes with hyphens between each section in place of the spaces.
3. Close any tables that have been left open.

Assessment

4 ADD RECORDS

1. With the **BenchmarkGolf.accdb** database open, add the following records. Type the text in the *State* field as shown to test your format code. Type ZIP codes, telephone numbers, and dates, being careful to watch the placeholders and enter in the required pattern.

Members Table

Field	Record 1	Record 2
ID Number	100	110
First Name	Hilary	Jesse
Last Name	Sampson	Reynolds
Street Address	300 South Saguaro Drive	7229 E University Drive
City	Apache Junction	Mesa
State	Az	Az
ZIP Code	85220 4956	85207 6501
Home Phone	602 555 1587	480 555 1385
Cell Phone	602 555 3496	480 555 1699

Birth Date	May 3, 1964	October 15, 1977
Category	Gold	Silver
Family Member?	Yes	No

Family_Members Table

Field	Record 1	Record 2
Supplementary ID	610	611
Main ID Number	100	100
First Name	Kayla	Roy
Last Name	Sampson	Sampson
Birth Date	July 18, 1992	March 16, 1994
Social Member?	No	No

Member_Types Table

Field	Record 1	Record 2	Record 3
Category	Gold	Silver	Bronze
Annual Fee	2725	1865	1480
Monthly Assessment	65	50	40
Restrictions	Unlimited weekdays and weekends; weekend ballot first	Unlimited weekdays; weekend ballot second	Unlimited weekdays; weekends after 3 P.M.

2. Adjust all column widths to Best Fit and print each table in landscape orientation.
3. Close any tables that have been left open saving layout changes.
4. Close the **BenchmarkGolf.accdb** database.

CASE study
Apply Your Skills

Part 1

You started an internship today at Bestar Plumbing Service. Examine the customer invoice shown in Figure 1.7. This is a typical invoice for which the owner would like to start using an Access database. Design tables for the data using the invoice and the following additional information from the owner:

- Customer numbers are assigned using the first three letters of the customer's last name all uppercase and are followed by three digits after a hyphen character.

- Some invoices include parts with a labor charge. Individual parts are not itemized on the customer invoice. The service technician shows a single line on the invoice for all parts used.

- Bestar has two labor rates: $38.75 for a senior service technician and $25.00 for an apprentice technician.

Using Microsoft Word, create a document that diagrams the tables including table names, field names, data types, and field sizes. Use the asterisk to denote the primary key field in each table. Ask your instructor for the required format of the diagram in text boxes or tables in Word, or, if a handwritten diagram is acceptable. Save the Word document and name it **AccessL2_C1_CS_P1**. Save, print, and close **AccessL2_C1_CS_P1.docx**.

Figure 1.7 Invoice for Case Study, Part 1

INVOICE

Bestar Plumbing Service

INVOICE NO. 1001
DATE February 12, 2009
CUSTOMER ID COL-104

TO
Diane Collier
2101 Lakeland Avenue
Madison, WI 53704
608-555-6377

QUANTITY	DESCRIPTION	UNIT PRICE	LINE TOTAL
1 hr labor	Service call to repair burst water pipe	$ 38.75	$ 38.75
	Service Technician: Jose Martinez		
	Date of Service: February 6, 2009		
		SUBTOTAL	$ 38.75
		5 % SALES TAX	1.94
		TOTAL	$ 40.69

Part 2

Using the table diagram created in Part 1, create a new database named **BestarService.accdb** and then create the tables.

Part 3

Consider the field properties learned in this chapter that can be used to ensure data integrity and consistency. Modify field properties in your tables that can be used to restrict data accepted into the field and display the data after it has been accepted. Use the data in Figure 1.7 to enter a sample record in each table to test your field properties. Print each table with all column widths set to Best Fit.

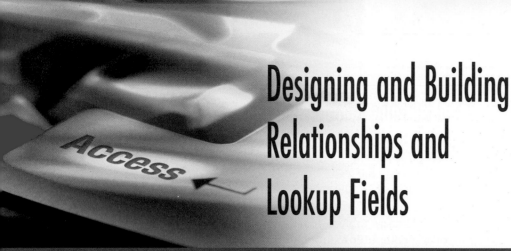

Designing and Building Relationships and Lookup Fields

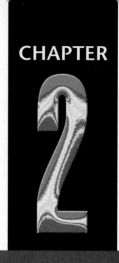

CHAPTER 2

Upon successful completion of Chapter 2, you will be able to:

- Design relationships between tables including one-to-many, one-to-one, and many-to-many relationships
- Edit relationship options, including specifying the join type
- Define a table with a multiple-field primary key
- Create a lookup field to populate records with data from another table
- Modify a lookup field's properties
- Create a field that allows multiple values
- Create single-field and multiple-field indexes
- Define what is meant by normalization
- Determine if a table is in first, second, and third normal form

access Chapter 2

Tutorial 2.1
Designing and Maintaining
Relationships
Tutorial 2.2
Lookup Fields

Once table design is completed, the task of defining relationships and relationship options involves analyzing the type of relationship that exists between two tables. This analysis is assisted by drawing a diagram to depict the primary table and the related table's matching record frequency. You will create and edit relationships and lookup fields, multiple-field primary keys, multivalued fields, and indexes in this chapter. The concept of database normalization and three forms of normalization are introduced to complete the examination of database design fundamentals.

Note: Before beginning computer projects, copy to your storage medium the Access2007L2C2 subfolder from the Access2007L2 folder on the CD that accompanies this textbook and then make Access2007L2C2 the active folder.

roject **1** Create and Edit Relationships

You will create relationships and edit relationship options for the tables designed to track work orders for RSR Computer Services.

Designing and Building Relationships

Continuing the process of designing tables discussed in Chapter 1, which included determining which tables would be related to each other, the next step is to examine the types of relationships that exist. A relationship is based upon an association between two tables. For example, in the computer service database created in Chapter 1 for RSR Computer Services there is an association between the Customers table and the Work_Orders table. A customer is associated with all of his or her work orders involving computer maintenance requests, and a work order is associated with the individual customer for which the service was requested.

When designing relationships, consider associations between tables and how the associations affect data that will be entered into the tables. In the database diagram presented in Chapter 1, relationships were shown by drawing arrows between tables. In this chapter, you consider the type of relationship that should exist between the tables, the relationship options that you want to use to place restrictions on data entry, and the type of join that will occur between the tables. Access provides for three types of relationships: one-to-many, one-to-one, and many-to-many.

Establishing a One-to-Many Relationship

In the computer service database in Chapter 1, the Customers table is related to the Work_Orders table. This relationship exists because a work order involves computer maintenance for a specific customer. The customer is identified by the customer's number stored in the Customers table. In the Customers table only one record exists per customer. In the Work_Orders table, the same customer number can be associated with several work orders. This means the relationship between the Customers table and the Work_Orders table is a one-to-many relationship.

One-to-many relationships are the most common type of relationship created in Access. A common field is needed to join the Customers table and the Work_Orders table, so the *Cust_ID* field was included in both tables. In the Customers table, *Cust_ID* is the primary key field because each customer has only one record with a unique identification number. In the Work_Orders table, *Cust_ID* cannot be the primary key because the same customer could be associated with several computer service work orders. In the Work_Orders table, *Cust_ID* is the *foreign key*. A foreign key is a field included in a table for the purpose of creating a relationship to a field that is a primary key in the other table. The Customers-to-Work_Orders one-to-many relationship can be illustrated using a diagram similar to the one shown in Figure 2.1.

Figure 2.1 One-to-Many Relationship between Customers Table and
Work_Orders Table

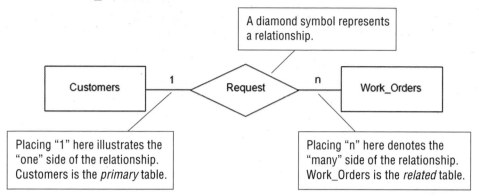

More than one method is used to diagram a relationship. Figure 2.1 displays
one variation of an entity-relationship diagram. Recall from Chapter 1 that tables
are considered *entities*. Table names are displayed in rectangles with lines drawn
to a diamond symbol that represents a relationship. Inside the diamond, a word
(usually a verb) describes the action that relates the two tables. For example, in
the relationship shown in Figure 2.1, the word *Request* is used to show that
"Customers *Request* Work_Orders."On the join line, a *1* is placed next to the table
that represents the primary table, or the "one" side in the relationship, and *n* is
placed next to the related table, or the "many" side of the relationship.

Project 1a Creating a One-to-Many Relationship

1. Open **RSRComputerServ2.accdb**. This database is the same structure as the database
   created in Chapter 1, however, additional field properties have been defined and several
   records have been added to each table to provide data with which to test relationships and
   lookup lists.
2. Click the Options button next to the Security Warning message in the Message bar. Click
   Enable this content at the Microsoft Office Security Options dialog box and then click OK.
3. Create a one-to-many relationship between the Customers table and the Work_Orders
   table by completing the following steps:
   a. Click the Database Tools tab.
   b. Click the Relationships button in the Show/Hide group.

c. At the Show Table dialog box with the Tables tab active and with *Customers* selected in the Tables list box, hold down the Ctrl key, click *Work_Orders* and then click the Add button.

d. Click the Close button to close the Show Table dialog box.

e. Drag the bottom border of each table's field list box to resize the box until all field names are shown.

f. Drag the *Cust_ID* field from the Customers table field list box to the *Cust_ID* field in the Work_Orders table field list box.

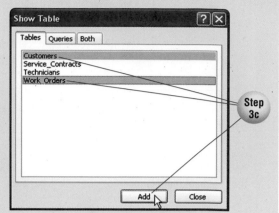

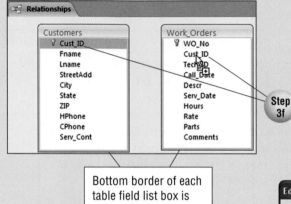

Bottom border of each table field list box is resized to show all field names at Step 3e.

g. At the Edit Relationships dialog box, notice *One-to-Many* appears in the *Relationship Type* section. Access detected the correct type of relationship because the field used to join the tables is a primary key in only one of the tables. Click the Create button.

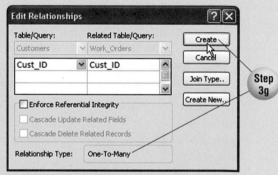

4. Click the Close button in the Relationships group of the Relationship Tools Design tab.

5. Click Yes at the Microsoft Office Access message box asking if you want to save changes to the layout of the 'Relationships' window.

Another one-to-many association exists between the Technicians table and the Work_Orders table. A technician is associated with all of the work orders that he or she has been assigned and a work order is associated with the technician that carried out the service request. The Technicians to Work_Orders relationship diagram is shown in Figure 2.2.

Figure 2.2 One-to-Many Relationship between Technicians Table and Work_Orders Table

Project 1b — Creating a Second One-to-Many Relationship

1. With the **RSRComputerServ2.accdb** database open, display the Relationships window by clicking the Database Tools tab and then clicking the Relationships button in the Show/Hide group.
2. Click the Show Table button  in the Relationships group in the Relationships Tools Design tab.
3. Click *Technicians* in the Tables list at the Show Table dialog box, click the Add button, and then click the Close button.
4. Drag the bottom border and the right border of the Technicians table field list box until all field names are fully visible.
5. Drag the *Tech_ID* field from the Technicians table field list box to the *Tech_ID* field in the Work_Orders table field list box.
6. Click the Create button at the Edit Relationships dialog box.
7. Click the Close button in the Relationships group of the Relationship Tools Design tab.
8. Click Yes at the Microsoft Office Access message box asking if you want to save changes to the layout of the 'Relationships' window.

One-to-many relationship created between Technicians and Work_Orders at Steps 1–6

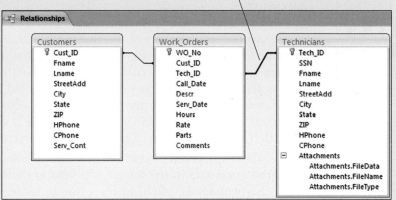

Editing Relationship Options

At the Edit Relationships dialog box shown in Figure 2.3 you can elect to turn on relationship options and/or specify the type of join to create. The *Cascade Update Related Fields* and *Cascade Delete Related Records* options do not become active unless referential integrity is turned on.

QUICK STEPS

Edit Relationship
1. Click Database Tools tab.
2. Click Relationships button.
3. Click black join line between tables.
4. Click Edit Relationships button.
5. Select desired options.
6. Click OK.

Edit Relationships

Figure 2.3 Edit Relationships Dialog Box

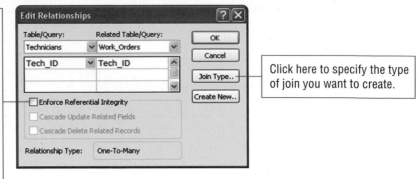

Enforce Referential Integrity places restrictions on data entry. A record will not be allowed in the related table (Work_Orders) with a value in the foreign key field (*Tech_ID*) for which no matching record is already in existence in the primary table (Technicians).

In other words, you cannot assign a technician to a work order if the technician does not exist in the Technicians table.

Click here to specify the type of join you want to create.

HINT

To enable referential integrity, the primary key and foreign key fields must be the same data type. If you receive an error message when attempting to activate referential integrity, open each table in Design view and compare the data type for each field used to join the tables.

HINT

Join properties can also be changed when creating a query by double-clicking the join line between tables in the query design grid.

Turning on referential integrity in a one-to-many relationship is a good idea to ensure that orphan records do not occur. An orphan record is a record in a related table for which no "parent" record exists in the primary table. Assigning a technician to a work order in the Work_Orders table with no matching technician record in the Technicians table creates an orphan record in the Work_Orders table. Once referential integrity is turned on, Access checks for the existence of a matching record in the primary table as a new record is added to the related table. If no match is found, Access does not allow the record to be saved.

With referential integrity active, Access can automatically update all occurrences of the same data in the foreign key field in the related table when a change is made to the primary key field in the primary table (Cascade Update Related Fields). If a record is deleted from the primary table for which related records exist in the related table, Access can automatically delete the related records (Cascade Delete Related Records).

Specifying the Join Type

Click the Join Type button at the Edit Relationships dialog box to open the Join Properties dialog box shown in Figure 2.4. By default, option 1 is selected, which is referred to as an **inner join**. In an inner join, only those records where the primary key field value in the primary table matches a foreign key field value in the related table are displayed.

Figure 2.4 Join Properties Dialog Box

Options 2 and 3 are referred to as *outer joins*. Option 2 is a *left outer join* where all records from the primary table are shown and only those records with a matching entry in the foreign key are shown from the related table. In this type of join, the primary table (or left table) displays all rows whereas the related table (or right table) shows only rows with a matching technician identification number. For example, those technicians who have not been assigned to a work order display with empty work order detail fields as shown in Figure 2.5.

Figure 2.5 Left Outer Join Example

Technician ID	First Name	Last Name	Work Order	Customer ID	Call Date	Description
01	Pat	Hynes	65020	1030	Wed Sep 16 2009	Troubleshoot noisy fan
02	Hui	Chen	65014	1005	Thu Sep 10 2009	Replace power supply
02	Hui	Chen	65019	1025	Tue Sep 15 2009	Upgrade to Vista Ultimate
03	Kayla	Blewett				
04	Mihir	Patel	65015	1008	Thu Sep 10 2009	Restore operating syst
04	Mihir	Patel	65022	1040	Mon Sep 21 2009	Customer reports scree
05	Madir	Sadiku				
06	Brody	Stewart	65016	1010	Fri Sep 11 2009	Install upgraded video
06	Brody	Stewart	65021	1035	Fri Sep 18 2009	Customer has blue scre
07	Ana	Takacs				
08	Marty	O'Leary	65017	1015	Mon Sep 14 2009	Replace DVD drive
09	Armando	Colacci				
10	Kelsey	Eastman	65013	1000	Tue Sep 08 2009	Replace keyboard
10	Kelsey	Eastman	65018	1020	Mon Sep 14 2009	Upgrade Office suite
11	Dana	Westman	65012	1000	Wed Sep 02 2009	Semiannual desktop computer cleaning and maintenance

Left outer join query results show related work order fields blank for technicians that have not yet been assigned to a work order.

Option 3 is a *right outer join* where all records from the related table are shown and only those records with a matching entry in the primary key are shown from the primary table. In this type of join, the related table (or right table) shows all work orders whereas the primary table (or left table) shows only rows with a matching technician identification number. For example, those work orders that have not yet been assigned to a technician display with empty technician detail fields as shown in Figure 2.6.

Figure 2.6 Right Outer Join Example

Technician ID	First Name	Last Name	Work Order	Customer ID	Call Date	Description
11	Dana	Westman	65012	1000	Wed Sep 02 2009	Semiannual desktop computer cleaning and maintenance
10	Kelsey	Eastman	65013	1000	Tue Sep 08 2009	Replace keyboard
02	Hui	Chen	65014	1005	Thu Sep 10 2009	Replace power supply
04	Mihir	Patel	65015	1008	Thu Sep 10 2009	Restore operating system
06	Brody	Stewart	65016	1010	Fri Sep 11 2009	Install upgraded video card
08	Marty	O'Leary	65017	1015	Mon Sep 14 2009	Replace DVD drive
10	Kelsey	Eastman	65018	1020	Mon Sep 14 2009	Upgrade Office suite
02	Hui	Chen	65019	1025	Tue Sep 15 2009	Upgrade to Vista Ultimate
01	Pat	Hynes	65020	1030	Wed Sep 16 2009	Troubleshoot noisy fan
06	Brody	Stewart	65021	1035	Fri Sep 18 2009	Customer has blue screen upon boot
04	Mihir	Patel	65022	1040	Mon Sep 21 2009	Customer reports screen is fuzzy
			65023	1045	Tue Sep 22 2009	Upgrade RAM
			65024	1005	Thu Sep 24 2009	Install malware protection
			65025	1010	Mon Sep 28 2009	Troubleshoot hard drive noise
			65026	1025	Tue Sep 29 2009	Upgrade memory

Right outer join query results display related technician fields blank for those work orders that have yet to be assigned to a technician.

The datasheets shown in Figures 2.5 and 2.6 were generated using the same tables and field specifications in a query. The difference between the two results is affected by the join type. Figure 2.7 displays the same query results datasheet with the default inner join (option *1*) in effect. Notice that fewer records display in the datasheet than in the previous two examples. Since an inner join displays only those records where a matching entry exists in both tables, records from either table that do not have a matching record in the other table are not displayed. Understanding that an inner join may not display all records that exist in the tables when you run a query is important.

Figure 2.7 Inner Join Example

Technician ID	First Name	Last Name	Work Order	Customer ID	Call Date	Description
01	Pat	Hynes	65020	1030	Wed Sep 16 2009	Troubleshoot noisy fan
02	Hui	Chen	65014	1005	Thu Sep 10 2009	Replace power supply
02	Hui	Chen	65019	1025	Tue Sep 15 2009	Upgrade to Vista Ultimate
04	Mihir	Patel	65015	1008	Thu Sep 10 2009	Restore operating system
04	Mihir	Patel	65022	1040	Mon Sep 21 2009	Customer reports screen is fuzzy
06	Brody	Stewart	65016	1010	Fri Sep 11 2009	Install upgraded video card
06	Brody	Stewart	65021	1035	Fri Sep 18 2009	Customer has blue screen upon boot
08	Marty	O'Leary	65017	1015	Mon Sep 14 2009	Replace DVD drive
10	Kelsey	Eastman	65013	1000	Tue Sep 08 2009	Replace keyboard
10	Kelsey	Eastman	65018	1020	Mon Sep 14 2009	Upgrade Office suite
11	Dana	Westman	65012	1000	Wed Sep 02 2009	Semiannual desktop computer cleaning and maintenance

An inner join displays a record only when a matching value in the joined field exists in both tables—no blanks appear in the query results. However, notice you are not viewing all records in *either* table. Technicians that have not been assigned to any work orders are not displayed, and work orders that have not yet been assigned to a technician are also not displayed.

Project 1c Editing Relationships

1. With the **RSRComputerServ2.accdb** database open, edit the one-to-many relationship between the Customers table and the Work_Orders table by completing the following steps:
   a. Open the Relationships window.
   b. Click to select the black join line between the Customers table and the Work_Orders table.
   c. Click the Edit Relationships button in the Tools group in the Relationship Tools Design tab.
   d. At the Edit Relationships dialog box, click the *Enforce Referential Integrity* check box, the *Cascade Update Related Fields* check box, and the *Cascade Delete Related Records* check box.
   e. Click the Join Type button.

Step 1d

Step 1e

Edit Relationships

Table/Query:	Related Table/Query:
Customers	Work_Orders
Cust_ID	Cust_ID

OK
Cancel
Join Type..
Create New..

☑ Enforce Referential Integrity
☑ Cascade Update Related Fields
☑ Cascade Delete Related Records

Relationship Type: One-To-Many

f. At the Join Properties dialog box, click option *2* and then click OK to create a left outer join. This join type will cause all records in the Customers table to display even if the customer has never placed a work order request.

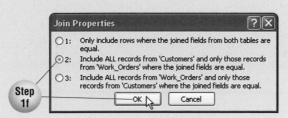

Step 1f

g. Click OK at the Edit Relationships dialog box. Access displays the arrowhead pointing towards the Work_Orders table indicating a left outer join relationship. The *1* at the primary table (one side) of the join line and the infinity symbol ∞ at the related table (many side) of the join line indicate referential integrity has been turned on.

2. Edit the one-to-many relationship between the Technicians table and the Work_Orders table by completing the following steps:

a. Double-click the black join line between the Technicians table and the Work_Orders table in the Relationships window.

b. At the Edit Relationships dialog box, turn on referential integrity and the two cascade options and create a left outer join by completing steps similar to those in Steps 1d–1g.

With referential integrity turned on, the 1 and infinity symbol display on the join line.

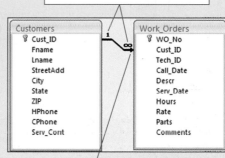

The arrowhead indicates the left outer join option.

Steps 2a–2b

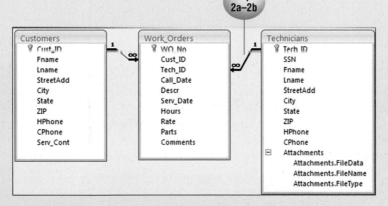

3. Close the Relationships window.

Establishing a One-to-One Relationship

Create One-to-One Relationship
1. Click Database Tools tab.
2. Click Relationships button.
3. Add tables from Show Table dialog box.
4. Close Show Table dialog box.
5. Drag primary key field name from primary table to primary key field name in related table.
6. Select desired relationship options.
7. Click Create button.

In the database for RSR Computer Services, a table is used to store service contract information for each customer. This table, named Service_Contracts, is associated with the Customers table. Only one record exists for a customer in the Customers table and each customer subscribes to only one service contract in the Service_Contracts table. This means the two tables are related in a one-to-one relationship as shown in Figure 2.8.

Figure 2.8 One-to-One Relationship between Customers Table and Service_Contracts Table

Project 1d Creating a One-to-One Relationship

1. With the **RSRComputerServ2.accdb** database open, create a one-to-one relationship between the Customers table and the Service_Contracts table by completing the following steps:

   a. Open the Relationships window.

   b. Click the Show Table button in the Relationships group.

   c. Double-click *Service_Contracts* in the Tables list box and then click the Close button.

   d. Drag the *Cust_ID* field from the Customers table field list box to the *Cust_ID* field in the Service_Contracts table field list box.

   e. At the Edit Relationships dialog box, notice *One-to-One* appears in the *Relationship Type* section. Access detected the correct type of relationship because the field used to join the tables is a primary key in both tables.

   f. Click the *Enforce Referential Integrity* check box, the *Cascade Update Related Fields* check box, and the *Cascade Delete Related Records* check box.

   g. Click the Create button.

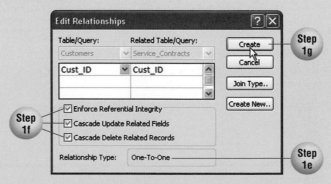

2. Drag the title bar of the Service_Contracts table field list box to the approximate location shown in the Relationships window. By moving the table field list box you are better able to view the join line and the 1 symbol at each end of the line between Customers and Service-Contracts.

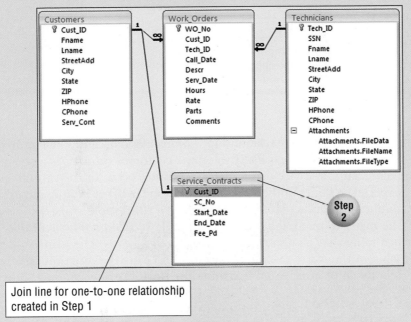

Join line for one-to-one relationship created in Step 1

3. Create and print a relationships report by clicking the Relationship Report button ![Relationship Report] in the Tools group of the Relationship Tools Design tab and then clicking the Print button on the Quick Access toolbar.
4. Close the Relationships for RSRComputerServ2 report. Click Yes to save the report and accept the default name at the Save As dialog box.
5. Close the Relationships window. Click Yes to save changes to the layout.

Establishing a Many-to-Many Relationship

Consider the association between the Customers table and the Technicians table in the RSR Computer Services database. Over time, any individual customer can have computer service work done by many different technicians and any individual technician can perform computer service work at any number of different customer locations. In other words, a record in the Customers table can be matched to many records in the Technicians table and a record in the Technicians table can be matched to many records in the Customers table. This is an example of a many-to-many relationship.

The diagram to show the many-to-many relationship between Customers and Technicians is depicted in Figure 2.9.

Figure 2.9 Many-to-Many Relationship between Customers Table and Technicians Table

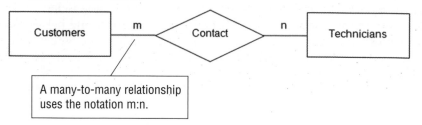

A many-to-many relationship is problematic because the nature of the relationship creates duplicate records. If the same customer number is associated with many technicians, and vice versa, many duplicates occur in the two tables and Access may experience data conflicts when trying to identify a unique record. To resolve the duplication and create unique entries, a third table is used to associate or link the many-to-many tables. The third table is called a ***junction table***. A junction table is a table that contains at least two foreign keys—the primary key field from each table in the many-to-many relationship. Using the junction table, two one-to-many relationships are created. Examine the Relationships window shown in Figure 2.10.

Figure 2.10 Relationships Window Showing Many-to-Many Relationship between Customers Table and Technicians Table

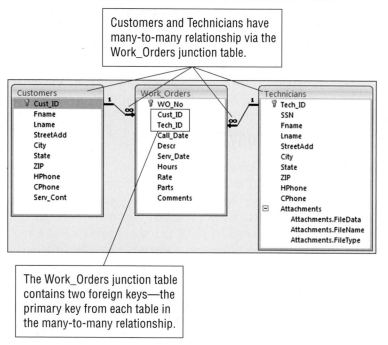

In Figure 2.10, the Work_Orders table is the junction table. Notice the Work_Orders table contains two foreign keys—*Cust_ID*, which is the primary key in the Customers table, and *Tech_ID*, which is the primary key in the Technicians table. A one-to-many relationship exists between Customers and Work_Orders and a one-to-many relationship also exists between Technicians and Work_Orders. These two one-to-many relationships create a many-to-many relationship between Customers and Technicians.

P roject ② Create a Table with a Multi-field Primary Key and Lookup Fields

You will create a new table that requires two fields to uniquely identify each record. To restrict data entry in the table, you will create fields that display a list from which the user selects the field value(s).

Defining a Multi-field Primary Key

In most tables one field is designated as the primary key. However, in some situations, a single field may not always be guaranteed to hold unique data. Look at the fields in the table shown in Figure 2.11. This is a new table you will create in the RSR Computer Services database to store computer profiles for RSR customers. The company stores the profiles as a service to RSR clients in case the client forgets his or her logon credentials. Technicians can also access the credentials data when troubleshooting at the customer's site.

Some customers may have more than one computer in their home or office and each computer can have a different profile. The *Cust_ID* field will not serve as the primary key field if the customer has more than one record in the Profiles table. However, a combination of the two fields *Cust_ID* and *Comp_ID* will uniquely identify each record. In this table, you will define both fields as a primary key. A primary key that is made up of two or more fields is called a ***composite key***.

Create Multiple-Field Primary Key
1. Open table in Design view.
2. Select first field.
3. Hold down Shift key (adjacent row) or Ctrl key (nonadjacent row) and select second field.
4. Click Primary Key button
5. Save table.

HINT

Delete a primary key by opening the table in Design view, activating the primary key field, and then clicking the Primary Key button to remove the key.

Primary Key

Figure 2.11 Project 2a Profiles Table

Profiles		
*Cust_ID	Text	4
*Comp_ID	Text	2
Username	Text	15
Password	Text	15
Rem_Access	Yes/No	

Project 2a | Creating a New Table with a Multiple-Field Primary Key

1. With the **RSRComputerServ2.accdb** database open, create a new table to store customer profiles by completing the following steps:
   a. Click the Create tab and then click the Table Design button in the Tables group.
   b. Type the field names, assign the data types, and change the field sizes as per the data structure shown in Figure 2.11.
2. Click in the field selector row next to *Cust_ID* to select the field.
3. Hold down the Shift key and click in the field selector row next to *Comp_ID*. Both fields are now selected.
4. Click the Primary Key button in the Tools group in the Table Tools Design tab. Access displays the key icon next to each field.
5. Click in any field to deselect the first two rows.
6. Save the table and name it **Profiles**.
7. Close the table.

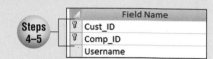

Steps 2–3

Field Name	Data Type
Cust_ID	Text
Comp_ID	Text
Username	Text
Password	Text
Rem_Access	Yes/No

Steps 4–5

Field Name
Cust_ID
Comp_ID
Username

QUICK STEPS

Create Lookup Field to Another Table
1. Open table in Design view.
2. Click in *Data Type* column of lookup field.
3. Click down-pointing arrow.
4. Click *Lookup Wizard.*
5. Click Next.
6. Choose table and click Next.
7. Choose fields to display in column.
8. Click Next.
9. Choose field by which to sort.
10. Click Next.
11. If necessary, expand column widths.
12. Clear *Hide key column* if desired.
13. Click Next.
14. Choose field value to store in table.
15. Click Next.
16. Click Finish.
17. Click Yes.

Creating a Field to Look Up Values in Another Table

A lookup field displays in a drop-down list the values found in records from another table that you connect to the lookup field. The user enters data by pointing and clicking rather than typing the field's entry. A lookup field has many advantages. Data can be restricted to items within the list, which avoids orphan records, data entry errors, or inconsistencies in spelling. The lookup list can display more than one clue to the user so that the correct data is selected. For example, assume a lookup field requires the user to select a customer's identification number. Looking at a drop-down list of identification numbers is not very helpful; however, if the lookup field displayed the identification number as well as the customer's name, the correct entry is easily identifiable. By choosing the field entry based on the name, the correct identification number is automatically entered by Access. To assist with creating lookup fields, Access provides the Lookup Wizard. Create lookup list fields before you create relationships. If a relationship already exists between the table for the lookup field and the source data table, Access prompts you to delete the relationship before the Lookup Wizard can run.

1. With the **RSRComputerServ2.accdb** database open, open the Profiles table in Design view.
2. Create a lookup field to enter a customer's identification number by selecting from a list of customers generated from the Customers table by completing the following steps:
   a. With *Cust_ID* the active field, click in the *Data Type* column, click the down-pointing arrow that appears, and then click *Lookup Wizard* at the drop-down list.
   b. At the first Lookup Wizard dialog box with *I want the lookup column to look up the values in a table or query* selected, click Next.

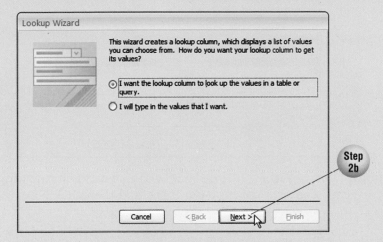

c. At the second Lookup Wizard dialog box with *Table: Customers* already selected in the *Which table or query should provide the values for your lookup column?* list box, click Next.

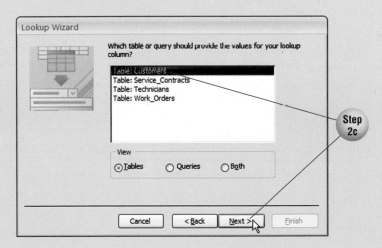

d. At the third Lookup Wizard dialog box you choose the fields you want to display in the drop-down list when the user clicks in the column. Double-click *Fname* in the *Available Fields* list box to move the field to the *Selected Fields* list box.

e. Double-click *Lname* in the *Available Fields* list box to move the field to the *Selected Fields* list box and then click Next.

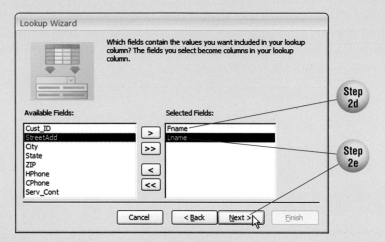

f. At the fourth Lookup Wizard dialog box, click the down-pointing arrow next to the first sort list box, click *Lname* at the drop-down list, and then click Next.

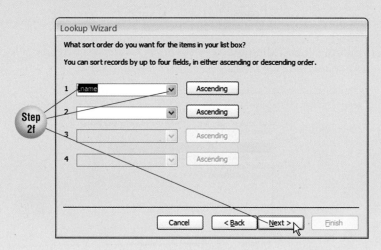

g. At the fifth Lookup Wizard dialog box you can expand column widths if necessary to display all data. Scroll down the list of entries in the dialog box. Notice the column widths are sufficient to show all of the text.

h. Click the *Hide key column (recommended)* check box to clear the check mark. Clearing the check mark displays the *Cust_ID* field values as the first column in the lookup list. You prefer to view the customer identification numbers with the names while the list is opened in a record.

i. Click Next.

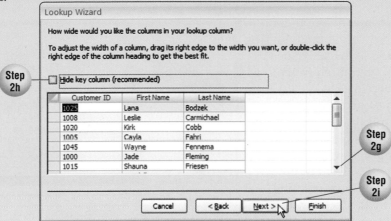

j. At the sixth Lookup Wizard dialog box with *Cust_ID* already selected in the *Available Fields* list box, click Next. At this dialog box you choose the field value that you want to store in the table when a row is selected in the drop-down list.

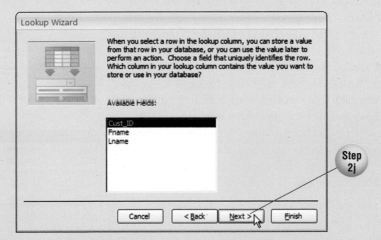

k. Click Finish at the last Lookup Wizard dialog box to accept the existing field name for the lookup field of *Cust_ID*.

l. Click Yes to save the table at the Lookup Wizard message box that states the table must be saved before relationships can be created. Access automatically creates a relationship between the Customers table and the Profiles table based on the *Cust_ID* field used to create the lookup field.

3. Close the Profiles table.

1. With the **RSRComputerServ2.accdb** database open, open the Profiles table in Design view.
2. Add the following text to the *Caption* property of the fields noted.

    Cust_ID   **Customer ID**
    Comp_ID   **Computer ID**
    Rem_Access   **Remote Access?**

3. Modify the lookup list properties to restrict entries in new records to an item within the list by completing the following steps:

    a. Make *Cust_ID* the active field.
    b. Click the Lookup tab in the *Field Properties* section.
    c. Look at the entries in each of the Lookup tab's property boxes. These entries were created by the Lookup Wizard.
    d. Click in the *Limit To List* property box, click the down-pointing arrow that appears, and then click *Yes* at the drop-down list. Changing *Limit To List* to *Yes* means that the field will accept data from existing customer records only. A user will not be able to type in an entry that is not in the list.
    e. Save the table.

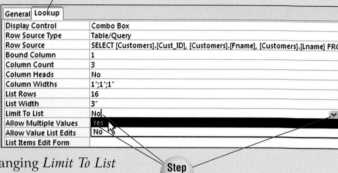

Step 3b

Step 3d

4. Switch to Datasheet view.
5. With *Customer ID* in the first row of the datasheet the active field, click the down-pointing arrow in the field and then click *Jade Fleming* at the drop-down list. Notice Access inserts *1000* as the field value in the first column. You were able to select the correct entry for *Customer ID* by clicking a customer's name and Access filled in the customer number associated with the name for you.
6. Type the remaining fields as indicated.

    Computer ID   **D1**
    Username   **jade47**
    Password   **P$ck7**
    Remote Access? **No**

7. Adjust all column widths to Best Fit.

Step 5

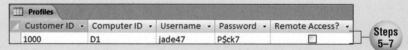

Steps 5–7

8. Print and then close the Profiles datasheet. Click Yes when prompted to save changes to the table layout.

Creating a Field That Allows Multiple Values

A new feature in Access 2007 is the ability to store multiple values in the same field. For example, assume you want to keep track of the industry certifications a technician has achieved. You could organize this data by creating a separate field for each certification. However, this approach might cause the table to require numerous fields in which only one or two technicians might have an entry. As an alternative, you can create a single field that displays a list of certifications with check boxes. Look at the fields in the table structure shown in Figure 2.12. In this table, for each technician, you would open a list in the *Certifications* field and click the check box next to the applicable certification title. In the field named *Op_Sys*, another list could be used to keep track of the operating systems for which the technician is considered an expert.

Create a field to store multiple values using the Lookup Wizard. You can choose to look up the values in a field in another table or create your own value list. At the last Lookup Wizard dialog box, click the *Allow Multiple Values* check box. Do not create a multivalued field if the possibility exists the Access database could be moved to Microsoft SQL Server in the future. An Access multivalued field upsizes to a memo field in a SQL database causing additional conversion work to be required.

QUICK STEPS

Create Multivalued Lookup List
1. Open table in Design view.
2. Start Lookup Wizard for desired field.
3. Create list by typing values or binding data to field in another table.
4. At last Lookup Wizard dialog box, click *Allow Multiple Values*.
5. Click Finish.
6. Click Yes.

HINT

Multivalued fields are suited to those occasions where you want to store more than one choice from a small list without having to create an advanced database design.

Figure 2.12 Project 2d Technicians_Skills Table

Technicians_Skills		
*Tech_ID	Text	2
Certifications	Text	20
Op_Sys	Text	20
Years_Exp	Number	

Project 2d Creating a Table with Lookup Fields Including a Multivalued Field

1. With the **RSRComputerServ2.accdb** database open, create a new table to store technician competencies by completing the following steps:
   a. Create a new table using Design view.
   b. Type the field names, assign the data types, and change the field sizes as per the data structure shown in Figure 2.12.
   c. Assign the primary key to the field denoted with the asterisk.
   d. Save the table and name it **Technicians_Skills**.
2. Create a lookup field to select the technician from a list of technician names in the Technicians table by completing the following steps:
   a. Click in the *Data Type* column for the *Tech_ID* field, click the down-pointing arrow that appears, and then click *Lookup Wizard*.
   b. Click Next to look up the values in a table or query.
   c. Click *Table: Technicians* and then click Next.
   d. Double-click *Lname* in the *Available Fields* list box to move the field to the *Selected Fields* list box.
   e. Double-click *Fname* in the *Available Fields* list box and then click Next. The *Selected Fields* list box shows the *Lname* field first followed by *Fname* because you want to view the technician names by last name first when you open a list.
   f. Sort by *Lname* and then click Next.

g. Click Next to accept the current column widths and hide the key column. In this lookup example, you are electing not to show the technician's ID field value. Although you will view and select by the names, Access stores the primary key value in the table. *Tech_ID* is considered the bound field, while *Lname* and *Fname* are considered display fields.

h. Click Finish and then click Yes to save the table.

3. Create a lookup field that allows multiple values for certification information by completing the following steps:

a. Click in the *Data Type* column for the *Certifications* field, click the down-pointing arrow that appears, and then click *Lookup Wizard*.

b. Click *I will type in the values that I want* and then click Next.

c. At the second Lookup Wizard dialog box, type the entries in *Col1* as shown.

d. Click Next.

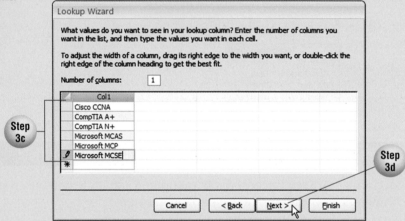

e. At the last Lookup Wizard dialog box, click the *Allow Multiple Values* check box and then click Finish.

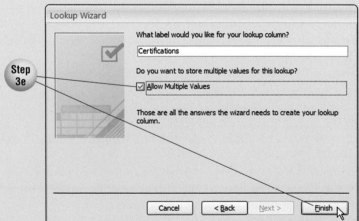

f. At the message box indicating that once the field is set to store multiple values, the action cannot be undone, click Yes to change the *Certifications* field to multiple values.

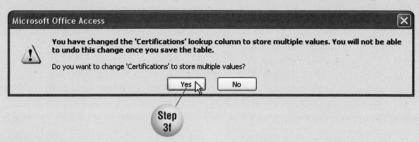

Step 3f

4. Create a lookup list to store multiple values in the *Op_Sys* field using the value list shown below by completing steps similar to those in Steps 3a–3f.

> Windows Vista
> Windows XP
> Windows 2000
> Linux
> Unix

5. Save and close the Technicians_Skills table.

Project 2e Assigning Multiple Values in a Lookup List

1. With the **RSRComputerServ2.accdb** database open, open the Technicians_Skills table in Design view.
2. Add the following text to the *Caption* property of the fields noted.

Tech_ID	Technician ID
Op_Sys	Operating Systems
Years_Exp	Years Experience

3. Save the table and then switch to Datasheet view.
4. Add a new record to the table by completing the following steps:
   a. With the insertion point positioned in the *Technician ID* column, click the down-pointing arrow and then click *Eastman Kelsey* at the drop-down list. Notice Access displays the technician's last name in the column. *Lname* is considered a display field for this column; however, the identification number associated with Kelsey Eastman is stored in the table.
   b. Press Tab and then click the down-pointing arrow in the *Certifications* column.
   c. Since *Certifications* is a multivalued field, the drop-down list displays with check boxes next to each item in the list. Click the *Cisco CCNA* check box and the *Microsoft MCP* check box and then click OK.

Step 4a

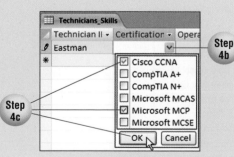

Step 4b

Step 4c

d. Press Tab and then click the down-pointing arrow in the *Operating System* column.
e. Click the *Windows Vista*, *Windows XP*, and *Linux* check boxes and then click OK.

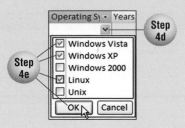

f. Press Tab, type 5, and then press Enter.
5. Adjust the width of all columns to Best Fit.
6. Print the Technicians_Skills table in landscape orientation.
7. Close the Technicians_Skills table. Click Yes when prompted to save changes to the layout.

Project ③ Create an Index

You will create indexes to speed up database processing.

QUICK STEPS

Create Single-Field Index
1. Open table in Design view.
2. Make desired field active.
3. Click in *Indexed* property box.
4. Click down-pointing arrow.
5. Click *Yes (Duplicates OK)* or *Yes (No Duplicates)*.
6. Save table.

HINT

An index cannot be generated for fields with a data type of OLE Object or Attachment.

Indexes

Creating Indexes

An index is a list created by Access containing pointers that direct Access to the location of a record in a table. A database index is very similar to an index you would find printed at the back of a textbook. You search an index for a keyword that is associated with the topic you want to find and are directed to the page number(s) in the book. You use a book's index because you want to find the information quickly and more directly. Access table indexes operate the same way. Access uses the index to locate a record in a table more quickly. A field that is specified as the primary key has an index generated by Access automatically. You can add additional indexed fields to the database to speed up sorting and searching. For example, in the Customers table in the RSR Computer Services database, creating an index for the *Lname* field is a good idea since the table data will be frequently sorted by last names.

An index can be created that restricts data in the field to unique values. This creates a field similar to a primary key in that Access will not allow two fields to hold the same data. For example, an e-mail field in a table that is frequently searched is a good candidate for an index. To avoid data entry errors in a field that should contain unique values (and is not the primary key), set up the index to not accept duplicates.

Create a multiple-field index if you frequently sort or search a large table by two or more fields at the same time. In Table Design view, click the Indexes button to open the Indexes window and create an index for the combination of fields. Up to 10 fields can be included in a multiple-field index in the Indexes window.

QUICK STEPS

Create Multiple-Field Index
1. Open table in Design view.
2. Click Indexes button.
3. Click in first blank row in *Index Name* column.
4. Type name for index.
5. Press Tab.
6. Click down-pointing arrow in *Field Name* column.
7. Click desired field.
8. If necessary, change sort order.
9. Click in *Field Name* column in next row.
10. Click down-pointing arrow.
11. Click desired field.
12. If necessary, change sort order.
13. Continue Steps 9–12 until finished.
14. Close Indexes window.

Project ③ Creating Indexes

1. With the **RSRComputerServ2.accdb** database open, open the Customers table in Design view.
2. Create a single-field index for the *ZIP* field by completing the following steps:
   a. Make *ZIP* the active field.
   b. Click in the *Indexed* property box, click the down-pointing arrow that appears, and then click *Yes (Duplicates OK)* at the drop-down list.

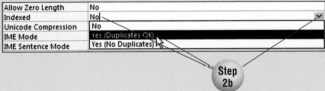

Step 2b

   c. Save the table.

3. Create a multiple-field index for the *Lname* and *Fname* fields by completing the following steps:
   a. Click the Indexes button 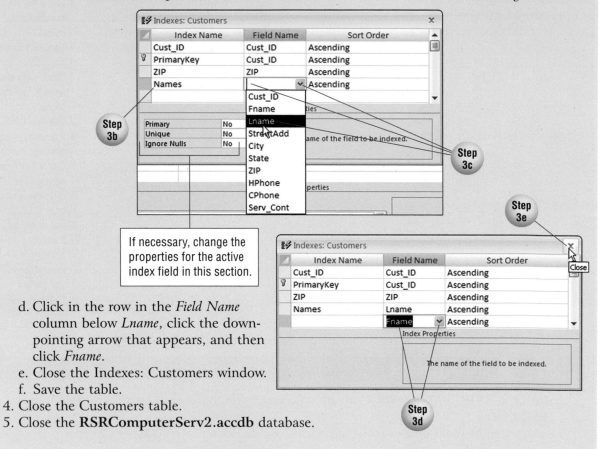 in the Show/Hide group in the Table Tools Design tab.
   b. At the Indexes: Customers window, click in the first blank row in the *Index Name* column (below *ZIP*) and then type **Names**.
   c. Press Tab, click the down-pointing arrow that appears in the *Field Name* column, and then click *Lname* at the drop-down list. The sort order for *Lname* defaults to *Ascending*.

Step 3b

Step 3c

Step 3e

If necessary, change the properties for the active index field in this section.

   d. Click in the row in the *Field Name* column below *Lname*, click the down-pointing arrow that appears, and then click *Fname*.
   e. Close the Indexes: Customers window.
   f. Save the table.
4. Close the Customers table.
5. Close the **RSRComputerServ2.accdb** database.

Step 3d

You cannot view an index. Access uses the index behind the scenes to work more efficiently. In a database with a large number of records, consider fields other than the primary key that are sorted or searched and create indexes for these fields.

Normalizing the Database

Normalizing a database involves reviewing the database structure and ensuring the tables are set up to eliminate redundancy. Three normalization states are tested: first normal form, second normal form, and third normal form.

First Normal Form

A table meets first normal form when the table does not contain any fields that could be broken down into smaller units and when the table does not have similar information stored in several fields. For example, a table that contains a single field called *Technician_Name* that stores the technician's first and last names in the same column is in violation of first normal form. To correct the structure, split *Technician_Name* into two fields.

A table that has multiple fields set up with each field containing similar data, such as *Week1*, *Week2*, *Week3*, and *Week4* violates first normal form. To correct this structure, delete the four week fields and replace them with a single field named *Week_Number*.

Second Normal Form

Second normal form is only of concern for a table that has a multiple-field primary key (composite key). A table with a composite key meets second normal form when the table is in first normal form and when all of the fields in the table are dependent on all of the fields that form the primary key. For example, assume a table is defined with two fields that form the primary key: *Cust_ID* and *Computer_ID*. A field in the same table is titled *EmailAdd*. The contents of the *EmailAdd* field are dependent on the customer only (not the computer). Since *EmailAdd* is not dependent on **both** *Cust_ID* **and** *Computer_ID*, the table is not in second normal form. To correct the structure, delete the *EmailAdd* field.

Third Normal Form

Third normal form applies to a table that has a single primary key and is in first normal form. If a field exists in the table for which the field value is not dependent on the field value of the primary key, the table is not in third normal form. For example, assume a table is defined with a single primary key titled *Technician_ID*. Two fields in the same table are titled *Pay_Code* and *Pay_Rate*. Assume also that a technician's pay rate is dependent on the pay code assigned to the technician. Since a pay rate is dependent on the field value in the pay code field and not on the technician's identification number, the table is not in third normal form. To convert the table to third normal form, delete the *Pay_Rate* field.

Normalizing a database often involves splitting fields into smaller units, and/or breaking larger tables down into smaller tables and creating relationships to remove repeating groups of data.

CHAPTER summary

- A relationship is based upon an association between two tables.
- When designing relationships consider the frequency of matching data in the common field in both tables to determine if the relationship is one-to-many, one-to-one, or many-to-many.
- One-to-many relationships are the most common type of relationship that involves joining the tables by dragging the primary key from the "one" table to the foreign key in the "many" table.
- In a one-to-many relationship, only one record for a matching field value exists in the primary table while many records for the same value can exist in the related table.
- A foreign key is a field included in a related table that is the primary key of another table needed to create a relationship.
- An entity-relationship diagram depicts the tables joined in the relationship. A diamond symbol is used to represent a relationship with join lines to rectangles that display the table names. Notations on the join line between the table name and the diamond shape indicate the type of relationship.
- At the Edit Relationships dialog box you can turn on referential integrity and the two cascade options and specify the join type.
- Referential integrity places restrictions on new data entered into the related table. A record is not allowed in the related table if a matching record does not already exist in the primary table.
- *Cascade Update Related Fields* and *Cascade Delete Related Records* are made available once referential integrity is turned on.
- *Cascade Update Related Fields* automatically updates all occurrences of the same data in the foreign key field when a change is made to the primary key data.
- *Cascade Delete Related Records* automatically deletes related records when a record is deleted from the primary table.
- Clicking the Join Type button at the Edit Relationships dialog box opens the Join Properties dialog box.
- By default, Access selects an inner join, which means only those records with matching values found in both tables are displayed.
- A left outer join displays all records in the primary table (left table) and matching records from the related table. Blank fields display in the datasheet for any records in the primary table that have no matching records in the related table.
- A right outer join displays all records in the related table (right table) and matching records from the primary table. Blank fields display in the datasheet for records in the related table that have no matching records in the primary table.
- In a one-to-one relationship only one record exists with a matching value in the joined field in both tables.
- In a many-to-many relationship many records can exist with a matching value in the joined field in both tables.

- Many-to-many relationships are problematic because the nature of the relationship means duplicates can occur.
- To create a many-to-many relationship, a junction table is used that contains a minimum of two fields which are the primary key fields from each table in the many-to-many relationship.
- Two one-to-many relationships using the junction table form a many-to-many relationship.
- In some tables, two or more fields are used to create the primary key if a single field is not guaranteed to hold unique data.
- To create a multiple-field primary key, select both fields in Table Design view and then click the Primary Key button in the Tools group in the Table Tools Design tab.
- A primary key that is made up of two or more fields is called a composite key.
- A lookup field displays a drop-down list in a field in which the user points and clicks to enter the field value. The list can be generated from records in a related table, or by typing in a value list.
- Access provides the Lookup Wizard to assist with creating a lookup field. The wizard is started by selecting *Lookup Wizard* from the *Data Type* drop-down list.
- Once the lookup field is created, use the Lookup tab in the *Field Properties* section in Table Design view to modify individual properties.
- The *Limit To List* property allows you to restrict entries in the field to items within the lookup list.
- A field that allows multiple entries to be selected from a drop-down list can be created by clicking *Allow Multiple Values* at the last Lookup Wizard dialog box.
- A field that is defined as a multivalued field cannot be changed back to a single value field.
- Access displays check boxes next to items in the drop-down list if the field has been set to allow multiple values.
- An index is a list generated by Access that includes pointers that direct Access to the location of records in a table.
- Access creates an index for a primary key field automatically.
- Create an index for fields in a table with many records that will be sorted or searched frequently.
- Create a single-field table index by changing the *Indexed* property to *Yes (Duplicates OK)* or *Yes (No Duplicates)*.
- A multiple-field index is created using the Indexes window.
- Normalizing a database involves reviewing the database structure to eliminate redundancy. Three normalization states are checked: first normal form, second normal form, and third normal form.
  - A table is in first normal form if no fields exist that should be split into smaller units and if the table does not have similar data in multiple fields.
  - Second normal form applies only to tables with composite keys and exists when the table is in first normal form and all of the fields are dependent on all of the primary key fields.
  - Third normal form occurs when the table is in first normal form and when all the fields in the table are dependent on the primary key field.

COMMANDS review

FEATURE	RIBBON TAB, GROUP	BUTTON
Edit relationships	Relationship Tools Design, Tools	
Indexes	Table Tools Design, Show/Hide	
Primary key	Table Tools Design, Tools	
Print relationships report	Relationship Tools Design, Tools	Relationship Report
Relationships window	Database Tools, Show/Hide	
Show table	Relationship Tools Design, Relationships	

CONCEPTS check

Test Your Knowledge

Completion: In the space provided at the right, indicate the correct term, command, or number.

1. This is the term for a field added to a related table for the purpose of creating a relationship that is the primary key in the other table.

   _____

2. The Relationships button is found in this tab in the ribbon.

   _____

3. Add a table to the Relationships window using this dialog box.

   _____

4. At the Edit Relationships dialog box, the two cascade options do not become active until this option is turned on.

   _____

5. By default, Access sets the join property to this type of join.

   _____

6. A join in which the primary table shows all records and blank fields display in related field columns if no matching record exists is referred to as this join type.

   _____

7. This type of relationship exists if only one matching record will be found in both tables in the relationship.

   _____

8. A many-to-many relationship is created by establishing two one-to-many relationships using a third table referred to by this term.

_____

9. A primary key that is made up of two or more fields is referred to by this term.

_____

10. A lookup field can be restricted to items within the list by setting this property to *Yes*.

_____

11. Specify a field as a multivalued field by clicking this check box at the last Lookup Wizard dialog box.

_____

12. Set the *Indexed* property to this option for an index field that is likely to contain more than one record with the same field value, such as a ZIP code.

_____

13. Open this window to create an index that uses two or more fields.

_____

14. These are the three normalization states that are tested.

_____

15. If a field exists in a table for which the field value is not dependent on the primary key, the table is not in this normalization state.

_____

SKILLS check
Demonstrate Your Proficiency

Assessment

1 CREATE A LOOKUP LIST

1. Open the database named **VantageVideos2.accdb** and enable the content.
2. Open each table in Datasheet view and review the table's fields and records to familiarize yourself with the database. Close all tables when finished.
3. Open the Relationships window and close the Show Table dialog box. Notice no relationships have been created in the database. Close the Relationships window.
4. The *Cust-ID* field in the WebOrders table can be made easier to use if the field is changed to a lookup list that presents customer names and numbers from the WebCustomers table. Open the WebOrders table in Design view, make *Cust-ID* the active field, and create a lookup list to display values from another table using the following information.
   a. Display the *Cust-ID, Fname,* and *Lname* fields from the WebCustomers table.
   b. Sort the list in ascending order by the *Lname* field.
   c. Clear the *Hide key column* check box.

d. Store the *Cust-ID* value.

e. Accept the default label for the column of *Cust-ID*.

f. Modify the *Lookup* property for the *Cust-ID* field that will ensure only items within the list are allowed to be entered into the field.

g. Save the table, switch to Datasheet view, and then enter the following record to test the lookup list.

Web Order ID	**10007**
Cust-ID	Select *106 Gary Gallagher* in the lookup list
Date Ordered	**Feb 26 2010**

7. Print the datasheet.
8. Close the WebOrders table.

Assessment

2 CREATE A TABLE WITH A MULTI-FIELD PRIMARY KEY AND LOOKUP LISTS

1. With the **VantageVideos2.accdb** database open, create a new table using Design view to track the videos ordered by a customer using the following information.

Field Name	Data Type	Field Size	Caption
WebOrdID	Text	5	Web Order ID
WebProdID	Text	7	Product ID
Qty	Number		Quantity

2. A customer can choose to buy more than one video on the same order. When this occurs, the same order number can be associated with more than one record in the table; therefore, the primary key cannot be based on the *WebOrdID* field alone. Assign a multi-field primary key using both the *WebOrdID* and *WebProdID* fields. The combination of the order identification number and product identification number will uniquely describe each record in the table.

3. Save the table and name it **WebOrderDetails**.

4. Create a lookup list for the *WebOrdID* field that connects to the *WebOrdID* field in the WebOrders table. You determine how to respond to each dialog box in the Lookup Wizard. Modify the *Lookup* property to ensure only items within the list are allowed to be entered into the field.

5. Create a lookup list for the *WebProdID* field that connects to the *WebProdID* field in the WebProducts table. Display the product name in the datasheet sorted in ascending order and make sure the column width is wide enough to display the entire video title. Modify the Lookup property that will ensure only items within the list are allowed to be entered into the field.

6. Save the table and switch to Datasheet view. Add the following records to the WebOrderDetails datasheet to test the lookup lists.

Web Order ID	Product ID	Quantity
10001	To Kill a Mockingbird	1
10001	Blue Hawaii	1
10002	The Great Escape	2
10003	Cool Hand Luke	1
10003	Doctor Zhivago	1
10003	The Longest Day	2
10004	Dial M for Murder	1

7. Adjust all column widths to Best Fit and print the datasheet.

8. Close the WebOrderDetails table. Click Yes when prompted to save changes to the layout.

Assessment

3 EDIT RELATIONSHIPS

1. With the **VantageVideos2.accdb** database open, open the Relationships window to view the relationships created by Access when the lookup lists were created.
2. Resize and move the table field list boxes to the approximate size and location shown in Figure 2.13.
3. Edit the relationships as follows:
   a. Edit the one-to-many relationship between WebCustomers and WebOrders to turn on referential integrity and the two cascade options and change the join type to a left outer join (show all records in WebCustomers and only those matching records in WebOrders where the joined fields are equal).
   b. Edit the one-to-many relationship between WebOrders and WebOrderDetails to turn on referential integrity and the two cascade options.
   c. Edit the one-to-many relationship between WebProducts and WebOrderDetails to turn on referential integrity and the two cascade options.
4. Create and print a relationship report.
5. On your relationship report printout write the type of relationship that exists between WebOrders and WebProducts.
6. Close the Relationships for VantageVideos2 report. Click Yes to save the report and accept the default name in the Save As dialog box.
7. Close the Relationships window.

Figure 2.13 Assessment 3

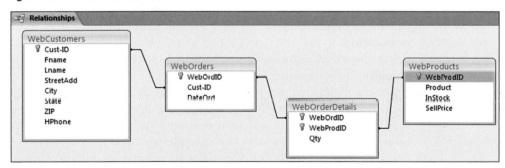

Assessment

4 CREATE A TABLE WITH A ONE-TO-ONE RELATIONSHIP

1. With the **VantageVideos2.accdb** database open, create a new table using Design view to store a customer's credit card information using the following information.

Field Name	Data Type	Field Size	Caption
Cust-ID	Text	3	**Customer ID**
CCType	Text	20	**Credit Card Type**
CCNumber	Text	16	**Credit Card Number**
CCExpMonth	Number		**Expiry Month**
CCExpYear	Number		**Expiry Year**
EmailAdd	Text	30	**Email Address**

2. Assign the primary key to the *Cust-ID* field.
3. Save the table and name it **WebCustomerPymnt**.
4. Create a lookup list for the *Cust-ID* field that connects to the *Cust-ID* field in the WebCustomers table by following steps similar to those in Assessment 1, Step 4. Modify the *Lookup* property to ensure only items within the list are allowed to be entered into the field.
5. Save the table, switch to Datasheet view, and enter the following record.

Customer ID	Select *106 Gary Gallagher* in the lookup list
Credit Card Type	Visa
Credit Card Number	0009100876453152
Expiry Month	7
Expiry Year	14
Email Address	gary_g@emcp.net

6. Adjust all column widths to Best Fit and print the datasheet in landscape orientation.
7. Close the WebCustomerPymnt table. Click Yes when prompted to save changes to the layout.
8. Open the Relationships window and open the Show Table dialog box.
9. Add the WebCustomerPymnt table to the window. Edit the one-to-one relationship between WebCustomers and WebCustomerPymnt to turn on referential integrity and the two cascade options.
10. Print a relationship report. Close the Relationships for the VantageVideos2 report. Click Yes to save the report and type **Relationships-Assessment4** as the report name in the Save As dialog box.
11. Close the Relationships window.
12. Close the **VantageVideos2.accdb** database.

CASE study

Apply Your Skills

You are working as an intern at Deering Sales. The intern that worked at the company before you started a database to be used for managing sales representatives, customers, and sales quotas. The previous intern did not have time to finish the database. Open **DeeringSales2.accdb** and enable the content. Open each table and review the fields and records to familiarize yourself with the database. The Representatives table is not in first normal form. The field named *RepName* contains both the first and last names of each sales representative. To improve the table design, modify the table so that two separate fields are used for representative names. Add captions to the name fields. Correct the data in the datasheet so that the names are correctly split into the two columns. Print the revised Representative table datasheet with all column widths adjusted to Best Fit. Close the table.

You decide to improve the efficiency of data entry by creating lookup lists as follows:

- In the Clients table you want to be able to select the correct sales representative ID by viewing the representative names in a drop-down list. Display the name in the column while storing the RepID as the value in the field.
- In the Representatives table you want to be able to select the quota code by viewing all of the quota codes and amounts in a drop-down list.

Open the Relationships window. Add all of the tables to the window. Resize and arrange boxes so that the join lines between tables are easy to follow and understand. Edit each relationship to turn on referential integrity and the two cascade options. Create, print, and save a relationships report. Close the relationships report and close the relationships window.

You have decided to add another table named **Sales** to the database. Create the table using the information below. You determine appropriate data types. Assign the primary key as a combination of three fields: *ClientID*, *RepID*, and *SaleDate*. Add a sample record to the table to test your lookup lists and multivalued field. Adjust all column widths to Best Fit, print the datasheet, and close the table saving the layout. Open the relationships window, add the new table, and arrange the layout so that join lines are not overlapping. Edit the relationships between Sales and Clients and Representatives to turn on referential integrity and the two cascade options. Create, print, and save a new relationships report named **Relationships-Part3**.

Field Name	Lookup Lists
ClientID	Create a lookup list to the Clients table
RepID	Create a lookup list to the Representatives table
SaleDate	
Amount	
Terms	Create a multivalued list that displays:
	2% 10 days
	1% 15 days
	Net 30 days
	Net 60 days

Advanced Query Techniques

CHAPTER 3

Upon successful completion of Chapter 3, you will be able to:

- Save a filter as a query
- Create and run a parameter query to prompt for criteria
- Add and remove tables to and from a query
- Create an inner join, left join, and right join to modify query results
- Create a self-join to match two fields in the same table
- Create a query that includes a subquery
- Assign an alias to a table and a field name
- Select records using a multivalued field in a query
- Create a new table using a make-table query
- Remove records from a table using a delete query
- Add records to the end of an existing table using an append query
- Modify records using an update query

Tutorial 3.1
Using Filters to Refine a Query
Tutorial 3.2
Using Advanced Queries and Expressions

In this chapter you create, save, and run queries that incorporate advanced query features such as saving a filter as a query, prompting for criteria on single and multiple fields, modifying join properties to view alternative query results, and using action queries to perform operations on groups of records. In addition to these topics, you will also create an alias for a table and a field and incorporate subqueries to manage multiple calculations.

Note: Before beginning computer projects, copy to your storage medium the Access2007L2C3 subfolder from the Access2007L2 folder on the CD that accompanies this textbook and then make Access2007L2C3 the active folder.

roject ❶ **Select Records Using Filtered Criteria and Prompted Criteria**

You will create queries to select records by saving a filter's criteria and by creating a query that prompts the user for the criteria when the query is run.

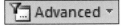

QUICK STEPS

Save Filter as Query
1. Open table.
2. Filter table as desired.
3. Click Advanced Filter Options button.
4. Click *Filter By Form.*
5. Click Advanced Filter Options button.
6. Click *Save As Query.*
7. Type desired query name.
8. Click OK.
9. Close Filter By Form datasheet.
10. Close table.

Extracting Records Using Select Queries

A select query is the query type that is most often used in Access. Select queries extract records from a single table or from multiple tables that meet criteria that you specify. The subset of records that is displayed can be edited, viewed, and/or printed. In Query Design view, the criteria used to select records are entered by typing expressions in the *Criteria* row for the required field(s). Access provides other methods for which criteria can be specified for a query.

Saving a Filter as a Query

A filter is used in a datasheet or form to temporarily hide records that do not meet specified criteria. For example, you can filter a Work_Orders datasheet to display only those work orders completed on a specified date. The subset of records can be edited, viewed, or printed. Use the Filter by Form feature to filter a datasheet by multiple criteria using a blank datasheet. A filter is active until the filter is removed or the datasheet or form is closed. When the object is reopened, all records are redisplayed.

If you filter a datasheet and then decide that you may want to reuse the criteria, save the filter as a query. To do this, display the criteria in the Filter by Form datasheet, click the Advanced Filter Options button in the Sort & Filter group in the Home tab and then click *Save as Query* at the drop-down list. Type a query name at the Save as Query dialog box and press Enter or click OK.

Saving a filter as a query means all columns in the table display in the query results datasheet. Use the Hide Columns feature to remove field(s) in the results.

HINT

Consider filtering a datasheet and saving the filter as a query if you are more comfortable using filters to select records than typing criteria expressions in Query Design view.

▼⊡ Advanced ▾

Project 1a ▏ **Saving a Filter as a Query**

1. Open the **RSRComputerServ3.accdb** database and enable the content.
2. Display only those service calls that required two or more hours of labor by technicians billed at $25.00 per hour using the Filter by Form feature by completing the following steps:
   a. Open the Work_Orders table in Datasheet view.
   b. Click the Shutter Bar Open/Close button ⟨⟨ to minimize the navigation pane.
   c. Hide the *Comments* field by right-clicking the *Comments* column heading in the datasheet and then clicking *Hide Columns* at the shortcut menu.
   d. Click the Advanced Filter Options button ▼⊡ Advanced ▾ in the Sort & Filter group in the Home tab and then click *Filter By Form* at the drop-down list.

Step 2d

e. Click in the empty record in the *Hours* column. A down-pointing arrow appears that you use if you want to filter the table by a specific value within the field. Type *>=2* and then press Tab.

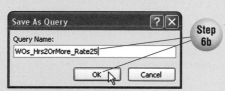

f. With the insertion point positioned in the *Rate* column, click the down-pointing arrow that appears and then click *25* at the drop-down list.

g. Click the Toggle Filter button (displays the ScreenTip *Apply Filter*) in the Sort & Filter group in the Home tab to apply the filter's criteria and display records that meet the filter conditions.

3. Review the nine filtered records in the datasheet.

4. Click the Toggle Filter button (displays the ScreenTip *Remove Filter*) to redisplay all records.

5. Click the Advanced Filter Options button and then click *Filter By Form* at the drop-down list. Notice the filter criteria in the *Hours* and *Rate* columns are intact.

6. Save the filter as a query so that you can reuse the criteria by completing the following steps:

a. Click the Advanced Filter Options button and then click *Save As Query* at the drop-down list.

b. At the Save As Query dialog box, type **WOs_Hrs2OrMore_Rate25** in the *Query Name* text box and then press Enter or click OK.

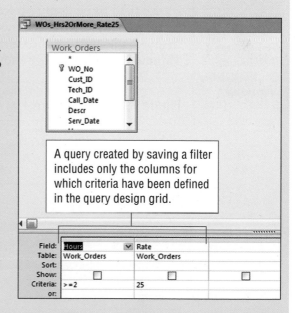

c. Click the Advanced Filter Options button and then click *Close* at the drop-down list to close the Filter By Form datasheet.

d. Close the Work_Orders table. Click No when prompted to save changes to the table design.

7. Click the Shutter Bar Open/Close button ≫ to redisplay the navigation pane. Notice the WOs_Hrs2OrMore_Rate25 query object in the Work_Orders section of the navigation pane.

8. Double-click the query object named *WOs_Hrs2OrMore_Rate25* to open the query and review the query results.

9. Right-click *CallDate* in the field name row and then click *Hide Columns* at the shortcut menu. Repeat this step to hide the *Comments* column.

10. Print the datasheet in landscape orientation.

11. Switch to Design view. Notice a query created from a filter creates columns in the query design grid for only those columns upon which a criterion has been defined.

12. Close the query. Click Yes when prompted to save changes to the query layout.

A query created by saving a filter includes only the columns for which criteria have been defined in the query design grid.

Prompting for Criteria Using a Parameter Query

In a parameter query, specific criteria for a field are not stored with the query design. Instead, the criteria field(s) have a parameter that displays a dialog box with a message when the query is run. The message prompts the user to type the criteria by which to select records. Figure 3.1 illustrates the Enter Parameter Value dialog box that is displayed when a parameter query is run. The message that is shown in the dialog box is created in the field for which the criterion will be applied. When the query is run, the user types the criterion at the Enter Parameter Value dialog box and Access selects the records based on the entry. If more than one field contains a parameter, Access prompts the user one field at a time.

Figure 3.1 Enter Parameter Value Dialog Box

A parameter query is useful if you run a query several times on the same field but use different criteria each time. For example, if you require a list of work orders by individual technician, you would have to create a separate query for each technician. This would create several query objects in the navigation pane. Creating a parameter query that prompts you to enter the technician's name means you only have to create one query.

To create a parameter query, start a new query in Design view and add the desired tables and fields to the query design grid. Type a message encased in square brackets to prompt the user for the required criterion in the *Criteria* row of the field to be used to select records. The text inside the square brackets is displayed in the Enter Parameter Value dialog box when the query is run. Figure 3.2 displays the entry in the *Criteria* row of the *Fname* field that generated the Enter Parameter Value message shown in Figure 3.1.

Figure 3.2 Criterion to Prompt for the Name in the *Fname* Field

Field:	WO_No	Fname
Table:	Work_Orders	Technicians
Sort:		
Show:	☑	☑
Criteria:		[Type the technician's first name]
or:		

Type a message in square brackets to prompt the user for the criterion by which to select records.

Project **1b** **Creating a Query to Prompt for Technician Names**

1. With the **RSRComputerServ3.accdb** database open, create a query in Design view to select records from the Technicians table and the Work_Orders table by completing the following steps:
   a. Click the Create tab and then click the Query Design button in the Other group.
   b. At the Show Table dialog box, add the Technicians table and the Work_Orders table to the query.

c. Close the Show Table dialog box.

d. Drag the bottom border of each table's field list box at the top of the query until all field names are visible in the box.

e. Add the following fields in order to the query design grid: *WO_No, Fname, Lname, Serv_Date, Hours, Rate*.

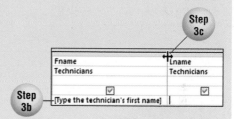

Field:	WO_No	Fname	Lname	Serv_Date	Hours	Rate
Table:	Work_Orders	Technicians	Technicians	Work_Orders	Work_Orders	Work_Orders
Sort:						
Show:	☑	☑	☑	☑	☑	☑

2. Click the Run button ❗ to run the query.

3. Add parameters to select records by a technician's first and last names by completing the following steps:

a. Switch to Design view.

b. Click in the *Criteria* row in the *Fname* column in the query design grid, type [Type the technician's first name], and then press Enter.

c. Position the pointer on the vertical line between *Fname* and *Lname* in the gray field selector bar above the field names until the pointer changes to a vertical line with a left- and right-pointing arrow and then double-click to expand the width of the *Fname* column so that you can see the entire criteria entry.

Step 3c

Step 3b

Fname	Lname
Technicians	Technicians
☑	☑
[Type the technician's first name]	

d. With the insertion point positioned in the *Criteria* row in the *Lname* column, type [Type the technician's last name] and then press Enter.

e. Expand the width of the *Lname* column so that you can see the entire criteria entry.

4. Click the Save button on the Quick Access toolbar, type **PromptedTechnicianLabor** in the *Query Name* text box at the Save As dialog box and then press Enter or click OK.

5. Close the query.

6. Run the prompted query and extract a list of work orders for the technician named Pat Hynes by completing the following steps:

a. Double-click the query named PromptedTechnicianLabor in the navigation pane.

b. Type **pat** at the Enter Parameter Value dialog box that displays the message *Type the technician's first name* and then press Enter or click OK. Note that Access is not case sensitive when typing text strings.

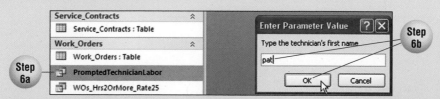

Step 6a

Step 6b

c. Type **hynes** at the second Enter Parameter Value dialog box that displays the message *Type the technician's last name* and then press Enter or click OK.

Step 6c

7. Review the records in the query results datasheet.

8. Adjust all column widths to Best Fit and then print the query results datasheet. If necessary, click in any field to deselect columns.

9. Close the query. Click Yes when prompted to save changes to the query layout.

1. With the **RSRComputerServ3.accdb** database open, create a query in Design view to prompt the user for a starting and ending date by which to select records using the Work_Orders table by completing the following steps:
   a. Click the Create tab and then click the Query Design button in the Other group.
   b. At the Show Table dialog box, add the Work_Orders table to the query and then close the Show Table dialog box.
   c. Drag the bottom border of the table's field list box until all field names are visible.
   d. Add the following fields in order to the query design grid: *WO_No*, *Cust-ID*, *Descr*, *Serv_Date*, *Hours*, *Rate*, *Parts*.
   e. Click in the *Criteria* row in the *Serv_Date* column, type the following entry, and then press Enter.
      Between [Type starting date] And [Type ending date]

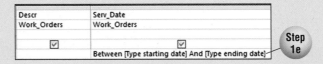

   f. Expand the *Serv_Date* column width until the entire criteria entry is visible.
2. Save the query and name it **PromptedServiceDate**.
3. Close the query.
4. Double-click the PromptedServiceDate query in the navigation pane. At the first Enter Parameter Value dialog box with *Type starting date* displayed, type **October 1, 2009** and press Enter or click OK. At the second Enter Parameter Value dialog box with *Type ending date* displayed, type **October 15, 2009** and press Enter or click OK.

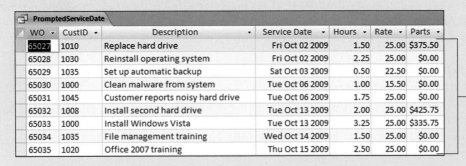

Records selected within the date range October 1, 2009 to October 15, 2009 for the *Service Date* column at Step 4

5. Print the query results datasheet in landscape orientation.
6. Close the query.

Project 2 — Modify Query Results by Changing the Join Property

You will create and modify queries that obtain various results based on changing the join properties for related tables.

Modifying Join Properties in a Query

Recall from Chapter 2 the join type can be changed when a relationship is created between two tables at the Edit Relationships dialog box. Access provides for three join types: an inner join, a left outer join, and a right outer join. By default, Access selects an inner join between the tables which means that records are selected for display in a query only when a match on the joined field value exists in both tables. If a record exists in either table with no matching record in the other table, the record is not displayed. Be aware that when viewing a query results datasheet that is generated from an inner join, you may not be viewing all records from both tables.

If you want to change the join type, you do not have to edit the relationship before creating a query. The join type can be changed at the query design window by double-clicking the black join line between tables to open the Join Properties dialog box shown in Figure 3.3. Select option *1* to create an inner join, option *2* to create a left outer join, or option *3* to create a right outer join and click OK.

QUICK STEPS

Create Query with Inner Join
1. Create new query in Design view.
2. Add tables to query window.
3. Double-click join line between tables.
4. Select option *1*.
5. Click OK.
6. Add desired fields to query design grid.
7. Save and run query.

HINT

Changing the join type at a query window does not alter the join type for other objects based on the relationship—the revised join property applies to the query only.

Figure 3.3 Join Properties Dialog Box

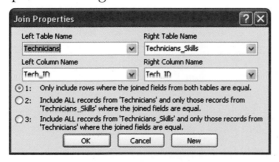

Project 2a — Selecting Records in a Query Using an Inner Join

1. With the **RSRComputerServ3.accdb** database open, create a query in Design view to display a list of technicians with each technician's certifications and operating system specialties by completing the following steps:
   a. Create a new query in Design view. At the Show Table dialog box, add the Technicians and the Technicians_Skills tables and then close the Show Table dialog box.
   b. Double-click the black join line between the two tables to open the Join Properties dialog box.

Step 1b

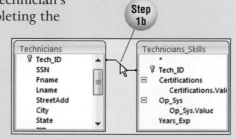

c. At the Join Properties dialog box, notice that *1* is selected by default. Option 1 selects records only when the joined fields from both tables are equal. This represents an inner join. Click OK.

d. Add the following fields in order to the query design grid: *Tech_ID*, *Fname*, *Lname*, *Certifications*, and *Op_Sys*.
Note: Be sure to select the Tech_ID field from the Technicians table field list box.
This is the primary table in the relationship and returns each technician's unique identification number in the query results. Selecting Tech_ID from the Technicians_Skills table will not supply the identification number since this table uses a lookup to the primary table and displays a last name in the field instead of a number. When the same field exists in more than one table, draw the field from the primary table in the relationship.

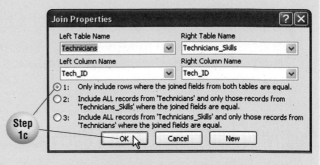

Step 1c

e. Run the query. Notice that eight records are displayed in the query results datasheet.

2. Minimize the navigation pane.

3. Save the query and name it **TechniciansWithCertAndOpSys**.

4. Adjust all column widths to Best Fit. Print the query results datasheet in landscape orientation with left and right margins of 0.5-inch. If necessary, click in any field to deselect columns.

Technician ID	First Name	Last Name	Certifications	Operating Systems
01	Pat	Hynes	Microsoft MCP, Microsoft MCSE	Windows 2000, Windows XP
02	Hui	Chen	CompTIA A+, CompTIA N+	Linux, Windows Vista
04	Mihir	Patel	CompTIA A+, CompTIA N+, Microsoft MCP	Unix, Windows Vista, Windows XP
05	Madir	Sadiku	Microsoft MCP, Microsoft MCSE	Windows 2000, Windows Vista, Windows XP
07	Ana	Takacs	Cisco CCNA	Windows XP
08	Marty	O'Leary	Cisco CCNA, CompTIA N+	Windows Vista
09	Armando	Colacci	Microsoft MCAS	Windows Vista, Windows XP
10	Kelsey	Eastman	Cisco CCNA, Microsoft MCP	Linux, Windows Vista, Windows XP

Step 4

5. Close the query. Click Yes to save changes.

6. Redisplay the navigation pane.

Project 2b   Selecting Records in a Query Using a Left Outer Join

1. With the **RSRComputerServ3.accdb** database open, modify the TechniciansWithCertAndOpSys query to a left outer join to check if any technicians do not have a matching record in the Technicians_Skills table by completing the following steps:

a. Open the TechniciansWithCertAndOpSys query in Design view.

b. Right-click the black join line between the two tables and then click *Join Properties* at the shortcut menu.

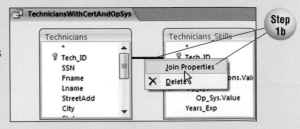

Step 1b

c. At the Join Properties dialog box, click *2* and then click OK. Option 2 includes all records from the Technicians table and only those records from Technicians_Skills where the joined fields are equal. The left table (Technicians) is the table that will show all records. If a technician does not have a matching record in the other table, the columns display empty fields next to the technician's name.

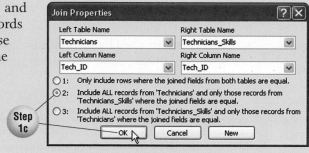

Step 1c

d. Notice the join line between the two tables now displays with an arrow pointing to the joined field in the Technicians_Skills table.

e. Run the query. Notice that 11 records display in the query results datasheet. Three records display blank fields in the *Certifications* and *Operating Systems* columns.

2. Minimize the navigation pane.

3. Adjust all column widths to Best Fit and then print the query results datasheet in landscape orientation and with a left margin set to 0.75-inch. If necessary, click in any field to deselect columns.

TechniciansWithCertAndOpSys

Technician ID	First Name	Last Name	Certifications	Operating Systems
01	Pat	Hynes	Microsoft MCP, Microsoft MCSE	Windows 2000, Windows XP
02	Hui	Chen	CompTIA A+, CompTIA N+	Linux, Windows Vista
03	Kayla	Blewett		
04	Mihir	Patel	CompTIA A+, CompTIA N+, Microsoft MCP	Unix, Windows Vista, Windows XP
05	Madir	Sadiku	Microsoft MCP, Microsoft MCSE	Windows 2000, Windows Vista, Windows XP
06	Brody	Stewart		
07	Ana	Takacs	Cisco CCNA	Windows XP
08	Marty	O'Leary	Cisco CCNA, CompTIA N+	Windows Vista
09	Armando	Colacci	Microsoft MCAS	Windows Vista, Windows XP
10	Kelsey	Eastman	Cisco CCNA, Microsoft MCP	Linux, Windows Vista, Windows XP
11	Dana	Westman		

Step 3

4. Close the query. Click Yes to save changes.

5. Redisplay the navigation pane.

Do not assume a left join always occurs with the table that is the left table in the query window. Although Technicians was the left table in the Project 2b query window, "left" refers to the table that represents the *one* side (primary table) in the relationship.

QUICK STEPS

Create Query with Left Outer Join

1. Create new query in Design view.
2. Add tables to query window.
3. Double-click join line between tables.
4. Select option *2*.
5. Click OK.
6. Add desired fields to query design grid.
7. Save and run query.

Adding Tables to and Removing Tables from a Query

Open a query in Design view to add a table to the query. Click the Show Table button in the Query Setup group in the Query Tools Design tab and then add the desired table using the Show Table dialog box. Close the Show Table dialog box when finished.

To remove a table from the query, click any field within the table field list box to activate the table in the query window and then press the Delete key. The table is removed from the window and all fields associated with the table that were added to the query design grid are automatically removed. You can also right-click the table in the query window and click *Remove Table* at the shortcut menu.

Project 2c Selecting Records in a Query Using a Right Outer Join

1. With the **RSRComputerServ3.accdb** database open, modify the TechniciansWithCertAndOpSys query to a right outer join to check for work orders that have not been assigned to a technician by completing the following steps:
   a. Open the TechniciansWithCertAndOpSys query in Design view.
   b. Right-click the Technicians_Skills table in the query window and then click *Remove Table* at the shortcut menu. Notice that the *Certifications* and *Op_Sys* columns are removed from the query design grid along with the table.

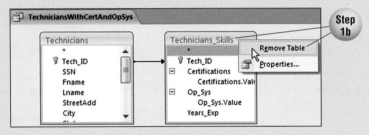

   c. Click the Show Table button 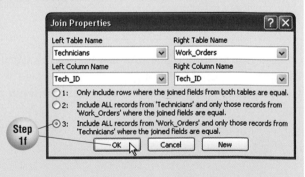 in the Query Setup group in the Query Tools Design tab.
   d. At the Show Table dialog box, double-click *Work_Orders* in the Tables list and then click the Close button.
   e. Double-click the black join line between the two tables.
   f. At the Join Properties dialog box, click *3* and then click OK. Option 3 includes all records from the Work_Orders table and only those records from the Technicians table where the joined fields are equal. The right table (Work_Orders) is the table that will show all records. If a work order does not have a matching record in the other table, the columns display empty fields next to the work order information.
   g. Notice the join line between the two tables now displays with an arrow pointing to the joined field in the Technicians table.
   h. Add the following fields in order from the Work_Orders table to the query design grid: *WO_No*, *Call_Date*, and *Descr*.

2. Save the revised query using a new name by completing the following steps:
   a. Click the Office button, point to Save As, and then click *Save Object As* at the drop-down list.
   b. At the Save As dialog box with the existing text already selected in the *Save 'TechniciansWithCertAndOpSys' to* text box, type **UnassignedWorkOrders** and then click OK. Access defaults to *Query* in the *As* list box since the source object was a query.

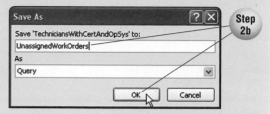

Step 2b

3. Run the query. Notice the first four records in the query results datasheet have empty fields in the *Technician ID*, *First Name*, and *Last Name* columns.
4. Adjust all column widths to Best Fit. If necessary, click in any field to deselect columns.

Technician ID	First Name	Last Name	WO	Call Date	Description
			65047	Tue Oct 27 2009	Set up automatic backup
			65048	Thu Oct 29 2009	Replace LCD monitor
			65049	Fri Oct 30 2009	Set up dual monitor system
			65050	Fri Oct 30 2009	Reinstall Windows XP
01	Pat	Hynes	65020	Wed Sep 16 2009	Troubleshoot noisy fan

Step 4

5. Change the page orientation to landscape.
6. Print the first page only of the datasheet. To do this, open the Print dialog box. Click *Pages* in the *Print Range* section, type 1 in the *From* text box, press Tab, type 1 in the *To* text box, and then press Enter or click OK to print the first page only of the query results datasheet.
7. Close the query. Click Yes to save changes.

Do not assume a right join always occurs with the table that is the right table in the query window. Although Work_Orders was the right table in the Project 2c query window, "right" refers to the table that represents the *many* side (related table) in the relationship.

Joining Two Copies of the Same Table in a Query

If you have a table that has matching values in two separate fields, you can create a query to display field values from a matched field instead of the stored content. For example, in the Technicians table, the field named *Tech_ID* storcs each technician's unique identification number. Another field in the table, named *Tier2Supv*, displays the technician identification number for the Tier 2 supervisor that is assigned to the technician. Tier 2 supervisors are senior technicians who are called in when a work order is too complex for the regular technician to solve. The *Tier2Supv* field stores the technician's number. You may prefer to see the last name of the technician instead of the number.

QUICK STEPS

Create Query with Right Outer Join
1. Create new query in Design view.
2. Add tables to query window.
3. Double-click join line between tables.
4. Select option *3*.
5. Click OK.
6. Add desired fields to query design grid.
7. Save and run query.

In a query window, add the same table to the query twice. The second occurrence of the table is named using the original table name with _*1* added to the end. Join the two tables by dragging the field with matching values from one table field list to the other. This join is called a *self-join query*. Add the required fields to the query design grid and then run the query.

Project 2d   Creating a Self-Join Query

1. With the **RSRComputerServ3.accdb** database open, open the Technicians table and review the datasheet. Notice the column titled *Tier 2 Supervisor* contains technician identification numbers. These numbers indicate the senior technician supervisor assigned to each technician. Close the Technicians table.

2. Create a self-join query to display the last name of the Tier 2 supervisor instead of the identification number by completing the following steps:
   a. Create a new query in Design view.
   b. At the Show Table dialog box, add the Technicians table to the query twice and then close the Show Table dialog box. Notice the second copy of the table is named *Technicians_1*.
   c. Drag the bottom border of both table field list boxes down until all field names are visible.
   d. Drag the field named *Tier2Supv* from the Technicians table field list box at the left to the field named *Tech_ID* in the Technicians_1 table field list box at the right.

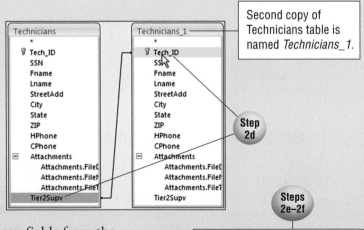

   e. Add the *Fname* and *Lname* fields from the Technicians table to the query design grid.
   f. Add the *Lname* field from the Technicians_1 table to the query design grid.

3. Run the query. The last names displayed in the second *Last Name* column represent the *Tier2Supv* name. This was the field used to join the two copies of the table and contained the matching values to the *Tech_ID* field.

4. Switch to Design view.
5. Right-click the second *Lname* column (from the Technicians_1 table) and click *Properties* at the shortcut menu. Click in the *Caption* property box in the Property Sheet task pane, type **Tier 2 Supervisor**, and press Enter. Close the Property Sheet task pane.
6. Save the query and name it **Tier2Supervisors**. Run the query.
7. Adjust all column widths to Best Fit and then print the query results datasheet. If necessary, click in any field to deselect columns.
8. Close the query. Click Yes to save changes.

First Name	Last Name	Tier 2 Supervisor
Pat	Hynes	Blewett
Hui	Chen	Stewart
Mihir	Patel	Westman
Madir	Sadiku	Blewett
Ana	Takacs	Westman
Marty	O'Leary	Westman
Armando	Colacci	Stewart
Kelsey	Eastman	Stewart

Tier2Supervisors

Step 7

Running a Query with No Established Relationship

If a query is created from two tables for which no join is established, Access will not know how to relate records in each table. For example, if one table contains 20 records and the other table contains 10 records and no join is established between the tables, Access produces a query results datasheet containing 200 records (20 × 10). Absent a relationship, Access produces a datasheet representing every combination of records between the two tables. This type of query is called a ***cross product*** or ***Cartesian product*** query. The results of such a query in most cases would provide data that serves no purpose.

If you add two tables to a query and no join line appears, create a join by dragging a field from one table to a compatible field in the other table. The two fields should contain the same data type and be logically related in some way.

oject **3** **Calculate Work Order Totals**

You will use a subquery nested within another query to calculate the total amount earned from each work order.

Creating and Using Subqueries

When performing multiple calculations based on numeric fields you may decide to create a separate query for each individual calculation and then use subqueries to generate the final total. A subquery is a query nested inside another query. Using subqueries to break the calculations into individual objects allows you to reuse a calculated field in multiple queries. For example, assume that you want to calculate the total amount for each work order. The Work_Orders table contains fields with the number of hours for each service call, the labor rate, and the total amount of the parts used. To find the total for each work order, you need to calculate the total labor by multiplying the hours times the rate and then add the parts value to the total labor value. However, you may want the total labor value

QUICK STEPS

Nest Query within a Query
1. Start new query in Design view.
2. At Show Table dialog box, click Queries tab.
3. Double-click query to be used as subquery.
4. Add other queries or tables as required.
5. Close Show Table dialog box.
6. Add fields as required.
7. Save and run query.

to be in a separate query so that you can perform other calculations such as finding the average, maximum, or minimum labor on work orders. To be able to reuse the total labor value, you will need to create the calculated field in its own query.

Once the query is created to calculate the total labor, you can nest the query inside another query to add the labor to the parts to calculate the total for all work orders. Creating subqueries provides you with the flexibility to reuse calculations, thus avoiding duplication of effort and reducing the potential for calculation errors.

Project 3a   Creating a Query to Calculate Total Labor

1. With the **RSRComputerServ3.accdb** database open, create a query to calculate the total labor for each work order by completing the following steps:
   a. Create a new query in Design view. At the Show Table dialog box, add the Work_Orders table to the query window and then close the Show Table dialog box.
   b. Drag the bottom border of the Work_Orders table field list box down until all fields are visible.
   c. Add the following fields in order to the query design grid: *WO_No*, *Serv_Date*, *Hours*, and *Rate*.
   d. Click in the blank *Field* row next to *Rate* in the query design grid, type **Total Labor: [Hours]*[Rate]**, and then press Enter.
   e. Expand the width of the calculated column until you can see all of the formula in the *Field* row.

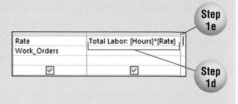

Step 1e

Step 1d

2. Run the query and view the query results. Notice the *Total Labor* column does not display a consistent number of decimal values.
3. Switch to Design view.
4. Format the *Total Labor* column by completing the following steps:
   a. Click the insertion point anywhere within the *Total Labor* field row to activate the field.
   b. Click the Property Sheet button [Property Sheet] in the Show/Hide group in the Query Tools Design tab.
   c. Click in the *Format* property box in the Property Sheet task pane, click the down-pointing arrow that appears, and then click *Standard* at the drop-down list.
   d. Click the Close button at the top right of the Property Sheet task pane.

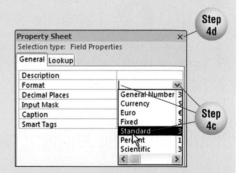

Step 4d

Step 4c

5. Save the query and name it **TotalLabor**.
6. Run the query. Notice the last four rows contain no values since the service calls have not yet been completed.
7. Switch to Design view. Click in the *Criteria* row in the *Hours* column, type **>0**, and then press Enter.
8. Save the revised query and then run the query.
9. Print the query results datasheet and then close the query.

Step 7

Project 3b Nesting a Query within a Query

1. With the **RSRComputerServ3.accdb** database open, create a new query to calculate the total value of all work orders using the TotalLabor query as a subquery by completing the following steps:

   a. Create a new query in Design view.

   b. At the Show Table dialog box, click the Queries tab.

   c. Double-click *TotalLabor* in the Queries list.

   d. Click the Tables tab.

   e. Double-click *Work_Orders* in the Tables list and then close the Show Table dialog box. Notice that Access has automatically joined the two objects on the *WO_No* field.

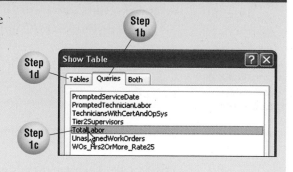

Step 1b

Step 1d

Step 1c

2. Add fields from the TotalLabor subquery and from the Work_Orders table by completing the following steps:

   a. Double-click the asterisk (*) at the top of the TotalLabor field list box. Access adds the entry *TotalLabor.** to the first column in the query design grid. This entry adds all of the fields from the query. Individual columns do not display in the grid; however, when you run the query, the datasheet will show all fields.

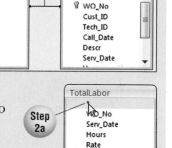

Step 1e

Subquery object

Step 2a

   b. Run the query. Notice the query results datasheet shows all five columns from the TotalLabor query.

   c. Switch to Design view. You decide to format the *Total Labor* column to Currency for this new query. In order to do this, you need to add the column to the query design grid.

   d. Right-click in the field selector bar (gray bar above the *Field* row) for the *TotalLabor.** column and then click *Cut* at the shortcut menu to remove the column from the design grid.

   e. Add the following fields in order to the query design grid: *WO_No*, *Serv_Date*, and *Total Labor*.

   f. Format the *Total Labor* column to *Currency*.

   g. Drag the bottom border of the Work_Orders table field list box down until all fields are visible and then double-click *Parts* to add the field to the query design grid.

3. Create the calculated field to add the total labor and parts by completing the following steps:

   a. Click in the blank *Field* row next to *Parts* in the query design grid, type **Total Work Order: [Total Labor]+[Parts]**, and then press Enter.

   b. Expand the width of the *Total Work Order* column until the entire formula is visible.

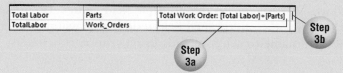

Step 3a

Step 3b

   c. Format the *Total Work Order* column to *Currency*.

4. Save the query naming it **TotalWorkOrders** and then run the query.

5. Adjust all column widths to Best Fit and then print the query results datasheet. If necessary, click in any field to deselect columns.
6. Close the query. Click Yes to save changes.

TotalWorkOrders				
WO	Service Date	Total Labor	Parts	Total Work Order
65012	Fri Sep 04 2009	$31.25	$10.15	$41.40
65013	Wed Sep 09 2009	$12.50	$42.75	$55.25
65014	Thu Sep 10 2009	$43.75	$62.77	$106.52

Step 5

Smaller queries are easier to build and troubleshoot. Another reason to use subqueries is when you need to create a complex query. Create subqueries to build and test each section individually and then combine the subqueries into the final query.

Project 4 Query a Multivalued Field and Assign Aliases

You will select records using a multivalued field in a query and assign an alias to a table and a field name to provide shorter names.

Selecting Records Using a Multivalued Field

You learned to create and use multivalued fields in Chapter 2. In a query, a multivalued field can display as it does in a table datasheet with the multiple field values in the same column separated by commas, or you can elect to show each field value in a separate row. To show each value in a separate row, add the multivalued field name with *.Value* at the end in the *Field* box in the query design grid. Figure 3.4 displays the query design grid for the query you will use in Project 4 that displays each entry in the *Op_Sys* field in a separate row in the datasheet.

To select records using criteria in a multivalued field, type the criteria using the same procedures you would for a single-value field. For example, in the TechniciansWithCertAndOpSys query, typing "Windows Vista" in the *Criteria* row in the *Op_Sys* column causes Access to return the records of any technician with Windows Vista as one of the multiple field values. If you assign an alias to the table in which the multivalued field resides, you will need to use the *.Value* property in the field name to select records using criteria statements.

Figure 3.4 Project 4 Query Design Grid

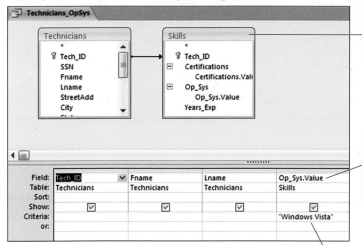

Technicians_Skills table with the alias *Skills* assigned to the table.

Adding *.Value* to the end of the multivalued field *Op_Sys* causes Access to display each value in a separate row in the datasheet.

Only those records with *Windows Vista* will be selected in the query results.

Creating an Alias for a Table or a Field

An alias is another name that you want to use to reference a table or a field in a query. The alias is temporary and applies to the query only. Generally, you create an alias if you want to assign a shorter name to a table or field or a more descriptive name if the table or field name is cryptic. For example, the table that you will use in the query in Project 4 is named Technicians_Skills. You can assign the table a shorter name such as Skills to make it easier to work with in the query. The shorter name requires less space in the design grid.

If you will be creating an SQL query, a shorter table name is easier to type in SQL statements. SQL stands for Structured Query Language and is the query programming language you use in Access to produce more advanced queries. Some queries can only be created using SQL statements. An SQL statement to select records begins with a structure similar to SELECT *tablename.fieldname1*, *tablename.fieldname2* . . . FROM *tablename*. Using a shorter table name makes these statements much easier to type into the SQL view window.

To assign an alias to a table, right-click the table name in the query window and click *Properties* at the shortcut menu to open the Property Sheet task pane. Click in the *Alias* property box, delete the existing table name and type the name by which you want the table referenced. Access replaces all occurrences of the table name with the alias in the query design grid.

QUICK STEPS

Assign Alias to Table in Query
1. Open query in Design view.
2. Right-click table.
3. Click *Properties*.
4. Click in *Alias* property box.
5. Delete existing text.
6. Type alias table name.
7. Close Property Sheet task pane.
8. Save query.

Assign Alias to Field in Query
1. Open query in Design view.
2. Click in *Field* box at beginning of field name.
3. Type alias field name.
4. Type colon :.
5. Press Enter.
6. Save table.

Show Multivalued Field in Separate Rows in Query
1. Open query in Design view.
2. Click in *Field* box of multivalued field in design grid.
3. Move insertion point to end of field name.
4. Type period ..
5. Press Enter to accept *.Value*.
6. Save query.

To assign an alias to a field, click at the beginning of the field name in the *Field* box in the query design grid and type the desired alias name followed by a colon. For example: typing *Operating Sys:Op_Sys* assigns the alias Operating Sys to the field named Op_Sys.

Project ④ Assigning Aliases and Using a Multivalued Field in a Query

1. With the **RSRComputerServ3.accdb** database open, open the TechniciansWithCertAndOpSys query in Design view.
2. Assign an alias to the Technicians_Skills table in the query by completing the following steps:

   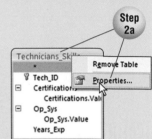

   Step 2a

   a. Right-click the Technicians_Skills table and click *Properties* at the shortcut menu.
   b. Select the current text in the *Alias* property box in the Property Sheet task pane and press the Delete key.
   c. Type **Skills** and press Enter.
   d. Close the Property Sheet task pane.
   e. Notice the table name in the field list box title bar is changed to *Skills* and the names in the *Table* row in the query design grid for the *Certifications* and *Op_Sys* fields display as *Skills*.

   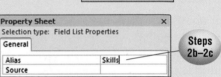

   Steps 2b–2c

3. Right-click in the field selector bar above the *Certifications* field and click *Cut* at the shortcut menu to remove the field from the query design grid.

   Step 3

4. Run the query. Notice each record in the *Operating Systems* column displays the multiple values separated by commas.
5. Switch to Design view.
6. Click in the *Op_Sys* field box in the query design grid, move the insertion point to the end of the file name and then type a period .. Access displays .*Value* in the *Field* box. Press Enter to accept the .*Value* property in the field name. ***Note: When creating a query from scratch, drag the multivalued field name with the .Value property already attached from the table's field list box to the query design grid.***

   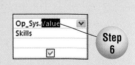

   Step 6

7. Use Save As to save the query using the name Technicians_OpSys.
8. Run the query. Notice that each entry in the multivalued field is now displayed in a separate row.
9. Switch to Design view.
10. Click in the *Criteria* row in the *Op_Sys.Value* column in the query design grid, type **Windows Vista**, and press Enter.
11. Run the query. Notice the column title for the multivalued field is now *Skills.Op_Sys.Value*. Assign an alias to the field by completing the following steps:

    Step 10

    a. Switch to Design view.

b. Click the insertion point at the beginning of the text in the *Op_Sys.Value* Field box in the query design grid.

c. Type **Operating_System:** and press Enter.

d. Expand the width of the *Op_Sys.Value* column until you can see the entire entry in the *Field* box.

e. Run the query.

12. Adjust all column widths to Best Fit and print the query results datasheet. If necessary, click in any field to deselect columns.

13. Close the query. Click Yes to save changes.

> **Step 11c**
>
> Operating_System: Op_Sys.Value
> Skills

Technicians_OpSys

Technician ID	First Name	Last Name	Operating_System
02	Hui	Chen	Windows Vista
04	Mihir	Patel	Windows Vista
05	Madir	Sadiku	Windows Vista
08	Marty	O'Leary	Windows Vista
09	Armando	Colacci	Windows Vista
10	Kelsey	Eastman	Windows Vista

> **Step 12**

Project 5 — Modify Records Using Action Queries

You will create a new table, add and delete records, and update field values using queries.

Performing Operations Using Action Queries

Action queries are used to perform an operation on a group of records. Building an action query is similar to building a select query with the extra step of specifying the action to perform on the group of selected records. Four types of action queries are available and are described in Table 3.1.

To create an action query, first build a select query by adding tables, fields, and criteria to the query design grid. Run the select query to make sure the desired group of records is being targeted for action. Once you are satisfied the correct records will be modified, change the query type using the Make Table, Append, Update, or Delete buttons in the Query Type group in the Query Tools Design tab shown in Figure 3.5.

Figure 3.5 Query Type Group in Query Tools Design Tab

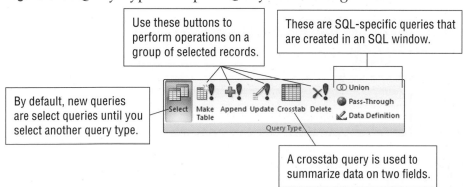

By default, new queries are select queries until you select another query type.

Use these buttons to perform operations on a group of selected records.

These are SQL-specific queries that are created in an SQL window.

A crosstab query is used to summarize data on two fields.

QUICK STEPS

Create Make Table Query
1. Create query in Design view.
2. Add desired table(s) to query.
3. Add desired fields to query design grid.
4. Enter criteria to select records.
5. Run query.
6. Switch to Design view.
7. Click Make Table button.
8. Type table name.
9. Select destination database.
10. Click OK.
11. Run the query.
12. Click Yes.
13. Save and close query.

Clicking the Run button once the query type has been changed to an action query causes Access to perform the make table, append, update, or delete operation. Once an Action query has been run, the results cannot be reversed.

Table 3.1 Action Query Types

Query Type	Description
Make Table	A new table is created from selected records in an existing table. For example, you could create a new table that combines fields from two other tables in the database.
Append	Selected records are added to the end of an existing table. This action is similar to performing a copy and paste.
Update	A global change is made to the selected group of records based on an update expression. For example, you could increase the selling price of a group of records by 10 percent in one step.
Delete	The selected group of records is deleted from a table.

HINT

Once you have run a make table query, do not double-click the query name in the navigation pane since doing so instructs Access to run the query again. Open the query in Design view to make changes to the criteria and/or query type if you need to use the query again.

Creating a New Table Using a Query

A make table query creates a new table from selected records placed in the same database or in another database. This type of query is useful to create a history table prior to purging old records that are no longer required. The history table can be placed in the same database or in another database used as an archive copy. Once you have created a select query that will extract the records you want to copy to a new table, click the Make Table button in the Query Type group in the Query Tools Design tab to open the Make Table dialog box shown in Figure 3.6. Enter a table name, choose the destination database and click OK.

Make Table

Figure 3.6 Make Table Dialog Box

Type a name for the new table to be generated from the query.

Specify another database in which to make the table by selecting this option and then using the Browse button to navigate to the other database file name.

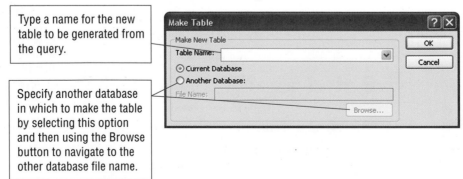

Project 5a Creating a New Table Using a Query

1. With the **RSRComputerServ3.accdb** database open, create a select query to select work order records for the month of September 2009 prior to September 15, 2009 by completing the following steps:

   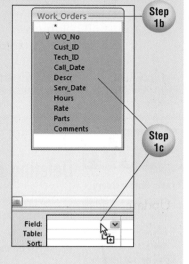

   Step 1b
   Step 1c

   a. Create a new query in Design view. Add the Work_Orders table to the query window and then close the Show Table dialog box. Increase the height of the table field list box until you can see all field names.
   b. Double-click the Work_Orders table field list box title bar. This selects all records within the table.
   c. Position the arrow pointer anywhere within the selected field names in the field list box and drag the pointer to the first column in the query design grid. All fields in the table are added to the query design grid.
   d. Click in the *Criteria* row in the *Serv_Date* column, type **Between September 1, 2009 and September 15, 2009**, and then press Enter.
   e. Run the query. The query results datasheet displays seven records.

WO	CustID	TechID	Call Date	Description
65012	1000	11	Wed Sep 02 2009	Semiannual computer maintenance
65013	1000	10	Tue Sep 08 2009	Replace keyboard
65014	1005	02	Thu Sep 10 2009	Replace power supply
65015	1008	04	Thu Sep 10 2009	Restore operating system
65016	1010	06	Fri Sep 11 2009	Install upgraded video card
65017	1015	08	Mon Sep 14 2009	Replace DVD drive
65018	1020	10	Mon Sep 14 2009	Upgrade Office suite

Records selected for make table query at Step 1e

   f. You decide you do not need to archive the *Comments* field data. Switch to Design view and then delete the *Comments* column from the query design grid.

2. Make a new table from the selected records and store the table in a history database used for archive purposes by completing the following steps:
   a. If necessary, switch to Design view.
   b. Click the Make Table button in the Query Type group in the Query Tools Design tab.
   c. With the insertion point positioned in the *Table Name* text box, type **Sept2009WorkOrders**.
   d. Click *Another Database* and then click the Browse button.
   e. At the Make Table dialog box, navigate to the Access2007L2C3 folder on your storage medium and then double-click the file named ***RSRComputerServ3_history.accdb***.

   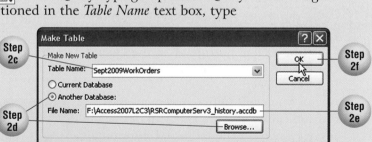

   Step 2c
   Step 2d
   Step 2f
   Step 2e

   f. Click OK.
   g. Click the Run button.
   h. Click Yes at the Microsoft Office Access message box indicating you are about to paste seven rows to a new table.

3. Save the query and name it Sept2009MakeTable.
4. Close the query.
5. Close the **RSRComputerServ3.accdb** database.

6. Open the **RSRComputerServ3_history.accdb** database. Click OK to continue if a message appears stating that Access has to update object dependencies.
7. Open the Sept2009WorkOrders table.
8. Adjust all column widths to Best Fit and then print the datasheet in landscape orientation. If necessary, deselect columns.
9. Close the table. Click Yes to save changes.
10. Close the **RSRComputerServ3_history.accdb** database.

QUICK
STEPS

Create Delete Query
1. Create query in Design view.
2. Add desired table(s) to query.
3. Add desired fields to query design grid.
4. Enter criteria to select records.
5. Run query.
6. Switch to Design view.
7. Click Delete button.
8. Run the query.
9. Click Yes.
10. Save query.

Deleting a Group of Records Using a Query

A delete query is used to delete a group of records that meet specified criteria in one step. You can use this action query in any instance where the records to be deleted can be selected using a criteria statement. Using a query to remove the records is more efficient and reduces the chances of removing a record in error if deleting is done manually in the table.

The make table query used in Project 5a created a duplicate copy of the records in the new table. The original records still exist in the Work_Orders table. The make table query used to archive the records can be modified by changing the query type to a delete query and then using it to remove the records from the original table.

Action query names display with a black exclamation mark in the navigation pane next to an icon that indicates the type of action that will be performed if the query is run.

Delete

Project 5b Deleting Records Using a Query

1. Open the **RSRComputerServ3.accdb** database and enable content.
2. Open the Sept2009MakeTable query in Design view.
3. Click the Delete button ![icon] in the Query Type group in the Query Tools Design tab.
4. Use Save As to save the revised query using the name Sept2009Delete.
5. Run the query.
6. At the Microsoft Office Access message box indicating you are about to delete seven rows from the table and informing you the action cannot be reversed, click Yes to delete the selected records.
7. Close the query.
8. Open the Work_Orders table. Notice that no records exist with a *Service Date* before September 15, 2009.
9. Print the first page of the datasheet only in landscape orientation.
10. Close the table.

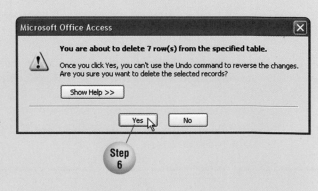

Step 6

Adding Records to a Table Using a Query

The append query is used to copy a group of records from one or more tables to the end of an existing table. Consider using an append query in any situation where you want to make a duplicate copy of records. For example, in Project 5a, the make table query was used to create a new table to store archive records. Once the table exists, you can use append queries to copy subsequent archive records to the end of the existing history table.

Clicking the Append button in the Query Type group in the Query Tools Design tab causes the Append dialog box to open with the same options as the Make Table dialog box, as shown in Figure 3.7.

The receiving table should have the same structure as the query from which the records are selected.

Figure 3.7 Append Dialog Box

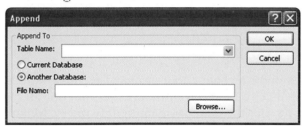

Create Append Query
1. Create query in Design view.
2. Add desired table(s) to query.
3. Add desired fields to query design grid.
4. Enter criteria to select records.
5. Run query.
6. Switch to Design view.
7. Click Append button.
8. Type table name.
9. Select destination database.
10. Click OK.
11. Run the query.
12. Click Yes.
13. Save and close query.

Project 5c — Adding Records to a Table Using a Query

1. With the **RSRComputerServ3.accdb** database open, open the Sept2009MakeTable query in Design view.
2. Modify the criteria to select work order records for the last half of September 2009 by completing the following steps:
   a. Expand the width of the *Serv_Date* column until you can see the entire criteria statement.
   b. Click the insertion point in the *Criteria* row in the *Serv_Date* column, insert and delete text as necessary to modify the criteria statement to the following text, and press Enter.

      Between #9/16/2009# And #9/30/2009#

3. Click the Append button in the Query Type group in the Query Tools Design tab.
4. Since the query is being changed from a make table query, Access inserts the same table name and database that was used to create the table in Project 5a. Click OK to accept the table name *Sept2009WorkOrders* and the *RSRComputerServ3_history.accdb* database located in the Access2007L2C3 folder on your storage medium.

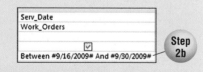

   If you are appending to a table in the existing database, you can select the table name from the drop-down list.

5. Use Save As to save the revised query using the name **Sept2009Append**.

6. Run the query.
7. Click Yes at the Microsoft Office Access message box indicating you are about to append eight rows and the action cannot be undone.
8. Close the query.
9. Close the **RSRComputerServ3.accdb** database.
10. Open the **RSRComputerServ3_history.accdb** database.
11. Open the Sept2009WorkOrders table and print the datasheet in landscape orientation.
12. Close the table.
13. Close the **RSRComputerServ3_history.accdb** database.

Create Update Query
1. Create query in Design view.
2. Add desired table(s) to query.
3. Add desired fields to query design grid.
4. Enter criteria to select records.
5. Run query.
6. Switch to Design view.
7. Click Update button.
8. Click in *Update To* box in field to be changed.
9. Type update expression.
10. Run the query.
11. Click Yes.
12. Save and close query.

Update

Modifying Records Using an Update Query

When you need to make a change to a group of records that can be selected in a query and the change to be incorporated is the same for all records, you can instruct Access to modify the data using an update query. Making a global change using an update query is efficient and reduces the potential for errors that could occur from manual editing of multiple records.

Clicking the Update button in the Query Type group in the Query Tools Design tab causes an *Update To* row to appear in the query design grid. Click in the *Update To* box in the column to be modified and type the expression that will change the field values as needed. Run the query to make the global change.

Project 5d Changing Labor Rates Using an Update Query

1. Open the **RSRComputerServ3.accdb** database and enable the content.
2. Open the table named Fees_ServiceContracts, print the datasheet, and then close the table.
3. Create an update query to increase Plan A service contract rates by 6% using an update query by completing the following steps:
   a. Create a new query in Design view.
   b. Add the table named Fees_ServiceContracts to the query and then close the Show Table dialog box.
   c. Add the *Plan* and *Rate* fields to the query design grid.
   d. Click in the *Criteria* row in the *Plan* column, type A, and press Enter.
   e. Run the query.
   f. Switch to Design view.

g. Click the Update button 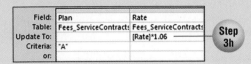 in the Query Type group in the Query Tools Design tab. Access adds a row labeled *Update To* in the query design grid between the *Table* and *Criteria* rows.

h. Click in the *Update To* row in the *Rate* column, type [Rate]*1.06, and press Enter.

4. Save the query and name it RateUpdate.

Field:	Plan	Rate
Table:	Fees_ServiceContract:	Fees_ServiceContract:
Update To:		[Rate]*1.06
Criteria:	"A"	
or:		

Step 3h

5. Run the query. Click Yes at the Microsoft Office Access message that says you are about to update four rows.

6. Close the query.

7. Open the Fees_ServiceContracts table. Notice the *Rate* values for Plan A records have increased. Print the datasheet.

8. Close the table and then close the **RSRComputerServ3.accdb** database.

CHAPTER summary

- Select queries are the query type used most often to select records to view, edit, or print based on criteria statements.

- A filter can be saved as a query by displaying the filter criteria in a Filter By Form window, clicking the Advanced Filter Options button, and then clicking *Save as Query* at the drop-down list.

- Parameter queries prompt the user for the criteria by which to select records when the query is run.

- To create a parameter query, type a prompt message encased in square brackets in the *Criteria* row in the field you want to use to select records.

- Multiple fields can be prompted in a parameter query; Access displays Enter Parameter Value dialog boxes with the prompt messages one after the other.

- To change a join type between two tables, double-click the black join line at the top of the query window to open the Join Properties dialog box.

- The join property defaults to the join type created at the Relationships window. Changing the join type at the query window affects the active query only.

- An inner join selects records only if a matching value is found in the joined field in both tables.

- A left outer join selects all records from the left table and matching records from the related table; empty fields display if no matching records exist in the related table.

- Click the Show Table button in the Query Setup group in the Query Tools Design tab to add a table or query to the query window.

- Remove a table from the query by clicking a field within the table's field list box and pressing the Delete key, or by right-clicking the table and clicking *Remove Table* at the shortcut menu.

- A right outer join selects all records from the right table and matching records from the primary table; empty fields display if no matching records exist in the primary table.

- A self-join query is created by adding two copies of the same table to the query window and joining the tables on a field containing matching field values.

- A query that contains two tables that are not joined creates a cross product or Cartesian product query, which means Access creates records for every possible combination from both tables, the results of which are generally not meaningful.

- A subquery is a query nested inside another query. Use subqueries to break down a complex query into manageable units. For example, a query with multiple calculations could be created by combining subqueries in which each calculation is built individually.

- Another reason for using subqueries is to have the ability to reuse a smaller query in many other queries, meaning you do not have to keep recreating the same structure.

- To nest a query inside another query, click the Queries tab at the Show Table dialog box, add the query to the window, and then add the required fields to the query design grid.

- Create select queries on multivalued fields using the same methods you would use for single-field criteria.
- Adding *.Value* to the end of a multivalued field name in the *Field* box in the query design grid causes Access to place each field value in a separate row in the query results datasheet.
- An alias is another name that you want to use to reference a table or a field in a query.
- Right-click a table name in the query window, click *Properties* at the shortcut menu, and then enter the alias for the table in the *Alias* property at the Property Sheet task pane.
- Add an alias to a field by clicking the insertion point at the beginning of the field name in the *Field* box in the query design grid, typing the alias and then a colon (:).
- Action queries are used to perform actions on a group of records.
- Click the desired action query button in the Query Type group in the Query Tools Design tab.
- A make table query creates a new table in the active database or in another database with the structure defined in the query design grid and containing records selected by a criteria statement.
- Delete a group of records in one step by creating and running a Delete query.
- Add a group of records to the bottom of an existing table in the active database or in another database using an append query.
- An update query allows you to make a global change to records by entering an expression such as a mathematical formula in the query design grid.

COMMANDS review

FEATURE	RIBBON TAB, GROUP	BUTTON
Advanced Filter Options	Home, Sort & Filter	Advanced
Append query	Query Tools Design, Query Type	
Create query in Design view	Create, Other	
Delete query	Query Tools Design, Query Type	
Make table query	Query Tools Design, Query Type	
Run query	Query Tools Design, Results	
Show Table	Query Tools Design, Query Setup	
Update query	Query Tools Design, Query Type	

CONCEPTS check

Test Your Knowledge

Completion: In the space provided at the right, indicate the correct term, command, or number.

1. Click this button at a Filter By Form datasheet to save the filter's criteria as a query. _____

2. This is the name for a query which prompts the user to type the criteria in a dialog box when the query is run. _____

3. Double-clicking the black join line between tables in a query window opens this dialog box. _____

4. Click this button in the Query Setup group in the Query Tools Design tab to add a table to an existing query. _____

5. This join type displays all records from the related table and empty fields if no matching record exists in the primary table. _____

6. This is the term for a query in which two copies of the same table are added to the query window and joined by two fields in the same table that contain matching field values. _____

7. This is the term for a query in which two tables are used in the query window with no join established to connect one table to the other. _____

8. This term describes a query nested inside another query. _____

9. Add this property to the end of a multivalued field name in the *Field* box in the query design grid to display each field value in a separate row. _____

10. This is the term used to describe another name with which you reference a table or a field. _____

11. Queries that perform operations on selected records are referred to by this term. _____

12. Create this type of query to create a new table from existing records to copy data to an archive database. _____

13. This query removes a group of records that meet specified criteria. _____

14. This query adds a group of records to the end of an existing table in the active database or in another database.   _____

15. Create this type of query to increase the prices in all records by 10%.   _____

SKILLS check
Demonstrate Your Proficiency

Assessment

1 EXTRACT RECORDS USING A FILTER AND PROMPTED QUERIES

1. Open the database named **VantageVideos3.accdb** and enable the content.
2. Open the table named WebCustomers.
3. Using the Filter By Form feature, display only those customers who reside in Burlington with a ZIP code that begins with 05401. *Hint: Type 05401* in the ZIP field to specify only the first five characters in the ZIP code. The asterisk is a wildcard that allows you to filter by specifying only a portion of the field value.*
4. Save the filter as a query named **Cust_Burlington05401**.
5. Close the Filter By Form datasheet and close the table. Click No when prompted to save changes to the table design.
6. Open the Cust_Burlington05401 query.
7. Adjust all column widths to Best Fit and print the query results datasheet in landscape orientation.
8. Close the query. Click Yes to save changes to the layout.
9. Create a new query in Design view using the following specifications:
   a. Add the tables WebOrders, WebOrderDetails, and WebProducts to the query.
   b. Add the fields *WebOrderID*, *DateOrd*, *Qty*, and *Product* to the query design grid. **Note: Add WebOrderID from the WebOrders table.**
   c. Create a parameter query to prompt the user to type the title of the video in the *Product* column. You determine the message that should display in the Enter Parameter Value dialog box.
   d. Save the query, name it **PromptedVideo**, and then close the query.
10. Run the PromptedVideo query. Type **The Longest Day** at the Enter Parameter Value dialog box. Print the query results datasheet and then close the query.
11. Open the PromptedVideo query in Design view. Delete the prompt message in the *Product* column. Create a parameter query to prompt the user to type a beginning and ending date to view Web orders in the *DateOrd* column. Use Save As to name the revised query **PromptedDates** and then close the query.
12. Run the PromptedDates query. Type **February 1, 2010** as the beginning date and **February 28, 2010** as the ending date. Print the query results datasheet and then close the query.

Assessment

2 MODIFY JOIN PROPERTIES AND REMOVE A TABLE FROM A QUERY

1. With the **VantageVideos3.accdb** database open, create a new query in Design view using the following specifications:
   a. Add the tables WebCustomers, WebOrders, and WebOrderDetails to the query.
   b. Add the fields *Cust-ID, Fname, Lname, WebOrderID, DateOrd, WebProdID*, and *Qty* to the query design grid.
   c. Modify the join type between the WebCustomers table and the WebOrders table to an inner join.
   d. Save the query and name it **WebSales**.
2. Run the query. Print the query results datasheet in landscape orientation and then close the query.
3. Open the WebSales query in Design view and modify the query as follows:
   a. Remove the WebOrderDetails table from the query.
   b. Modify the join type between the WebCustomers table and the WebOrders table to a left outer join.
   c. Use Save As to name the revised query **CustomersIncNoOrders**.
4. Run the query. Print the query results datasheet and then close the query.

Assessment

3 ADD A TABLE TO A QUERY AND CREATE AND USE A SUBQUERY TO PERFORM CALCULATIONS

1. With the **VantageVideos3.accdb** database open, open the WebSales query in Design view and modify the query as follows:
   a. Add the WebProducts table to the query and then add the field named *SellPrice* to the query design grid.
   b. Delete the *Cust-ID* field from the query.
   c. Create a calculated field with the column label **Total Sale** that multiplies the quantity ordered times the selling price. Format the calculated column to *Currency*.
   d. Use Save As to name the revised query **WebSalesWithTotal**.
2. Run the query. Print the query results datasheet in landscape orientation with a left and right margin set to 0.5 inch and then close the query.
3. Create a new query in Design view that calculates the total sale with tax as follows:
   a. Nest the WebSalesWithTotal query in the new query.
   b. Add the fields *WebOrdID, DateOrd*, and *Total Sale* to the query design grid.
   c. Create a calculated field with the column label **Tax** that multiples the value in the *Total Sale* column times .06 (decimal equivalent of 6%). Format the calculated column to *Standard*.
   d. Create a second calculated column with the column label **Total Sale with Tax** that adds the *Total Sale* column to the *Tax* column.
   e. Save the query and name it **WebSalesWithTotalAndTax**.
4. Run the query. Adjust all column widths to Best Fit, print the query results datasheet in landscape orientation, and then close the query. Click Yes to save changes.

Assessment

4 USE ACTION QUERIES TO ARCHIVE RECORDS AND UPDATE SELLING PRICES

1. With the **VantageVideos3.accdb** database open, open the WebSales query in Design view and modify the query as follows:
   a. Add a criterion to select the records for sales during the month of February 2010.
   b. Run the query to make sure the correct records are being selected.
   c. Change the query to a make table query, name the new table **Feb2010WebSales**, and store the table in the database named *VantageVideos3_archive.accdb* on your storage medium.
   d. Use Save As to name the revised query **Feb2010SalesMakeTable**.
   e. Run the query.
2. Close the query and then close the **VantageVideos3.accdb** database.
3. Open the database named **VantageVideos3_archive.accdb**. Click OK to continue if a message appears stating Access has to update object dependencies. Open the table named Feb2010WebSales.
4. Print the datasheet in landscape orientation. Close the table and then close the **VantageVideos3_archive.accdb** database.
5. Open the **VantageVideos3.accdb** database and enable the content.
6. Open the Feb2010SalesMakeTable query in Design view and modify the query as follows:
   a. Change the query to a delete query.
   b. Remove the WebCustomers and WebOrderDetails tables from the query.
   c. Use Save As to name the revised query **Feb2010SalesDelete**.
   d. Run the query and then close the query window.
7. Open the WebSales query. Print the query results datasheet in landscape orientation and then close the query.
8. Create a new query in Design view to update the selling prices of all videos as follows:
   a. Add the *WebProducts* table to the query.
   b. Add the *SellPrice* field to the query design grid.
   c. Change the query to an update query and add a formula that will add $1.00 to the selling price of all videos.
   d. Save the query and name it **PriceUpdate**.
   e. Run the query and then close the query window.
9. Open the WebProducts table. Print the datasheet and then close the table.
10. Close the **VantageVideos3.accdb** database.

CASE study

Apply Your Skills

Part 1

You are continuing your work as an intern at Deering Sales. The sales manager has requested a series of printouts with information from the database. Open the database named **DeeringSales3.accdb** and enable the content. Design, create, save, run, and print query results to provide the required information. You determine appropriate descriptive names for each query.

- A list of sales by client that includes the date of sale, amount, and terms.
- Modify the first query to allow the sales manager to type the customer's name for the query. To test your query, run the query using the customer name *Madison Electrics*. Save the revised query using a new name.
- Modify the first query to display only those sales with a discount of *2% 10 days* or *1% 15 days*. Save the revised query using a new name.
- A list of sales by representative that includes the date of sale and amount and shows all representative names so that the manager can see if there is a representative who has not recorded any sales to date.
- Modify the sales representative query to allow the sales manager to enter a value in the amount column when the query is run that displays sales below a specified threshold value. **Hint: Type a less than symbol in the Criteria box before the prompt message**. To test your query, run the query using the value *5000.00*. Save the revised query using a new name.
- Print the Quotas table datasheet and then use a query to update all quota values to add 15% to the existing quotas. After updating the values, create a new query to show each sales representative name and his or her respective quota.

Part 2

The sales manager would like a printout of the five highest sales to date. Research in Help how to create a top values query. Using the information you learned in Help, modify the query that contains the sales by representative created in Part 1. Save the revised query using a new name and print the query results.

Part 3

The sales manager would like a printout of the sales representatives with multiple sales recorded to date. Include in the printout the date of sale and the amount of sale along with the representative names. **Hint: Use the Find Duplicates Query Wizard and select the query you created in Part 1 that lists the sales by representative at the first dialog box.**

Creating and Using Custom Forms

CHAPTER 4

Upon successful completion of Chapter 4, you will be able to:

- Create a custom form in Design view using all three form sections
- Add fields individually and as a group
- Move, size, and format control objects
- Change the tab order of fields
- Create tabbed pages in a form and insert a subform on each page
- Add and format a calculation to a custom form
- Group and ungroup multiple controls
- Adjust the alignment and spacing of controls
- Add graphics to a form
- Anchor a control to a position in the form
- Create a datasheet form
- Modify form properties to restrict actions allowed in records
- Sort records in a form and locate a record using a wildcard character

access Chapter 4

Tutorial 4.1
Working with Forms and Subforms
Tutorial 4.2
Adding Visual Appeal to Forms

Forms provide an interface for data entry and maintenance that allows end users to work with data stored in the underlying tables more efficiently. For example, forms can be designed using a layout that uses the screen space more effectively than the tabular layout of a datasheet. Forms can include fields from multiple tables allowing data to be entered in one object that updates several tables. Generally, database designers provide forms for end users to use to perform data maintenance and restrict access to tables to protect the structure and integrity of the database. In this chapter you will learn how to build a custom form using Design view.

Note: Before beginning computer projects, copy to your storage medium the Access2007L2C4 subfolder from the Access2007L2 folder on the CD that accompanies this textbook and then make Access2007L2C4 the active folder.

Project ① Design and Create a Custom Form

You will create a custom form in Design view that includes subforms in tabbed pages to provide a single object in which data stored in four tables can be entered, viewed, and printed.

QUICK STEPS

Start New Form in Design View
1. Click Create tab.
2. Click Form Design button.

Form Design

Creating Custom Forms Using Design View

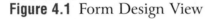

Access provides several tools with which you can create forms such as the Form tool, the Split Form tool, and the Form Wizard. These features allow you to build a form quickly. A form generated using one of these tools can be modified in Layout view or Design view to customize the content, format, or layout. If you require a form with several custom options, you can begin in Design view and build the form from scratch. Click the Create tab and click the Form Design button in the Forms group to begin a new form using the Design view window shown in Figure 4.1.

Figure 4.1 Form Design View

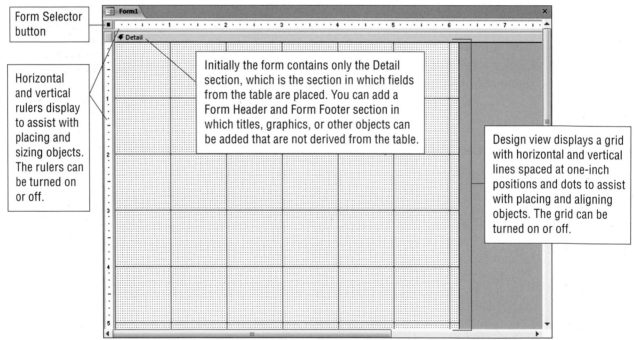

Form Selector button

Horizontal and vertical rulers display to assist with placing and sizing objects. The rulers can be turned on or off.

Initially the form contains only the Detail section, which is the section in which fields from the table are placed. You can add a Form Header and Form Footer section in which titles, graphics, or other objects can be added that are not derived from the table.

Design view displays a grid with horizontal and vertical lines spaced at one-inch positions and dots to assist with placing and aligning objects. The grid can be turned on or off.

The form displays the Detail section, which is used to display fields from the table associated with the form. You can add the Form Header and Form Footer sections in which control objects are added to hold text or graphics. To do this, click the Form Design Tools Arrange tab and then click the Form Header/Footer button in the Show/Hide group.

Form Header/Footer

The Form Header section is used to create objects that you want to display at the top of the form while scrolling records in Form view and printed at the top of the page when a record or group of records is printed from Form view. Titles and company logos are generally placed in the Form Header section. The Form Footer section is used to create objects that you want to display at the bottom of the form while scrolling records in Form view and printed at the end of a printout when a record or group of records is printed from Form view. Consider adding a creation date and/or revision number in the Form Footer section.

Objects are added to the form using buttons in the Controls and Tools groups in the Form Design Tools Design tab shown in Figure 4.2.

Figure 4.2 Controls and Tools Groups in Form Design Tools Design Tab

Bound, Unbound, and Calculated Control Objects

A control object in a form is **bound**, **unbound**, or **calculated**. Bound objects draw data displayed in the control from the field in the table to which the control is associated. In other words, the content that is displayed in the control object in Form view is drawn from a field in a record in a table. Unbound objects are used to display text or graphics that are not associated with a field in the table. For example, an object that contains instructions to the user on how to use the form is an unbound object. A calculated object displays the result of a mathematical formula.

Creating Titles and Label Objects

Click the Title button in the Controls group of the Form Design Tools Design tab to display the Form Header and Form Footer sections and automatically insert a label object with the name of the form inside the Form Header section. The text inside the title object is selected in order to insert, delete, or otherwise modify the title text. Click the Label (Form Control) button in the Controls group to draw a label control object within any section in the form and type descriptive or explanatory text inside the object.

Once a title or label control object has been created, the text can be formatted using buttons in the Font group in the Form Design Tools Design tab. You can also move and resize the control object to reposition it on the form.

QUICK STEPS

Add Form Title
1. Open form in Design view.
2. Click Title button.
3. Type title text.
4. Press Enter.

Add Label Object
1. Open form in Design view.
2. Click Label (Form Control) button.
3. Drag to create object the desired height and width.
4. Type label text.
5. Press Enter.

HINT

Before starting a new custom form in Design view it is a good idea to draw a sketch on a piece of paper that indicates the rough layout of the form. This will help you place the fields and determine other objects you need to create.

Title

Label

1. Open **RSRComputerServ4.accdb** and enable the content.
2. Click the Create tab and then click the Form Design button in the Forms group.

Step 2

3. Add a title in the Form Header section of the form and position the title object using the ruler for a guide by completing the following steps:

   a. With the Form Design Tools Design tab active, click the Title button in the Controls group. Access displays the Form Header section above the Detail section and places a title object with the text *Form1* selected.

   b. Type **Customer Data Maintenance Form**. Notice the width of the object automatically expands to accommodate the length of the typed text.

Step 3a

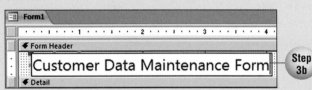

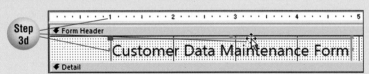

Step 3b

   c. Press Enter.

   d. Position the mouse pointer on the orange border of the control object until the pointer displays with a four-headed arrow move icon attached and then drag the object to the right until the left edge of the control object is aligned at the 1-inch position in the horizontal ruler.

Step 3d

4. Scroll down the form until you can see the Form Footer section.
5. Position the mouse pointer at the bottom border of the form's grid until the pointer changes to a horizontal line with an up- and down-pointing arrow and then drag the bottom of the form down to the 0.5-inch position in the vertical ruler.

Step 5

6. Add a label control object at the left edge of the form that contains a revision number and another label control object at the right edge of the form that contains your name by completing the following steps:

   a. Click the Label (Form Control) button *Aa* in the Controls group.

   b. Position the crosshairs with the label icon attached at the left side of the Form Footer section and drag to draw a label control object the approximate height and width shown. When you release the mouse, an insertion point appears inside the label control object.

Step 6b

   c. Type **Revision number 1.0** and press Enter.

   d. Create another label control object at the right side of the Form Footer section similar in height and width to the one shown, type your first and last names inside the label control object, and press Enter. If necessary, refer to Steps 6a–6c if you need help with this step.

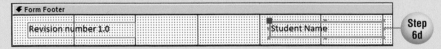

Step 6d

e. Click in any blank area of the form to deselect the label control object.

7. Click the Save button on the Quick Access toolbar, type **Customer_Maintenance** in the *Form Name* text box at the Save As dialog box, and press Enter or click OK.

Adding Fields to a Form

Before you can add fields to the Detail section, you need to first bind a table to the form. The table to be associated with the form is specified in the *Record Source* property in the Data tab of the Form Property Sheet. Double-click the Form Selector button located above the vertical ruler and left of the horizontal ruler to open the form's Property Sheet at the right side of the work area. Click the Data tab, click the down-pointing arrow in the *Record Source* property box, click the desired table at the drop-down list, and then close the Property Sheet.

Click the Add Existing Fields button in the Tools group in the Form Design Tools Design tab to open the Field List pane. Select and drag a group of field names or an individual field name from the Field List pane to the desired location on the form. Position the pointer on the form near the location at which you want to display the data from the record keeping in mind that for each field added to the form, Access places a label control object with the caption or field name (if no caption exists) to the left of where you release the mouse. A text box control object that is bound to the field is placed where you release the mouse. This is the object that displays table data in Form view. Figure 4.3 displays the fields from the Customers table that you will add to the Customer_Maintenance form in Project 1b.

Bind Table to Form
1. Open form in Design view.
2. Double-click Form Selector button.
3. Click Data tab in Property Sheet.
4. Click down-pointing arrow in *Record Source* property box.
5. Click desired table.
6. Close Property Sheet.

Add Fields to Form
1. Click Add Existing Fields button.
2. Drag field name from Field List pane to desired location in Detail section.
OR
1. Click first field name in Field List pane.
2. Hold down Shift key.
3. Click last field name in Field List pane.
4. Drag selected fields from Field List pane to desired location in Detail section.

HINT

Do not be overly concerned with exact placement and alignment as you initially add fields to the form. You will learn how to use alignment and spacing tools in the Form Design Tools Arrange tab to assist with layout.

Figure 4.3 Fields from Customer Table Added to Form in Project 1b

Customer Data Maintenance Form					
Customer ID:	Cust_ID	First Name:	Fname	Last Name:	Lname
Street Address:	StreetAdd				
City:	City	State:	State	ZIP Code:	ZIP
Home Phone:	HPhone				
Cell Phone:	CPhone				
	☑ Service Contract?				

Form Selector

Add Existing Fields

1. With the **RSRComputerServ4.accdb** database open and the Customer_Maintenance form open in Design view, scroll up to the top of the form in the work area.
2. Bind the Customers table to the form by completing the following steps:
   a. Double-click the Form Selector button (displays as a black square) located at the top of the vertical ruler and left of the horizontal ruler to open the form's Property Sheet.
   b. Click the Data tab in the Property Sheet.
   c. Click the down-pointing arrow in the *Record Source* property box and then click *Customers* at the drop-down list.
   d. Close the Property Sheet.

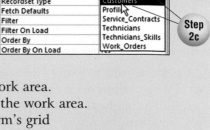

3. Add fields individually from the Customers table to the Detail section of the form by completing the following steps:
   a. Click the Add Existing Fields button in the Tools group in the Form Design Tools Design tab. The Field List pane opens at the right side of the work area.
   b. Minimize the navigation pane to provide more space in the work area.
   c. Position the mouse pointer at the right border of the form's grid until the pointer changes to a vertical line with a left- and right-pointing arrow and then drag the right edge of the form to the 6.5-inch position in the horizontal ruler.

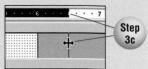

   d. If necessary, click *Cust_ID* in the Field List pane to select the field and then drag the field name to the Detail section, releasing the mouse with the pointer near the top of the section at the 1-inch position in the horizontal ruler.

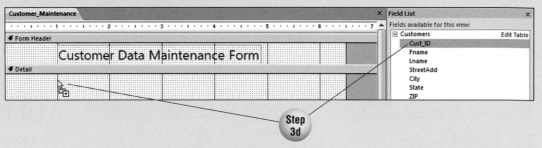

   e. Click to select *Fname* in the Field List pane and then drag the field to the same horizontal position as *Cust_ID* in the Detail section, releasing the mouse with the pointer at the 3-inch position in the horizontal ruler.
   f. Click to select *Lname* in the Field List pane and then drag the field to the same horizontal position as *Cust_ID* in the Detail section, releasing the mouse with the pointer at the 5-inch position in the horizontal ruler.

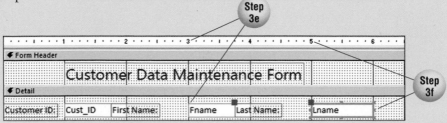

g. Drag the *StreetAdd* field from the Field List pane to the Detail section below *Cust_ID*, releasing the mouse at the 1-inch position in the horizontal ruler approximately 3 rows of grid dots below *Cust_ID*.

h. Drag the *City* field from the Field List pane to the Detail section below *StreetAdd*, releasing the mouse at the 1-inch position in the horizontal ruler approximately 3 rows of grid dots below *StreetAdd*.

i. Drag the *State* field from the Field List pane to the Detail section at the same horizontal position as *City*, releasing the mouse at the 3-inch position in the horizontal ruler.

j. Drag the *ZIP* field from the Field List pane to the Detail section at the same horizontal position as *City*, releasing the mouse at the 5-inch position in the horizontal ruler.

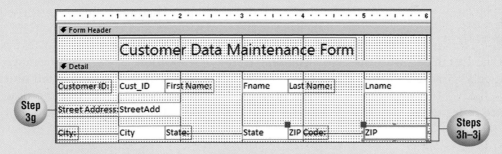

4. Add a group of fields from the Customers table to the Detail section of the form by completing the following steps:

   a. Click the *HPhone* field name in the Field List pane.

   b. Hold down the Shift key and click the *Serv_Cont* field name in the Field List pane. Access selects all fields from the first field name clicked to the last field name clicked when Shift is used.

   c. Position the mouse pointer within the selected group of fields in the Field List pane and then drag the group to the Detail section below *City*, releasing the mouse at the 1-inch position in the horizontal ruler approximately 3 rows of grid dots below *City*.

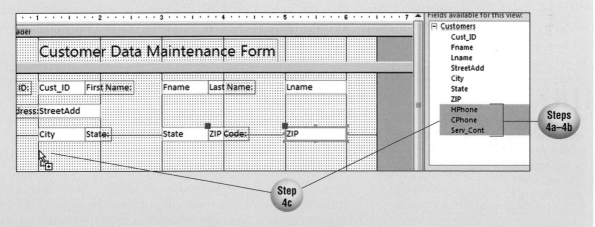

5. Click in any blank area to deselect the group of fields.
6. Compare your form with the one shown in Figure 4.3.
7. Click the Save button on the Quick Access toolbar.
8. Close the Field List pane.
9. Redisplay the navigation pane.

Moving and Resizing Control Objects

Move Objects in Design View
1. Select control object.
2. Drag using orange border or move handle to desired location.

Resize Objects in Design View
1. Select control object.
2. Drag middle top, bottom, left, or right sizing handle to resize the height or width.
OR
1. Select control object.
2. Drag corner sizing handle to resize the height and width at the same time.

Once fields are placed on the form, move or resize objects to change the layout. In Project 1b, you saw that Access places two control objects for each field on the form. A label control object which contains the caption or field name is placed left of a text box control object which displays the field value from the record or a blank entry box when adding a new record. Click the label control object or the text box control object for the field you want to move or resize to display an orange border with eight handles. Access displays a large black square (called the move handle) at the top left of the selected field's label control object or text box control object.

Point to the orange border of the selected control object until the pointer displays with the four-headed arrow move icon and then drag the field to the new position on the form. Access moves the connected label control or text box control along with the object you drag to the new location. If you want to move a selected label control or text box control independently from its connected object, point to the large black handle at the top left of the selected control and drag using the move handle to the new position as described in Figure 4.4.

Figure 4.4 Moving a Control Object in Design View

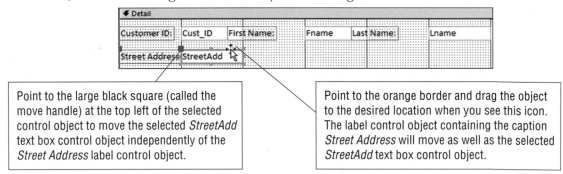

Point to the large black square (called the move handle) at the top left of the selected control object to move the selected *StreetAdd* text box control object independently of the *Street Address* label control object.

Point to the orange border and drag the object to the desired location when you see this icon. The label control object containing the caption *Street Address* will move as well as the selected *StreetAdd* text box control object.

HINT

You can apply an AutoFormat to a form in Design view using the AutoFormat button in the AutoFormat group in the Form Design Tools Arrange tab. AutoFormat options apply fonts and colors to controls and backgrounds within the form.

To resize a selected control object, point to one of the sizing handles (small orange squares) in the border of the selected object until the pointer displays with an up- and down-pointing arrow, a left- and right-pointing arrow, or a two-headed diagonal arrow to resize the height and/or width.

By default, the Snap to Grid feature is turned on in Design view. This feature pulls a control to the nearest grid point when moving or resizing objects. If you want to move or resize an object very precisely in small increments, you may want to turn the feature off. To do this, click the Form Design Tools Arrange tab and then click the Snap to Grid button in the Control Layout group. Snap to Grid is a toggle feature which is turned on or off by clicking the button.

Snap to Grid

Formatting Controls

Use the buttons in the Font group in the Form Design Tools Design tab to change the font, font size, font color, background color, alignment, or apply bold, italic, or underline formatting to the selected control object. Use the Conditional button to apply conditional formatting to the selected object.

Multiple control objects can be formatted at the same time by holding down the Shift key while clicking individual controls. You can also use the mouse pointer to draw a selection rectangle around a group of controls to select multiple objects inside the rectangle.

Applying an AutoFormat option to a form overrides individual object formatting—if you plan to use an AutoFormat, apply the desired option before making individual font, color, or size changes.

QUICK STEPS

Format Controls Using Selection Rectangle
1. Open form in Design view.
2. Position pointer above top left control to be selected.
3. Drag down and right to draw a rectangle around controls to be formatted.
4. Release mouse.
5. Click desired formatting options.
6. Deselect controls.

Format Multiple Controls Using Shift
1. Open form in Design view.
2. Click to select first control object.
3. Hold down Shift key.
4. Click remaining control objects.
5. Release Shift key.
6. Click desired formatting options.
7. Deselect controls.

Project 1c — Moving and Resizing Controls

1. With the **RSRComputerServ4.accdb** database open and the Customer_Maintenance form open in Design view, preview the form to determine the controls that need to be moved or resized by clicking the View button in the Views group of the Form Design Tools Design tab. (Do not click the down-pointing arrow on the button.)
2. The form is displayed in Form view with data from the first record displayed in the text box control objects. Notice that some label control objects are overlapping text box control objects and that the street address in the first record is not entirely displayed.
3. Click the Design view button located at the right end of the Status bar (last button in View buttons group).
4. Move the controls for those objects that are overlapping other objects by completing the following steps:
   a. Click the *First Name* label control object.
   b. Point to the large black square (move handle) at the top left of the selected label control object and then drag right to the 2-inch position in the horizontal ruler. Notice the connected *Fname* text box control object does not move because you are dragging using the move handle.

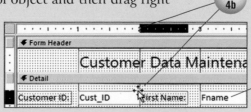

Step 4b

Connected *Fname* text box control does not move when you drag using the move handle.

c. Click the *Last Name* label control object and then drag right using the move handle to the 4-inch position in the horizontal ruler.

d. Move the *State* label control object right to the 2-inch position in the horizontal ruler.

e. Move the *ZIP Code* label control object right to the 4-inch position in the horizontal ruler.

f. Click in any blank area to deselect the *ZIP Code* label control.

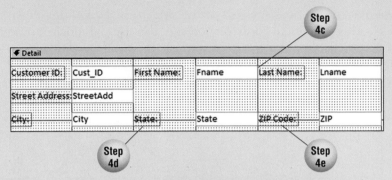

5. Click the *StreetAdd* text box control object. Drag the right middle sizing handle to the right to the 3-inch position in the horizontal ruler.

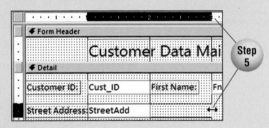

6. Click the *State* text box control object and then drag the right middle sizing handle to the left to the 3.5-inch position in the horizontal ruler.

7. Resize the *Cust_ID* text box control so that the right edge of the control is at the 1.5-inch position in the horizontal ruler.

8. Click the *Service Contract?* label control object. Point to any side of the selected object's orange border and then drag the object until the left edge is at the 3-inch position in the horizontal ruler adjacent to the *HPhone* field. Notice that both the label control object and the text box control object moved since you dragged the border (not the move handle).

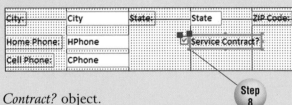

9. Deselect the *Service Contract?* object.

10. Save the form.

Project 1d Formatting Multiple Controls

1. With the **RSRComputerServ4.accdb** database open and the Customer_Maintenance form open in Design view, click the View button to preview the form in Form view.
2. Switch back to Design view.
3. Format multiple controls using a selection rectangle by completing the following steps:
   a. Position the arrow pointer at the top left corner in the Detail section above the *Customer ID* label control object and then drag down and right until you have drawn a rectangle around all of the controls in the section as shown below and then release the mouse.

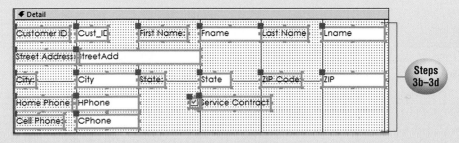

Step 3a

   b. Notice all objects contained with the rectangle are selected.
   c. Use the Font button in the Font group in the Form Design Tools Design tab to change the font to Century Gothic.
   d. Use the Font Size button to change the font size to 10.

Steps 3b–3d

   e. Click in any blank area to deselect the controls.
4. Format by selecting multiple controls using the Shift key by completing the following steps:
   a. Click the *Cust_ID* text box control object.
   b. Hold down the Shift key and click each of the other text box control objects in the Detail section.

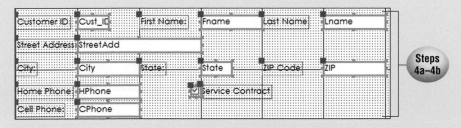

Steps 4a–4b

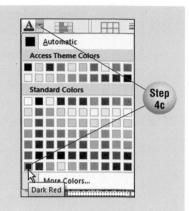
c. Click the down-pointing arrow on the Font Color button and then click *Dark Red* at the color palette (first option in last row).
d. Click the Bold button.
5. Click in any blank area to ungroup the selected controls.
6. Switch to Form view to view the formatting changes applied to the form.
7. Switch to Design view. Adjust the width of the *Service Contract?* label control object until the question mark is redisplayed at the end of the label.
8. Deselect the *Service Contract?* label control and then save the form.

Changing the Tab Order of Fields

Tab order refers to the order in which fields are selected when you press the Tab key while entering data in Form view. You do not have to enter data into a record in the order in which the fields are presented. Click the Form Design Tools Arrange tab and click the Tab Order button in the Control Layout group to open the Tab Order dialog box shown in Figure 4.5.

Figure 4.5 Tab Order Dialog Box

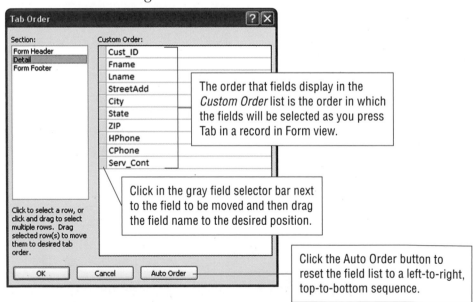

The order that fields display in the *Custom Order* list is the order in which the fields will be selected as you press Tab in a record in Form view.

Click in the gray field selector bar next to the field to be moved and then drag the field name to the desired position.

Click the Auto Order button to reset the field list to a left-to-right, top-to-bottom sequence.

Position the pointer in the gray field selector bar next to the field name that you want to move until the pointer displays as a right-pointing black arrow and click to select the field. Drag the selected field up or down to the desired position. The order of fields in the *Custom Order* list box in the Tab Order dialog box is the order in which the fields will be selected as the Tab key is pressed in a record in Form view. Click OK when you have finished relocating the fields.

Project 1e | Changing the Tab Order of Fields

1. With the **RSRComputerServ4.accdb** database open and the Customer_Maintenance form open in Design view, click the View button to display the form in Form view.
2. With the insertion point positioned in the *Cust_ID* field in the first record in the table, press the Tab key seven times. As you press Tab notice that the order in which the fields are selected is a left-to-right, top-to-bottom sequence.
3. With the insertion point in the *HPhone* field, press Tab. Notice the selected field moves down to the *CPhone* field instead of moving right to the *Serv_Cont* field.
4. With the insertion point in the *CPhone* field, press Tab to move to the *Serv_Cont* field.
5. Switch to Design view.
6. Change the tab order of the fields so that the *Serv_Cont* field is selected after the *HPhone* field by completing the following steps:
   a. Click the Form Design Tools Arrange tab.
   b. Click the Tab Order button  in the Control Layout group.
   c. At the Tab Order dialog box, move the pointer to the gray field selector bar next to *Serv_Cont* until the pointer displays as a right-pointing black arrow.
   d. Click to select the field.
   e. With the pointer now displayed as white arrow in the field selector bar, drag *Serv_Cont* up until the horizontal black line indicating the location at which the field will be moved is positioned between *HPhone* and *CPhone* in the *Custom Order* list and then release the mouse.
   f. Click OK.
7. Switch to Form view.
8. Press the Tab key nine times to move through the fields in the first record. Notice when you reach the *HPhone* field and press Tab the *Serv_Cont* field is active next instead of the *CPhone* field.
9. Switch to Design view.
10. Save the form.

Step 6c

Step 6e

Adding a Tab Control to a Form

Add a tab control to a form to organize fields in a large table into smaller related groups or to insert multiple subforms that display on separate pages within the tab control object. A tab control displays pages with a tab at the top of each page which the user clicks to display the page contents. Examine the tab control shown in Figure 4.6. You will create this object in Projects 1f–1g. The tab control contains three pages. The tabs across the top of the control display the caption assigned to each page. Click a tab to display the page's contents.

QUICK STEPS

Add Tab Control to Form
1. Open form in Design view.
2. Click Tab Control button.
3. Position crosshairs in Detail section at desired location for top left of object.
4. Drag down and right to draw object desired height and width.
5. Release mouse.

Figure 4.6 Tab Control with Three Pages Created in Projects 1f–1g

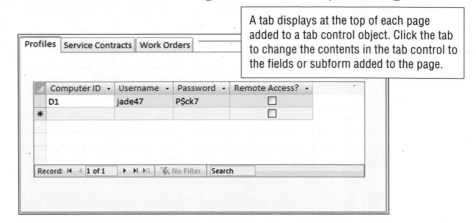

A tab displays at the top of each page added to a tab control object. Click the tab to change the contents in the tab control to the fields or subform added to the page.

In Projects 1f–1g you will create a subform on each page within the tab control to display fields from a related table. When completed, the Customer_Maintenance form can be used to enter or view data related to customers that includes fields from four tables.

Tab Control

To add a tab control object to a form, click the Tab Control button in the Controls group in the Form Design Tools Design tab. Position the crosshairs with the tab control icon attached at the top left of the area in the Detail section where you want to begin the tab control and then drag down and right to draw the control the size that you want to make the tabbed pages. When you release the mouse, the tab control object initially displays with two pages as shown in Figure 4.7.

Figure 4.7 New Tab Control Object with Two Pages

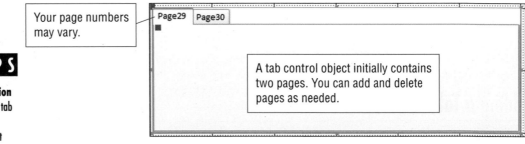

Your page numbers may vary.

A tab control object initially contains two pages. You can add and delete pages as needed.

Change Page Caption
1. Click desired tab in tab control.
2. Click Property Sheet button.
3. Click in *Caption* property.
4. Type desired text.
5. Close Property Sheet.

Add New Page to Tab Control
1. Select tab control object.
2. Click Insert Page button in Controls group.

Insert Page

Change the text displayed in the tab at the top of the page by changing the *Caption* property in the page's Property Sheet. Add fields or create a subform on each page as needed. Add an additional page to the tab control by selecting the tab control object and then clicking the Insert Page button in the Controls group. To remove a page from the tab control, right-click the tab to be deleted and then click *Delete Page* at the shortcut menu.

Creating a Subform

The Subform/Subreport button in the Controls group of the Form Design Tools Design tab is used to add a subform to a form. Create a subform to display fields from another related table within the existing form. The form in which a subform is created is called the main form. Adding a related table as a subform creates a control object within the main form that can be moved, formatted, and resized independently of other objects. The subform displays as a datasheet within the main form in Form view. Data can be entered or updated in the subform while the main form is being viewed. Make sure the Use Control Wizards button is toggled on in the Controls group before clicking the Subform/Subreport button so that you can add the subform using the Subform Wizard shown in Figure 4.8.

Figure 4.8 First Dialog Box in Subform Wizard

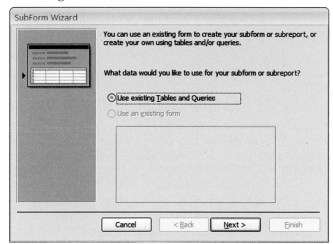

A subform is stored as a separate object outside the main form. You will notice an additional form name added in the navigation pane with *subform* at the end of the name when you finish the steps in the Subform Wizard.

Add Subform to Page
1. Click desired page tab in tab control.
2. Make sure Use Control Wizards is active.
3. Click Subform/ Subreport button.
4. Click crosshairs inside selected page.
5. Click Next.
6. Choose table and fields.
7. Click Next.
8. Click Next.
9. Click Finish.
10. Delete subform label control object.
11. Move and resize subform object as required.

Subform/Subreport

Control Wizard

HINT
Do not delete a subform object in the navigation pane. If the subform object is deleted, the main form will no longer display the fields from the related table in the tab control.

1. With the **RSRComputerServ4.accdb** database open and the Customer_Maintenance form open in Design view, add a tab control object to the form by completing the following steps:
   a. If necessary, click the Form Design Tools Design tab.
   b. Click the Tab Control button ⬚ in the Controls group.
   c. Position the crosshairs with the tab control icon attached at the left edge of the grid in the Detail section at the 2-inch position in the vertical ruler, drag down to the 4-inch position in the vertical ruler and right to the 6-inch position in the horizontal ruler and then release the mouse.

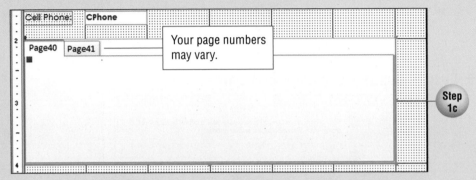

2. Change the page caption and add a subform to the first page within the tab control by completing the following steps:
   a. Click the first tab in the tab control that displays *Pagexx* where *xx* is the page number to select the page.
   b. Click the Property Sheet button in the Tools group.
   c. With the Format tab active in the Property Sheet, click in the *Caption* property box, type **Profiles**, and then close the Property Sheet. The tab displays the caption text in place of *Pagexx*.

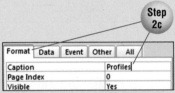

   d. By default, the Use Control Wizards button ⚟ is toggled on in the Controls group. The button displays with an orange background when the feature is active. If the feature is not active, click the Use Control Wizards button to turn the feature on.
   e. Click the Subform/Subreport button ⬚ in the Controls group.
   f. Move the crosshairs with the subform icon attached to the Profiles page in the tab control. The background of the page turns black. Click the mouse to start the Subform Wizard.

   g. Click Next at the first Subform Wizard dialog box with *Use existing Tables and Queries* already selected.

h. At the second Subform Wizard dialog box select the table and fields to be displayed in the subform by completing the following steps:
   1) Click the down-pointing arrow next to the *Tables/Queries* list box and then click *Table: Profiles* at the drop-down list.
   2) Move all of the fields except *Cust_ID* from the *Available Fields* list box to the *Selected Fields* list box.
   3) Click Next.

i. Click Next at the third Subform Wizard dialog box with *Show Profiles for each record in Customers using Cust_ID* selected. Since the two tables have a relationship created with *Cust_ID* as the joined field, Access knows the field that links records in the main form with the subform.

j. Click Finish at the last Subform Wizard dialog box to accept the default subform name *Profiles subform*.

3. Access creates the subform within the active page in the tab control with a label control object above the subform control. Click the label control object displaying the text *Profiles subform* to select the object and then press the Delete key.

4. Click the border of the subform control object to display the orange border and sizing handles and then move and resize the object as shown.

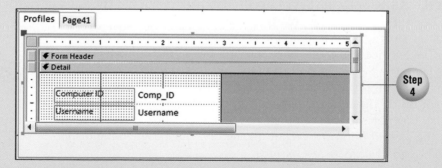

5. Deselect the subform control object and then switch to Form view. Notice the subform displays as a datasheet within the tab control object in the Customer_Maintenance form.

6. Position the pointer on the column boundary line in the field names row in the datasheet between each column and then double-click to adjust each column's width to Best Fit.

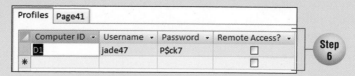

7. Notice that two sets of navigation buttons are displayed—one set at the bottom of the main form and another set at the bottom of the datasheet in the subform. Use the navigation bar at the bottom of the main form to scroll a few records and watch the fields update in both the main form and the subform as you move to the next customer record.
8. Switch to Design view.
9. Save the form.
10. Notice in the navigation pane a form object exists with the name *Profiles subform* below the Profiles: Table object. Subforms are separate objects within the database. If the main form is closed, you can open the subform individually to edit data.

In Design view the controls within the subform display one below another; however in Form view, the subform displays using a datasheet layout. If desired, you can change the *Default View* property in the subform's Property Sheet to *Single Form*. This view matches the layout of the controls in Design view to the layout of the fields in Form view. The fields display one below another in a single column in Form view. To do this, open the subform Property Sheet by double-clicking the Form Selector button at the top of the vertical ruler and left of the horizontal ruler in the subform control object in Design view. Click the down-pointing arrow in the *Default View* property in the Format tab and click *Single Form* at the drop-down list.

Project 1g   Adding More Subforms and Adding a New Page to the Tab Control

1. With the **RSRComputerServ4.accdb** database open and the Customer_Maintenance form open in Design view, change the caption for the second page in the tab control to **Service Contracts** by completing steps similar to those in Steps 2a–2c of Project 1f.
2. With the Service Contracts page selected in the tab control, add a subform to display the fields from the Service_Contracts table on the page by completing the following steps:
   a. Click the Subform/Subreport button in the Controls group.
   b. Click inside the selected Service Contracts page in the tab control.
   c. Click Next at the first Subform Wizard dialog box.
   d. At the second Subform Wizard dialog box change the table displayed in the *Tables/Queries* list box to *Table: Service_Contracts*.
   e. Move all fields from the table except the *Cust_ID* field to the *Selected Fields* list box.
   f. Click Next.
   g. Click Next at the third Subform Wizard dialog box with *Show Service_Contracts for each record in Customers using Cust_ID* selected.
   h. Click Finish at the last Subform Wizard dialog box to accept the default subform name *Service_Contracts subform*.
3. Select and then delete the label control object above the subform displaying the text *Service_Contracts subform*.

4. Click the subform control object to display the orange border and sizing handles and move and resize the form as shown.

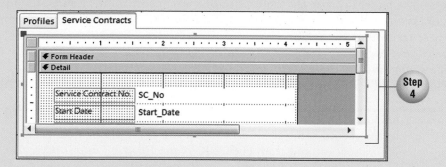

Step 4

5. Deselect the subform control object and then switch to Form view.
6. Click the Service Contracts tab and adjust the column width for each column in the datasheet to Best Fit.
7. Switch to Design view and save the form.
8. Add a new page to the tab control and add a subform to display selected fields from the Work_Orders table in the new page by completing the following steps:
   a. Click in the blank white area to the right of the Service_Contracts tab to deselect the Service_Contracts page and display the orange border and sizing handles around the entire tab control object.
   b. Click the Insert Page button in the Controls group.
   c. With the new page selected, change the page caption to **Work Orders**.
   d. Click the Subform/Subreport button and then click inside the selected Work Orders page. Create a subform to display selected fields from the Work_Orders table by completing the following steps:
      1) Click Next at the first Subform Wizard dialog box.
      2) At the second Subform Wizard dialog box change the table displayed in the *Tables/Queries* list box to *Table: Work_Orders*.
      3) Move the following fields from the *Available Fields* list box to the *Selected Fields* list box.
         WO_No
         Call_Date
         Descr
      4) Click Next.
      5) Click Next at the third Subform Wizard dialog box.
      6) Click Finish at the last Subform Wizard dialog box to accept the default subform name.
9. Select and then delete the label control object above the subform displaying the text *Work_Orders subform*.
10. Click the subform control object to display the orange border and sizing handles and move and resize the form as shown.

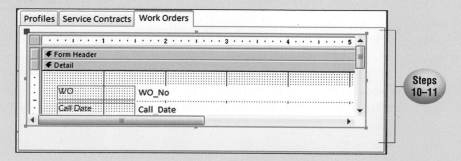

Steps 10–11

11. Access will automatically extend a form's width and widen the tab control object if a table with many fields is added in a subform. If necessary, select the tab control object and decrease the width so that the right edge of the tab control is at the 6-inch position in the horizontal ruler. If necessary, decrease the width of the form so that the right edge of the grid is at the 6.5-inch position in the horizontal ruler. ***Hint: If Access resizes the tab control to the edge of the form, you may have to temporarily widen the grid in order to see the middle sizing handle at the right edge of the tab control object.***

12. Deselect the subform control object, switch to Form view, click the Work Orders tab and adjust the column width for each column in the datasheet to Best Fit.

13. Compare your Customer_Maintenance form with the one shown in Figure 4.9.

14. Print the selected record only. To do this, open the Print dialog box, click *Selected Record(s)* in the *Print Range* section and then click OK. ***Note: Printing may take a few moments while this complex form is rendered. Skip this step if you do not need to print.***

15. Save and close the form.

Figure 4.9 Completed Customer_Maintenance Form

Adding the tab control with a separate page displaying a subform for each table related to the Customers table in the Customer_Maintenance form allowed you to create one object which can be used to view and update fields in multiple tables.

Project 2 Create a New Form with Calculations and Graphics

You will create a new form using the Form Wizard, add two calculations to the form, use features that assist with alignment and spacing of multiple control objects, and add graphics to the form.

Adding Calculations to a Form in Design View

To display a calculated value in a form, you can create a query that includes a calculated column and then create a new form based on the query. Alternatively, you can create a calculated control object in an existing form using Design view. To do this, click the Text Box button in the Controls group in the Form Design Tools Design tab and then drag the crosshairs in the Detail section to create a control object the approximate height and width required to show the calculation. Access displays a text box control with *Unbound* displayed inside the object and a label control to the left displaying *Textxx* inside the object (where *xx* is the text box object number). A calculated control is considered an unbound object since the data displayed in the control is not drawn from a stored field value in a record. Click inside the text box control object (*Unbound* disappears when you click inside the control) and type the formula beginning with an equals sign. For example, the formula *=[Hours]*[Rate]* multiplies the value in the *Hours* field times the value in the *Rate* field. Field names in a formula are encased in square brackets.

Open the Property Sheet for the calculated control object to format the calculated values to *Fixed*, *Standard*, or *Currency* depending on the calculated value. Edit the label control object next to the calculated control to add a descriptive label that describes the calculated value.

QUICK STEPS

Add Calculated Control to Form
1. Open form in Design view.
2. Click Text Box button.
3. Position crosshairs in Detail section at desired location.
4. Drag to create control object the required height and width.
5. Release mouse.
6. Click in text box control (displays *Unbound*).
7. Type formula.
8. Press Enter.
9. Format as required.
10. Delete existing text in associated label control object.
11. Type descriptive label text.
12. Press Enter.

abl
Text Box

Project 2a Adding and Formatting Calculated Control Objects

1. With the **RSRComputerServ4.accdb** database open, create a new form based on the Work_Orders table using the Form Wizard by completing the following steps:
   a. Click the Work_Orders : Table object name in the navigation pane and then click the Create tab.
   b. Click the More Forms button in the Forms group and then click *Form Wizard* at the drop-down list.
   c. With *Table: Work_Orders* selected in the *Table/Queries* list box, complete the steps in the Form Wizard as follows:
      1) Move the following fields from the *Available Fields* list box to the *Selected Fields* list box and then click Next.
         WO_No, Descr, Serv_Date, Hours, Rate, Parts
      2) With *Columnar* layout selected, click Next.

3) Choose the *Solstice* AutoFormat and then click Next.

4) Click *Modify the form's design* at the last dialog box and click Finish.

2. With the Work_Orders form displayed in Design view, add a calculated control object to display the total labor for the work order by completing the following steps:

a. Position the pointer on the top border of the blue Form Footer section bar until the pointer displays as a horizontal line with an up- and down-pointing arrow and then drag down to the 3-inch position in the vertical ruler. This creates more grid space in the Detail section in which you can add controls.

b. Click the Text Box button in the Controls group.

c. Position the crosshairs with the text box icon attached below the *Parts* text box control, drag to create an object the approximate height and width shown, and then release the mouse.

d. Click in the text box control (displays *Unbound*) and type **=[Hours]*[Rate]**.

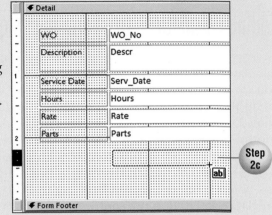

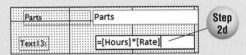

e. Press Enter.

f. With the calculated control object selected, click the Property Sheet button in the Tools group. Click the down-pointing arrow in the *Format* property box, click *Standard* at the drop-down list, and then close the Property Sheet.

g. With the calculated control object still selected, click the Align Text Left button in the Font group.

h. Click to select the label control object to the left of the calculated control object (displays *Textxx* [where *xx* is the text box label number]). Click inside the selected label control object a second time to display an insertion point. Delete *Textxx:*, type **Total Labor**, and press Enter. Notice the label control automatically expands to accommodate the width of the typed text.

3. Display the form in Form view and scroll a few records to view the calculated field. Do not be concerned with alignment and spacing since this will be fixed at a later step.

4. Switch to Design view and save the form.

5. A calculated control object can be used as a field in another formula. To do this, reference the calculated object in the formula by its *Name* property encased in square brackets. Change the name for the calculated object created in Step 2 to a more descriptive name by completing the following steps:

a. Click the calculated control object (displays the formula =[Hours]*[Rate]).

b. Click the Property Sheet button in the Tools group.

c. Click the Other tab in Property Sheet.

d. Select and delete the existing text in the *Name* property box.

e. Type **LaborCalc**.

f. Close the Property Sheet.

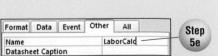

6. Add another calculated control object to the form to add the labor and parts to display the total value for the work order by completing the following steps:

a. Click the Text Box button.

b. Position the crosshairs with the text box icon attached below the existing calculated control, drag to create an object the same height and width as the first calculated control, and then release the mouse.

c. Click in the text box control (displays *Unbound*), type =[LaborCalc]+[Parts], and press Enter.

d. Format the calculated control to *Currency* and align the text at the left side of the control.

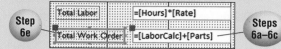

e. Change the entry in the label control object to **Total Work Order**.

7. Save the form. Display the form in Form view and scroll a few records to view the calculations.

8. Close the form.

Grouping Multiple Objects

When working in Design view to add objects to an existing form, Access provides tools to assist with positioning, aligning, and spacing multiple controls. Select multiple control objects and click the Group button in the Control Layout group in the Form Design Tools Arrange tab to add a border around the objects joining the controls together and allowing you to perform a change on the entire group. When you no longer need to work on the controls as a group, use the Ungroup button to separate the control objects back into individual fields.

Aligning Multiple Controls at the Same Position

The buttons in the Control Alignment group in the Form Design Tools Arrange tab shown in Figure 4.10 can be used to align multiple selected controls at the same horizontal or vertical position. Using the control alignment buttons saves the work of adjusting each control individually to the same position on the form.

Figure 4.10 Control Alignment Buttons in Form Design Tools Arrange Tab

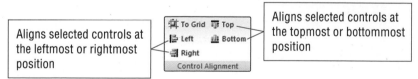

Aligns selected controls at the leftmost or rightmost position

Aligns selected controls at the topmost or bottommost position

Adjusting the Spacing between Controls

Use buttons in the Position group in the Form Design Tools Arrange tab shown in Figure 4.11 to adjust the horizontal and vertical spacing between controls. These tools are helpful when creating a new form by adding controls manually to the grid or after editing an existing form since the space between controls can easily change after adding or deleting objects. To precisely move individual control objects to adjust the spacing would be time-consuming. Access provides buttons that allow you to adjust the amount of vertical or horizontal space between control objects to increase the space, decrease the space, or make all of the spaces between objects equal.

QUICK STEPS

Group Objects
1. Open form in Design view.
2. Select desired control objects.
3. Click Form Design Tools Arrange tab.
4. Click Group button.

Align Multiple Objects
1. Open form in Design view.
2. Select desired control objects.
3. Click Form Design Tools Arrange tab.
4. Click desired button in Control Alignment group.
5. Deselect controls.

Group   Ungroup

QUICK STEPS

Adjust Spacing between Objects
1. Open form in Design view.
2. Select desired control objects.
3. Click Form Design Tools Arrange tab.
4. Click desired button in Position group.
5. Deselect controls.

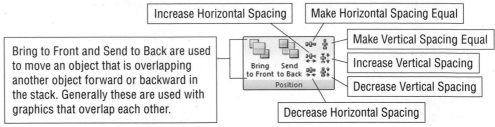
Figure 4.11 Position Buttons in Form Design Tools Arrange Tab

Increase Horizontal Spacing

Make Horizontal Spacing Equal

Make Vertical Spacing Equal

Increase Vertical Spacing

Decrease Vertical Spacing

Decrease Horizontal Spacing

Ungroup Objects
1. Open form in Design view.
2. Select group.
3. Click Ungroup button.
4. Deselect controls.

Bring to Front and Send to Back are used to move an object that is overlapping another object forward or backward in the stack. Generally these are used with graphics that overlap each other.

Project 2b Grouping, Aligning, and Spacing Controls

1. With the **RSRComputerServ4.accdb** database open, open the Work_Orders form in Design view.
2. Edit the title in the Form Header section to **Work Orders with Calculations**, widen the control object to fit the title text on one line, and position the control in the center of the Form Header section.
3. Point to the bottom blue border in the Form Footer section bar until the pointer displays as a horizontal line with an up- and down-pointing arrow and then drag down approximately 0.5-inch to create space in the form footer section. Create a label control object with your name in the center of the Form Footer section.
4. Select the six text box control objects for the fields added to the form above the two calculated controls. Drag any one of the middle sizing handles left until the right edge of the selected controls is approximately at the 4-inch position in the horizontal ruler.
5. With the six text box control objects still selected, click the Form Design Tools Arrange tab and then click the Group button in the Control Layout group (located left of Snap to Grid button). Access displays a brown border with a move handle and sizing handles around the perimeter of the selected controls.

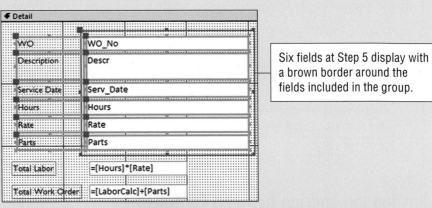

Six fields at Step 5 display with a brown border around the fields included in the group.

6. Point to the move handle (large square) at the top left of the grouped fields (in brown border) and then drag the grouped fields right to approximately the 2-inch position in the horizontal ruler.
7. Click in any blank area to deselect the controls.

Step 6

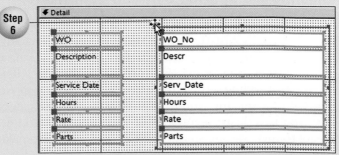

8. Use buttons in the Control Alignment group to align multiple
   controls by completing the following steps:
   a. Draw a selection rectangle around all of the label control objects
      at the left side of the form to select all eight label controls.
   b. Click the Align Left button ⊫ Left in the Control Alignment
      group. All of the control objects align at the left edge of the
      leftmost control.
   c. Deselect the controls.
   d. Click any of the grouped fields to select the group. Hold down
      the Shift key and click each of the calculated control objects
      below the grouped fields.
   e. Click the Align Right button ⊒ Right in the Control Alignment
      group. All of the control objects align at the right
      edge of the rightmost control.
   f. Deselect the controls.
9. Adjust the vertical space between controls to make
   all of the control objects equally spaced in the
   Detail section by completing the following steps:
   a. Draw a selection rectangle around all of the
      control objects in the Detail section.
   b. Click the Make Vertical Spacing Equal button
      ⊟ in the Position group. All of the control
      objects now have the same amount of vertical
      space between each object.

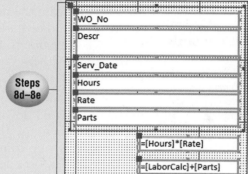

Steps
8a–8b

Steps
8d–8e

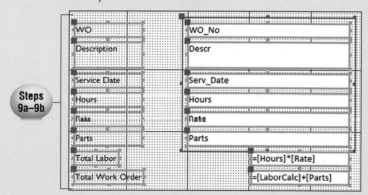

Steps
9a–9b

   c. Deselect the controls.
10. Save the form.
11. Display the form in Form view to see the revised alignment and spacing options.
12. Switch to Design view.

Adding Graphics to a Form in Design View

Add Clip Art to Form
1. Open form in Design view.
2. Start Microsoft Word.
3. Click Insert, Clip Art.
4. Locate and insert desired clip art into document.
5. Copy clip art image to clipboard.
6. Switch to Microsoft Access.
7. Paste image into desired form section.
8. Move and resize as required.
9. If necessary, display Property Sheet and change *Size Mode* property.
10. Switch to Microsoft Word.
11. Exit Word without saving.

Draw Horizontal Line on Form
1. Open form in Design view.
2. Click Line button.
3. Position crosshairs at starting point for line.
4. Hold down Shift key.
5. Drag to desired width.
6. Release mouse.
7. Release Shift key.
8. Change thickness, type, or color as required.

A picture that is saved in a graphic file format can be added to a form using the Logo button or the Image button in the Controls group in the Form Design Tools Design tab. Click the Logo button and Access opens the Insert Picture dialog box. Navigate to the drive and/or folder in which the graphic file is stored and then double-click the image file name. Access automatically adds the image to the left side of the Form Header section. Move and/or resize the image as needed.

Use the Image button when you want to place the picture in another section or prefer to draw a larger control object to hold the picture at the start. Click the Image button, position the crosshairs pointer with the image icon attached at the desired location in the form where you want to place the image, and then drag the crosshairs to draw a control object the approximate height and width desired. When you release the mouse, Access displays the Insert Picture dialog box. Navigate to the drive and/or folder in which the graphic file is stored and then double-click the image file name to insert the picture within the image control object. Access 2007 supports these popular graphic file formats for a logo control or an image control object: *bmp*, *gif*, *jpeg*, *jpg*, and *png*.

Use the Line button in the Controls group to draw horizontal or vertical lines in the form. Hold down the Shift key while dragging to draw a straight line. Once the line is drawn, use the Line Thickness, Line Type, and Line Color buttons in the Controls group to modify the line.

You can also add clip art images to a form. Access does not provide a clip art button in the Controls group; however, you can use Microsoft Word to insert a clip art image in a document and use standard Windows commands to copy the image to the clipboard and paste the clip art into a form. Access inserts the clip art in an unbound OLE control object.

Logo

Image   Line

1. With the **RSRComputerServ4.accdb** database open and the Work_Orders form open in Design view, start Microsoft Word.
2. Locate and insert a clip art image in a new document and copy and paste the image to the form in Microsoft Access by completing the following steps:
   a. At a blank Word document screen, click the Insert tab and then click the Clip Art button in the Illustrations group to open the Clip Art task pane.
   b. Select and delete existing text in the *Search for* text box, type repairs, and press Enter.
   c. Scroll down the results list box and click the image shown to insert the clip art in the current document. If the image shown is not available, select a suitable alternative image.
   d. Right-click the clip art image in the Word document and click *Copy* at the shortcut menu.
   e. Click the button on the Taskbar representing Microsoft Access.
   f. If necessary, drag the right border of the grid to the 6.5-inch position in the horizontal ruler to expand the width of the form before adding the clip art image.
   g. Right-click in the Detail section of the form and click *Paste* at the shortcut menu. Access inserts the image overlapping existing controls and displays the orange border with selection handles.
   h. Move and resize the image to the approximate position and size shown below (your size and image may vary). You will notice when you resize the control object that Access cuts off parts of the image as you make the control object smaller. This action reflects the default *Clip* property for the object. You will correct this in Step 3.

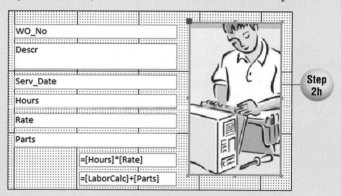

   i. Click the button on the Taskbar representing Microsoft Word and exit Word. Click No when prompted to save the document.
3. Right-click the clip art image pasted at the right side of the Detail section in the form and click *Properties* at the shortcut menu. With Format the active tab in the Property Sheet, click in the *Size Mode* property box, click the down-pointing arrow that appears, and then click *Zoom* at the drop-down list. Close the Property Sheet. Changing *Size Mode* to *Zoom* instructs Access to resize the image within the control object maintaining the original proportions to height and width. The *Size Mode* drop-down list also contains the *Stretch* option. Use this option to stretch the image to fit the height and width of the control object. Using *Stretch* may cause a skewed appearance to the image.

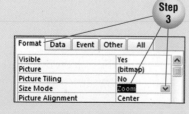

4. Deselect the control object containing the clip art image and display the form in Form view. Notice a thin border surrounds the image. Remove the border by completing the following steps:
   a. Switch to Design view.
   b. Click to select the control object containing the clip art image.
   c. Click the Line Type button [icon] in the Controls group.
   d. Click *Transparent* (first option that displays no line) in the drop-down list.
   e. Deselect the control object.
   f. Display the form in Form view. Notice the border is removed.
   g. Switch to Design view.

5. Draw a line below the form title and modify the line by completing the following steps:
   a. Click the Line button [icon] in the Controls group.
   b. Position the crosshairs with the line icon attached below the title in the Form Header section beginning a few rows of grid dots below the first letter in the title, hold down the Shift key, drag right releasing the mouse below the last letter in the title, and then release the Shift key.
   c. Click the Line Thickness button [icon] in the Controls group and click 3 pt at the drop-down list (fourth option from top).
   d. Deselect the line object.

6. Display the form in Form view to view the line under the title.
7. Switch to Design view.
8. If necessary, adjust the length and/or position of the line as desired.
9. Ungroup the grouped control objects and adjust alignment and formatting options of numeric fields by completing the following steps:
   a. Click the *Hours* text box control object. Since the *Hours* text box control object is part of a set of grouped fields, the entire group is selected.
   b. Click the Form Design Tools Arrange tab.
   c. Click the Ungroup button [icon] in the Control Layout group.
   d. Click to deselect the fields included in the group.
   e. Select the *Hours, Rate, Parts*, and both calculated text box control objects.
   f. Click the Form Design Tools Design tab and then click the Align Text Right button in the Font group.
   g. Deselect the controls.
   h. Select the *Parts* text box control and the bottom calculated control object that displays the formula *=[LaborCalc]+[Parts]*.
   i. Click the Property Sheet button in the Tools group. Change the *Format* property to *Standard* and then close the Property Sheet.
   j. Deselect the controls.
10. Save the form.
11. Display the form in Form view and compare your form with the one shown in Figure 4.12.
12. Print the selected record only.
13. Close the form.

Figure 4.12 Completed Work_Orders Form

Work_Orders

Work Orders with Calculations

WO	65012
Description	Semiannual computer maintenance
Service Date	Fri Sep 04 2009
Hours	1.25
Rate	25.00
Parts	10.15
Total Labor	31.25
Total Work Order	41.40

Your image position and size may vary.

Student Name

Anchoring Controls to a Form

A control object in a form can be anchored to a section or to another control object using the Anchoring button in the Size group in the Form Design Tools Arrange tab. When a control object is anchored, the object's position is maintained when the form is resized. For example, if a clip art image is anchored to the top right of the Detail section, when the form is resized in Form view, the image automatically moves in conjunction with the new form size so that the original distance between the image and the top right of the Detail section is maintained. If an image is not anchored and the form is resized, the position of the image relative to the edges of the form can change.

By default, *Top Left* is selected as the anchor position for each control object in a form. To change the anchor position, select the object(s), click the Form Design Tools Arrange tab, click the Anchoring button and then click *Stretch Down, Bottom Left, Stretch Across Top, Stretch Down and Across, Stretch Across Bottom, Top Right, Stretch Down and Right,* or *Bottom Right.* Click the option that represents how you want the object to dynamically move as a form is resized. Some options will cause a control object to resize as well as move when the form is changed.

1. With the **RSRComputerServ4.accdb** database open, open the Work_Orders form in Form view. Note the clip art image's current position in the form.
2. Switch to Design view.
3. Anchor the clip art image to the bottom of the Detail section of the form by completing the following steps:
   a. Click to select the clip art image.
   b. Click the Form Design Tools Arrange tab.
   c. Click the Anchoring button in the Size group.
   d. Click *Stretch Across Bottom* at the drop-down list.

Step 3c

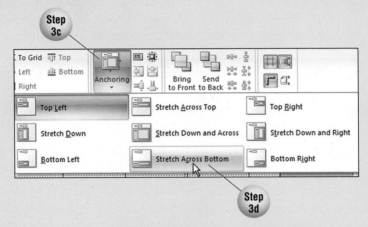

Step 3d

   e. Take note of the distance between the bottom border of the selected clip art image and the bottom of the Detail section.
4. Display the form in Form view. Notice the image has shifted down to maintain the distance between the bottom of the control object's boundary and the bottom of the Detail section.

Clip art image has shifted down to maintain position that control object is to the bottom of Detail section in Design view.

5. Compare the revised position of the clip art image with the completed form shown in Figure 4.12. After comparing the two forms, assume you decide that you prefer the original form layout.
6. Close the form. Click No when prompted to save changes.

Project 3 Create a Restricted-Use Datasheet Form

You will create a datasheet form to be used to enter information into a table and set the form's properties to prevent records from being deleted in the form.

Creating a Datasheet Form

A form can be created that looks just like a table's datasheet. Click the table for which you want to create the datasheet form in the navigation pane, click the Create tab, click the More Forms button in the Forms group, and then click *Datasheet* at the drop-down list. Access creates a form including all fields from the selected table presented in a datasheet layout.

Although the datasheet form has the look and feel of a table datasheet, the form object prevents end users from accessing and modifying the underlying table's structure.

Modifying Form Properties

Using options available in the Data tab of a form's Property Sheet shown in Figure 4.13, you can restrict actions that can be performed while a form is displayed in Form view. For example, you can prevent new records from being added and/or existing records from being deleted and/or edited and/or filtered. Setting the *Data Entry* property to *Yes* means the end user will see a blank form only when the form is opened. A data entry form is intended to be used to add new records only; the user is prevented from scrolling through existing records in the form.

QUICK STEPS

Create Datasheet Form
1. Select table in navigation pane.
2. Click Create tab.
3. Click More Forms button.
4. Click *Datasheet*.
5. Save form.

Restrict Record Actions for Form
1. Open form in Design view.
2. Double-click Form Selector button.
3. Click Data tab.
4. Change *Allow Additions, Allow Deletions, Allow Edits,* or *Allow Filters* to *No.*
5. Close Property Sheet.
6. Save form.

Figure 4.13 Form Property Sheet with Data Tab Selected

Use these form properties to restrict the usage of the form.

1. With the **RSRComputerServ4.accdb** database open, click the Technicians table object in the navigation pane, and then click the Create tab.
2. Click the More Forms button in the Forms group and then click *Datasheet* at the drop-down list.
3. Review the Technicians form in the work area. Notice the form resembles a table datasheet.
4. Switch to Design view.
5. Modify the Technician's form properties to prevent users from deleting records using the form by completing the following steps:
   a. Click in a blank area to deselect the controls.
   b. Double-click the Form Selector button located at the top of the vertical ruler and left of the horizontal ruler to open the form's Property Sheet.
   c. Click the Data tab.
   d. Click in the *Allow Deletions* property box, click the down-pointing arrow that appears, and then click *No* at the drop-down list.

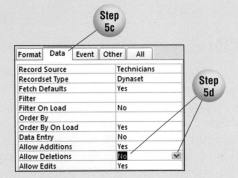

e. Close the Property Sheet.
6. Click the Save button and then click OK to accept *Technicians* as the *Form Name*.
7. Click the down-pointing arrow on the View button in the Views group in the Form Design Tools Design tab. Notice that *Datasheet View* and *Design View* are the only views available. The *Form View* option is dimmed, meaning this view is unavailable.
8. Click in a blank area to remove the drop-down list and then close the form.
9. Double-click the Technicians form object in the navigation pane. Be careful to open the form object and not the table object.
10. Click in the record selector bar next to the first row in the datasheet for Technician ID 01 to select the record.
11. Look in the Records group in the Home tab. Notice the Delete button is dimmed. The feature is unavailable since the *Allow Deletions* form property was set to *No*.

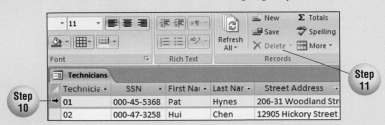

12. Close the form.

13. Right-click the Technicians form object in the navigation pane and then click *Layout View* at the shortcut menu. Notice the datasheet form displays in a columnar layout in Layout view. The Technicians table includes a field named *Attachments*. In this field in some records a picture of the technician has been attached to the record. In Layout View, Access automatically opens the image file and displays the contents.

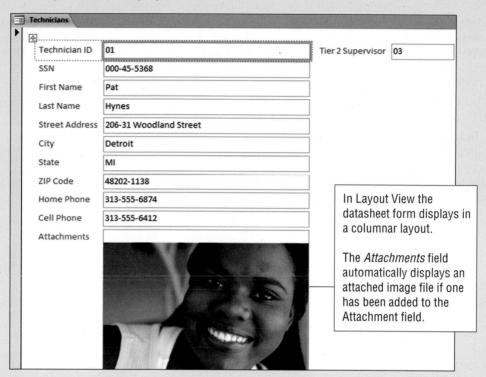

In Layout View the datasheet form displays in a columnar layout.

The *Attachments* field automatically displays an attached image file if one has been added to the Attachment field.

14. Close the form.

Project ④ Sort and Find Records within a Form

You will open a custom-built form and use the form to sort and find records using a wildcard character and by searching backwards by date.

Sorting and Finding Records in Forms

Sort Records in Form
1. Open form in Form view.
2. Click in field by which to sort.
3. Click Ascending or Descending button.

Find Records Using Wildcard
1. Open form in Form view.
2. Click in field by which to search.
3. Click Find button.
4. Type search string including an asterisk for any variable text.
5. Click Find Next.
6. Continue clicking Find Next until search is finished.
7. Click OK.
8. Close Find and Replace dialog box.

One of the advantages to using a form for data entry and maintenance is that the form displays a single record at a time within the work area. This prevents distractions from viewing records other than the one for which you need to focus at the moment, reducing the likelihood of editing the wrong record.

In a table with many records, finding the one you need to maintain quickly is important. Use the Sort and Find features to move to the desired record quickly. In Project 4, you will use a wildcard character, the asterisk (*), to locate a record without specifying the entire field value.

Ascending

Find

Project 4   Sorting and Finding Records in a Form

1. With the **RSRComputerServ4.accdb** database open, open the Customer_Maintenance form in Form view.
2. Click in the *Last Name* field to place an insertion point in the field and then click the Ascending button in the Sort & Filter group in the Home tab. The records are now arranged in alphabetic order by the customer's last name in ascending order.

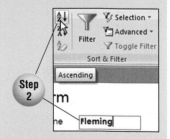

3. Assume that you now need to locate the name of the customer that resides on Roselawn Street. You do not know the exact house number or the customer's name. Complete the following steps to find the record using a wildcard character in the criterion:
   a. Click the insertion point in the *Street Address* field to activate the field by which you want to search records.
   b. Click the Find button in the Find group.

c. With the insertion point positioned in the *Find What* text box, type ***roselawn*** and then click the Find Next button. Access displays the first record in the form in which a match was made. Insert an asterisk within a criterion at each point where any number of variable characters can exist in the field. For example, the entry **roselawn** means "Find any record in which any number of characters before roselawn and any number of characters after roselawn exist in the active field."

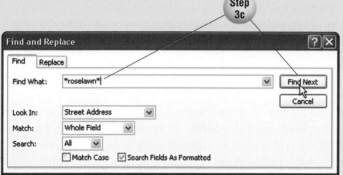

Step 3c

d. Click the Find Next button a second time to see if any other records exist for customers on Roselawn Street.

e. At the Microsoft Office Access message box indicating that Access has finished searching records, click OK.

f. Close the Find and Replace dialog box.

g. Print the selected record. ***Note: Printing may take a few moments to render this complex form. Skip this step if you do not need to print.***

4. Close the Customer_Maintenance form.

5. Open the Work_Orders form in Form view.

6. Click in the *Service Date* field and then click the Descending button ![Z A down arrow] in the Sort & Filter group to sort the records from the most recent service date to the oldest service date.

7. Find the records for work orders completed on October 19, 2009 by completing the following steps:

a. With the insertion point active in the *Service Date* field, click the Find button.

b. With the existing text in the *Find What* text box already selected, press Delete to remove the entry and then type **10/19/2009**.

c. Click the down-pointing arrow next to the *Search* list box and click *Down* at the drop-down list. Since the records are arranged in descending order you need Access to search in a downward direction.

d. Click the *Search Fields As Formatted* check box to clear the check mark. Since the date entered in the *Find What* text box does not match the date format in the Service Date field, this check box must be cleared or Access will not match any records.

e. Click the Find Next button. Access moves to the first record for the specified date (WO 65039). If necessary, drag the Find and Replace dialog box down towards the bottom of the work area so that you can view the record details.

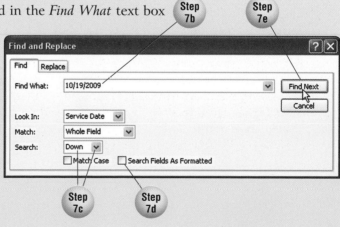

Step 7b   **Step 7e**

Step 7c   **Step 7d**

f. Click the Find Next button. Access moves to the next record (WO 65038).

g. Click the Find Next button. Access moves to the next record (WO 65037).

h. Click the Find Next button. At the message box indicating Access has finished searching records, click OK.

i. Close the Find and Replace dialog box.

j. Print the selected record.

8. Close the Work_Orders form.

9. Close the **RSRComputerServ4.accdb** database.

Clear All Sorts

Once a form has been sorted, Access displays the records in the sorted order whenever you open the form. To remove a sort and have the order revert to the order of the primary key, open the form in Form view and then click the Clear All Sorts button in the Sort & Filter group in the Home tab. Access clears the sort order and the table's records are rearranged in ascending order by the primary key field value.

In this chapter you have learned techniques for building a custom form using Design view. As you learned in Project 2, you can create a form using one of the form tools such as the Form Wizard and then make changes to the form in Design view. As you become more experienced with Access, you will likely use a combination of three methods to build custom forms: a form tool to build the basic table and field structure of the form; Layout view to apply formatting options, add a title and logo, and make other appearance changes; and Design view to add advanced control objects such as tab controls, subforms, and calculations.

CHAPTER summary

- Build a new form using Design view by clicking the Form Design button in the Forms group in the Create tab.

- A new form in Design view initially displays only the Detail section, which is the section in which fields are placed to display record data.

- A Form Header and Form Footer section can be added to the form. Objects placed in the Form Header display at the top of the form or print at the beginning of a printout of records from Form view. Objects placed in the Form Footer section display at the bottom of the form or print at the end of the printout of records from Form view.

- A form can contain three types of control objects: bound, unbound, and calculated.

- Click the Title button in the Controls group of the Form Design Tools Design tab to display the Form Header and Form Footer sections and add a label control object in the Form Header that contains the form name.

- Click the Label button in the Controls group to add a label control object containing unbound text to any section within the form.

- Double-click the Form Selector button in Design view to open the form's Property Sheet and specify the table to be bound to the form in the *Record Source* property.

- Once a table has been associated with a form, click the Add Existing Fields button to open the Field List pane.

- Drag individual field names or a group of selected field names from the Field List pane to the Detail section in the form to add fields to the form.

- Click a control object in Design view to select the object and then move or resize as needed.

- Use the move handle (large black square at top left of selected control) to move a selected object independently of the control's associated label control or text box control.

- By default, the Snap to Grid feature is active which pulls a control object to the nearest grid point when moving or resizing.

- Use buttons in the Font group in the Form Design Tools Design tab to apply formatting options to selected controls.

- Multiple control objects can be selected in Design view by drawing a selection rectangle around a group of adjacent control objects or by holding down the Shift key while clicking controls.

- Open the Tab Order dialog box to change the order in which fields are selected as you press Tab to move from field to field in Form view.

- A tab control object in a form allows you to organize groups of related fields in pages.

- Change the text displayed in the tab at the top of a page within a tab control object by clicking the tab and changing the *Caption* property in the page's Property Sheet.

- Click the Subform/Subreport button in the controls group to create a subform in a page within a tab control object.
- Make sure the Use Control Wizards button is active before clicking the Subform/Subreport button in order to use the Subform Wizard when adding a subform.
- A subform is stored as a separate object outside the main form.
- By default, subforms display as a datasheet within the form. If you prefer a columnar layout for the subform's fields, you can change the *Default View* property to *Single Form*.
- Create a calculated control object in a form using the Text Box button in the Controls group.
- Type a formula in the text box control object (displays *Unbound*) beginning with an equals sign (=). Field names within the formula are encased in square brackets.
- Use buttons in the Control Alignment group in the Form Design Tools Arrange tab to align multiple selected control objects at the same horizontal or vertical position.
- Buttons in the Position group in the Form Design Tools Arrange tab are used to adjust the horizontal and/or vertical spacing between multiple selected control objects.
- Multiple selected control objects can be joined together in a group in order to perform a change that affects all objects within the group.
- Images can be added to a form in Design view using the Logo button or the Image button in the Controls group.
- The Logo button adds the image to the Form Header section.
- Draw a horizontal or vertical line in a form using the Line button in the Controls group. Hold down the Shift key while dragging to draw a straight line.
- Use the Line Thickness, Line Type, and Line Color buttons in the Controls group to modify a line.
- Clip art images can be copied to the clipboard from another Microsoft Office program such as Microsoft Word and then pasted to a form in Design view.
- Change a control object's *Size Mode* property if a clip art image has become truncated after resizing to *Zoom* or *Stretch*.
- A control object can be anchored to a position in a form so that the object's position relative to the edges of the form is maintained when the form is resized.
- A datasheet form is a form that looks like a table datasheet.
- Create a datasheet form by selecting the table for which the form is to be generated, clicking the Create tab, clicking the More Forms button, and then clicking *Datasheet*.
- Modify properties in the Data tab of a form's Property Sheet to restrict the actions a user can perform when viewing records in Form view.
- Sort a form in Form view by clicking in the field by which to sort records and then clicking the Ascending or Descending button.
- Click in a field by which to search records in Form view, click the Find button, and then enter the search criterion in the *Find What* text box. Typing an asterisk in the criterion allows you to search records using a wildcard character inserted for variable data within the search string.

COMMANDS review

FEATURE	RIBBON TAB, GROUP	BUTTON	KEYBOARD SHORTCUT
Add existing fields	Form Design Tools Design, Tools		
Align multiple controls at same position	Form Design Tools Arrange, Control Alignment	Left / Right	
Change tab order of fields	Form Design Tools Arrange, Control Layout	Tab Order	
Create datasheet form	Create, Forms	More Forms ▾	
Design view	Home, Views		
Find	Home, Find		Ctrl + F
Form view	Form Design Tools Design, Views		
Group selected controls	Form Design Tools Arrange, Control Layout		
Image	Form Design Tools Design, Controls		
Insert page in tab control	Form Design Tools Design, Controls		
Label control object	Form Design Tools Design, Controls	Aa	
Line	Form Design Tools Design, Controls		
Logo	Form Design Tools Design, Controls		
Make Vertical Spacing Equal	Form Design Tools Arrange, Position		
Property Sheet	Form Design Tools Design, Tools		F4
Sort ascending order	Home, Sort & Filter		
Sort descending order	Home, Sort & Filter		
Subform	Form Design Tools Design, Controls		
Tab control object	Form Design Tools Design, Controls		
Text box control object	Form Design Tools Design, Controls	abl	
Title	Form Design Tools Design, Controls		

continued

FEATURE	RIBBON TAB, GROUP	BUTTON	KEYBOARD SHORTCUT
Ungroup fields	Form Design Tools Arrange, Control Layout		
Use control wizards	Form Design Tools Design, Controls		

CONCEPTS check

Test Your Knowledge

Completion: In the space provided at the right, indicate the correct term, command, or number.

1. A new form in Design view initially displays only this section in the form.

2. These are the three types of control objects found in a form.

3. Use this button from the Controls group to create an object in the Form Footer section in which to display a form's version number.

4. Before you can add fields to the table you must first bind a table to the form in this property box in the form's Property Sheet.

5. The large black handle at the top left of a selected control is referred to by this name.

6. Hold down this key while clicking controls to select multiple control objects to be formatted.

7. Open this dialog box to change the order in which fields are selected when the Tab key is pressed in Form view.

8. Add this object to the bottom of a form to display subforms in individual pages.

9. Make sure this button is active in the Controls group before clicking the Subform/Subreport button so that the Subform Wizard is available.

10. Click this button in the Controls group to add a calculation to a form.

11. The Make Vertical Spacing Equal button is found in this group in the Form Design Tools Arrange tab.

_____

12. Change this property for a control object containing a clip art image to *Zoom* to proportionately adjust the image to the resized object's height and width.

_____

13. The *Datasheet* form is available from this button's drop-down list in the Forms group in the Create tab.

_____

14. Click this tab in a form's Property Sheet to locate the *Allow Deletions* property.

_____

15. Type this entry in the *Find What* text box to search for all records in the active field that begin with the ZIP code 48221 and have any other four-character extension.

_____

SKILLS check
Demonstrate Your Proficiency

Assessment

1 CREATE A CUSTOM FORM USING DESIGN VIEW

1. Open the database named **VantageVideos4.accdb** and enable the content.
2. Create a query named **CustWebOrders** using the following specifications:
   a. Add the WebOrders, WebOrderDetails, and WebProducts tables to the query.
   b. Add the following fields in order:
      WebOrders table
         WebOrdID
         Cust-ID
         DateOrd
      WebOrderDetails table
         Qty
      WebProducts
         Product
         SellPrice
   c. Run the query and then close the query results datasheet.
3. Create a new form using Design view and build the form using the following specifications:
   a. Expand the width of the form in the grid to the 6.5-inch position in the horizontal ruler.
   b. Add a title in the center of the form header section with the text **Web Customer Orders**.
   c. Add your name in a label control object centered in the form footer section.

d. Bind the WebCustomers table to the form and add all of the fields to the Detail section in the layout shown in Figure 4.14. Adjust the width of the *Cust-ID*, *StreetAdd*, and *State* text box control objects as shown.

e. Change the tab order of the fields so that the *HPhone* field is selected after *Cust-ID*.

f. Add a tab control object below the existing fields that is approximately two inches in height and with the width extended to the right edge of the form.

1) On the first page, change the caption to **Web Orders** and add all fields from the CustWebOrders query in a subform. Delete the subform label control object and move and resize the subform to fit the width of the page. Adjust column widths in Form view as needed to view all columns within the page. *Note: Expand the width of the first column until the column title reads Web Order (do not use Best Fit).*

2) On the second page, change the caption to **Payment Information** and add all fields except *EmailAdd* from the WebCustomerPymnt table in a subform. Delete the subform label control object and move and resize the subform to fit the width of the page. Adjust column widths in Form view as needed.

4. Make any formatting changes you think would improve the appearance of the form.

5. Save the form and name it **WebCustOrders**.

6. Print the form in Form view with the first record displayed and the Web Orders page active. *Note: Printing may take a few moments while the complex form is rendered.*

7. Close the form.

Figure 4.14 Assessment 1

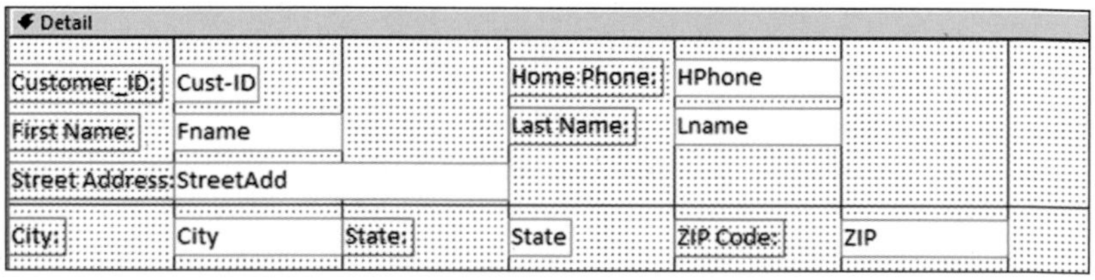

Assessment

2 CREATE A FORM USING THE FORM WIZARD; ADD A CALCULATION AND GRAPHICS

1. With the **VantageVideos4.accdb** database open, create a new form using the Form Wizard as follows:
   a. Select all fields from the WebProducts table.
   b. Select the *Columnar* style.
   c. Select the *Trek* style.
   d. Accept the default form name *WebProducts*.

2. View the completed form in Form view.

3. Switch to Design view and edit the form to resemble the form shown in Figure 4.15 using the following additional information:
   a. Retail Value is a calculated field that uses a formula to multiply the quantity of videos that are in stock times the selling price.

b. The clip art image can be found by searching using the keyword *Movies*.

c. Use your best judgment for other formatting options to match as closely as possible the form shown in Figure 4.15.

4. Print the form in Form view with the first record displayed.

5. Save and close the form.

Figure 4.15 Assessment 2

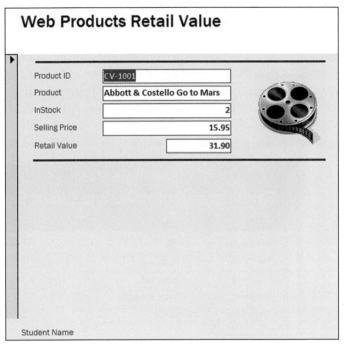

Web Products Retail Value

Product ID	CV-1001
Product	Abbott & Costello Go to Mars
InStock	2
Selling Price	15.95
Retail Value	31.90

Student Name

Assessment

3 CREATE A RESTRICTED-USE FORM

1. With the **VantageVideos4.accdb** database open, create a datasheet form using the WebCustomerPymnt table.

2. Modify the form so that records cannot be deleted when using the form.

3. Display the form in Datasheet view and select a record.

4. Use PrintScreen to capture an image of the screen with the Delete button dimmed while the record is selected.

5. Paste the screen image into a blank Word document. Type your name, the chapter number and assessment number and any other identification information required by your instructor above or below the screen image.

6. Print the document.

7. Save the Word document and name it **Access2007L2C4-Assessment3.docx**.

8. Exit Word.

9. Save the form using the default form name *WebCustomerPymnt* and then close the form.

10. Close the **VantageVideos4.accdb** database.

CASE study

Apply Your Skills

Part 1

You are continuing your work as an intern with Deering Sales. The office manager has requested that you create a form for easier data entry and maintenance of the sales representative information. Open the database named **DeeringSales4.accdb** and enable the content. Design and create the form similar to the one shown in Figure 4.16 using the Representatives and Sales tables. *Hint: Search for the clip art image using the keyword "chart."*

Save the form and name it appropriately. Print the form as shown in Figure 4.16 with record 10 in the Representatives table displayed.

Figure 4.16 Case Study Part 1 Form

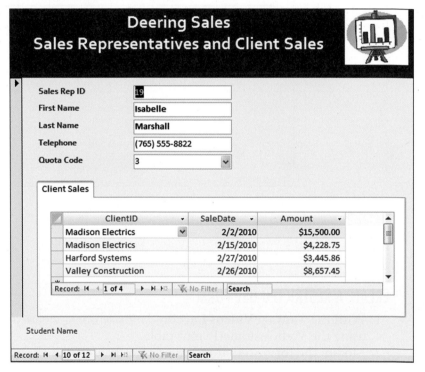

Part 2

The office manager would like another form created that displays the information from the Clients table along with the *RepID*, *SaleDate*, and *Amount* from the Sales table in a subform. Design and create a form. You determine the form design, layout, and formatting options. Save the form and name it appropriately. Print the form with the first record displayed in the main form.

Part 3

Modify the main form created in Part 1 so that representative records cannot be added or deleted. Display the form in Form view. Click the down-pointing arrow at the right of the Delete button in the Records group to show the *Delete Record* option dimmed in the drop-down list. Capture an image of the screen with the New button dimmed and the Delete drop-down list in the Records group displayed. Paste the image into a Word document, type your name, the chapter number and case study identification information above or below the screen image. Print the document. Exit Word without saving. Save and close the Representatives form.

Part 4

Research in Help how to create a new form using the Blank Form tool. Using the information you learned in Help, create a new form using the Blank form tool that includes all of the fields in the Sales table. Add a title to the form to describe the form as displaying Sales with taxes. Switch to Design view and create a calculated control object to show the total sale with taxes. Calculate taxes as the amount of the sale with 6% added. You determine other formatting and design options. Save the form and name it appropriately. Print the form with the first record displayed. Close the form. Close the **DeeringSales4.accdb** database.

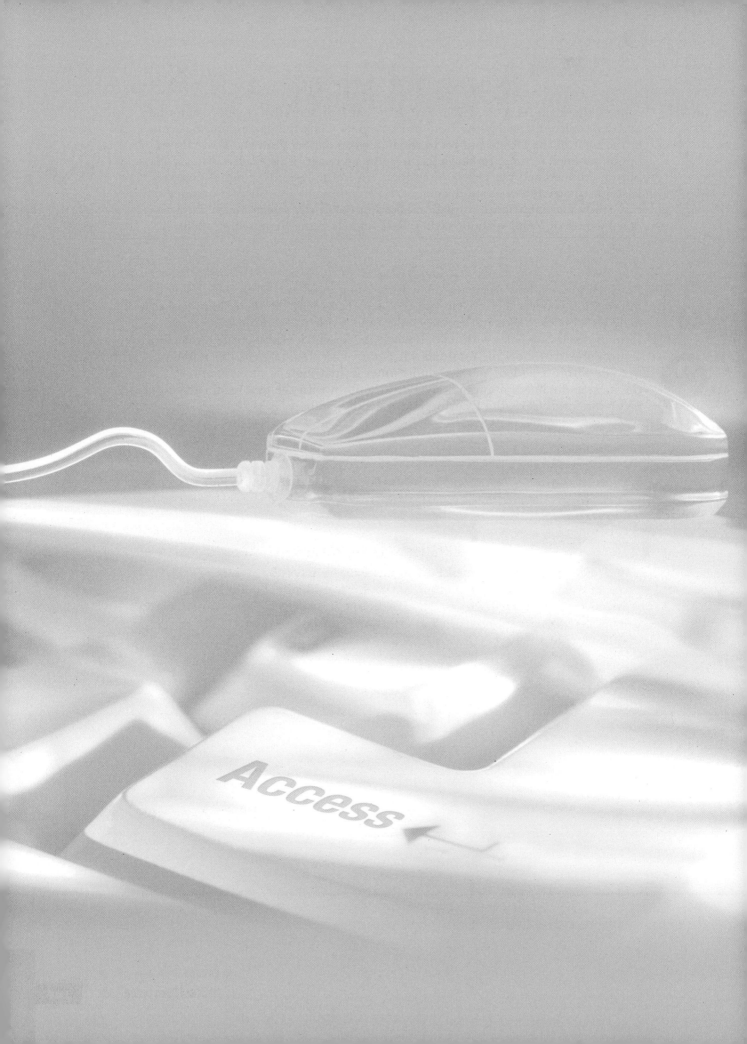

Advanced Tables, Relationships, Queries, and Forms

ASSESSING proficiency

In this unit you have learned to design advanced tables that incorporate best practices in database design. You have created tables with multiple-field primary keys, multivalued fields, attachment fields, and lookup fields to retrieve data from another table. You have learned to modify the join type in a relationship to achieve various query results and understand the concept of normalization as it applies to table design. You have created select queries, parameter queries, and action queries. Finally, you learned how to build a custom form using Design view that includes calculations, multiple pages, and subforms.

Note: The Student Resources CD does not include an Access Level 2, Unit 1 subfolder of files because no data files are required for the Unit 1 assessments. You will create all of the files yourself. Before beginning the assessments, create a folder called Access2007L2U1 for the new files.

Assessment 1 Create Tables for a Property Management Database

1. Create a new database named **BenchmarkPropMgt.accdb**.
2. Create the tables shown in Figure U1.1 to store residential building management and tenant information including setting the primary key, assigning data types and field sizes. Leave field sizes at the default setting for those fields that do not have a field size specified in Figure U1.1.
3. Close any tables that have been left open.

Figure U1.1 Assessment 1

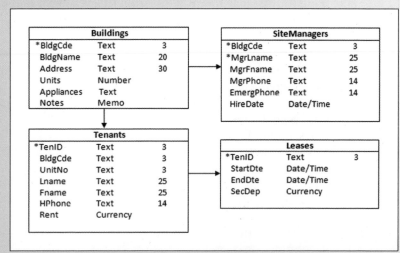

Buildings		
*BldgCde	Text	3
BldgName	Text	20
Address	Text	30
Units	Number	
Appliances	Text	
Notes	Memo	

SiteManagers		
*BldgCde	Text	3
*MgrLname	Text	25
MgrFname	Text	25
MgrPhone	Text	14
EmergPhone	Text	14
HireDate	Date/Time	

Tenants		
*TenID	Text	3
BldgCde	Text	3
UnitNo	Text	3
Lname	Text	25
Fname	Text	25
HPhone	Text	14
Rent	Currency	

Leases		
*TenID	Text	3
StartDte	Date/Time	
EndDte	Date/Time	
SecDep	Currency	

Assessment 2 Add Captions and Modify Field Properties

1. With the **BenchmarkPropMgt.accdb** database open, create captions for the fields as follows:

Buildings Table

Field Name	Caption
BldgCde	Bldg Code
BldgName	Name

SiteManagers Table

Field Name	Caption
BldgCde	Bldg Code
MgrLname	Last Name
MgrFname	First Name
MgrPhone	Telephone
EmergPhone	Emergency
HireDate	Hire Date

Tenants Table

Field Name	Caption
TenID	Tenant ID
BldgCde	Bldg Code
UnitNo	Unit No
Lname	Last Name
Fname	First Name
HPhone	Telephone

Leases Table

Field Name	Caption
TenID	Tenant ID
StartDte	Start Date
EndDte	End Date
SecDep	Security Deposit

2. Make *UnitNo* in the Tenants table a required field including disallowing zero-length strings.
3. Create a custom format for all date fields that displays dates in the short date format with leading zeroes for months and days. Use a slash to separate each section in the date, for example, *10/05/2010*.
4. Create the following custom input masks:
   a. In *BldgCde* in the Buildings table, require three digits and display the underscore character as the placeholder.
   b. In *TenID* in the Tenants table, require three digits and display the underscore character as the placeholder.
   c. In all of the date fields, create an input mask that will require dates to be entered using the short date format created in Step 3 with all digits required. *Hint: You can use the Input Mask Wizard to create the input mask and then modify the code created by the wizard to change optional digits to required digits.*
   d. Require all telephone numbers to include the area code with hyphens between each section of the number. Display the pound symbol (#) as the placeholder character.

5. Enable rich text formatting in the *Notes* field in the Buildings table.
6. Make *875.00* the default value in the *Rent* field in the Tenants table.
7. Close any tables that have been left open.

Assessment 3 Add Records

1. With the **BenchmarkPropMgt.accdb** database open, add the following records:

Buildings Table

Field	Record 1	Record 2	Record 3
Bldg Code	115	120	125
Name	Coventry Park	Mornington Place	Bayview Towers
Address	33 Westview Road	1100 Forrester Lane	12 Lakeview Circle
Units	38	60	110
Appliances	(leave blank)	(leave blank)	(leave blank)
Notes	New roof in 2007	Furnace and air conditioning units under warranty until 2013	Parking lot resurfaced in 2008

SiteManagers Table

Field	Record 1	Record 2	Record 3
Bldg Code	115	120	125
Last Name	Jenkins	Hernandez	Doxtator
First Name	Blair	Maria	Cody
Telephone	800 555 3485	800 555 8675	800 555 9677
Emergency	800 555 3748	800 555 3996	800 555 7795
Hire Date	02 08 2007	04 23 2007	09 15 2007

Tenants

Field	Record 1	Record 2	Record 3
Tenant ID	101	102	103
Bldg Code	115	115	115
Unit No	110	215	320
Last Name	Chen	Ayoub	Reiser
First Name	Wei	Mona	Helena
Telephone	800 555 8776	800 555 2286	800 555 7668
Rent	875	875	1125

Leases Table

Field	Record 1	Record 2	Record 3
Tenant ID	101	102	103
Start Date	01 01 2009	02 01 2009	02 01 2009
End Date	12 31 2009	01 31 2010	01 31 2010
Security Deposit	875	875	1125

2. Apply bold and red font color to the years entered in the *Notes* field in each record.
3. For each table, adjust column widths until all data is entirely visible and print the table, adjusting print options as necessary to fit the table on one page.
4. Close any tables that have been left open saving layout changes.

Assessment 4 Create Lookup Lists and Edit Relationships

1. With the **BenchmarkPropMgt.accdb** database open, create the following lookup lists to display values from another table:
   a. In the SiteManagers table, create a lookup list for *BldgCde* that displays the building codes and names from the Buildings table. Sort the list by the building names and show the key column. Widen the column displaying the building names to accommodate longer names that may be added to the table in the future. Store the *BldgCde* value in the field.
   b. In the Tenants table, create a lookup list for *BldgCde* using the same specifications as Step 1a.
   c. In the Leases table, create a lookup list for *TenID* that displays the tenant IDs, first names, and last names from the Tenants table. Sort the list by the last names and show the key column. Store the *TenID* value in the field.

2. Create a multivalued drop-down list for the *Appliances* field in the Buildings table with the following items. Limit entries in the field to only those items in the list.
   Refrigerator
   Stove
   Microwave
   Dishwasher
   Washer
   Dryer

3. Edit the three records to populate the *Appliances* field as follows:

BldgCde	Appliances
115	Refrigerator, Stove, Microwave
120	Refrigerator, Stove, Microwave, Dishwasher
125	Refrigerator, Stove, Washer, Dryer

4. Adjust the column width of the *Appliances* column to Best Fit, change the column width of the *Notes* column to 35, and then print the Buildings table in landscape orientation with left and right margins set to 0.25-inch.

5. Close the Buildings table, saving changes to the table layout.

6. Open the Relationships window. Edit all relationships to turn on referential integrity and the two cascade options.

7. Arrange the table field list boxes in the window to show the relationships with the primary tables on the left and the related tables on the right. Make sure no join lines are overlapping each other so that each relationship is easily distinguished from others. Create, save, and print a relationships report using the default report name.

8. Close the relationship report window and the relationships window.

Assessment 5 Create Select Queries

1. With the **BenchmarkPropMgt.accdb** database open, design and create the following select queries:
   a. A query named *PromptedTenant* that displays the *BldgCde* and *BldgName* fields from the Buildings table and the *UnitNo, Fname, Lname,* and *HPhone* fields from the Tenants table. Include prompts to specify the building name and the unit number criteria when the query is run.
   b. A query named *PromptedLease* that displays the *TenID, UnitNo, Fname,* and *Lname* fields from the Tenants table and the *StartDte, EndDte,* and *SecDep* fields from the Leases table. Include prompts to specify the starting date and ending date criteria when the query is run.

    c. A query named *TenantsList* that displays the *BldgCde* and *BldgName* fields from the Buildings table and the *UnitNo*, *Fname*, *Lname* and *Rent* fields from the Tenants table. Sort in ascending order by the building names. Modify the join properties to show all records from the Buildings table in a left outer join.

    d. A query named *BuildingsList* that displays all of the fields in the Buildings table except the *Notes* field. Show each entry in the multivalued *Appliances* field in a separate row in the query results datasheet and assign the field the alias *Supplied Appliances*.

2. Run the PromptedTenant query. Type **coventry park** when prompted for the building name and **110** when prompted for the unit number. Print the query results datasheet and then close the query.

3. Run the PromptedLease query. Type **02-01-2009** when prompted for the starting date and **01-31-2010** when prompted for the ending date. Print the query results datasheet in landscape orientation and then close the query.

4. Run the TenantsList query, print the query results datasheet, and then close the query.

5. Run the BuildingsList query, print the query results datasheet, and then close the query.

Assessment 6 Calculate in a Query and Use an Update Query to Increase Rents

1. With the **BenchmarkPropMgt.accdb** database open, create a query to calculate the total rental income from each unit as follows:
    a. Open the TenantsList query and use Save As to name the query *RentalIncome*.
    b. Modify the join properties to show records only when the joined fields are equal in both tables using an inner join.
    c. Add a calculated field to the query with the column heading *Annual Rent* that calculates twelve months of rental income.
    d. Run the query and add a total row in the query results datasheet with a sum function in the *Rent* and *Annual Rent* columns.
    e. Print the query results datasheet in landscape orientation and then close the query.

2. Create an update query named *RentIncrease* to increase all rents by 4%. Run the query.

3. Close the RentIncrease query.

4. Open the RentalIncome query, print the query results datasheet in landscape orientation, and then close the query.

Assessment 7 Design and Create Forms

1. With the **BenchmarkPropMgt.accdb** database open, design and create a form to enter data into the Buildings table as a main form with the SiteManagers table in a subform. Name the main form *BldgsAndMgrs*. You determine the form design, layout, and formatting options. Include an appropriate clip art image in the form. Add your name in the form footer section. Print the first record in the Buildings table displayed in Form view.

2. Design and create a form to enter data into the Tenants table as a main form with the Leases table in a subform similar to the one shown in Figure U1.2. Name the form *TenantsAndLeases*. Make sure the tab order moves to the fields in the order the fields are arranged in the form. The *Annual Rent* field is a calculated column.

3. Print all records using the TenantsAndLeases form and then close the form saving changes.

4. Close the **BenchmarkPropMgt.accdb** database.

Figure U1.2 Assessment 7, Step 2

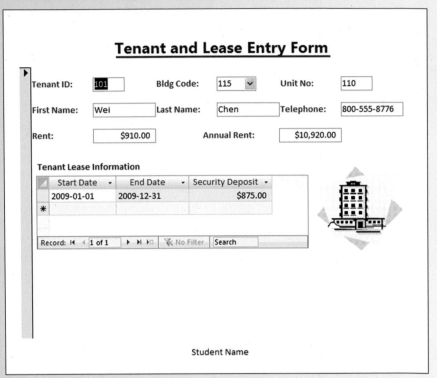

WRITING activities

The following activities give you the opportunity to practice your writing skills along with demonstrating an understanding of some of the important Access features you have mastered in this unit. Use correct grammar, appropriate word choices, and clear sentence constructions when required.

Activity 1 Design Tables for Parking Information in the Property Management Database

The office manager at Benchmark Property Management would like to add tables to the **BenchmarkPropMgt.accdb** database to store information about assigned parking at each of the buildings. Design and create a table to store parking rates and another table to track rental information for each parking spot using the information provided below. Create two lookup lists in the assigned parking table, one to look up the correct parking rate in the rates table and another to look up the tenant's ID in the Tenants table. Add at least three records to test your tables.

Use the following information to assist you with the table design:

Parking Rates
- Coventry Park charges $28 per month for parking.
- Mornington Place charges $35 per month for parking.
- Bayview Towers charges $55 per month for parking.

Assigned Parking Table
- Include fields to store the vehicle make, model, color, and license plate number of the tenant's vehicle that will be parked in the spot.
- Include a field to store the date the tenant began renting the spot.

In Microsoft Word, document your table design by including each table's name and the fields created in each table including the data type and field properties that you set such as field size, caption, input mask, and so on. Indicate the primary key(s) in each table by typing an asterisk preceding the field name. Save the Word document and name it **Access2007L2_U1_Act01.docx**. Print the document and then exit Word.

Activity 2 Design Tables for a Soccer League Database

You are assisting the volunteer registration coordinator for a local soccer league. The registration coordinator would like to create an Access database in which to store information about this season's soccer players so that he can extract reports by age category to develop team lists and generate financial reports for the league treasurer. Design and create tables in a new database named **SoccerRegn.accdb**. The registration coordinator has given you a sample registration form to help you design the tables. Refer to the sample form shown in Figure U1.3.

Create one data entry form to enter information into the tables and add at least five records to test your table and form design. Print all of the records using the form. Design and create a prompted query that will print a list of soccer players selecting records by age category. Design and create another query to print the soccer players registered for the current season including the registration fee paid. Add a total row in the query results datasheet to show the total registration fees collected. Run each query to test your query design and print the query results datasheets.

In Microsoft Word, create a one-page quick reference guide for the registration coordinator and the treasurer that provides instructions on how to open the database and use the data entry form, the prompted query, and the registration fee query. Include in your instructions how to print objects in the database, including how to print a selected form. Save the Word document and name it **Access2007L2_U1_Act02.docx**. Print the document and exit Word.

Figure U1.3 Activity 2

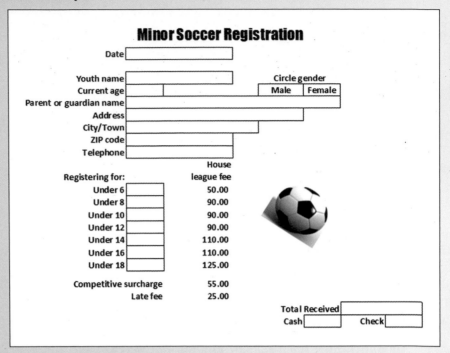

INTERNET research

Plan a Road Trip

On your next vacation you intend to drive across country, staying at a campground or bed and breakfast accommodation each night. As you begin planning for this trip, you decide to research on the Internet campgrounds and/or bed and breakfast facilities along the way. You want to assemble the information in a database so that you can select records by category—campground or bed and breakfast—as you determine the budget you need for the trip. Begin in your home state or province looking for information on both types of accommodation locations near major highways or near destinations you want to visit. Continue your search in your neighboring state or province. Design tables in a new Access database named **CCRoadTrip.accdb** in which to store the name, address, telephone number, and overnight rate. Include Yes/No fields for electricity and water hookups at campgrounds. Include a memo field in which to store amenities provided at each facility. Design and create a form for data entry and use the form to input ten records. Print all of the records using the form.

Level 2

Microsoft®
access

Unit 2: Advanced Reports, Access Tools, and Customizing Access

➤ Creating and Using Custom Reports

➤ Using Access Tools and Managing Objects

➤ Automating, Customizing, and Securing Access

➤ Integrating Access Data

Benchmark Microsoft® Access 2007 Level 2

Microsoft Certified Application Specialist Skills—Unit 2

Reference No.	Skill	Pages
1	**Structuring a Database**	
1.4	Split databases	217-220
2	**Creating and Formatting Database Elements**	
2.1	Create databases	
2.1.1	Create databases using templates	201-205
2.2	Create tables	
2.2.2	Create tables by copying the structure of other tables	207-209
2.2.3	Create tables from templates	205-207
2.3	Modify tables	
2.3.2	Evaluate table design using the Table Analyzer	210-214
2.3.3	Rename tables	222-223
2.3.4	Delete tables	222-223
2.6	Create reports	
2.6.3	Create reports using Design view	162-164
2.6.4	Define group headers	177-180
2.6.5	Create aggregate fields	181-183
2.6.6	Set the print layout	183-186
2.7	Modify the design of reports and forms	
2.7.1	Add controls	164-165, 171-174
2.7.2	Bind controls to fields	164-165
2.7.7	Apply AutoFormats to forms and reports	167-168
3	**Entering and Modifying Data**	
3.5	Import data	
3.5.1	Import data from a specific source	271-275
3.5.2	Link to external data sources	275-284
3.5.3	Save and run import specifications	281-285
5	**Presenting and Sharing Data**	
5.1	Sort data	
5.1.3	Sort data within reports	177-180
5.3	Create and modify charts	
5.3.1	Create charts	187-190
5.3.2	Format charts	190-192
5.3.3	Change chart types	190-192
5.4	Export data	
5.4.1	Export data from tables	286, 301-302
5.4.2	Export data from queries	285-288
5.4.3	Save and run export specifications	289-291
5.5	Save database objects as other file types	285-288
6	**Managing and Maintaining Databases**	
6.1	Perform routine database operations	
6.1.1	Open databases	257-258
6.2	Manage databases	
6.2.1	Encrypt databases using passwords	257-258
6.2.2	Configure database options	250-256
6.2.5	Print database information using the Database Documenter	220-222
6.2.6	Reset or refresh table links using the Linked Table Manager	278-280

Note: The Level 1 and Level 2 texts each address approximately half of the Microsoft Certified Application Specialist skills. Complete coverage of the skills is offered in the combined Level 1 and Level 2 text titled *Benchmark Series Microsoft® Access 2007: Levels 1 and 2,* which has been approved as certified courseware and which displays the Microsoft Certified Application Specialist logo on the cover.

Creating and Using Custom Reports

Upon successful completion of Chapter 5, you will be able to:

- Create a custom report in Design view using all five report sections
- Add bound and unbound control objects to a report
- Move, size, format, and align control objects
- Apply an AutoFormat to a report
- Insert a subreport into a report
- Add page numbering, date and time controls
- Add graphics to a report
- Group records and add aggregate functions and grand totals to a group
- Modify section or group properties to control print options
- Create and modify charts in a report

access Chapter 5

Tutorial 5.1
Creating and Using Advanced Reports

Reports are used to generate printouts from the tables in a database. Although data can be printed from a table datasheet, query results datasheet, or form using the Print feature, these printouts do not allow you to customize the output and do not offer formatting options to present the data in a different manner. The Report feature provides tools and options that can be used to control the content and formatting in order to produce professional-quality reports that serve a particular purpose. In this chapter you will learn how to build a custom report using Design view.

Note: Before beginning computer projects, copy the Access2007L2C5 subfolder from the Access2007L2 folder on the CD that accompanies this textbook to your storage medium and then make Access2007L2C5 the active folder.

Project 1 Design and Create a Custom Report

You will create a custom report in Design view with fields from two tables, apply an AutoFormat to the report, and insert a subreport.

Creating Custom Reports Using Design View

Start New Report in Design View
1. Click Create tab.
2. Click Report Design button.

Add Report Title
1. Open report in Design view.
2. Click Title button.
3. Type title text.
4. Press Enter.

Add Label Object
1. Open report in Design view.
2. Click Label (Form Control) button.
3. Drag to create object the desired height and width.
4. Type label text.
5. Press Enter.

Access provides the Report tool and the Report Wizard that can be used to create reports. These features allow you to build a report quickly that can be modified in Layout view or Design view to customize the content, format, or layout. In most cases, you will want to use one of the report tools to generate the report structure and then customize the report; however, if you require a report with several custom options, you can begin in Design view and build the report from scratch. Click the Create tab and click the Report Design button in the Reports group to begin a new report using the Design view window shown in Figure 5.1.

Creating a report in Design view involves using the same techniques that you learned in Chapter 4 for designing and building a custom form. You will add a title, bind a table or query to the report, add fields, align, move, resize, and format controls the same way that you learned to do these tasks in a form.

A report can contain up to five sections, each of which is described in Table 5.1. You can also add a Group Header and a Group Footer section which are used when you group records that contain repeating values in a field such as a department or city. You will learn how to use these additional sections in Project 3. A report that is grouped by more than one field can have multiple group header and group footer sections.

Report Design

Figure 5.1 Report Design View

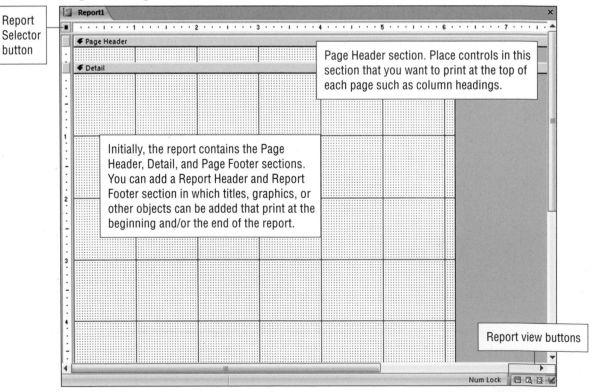

Report Selector button

Page Header section. Place controls in this section that you want to print at the top of each page such as column headings.

Initially, the report contains the Page Header, Detail, and Page Footer sections. You can add a Report Header and Report Footer section in which titles, graphics, or other objects can be added that print at the beginning and/or the end of the report.

Report view buttons

Table 5.1   Report Sections

Report Section	Description
Report Header	Content in the report header section prints at the beginning of the report and generally includes controls for the report title and company logo or other image.
Page Header	Content in the page header section prints at the top of each page in the report. Place controls for column headings in a tabular report format in the page header.
Detail	Place controls for the body of the report with the fields from the table or query in the Detail section.
Page Footer	Content in the page footer section prints at the bottom of each page in the report. Add a control to this section to print a page number at the bottom of each page.
Report Footer	Content in this section prints at the end of the report. Add controls in this section to print grand totals or perform another aggregate function such as average, max, min, or count.

Project 1a   Starting a New Report Using Design View and Adding a Title and Label Object

1. Open **RSRComputerServ5.accdb** and enable the content.
2. Click the Create tab and then click the Report Design button in the Reports group.
3. Add a title in the Report Header section of the report by completing the following steps:
   a. With the Report Design Tools Design tab active, click the Title button in the Controls group. Access adds the Report Header section above the Page Header section and places a title object with the text *Report1* selected.
   b. Type **RSR Computer Service Work Orders** and press Enter.

Step 2

New Object: Report

Create a new blank report in Design view.

In Design view, you can make advanced design changes to reports, such as adding custom control types and writing code.

Steps 3a–3b

4. Minimize the navigation pane to provide more room in the work area.
5. Widen the report to provide more space in the design grid by dragging the right edge of the grid until the width is aligned at the 8-inch position in the horizontal ruler.

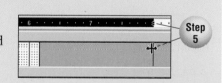

Step 5

6. Scroll down the report until you can see the Page Footer and Report Footer sections. The Report Footer section was added to the design grid at the same time the Report Header section was added when the title was created in Step 3.

7. Drag the bottom edge of the grid down until the bottom of the report is at the 0.5-inch position in the vertical ruler.

8. Add a label control object at the left edge of the Report Footer section that contains your first and last names.

9. Click in any blank area of the report to deselect the label control object.

10. Save the report and name it **Work_Orders**.

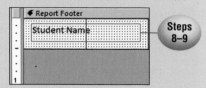

Steps 8–9

Bind Table or Query to Report
1. Open report in Design view.
2. Double-click Report Selector button.
3. Click Data tab in Property Sheet.
4. Click down-pointing arrow in *Record Source* property box.
5. Click desired table or query.
6. Close Property Sheet.

Add Fields to Report
1. Click Add Existing Fields button.
2. Drag field name(s) from Field List pane to Detail section.

Add Fields from Related Table
1. Open Field List pane.
2. Click <u>Show all tables</u> hyperlink.
3. Click expand button next to desired table name in *Fields available in related tables* section.
4. Drag field name from related table list to Detail section.

Binding a Table or Query to the Report and Adding Fields

A table or query's fields can be added to the Detail section in the design grid by first binding the desired table or query to the report using the same process that you learned to bind a table to a form. Double-click the Report Selector button located above the vertical ruler and left of the horizontal ruler to open the report's Property Sheet. Click the Data tab and then select the table or query name in the drop-down list in the *Record Source* property.

Display the Field List pane and drag individual fields from the table or query or a group of fields to the Detail section. After fields have been added you can move and resize the control objects as needed.

The Field List pane displays in one of two states: with one section only with the fields from the table or query bound to the report, or, with two additional sections with fields from other tables in the database. If the Field List pane contains only the fields from the bound table or query, you can add fields from other tables by displaying other table names from the database within the Field List pane. At the bottom of the pane, Access displays a hyperlink with the text <u>Show all tables</u>. Click the hyperlink to display two additional sections within the pane: *Fields available in related tables* and *Fields available in other tables*. Next to each table name is an expand button (displays as a plus symbol). Click the expand button next to a table name to display the fields stored within the table and then drag the field name to the Detail section of the report. You will perform these steps in Project 1b.

Report Selector

Add Existing Fields

Project 1b Binding a Table to a Report and Adding Fields

1. With the **RSRComputerServ5.accdb** database open and the Work_Orders report open in Design view, scroll up to the top of the report in the work area.

2. Bind the Work_Orders table to the report by completing the following steps:

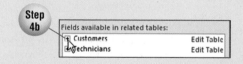

   a. Double-click the Report Selector button located at the top of the vertical ruler and left of the horizontal ruler to open the report's Property Sheet.

   b. Click the Data tab in the Property Sheet, click the down-pointing arrow in the *Record Source* property box, and then click *Work_Orders* at the drop-down list.

   c. Close the Property Sheet.

3. Click the Add Existing Fields button in the Tools group in the Report Design Tools Design tab to open the Field List pane.

4. Add fields from the Work_Orders table and related fields from the Customers table by completing the following steps:

   a. Click the <u>Show all tables</u> hyperlink at the bottom of the Field List pane. Access adds two sections to the pane. One section contains related tables and the other section contains other tables in the database which do not have an established relationship with the bound table. Next to each table name is an expand button (displays as a plus symbol) which is used to display field names for the table. ***Note: Skip this step if the hyperlink at the bottom of the Field List pane displays <u>Show only fields in the current record source</u> since the additional sections are already added to the pane.***

   b. Click the expand button next to *Customers* in the *Fields available in related tables* section of the Field List pane. Access expands the list to display the field names in the Customers table below the Customers table name.

   c. Drag the *WO_No*, *Cust_ID*, *Call_Date*, and *Descr* fields from the Work_Orders table to the design grid as shown.

   d. Drag the *Fname* and *Lname* fields from the Customers table to the design grid as shown.

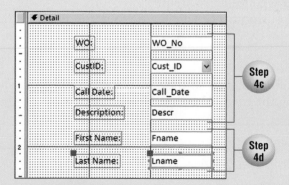

5. Close the Field List pane.

6. Save the report.

![QUICK STEPS]

Move Controls to Another Section
1. Open report in Design view.
2. Select controls to be moved.
3. Click Home tab.
4. Click Cut button.
5. Click section bar in which to move controls.
6. Click Paste button.
7. Deselect controls.

Moving Control Objects to Another Section

As with a form, when a field is added to the Detail section in a report, a label control object containing the caption or field name is placed left of a text box control object that displays the field value from the record when the report is viewed or printed. In the Work_Orders report, the label control object for each field needs to be moved to the Page Header section so that the field names or captions print at the top of each page as column headings. To do this, you will cut and paste the controls from the Detail section to the Page Header section in Project 1c.

Project 1c   Moving Controls to Another Section

1. With the **RSRComputerServ5.accdb** database open and the Work_Orders report open in Design view, move the label control objects from the Detail section to the Page Header section by completing the following steps:
   a. Click to select the *WO* label control object.
   b. Hold down the Shift key and click to select each of the other label control objects.

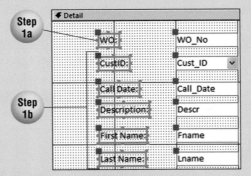

   c. Click the Home tab and then click the Cut button in the Clipboard group.
   d. Click the blue Page Header section bar.
   e. Click the Paste button in the Clipboard group (do not click the down-pointing arrow on the button). Access pastes the label control objects and expands the Page Header section.
   f. Deselect the controls.
2. Move the label control objects so they are placed in the order shown below in a horizontal arrangement along the top of the Page Header section.

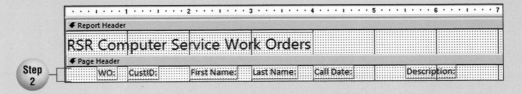

3. Edit the text in each label control object to delete the colon (:) at the end of each caption or field name.
4. Drag the top of the blue Detail section bar up until the top of the bar is aligned at the bottom edge of the label control objects in the Page Header section.

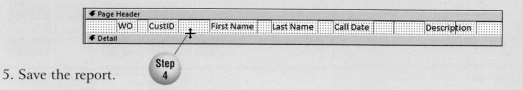

5. Save the report.

Step 4

Applying an AutoFormat

Click the AutoFormat button in the AutoFormat group in the Report Design Tools Arrange tab to apply one of the predefined formats to the report in Design view. The AutoFormat options align with the themes available in Word, Excel, and PowerPoint so that you can maintain a consistent look for Access reports that you use for other documents, worksheets, or presentations. Make sure a control object or group of control objects is not selected before applying an AutoFormat to the report since Access will apply the AutoFormat option to the selected controls instead of the entire report.

QUICK STEPS

Apply AutoFormat
1. Open report in Design view.
2. Click Report Design Tools Arrange tab.
3. Click AutoFormat button.
4. Click desired AutoFormat option.

AutoFormat

Project 1d Moving Controls, Resizing Controls, and Applying an AutoFormat

1. With the **RSRComputerServ5.accdb** database open and the Work_Orders report open in Design view, move each text box control object in the Detail section below the object's associated label control object in the Page Header section so that the field values will align below the correct column headings in the report.

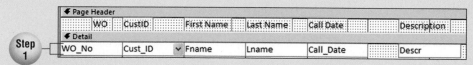

Step 1

2. Click the Print Preview button in the View group at the right end of the Status bar to view the report in the Print Preview window. Notice the field value in the *Call Date* column is displaying pound symbols indicating the field's text box control object needs to be widened.

Step 2

3. Click the Design View button in the View group to return to Design view.
4. Resize the *Call_Date* text box control in the Detail section until the right edge of the control is aligned at the 5.25-inch position in the horizontal ruler.
5. Resize the *Descr* text box control in the Detail section until the right edge of the control is aligned at the 7.75-inch position in the horizontal ruler.

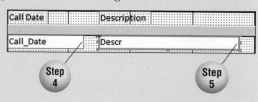

Step 4

Step 5

6. Deselect the *Descr* control object.
7. Apply the *Trek* AutoFormat to the report by completing the following steps:
   a. Click the Report Design Tools Arrange tab.
   b. Click the AutoFormat button in the AutoFormat group.
   c. Click *Trek* at the drop-down list (second option from left in last row).
8. Save the report.
9. Display the report in Print Preview to review the changes made in this project. Switch back to Design view when finished previewing the report.

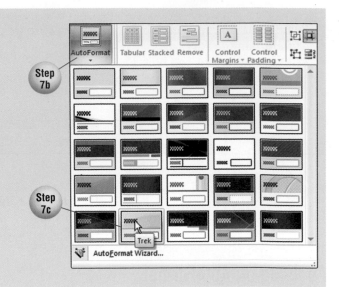

Step 7b

Step 7c

QUICK STEPS

Inserting a Subreport

Insert Subreport
1. Open report in Design view.
2. Make sure Use Control Wizards is active.
3. Click Subform/Subreport button.
4. Drag crosshairs desired height and width in Detail section.
5. Click Next.
6. Choose table or query and fields.
7. Click Next.
8. Choose field by which to link main report with subreport.
9. Click Next.
10. Click Finish.
11. If desired, delete subreport label control object.
12. Move and/or resize subreport object as required.

Subform/Subreport

Control Wizards

The Subform/Subreport button in the Controls group of the Report Design Tools Design tab is used to insert a subreport into a report. The report into which the subreport is embedded is called the main report. Adding a related table or query as a subreport creates a control object within the main report that can be moved, formatted, and resized independently of the other control objects. Make sure the Use Control Wizards button is toggled on in the Controls group before clicking the Subform/Subreport button so that you can add the subreport using the SubReport Wizard shown in Figure 5.2.

A subreport is stored as a separate object outside the main report. You will notice an additional report name added in the navigation pane with *subreport* at the end of the name when you finish the steps in the SubReport Wizard. Do not delete a subreport object in the navigation pane. If the subreport object is deleted, the main report will no longer be able to display the fields from the related table or query in the report.

Figure 5.2 First Dialog Box in SubReport Wizard

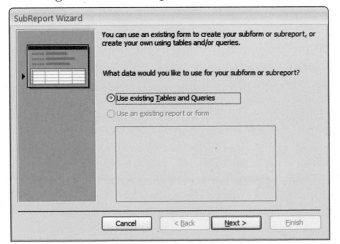

Project 1e   Inserting a Subreport

1. With the **RSRComputerServ5.accdb** database open and the Work_Orders report open in Design view, insert a subreport into the Work_Orders report with fields from a query for the service date, labor, and parts for each work order by completing the following steps:

   a. Click the Report Design Tools Design tab.

   b. By default, the Use Control Wizards button is toggled on in the Controls group. If the feature is not active, click the Use Control Wizards button to turn the feature on.

   c. Click the Subform/Subreport button in the Controls group.

   d. Move the crosshairs with the subreport icon attached to the Detail section below the *WO_No* text box control object and drag down and right to create a subreport object the approximate height and width shown. When you release the mouse, the SubReport Wizard begins.

   e. With *Use existing Tables and Queries* already selected, click Next at the first SubReport Wizard dialog box.

   f. At the second SubReport Wizard dialog box, select the query fields to be displayed in the subreport by completing the following steps:

      1) Click the down-pointing arrow next to the *Tables/Queries* list box and then click *Query: TotalWorkOrders* at the drop-down list.

      2) Move all of the fields from the *Available Fields* list box to the *Selected Fields* list box.

      3) Click Next.

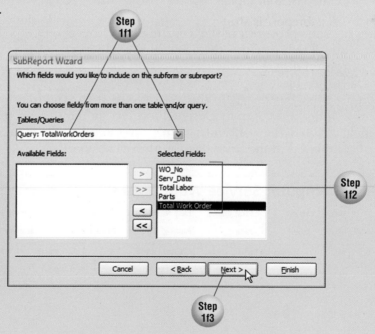

g. At the third SubReport Wizard dialog box, choose the field by which to link the main report with the subreport by completing the following steps:

1) With *Choose from a list* and the first option in the list box selected, read the text that displays below the list box describing the linked field. The text indicates that the main report will be linked to the subreport using the *Cust_ID* field. This is not the correct field since you want your report to show the service date, labor, and parts based on the work order number.

2) Click the second option in the list box and then read the text below the list box.

3) Since the second option indicates the two reports will be linked using *WO_No*, click Next.

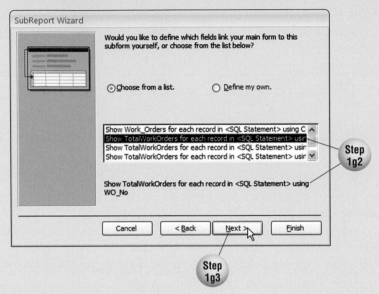

h. Click Finish at the last SubReport Wizard dialog box to accept the default subreport name *TotalWorkOrders subreport*.

2. Access inserts the subreport with a label control object above the subreport control that contains the name of the subreport. Click the label control displaying the text *TotalWorkOrders subreport* to select the object and then press the Delete key.

3. Click the Report View button 📇 in the View group at the right end of the Status bar or in the Views group in the Report Design Tools Design tab to view the subreport with data in the fields. Notice the work order number in the subreport is the same work order number that is displayed in the first record in the main report.

The main report and the subreport are linked by the *WO_No* field.

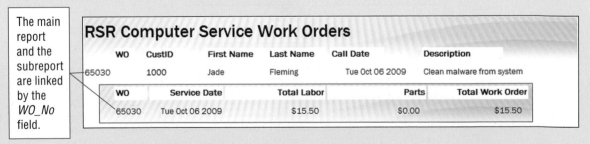

RSR Computer Service Work Orders

WO	CustID	First Name	Last Name	Call Date	Description
65030	1000	Jade	Fleming	Tue Oct 06 2009	Clean malware from system

WO	Service Date	Total Labor	Parts	Total Work Order
65030	Tue Oct 06 2009	$15.50	$0.00	$15.50

4. Switch back to Design view.

5. Now that you know the subreport is linked correctly to the main report, you do not need to display the work order number in the subreport. Delete the work order number control objects in the subreport by completing the following steps:

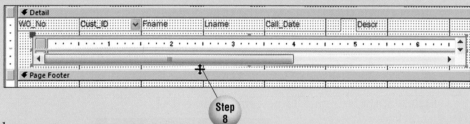

   a. Click to select the subreport control object and then drag the bottom middle sizing handle down to increase the height of the subreport until you can see all of the controls in the Report Header and Detail sections.
   b. Click to select the *WO* label control object in the Report Header section, hold down the Shift key, and click the *WO_No* text box control object in the Detail section in the subreport.
   c. Press Delete.
6. Click to select the subreport control object and drag the bottom middle sizing handle of the control up until the height of the subreport is approximately one-half inch.
7. Scroll down the report until you can see the blue Page Footer section bar.
8. Drag the top of the Page Footer section bar up until the section bar is just below the subreport control object in the Detail section.

9. Save the report.
10. Switch to Report view to view the revised report. Resizing the Detail section at Step 8 allowed the report to show more records and related subreport records on the page since the spacing between sections was reduced.
11. Close the report and redisplay the navigation pane.

Project 2 Add Features and Enhance a Report

You will modify the Work_Orders report to add page numbering, date and time controls, and graphics.

Adding Page Numbering and Date and Time Controls

Add page numbering to a report using the Insert Page Number button in the Controls group in the Report Design Tools Design tab. Clicking the button opens the Page Numbers dialog box shown in Figure 5.3. Choose the desired format, position, and alignment for the page number and click OK. Access inserts a control object in either the Page Header or the Page Footer section depending on the *Position* option selected in the dialog box.

QUICK STEPS

Add Page Numbers
1. Open Report in Design view.
2. Click Insert Page Number button.
3. Select desired format, position, and alignment options.
4. Click OK.

Figure 5.3 Page Numbers Dialog Box

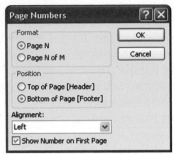

Add Date and/or Time
1. Open report in Design view.
2. Click Date & Time button.
3. Select desired date and/or time options.
4. Click OK.
5. If necessary, move and or resize controls as required.

Insert Page Number

Date and Time

Add the current date and/or time in the Report Header section by clicking the Date & Time button in the Controls group to open the Date and Time dialog box shown in Figure 5.4. By default both the *Include Date* and *Include Time* check boxes are selected. Access creates one control object for the desired date format and a separate control object for the desired time format. Access places the control objects with the date above the time aligned at the right edge of the Report Header section. Once inserted, you can move the controls to another section in the report.

Figure 5.4 Date and Time Dialog Box

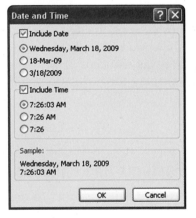

Project 2a   Adding Page Numbering and the Date and Time to a Report

1. With the **RSRComputerServ5.accdb** database open, right-click the Work_Orders report object name in the navigation pane and click *Design View* at the shortcut menu.
2. Minimize the navigation pane.
3. When the subreport was inserted in Project 1e, the width of the report may have been automatically extended beyond the page width. Look at the Report Selector button. If a green diagonal triangle displays in the upper left corner of the button, correct the page width by completing the following steps; otherwise, skip this step if your Report Selector button does not display with a green diagonal triangle.

a. Click the green triangle to display the error checking options button 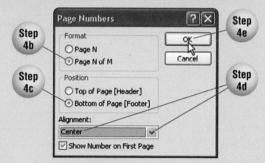 and then click the error checking options button to display the drop-down list of options.

b. Click *Remove Extra Report Space* at the drop-down list to automatically decrease the width of the report.

4. Add page numbering at the bottom center of each page by completing the following steps:

a. Click the Insert Page Number button in the Controls group in the Report Design Tools Design tab.

b. Click *Page N of M* in the *Format* section of the Page Numbers dialog box.

c. Click *Bottom of Page [Footer]* in the *Position* section.

d. Click the down-pointing arrow at the right of the *Alignment* list box and then click *Center* at the drop-down list.

e. Click OK. Access adds a control object in the center of the Page Footer section with the codes required to print the page numbers in the desired format.

Step 3a
Step 3b

Work_Orders
Report Header
Common Report Error
Report width is greater than page width
Edit Margins
Remove Extra Report Space
Select the Control Farthest to the Right
Help on This Error
Ignore Error
Error Checking Options...

Step 4b
Step 4c
Step 4e
Step 4d

Page Numbers
Format
○ Page N
⊙ Page N of M
OK
Cancel
Position
○ Top of Page [Header]
⊙ Bottom of Page [Footer]
Alignment:
Center
☑ Show Number on First Page

5. Add the current date and time to the end of the report along with a label control object containing the text *Date and Time Printed:* by completing the following steps:

a. Click the Date & Time button in the Controls group.

b. Click the second option in the *Include Date* section in the Date and Time dialog box that displays the date in the format dd-mmm-yy. For example, *18-Mar-09*.

c. Click the second option in the *Include Time* section that displays the time in the format hh:mm a.m./p.m. For example, *8:09 AM*.

d. Click OK. Access adds two control objects one above the other at the right end of the Report Header section with the date code *=Date()* and the time code *=Time()*.

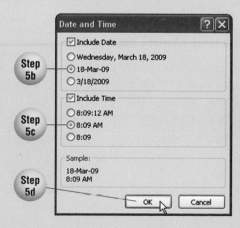

Step 5b
Step 5c
Step 5d

Date and Time
☑ Include Date
○ Wednesday, March 18, 2009
⊙ 18-Mar-09
○ 3/18/2009
☑ Include Time
○ 8:09:12 AM
⊙ 8:09 AM
○ 8:09
Sample:
18-Mar-09
8:09 AM
OK   Cancel

e. Select both control objects added to the Report Header section containing the date and time codes.

f. Position the mouse pointer on the orange border of the selected control objects until the pointer displays with the four-headed arrow move icon and then drag the controls to the bottom of the report at the right end of the Report Footer section.

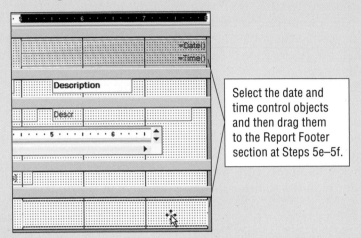

Select the date and time control objects and then drag them to the Report Footer section at Steps 5e–5f.

g. Resize and then move the date and time controls to arrange them side-by-side as shown.

h. Create the label control object with the text **Date and Time Printed:** left of the date control object as shown. *Note: Ignore the green error flag that appears at the top left of the label control object. The error flag appears because the label control object is not associated with any other object.*

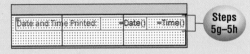

Steps 5g–5h

6. Save the report.

7. Display the report in Print Preview.

8. Scroll to the bottom of the report to view the page numbering at the bottom center of the page.

9. Click the Last Page button in the page navigation bar to scroll to the last page in the report and view the date and time at the end of the report.

10. Switch back to Design view.

Adding Graphics to a Report

The same techniques that you learned in Chapter 4 to add pictures or clip art or to draw lines in a form in Design view can be applied to a report. Recall from Chapter 4 that clip art when resized is truncated to fit within the resized control object. Display the Property Sheet for the clip art object and change the *Size Mode* property to *Zoom* or *Stretch* to resize the image to the height and width of the control object.

1. With the **RSRComputerServ5.accdb** database open, start Microsoft Word.
2. Locate and insert a clip art image in a new document and copy and paste the image to the Report Header section in the Access report by completing the following steps:
   a. At a blank Word document screen, click the Insert tab and then click the Clip Art button in the Illustrations group to open the Clip Art task pane.
   b. Select and delete existing text in the *Search for* text box, type **computer**, and press Enter.
   c. Locate and click the image shown in the Clip Art task pane to insert the clip art in the current document. If the image shown is not available, select a suitable alternative image.

Step 2c

   d. Right-click the clip art image in the Word document and click *Copy* at the shortcut menu.
   e. Click the button on the taskbar representing Microsoft Access.
   f. Right-click in the Report Header section of the report and click *Paste* at the shortcut menu. Access inserts the image overlapping the title and expands the height of the section to accommodate the height of the image.
   g. Move and resize the image as shown, placing the object at the right edge of the Report Header section.
   h. With the clip art image selected, open the Property Sheet, change the *Size Mode* property to *Zoom*, and then close the Property Sheet.
   i. Change the *Line Type* option to *Transparent* for the clip art image. If necessary, change the *Line Type* option to *Transparent* for the clip art image. ***Note: If you inserted an alternative image, the* Line Type *option may display as* Border Styles.**
   j. Drag the top of the blue Page Header section bar to decrease the height of the section as shown.

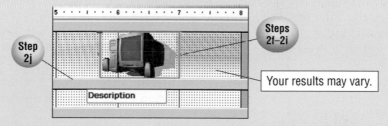

Step 2j

Steps 2f–2i

Your results may vary.

Description

   k. Click the button on the taskbar representing Microsoft Word and exit Word. Click No when prompted to save the document.

3. Draw and format horizontal lines below the title and below the column headings by completing the following steps:

   a. Click the Line button ◥ in the Controls group.

   b. Position the crosshairs with the line icon attached below the first letter in the title in the Report Header section, hold down the Shift key, drag right releasing the mouse below the last letter in the title, and then release the Shift key.

   c. Change the Line Thickness to *3 pt*.

   d. Change the Line Color to *Green* (sixth option in last row in *Standard Colors* section of color palette).

   e. Deselect the line.

   f. Draw another straight horizontal line that extends the width of the report along the bottom of the label control objects in the Page Header section.

   g. Change the Line Thickness to *1 pt*.

   h. Change the line color to the same green applied to the line below the report title.

   i. Deselect the line.

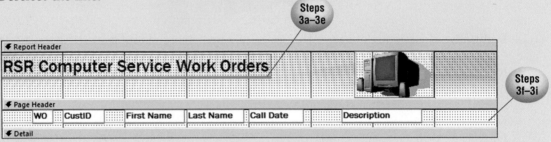

4. Format, move, and resize control objects as follows:

   a. Select all of the label control objects in the Page Header section and change the font size to 12.

   b. Resize the controls as needed to show all of the label text after increasing the font size.

   c. Drag the horizontal line to the bottom edge of the Page Header section.

   d. Select the *WO_No* text box control object in the Detail section, change the font size to 12, and center-align the text within the control.

   e. Select all of the text box control objects in the Detail section and apply bold.

   f. Move the report title and the line below the title until the left edges of the objects align at the 1-inch position in the horizontal ruler and are approximately vertically centered within the section.

   g. Move the *Call Date* label control object in the Page Header section until the left edge of the object is aligned at the 4.5-inch position in the horizontal ruler.

5. Display the report in Print Preview.

6. Compare your report with the one shown in Figure 5.5. If necessary, return to Design view, make adjustments to formats, alignment, or position of control objects, and then redisplay the report in Print Preview.

7. Save the report.

8. Print the report. **Note: This report is four pages long. Print only if required by your instructor.**

9. Close the Work_Orders report.

10. Redisplay the navigation pane.

Figure 5.5 Partial View of Completed Work_Orders Report

RSR Computer Service Work Orders

WO	CustID	First Name	Last Name	Call Date	Description
65030	1000	Jade	Fleming	Tue Oct 06 2009	Clean malware from system

Service Date	Total Labor	Parts	Total Work Order
Tue Oct 06 2009	$15.50	$0.00	$15.50

WO	CustID	First Name	Last Name	Call Date	Description
65033	1000	Jade	Fleming	Mon Oct 12 2009	Install Windows Vista

Service Date	Total Labor	Parts	Total Work Order
Tue Oct 13 2009	$81.25	$335.75	$417.00

WO	CustID	First Name	Last Name	Call Date	Description
65024	1005	Cayla	Fahri	Thu Sep 24 2009	Install malware protection

Service Date	Total Labor	Parts	Total Work Order
Thu Sep 24 2009	$15.50	$75.50	$91.00

Project ③ Group Records and Add Functions to Count and Sum

You will create a new report using the Report Wizard and then modify the report in Design view to add sum and count functions.

Grouping Records in a Report

You can group records in a report if a field included in the report contains repeating field values. For example, a field for a department name, a city name, or a salesperson name is likely to contain several records with the same field value. You can group all of the records for the same department or city together and add totals with aggregate functions to calculate the sum, average, max, min, or count for each group. At the second Report Wizard dialog box shown in Figure 5.6, you can specify how you want to group the report. Double-click a field name in the field list box to add a grouping level. The preview window updates to display the grouped field in blue. More than one grouping level can be added to a report.

If you change your mind after adding a grouping level, use the Remove Field button (button with left-pointing arrow) to remove the grouped level. Use the Priority buttons (buttons with up- and down-pointing arrows) to change the grouping order when you have multiple grouped fields.

QUICK STEPS

Group Records Using Report Wizard
1. Click Create tab.
2. Click Report Wizard button.
3. Choose table or query and fields.
4. Click Next.
5. If necessary, remove default grouped field name.
6. Double-click field name by which to group records.
7. Click Next.
8. Choose field(s) by which to sort.
9. Click Next.
10. Choose layout options.
11. Click Next.
12. Choose style option.
13. Click Next.
14. Enter title for report.
15. Click Finish.

Figure 5.6 Grouping by a Field Using the Report Wizard

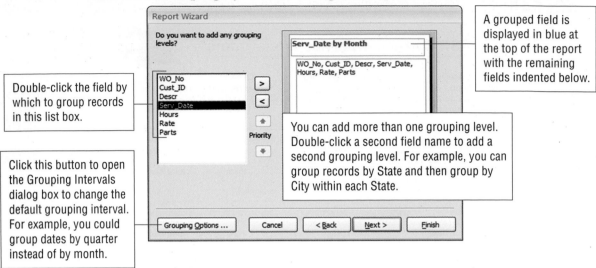

Double-click the field by which to group records in this list box.

A grouped field is displayed in blue at the top of the report with the remaining fields indented below.

You can add more than one grouping level. Double-click a second field name to add a second grouping level. For example, you can group records by State and then group by City within each State.

Click this button to open the Grouping Intervals dialog box to change the default grouping interval. For example, you could group dates by quarter instead of by month.

HINT

Use Layout view to group records using the Group, Sort, and Total pane since Access does all of the work for you after you select the group field. In Design view, Access creates the group header section but does not automatically place the field's text box control within the group section—you have to do this manually.

 Group & Sort

If you created a report using the wizard and did not specify a grouping level, you can group records after the report has been generated using Layout view or Design view. In Layout view, click the Group & Sort button in the Grouping & Totals group of the Report Layout Tools Format tab. In Design view, click the Group & Sort button in the Grouping & Totals group in the Report Design Tools Design tab. Clicking the button in either view opens the Group, Sort, and Total pane shown in Figure 5.7 at the bottom of the work area. Click the Add a group button and then click the field name by which to group records in the pop-up list.

Figure 5.7 Group, Sort, and Total Pane

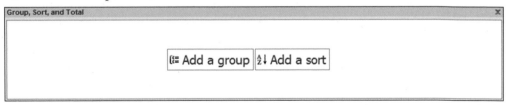

Project 3a Creating a Report with a Grouping Level Using the Report Wizard

1. With the **RSRComputerServ5.accdb** database open, modify the TotalWorkOrders query to add two fields you want to include in a report by completing the following steps:
   a. Open the TotalWorkOrders query in Design view.
   b. Drag the *Cust_ID* field from the Work_Orders field list box to the *Field* box in the second column in the design grid. The existing *Serv_Date* and other fields will shift right to accommodate the new field.

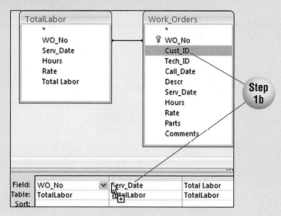

   c. Drag the *Descr* field from the Work_Orders table to the *Field* box in the third column in the design grid.
   d. Save the revised query.
   e. Run the query.

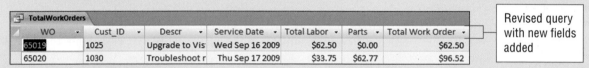

Revised query with new fields added

   f. Close the query.
2. Create a report based on the TotalWorkOrders query that is grouped by the service dates by month using the Report Wizard by completing the following steps:
   a. Click the Create tab and then click the Report Wizard button in the Reports group.
   b. At the first Report Wizard dialog box with *Query: TotalWorkOrders* already selected in the *Tables/Queries* list box, move all of the fields from the *Available Fields* list box to the *Selected Fields* list box and then click Next.
   c. At the second Report Wizard dialog box, specify the grouping level by the *Serv_Date* field by completing the following steps:
      1) With *Cust_ID* displayed in blue in the preview section indicating the report will be grouped by customer number, click the Remove field button (displays as a left-pointing arrow) to remove the grouping level.
      2) Double-click *Serv_Date* in the field list box to add a grouping level by the service date field. By default, Access groups the date field by month.

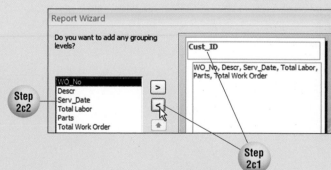

3) With the preview section now displaying the report will be grouped by *Serv_Date by Month*, click Next.

Step 2c3

d. At the third Report Wizard dialog box, click the down-pointing arrow at the right of the first sort list box, click *WO_No* at the drop-down list to sort within each group by the work order numbers in ascending order, and then click Next.

e. At the fourth Report Wizard dialog box, click *Landscape* in the *Orientation* section and then click Next.

f. At the fifth Report Wizard dialog box, click *Concourse* in the *Report AutoFormats* list box and then click Next.

g. At the last Report Wizard dialog box, select the existing text in the *What title do you want for your report?* text box, type **WorkOrdersbyMonth**, and click Finish.

3. Minimize the navigation pane.

4. Preview the report and then switch to Layout view or Design view. Edit text in the report title and column heading labels and adjust widths as necessary until the report looks similar to the one shown below.

Step 4

5. Save the report.

Adding Aggregate Functions to a Group

When a report is grouped, the Group, Sort, and Total pane can be used to add a calculation below a numeric field at the end of each group. You can add a function to more than one field within the group. For example you can calculate a sum function on a sales field and a count function on an invoice field. The following functions are available for numeric fields: Sum, Average, Count Records, Count Values, Maximum, Minimum, Standard Deviation, and Variance. A non-numeric field can have a Count Records or Count Values function added.

The Group, Sort, and Total pane for a report with an existing grouping level displays similar to the one shown in Figure 5.8. Click the More Options button next to the group level to which a total is to be added to expand the available group options.

QUICK STEPS

Add Functions to Group
1. Open report in Design view.
2. Click Group & Sort button.
3. Click More Options button.
4. Click down-pointing arrow next to *with no totals.*
5. Choose field in *Total On* list box.
6. Choose function in *Type* list box.
7. If desired, click *Show grand total* check box.
8. If desired, click *Show group totals as % of Grand Total* check box.
9. Click *Show in group header* or *Show in group footer* check box.
10. Repeat Steps 5–9 as needed for other fields.
11. Click outside Totals option box.
12. Close Group, Sort, and Total pane.

Figure 5.8 Group, Sort, and Total Pane with a Grouping Level Added

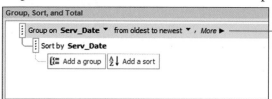

Click the More Options button to expand the pane to show group interval options, the totals option, and other group options.

Click the down-pointing arrow next to *with no totals* to open the Totals option box. Select the field to which a function should be added and the type of aggregate function to calculate using the drop-down list boxes. Use the check boxes to choose to add a grand total to the end of the report, calculate group totals as a percentage of the grand total, and whether to add the calculated function to the group header or group footer section. Continue adding functions to other fields as needed and click outside the Totals option box when finished to close the box.

Figure 5.9 Totals Option Box in Group, Sort, and Total Pane

Click here in the expanded options list to open the Totals option box in which you specify the field(s) and aggregate function(s) to add to the report. You can also add functions to calculate a grand total at the end of the report and calculate group totals as a percentage of the grand total.

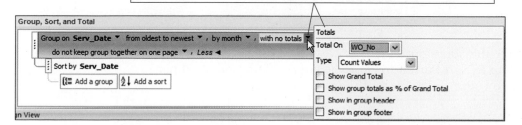

1. With the **RSRComputerServ5.accdb** database open, display the WorkOrdersbyMonth report in Design view.
2. Add two functions at the end of each month to show the number of work orders and the total value of work orders by completing the following steps:
   a. In the Grouping & Totals group of the Report Design Tools Design tab, click the Group & Sort button.
   b. At the Group, Sort, and Total pane located at the bottom of the work area, click the More Options button located next to *from oldest to newest* in the *Group on Serv_Date* group options.

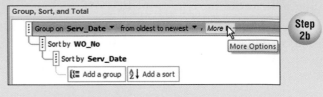

Step 2b

   c. Click the down-pointing arrow next to *with no totals* in the expanded group options.
   d. At the Totals option box, with *WO_No* in the *Total On* list box, specify the type of function and the placement of the result by completing the following steps:

Step 2d1

Step 2d2

Step 2d3

   1) Click the down-pointing arrow next to *Type* and then click *Count Records* at the drop-down list.
   2) Click the *Show Grand Total* check box to insert a check mark. Access adds a count function in a control object in the Report Footer section below the *WO_No* column.
   3) Click the *Show in group footer* check box to insert a check mark. Access displays a new section with the title *Serv_Date Footer* in the blue section bar below the Detail section and inserts a count function in a control object below the *WO_No* column.
   e. With the Totals option box still open, click the down-pointing arrow next to *Total On* and select *Total Work Order* at the drop-down list. The *Type* option defaults to *Sum* for a numeric field.
   f. Click the *Show Grand Total* check box to insert a check mark. Access adds a sum function in a control object in the Report Footer section below the *Total Work Order* column.
   g. Click the *Show in group footer* check box to insert a check mark. Access adds a sum function in a control object in the *Serv_Date Footer* section below the *Total Work Order* column.

Step 2e

Step 2f

Step 2g

   h. Click outside the Totals option box to close the box.
3. Click the Group & Sort button to close the Group, Sort, and Total pane.
4. Review the two count functions and the two sum functions added to the report in Design view.

5. Display the report in Print Preview to view the calculated results. Notice the printout requires two pages with the report's grand totals printing on page 2. You will correct this in Project 4.

6. Switch back to Design view.

7. Add a label control object left of the count function in the Serv_Date Footer section that displays the text **Work Order Count:** and another label control object left of the sum function that displays the text **Month Total:**. Apply bold and right-align the text in the two label control objects. Ignore the error flags that display indicating the label control is not associated with another control object. Resize and align the two labels as necessary.

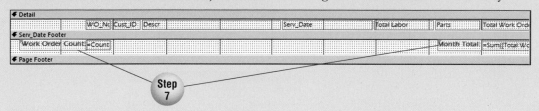

8. Display the report in Print Preview to view the labels. If necessary, return to Design view to make further size and alignment adjustments.

Partial report displayed in Print Preview with labels and functions added

Serv_Date by Month	WO	Cust_ID	Description of Call	Service Date	Total Labor	Parts	Total Work Order
September 2009							
	65019	1025	Upgrade to Vista Ultimate	Wed Sep 16 2009	$62.50	$0.00	$62.50
	65020	1030	Troubleshoot noisy fan	Thu Sep 17 2009	$33.75	$62.77	$96.52
	65021	1035	Customer has blue screen upon boot	Fri Sep 18 2009	$81.25	$0.00	$81.25
	65022	1040	Customer reports screen is fuzzy	Tue Sep 22 2009	$37.50	$55.47	$92.97
	65023	1045	Upgrade RAM	Wed Sep 23 2009	$31.25	$62.50	$93.75
	65024	1005	Install malware protection	Thu Sep 24 2009	$15.50	$75.50	$91.00
	65025	1010	Troubleshoot hard drive noise	Mon Sep 28 2009	$37.50	$0.00	$37.50
	65026	1025	Upgrade memory	Tue Sep 29 2009	$18.75	$75.75	$94.50
Work Order Count:	8					Month Total:	$649.99

9. Save and close the report.

10. Redisplay the navigation pane.

Project 4 Modify Section and Group Properties

You will change a report's page setup and then modify section and group properties to control print options.

Modifying Section Properties

A report has a Property Sheet, each control object within the report has a Property Sheet, and each section within the report has a Property Sheet. Section properties control whether the section is visible when printed, the section's height, background color, special effects, and so on. Figure 5.10 displays the Format tab in the Property Sheet for the Report Header section. Some of the options can be changed without opening the Property Sheet. For example, you can increase or decrease the height of a section by dragging the top or bottom of a blue section bar in Design view. You can also set the background color using the Fill/Back Color button in the Font group.

QUICK STEPS

Modify Section Properties
1. Open report in Design view.
2. Double-click blue section bar.
3. Change desired properties.
4. Close Property Sheet.

Use the *Keep Together* property to ensure that a section is not split over two pages by a page break. If necessary, Access starts printing the section at the top of the next page. If the section is longer than can fit on the page, Access continues printing the section on the following page. In that case, you can decrease margins and/or apply a smaller font size to fit the text all on one page.

Use the *Force New Page* property to insert a page break before a section begins *(Before Section)*, after a section is finished *(After Section)*, or before and after a section *(Before & After)*.

Figure 5.10 Report Header Section Property Sheet with Format Tab Selected

Keep Group Together on One Page

1. Open report in Design view.
2. Click Group & Sort button.
3. Click More Options button.
4. Click down-pointing arrow next to *do not keep group together on one page*.
5. Click desired print option.
6. Close Group, Sort, and Total pane.

Keeping a Group Together on the Same Page

Open the Group, Sort, and Total pane and click the More Options button for a group to specify whether you want to keep an entire group together on the same page. By default, Access does not keep a group together. Click the down-pointing arrow next to *do not keep group together on one page* and then click the desired option as shown in Figure 5.11.

Figure 5.11 Group, Sort, and Total Pane with Keep Group Together Print Options

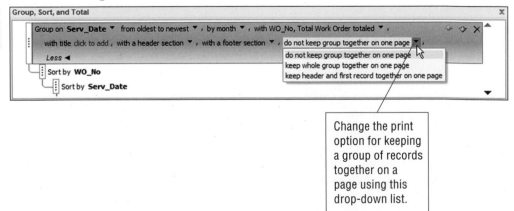

Change the print option for keeping a group of records together on a page using this drop-down list.

1. With the **RSRComputerServ5.accdb** database open, display the WorkOrdersbyMonth report in Print Preview. Zoom the report to *Fit to window* in order to view the report in context with the page margins and page footer options.

2. Modify the page setup to print wider margins by completing the following steps:
   a. Click the Margins button in the Page Layout group.
   b. Click *Wide* at the drop-down list. The *Wide* option sets the top and bottom margins to 1-inch and the left and right margins to 0.75-inch.
   c. Use the Next Page button in the Page Navigation bar to scroll through the report. Notice the wider left and right margins means the report's width needs to be decreased.
   d. Close Print Preview and switch to Design view.

3. Notice the green diagonal triangle in the Report Selector button. The error flag has occurred because the report width is now greater than the page width. Adjust the width of the report by completing the following steps:
   a. Minimize the navigation pane.
   b. Scroll right until you can see the right edge of the report. Notice the report ends at the 10.5-inch position in the horizontal ruler. With a left and right margin of 0.75-inch, the maximum width that can fit on the page in landscape orientation is 9.5 inches (11.0 – 1.5).
   c. Switch to Layout view. Decreasing the width of multiple columns to accommodate a shorter page width is easier done in Layout view.
   d. Select the *Description of Call* column, point to the right edge of the column, and decrease the column width by dragging the right boundary left approximately 0.25 inch.
   e. Select the *Service Date* column and decrease the width of the column until the vertical dashed line indicating a page break is positioned right of the *Total Work Order* column.
   f. Scroll to the bottom of the page, select the *Page 1 of 1* control at the bottom right, and drag the control left until the right edge of the page number control is aligned below the right edge of the values.
   g. If necessary, select the *Month Total* label control and drag the control to the left of the calculated sum function.
   h. Switch to Design view. Notice the right edge of the report is now at the 9.5-inch position in the horizontal ruler and the green error flag has been removed.

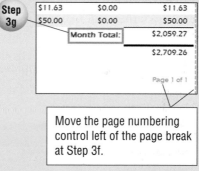

Move the page numbering control left of the page break at Step 3f.

4. Display the report in Print Preview and scroll the report to view both pages. Switch back to Design view.

5. Change the section properties for the group footer and the report footer sections displaying the count and sum functions by completing the following steps:
   a. Double-click the blue Serv_Date Footer section bar to open the section's Property Sheet.
   b. Click in the *Back Color* property box and click the Build button [...] to open the color palette.
   c. Click the *Green* color box (seventh color in first row of *Standard Colors* section).

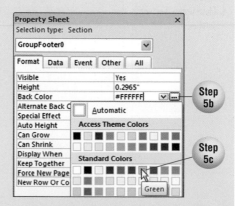

d. Close the Property Sheet.

e. Bold the control object containing the Count function and the control object containing the Sum function in the Serv_Date Footer section.

f. Double-click the blue Report Footer section bar, change the *Back Color* to *Maroon* (sixth color in first row of *Standard Colors* section) and then close the Property Sheet.

g. Bold the two control objects in the Report Footer section containing the functions.

6. Print each month's work orders on a separate page by completing the following steps:

a. Click the Group & Sort button.

b. Click the More Options button in the Group, Sort, and Total pane.

c. Click the down-pointing arrow next to *do not keep group together on one page* and then click *keep whole group together on one page* at the drop-down list.

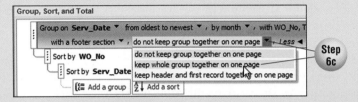

d. Close the Group, Sort, and Total pane.

7. Create a label control object in the center of the Report Footer section with your first and last name. Bold the label control object and apply black font color.

8. Display the report in Print Preview and zoom to One Page. Compare your report with the one shown in Figure 5.12. Scroll to page 2 to view all of October's work orders together on the same page.

9. Save, print, and then close the report.

10. Redisplay the navigation pane.

Figure 5.12 Page 1 of Completed Report in Project 4

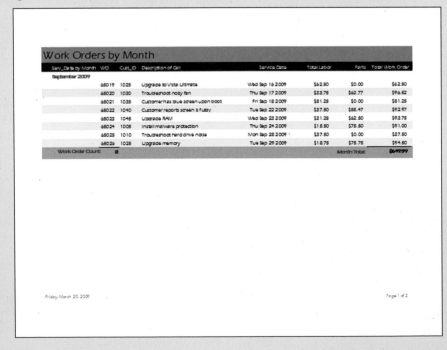

Project **5** **Create and Format a Chart**

You will create and format a chart in a customers report to show the total parts and labor on work orders by month.

Inserting a Chart into a Report

A chart can be added to a report to graphically display numerical data from a table or query linked to a field in the report that is common to both objects. Access summarizes and graphs the data from the charted table or query based on the fields you select for each record in the report.

With a report open in Design view, increase the height or width of the Detail section to make room for the chart, click the Insert Chart button in the Controls group of the Report Design Tools Design tab and drag the crosshairs with the chart icon attached the approximate height and width for the chart. When you release the mouse, Access launches the Chart Wizard with the first of six dialog boxes shown in Figure 5.13 that guide you through the steps of creating a chart.

Figure 5.13 First Dialog Box in Chart Wizard

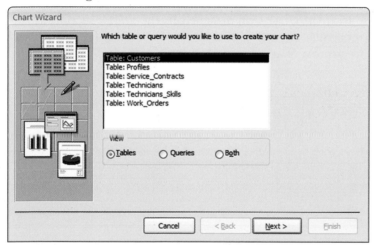

QUICK STEPS

Insert Chart in Report
1. Open report in Design view.
2. Click Insert Chart button.
3. Drag to create control object the height and width desired.
4. Select table or query for chart data.
5. Click Next.
6. Add fields to use in chart.
7. Click Next.
8. Click desired chart type.
9. Click Next.
10. Add fields as needed to chart layout.
11. Click Preview Chart.
12. Close Sample Preview window.
13. Click Next.
14. Select field to link report with chart.
15. Click Next.
16. Type chart name.
17. Click Finish.

HINT

The chart feature in Access is not the same Chart tool that is included with Word, Excel, and PowerPoint.

Chart

In Project 5 you will use the Chart Wizard to insert a chart in a customer report that depicts the total value of work orders for each customer by month. The data for the chart will be drawn from a related query. A chart can also be inserted into a form and formatted by completing steps similar to those in Project 5a and 5b.

1. With the **RSRComputerServ5.accdb** database open, create a new report using the Report Wizard by completing the following steps:
   a. Select the Customers table in the navigation pane, click the Create tab and then click the Report Wizard button.
   b. At the first Report Wizard dialog box with *Table: Customers* selected in the *Tables/Queries* list box, move *Cust_ID*, *Fname*, *Lname*, and *Serv_Cont* from the *Available Fields* list box to the *Selected Fields* list box and then click Next.
   c. Click Next at the second Report Wizard dialog box with no group field selected.
   d. Click Next at the third Report Wizard dialog to choose not to sort the report.
   e. Click *Columnar* at the fourth Report Wizard dialog box and then click Next.
   f. Click *Solstice* at the fifth Report Wizard dialog box and then click Next.
   g. Click at the end of the current text in the *What title do you want for your report?* text box, type **WOChartByMonth** so that the report title is *CustomersWOChartByMonth*, and then click Finish.
2. Minimize the navigation pane and display the report in Design view.
3. Edit the report title in the Report Header section to **Customers with Work Orders by Month**.
4. Drag the top of the Page Footer section bar down until the Detail section ends at the 2-inch position in the vertical ruler.
5. Insert a chart at the right side of the report to show the value of the work orders for each customer by month by completing the following steps:
   a. Click the Insert Chart button in the Controls group.
   b. Position the crosshairs with the chart icon attached in the Detail section at the 4-inch position in the horizontal ruler aligned near the top of the *Cust_ID* control object and drag down and right to create a chart object the approximate height and width shown.

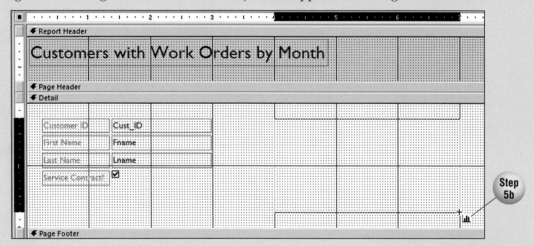

Step 5b

c. At the first Chart Wizard dialog box, click *Queries*, click *Query: TotalWorkOrders* in the list box, and then click Next.

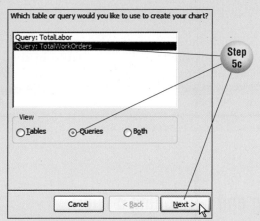

Which table or query would you like to use to create your chart?

Query: TotalLabor
Query: TotalWorkOrders

View
○ <u>T</u>ables   ◉ <u>Q</u>ueries   ○ B<u>o</u>th

Cancel   < <u>B</u>ack   <u>N</u>ext >

Step 5c

d. At the second Chart Wizard dialog box, double-click *Serv_Date* and *TotalWorkOrder* in the *Available Fields* list box to move the fields to the *Fields for Chart* list box and then click Next.

e. At the third Chart Wizard dialog box, click the second chart type in the first row (3-D Column Chart) and then click Next.

f. At the fourth Chart Wizard dialog box, look at the fields that Access has already placed to lay out the chart. Since only two fields were added, Access automatically used the numeric field with a sum function as the data series for the chart and the date field as the x-axis category axis.

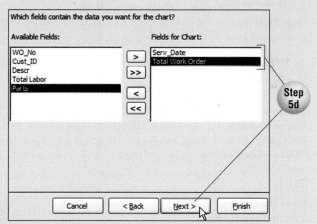

Which fields contain the data you want for the chart?

Available Fields:

WO_No
Cust_ID
Descr
Total Labor
Parts

Fields for Chart:

Serv_Date
Total Work Order

>   >>   <   <<

Cancel   < <u>B</u>ack   <u>N</u>ext >   <u>F</u>inish

Step 5d

g. Click the Preview Chart button located at the top left of the dialog box to preview a sample chart.

h. Review the sample chart and then click the Close button in the Sample Preview dialog box.

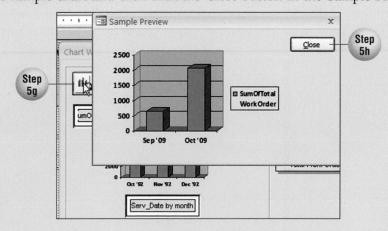

Sample Preview   ✕

Close

Step 5h

Chart W

2500
2000
1500
1000
500
0

Sep '09   Oct '09

☐ SumOfTotal Work Order

Step 5g

umO

2000
0

Oct '92   Nov '92   Dec '92

Serv_Date by month

i. Click Next.

j. At the fifth Chart Wizard dialog box notice that Access has correctly detected the field to link records in the Customers report with the chart (based on the TotalWorkOrders query) as *Cust_ID*. Click Next.

k. At the last Chart Wizard dialog box, click Finish. Access inserts a chart within the height and width of the chart control. The chart displayed in the control in Design view is not the actual chart based on the query data—it is only a sample to show the chart elements.

6. Display the report in Print Preview and scroll through the three pages in the report.

7. Save the report.

QUICK STEPS

Change Chart Type
1. Open report in Design view.
2. Double-click chart.
3. Click Chart on Menu bar.
4. Click *Chart Type*.
5. Click desired chart type in list box.
6. Click desired chart sub-type.
7. Click OK.

Change Chart Options
1. Open report in Design view.
2. Double-click chart.
3. Click Chart on Menu bar.
4. Click *Chart Options*.
5. Click tab for options to be changed.
6. Change options as required.
7. Click OK.

Format Chart Element
1. Open report in Design view.
2. Double-click chart.
3. Right-click chart element.
4. Click *Format* for selected chart element.
5. Change format options as required.
6. Click OK.

Editing and Formatting a Chart

The chart application within Access is not the same chart feature that is available in Microsoft Word, Microsoft Excel, and Microsoft PowerPoint. Access uses the Microsoft Graph application for charts. Open a report in Design view and double-click a chart object to edit the chart. In chart editing mode, a Menu bar and a toolbar display at the top of the Access window as well as a datasheet for the chart in the work area. You can change the chart type, add, remove, or change chart options, and format chart elements.

Click Chart on the Menu bar and click Chart Options to add, delete, or edit text in chart titles, to add or remove chart axes, gridlines, the legend, data labels, or a data table at the Chart Options dialog box. Click Chart and click Chart Type to open the *Chart Type* dialog box and choose a different chart such as a bar chart or a pie chart.

Right-click an object within the chart such as the chart title, legend, chart area, or data series and a format option displays in the shortcut menu for the selected chart element. Click the Format option to open a Format dialog box for the selected element. Make the desired changes and click OK.

When you have finished editing the chart, click outside the chart object to exit chart editing mode. Sometimes Access displays a sample chart within the control object in chart editing mode instead of the actual chart which can make editing specific chart elements difficult if your actual chart does not match the sample. If this occurs, exit chart editing mode, close and reopen the report in Design view, or switch views to cause Access to update the chart displayed in the control object.

Project 5b Changing the Chart Type, Chart Options, and Formatting a Chart

1. With the **RSRComputerServ5.accdb** database open, display the CustomersWOChartByMonth report in Design view.
2. Change the chart type, edit the chart title, and remove the legend in the chart by completing the following steps:
   a. Double-click within the chart to open the chart in chart editing mode. Access displays a datasheet with the chart and opens the Microsoft Graph application in which you edit charts.
   b. Click Chart on the Menu bar and then click *Chart Type*.

   Step 2b

   c. At the Chart Type dialog box with Standard Types selected, click *Bar* in the *Chart type* list box and click the first chart in the second row in the *Chart sub-type* section.

   Step 2c

   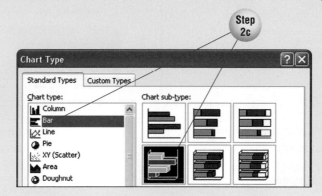

   d. Click OK.
   e. Click Chart on the Menu bar and then click Chart Options.
   f. At the Chart Options dialog box with the Titles tab selected, edit the text in the *Chart title* text box by inserting a space between the words so that the title text reads *Total Work Orders*.
   g. Click the Legend tab.
   h. Click the *Show legend* check box to clear the check mark. Since there is only one data series, the chart title sufficiently describes the data and the legend can be removed from the chart.
   i. Click OK.
3. Format the bars in the chart to change the shape and colors by completing the following steps.
   Note: If the chart shown is not the actual chart but the sample chart showing multiple data bars, click outside the chart object to exit chart editing mode, save, and then close the report. Reopen the report in Report view, switch to Design view, and then double-click the chart to open Microsoft Graph.

   Step 3b

   a. Right-click the bar in the chart and click *Format Data Series* at the shortcut menu.
   b. At the Format Data Series dialog box, click the Shape tab.

   Step 3d

   c. Click *4* in the *Bar shape* section (cylinder shape).
   d. Click the Patterns tab.

   Step 3c

   e. Click the dark blue color box (first square in last row).
   f. Click OK.

   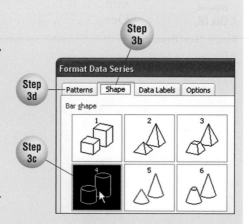

4. Right-click the chart title, click *Format Chart Title* at the shortcut menu, click the Font tab, change the *Color* to red (first square in third row at drop-down list), and then click OK.
5. Click outside the chart object to exit Microsoft Graph.
6. Create a label control object with your first and last names in the Report Header section with the right edge of the control aligned with the right edge of the chart in the Detail section.
7. Display the report in Print Preview.

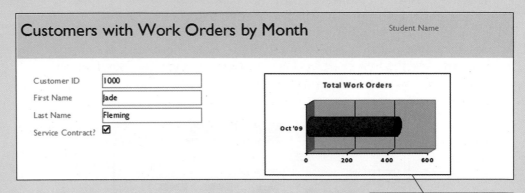

8. Print the first page only of the report.
9. Save and close the report.
10. Redisplay the navigation pane.
11. Close the **RSRComputerServ5.accdb** database.

Edited and formatted chart for first customer record displayed in Print Preview

In this chapter you have learned how to build a custom report from scratch using Design view. You have also created reports using the Report Wizard and used options in Layout view and Design view to customize the report. As you become more comfortable with reports, explore other tools available in the three Report Layout Tools and three Report Design Tools tabs. More features are available to assist you with creating professional-quality reports.

CHAPTER summary

- A report can contain up to five sections: Report Header, Page Header, Detail, Page Footer, and Report Footer.

- Items in the Report Header and Report Footer section print once at the beginning and end of the report.

- Items in the Page Header and Page Footer section print at the top and bottom of each page.

- Drag a field or group of fields from the Field List pane to the Detail section of the report which represents the body of the report.

- An additional group header and group footer section can be added if the report is grouped by a field containing repeating values such as a department or city.

- Click the Create tab and click the Report Design button to build a custom report from scratch.

- Double-click the Report Selector button to open a report's Property Sheet.

- Bind a table or query to a report using the *Record Source* property in the Data tab of the report's Property Sheet.

- Place label control objects to be used as column headings in a tabular report within the Page Header section in Design view.

- Click the AutoFormat button in the AutoFormat group in the Report Design Tools Arrange tab to apply a predefined set of formats for colors and fonts to a report.

- A related table or query can be inserted as a subreport within a main report.

- A subreport is stored as a separate object outside the main report.

- Click the Insert Page Number button in the Controls group to open the Page Numbers Dialog box in which you specify the format, position, and alignment options for page numbering in a report.

- The current date and/or time can be added as a control object within the Report Header section using the Date & Time button in the Controls group.

- Add pictures, clip art images, or draw lines in a report using the same techniques that you learned for adding graphics to forms.

- A report can be grouped by a field at the second Report Wizard dialog box by double-clicking the field name for the field that contains repeating data.

- More than one grouping level can be added to a report.

- Group an existing report by opening the report in Layout view or Design view and opening the Group, Sort, and Total pane.

- Click the Add a group button in the Group, Sort, and Total pane to select the field by which the report should be grouped from a pop-up field list.

- Aggregate functions such as sum, average, or count can be added to each group within a report and grand totals added to the end of a report by expanding the group options in the Group, Sort, and Total pane.

- Each section within a report has a set of properties that can be viewed or changed by opening the section's Property Sheet.

- Double-click a section bar to open the Property Sheet for the section.
- The *Keep Together* property for a section is used to prevent a section from being split by a page break.
- The *Force New Page* option in a section Property Sheet can be used to automatically insert a page break before a section begins, after the section ends, or before and after a section.
- At the Group, Sort, and Total pane, you can specify to keep an entire group together on the same page.
- A chart can be added to a report to graphically display numerical data from another table or query related to the report.
- Open a report in Design view, click the Insert Chart button in the Controls group to create a chart control object in a report or form, and use the Chart Wizard to generate the chart.
- Double-click a chart control object in Design view to edit the chart using Microsoft Graph by changing the chart type; adding, removing, or changing chart options; and formatting chart elements.
- Click outside the chart to exit the Microsoft Graph application when finished editing a chart.

COMMANDS review

FEATURE	RIBBON TAB, GROUP	BUTTON
Add existing fields	Report Design Tools Design, Tools	
AutoFormat	Report Design Tools Arrange, AutoFormat	
Date and Time	Report Design Tools Design, Controls	
Design view	Home, Views	
Group & Sort	Report Design Tools Design, Grouping & Totals OR Report Layout Tools Format, Grouping & Totals	Group & Sort OR
Insert a chart	Report Design Tools Design, Controls	
Layout view	Home, Views	
Page numbering	Report Design Tools Design, Controls	
Property Sheet	Report Design Tools Design, Tools	
Report Design	Create, Reports	
Report Wizard	Create, Reports	Report Wizard
Report view	Home, Views	
Subreport	Report Design Tools Design, Controls	
Title	Report Design Tools Design, Controls	

CONCEPTS check

Test Your Knowledge

Completion: In the space provided at the right, indicate the correct term, command, or number.

1. Add controls in this section to print grand totals at the end of a report.

2. Double-click this button to open the Property Sheet for a report.

3. The Subform/Subreport button is found in this group within the Report Design Tools Design tab.

4. Click this button to open the Page Numbers dialog box in Design view for a report.

5. If the date and time are added to a report using the Date and Time dialog box, Access creates the control objects in this report section.

6. At the second Report Wizard dialog box, Access displays a grouped field in this color in the preview section.

7. An existing report can have grouping added by opening this pane.

8. Click this button to expand the group options for a grouped field in order to add a sum function to each group.

9. Double-click this element in report Design view to open the Property Sheet for a section.

10. Modify this section property to instruct Access to insert a page break after the section is finished printing.

11. Use this button to insert a bar chart into a report.

12. Launch the Microsoft Graph application to edit a chart by doing this action with the mouse.

13. When finished editing a chart, exit Microsoft Graph by doing this action with the mouse.

SKILLS check
Demonstrate Your Proficiency

Assessment

1 CREATE A CUSTOM REPORT USING DESIGN VIEW

1. Open the database named **VantageVideos5.accdb** and enable the content.
2. Create a new report using Design view and build the report using the following specifications:
   a. Expand the width of the report in the grid to the 7.5-inch position in the horizontal ruler.
   b. Add a title at the left side of the report with the text **Web Products and Orders**.
   c. Add your name in a label control object in the center of the Report Footer section.
   d. Bind the WebProducts table to the report. Add all of the fields from the table to the report.
   e. Move the label control objects for each field from the Detail section to the Page Header section arranging the controls horizontally in the order the fields appeared in the table. You determine the amount of space to leave between controls. Edit each label to remove the colon (:) at the end of the caption or field name. Resize the Page Header section when finished so that the extra space is removed.
   f. Align each text box control object in the Detail section below the object's associated label control object in the Page Header section.
   g. Use Report view to check alignment and width of controls to make sure data is not truncated in any of the control objects. Make adjustments as needed in Design view or Layout View.
   h. Apply the *Equity* AutoFormat (fourth AutoFormat in second row).
   i. Insert a subreport into the report as follows:
      1) Use the WebSaleswithTotal query and add the fields *Cust-ID, WebOrdID, DateOrd, WebProdID,* and *Qty* to the subreport.
      2) Accept the default link option to link the main report to the subreport on the *WebProdID* field.
      3) Accept the default subreport name.
      4) Edit the text in the subreport label control object to *Web Sales*.
      5) View the report to ensure the data is properly linked.
      6) Remove the *WebProdID* field from the subreport since this data is duplicated in the main report.
      7) Move and/or resize the subreport control object as desired.
   j. Resize the Detail section so that the section ends just below the subreport.
   k. Format the *WebProdID* and *Product* fields in the Detail section to 12-point bold.
   l. Make any additional formatting changes you think would improve the appearance of the report.
3. Save the report and name it **WebProductsWithOrders**.
4. Print and then close the report.

Assessment

2 ENHANCE THE REPORT

1. With the **VantageVideos5.accdb** database open, display the WebProductsWithOrders report in Design view.
2. Add page numbering using the *Page N of M* format to the bottom left of each page.
3. Add the current date to the bottom right of each page. You determine the date format. Resize the design grid to the 7.5-inch position on the ruler if Access widens the page after inserting the current date control object.
4. Insert an appropriate clip art image to the top right of the report.
5. Draw a horizontal line under the report title. You determine the line thickness, line type, and line color.
6. Save the report.
7. Print page 1 only of the revised report.
8. Close the report.

Assessment

3 CREATE A NEW REPORT WITH GROUPING AND TOTALS

1. With the **VantageVideos5.accdb** database open, create a new report using the Report Wizard as follows:
   a. Use the WebSalesWithTotal query and add all fields to the report.
   b. Remove the *WebProdID* as the grouped field and instead group by the *Date_Ord* field by month.
   c. Sort by the *Lname* field in ascending order.
   d. Use a *Stepped* layout in *Landscape* orientation.
   e. Use the *Equity* AutoFormat.
   f. Edit the report title to *WebSalesWithTotalByDate*.
2. Preview the report and then change the margins to *Normal*.
3. Minimize the navigation pane and use Layout view to edit the column widths and move the *Last Name* column after the *First Name* column. If necessary, edit long labels to abbreviate text in order to make sure the revised report fits on one page.
4. Add your name in a label control object in the center of the Report Footer section.
5. Add a sum function to show the total of each month's sales at the end of the group, and show a grand total at the end of the report. Add an appropriate label next to the sum function in the group footer and next to the sum function in the report footer.
6. Edit the report title to *Web Sales with Total by Date*.
7. Change the margins as necessary to fit the report on one page and then print the report.
8. Save and close the report.
9. Redisplay the navigation pane.

Assessment

4 CREATE AND FORMAT A REPORT WITH A CHART

1. With the **VantageVideos5.accdb** database open, create a new report using the Report Wizard as follows:
   a. Use the WebCustomers table and add the customer number, customer name, and home telephone fields to the report.
   b. Do not group or sort the report.
   c. Use a *Columnar* layout in *Portrait* orientation.
   d. Use the *Equity* AutoFormat.
   e. Edit the report title to *WebCustomersWithChart*.
2. Preview the report.
3. Minimize the navigation pane and switch to Design view.
4. Insert a chart at the right side of the page next to each customer record using the following information:
   a. Use the WebSalesWithTotal query.
   b. Add the *DateOrd* and *TotalSale* fields to the chart field list.
   c. Select a bar chart style. You determine which style to use.
   d. Preview the chart. The category axis should display the date ordered by month and the data series axis should display the total sale amount for each month.
   e. Make sure *Cust-ID* is the linked field for the report and the chart.
   f. Use the title **Web Sales** for the chart.
5. Preview the report with the bar chart.
6. Edit the chart as follows:
   a. Change the chart type to a column chart. You determine the sub-type.
   b. Delete the legend.
   c. Change the color of the bar to dark brown.
7. Edit the report title to *Customers with Web Sales Chart*.
8. Add your name in a label control object at the bottom left of the report.
9. Make any other formatting changes you think would improve the appearance of the report.
10. Save, print, and then close the report.
11. Close the **VantageVideos5.accdb** database.

CASE study
Apply Your Skills

Part 1

Continuing your work as an intern at Deering Sales, your next task is to create reports for management. Open the database named **DeeringSales5.accdb** and enable the content. For each report created, add your name in a label control object in the Report Footer. The first report has been requested by the sales manager. The sales manager uses the SalesbyRep query frequently but has asked for a report that provides the information in a more useful format. Specifically, the sales manager would like the report to group the records by the individual sales representative with the sale date and sale amount records provided in each group. Show two totals for each representative—a total of each sale amount and the total as a percent of the grand total. Include a grand total of all sales at the end of the report. Design and create the report including features such as page numbering, date and time controls, and graphics. Save the report and name it appropriately. Print the report.

Part 2

The office manager would like a printout of Deering Sales customers grouped by city with each customer name and telephone number as well as the customer's assigned sales representative name and telephone number. Design and create the report. Save the report and name it appropriately. Print the report. *Hint: Consider creating a query first with the fields needed from the two tables and base the report on the query*.

Part 3

The accountant would like the report you created in Part 2 to be modified to show the sales for each customer. Open the report from Part 2 and use Save As to create a new report. Choose an appropriate new name. Modify the report title to indicate the report includes sales for each customer and insert a subreport using the ClientSales query to show the sale date and amount records linked to the customer. The accountant would also like to see a sales total for each customer. *Hint: Add the total in the subreport object*. Save the revised report. Print the report.

Part 4

Research in Help how to calculate a running sum (cumulative total) in a report. Use Save As to create a new report from the report created in Part 3. Choose an appropriate new name. Within the subreport, remove the total and then create a control object placed next to the Amount field that calculates a running sum of the amounts. Save the revised report. Print the report. Close the **DeeringSales5.accdb** database.

Using Access Tools and Managing Objects

Upon successful completion of Chapter 6, you will be able to:

- Create a new database using a template
- Create a new table using a table template
- Create a table by copying the structure of another table
- Evaluate a table using the Table Analyzer Wizard
- Evaluate a database using the Performance Analyzer
- Split a database
- Print documentation about a database using the Database Documenter
- Rename and delete objects

access Chapter 6

Tutorial 6.1
Protecting and Customizing
Databases
Tutorial 6.2
Splitting a Table

Access provides tools to assist you with creating and managing databases and objects within databases. Templates are provided that can be used to create a new database or create a new table. Access provides wizards to assist with analyzing a table and a database in order to improve performance. A database can be split into two files to store the tables separate from the queries, forms, and reports. The Database Documenter can be used to print a report that provides details about objects and object properties. In this chapter you will learn how to use these Access tools and rename and delete objects in the navigation pane.

Note: Before beginning computer projects, copy the Access2007L2C6 subfolder from the Access2007L2 folder on the CD that accompanies this textbook to your storage medium and then make Access2007L2C6 the active folder.

Project ① Create a Database Using a Template

You will create a new database using one of the database templates supplied with Access.

Creating a Database Using a Template

At the Getting Started with Microsoft Office Access window you can create a new database using one of the professionally-designed templates provided by Microsoft. The database templates provide a complete series of objects including predefined tables, forms, reports, queries, and relationships. You can use a template as provided and immediately start entering data or you can base a new database on a template and modify the objects to suit your needs. If a template exists for a database application that you need, you can save time by creating the database based on one of the template designs.

To create a new database using a template, start Access and click *Local Templates* in the *Template Categories* section in the left pane at the *Getting Started with Microsoft Office Access* window. The available template designs display in the center pane. Click a template to read a description about the type of data the database template is designed to track in the right pane as shown in Figure 6.1. Use the Browse button to navigate to the drive and/or folder in which you want to store the database and enter a file name. Click the Create button in the right pane of the *Getting Started with Microsoft Office Access* window to create the database.

Figure 6.1 Local Templates at *Getting Started with Microsoft Office Access* Window

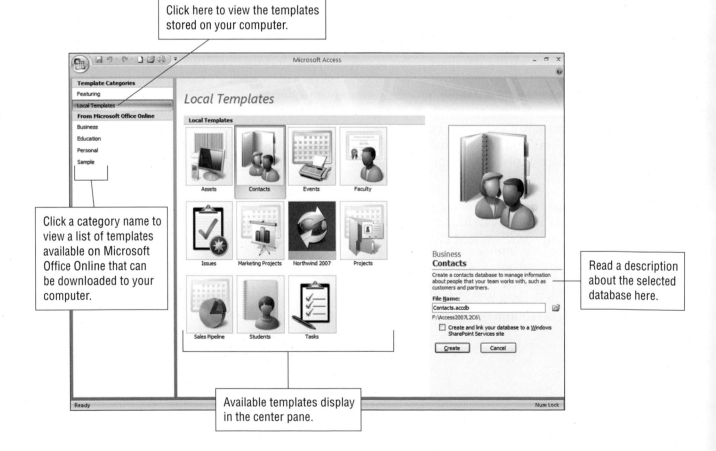

Click here to view the templates stored on your computer.

Click a category name to view a list of templates available on Microsoft Office Online that can be downloaded to your computer.

Read a description about the selected database here.

Available templates display in the center pane.

If one of the local templates does not provide the type of application that you need, click one of the categories below *From Microsoft Office Online* to view a list of database templates that can be downloaded from the Microsoft Office Online Web site to your computer.

Project ⓵ᵃ Creating a New Contacts Database Using a Template

1. Start Microsoft Office Access 2007.
2. At the *Getting Started with Microsoft Office Access* window, click *Local Templates* in the left pane.
3. Click *Assets* in the center pane and read the description of the database template that displays below the icon in the right pane.
4. Click *Contacts* in the center pane and then read the description of the database template that displays below the icon in the right pane.
5. Create a new database based on the *Contacts* template by completing the following steps:
   a. Click the Browse button (displays as a file folder icon) next to the *File Name* text box in the right pane.
   b. At the File New Database dialog box, navigate to the Access2007L2C6 folder on your storage medium.
   c. Click at the beginning of *Contacts* in the *File name* text box and then type **RSR** so that the database file name is *RSRContacts.accdb*.
   d. Click OK.

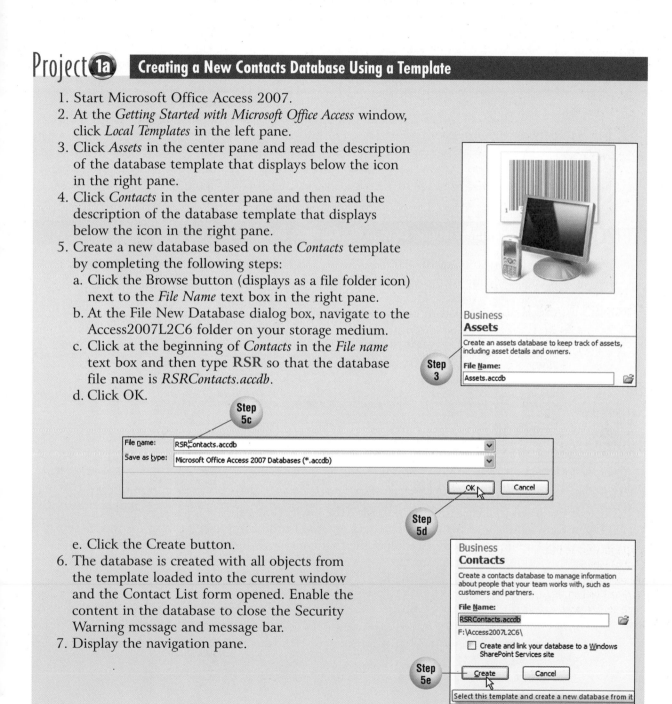

   e. Click the Create button.
6. The database is created with all objects from the template loaded into the current window and the Contact List form opened. Enable the content in the database to close the Security Warning message and message bar.
7. Display the navigation pane.

8. Expand the *Supporting Objects* group in the navigation pane to view the name of the table and query created in the database.

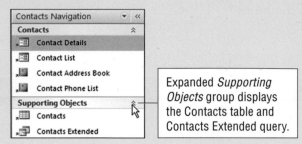

Expanded *Supporting Objects* group displays the Contacts table and Contacts Extended query.

9. Minimize the navigation pane.

Project 1b Entering and Viewing Data in the Contacts Database

1. With the **RSRContacts.accdb** database open, and the Contact List form open in Form view, add the following record using the form:

First Name	**Ariel**
Last Name	**Grayson**
E-mail Address	**ariel@emcp.net**
Business Phone	**800-555-4988**
Company	**Grayson Accounting Services**
Job Title	**Accountant**

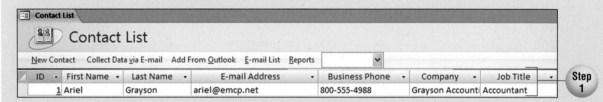

Step 1

2. Close the Contact List form and redisplay the navigation pane.
3. Open the Contact Details form. The data entered in the Contact List form for the first record appears in this form. Complete the first contact record in the Contact Details form using the following information:

Home Phone	**313-555-6811**
Mobile Phone	**800-555-3472**
Fax Number	**313-555-9648**
Street	**17399 Windsor Avenue**
City	**Detroit**
State/Province	**MI**
Zip/Postal Code	**48214-3274**
Country/Region	**USA**
Web Page	**www.emcp.net/grayson**
Notes	**Ariel recommended to RSR by Pat Hynes**

4. Add a picture of the contact using the Attachments field to the Contact Details form by completing the following steps:
   a. Double-click the picture icon in the Attachments box at the left of the *E-mail* and *Web Page* fields.

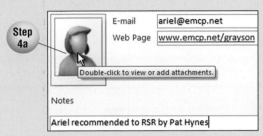

   b. At the Attachments dialog box, click the Add button.
   c. At the Choose File dialog box, navigate to the Access2007L2C6 folder on your storage medium.
   d. Double-click *Ariel_Grayson.jpg* to add the file to the Attachments dialog box.
   e. Click OK.

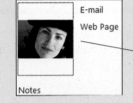

Picture displays in form after adding a jpg file to Attachments dialog box. If you add a Word document in the Attachments box, a Word icon diplays.

5. Close the Contact Details form.
6. Open each of the other objects in the database and view the data for Ariel Grayson in the form, report, query, or table. Close each object when finished.
7. Print the Contact Phone List report.
8. Close the **RSRContacts.accdb** database.

Project ② Create a Table Using a Template

You will create a new table using a table template.

Creating a Table Using a Table Template

Access provides table templates designed to store information about Contacts, Tasks, Issues, Events, or Assets. If you need to add a table to an existing database file that is about one of these topics, consider creating the table using the table template. Once the table is added, you can modify the table design to suit your needs.

To create a table based on a table template, click the Create tab and click the Table Templates button in the Tables group. Click the desired table template from the drop-down list shown in Figure 6.2. Access creates the table structure and opens a table datasheet in which you can begin entering data. Save the table and switch to Design view to add, delete, or modify fields as required. Consider modifying the table design of a table based on a table template using the techniques learned in Chapters 1–2 to apply validation and data restriction rules.

Create Table Using Table Template
1. Open database.
2. Click Create tab.
3. Click Table Templates button.
4. Click desired template.
5. Save table.

Figure 6.2 Table Templates Drop-down List

Project ② Creating a Table Using a Table Template

1. Open **RSRComputerServ6.accdb** and enable the content.
2. Create a new table to store contacts using the predefined *Contacts* table template by completing the following steps:
   a. Click the Create tab.
   b. Click the Table Templates button  in the Tables group and click Contacts at the drop-down list. Access creates the table using the predefined fields for Contacts and opens a table datasheet.

Step
2a

Step
2b

3. Click the Save button, type **SupplierContacts** in the *Table Name* text box at the Save As dialog box, and press Enter or click OK.

Step
3

4. Click the Home tab and then click the View button to switch to Design view.
5. Modify the table design to change a field name and delete fields by completing the following steps:
   a. Change the *Mobile Phone* field name to *Cell Phone*.
   b. Select the *Country/Region*, *Web Page*, *Notes*, and *Attachments* fields and click the Delete Rows button in the Tools group in the Table Tools Design tab to delete the fields.
   c. Delete the *Home Phone* field.
   d. Save the table.

6. Switch to Datasheet view and enter the following data in a new record:

Company	**Cityscape Electronics**
Last Name	**Silver**
First Name	**Terry**
E-mail Address	**terry_s@emcp.net**
Job Title	**Sales Manager**
Business Phone	**800-555-4968**
Cell Phone	**313-555-3442**
Fax Number	**800-555-6941**
Address	**3700 Woodward Avenue**
City	**Detroit**
State/Province	**MI**
ZIP/Postal Code	**48201-2006**

7. Adjust all column widths to Best Fit.
8. Save and close the table.
9. Select SupplierContacts in the navigation pane, click the Create tab, and click the Form button in the Forms group to create a form based on the table.

SupplierContacts form created at Step 9 (Your form may show fields in a single column instead of two as shown.)

10. Display the form in Print Preview, change the page orientation to landscape and then close Print Preview.
11. Save the form using the default name SupplierContacts.
12. Print the selected record and then close the form.

Project 3 Copy Table Structure

You will create a new table to store contact information for manufacturer sales representatives by copying an existing table's field names and field properties.

Copying Table Structure to Create a New Table

Using copy and paste commands you can copy an existing table's structure if you need to create a new table that uses the same or similar fields as an existing table. For example, in Project 3 you will copy the SupplierContacts table structure to create a new table for manufacturer contacts. Since the fields needed for manufacturer contact records are the same as those that already exist for the supplier contact records, you can base the new table on the existing table.

To copy a table's structure, click the existing table name in the navigation pane and click the Copy button in the Clipboard group in the Home tab. Next, click the Paste button in the Clipboard group. When a table has been copied to the clipboard, clicking the Paste button causes the Paste Table As dialog box shown in Figure 6.3 to appear.

Figure 6.3 Paste Table As Dialog Box

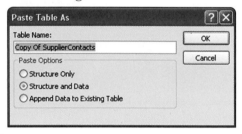

Type the desired name for the new table in the *Table Name* text box, click *Structure Only* in the *Paste Options* section, and then click OK. Once the table is created you can add, delete, or modify fields as needed.

Project 3 Copying Table Structure to Create a New Table

1. With the **RSRComputerServ6.accdb** database open, make sure the SupplierContacts table is selected in the navigation pane.
2. Click the Copy button in the Clipboard group in the Home table.
3. Click the Paste button in the Clipboard group. (Do not click the down-pointing arrow on the button.)
4. At the Paste Table As dialog click, type **MfrContacts** in the *Table Name* text box, click *Structure Only* in the *Paste Options* section, and then press Enter or click OK.

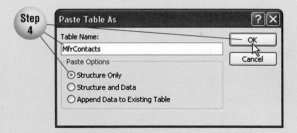

Step 4

5. Open the MfrContacts table in Datasheet view. The table structure contains the same fields as the SupplierContacts table.

6. Enter the following data in a new record:

Company	Dell Inc.
Last Name	Haldstadt
First Name	Cari
E-mail Address	haldstadt_c@emcp.net
Job Title	Northeast Sales Manager
Business Phone	800-555-9522
Cell Phone	800-555-4662
Fax Number	800-555-7781
Address	One Dell Way
City	Round Rock
State/Province	TX
ZIP/Postal Code	78682

7. Adjust all column widths to Best Fit.
8. Save and close the table.
9. With MfrContacts selected in the navigation pane, click the Create tab and create a new form based on the table.

MfrContacts form created at Step 9 (Your form may show fields in a single column instead of two as shown.)

10. Display the form in Print Preview, change the page orientation to landscape, and then close Print Preview.
11. Save the form using the default name *MfrContacts*.
12. Print the selected record and then close the form.

Project 4 Use Access Tools to Optimize and Document a Database

You will use the Table Analyzer Wizard to improve a table's design, the Performance Analyzer to optimize database design, and split a database by separating tables from queries, forms, and reports. Finally, you will use the Database Documenter to print a report documenting table structure.

Modifying a Table Using the Table Analyzer Wizard

The Table Analyzer Wizard is used to examine a table and determine if duplicate information in the table can be split into smaller related tables to improve the table design. Repeated information in tables can result in inconsistencies and wasted storage space. The wizard presents a solution with fields that can be separated into a new table related to the original table with a lookup field. You can accept the proposed solution or modify the suggestion. In Project 4a you will use the Table Analyzer Wizard in a new Parts table. The table was created to store information about parts that are commonly used by the technicians at RSR Computer Service. Access will examine the table and propose that the *Supplier* field be moved to a separate table. The reason this solution is a better design is that several parts records can be associated with the same supplier. In the current table design, the supplier name is typed into a field in each record. With several parts associated with the same supplier name, the field contains many duplicated entries that use disk space. Furthermore, the potential exists for a typing mistake in a record, which could result in a query not producing the correct list.

To begin the Table Analyzer Wizard, click the Database Tools tab and then click the Analyze Table button in the Analyze group. This presents the first Table Analyzer Wizard dialog box shown in Figure 6.4. The first two dialog boxes in the wizard explain what the Table Analyzer does to improve the table design. At the third dialog box in the wizard you select the table to be analyzed and at the fourth dialog box you choose to let the wizard decide which fields to group together in the smaller tables or manually split the tables by dragging and dropping fields.

HINT

The Table Analyzer Wizard helps you normalize a table.

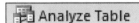

Figure 6.4 First Table Analyzer Wizard Dialog Box

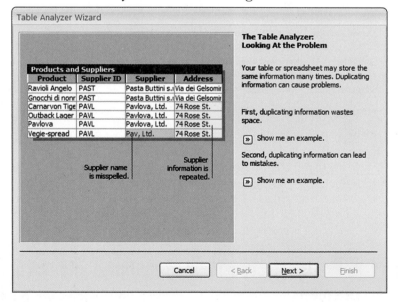

The wizard looks for fields with repetitive data and suggests a solution. You confirm the grouping of fields and the primary keys in the new tables and at the final step in the wizard, you can elect to have Access create a query so that the fields in the split tables are presented together in a datasheet that resembles the original table.

Project 4a   Splitting a Table Using the Table Analyzer Wizard

1. With the **RSRComputerServ6.accdb** database open, open the Parts table in Datasheet view and review the table structure and data. Notice the table includes four fields: *PartNo*, *PartName*, *Supplier*, and *Cost*. Also notice that supplier names are repeated in the *Supplier* field.
2. Close the Parts table.
3. Use the Table Analyzer Wizard to evaluate the Parts table design to determine if the table can be improved by completing the following steps:
   a. Click the Database Tools tab.
   b. Click the Analyze Table button Analyze Table in the Analyze group.
   c. Read the information at the first Table Analyzer Wizard dialog box and click Next.
   d. Read the information at the second Table Analyzer Wizard dialog box and click Next.
   e. With *Parts* selected in the *Tables* list box at the third Table Analyzer Wizard dialog box, click Next.

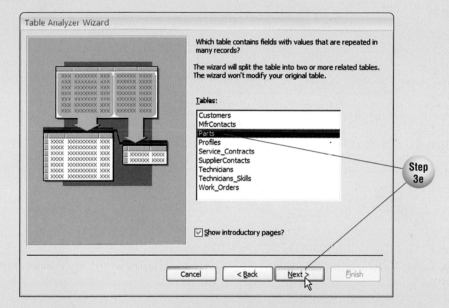

   f. With *Yes, let the wizard decide* for *Do you want the wizard to decide what fields go in what tables?* at the fourth Table Analyzer Wizard dialog box, click Next.
   g. At the fifth Table Analyzer Wizard dialog box, look at the two tables the wizard is proposing. Notice that the *Supplier* field has been moved to a new table with a one-to-many relationship created between the table with the supplier names ("one" table) and a new table with the remaining fields ("many" table). Access names the new tables Table1 and Table2 and asks two questions: *Is the wizard grouping information correctly?* and *What name do you want for each table?* **Note: If necessary, resize the table list boxes in order to see the proposed fields.**

h. The proposed tables have the fields grouped correctly. Rename the first table by double-clicking the Table1 title bar.

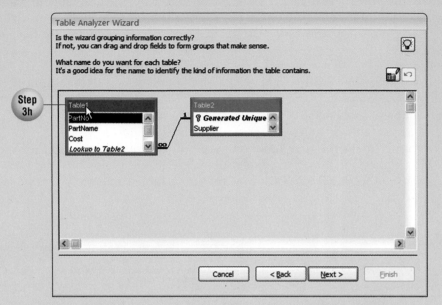

i. Type **PartsAndCosts** in the *Table Name* text box and press Enter or click OK.

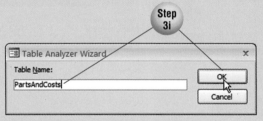

j. Click the Table2 title bar and click the Rename Table button 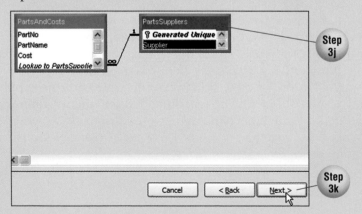 located near the top right of the dialog box above the table list boxes. Type **PartsSuppliers** in the *Table Name* text box and press Enter or click OK.

k. Click Next.

l. At the sixth Table Analyzer Wizard dialog box, the primary key fields for each table are set and/or confirmed. The primary key fields are displayed in bold in the table list boxes. Notice the PartsAndCosts table does not have a primary key defined. Click *PartNo* in the PartsAndCosts table list box and click the Primary Key button located near the top right of the dialog box. Access sets *PartNo* as the primary key field, displays a key icon, and applies bold to the field name.

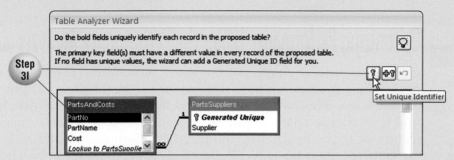

m. Click Next.

n. At the last Table Analyzer Wizard dialog box, you can choose to have Access create a query with the original table name that includes the fields from the new tables. Creating the query means existing forms or reports that were based on the original table will still operate. With *Yes, create the query* selected, click Finish. Access renames the original table *Parts_OLD*, creates the query with the name *Parts*, and opens the Parts query results datasheet with the Access Help window in the foreground.

o. Close the Help window.

4. Examine the Parts query datasheet and the object names added in the navigation pane including the new tables PartsAndCosts and PartsSuppliers along with the original table named Parts_OLD. The Parts query looks just like the original table you opened at Step 1 with the exception of the additional field named *Lookup to PartsSupplier*. The lookup field displays the supplier name which is also displayed in the original *Supplier* field. The second *Supplier* field can be deleted from the query.

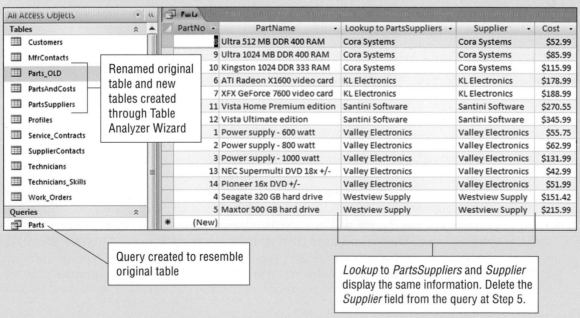

5. Switch to Design view and delete the *Supplier* field.
6. Save the revised query. Switch to Datasheet view, adjust all column widths to Best Fit, and print the query results datasheet.
7. Close the query saving changes to the layout.

Optimizing Performance Using the Performance Analyzer

QUICK STEPS

Optimize Database Performance
1. Click the Database Tools tab.
2. Click Analyze Performance button.
3. Click All Objects tab.
4. Click Select All button.
5. Click OK.
6. Review *Analysis Results* items.
7. Optimize desired *Recommendation* or *Suggestion* items.
8. Click Close button.

The Performance Analyzer can evaluate an individual object, a group of objects, or the entire database for ways that objects can be modified to optimize the use of system resources such as memory and improve the speed of data access. If you find the database seems to run slowly, consider running tables, queries, forms, reports, or the entire database through the Performance Analyzer. To do this, click the Database Tools tab and click the Analyze Performance button in the Analyze group to open the Performance Analyzer dialog box shown in Figure 6.5. Select a tab for the object type, click the check box next to an object to have the object analyzed, and click OK. You can select multiple objects or click the Select All button to select all objects in the current tab for analysis. To evaluate the entire database, click the All Object Types tab and then click the Select All button. Click OK to begin the analysis.

HINT
Make sure objects are closed that will be evaluated using the Performance Analyzer —open objects are skipped when the evaluation is run.

Figure 6.5 Performance Analyzer Dialog Box

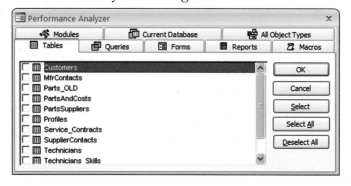

Three types of results are presented to optimize the selected objects: *Recommendation*, *Suggestion*, and *Idea*. Click an item in the *Analysis Results* list to read a description of the proposed optimization method in the *Analysis Notes* section. Click a recommendation or suggestion in the *Analysis Results* list box and then click the Optimize button to instruct Access to carry out the recommendation or suggestion. Access will modify the object and mark the item as *Fixed* when completed. The Performance Analyzer may provide items to improve the design such as assigning a different data type for a field based on the type of data that has been entered into records or creating relationships between tables that are not related.

1. With the **RSRComputerServ6.accdb** database open, use the Performance Analyzer to evaluate the database for optimization techniques by completing the following steps:
   a. If necessary, click the Database Tools tab.
   b. Click the Analyze Performance button 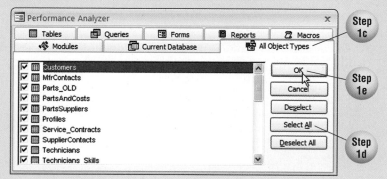 in the Analyze group.
   c. At the Performance Analyzer dialog box, click the All Object Types tab.
   d. Click the Select All button.
   e. Click OK. The Performance Analyzer displays the name of each object as the object is evaluated and presents the *Analysis Results* when completed.

2. Review the items in *Analysis Results* and optimize a relationship by completing the following steps:
   a. Click the first entry in the *Analysis Results* list with the text *Application: Save your application as an MDE file* and read the description of the idea in the *Analysis Notes* section. You will learn about saving the application as an MDE file in the next chapter.

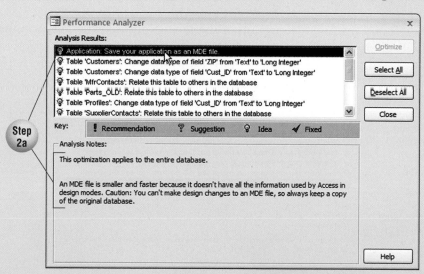

   b. Click the fourth entry in the *Analysis Results* with the text *Table 'MfrContacts': Relate this table to others in the database* and read the description of the idea in the *Analysis Notes* section. The contact information stored in this table is for manufacturer sales representatives and cannot be related to any other tables.

c. Scroll down the *Analysis Results* list box and click the item with the green question mark representing a Suggestion with the text *Table 'Work_Orders': Relate to table 'Work_Orders'*. Read the description of the suggestion in the *Analysis Notes* section. Note that the optimization will benefit the query named TotalWorkOrders. This optimization refers to a query that contains a subquery with two levels of calculations. The suggestion is referring to creating a relationship to speed up the query calculations.

d. Click the Optimize button.

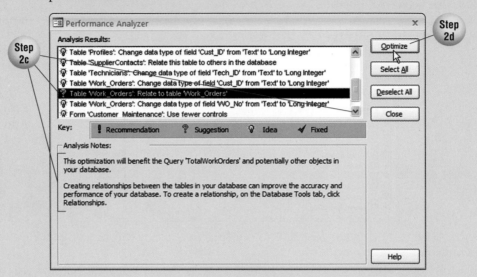

e. Access creates the relationship and changes the question mark next to the item in the *Analysis Results* to a check mark. The check mark indicates the item has been fixed.

f. Click the last item in the *Analysis Results* list box with the text *Form 'Customer_Maintenance': Use fewer controls* and read the description of the idea. Note that the idea is to break the form into multiple forms with information used often retained in the existing form. Information viewed less often should be split out into individual forms. To implement this optimization idea, you would need to redesign the form.

3. Click the Close button to close the Performance Analyzer dialog box.

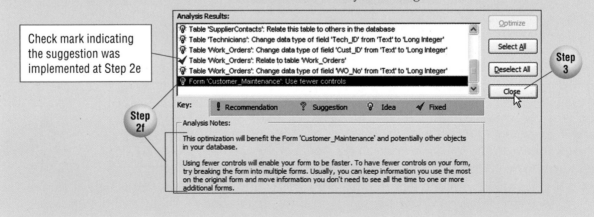

Splitting a Database

If a database is placed in a network where multiple users access the database simultaneously, the speed with which the data is accessed may decrease. One solution to improve the performance of the database is to split the database into two files: one file containing the tables (called the **back-end**) is stored in the network share folder, and the other file containing the queries, forms, and reports (called the *front-end*) is stored on the individual end-user computers. The individual end users can create and/or customize their own queries, forms, and reports, to serve their individual purposes. The front-end database contains linked tables to the back-end data so that each user is updating a single data source.

To split an existing database into a back-end and a front-end database, Access provides the Database Splitter Wizard. Click the Database Tools tab and click the Access Database button in the Move Data group to begin the Database Splitter Wizard shown in Figure 6.6.

Split a Database
1. Click Database Tools tab.
2. Click Access Database button.
3. Click Split Database button.
4. If necessary, navigate to desired drive and/or folder.
5. If necessary, edit the *File name*.
6. Click Split button.
7. Click OK.

Access Database

Figure 6.6 First Database Splitter Wizard Dialog Box

Click the Split Database button to open the Create Back-end Database dialog box where you navigate to the drive and/or folder in which to store the database file containing the original tables. By default, Access uses the original database file name with *_be* appended to the end of the name. Change the file name if desired and then click the Split button. Access moves the table objects to the back-end file, creates links to the back-end tables in the front-end file, and displays a message when the process is complete that the database was successfully split.

1. With the **RSRComputerServ6.accdb** database open, split the database to create a back-end and a front-end database by completing the following steps:

   a. If necessary, click the Database Tools tab.

   b. Click the Access Database button 🕸 in the Move Data group.

   c. Click the Split Database button at the first Database Splitter Wizard dialog box.

   d. At the Create Back-end Database dialog box with the default option to save the back-end database in the same folder from which the original database originated (Access2007L2C6) and the file name *RSRComputerServ6_be.accdb* in the *File name* text box, click the Split button.

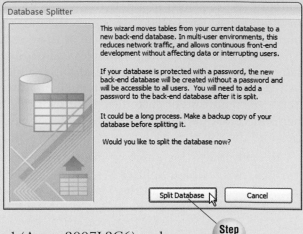

Step 1c

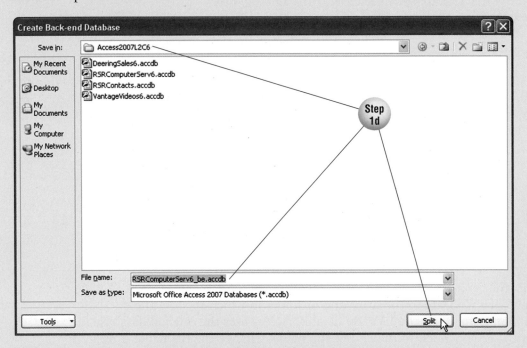

Step 1d

   e. Click OK at the Database Splitter message box indicating the database was successfully split.

Step 1e

2. When the database was split, Access moved the tables to the back-end file and created links to the tables in the front-end file. Notice the table names in the navigation pane are all preceded with a right-pointing arrow. The arrow indicates the table is a linked object. Opening a linked table causes Access to retrieve the records from the back-end database to display in the table datasheet. Open the linked Customers table datasheet and review the data.

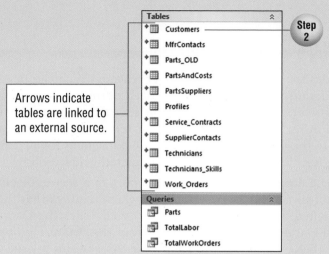

Arrows indicate tables are linked to an external source.

3. Switch to Design view. Since the table is linked to an external source, Access displays a message indicating the table design cannot be modified; changes to fields or field properties have to be made in the source database. Click No at the Microsoft Office Access message box asking if you want to open the table anyway.

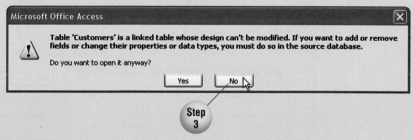

4. Close the table and then close the **RSRComputerServ6.accdb** database.
5. Open the **RSRComputerServ6_be.accdb** database and enable the content.
6. Notice the back-end database file contains only the tables. Open the Customers table in Datasheet view and review the data.
7. Switch to Design view. Notice in the back-end database you can switch to Design view to make changes without receiving the message box you saw at Step 3 since this database contains the original source table.
8. Close the table.

Another reason to split a database may be to overcome the file size restriction in Access 2007. Database specifications for Access 2007 place the maximum file size at 2 gigabytes. This size includes any space needed by Access to open system objects while working with the database; therefore, the actual maximum file size is less than 2 gigabytes. However, the size restriction does not include links to external data sources. By splitting a database you can extend the size beyond the 2-gigabyte limitation.

QUICK STEPS

Print Object Documentation
1. Click Database Tools tab.
2. Click Database Documenter button.
3. Click Options button.
4. Choose desired report options.
5. Click OK.
6. Click desired object name.
7. Click OK.
8. Print report.
9. Close report.

Documenting a Database

Access provides the Database Documenter feature which can be used to print a report with details about a database object's definition. The report is used to obtain hard copy documentation of a table's structure with field properties or documentation regarding a query, form, or report definition. You can add the relationships to the report to include relationship diagrams for all defined relationships for the table. Relationship options are documented below each relationship diagram.

Storing the database documentation report in a secure place is a good idea in case of data corruption or other disaster which requires that the database be manually repaired, rebuilt, or otherwise recovered. Click the Database Tools tab and click the Database Documenter button in the Analyze group to open the Documenter dialog box shown in Figure 6.7. As you did for the Performance Analyzer, select the object for which you want to generate a report and then click OK.

Figure 6.7 Documenter Dialog Box

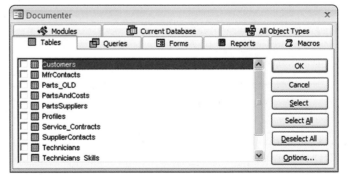

Project 4d Generating a Table Definition Documentation Report

1. With the **RSRComputerServ6_be.accdb** database open, generate a report providing details of the table structure, field properties, and relationships for an individual table by completing the following steps:
   a. Click the Database Tools tab.
   b. In the Analyze group, click the Database Documenter button.
   c. At the Documenter dialog box, click the Options button.

d. At the Print Table Definition dialog box, click the *Permissions by User and Group* check box in the *Include for Table* section to clear the check mark.

e. Make sure *Names, Data Types, Sizes, and Properties* is selected in the *Include for Fields* section.

f. Click *Nothing* in the *Include for Indexes* section.

g. Click OK.

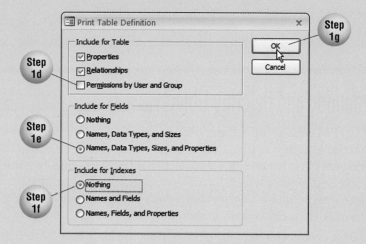

h. With Tables the active tab in the Documenter dialog box, click the *PartsSuppliers* check box to select the object.

i. Click OK.

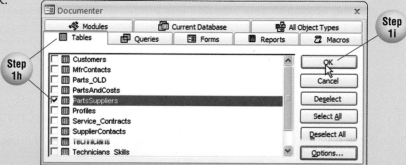

2. Access generates the table definition report and displays the report in Print Preview. Print the report.

3. Notice the Save option is dimmed. You cannot save a report generated by the Documenter.

4. Click the Close Print Preview button in the Close Preview group in the Print Preview tab.

5. Generate another report providing details of all of the tables, view the report, and print selected pages by completing the following steps:

a. Click the Database Documenter button.

b. With Tables the active tab at the Documenter dialog box, click the Select All button to select all table objects and then click OK to generate the report.

c. Change the Zoom to 100% and maximize the report window.

d. Scroll down the first page of the report and review the data.

e. Click the Last Page button in the Page navigation bar to navigate to the last page in the report. Review the relationship diagrams and relationship options documented on the last page of the report. Notice the page number is 44.

f. Click the Print button in the Print group in the Print Preview tab. Change *Pages* in the *Print Range* section to print *From* 1 *To* 1 and click OK.

g. Print page 44 only by completing a step similar to Step 5f.

6. Close the report.

Rename Object
1. Right-click object in navigation pane.
2. Click *Rename*.
3. Type new name.
4. Press Enter.

Delete Object
1. Right-click object in navigation pane.
2. Click *Delete*.
3. Click Yes.

Renaming and Deleting Objects

As part of managing a database you may decide to rename or delete objects within the database file. To do this, right-click the object name in the navigation pane and click *Rename* or *Delete* at the shortcut menu. Be cautious with renaming or deleting objects which have dependencies to other objects. For example if you delete a table and a query exists which is dependent on fields within the table deleted, the query will no longer run.

You can also delete an object from the database by selecting the object in the navigation pane and pressing the Delete key. Click Yes at the Microsoft Office Access message box that displays asking you to confirm you want to delete the object. Consider making a backup copy of a database before renaming or deleting objects in case several object dependencies are broken afterwards and you want to restore the database to its previous state.

HINT

Undo can undo a rename operation but not a delete command.

Project 4e — Renaming and Deleting Database Objects

1. With the **RSRComputerServ6_be.accdb** database open, rename the MfrContacts table by completing the following steps:
   a. Right-click *MfrContacts : Table* in the navigation pane.
   b. Click *Rename* at the shortcut menu.
   c. Type **Manufacturer_Contacts** and press Enter.

2. Delete the original table that was split using the Table Analyzer Wizard in Project 4a by completing the following steps:
   a. Right-click *Parts_OLD : Table* in the navigation pane.
   b. Click *Delete* at the shortcut menu.

c. Click Yes at the Microsoft Office Access message box asking if you want to delete the table 'Parts_OLD'.

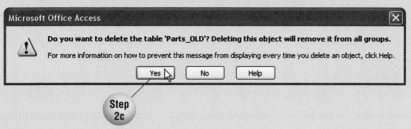

Step
2c

3. Close the **RSRComputerServ6_be.accdb** database.
4. Open the **RSRComputerServ6.accdb** front-end database and enable the content.
5. When the database was split in Project 4c, Access created links to the existing table objects at the time the database was split. Since you have now renamed and deleted a table object in the back-end database, the linked objects will no longer work.
6. Double-click the link to MfrContacts in the navigation pane. Since the table was renamed at Step 1, Access can no longer find the source data. At the Microsoft Office Access message box informing you that the database engine cannot find the input table, click OK. The link would have to be recreated to establish a new connection to the renamed table. You will learn how to link to external tables in Chapter 8.

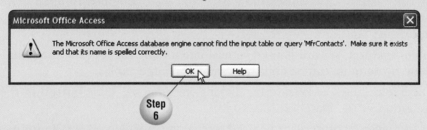

Step
6

7. Double-click the link to Parts_OLD. Since this table was deleted, the same message appears. Click OK to close the message box.
8. Right-click *Parts_OLD* in the navigation pane and click *Delete* at the shortcut menu. Click Yes at the Microsoft Office Access message asking if you want to remove the link.

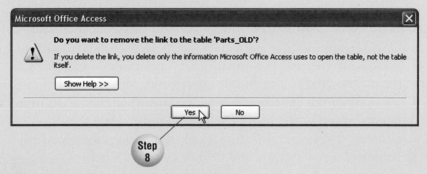

Step
8

9. Close the **RSRComputerServ6.accdb** database.

In this chapter you have learned to use some of the tools that Access provides to create a new database, create new tables, improve database or individual object design and performance, and document the database. You have also learned how to rename and delete objects.

CHAPTER summary

- Access includes predefined database templates that include tables, queries, forms, and reports which can be used to create a new database.

- You can choose a database template from local templates stored on your computer or you can download a database template from Microsoft Office Online.

- Create a new database from a template at the Getting Started with Microsoft Office Access window.

- Predefined table templates for Contacts, Tasks, Issues, Events, or Assets are available from the Table Templates drop-down list in the Tables group in the Create tab.

- A database created from a template or a table created from a template can be modified to suit your needs.

- Using Copy and Paste commands, you can copy a table structure to create a new table.

- When a table has been copied to the clipboard from the navigation pane, clicking the Paste button causes the Paste Table As dialog box to open in which you choose to paste *Structure Only*, *Structure and Data*, or *Append Data to Existing Table*.

- The Table Analyzer Wizard is used to evaluate a table for repeated data and determine if the table can be split into smaller related tables.

- Start the Table Analyzer Wizard by clicking the Analyze Table button in the Analyze group in the Database Tools tab.

- The Performance Analyzer can be used to evaluate a single object, a group of objects, or the entire database for ways to optimize the use of system resources or disk space.

- The Performance Analyzer provides three types of results in the *Analysis Results* list: *Recommendation*, *Suggestion*, or *Idea*.

- Click an item in the *Analysis Results* list that is a recommendation or suggestion and click the Optimize button to instruct Access to carry out the modification.

- A database can be split into two individual files, a back-end database and a front-end database to improve performance for a multi-user database or to overcome the maximum database file size restriction.

- Split a database using the Database Splitter Wizard which is started from the Access Database button in the Move Data group in the Database Tools tab.

- Access provides the Documenter feature which is used to obtain hard copy reports providing object definition and field or control properties.

- Open the Documenter dialog box by clicking the Database Documenter button in the Analyze group in the Database Tools tab.

- Rename an object by right-clicking the object name in the navigation pane, clicking *Rename* at the shortcut menu, typing a new name, and then pressing Enter.

- Delete an object by right-clicking the object name in the navigation pane, clicking *Delete* at the shortcut menu, and then clicking Yes at the message box asking if you want to delete the object.

COMMANDS review

FEATURE	RIBBON TAB, GROUP	BUTTON	KEYBOARD SHORTCUT
Documenter	Database Tools, Analyze	Database Documenter	
Paste Table As	Home, Clipboard		Ctrl + V
Performance Analyzer	Database Tools, Analyze	Analyze Performance	
Split database	Database Tools, Move Data		
Table Analyzer Wizard	Database Tools, Analyze	Analyze Table	
Table templates	Create, Tables		

CONCEPTS check

Test Your Knowledge

Completion: In the space provided at the right, indicate the correct term, command, or number.

1. Click this option in *Template Categories* to view the database templates stored on the computer you are using.

2. A predefined table to store information about Contacts, Tasks, Issues, Events, or Assets can be created from this button in the Tables group in the Create tab.

3. Clicking the Paste button after copying a table in the Navigation pane causes this dialog box to open.

4. This wizard analyzes a table for repeated information and proposes a solution where the table can be split into smaller related tables.

5. Optimize a database using this button in the Analyze group in the Database Tools tab.

6. List the three types of solutions the Performance Analyzer provides to optimize the selected objects.

_____

7. Click an item in the *Analysis Results* list and read a description of the optimization method in this section of the Performance Analyzer dialog box.

_____

8. A database can be split into a front-end database file and a back-end database file using this button in the Move Data group in the Database Tools tab.

_____

9. When a database has been split, the back-end database file contains these objects.

_____

10. When a database has been split, the front-end database file contains links to these objects.

_____

11. Open this dialog box to print a report with a table's definition and field properties.

_____

12. Rename a database object in the Navigation pane by performing this action.

_____

13. Remove a selected object from the database by pressing this key.

_____

SKILLS check
Demonstrate Your Proficiency

Assessment

1 CREATE A DATABASE USING A TEMPLATE

1. Create a new database named **VantageAssets.accdb** using the Assets database template.
2. Enable the content, close the Asset List form, and display the navigation pane.
3. Open the Assets table in Design view and make the following changes:
   a. Make *Category* the active field and click the Lookup tab.
   b. Click in the *Row Source* property box and click the Build button (button with three dots at end of property box).
   c. At the Edit List Items dialog box, edit the list so that the items read as follows:
      (1) *Office Equipment*
      (2) *Store Equipment*
      (3) *Warehouse Equipment*
   d. Click OK.

     e. Make *Location* the active field and edit the lookup list to the following items by completing steps similar to those in Steps 3b–3d.

        (1)   *Store 110*

        (2)   *Store 120*

        (3)   *Store 130*

4. Save and close the table.
5. Open the Contact List form, add a record using the following information, and then close the form.

    Jon Rodriguez

    jon@emcp.net

    800-555-3346

    Vantage Videos

    Store manager

6. Open the Asset List form, add a record using the following information, and then close the form.

    HP Pavilion Computer

    (1)   *Office Equipment*

    (1)   *Great*

    (1)   *Store 110*

    Jon Rodriguez

    03-15-2010

7. Print the Assets Details report.
8. Close the **VantageAssets.accdb** database.

Assessment

2 CREATE A TABLE USING A TABLE TEMPLATE

1. Open **VantageVideos6.accdb** and enable the content.
2. Create a new table using the Tasks table template.
3. Save the table naming it TaskList and then close the table.
4. Create a form based on the TaskList table and add a record using the following information.

    Set up backup Web server

    High priority

    Not started (0% complete)

    Configure hot server to be on standby in event of failover

    Accept the current date for the *Start Date* field

    Enter a due date that is one week from the current date

5. Decrease the width of the controls in Layout view by a few inches.
6. Save the form using the default name *TaskList* and print the selected record.
7. Close the form.

Assessment

3 USE ACCESS TOOLS TO IMPROVE DESIGN AND PERFORMANCE

1. With the **VantageVideos6.accdb** database open, use the Table Analyzer Wizard to analyze the WebCustomerPymnt table using the following information.

   a. Rename the new table with all of the fields except the *CCType* field to **WebCustCreditCards**.

   b. Rename the new table with the *CCType* field to **CreditCardsAccptd**.

   c. Choose an appropriate field for the primary key in the WebCustCreditCards table.

   d. Create the query.

2. Close the Help window.

3. Delete the *CCType* field in the WebCustomerPymnt query. Adjust all column widths to Best Fit and print the query results datasheet using left and right margins of 0.25-inch. ***Hint: You can change margins using the Setup button in the Print dialog box.***

4. Close the query saving the layout changes.

5. Delete the WebCustomerPymnt_OLD table.

6. Split the database to create a front-end database and a back-end database file. Accept the default file name for the back-end database.

7. Close the **VantageVideos6.accdb** database.

8. Open the **VantageVideos6_be.accdb** database and enable the content.

9. Generate and print a report that provides the table and field property definitions for the CreditCardsAccptd table. Include the relationships in the report.

10. Close the **VantageVideos6_be.accdb** database.

CASE study

Apply Your Skills

Part 1

As an intern at Deering Sales, you have been building a sales database over the past weeks. You have been learning about Access tools that assist with creating tables and improving design and performance and decide to apply these tools to the database. Open the database named **DeeringSales6.accdb** and enable the content. As your first task, you decide to create a table to store information about trade shows that Deering Sales attends as an exhibitor. Using a table template, create a new table named *TradeShows* using the Events table template. Add the following two trade show events to the table. Delete any unused fields based on the data entered.

- The three-day Homebuilders Association Trade Show begins April 14, 2010 at the Colorado Convention Center.
- The four-day Green Home Design Conference begins October 12, 2010 at the University of Chicago Gleacher Center.

Create a form for the TradeShows table and print the form for both records. Save and close the form.

The office manager likes the idea of tracking the trade shows in the database and would like you to create a similar table to keep track of manufacturer trade shows that the company attends as a visitor. Copy the structure of the TradeShows table to create a new table named *MfrShows*. Modify the table to add a new field to store the number of people the company will send to the show. Create a form for the MfrShows table and add the following record.

- Five employees will attend the three-day Window and Door Manufacturers Association Trade Show beginning February 25, 2010 at the Georgia International Convention Center.

Preview the form in Print Preview. If necessary, adjust margins to fit the form on one page. Print the form with the first record displayed and then save and close the form.

Part 2

You want to see if Access tools can help you improve the database design. A new table was added to the database to keep track of sales returns by customer. Use the Table Analyzer Wizard to analyze the SalesReturns table. Accept the proposed table split, create appropriate table names, assign primary key fields, and create the query. Modify the query as needed to remove duplicate columns. Print the query results datasheet with all column widths adjusted to Best Fit. Delete the original table.

Part 3

Use the Performance Analyzer to analyze the entire database. All of the fields that store identification numbers such as *ClientID*, *RepID*, and *QuotaID* have the idea proposed that the data type should be changed from Text to Long Integer. Long Integer is not actually a data type but a field size setting for a numeric field. Research data types in Help. Specifically find out the difference between assigning a field the Text data type and the Number data type. Using Microsoft Word, compose a memo to your instructor with the following information:

- An explanation of the use of the Text data type
- An explanation of the use of the Number data type
- Your recommendation of which data type should be used for the three ID fields in the database and why

Save the memo and name it **Access2007_L2_C6-DeeringMemo.docx**. Print the memo and exit Word.

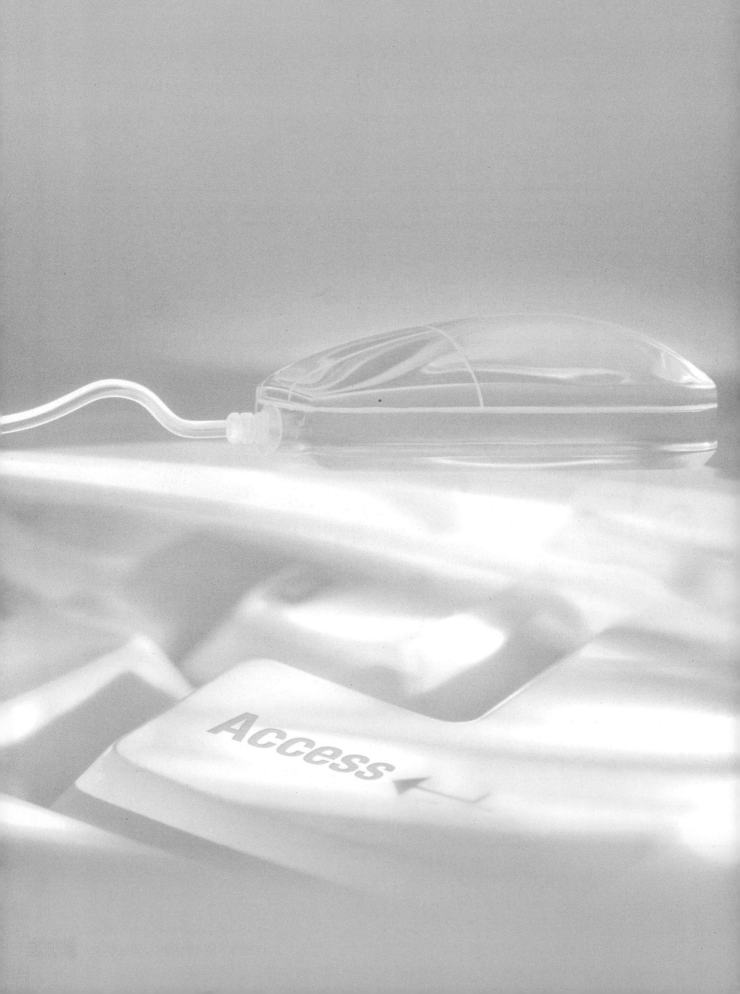

Automating, Customizing, and Securing Access

Upon successful completion of Chapter 7, you will be able to:

- Create, edit, and run a macro
- Assign a macro to a command button on a form
- Create and edit a switchboard form
- Configure the database to display a form at startup and show an application title
- Show and hide the navigation pane
- Customize the navigation pane by hiding objects
- Define error checking options
- Encrypt a database by assigning a password
- Create an .accde database file
- View trust center settings

access Chapter 7

SNAP

Tutorial 7.1
Using Advanced Database Features
Tutorial 7.2
Customizing and Securing a Database

Macros are used to automate repetitive tasks or to store actions that can be executed by clicking a button in a form. A switchboard form is a form used as a menu that provides an interface between the end user and the objects within the database file. In this chapter you will learn how to automate a database using macros and a switchboard form. You will also learn methods to secure and customize the Access environment to prevent unauthorized access and/or changes to the design of objects.

Note: Before beginning computer projects, copy the Access2007L2C7 subfolder from the Access2007L2 folder on the CD that accompanies this textbook to your storage medium and then make Access2007L2C7 the active folder.

Project 1 — Create Macros and Assign Macros to Command Buttons

You will create macros to automate routine tasks and add macros to command buttons in forms that run the macros.

QUICK STEPS

Create Macro
1. Click Create tab.
2. Click Macro button.
3. Click down-pointing arrow in *Action* column.
4. Click desired action.
5. If desired, type documentation in *Comment* column.
6. Enter arguments as required in *Action Arguments* section.
7. Click Save button.
8. Type name for macro.
9. Press Enter or click OK.

Run Macro
Double-click macro name in navigation pane.
OR
1. Right-click macro name.
2. Click *Design View*.
3. Click Run button.

HINT

For a complex macro, consider working through the steps you want to save, writing down all of the parameters as you go before attempting to create the macro.

Creating a Macro

Macros are used to automate repetitive tasks within the database. For example, a macro could be created to open a query, form, or report. The macro object stores a series of instructions (called ***actions***) in the sequence in which the actions are to be performed. Macros appear as objects within the Navigation pane. Double-clicking the macro name causes Access to execute the instructions. A macro can also be assigned to a command button to enable the macro to be run using a single mouse click. For example, you could create a macro in a form that automates the process of finding a record by the last name field and assign the macro to a button. The macro would contain two instructions, the first instruction to move to the field in which the last name is stored, and the second instruction to open the Find dialog box.

To create a macro, click the Create tab and then click the Macro button in the Other group. This opens the Macro builder window shown in Figure 7.1. The insertion point is positioned in the first row in the *Action* column. Each row in the Macro builder window is used to enter a command to be executed when the macro is run. Click the down-pointing arrow in the *Action* column and click the desired instruction at the drop-down list.

Figure 7.1 Macro Builder Window

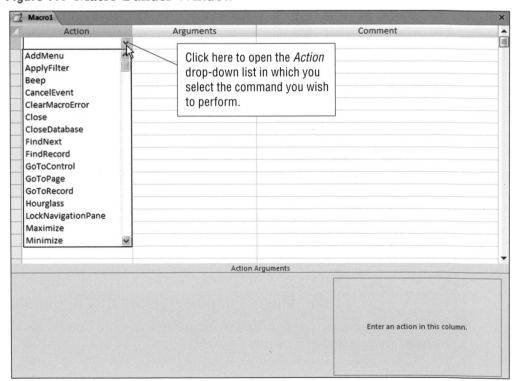

Type documentation in the *Comment* column that explains the purpose of the action within the macro. Text typed within the *Comment* section is optional and used for informational purposes only. Each action entered in the top section of the Macro builder window is associated with a set of *Arguments* that displays at the bottom of the window. Similar to field properties in Table Design view, the arguments displayed in the *Action Arguments* section vary depending on the active action in the top half of the window. For example, Figure 7.2 displays the *Action Arguments* section for the OpenReport action.

Figure 7.2 Macro Builder Window with Action Arguments for OpenReport Action

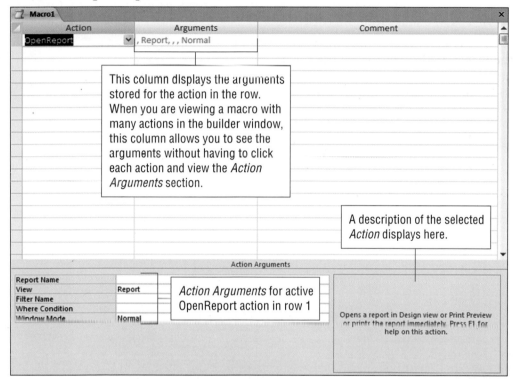

The OpenReport action is used to open a report similar to double-clicking a report name in the navigation pane. Within the *Action Arguments* section you specify the name of the report to open and the view in which the report is to be presented. You can choose to open the report in Design view, Print Preview, Report view, Layout view, or to send the report directly to the printer. Use the *Filter Name* or *Where Condition* arguments to restrict the records displayed in the report. The *Window Mode* argument is used to instruct Access to open the report in *Normal*, *Hidden*, *Icon*, or *Dialog* mode.

The *Arguments* column in the top half of the Macro builder window displays the arguments for an action in dimmed text, indicating you cannot directly enter or edit an argument using this column. Arguments are entered or edited by making the desired action row active in the top half of the builder window and then entering the arguments using the bottom *Action Arguments* section (similar to entering or editing field properties in table Design view). In a macro with more than one action, this column is very useful because you can view the arguments without having to activate the action row and view the bottom section of the builder window.

1. Open **RSRComputerServ7.accdb** and enable the content.
2. Create a macro to open the Work_Orders report in a Print Preview window by completing the following steps:
   a. Click the Create tab.
   b. Click the Macro button 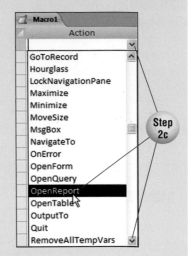 in the Other group (do not click the down-pointing arrow on the button).
   c. With the insertion point positioned in the first row in the Macro builder window, click the down-pointing arrow at the right of the *Action* column, scroll down the list box, and then click *OpenReport*.
   d. Click in the *Comment* column in the first row and type **Open Work_Orders report in Print Preview window**.

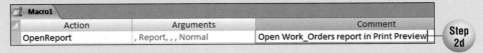

   e. Click in the *Report Name* argument box in the *Action Arguments* section, click the down-pointing arrow that appears, and click *Work_Orders* at the drop-down list.

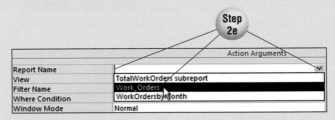

   f. Click in the *View* argument box in the *Action Arguments* section, click the down-pointing arrow that appears, and click *Print Preview* at the drop-down list.

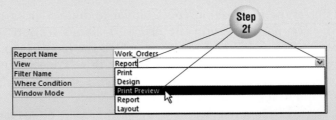

3. Click the Save button, type **Rpt_WO_PrintPreview** in the *Macro Name* text box at the Save As dialog box, and press Enter or click OK.

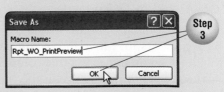

4. Click the Run button in the Tools group in the Macro Tools Design tab to instruct Access to carry out the macro instructions. The Work_Orders report opens in a new tab in the work area in a Print Preview window.

5. Close the report.
6. Close the macro.
7. The navigation pane is set to display objects by object type. If necessary, scroll down the navigation pane to view the group titled Macros and the Rpt_WO_PrintPreview macro object within the group.

To create a macro with multiple actions, add the next instruction in the *Action* column in the row immediately below the last instruction. Access executes each action in the order they appear in the Macro builder window. In Project 1b you will create a macro with multiple actions that will instruct Access to open a form, make active a control within the form, and then open the Find dialog box in order to search for a record. The *GoToControl* action is used to make active a control within a form or report and the *RunCommand* action is used to execute an Access command. For each of these actions, a single argument specifies the name of the control to move to and the name of the command you want to run.

Project 1b · Creating a Macro to Open a Form and Find a Record

1. With the **RSRComputerServ7.accdb** database open, create a macro to open the Technician_Maintenance form by completing the following steps:
   a. Click the Create tab.
   b. Click the Macro button in the Other group.
   c. With the insertion point positioned in the first row in the Macro builder window, click the down-pointing arrow at the right of the *Action* column, scroll down the list box, and then click *OpenForm*.
   d. Click in the *Comment* column in the first row and type **Open Technician_Maintenance form**.
   e. Click in the *Form Name* argument box in the *Action Arguments* section, click the down-pointing arrow that appears, and click *Technician_Maintenance* at the drop-down list.

2. Add additional instructions to move to the technician's last name field and then open the Find dialog box by completing the following steps:
   a. Click in the second row in the *Action* column, click the down-pointing arrow that appears, and then click *GoToControl* at the drop-down list.
   b. Click in the *Comment* column in the second row and type **Move to Last Name field**.

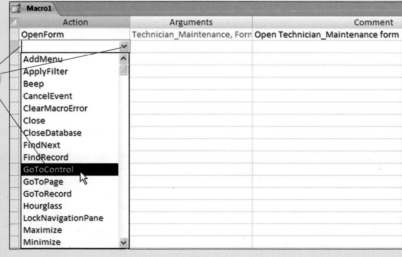

c. Click in the *Control Name* argument box in the *Action Arguments* section and type **Lname**. At the *Control Name* argument box, type the field name that you want to make active in the form.

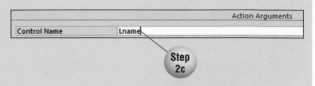

Step 2c

d. Click in the third row in the *Action* column, click the down-pointing arrow that appears, scroll down the list box, and then click *RunCommand* at the drop-down list.

e. Click in the *Comment* column in the third row and type **Open Find dialog box**.

f. Click in the *Command* argument box in the *Action Arguments* section, click the down-pointing arrow that appears, scroll down the list box, and click *Find*.

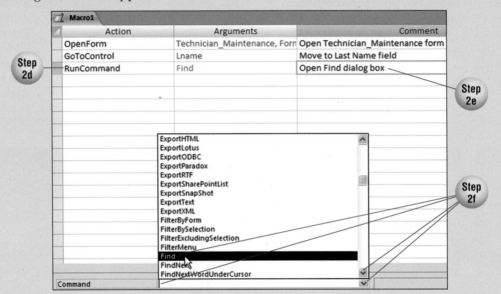

Step 2d

Step 2e

Step 2f

3. Click the Save button, type **Form_Tech_Find** in the *Macro Name* text box at the Save As dialog box and press Enter or click OK.

4. Click the Run button. The Technician_Maintenance form opens, the active field is *Last Name* and the Find and Replace dialog box appears with the last name of the first technician entered in the *Find What* text box. Type **Sadiku** and click the Find Next button.

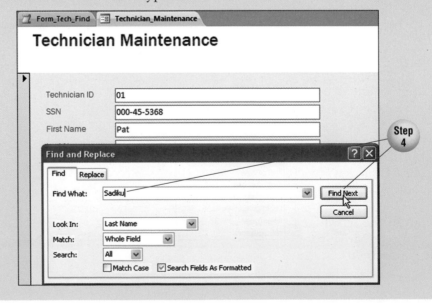

Step 4

5. Access moves to record 4. Close the Find and Replace dialog box. Notice the record for the technician named *Madir Sadiku* is the active record.

6. Close the form.

7. Close the macro.

A macro can also be created by dragging and dropping an object name from the navigation pane to the *Action* column in a Macro builder window. By default, Access creates an *OpenTable*, *OpenQuery*, *OpenForm*, or *OpenReport* action depending on the object dragged to the window. The object name is also automatically entered in the *Action Arguments* section.

Create Macro by Drag and Drop
1. Click Create tab.
2. Click Macro button.
3. Drag desired object name from navigation pane to first row in *Action* column.
4. Save macro.

Project 1c Creating a Macro by Dragging and Dropping an Object

1. With the **RSRComputerServ7.accdb** database open, create a macro to open the WorkOrdersbyMonth report using the drag and drop method by completing the following steps:

   a. Click the Create tab.
   b. Click the Macro button in the Other group.
   c. Position the mouse pointer on the WorkOrdersbyMonth report name in the navigation pane, hold down the left mouse button, drag the object name to the *Action* column in the first row of the Macro builder window, and then release the mouse. Access inserts an OpenReport action with *WorkOrdersbyMonth* entered in the *Report Name* argument box.

2. Save the macro and name it **Rpt_WOsbyMonth**.

3. Run the macro.

4. Close the report.

5. Close the macro.

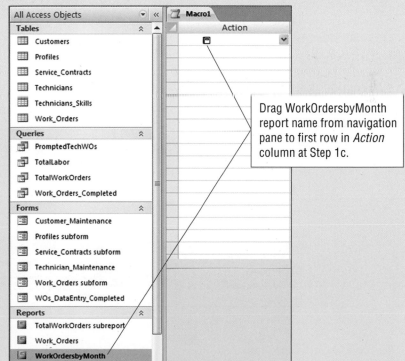

Drag WorkOrdersbyMonth report name from navigation pane to first row in *Action* column at Step 1c.

Editing a Macro

To edit a macro, right-click the macro name in the navigation pane and click *Design View* at the shortcut menu. The macro opens in the Macro builder window. Edit an action and/or the action's arguments, insert new actions, or delete actions as required. Save the revised macro and close the Macro builder window when finished.

Project 1d — Editing a Macro to Delete an Instruction

1. With the **RSRComputerServ7.accdb** database open, assume you decide that the macro to find a technician record will begin with the form already opened. This means you have to delete the first macro instruction to open the Technician_Maintenance form in the Form_Tech_Find macro. To do this, complete the following steps:

   a. If necessary, scroll down the navigation pane to view the macro object names.

   b. Right-click the macro named *Form_Tech_Find* and then click *Design View* at the shortcut menu. The macro opens in the Macro builder window.

   c. Move the pointer to the selector bar next to *OpenForm* in the first row in the Macro builder window until the pointer displays as a right-pointing black arrow and then click the left mouse button to select the action row.

   d. Click the Delete Rows button in the Rows group in the Macro Tools Design tab. The action is removed from the Macro builder window.

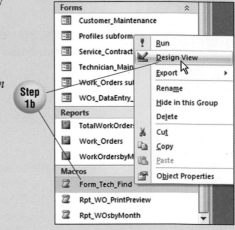

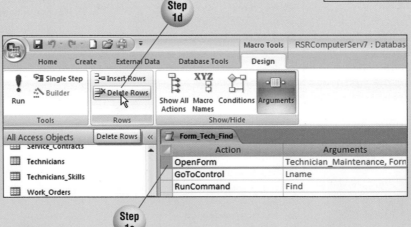

2. Save the revised macro.
3. Close the macro.

Creating a Command Button to Run a Macro

A macro can be assigned to a button added to a form so that the macro can be executed with a single mouse click. This method of running a macro makes macros more accessible and efficient. Open a form in Design view to add a button to the form to be used to run a macro. Click the Button (Form Control) button in the Controls group in the Form Design Tools Design tab and drag to create the button the approximate height and width in the desired form section. When you release the mouse, the Command Button Wizard launches if the Use Control Wizards button is active. At the first Command Button Wizard dialog box shown in Figure 7.3, you begin by choosing the type of command to assign to the button.

Figure 7.3 First Command Button Wizard Dialog Box

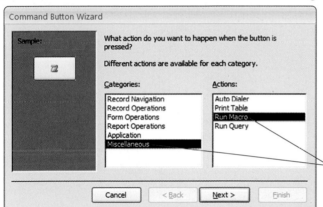

Select the *Miscellaneous* category and the *Run Macro* action to assign a macro to the button at the first Command Button Wizard dialog box.

Click *Miscellaneous* in the *Categories* list box and *Run Macro* in the *Actions* list box and click Next. At the second Command Button Wizard dialog box you choose the name of the macro to assign to the button. At the third dialog box shown in Figure 7.4, specify text to display on the face of the button or choose to display a picture as an icon. The button in the *Sample* section of the dialog box updates to show how the button will appear as you enter text or select a picture file. At the last Command Button Wizard dialog box, assign a name to associate with the command button and click Finish.

Figure 7.4 Third Command Button Wizard Dialog Box

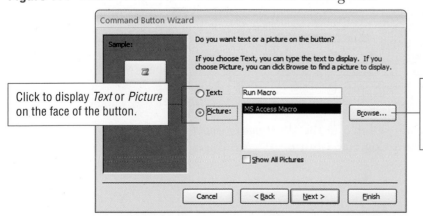

Click to display *Text* or *Picture* on the face of the button.

Click the Browse button to locate a picture you want to display on the face of the button.

QUICK
STEPS

Create Command Button in Form

1. Open form in Design view.
2. Click Button (Form Control) button.
3. Drag to create button desired height and width.
4. Click *Miscellaneous*.
5. Click *Run Macro*.
6. Click Next.
7. Click desired macro name.
8. Click Next.
9. Click *Text*.
10. Select current text in *Text* text box.
11. Type desired text to appear on button.
12. Click Next.
13. Type name for command button.
14. Click Finish.

HINT

Actions can be assigned to a command button without using a macro. Explore the categories and actions for each category at the first Command Button Wizard dialog box.

Button

Control Wizards

1. With the **RSRComputerServ7.accdb** database open, create a command button to run the macro to locate a technician record by last name in the Technician_Maintenance form by completing the following steps:

   a. Open the Technician_Maintenance form in Design view.

   b. Make sure the Use Control Wizards button is active. If necessary, click the button to turn the feature on.

   c. Click the Button (Form Control) button [icon] in the Controls group in the Form Design Tools Design tab.

   d. Position the crosshairs with the button icon attached in the Form Header section, drag to create a button the approximate height and width shown, and then release the mouse.

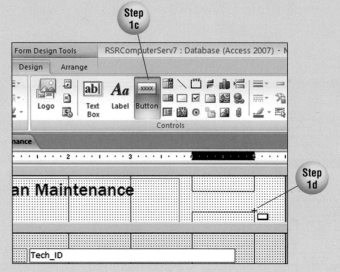

   e. At the first Command Button Wizard dialog box, click *Miscellaneous* in the *Categories* list box.

   f. Click *Run Macro* in the *Actions* list box and then click Next.

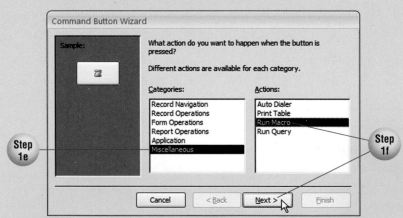

   g. With *Form_Tech_Find* already selected in the *What macro would you like the command button to run?* list box at the second Command Button Wizard dialog box, click Next.

h. At the third Command Button Wizard dialog box, click *Text*.

i. Select the current text in the *Text* text box, type **Find Technician Record**, and click Next.

j. With *Command##* (where *##* is the number of the command button) already selected in the *What do you want to name the button?* text box, type **FindTechRec** and click Finish. Access automatically resizes the width of the button to accommodate the text to be displayed on the face of the button.

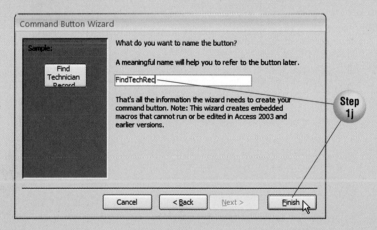

2. Save the revised form.
3. Switch to Form view.
4. Click the Find Technician Record button to run the macro.

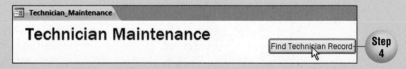

5. Type **Colacci** in the *Find What* text box at the Find and Replace dialog box and press Enter or click the Find Next button. Access moves the active record to record 7.
6. Close the Find and Replace dialog box.
7. Close the form.

1. With the **RSRComputerServ7.accdb** database open, create a command button to run the macro to display the Work_Orders report in the WOs_DataEntry_Completed form by completing the following steps:
   a. Open the WOs_DataEntry_Completed form in Design view.
   b. Drag the top of the Form Footer section bar down approximately 0.5 inch to create more space in the Detail section below the *Comments* control objects.
   c. Click the Button (Form Control) button in the Controls group in the Form Design Tools Design tab.
   d. Position the crosshairs with the button icon attached at the bottom left of the Detail section, drag to create a button the approximate height and width shown, and then release the mouse.
   e. Click *Miscellaneous* in the *Categories* list box, click *Run Macro* in the *Actions* list box, and click Next.
   f. Click *Rpt_WO_PrintPreview* and click Next.
   g. Click *Text*, select the current text in the *Text* text box, type **Open Work Orders Report**, and click Next.
   h. Type **WORpt** and click Finish.

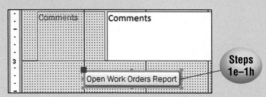

2. Save the revised form.
3. Create a second button at the right side of the form at the same horizontal position as the first command button to run the macro that displays the WorkOrdersbyMonth report by completing steps similar to those in Steps 1c–1h and with the following additional information:
   • Select *Rpt_WOsbyMonth* as the macro to assign to the button.
   • Display the text *Open Work Orders by Month Report* on the button.
   • Name the button **Rpt_WOsMth**.
4. If necessary, move the button to position it as shown.

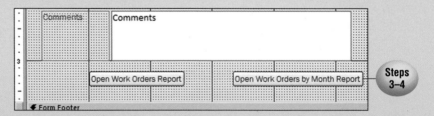

5. Save the revised form.
6. Switch to Form view.
7. Click the Open Work Orders Report button to view the report and then close the report.
8. Click the Open Work Orders by Month Report button to view the report and then close the report.
9. Close the form.

Project 2 Create a Switchboard

You will create a switchboard form to be used as a menu. The menu will contain two pages: one page that provides access to available forms, and another page to provide access to available reports.

Creating a Switchboard Form

Database files are often accessed by multiple users who need to enter the file for a specific purpose such as updating a customer record or entering details related to a completed work order. These individuals may not be well versed in database applications and simply want an easy method with which to accomplish the data entry or maintenance task. A switchboard is a form used to present a menu with command buttons which end users click to open the forms and reports needed to update, view, or print data. The switchboard form can be set to display automatically when the database file is opened so that end users do not need to know which objects are needed from the navigation pane. Access provides a utility called the switchboard manager which allows you to easily create a switchboard form by selecting options in a series of dialog boxes.

To create a new switchboard, click the Database Tools tab and then click the Switchboard Manager button in the Database Tools group. If a switchboard form does not currently exist within the database, Access displays a message box asking if you want to create a new switchboard. Click Yes to instruct Access to create a new Switchboard form and display the dialog box shown in Figure 7.5.

Figure 7.5 Switchboard Manager Dialog Box

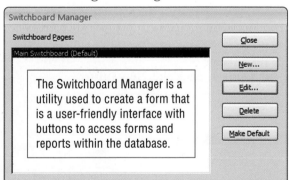

A switchboard form can contain all menu items on a single switchboard page or you can create additional switchboard pages to group related items together. From the main switchboard you can create a button that, when clicked, displays another switchboard page with additional menu options. For example, you may decide to group all of the forms in a database together in one menu and all of the reports in another menu. In this example, the switchboard would contain three pages: the main switchboard, the forms switchboard, and the reports switchboard. The main switchboard page would contain a button to open the forms switchboard and

QUICK STEPS

Create New Switchboard
1. Click Database Tools tab.
2. Click Switchboard Manager button.
3. Click Yes.

Create New Switchboard Page
1. At Switchboard Manager dialog box, click New button.
2. Type name for new page.
3. Click OK.

Add Items to Switchboard Page
1. At Switchboard Manager dialog box, click desired page name.
2. Click Edit button.
3. Click New button.
4. Type text to display for item.
5. Click down-pointing arrow next to *Command.*
6. Click desired command.
7. Click down-pointing arrow next to *Switchboard, Form,* or *Report.*
8. Click desired object name.
9. Click OK.

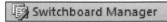

another button to open the reports switchboard. When you want to use multiple switchboard pages, create the pages for the submenu items first before creating the items on the main switchboard. In Project 2a you will create a new switchboard and then create the forms switchboard page for the database. In Project 2b you will create the reports switchboard page and in Project 2c you will assemble the main switchboard. You will notice that Access creates a table named *Switchboard Items.* This table is used by the Switchboard Manager to store the menu options and arguments—do not delete or rename this object.

Project 2a Creating a Switchboard and Adding a Switchboard Page

1. With the **RSRComputerServ7.accdb** database open, create a new switchboard form using the Switchboard Manager utility by completing the following steps:
   a. Click the Database Tools tab.
   b. Click the Switchboard Manager button 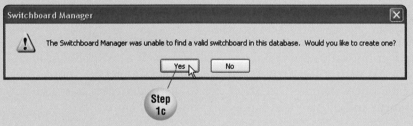 in the Database Tools group.
   c. At the Switchboard Manager message box indicating a valid switchboard was not found, click Yes to create a new switchboard. Access creates a form with the object name *Switchboard* and opens the Switchboard Manager dialog box.

   Switchboard Manager

   ⚠ The Switchboard Manager was unable to find a valid switchboard in this database. Would you like to create one?

   [Yes]   [No]

   Step 1c

2. A Main Switchboard form is created by default and is displayed in the *Switchboard Pages* list box as *Main Switchboard (Default)*. You want the main switchboard to contain a button to open another switchboard page that is a menu to access each form used in the database. Before you can add a button to the main switchboard to open the forms switchboard page, you first have to create the forms page. Create a new switchboard page by completing the following steps:
   a. At the Switchboard Manager dialog box, click the New button.

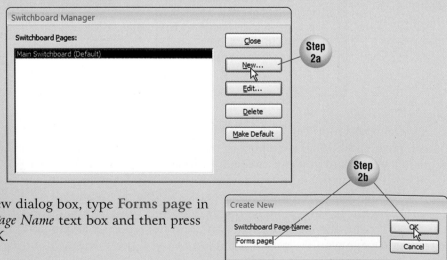

   Switchboard Manager

   Switchboard Pages:

   Main Switchboard (Default)

   [Close]
   [New...] Step 2a
   [Edit...]
   [Delete]
   [Make Default]

   Step 2b

   b. At the Create New dialog box, type **Forms page** in the *Switchboard Page Name* text box and then press Enter or click OK.

   Create New

   Switchboard Page Name:
   [Forms page]

   [OK]
   [Cancel]

3. Add three items to the Forms switchboard page by completing the following steps:
   a. At the Switchboard Manager dialog box, click *Forms page* in the *Switchboard Pages* list box.
   b. Click the Edit button. Access opens the Edit Switchboard Page dialog box.
   c. At the Edit Switchboard Page dialog box with *Forms page* displayed in the *Switchboard Name* text box, click the New button.

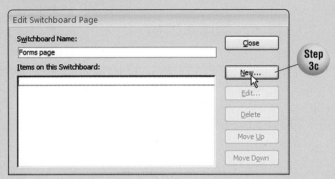

   d. At the Edit Switchboard Item dialog box with the existing text selected in the *Text* text box, type **Open form for Customer Maintenance**. The text entered in the *Text* text box displays next to a command button in the switchboard form. The text should describe for the end user the action that will occur if the command button is clicked.
   e. Click the down-pointing arrow next to the *Command* list box and then click *Open Form in Edit Mode* at the drop-down list.
   f. Click the down-pointing arrow next to the *Form* list box and then click *Customer_Maintenance* at the drop-down list.
   g. Click OK.

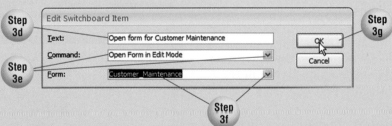

   h. Click the New button to add a second item to the Forms page.
   i. At the Edit Switchboard Item dialog box, type **Open form for Technician Maintenance** in the *Text* text box.
   j. Click the down-pointing arrow next to *Command* and click *Open Form in Edit Mode*.
   k. Click the down-pointing arrow next to *Form* and click *Technician_Maintenance*.
   l. Click OK.

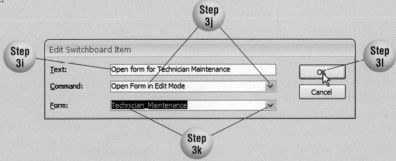

   m. Click New and add a third item to the Forms page with the text **Open form for completed Work Order data** that opens the *WOs_DataEntry_Completed* form in edit mode.

4. Click the Close button at the Edit Switchboard Page dialog box to close the Forms page.

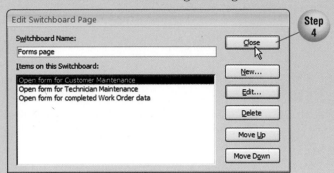

Step 4

5. Leave the Switchboard Manager dialog box open for the next project.

Project 2b Creating a New Switchboard Page

1. With the **RSRComputerServ7.accdb** database open and the Switchboard Manager dialog box open, create a new page for the report items by completing the following steps:
   a. Click the New button.
   b. At the Create New dialog box, type **Reports page** and press Enter or click OK.
2. Add two items to the Reports page by completing the following steps:
   a. At the Switchboard Manager dialog box, click *Reports page* in the *Switchboard Pages* list box and click the Edit button.
   b. At the Edit Switchboard Page dialog box with *Reports page* displayed in the *Switchboard Name* text box, click the New button.
   c. At the Edit Switchboard Item dialog box, type **Open Work Orders report** in the *Text* text box.
   d. Click the down-pointing arrow next to the *Command* list box and then click *Open Report*.
   e. Click the down-pointing arrow next to the *Report* list box and then click *Work_Orders*.
   f. Click OK.

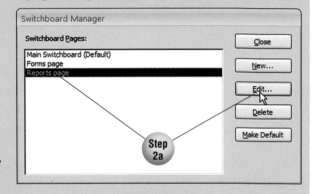

Step 2a

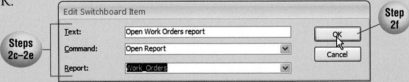

Steps 2c–2e

Step 2f

   g. Click the New button to add a second item to the Reports page with the text **Open Work Orders by month report** that opens the *WorkOrdersbyMonth* report.

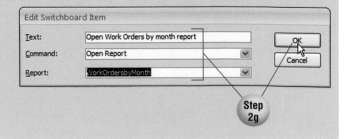

Step 2g

3. Click the Close button at the Edit Switchboard Page dialog box to close the Reports page.
4. Leave the Switchboard Manager dialog box open for the next project.

Now that the two switchboard pages have been created, you are ready to edit the main switchboard page that displays when the switchboard form is opened. You will add two items to the main switchboard, each of which instructs Access to go to another switchboard page. The main switchboard page also generally includes a button at the bottom of the menu that is used to close the database. The *Exit Application* command is used to close the active database.

Project 2c   Editing the Main Switchboard Page

1. With the **RSRComputerServ7.accdb** database open and the Switchboard Manager dialog box open, edit the main switchboard page to add commands to open the Forms page and the Reports page by completing the following steps:
   a. At the Switchboard Manager dialog box, click *Main Switchboard (Default)* in the *Switchboard Pages* list box and click the Edit button.
   b. At the Edit Switchboard Page dialog box with *Main Switchboard* displayed in the *Switchboard Name* text box, click the New button.
   c. At the Edit Switchboard Item dialog box, type **Forms menu** in the *Text* text box.
   d. Look at the option in the *Command* list box. The *Go to Switchboard* command is the correct action to replace the menu with another switchboard page.
   e. Click the down-pointing arrow next to the *Switchboard* list box and then click *Forms page*.
   f. Click OK.

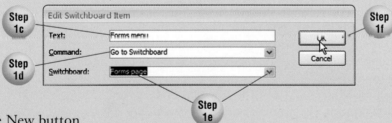

   g. Click the New button.
   h. Type **Reports menu** in the *Text* text box.
   i. Click the down-pointing arrow next to the *Switchboard* list box and click *Reports page*.
   j. Click OK.

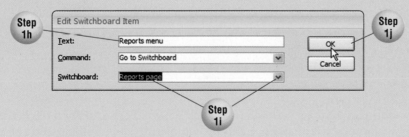

2. Add an item to the main switchboard page to exit Access by completing the following steps:
   a. At the Edit Switchboard Page dialog box, click the New button.
   b. Type **Exit RSR Computer Maintenance database** in the *Text* text box.
   c. Click the down-pointing arrow next to the *Command* list box and click *Exit Application*.
   d. Click OK.

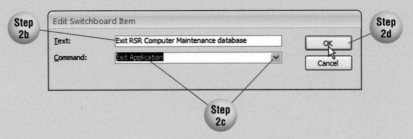

3. At the Edit Switchboard Page dialog box, select the current text in the *Switchboard Name* text box and type **Main Menu**.
4. Click the Close button.

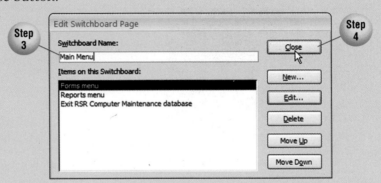

5. Once the Main Menu switchboard form is opened and the end user clicks the button to go to the Forms page, you need to include a way for the end user to return back to the main menu. To do this, a button needs to be added to the Forms page and the Reports page that returns to the main switchboard page. To do this, complete the following steps:
   a. At the Switchboard Manager dialog box, click *Forms page* and then click the Edit button.
   b. Click the New button.
   c. Type **Return to Main Menu** in the *Text* text box.
   d. Click the down-pointing arrow next to the *Switchboard* list box and click *Main Menu*.
   e. Click OK.

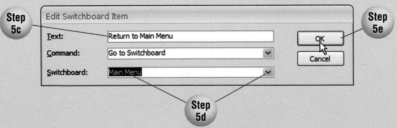

   f. Click the Close button.
   g. At the Switchboard Manager dialog box, click *Reports page* and then click the Edit button.
   h. Add an item to return to the main menu by completing steps similar to those in Steps 5b–5e.
   i. Click the Close button.

6. The switchboard pages are now complete. At the Switchboard Manager dialog box, click the Close button.
7. Use the switchboard form to navigate among the objects in the database by completing the following steps:
   a. Double-click the Switchboard form in the navigation pane.
   b. Click the command button next to *Forms menu* to open the Forms page.
   c. At the Forms page, click each button next to a form, view the form, and then close the form to return to the Switchboard.
   d. Click the button next to Return to Main Menu.
   e. Click the button to open the Reports menu.
   f. At the Reports page, click each button next to a report, view the report, and then close the report to return to the Switchboard.
   g. Click the button next to Return to Main Menu.
8. Click the button next to Exit the RSR Computer Maintenance database. Access closes the switchboard form and closes the database.

Step 7b

Switchboard

Main Menu

Forms menu
Reports menu
Exit RSR Computer Maintenance database

Editing an Existing Switchboard Form

Once a switchboard form has been created, clicking the Switchboard Manager button in the Database Tools group in the Database Tools tab opens the Switchboard Manager dialog box. You can add, delete, or modify switchboard pages and items on switchboard pages using similar techniques to those learned in Projects 2a–2c.

The Switchboard form can also be opened in Layout view or Design view in order to change fonts, colors, or insert a logo in the form. Be careful not to delete or edit the command buttons or text next to the command buttons—these items should be edited using the Switchboard Manager utility. Do not delete or rename the Switchboard object in the navigation pane. Doing so means Switchboard Manager will be unable to locate the form to edit pages and deleting the form does not allow you to create a new one.

QUICK STEPS

Edit Switchboard
1. Click Database Tools tab.
2. Click Switchboard Manager button.
3. Select switchboard page to be edited.
4. Click Edit button.
5. Add, delete, or modify items as required.
6. Click Close button twice.

Project 2d Editing a Switchboard

1. Open the **RSRComputerServ7.accdb** database and enable content.
2. You decide you want to rename *Forms page* to *Forms Menu*. To do this, complete the following steps:
   a. Click the Database Tools tab.
   b. Click the Switchboard Manager button in the Database Tools group.

c. At the Switchboard Manager dialog box, click *Forms page* and click the Edit button.

d. At the Edit Switchboard Page dialog box, edit the entry in the *Switchboard Name* text box to *Forms Menu* and then click the Close button.

3. Rename *Reports page* to *Reports Menu* by completing steps similar to those in Steps 2c–2d.

4. Close the Switchboard Manager dialog box.

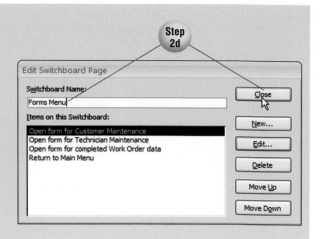

Step 2d

Edit Switchboard Page

Switchboard Name:
Forms Menu

Items on this Switchboard:
Open form for Customer Maintenance
Open form for Technician Maintenance
Open form for completed Work Order data
Return to Main Menu

Close
New...
Edit...
Delete
Move Up
Move Down

Project ③ Configure Database Options

You will configure database options for the active database and error checking options for all databases.

QUICK STEPS

Set Startup Form
1. Click Office button.
2. Click Access Options button.
3. Click *Current Database* in left pane.
4. Click down-pointing arrow next to *Display Form*.
5. Click desired form.
6. Click OK.

Specify Application Title
1. Click Office button.
2. Click Access Options button.
3. Click *Current Database* in left pane.
4. Click in *Application Title* text box.
5. Type desired title.
6. Click OK.

Access Options

Customizing the Access Environment

Click the Office button and then click the Access Options button located near the bottom right of the drop-down list to open the Access Options dialog box in which you can customize the Access environment. You can specify database options for all databases or for the current database. You can also define behavior for certain keys and set the default margins for printing. A form such as the switchboard form can be set to display automatically whenever the database file is opened. You can also choose to show or hide the navigation pane in the current database. For example, if you have created a switchboard which provides limited access to the objects that you want to make available, you may choose to hide the navigation pane to prevent users from being able to open other objects within the database. Databases can be set to open by default in shared use or exclusive use. Exclusive use means the file is restricted to one individual user.

Figure 7.6 displays the Access Options dialog box with *Current Database* selected in the left pane. In the Current Database pane, you can define a startup form to open automatically when the database is opened. In Project 3a you will configure the current database to display the switchboard automatically when the database is opened and in Project 3b you will customize the navigation pane.

Figure 7.6 Access Options Dialog Box with Current Database Pane Selected

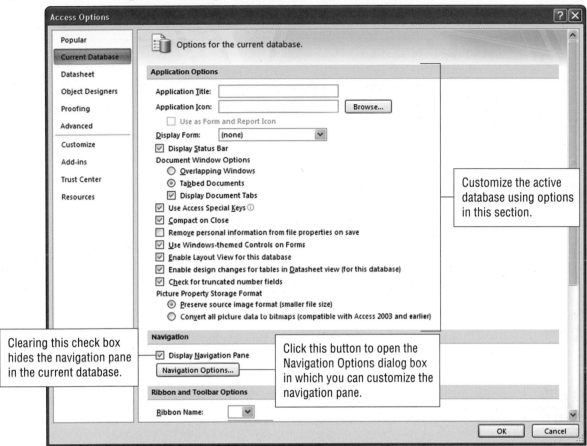

Customize the active database using options in this section.

Clearing this check box hides the navigation pane in the current database.

Click this button to open the Navigation Options dialog box in which you can customize the navigation pane.

Project 3a   **Configuring a Startup Form and Application Title**

1. With the **RSRComputerServ7.accdb** database open, configure the switchboard form to open automatically when the database file is opened by completing the following steps:

a. Click the Office button.

b. Click the Access Options button located near the bottom right of the drop-down list.

c. Click *Current Database* in the left pane.

d. Click the down-pointing arrow next to the *Display Form* list box (currently displays *[none]*) in the *Application Options* section, and then click *Switchboard* at the drop-down list.

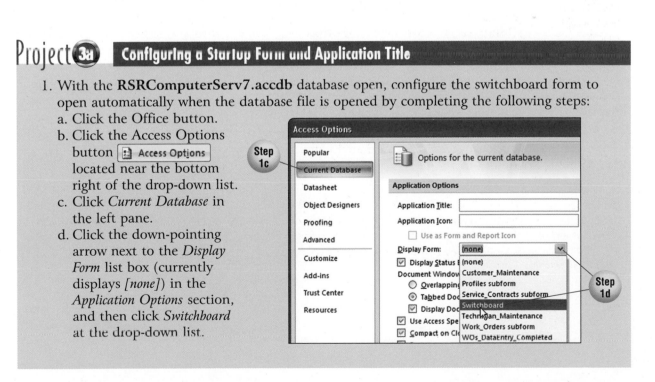

Step 1c

Step 1d

2. Click in the *Application Title* text box and type **RSR Computer Service Database**.

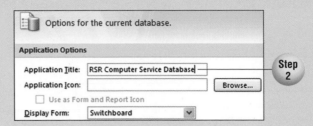

3. Click OK.
4. Click OK at the Microsoft Office Access message box indicating you have to close and reopen the database for the options to take effect.

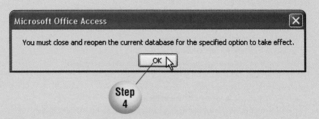

5. Close the **RSRComputerServ7.accdb** database.
6. Reopen the **RSRComputerServ7.accdb** database and enable the content. The Switchboard form displays automatically in the work area and the Title bar displays the application title *RSR Computer Service Database*.

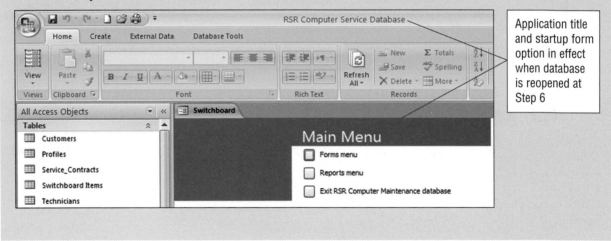

Application title and startup form option in effect when database is reopened at Step 6

Figure 7.7 Navigation Options Dialog Box

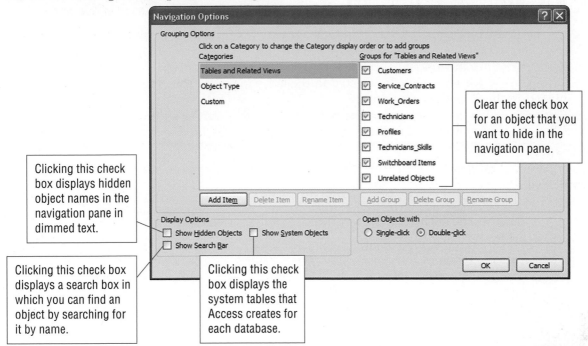

Clicking this check box displays hidden object names in the navigation pane in dimmed text.

Clear the check box for an object that you want to hide in the navigation pane.

Clicking this check box displays a search box in which you can find an object by searching for it by name.

Clicking this check box displays the system tables that Access creates for each database.

Customizing the Navigation Pane

Often, when a startup form is used in a database, the Navigation pane is hidden to prevent users from accidentally making changes to other objects by opening an object from the Navigation pane. To hide the Navigation pane, open the Access Options dialog box, click *Current Database* in the left pane, and clear the *Display Navigation Pane* check box in the *Navigation* section.

Click the Navigation Options button in the *Navigation* section to open the Navigation Options dialog box shown in Figure 7.7. At this dialog box you can elect to hide individual objects or groups of objects, set display options for the pane, and define whether objects are opened using a single mouse click or a double mouse click. For example, to prevent changes from being made to table design, you can hide the Tables group.

QUICK STEPS

Customize Navigation Pane
1. Click Office button.
2. Click Access Options button.
3. Click *Current Database* in left pane.
4. Click Navigation Options button.
5. Select desired options.
6. Click OK.
7. Click OK.

Hide Navigation Pane
1. Click Office button.
2. Click Access Options button.
3. Click *Current Database* in left pane.
4. Clear *Display Navigation Pane* check box.
5. Click OK.
6. Click OK.

HINT
Press F11 to display a hidden navigation pane.

1. With the **RSRComputerServ7.accdb** database open, customize the navigation pane to hide all of the table and macro objects by completing the following steps:
   a. Click the Office button and then click the Access Options button.
   b. With *Current Database* already selected in the left pane, click the Navigation Options button in the *Navigation* section.
   c. Click *Object Type* in the *Categories* list box.
   d. Click the *Tables* check box in the *Groups for 'Object Type'* list box to clear the check mark.
   e. Clear the check mark in the *Macros* check box.
   f. Click OK to close the Navigation Options dialog box.

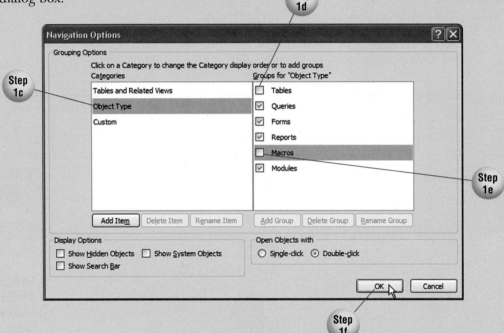

g. Click OK to close the Access Options dialog box.
2. Notice the Tables and Macros groups are removed from the navigation pane.

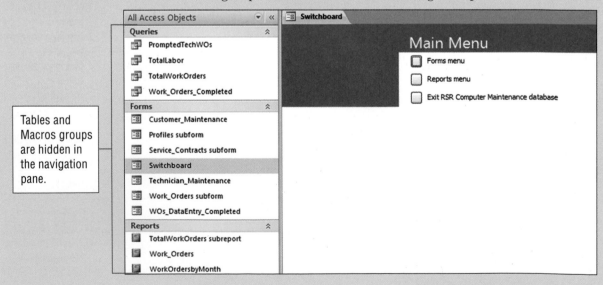

Tables and Macros groups are hidden in the navigation pane.

3. After reviewing the customized navigation pane, you decide the database would be more secure if the pane were hidden when the database is opened. To do this, complete the following steps:

a. Click the Office button and click the Access Options button.

b. With *Current Database* already selected in the left pane, click the *Display Navigation Pane* check box in the *Navigation* section to clear the check mark.

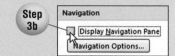

c. Click OK.

d. Click OK at the message box indicating you have to close and reopen the database for the option to take effect.

4. Close the **RSRComputerServ7.accdb** database.

5. Reopen the **RSRComputerServ7.accdb** database and enable the content. The navigation pane is now hidden from view and only the Switchboard form displays in the work area.

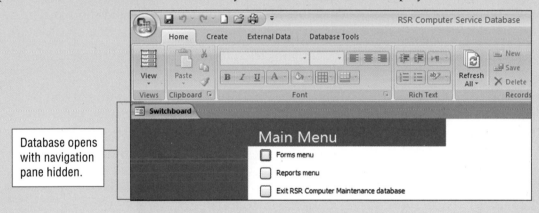

Database opens with navigation pane hidden.

Configuring Error Checking Options

Recall from Chapter 6 that a green triangle displayed in the Report Selector button when the report width was wider than the page would allow. Clicking the error checking options button allowed you to instruct Access to automatically fix the report's spacing. A green triangle also appeared in a new label you added to a report to describe another control. Access flagged the label as an error because the label control object was not associated with another object.

By default, Access has error checking turned on with all error checking options active. Figure 7.8 displays the error checking option parameters that you can configure in Access. Open the Access Options dialog box and select *Object Designers* in the left pane. Scroll down the right pane to locate the *Error checking* section. Clear check boxes for those options for which you want to disable error checking and click OK. Table 7.1 provides a description of each option.

QUICK STEPS

Customize Error Checking Options
1. Click Office button.
2. Click Access Options button.
3. Click *Object Designers* in left pane.
4. Scroll down right pane to *Error checking* section.
5. Clear check boxes as required.
6. Click OK.

Figure 7.8 Error Checking Options in Access

Table 7.1 Error Checking Options

Error checking option	Description
Enable error checking	Turn on or off error checking in forms and reports. An error is indicated by a green triangle in the upper left corner of a control.
Check for unassociated label and control	Access checks a selected label and text box control object to make sure the two objects are associated with each other. A Trace Error button appears if Access detects an error.
Check for new unassociated labels	New label control objects are checked for association with a text box control object.
Check for keyboard shortcut errors	Duplicate keyboard shortcuts or invalid shortcuts are flagged.
Check for invalid control properties	Invalid properties, formula expressions, or field names are flagged.
Check for common report errors	Reports are checked for errors such as invalid sort orders or reports that are wider than the selected paper size.
Error indicator color	A green triangle indicates an error in a control. Click the Color Picker button to change to a different color.

Project **3c** **Customizing Error Checking Options**

1. With the **RSRComputerServ7.accdb** database open, assume you frequently add label control objects to forms and reports to add explanatory text to users. You decide to customize the error checking options to prevent Access from flagging these independent label controls as errors. To do this, complete the following steps:

   a. Click the Office button and then click the Access Options button.
   b. Click *Object Designers* in the left pane.
   c. Scroll down the right pane to the *Error checking* section.
   d. Click the *Check for new unassociated labels* check box to clear the check mark.
   e. Click OK.

2. Close the **RSRComputerServ7.accdb** database.

Step 1d

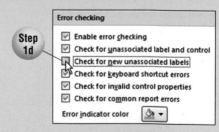

Project **4** **Secure a Database**

You will secure a database by encrypting the database with a password and by making an ACCDE file. You will also explore the default settings in the Trust Center.

Encrypting a Database

Microsoft Office Access 2007 includes an encryption tool that can be used to secure a database that you want to protect from unauthorized access. Encryption is a process of encoding the database by transforming the data into a format that renders the data meaningless. In Access, encryption takes place when you assign a password to the database. When the database is opened using the correct password, the database is decoded which involves transforming the data back to its original state.

Encryption in Access 2007 was updated to a stronger tool than the encoding feature used in earlier versions of Access; therefore, only database files that end in .accdb use the new encryption feature. Older database files will use the prior versions of encoding and decoding from Access 2003. If you have a confidential database file that ends with .mdb, consider converting the database to the new file format to take advantage of the stronger encryption feature.

Opening a Database in Exclusive Mode

A database is encrypted by assigning a password. In order to assign a password to the database, the database has to be opened in exclusive mode. Exclusive mode means that no other copies of the database are currently being shared. To open the database exclusively, begin by closing the current database and making sure no one else is currently sharing the database. Display the Open dialog box and click once to select the database file name in the file list. Next, click the down-pointing arrow on the Open button and then click *Open Exclusive* at the drop-down list as shown in Figure 7.9.

Figure 7.9 Open Button Drop-down List

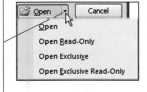

Click the Open button arrow to display a drop-down list with options in which you can open the currently selected database file. *Open Exclusive* means the database is opened without shared access.

Assigning a Password to a Database

Once the database that you want to encrypt has been opened exclusively, click the Database Tools tab and then click the Encrypt with Password button in the Database Tools group. At the Set Database Password dialog box shown in Figure 7.10 with the insertion point positioned in the *Password* text box, type the password to assign to the file, press tab to move to the *Verify* text box, type the same password again, and then click OK. Once assigned a password, the database cannot be opened without the password—store the password in a secure location away from the computer.

Figure 7.10 Set Database Password Dialog Box

Project 4a · Encrypting a Database Using a Password

1. Open the **RSRComputerServ7.accdb** database in exclusive mode by completing the following steps:
   a. Display the Open dialog box.
   b. If necessary, navigate to your storage medium and the Access2007L2C7 folder.
   c. Click once to select the file named *RSRComputerServ7.accdb*.
   d. Click the down-pointing arrow at the right of the Open button.
   e. Click *Open Exclusive* at the drop-down list.
2. Remove the security warning message by enabling content.
3. Encrypt the database by assigning a password to the file by completing the following steps:
   a. Click the Database Tools tab.
   b. Click the Encrypt with Password button [Encrypt with Password] in the Database Tools group.
   c. At the Set Database Password dialog box with the insertion point positioned in the *Password* text box, type **r$S3m** and press Tab.
   d. With the insertion point positioned in the *Verify* text box, type **r$S3m** and then press Enter or click OK.
4. Close the **RSRComputerServ7.accdb** database.
5. Reopen the **RSRComputerServ7.accdb** as you normally would. At the Password Required dialog box, type **r$S3m** in the *Enter database password* text box and press Enter or click OK.
6. Remove the security warning message by enabling the content.

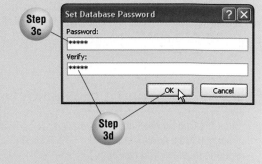

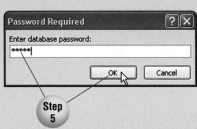

Removing a Database Password

[Decrypt Database]

The database is decrypted each time the database is opened using the correct password. If you decide you want to permanently decrypt the database, remove the database password. To do this, open the database in exclusive mode. Click the Database Tools tab and then click the Decrypt button (the Encrypt with Password button changes to Decrypt Database when the database has been assigned a password). At the Unset Database Password dialog box shown in Figure 7.11, type the password and click OK.

Figure 7.11 Unset Database Password Dialog Box

Creating an ACCDE Database File

In Chapter 6 you learned how to split a database into two files to create a front-end and a back-end database. This method allowed you to improve performance and protect the table objects from changes by separating the tables from the queries, forms, and reports. Another method with which you can protect an Access database is to create an ACCDE file. In an ACCDE file, end users are prevented from making changes to the design of objects. An Access database stored as an ACCDE file is a locked-down version of the database that does not provide access to Design view or Layout view. In addition, if the database contains any Visual Basic for Application (VBA) code, the code cannot be modified or changed.

To save an Access database as an ACCDE file, click the Database Tools tab and then click the Make ACCDE button in the Database Tools group. At the Save As dialog box, navigate to the drive and/or folder in which to save the database, type the desired file name in the *File Name* text box, and click the Save button. Once the file is created, move the original database in .accdb format to a secure location and provide end users with the path to the .accde file for daily use.

QUICK STEPS

Make ACCDE File
1. Open database.
2. Click Database Tools tab.
3. Click Make ACCDE button.
4. Navigate to required drive and/or folder.
5. Type name in *File name* text box.
6. Click Save button.

Make ACCDE

Project 4b Making an ACCDE Database File

1. With the **RSRComputerServ7.accdb** database open, create an ACCDE file by completing the following steps:
   a. Click the Database Tools tab.
   b. Click the Make ACCDE button in the Database Tools group.
   c. At the Save As dialog box with the default location the Access2007L2C7 folder on your storage medium and **RSRComputerServ7.accde** the default name in the *File name* text box, click the Save button.

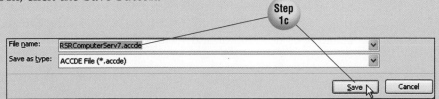

Step 1c

| File name: | RSRComputerServ7.accde |
| Save as type: | ACCDE File (*.accde) |

Save Cancel

2. Close the **RSRComputerServ7.accdb** database.
3. Open the **RSRComputerServ7.accde** database. Type r$S3m in the *Enter database password* text box and press Enter or click OK.
4. At the Microsoft Office Access Security Notice dialog box informing you the file might contain unsafe content, click the Open button.
5. Click the Forms menu button and then click the button to Open form for completed Work Order data.

6. With the WOs_DataEntry_Completed form open, look at the View button in the Views group in the Home tab. Notice the button is dimmed. Also notice only one view button is available in the View group located at the right end of the Status bar.

7. Click the Open Work Orders by Month Report button at the bottom of the form. Access opens the WorkOrdersbyMonth report. Notice the View group at the right end of the Status bar contains only a Report view and Print Preview button.
8. Close the report and close the form.
9. Close the **RSRComputerServ7.accde** database.

Viewing Trust Center Settings for Access

QUICK STEPS

View Trust Center Options
1. Click Office button.
2. Click Access Options.
3. Click *Trust Center* in left pane.
4. Click Trust Center Settings button.
5. Click desired trust center category in left pane.
6. View and/or modify required options.
7. Click OK twice.

HINT

Changing the macro security setting in Access does not affect the macro security setting in other Microsoft programs such as Word or Excel.

Access Options

In Access 2007, the Trust Center is set to block unsafe content when you open a database file. As you have been working with Access you have closed the Security Warning that appears in the message bar when you open a database by clicking the Options button and enabling the content. Access provides the Trust Center in which you can view and/or modify the security options that are in place to protect your computer from malicious content.

The Trust Center maintains a Trusted Locations list with content stored within the location considered a trusted source. You can add a path to the trusted locations list and Access will treat any files opened from the drive and folder as safe. Databases opened from trusted locations do not display the Security Warning in the message bar and do not have content blocked.

Before a database can have macros enabled, the Trust Center checks for a valid and current digital signature signed by an entity that is stored in the Trusted Publishers list. The Trusted Publishers list is maintained by you on the computer you are using. A trusted publisher is added to the list when you enable content from an authenticated source and click the option to *Trust all content from this publisher*. Depending on the active macro security setting, if the Trust Center cannot match the digital signature information with an entity in the Trusted Publishers list or the macro does not contain a digital signature, the security warning displays in the message bar.

The default Macro Security option is *Disable all macros with notification*. Table 7.2 describes the four options for macro security. In some cases, you may decide to change the default macro security setting by opening the Trust Center dialog box. You will explore the Trust Center in Project 4c.

Table 7.2 Macro Security Settings for Databases Not Opened from a Trusted Location

Macro Setting	Description
Disable all macros without notification	All macros are disabled; security alerts will not appear.
Disable all macros with notification	All macros are disabled; security alert appears with the option to enable content if you trust the source of the file. This is the default setting.
Disable all macros except digitally signed macros	A macro that does not contain a digital signature is disabled; security alerts do not appear. If the macro is digitally signed by a publisher in your Trusted Publishers list, the macro is allowed to run. If the macro is digitally signed by a publisher not in your Trusted Publishers list, you receive a security alert.
Enable all macros (not recommended, potentially dangerous code can run)	All macros are allowed; security alerts do not appear.

Project 4c Exploring Trust Center Settings

1. At the *Getting Started with Microsoft Office Access* window, explore the current settings in the Trust Center by completing the following steps:
   a. Click the Office button and click the Access Options button.
   b. Click *Trust Center* in the left pane of the Access Options dialog box.
   c. Click the Trust Center Settings button in the *Microsoft Office Access Trust Center* section.

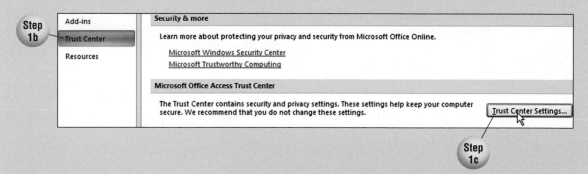

d. At the Trust Center dialog box, click *Macro Settings* in the left pane.

e. Review the options under the section titled *For macros in documents not in a trusted location.* Note which option is active on the computer you are using. The default option is *Disable all macros with notification.* **Note: The security setting on the computer you are using may be different than the default option. Do not change the security setting without the permission of your instructor.**

f. Click *Trusted Publishers* in the left pane. If any publishers have been added to the list on the computer you are using, the names of the entities will be shown in the list box. If the list box is empty, no trusted publishers have been added.

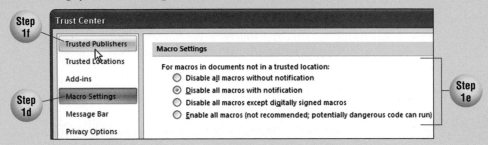

g. Click *Trusted Locations* in the left pane. Review the path and description of any folders added to the trusted locations list. By default, Access adds the folder created upon installation of Microsoft Office Access that contains the database templates provided by Microsoft. Additional folders may also appear that have been added by a system administrator or network administrator.

h. Click OK to close the Trust Center dialog box.

2. Click OK to close the Access Options dialog box.

In this chapter you have learned some techniques to automate, customize, and secure an Access database. As you gain more experience with Access, explore further Access options to customize the environment that allow you to change behavior of actions and keys while editing. Also consider experimenting with the OpenQuery action to automate queries and the MsgBox action to display messages to end users as a macro is run.

CHAPTER summary

- A macro is used to automate actions within a database such as opening a form or report.
- Click the Database Tools tab and click the Macro button in the Other group to open a Macro builder window in which you create the actions you want to store.
- Each macro action is entered in a separate row in the Macro builder window.
- Type documentation to describe the action in the *Comment* column. Comments are optional and used for informational purposes only.
- The bottom section of the Macro builder window is where *Action Arguments* are entered.
- Action arguments are parameters for the action such as the object name, the mode in which the object opens, and other restrictions placed on the action.
- The available arguments displayed in the *Action Arguments* section are dependent on the active action.
- To create a macro with multiple actions, enter each action one below the other in the Macro builder window in the desired sequence.
- Run a macro by clicking the Run button in the Macro Builder window or by double-clicking the macro name in the navigation pane.
- A macro can also be created by dragging and dropping an object name from the navigation pane to the *Action* column in the Macro builder window.
- Edit a macro by right-clicking the macro name and clicking *Design View* at the shortcut menu.
- A macro can be assigned to a button in a form to provide single-click access to run the macro.
- Use the Button (Form Control) tool to create a command button in a form.
- Make sure the Use Control Wizards button is active before creating a command button to use the Command Button Wizard to assist with assigning the macro and creating the text or picture on the face of the button.
- A switchboard is a form that is used to present a menu to an end user with command buttons that provide single-click access to objects within the database.
- A switchboard can have multiple pages that display submenus in order to group related items.
- Click the Database Tools tab and then click the Switchboard Manager button to create a new switchboard or edit an existing switchboard.
- The Switchboard Manager is a utility that allows you to create the menu items by selecting options in dialog boxes.
- If the switchboard is to include subpages for menus, create the individual switchboard pages for the submenu items first before editing the main switchboard page.
- Create a new switchboard page at the Switchboard Manager dialog box by clicking the New button and typing a name for the new page.

- Add items to a switchboard page by selecting the page name at the Switchboard Manager dialog box and clicking the Edit button. At the Edit Switchboard Page dialog box, click the New button to add an item to the page.
- A switchboard can be set to display automatically whenever the database is opened by setting the switchboard as the *Display Form* at the Access Options dialog box with *Current Database* selected in the left pane.
- Change the title that appears in the Title bar for the active database by typing an entry in the *Application Title* text box at the Access Options dialog box with *Current Database* selected in the left pane.
- You can set options for the navigation pane such as hiding individual objects or groups of objects at the Navigation Options dialog box.
- Hide the navigation pane by clearing the *Display Navigation Pane* check box at the Access Options dialog box with *Current Database* selected in the left pane.
- Change default error checking options in the Access Options dialog box with *Object Designers* selected in the left pane.
- To open a database exclusively (without shared access), display the Open dialog box, click once to select the database name, click the down-pointing arrow on the Open button, and click *Open Exclusive*.
- Encrypt a database by assigning a database password.
- To assign a database password, open the database in exclusive mode, click the Database Tools tab, and then click the Encrypt with Password button. Type the password to assign to the database twice and click OK.
- Opening a password-protected database by typing the correct database password decrypts the database.
- To permanently decrypt the database, remove the database password.
- Create an ACCDE database file to create a locked-down version of the database in which objects are prevented from being opened in Design view or Layout view.
- Click the Database Tools tab and click the Make ACCDE button to save a copy of the active database as an .accde database file.
- By making the .accde database file available to end users for daily use, your object designs are kept secure.
- Open the Access Options dialog box, click *Trust Center* in the left pane, and then click the Trust Center Settings button to view and/or modify trust center options.

COMMANDS review

FEATURE	RIBBON TAB, GROUP	BUTTON	OFFICE BUTTON DROP-DOWN LIST
Create ACCDE file	Database Tools, Database Tools		
Create command button	Form Design Tools Design, Controls	xxxx	
Create macro	Create, Other		
Customize Access options			Access Options
Customize Navigation pane			Access Options
Encrypt database	Database Tools, Database Tools	Encrypt with Password	
Run macro	Macro Tools Design, Tools	!	
Switchboard Manager	Database Tools, Database Tools	Switchboard Manager	

CONCEPTS check

Test Your Knowledge

Completion: In the space provided at the right, indicate the correct term, command, or number.

1. This is the name of the window in which you create actions with associated action arguments for a macro.

2. Type documentation for a macro action in this column.

3. To cause Access to display the Find dialog box in a macro, specify this option in the *Action* column.

4. Dragging a report name from the Navigation pane to the *Action* column in a macro causes Access to insert this option in the column.

5. Edit a macro by right-clicking the macro name in the Navigation pane and selecting this option at the shortcut menu.

6. At the first Command Button Wizard dialog box, click this option in the *Categories* list box to locate the *Run Macro* action.

7. A switchboard form is created using this utility. _____

8. This *Command* option at the Edit Switchboard Item dialog box instructs Access to replace the current menu with another switchboard page. _____

9. This *Command* option at the Edit Switchboard Item dialog box instructs Access to close the active database. _____

10. Open this dialog box to specify a display form to open whenever the database is opened. _____

11. Hide the Tables group in the Navigation pane by opening this dialog box. _____

12. A database is encrypted by doing this action. _____

13. A database by default opens in Shared mode. Open a database in this mode to restrict file access to one person. _____

14. Save a database as this type of file to disallow Design view and Layout view for the database objects. _____

15. View and/or change the macro security setting at this dialog box. _____

SKILLS check
Demonstrate Your Proficiency

Assessment

1 CREATE AND RUN MACROS

1. Open the database named **VantageVideos7.accdb** and enable the content.
2. Create the following macros. You determine appropriate comment text to document each action. Run each macro to make sure the macro works properly and then close the macro.
   a. A macro named Rpt_OrdbyProd that opens the WebProductsWithOrders report in Print Preview.
   b. A macro named Form_CustOrd that opens the WebCustOrders form, activates the control named *Lname*, and then opens the Find dialog box. Test the macro using the customer last name **Yiu**.
   c. A macro named Rpt_WebSales that opens the WebSalesWithTotalByDate report in report view.

3. Open the Rpt_OrdbyProd macro in Design view. Click the Office button and then click *Print*. At the Print Macro Definition dialog box, clear check marks as necessary until only the *Actions and Arguments* check box is checked and then click OK.
4. Print the Form_CustOrd macro and the Rpt_WebSales macro by completing a step similar to Step 3.

Assessment

2 EDIT A MACRO AND ASSIGN MACROS TO COMMAND BUTTONS

1. With the **VantageVideos7.accdb** database open, edit the Form_CustOrd macro to remove the OpenForm action. Save and close the revised macro.
2. Create command buttons to run macros as follows:
   a. Open the WebCustOrders form in Design view and create a command button at the right side of the Form Header section that runs the Form_CustOrd macro. You determine appropriate text to display on the face of the button. Save and close the form.
   b. Open the WebProducts form in Design view and create two command buttons as follows. Place each button at the bottom of the Detail section and determine appropriate text to display on the face of the button. Save and close the form.
      • A button at the left side of the form that runs the Rpt_OrdbyProd macro
      • A button at the right side of the form that runs the Rpt_WebSales macro
3. Open each form and test the buttons to make sure the macros display the correct form and reports.
4. Open each form in Form view. Use Print Screen to make a copy of the screen image. At a blank Word document, paste the image. Type your name, the chapter number, and the assessment number, and then print the document. Exit Word without saving.
5. Make sure all objects are closed.

Assessment

3 CREATE A SWITCHBOARD AND CONFIGURE DATABASE OPTIONS

1. With the **VantageVideos7.accdb** database open, create a switchboard form using the following information.
   a. The switchboard will be a single page only with command buttons for the following items in order. You determine appropriate text to display next to each command button.
      • Open the WebCustOrders form in Edit mode.
      • Open the WebProducts form in Edit mode.
      • Open the WebProductsWithOrders report.
      • Open the WebSalesWithTotalByDate report.
      • Exit the database.
   b. Edit the switchboard page name to *Main Menu*.
2. Set the switchboard form as the startup display form.
3. Create an application title for the database with the text **Vantage Videos Web Orders Database**.

4. Hide the navigation pane.
5. Turn on the *Check for new unassociated labels* error checking option. ***Note: Skip this step if you did not complete Project 3c where this option was turned off***.
6. Close and reopen the database to test your startup options. Click each button in the switchboard to make sure the option works correctly.
7. With the database open at the Main Menu, use Print Screen to make a copy of the screen image. At a blank Word document, paste the image. Type your name, the chapter number, and the assessment number, and then print the document. Exit Word without saving.
8. Close the **VantageVideos7.accdb** database.

Assessment

4 SECURE THE DATABASE

1. Open the **VantageVideos7.accdb** database in exclusive mode and enable the content.
2. Assign the database the password **v@18Wb**.
3. Save a copy of the database in the same folder and using the same name as an ACCDE file.
4. Close the **VantageVideos7.accdb** database.
5. Open the **VantageVideos7.accde** database using the correct password.
6. Use the last button in the switchboard form to exit the database.

CASE study
Apply Your Skills

Part 1

As you near completion of your work as an intern at Deering Sales, you decide to automate the database to make the application easier for the next intern to use. Open **DeeringSales7.accdb** and enable the content. Create four macros to accomplish the tasks in the bulleted list. You determine macro names and comment text.

- Open the ClientSales query in Datasheet view and in Edit mode.
- Open the ClientsWithSalesRepsAndSales report in Print Preview.
- Open the RepresentativesWithSales report in Report view.
- Move the control in a form to the *Customer* field and then open the Find dialog box. Assign this macro to a command button in the Clients form.

Check with your instructor for instructions on whether you need to print the macros and a screen image of the form with the command button.

Create a switchboard form for the database and set the form to display automatically when the database is opened. Add an appropriate application title for the database and hide the navigation pane. The switchboard should contain two pages as follows. You determine appropriate text to display for each menu item.

Page 1 – Main Menu

- Run the ClientSales query by executing the macro created in Part 1.
- Open the Clients form in edit mode.
- Open the Representatives form in edit mode.
- Go to the Reports Menu.
- Exit the database.

Page 2 – Reports Menu

- Open ClientsWithSalesRepsAndSales report.
- Open RepresentativesWithSales report.
- Return to Main Menu.

Close and reopen the database to test your startup options. Test each menu item to make sure each option works.

Check with your instructor for instructions on whether you need to print a screen image of each switchboard page.

Open a Help window and search for help content using the text **accdc** in the *Search* text box. Click the link to <u>Help Secure an Access 2007 database</u> and then find the information on *Package, sign, and distribute an Office Access 2007 database*. Read the information in Help and then compose a memo in your own words addressed to your instructor using Microsoft Word that provides the following answers.

- What type of file is an .accdc file?
- Why would you create an .accdc file?
- What must you have available in order to run this feature?
- Where is the Package and Sign feature located in Microsoft Office Access 2007?
- What does the recipient of a signed package have to do before he or she can use the database?

Save the memo in Word and name it **Access2007L2_C7_CS_P3-Memo.docx**. Print the memo and then exit Word.

Integrating Access Data

Upon successful completion of Chapter 8, you will be able to:

- Import data from another Access database
- Link to a table in another Access database
- Determine when to import versus link from external sources
- Reset or refresh links using Linked Table Manager
- Import data from a text file
- Save import specifications
- Export data in an Access table or query as a text file
- Save and run export specifications
- Save an object as an XPS file

Tutorial 8.2
Importing, Exporting, and
Linking Data

Integrating data between the applications within the Microsoft Office 2007 suite is easily accommodated with buttons in the External Data tab to import from Word and Excel and export to Word and Excel. Data is able to be exchanged between the Microsoft programs with formatting and data structure maintained. In some cases however, you may need to exchange data between Access and a non Microsoft program. In this chapter you will learn how to integrate data between individual Access database files and how to import and export in a text file format recognized by nearly all applications. You will also learn how to publish an Access object as an XPS file which is an XML document format.

Note: Before beginning computer projects, copy the Access2007L2C8 subfolder from the Access2007L2 folder on the CD that accompanies this textbook to your storage medium and then make Access2007L2C8 the active folder.

Project ① Import Data from External Sources

You will link and import data from a table in another Access database and from a comma delimited text file. You will also save import specifications for an import routine you expect to repeat often.

Importing Data from Another Access Database

Data stored in another Access database can be integrated into the active database by importing a copy of the source object(s). You can choose to copy multiple objects including duplicating the relationships between tables. When importing, you can specify to import the definition only or the definition and the data. To begin an import operation, click the External Data tab and then click the Import Access database button in the Import group to open the Get External Data - Access Database dialog box shown in Figure 8.1.

Figure 8.1 Get External Data - Access Database Dialog Box with Import Option Selected

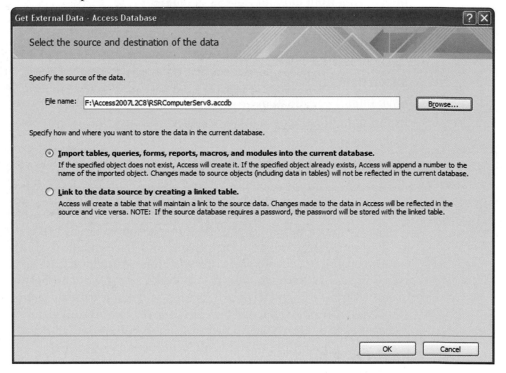

Access

Specify the source database containing the object(s) that you want to import by clicking the Browse button to open the File Open dialog box. Navigate to the drive and/or folder containing the source database and double-click the desired Access database file name to insert the database file name in the *File name* text box below *Specify the source of the data*. With *Import tables, queries, forms, reports, macros, and modules into the current database* selected by default, click OK. This opens the Import Objects dialog box shown in Figure 8.2. Select the objects to be imported, change options if necessary and click OK.

Figure 8.2 Import Objects Dialog Box

Click tab for object type to be imported, click object name, and then click OK. Use standard Windows selection keys Shift (adjacent objects) or Ctrl (nonadjacent objects) to select multiple objects.

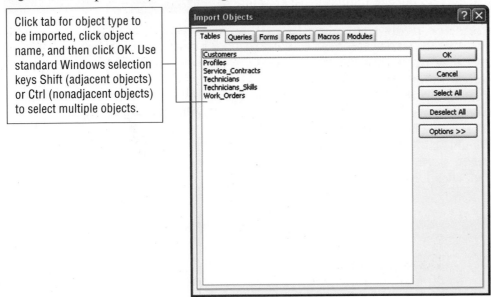

Click the Options button to display the *Import*, *Import Tables*, and *Import Queries* options shown in Figure 8.3. By default, Access imports relationships between tables; imports table structure definition and data; and imports a query as a query as opposed to importing the query as a table. Select or clear the options as required before clicking OK to begin the import operation.

Figure 8.3 Import Objects Dialog Box with Options Displayed

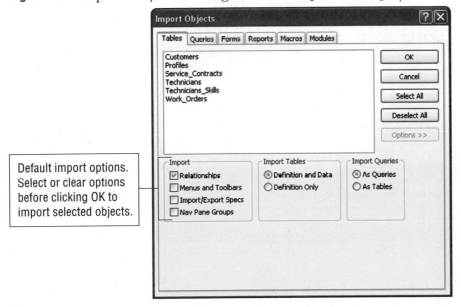

Default import options. Select or clear options before clicking OK to import selected objects.

1. Open the **RSRTechPay8.accdb** database and enable content.
2. Import the Technicians form from the *RSRComputerServ8.accdb* database by completing the following steps:
   a. Click the External Data tab.
   b. Click the Import Access database button [img] in the Import group.
   c. At the Get External Data - Access Database dialog box, click the Browse button.
   d. At the File Open dialog box, navigate to the Access2007L2C8 folder on your storage medium and double-click the file named *RSRComputerServ8.accdb*.
   e. With *Import tables, queries, forms, reports, macros, and modules into the current database* already selected, click OK.

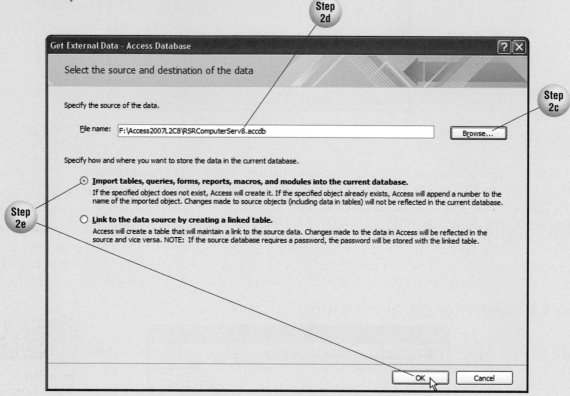

f. At the Import Objects dialog box, click the Forms tab.
g. Click *Technician_Maintenance* in the Forms list box and click OK.

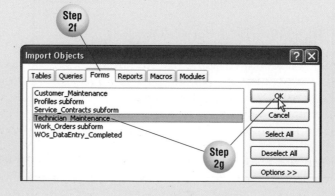

h. At the Get External Data - Access Database dialog box with the *Save import steps* check box cleared, click Close.

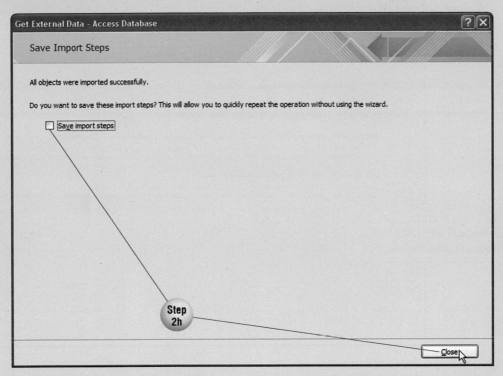

3. Access imports the Technician_Maintenance form and adds the object name to the navigation pane. The form will not be operational until after Project 1b since the tables needed to populate data in the form do not yet reside in the database. You did not import the dependent tables in this project because you want the tables that contain the records to be linked.

You can also copy an object by opening two copies of Access, one with the source database opened and the other with the destination database opened. With the source database window active, right-click the source object in the navigation pane and click Copy. Switch to the window containing the destination database, right-click in the navigation pane, and then click Paste. Close the Access window containing the source database.

Linking to a Table in Another Access Database

In Project 1a you imported a form which duplicates the source object from one database to another. If the source object is modified, the imported copy of the object is not altered. Link the data when importing if you want to ensure that the table in the destination database inherits any changes made to the source table. To create a linked table in the destination database, click the External Data tab and then click the Import Access database button. Click the Browse button, navigate to the drive and/or folder in which the source database is stored, and then double-click the source database file name. Click *Link to the data source by creating a linked table* at the Get External Data - Access Database dialog box and click OK as shown in Figure 8.4.

Link to Table in Another Database
1. Open destination database.
2. Click External Data tab.
3. Click Import Access database button.
4. Click Browse button.
5. Navigate to drive and/or folder.
6. Double-click source file name.
7. Click *Link to the data source by creating a linked table*.
8. Click OK.
9. Select desired table(s).
10. Click OK.

Figure 8.4 Get External Data - Access Database Dialog Box with Link
Option Selected

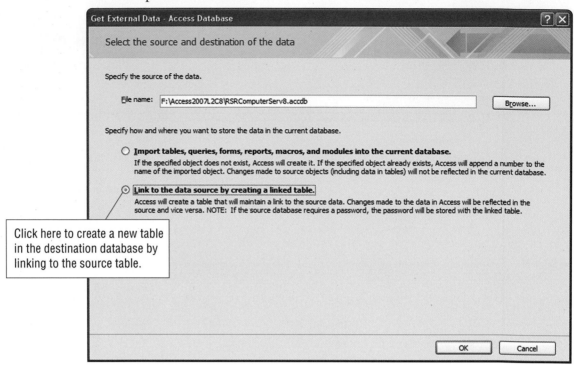

Click here to create a new table
in the destination database by
linking to the source table.

The Link Tables dialog box shown in Figure 8.5 opens with the Tables list box in which you select the tables to be linked. You can use the Shift key or the Ctrl key to select multiple tables to link all in one step. Linked tables are indicated in the navigation pane with a right-pointing blue arrow.

Figure 8.5 Link Tables Dialog Box

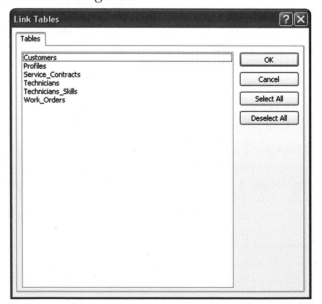

1. With the **RSRTechPay8.accdb** database open, link to two tables in the *RSRComputerServ8.accdb* database by completing the following steps:
   a. With the External Data tab still active, click the Import Access database button.
   b. Click the Browse button and double-click the file named *RSRComputerServ8.accdb*.
   c. Click *Link to the data source by creating a linked table* and click OK.

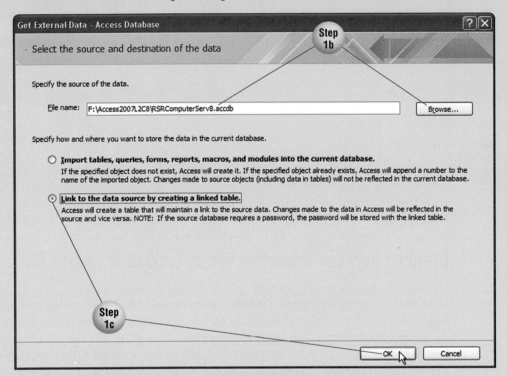

   d. At the Link Tables dialog box, click *Technicians* in the Tables list box.
   e. Hold down the Shift key and click *Technicians_Skills* in the Tables list box.
   f. Click OK.

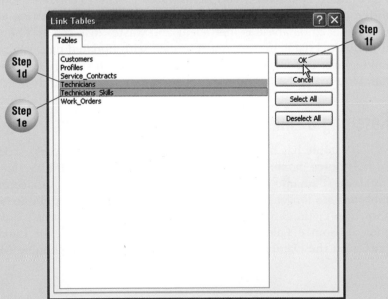

2. Access links the two tables to the source database and adds the table names to the navigation pane. Linked tables display with a blue right-pointing arrow next to the table icon.
3. Double-click the Technician_Maintenance form to view the form with the first record displayed. Print the form for the selected record only and then close the form.
4. Double-click the Technicians table to view the table datasheet and then close the datasheet.
5. Double-click the Technicians_Skills table to view the table datasheet and then close the datasheet.

> Linked table names display with a blue right-pointing arrow next to the table icon.

When a table is linked, the source data does not reside in the destination database. Opening a linked table causes Access to dynamically update the datasheet with the information in the source table. You can edit the source data in either the source database table or the linked table in the destination database.

Deciding between Importing versus Linking to Source Data

In most cases you would import data into Access from another Access database or some other external source if the source data is not likely to be updated. Since importing creates a copy of the data in two locations, changes or updates to the data must be duplicated in both copies. Duplicating the change or update increases the risk of data entry error or missed updates in one or the other location.

If the data is updated frequently, link to the external data source so that all changes are only required to be entered once. Since the data exists only in the source location, the potential for error or missed updates is reduced.

In another situation you may choose to link to the data source when several different databases require a common table such as Inventory. To duplicate the table in each database is inefficient and wastes disk space. The potential for error if individual databases are not refreshed with updated data is also a risk that favors linking over importing. In this scenario a master Inventory table in a separate shared database would be linked to all of the other databases that need to use the data.

Resetting a Link Using Linked Table Manager

When a table has been linked to another database, Access stores the full path to the source database file name along with the linked table name. Changing the database file name or folder location for the source database means the linked table will no longer function. Access provides the Linked Table Manager dialog box shown in Figure 8.6 to allow you to reset or refresh a table's link to reconnect to the data source. Click the Database Tools tab and click the Linked Table Manager button in the Database Tools group to open the Linked Table Manager dialog box.

Refresh Link(s)
1. Click Database Tools tab.
2. Click Linked Table Manager button.
3. Click Select All button or click individual linked table.
4. Click OK.
5. Navigate to drive and/or folder.
6. Double-click source database file name.
7. Click OK.
8. Click Close button.

Linked Table Manager

Figure 8.6 Linked Table Manager Dialog Box

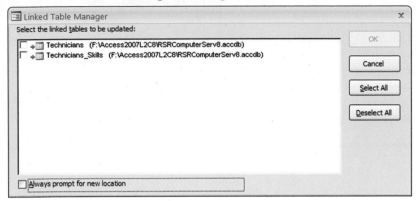

Click the check box next to the link you want to refresh and then click OK.
Access displays a message box stating that the link was successfully refreshed or
displays a dialog box in which you navigate to the new location for the data source.

Project 1c Refreshing a Link

1. With the **RSRTechPay8.accdb** database open, move the location of the
   RSRComputerServ8.accdb database by completing the following steps:
   a. Display the Open dialog box.
   b. Right-click *RSRComputerServ8.accdb* in the file list box and then click *Cut* at the
      shortcut menu.
   c. Click the Up One Level button [icon] in the Open dialog box toolbar to move to the
      parent folder in your storage medium.
   d. Right-click in a blank area of the file list box and click *Paste*.
   e. Close the Open dialog box. With the location of the source database now moved, the
      linked tables are no longer connected to the correct location.
2. Refresh the links to the two tables by completing the following steps:
   a. Click the Database Tools tab.
   b. Click the Linked Table Manager button [icon] in the Database Tools group.
   c. At the Linked Table Manager dialog box, click the Select All button to select all
      linked objects.
   d. Click OK. Access attempts to refresh the links. Since the source database has been
      moved, Access displays a dialog box in which you select the new location.

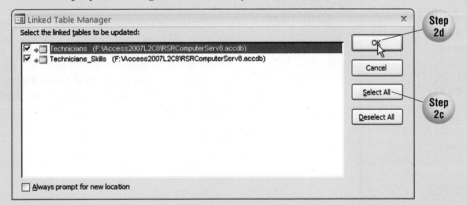

e. At the Select New Location of Technicians dialog box, locate and then double-click *RSRComputerServ8.accdb*.

f. Click OK at the Linked Table Manager message box that indicates all selected links were successfully refreshed.

3. Click the Close button at the Linked Table Manager dialog box.

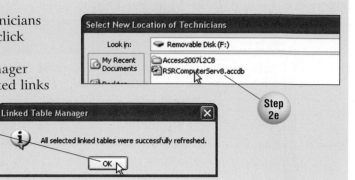

Step 2e

Step 2f

Linked Table Manager
All selected linked tables were successfully refreshed.
OK

Import Data from Comma Separated Text File
1. Click External Data tab.
2. Click Import text file button.
3. Click Browse button.
4. Navigate to drive and/or folder.
5. Double-click .csv file name.
6. Click OK.
7. Click Next.
8. If applicable, click *First Row Contains Field Names* check box.
9. Click Next.
10. Choose primary key field.
11. Click Next.
12. Click Finish.

Importing Data to Access from a Text File

A text file is often used to exchange data between dissimilar programs since the file format is recognized by nearly all applications. Text files contain no formatting and consist of letters, numbers, punctuation symbols, and a few control characters only. Two commonly used text file formats separate fields with either a tab character (delimited file format) or a comma (comma separated file format). The text file you will use in Project 1d is shown in a Notepad window in Figure 8.7. If necessary, you can view and edit a text file in Notepad prior to importing if the source application inserts characters that you wish to delete.

To import a text file into Access, click the Import text file button in the Import group of the External Data tab. Access opens the Get External Data - Text File dialog box which is similar to the dialog box used to import data from another Access database. When importing a text file, Access adds an append option in addition to the import and link options in the *Specify how and where you want to store the data in the current database* section. Click the Browse button to navigate to the location of the source file and double-click the source file name to launch the Import Text Wizard which guides you through the import process through four dialog boxes.

Figure 8.7 Project 1d Text File Contents in Notepad

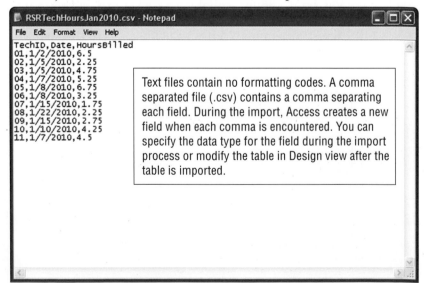

RSRTechHoursJan2010.csv - Notepad
File Edit Format View Help

```
TechID,Date,HoursBilled
01,1/2/2010,6.5
02,1/5/2010,2.25
03,1/5/2010,4.75
04,1/7/2010,5.25
05,1/8/2010,6.75
06,1/8/2010,3.25
07,1/15/2010,1.75
08,1/22/2010,2.25
09,1/15/2010,2.75
10,1/10/2010,4.25
11,1/7/2010,4.5
```

Text files contain no formatting codes. A comma separated file (.csv) contains a comma separating each field. During the import, Access creates a new field when each comma is encountered. You can specify the data type for the field during the import process or modify the table in Design view after the table is imported.

HINT

Most programs can export data in a text file. If you need to use data from a program that is not compatible with Access, check the source program's export options for a text file format.

Text File

Saving Import Specifications

QUICK STEPS

In Access 2007 you can save import specifications for an import routine that you are likely to repeat. The last step in the Get External Data dialog box displays a *Save import steps* check box. Click the check box to expand the dialog box to display the *Save as* and *Description* text boxes. Type a unique name to assign to the import routine and a brief description that describes the steps. Click the Save Import button to complete the import and store the specifications. Click the *Create Outlook Task* check box if you want to create an Outlook 2007 task that you can set up as a recurring item for an import or export operation that is repeated at fixed intervals.

Save Import Specifications
1. At last Get External Data dialog box, click *Save import steps*.
2. If necessary, edit name in *Save as* text box.
3. Type description in *Description* text box.
4. Click Save Import button.

Project 1d Importing Data from a Comma Separated Text File and Saving Importing Specifications

1. With the **RSRTechPay8.accdb** database open, select a text file to import containing hours billed for each technician by completing the following steps:
   a. Click the External Data tab.
   b. Click the Import text file button ▶️ Text File in the Import group.
   c. At the Get External Data - Text File dialog box, click the Browse button.
   d. At the File Open dialog box, navigate to the Access2007L2C8 folder on your storage medium if necessary.
   e. Double-click the file named *RSRTechHoursJan2010.csv*.
   f. With *Import the source data into a new table in the current database* already selected, click OK. This launches the Import Text Wizard.

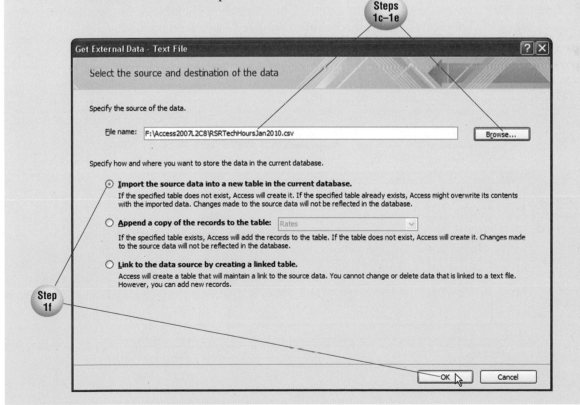

2. Import the comma separated data using the Import Text Wizard by completing the following steps:
   a. At the first Import Text Wizard dialog box, with *Delimited* selected as the format, click Next. Notice the preview window in the lower half of the dialog box displays a sample of the data in the source text file. Delimited files use commas or tabs as separators while fixed width files use spaces.

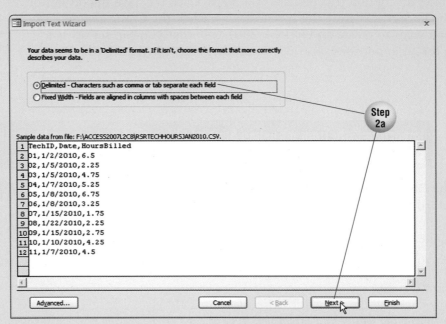

   b. At the second Import Text Wizard dialog box, with *Comma* already selected as the delimiter, click the *First Row Contains Field Names* check box and then click Next. Notice the preview section already shows the data set in columns similar to a table datasheet.

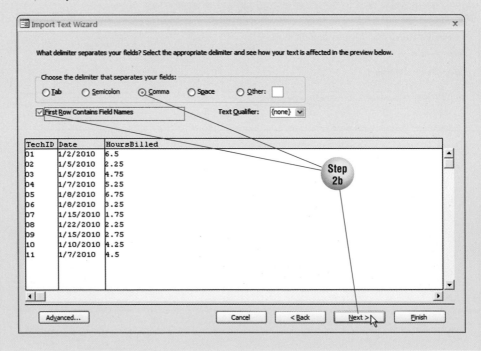

c. At the third Import Text Wizard dialog box with the *TechID* column in the preview section selected, click the down-pointing arrow next to *Data Type* in the *Field Options* section and then click *Text* at the drop-down list.

d. Click Next.

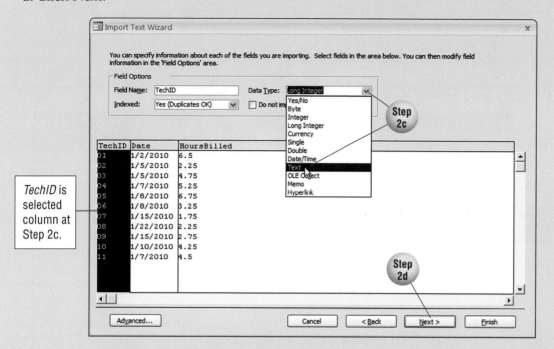

TechID is selected column at Step 2c.

e. At the fourth Import Text Wizard dialog box, click *Choose my own primary key*. Access automatically inserts the first field name, *TechID*, in the list box which is the correct primary key field.

f. Click Next.

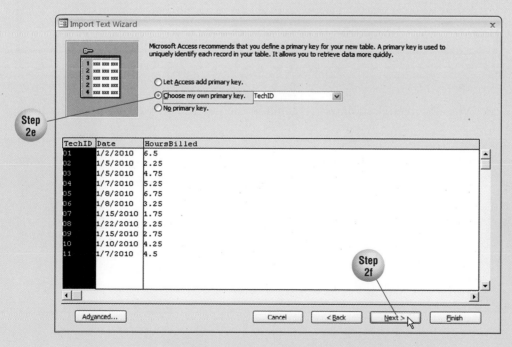

g. At the last Import Text Wizard dialog box, with *RSRTechHoursJan2010* entered in the *Import to Table* text box, click Finish.
3. Save the import specifications in case you want to run this import again at a future date by completing the following steps:
a. At the Get External Data - Text File dialog box, click the *Save import steps* check box. This causes the *Save as* and *Description* text boxes to appear as well as the *Create an Outlook Task* section. By default Access creates a name in the *Save as* text box with *Import-* preceding the file name containing the imported data.
b. Click in the *Description* text box and type **CSV file with hours billed by technicians**.
c. Click the Save Import button.

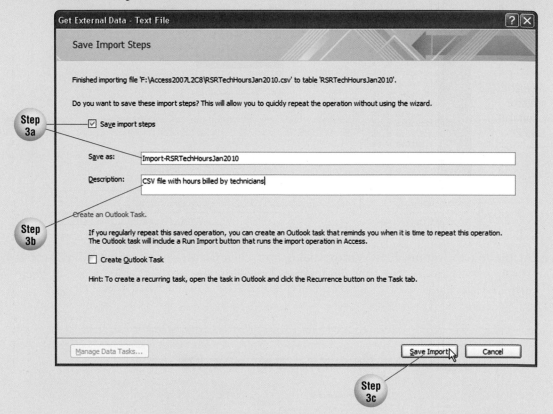

4. Double-click the RSRTechHoursJan2010 table in the navigation pane to open the table datasheet.
5. Print and then close the datasheet.
6. Close the **RSRTechPay8.accdb** database.

Repeating a Saved Import Process

Once an import routine has been saved, you can repeat the import process by opening the Manage Data Tasks dialog box with the Saved Imports tab selected shown in Figure 8.8. To do this, click the External Data tab and click the Saved Imports button in the Import group. Click the desired import name and click the Run button to instruct Access to repeat the import operation.

Saved
Imports

Figure 8.8 Manage Data Tasks Dialog Box with Saved Imports Tab Selected

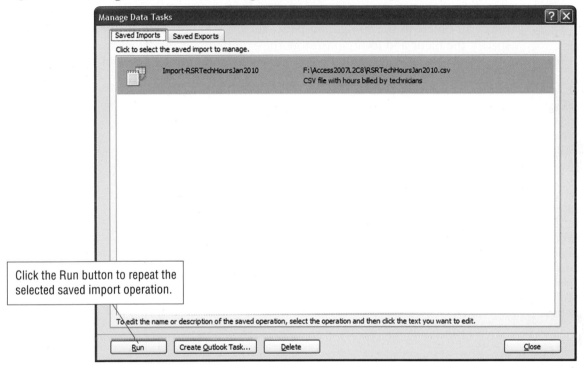

Click the Run button to repeat the selected saved import operation.

Exporting Access Data in a Text File

The Export group in the External Data tab contains buttons with which you can export Access data from a table, query, form, or report to other applications such as Excel or Word. If you need to work with data from Access in a program that is not part of the Microsoft Office suite, you can click the More button in the Export group to see if a file format converter exists for the application that you will be using. For example, the More button contains options to export in dBase, Paradox, or Lotus 1-2-3 file formats.

If a file format converter does not exist for the program that you will be using, export the data as a text file since most applications recognize and can import a text data file. Access includes the Export Text Wizard which is launched after you select an object in the navigation pane, click the Export to text button, and then specify the name and location to store the exported text file. The Export Text Wizard uses similar steps as those that you used when you imported a text file in Project 1d.

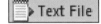

Project 2a   Exporting a Query as a Text File

1. Display the Open dialog box and move the *RSRComputerServ8.accdb* database back to the Access2007L2C8 folder on your storage medium.
2. Open the **RSRComputerServ8.accdb** database and enable content.
3. Export the TotalWorkOrders query as a text file by completing the following steps:
   a. Select the query named TotalWorkOrders in the navigation pane.
   b. Click the External Data tab.
   c. Click the Export to text file button in the Export group.

d. At the Export - Text File dialog box, click the Browse button.

e. At the File Save dialog box, navigate to the Access2007L2C8 folder on your storage medium.

f. With the default file name of *TotalWorkOrders.txt* in the *File name* text box, click the Save button.

g. Click OK.

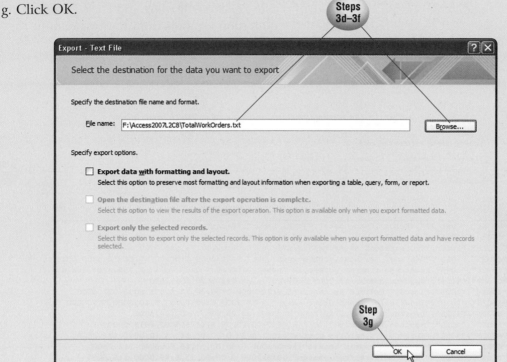

h. At the first Export Text Wizard dialog box with *Delimited* selected as the format, click Next. Notice in the preview section of the dialog box a comma separates each field and data in a field defined with the text data type is encased in quotation symbols.

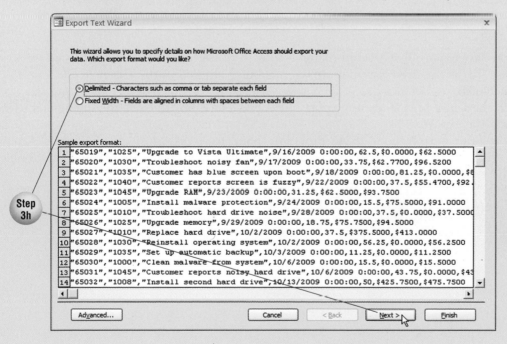

i. At the second Export Text Wizard dialog box, with *Comma* selected as the delimiter character that separates the fields, click the *Include Field Names on First Row* check box. Access adds a row to the top of the data in the preview section with the field names. Each field name is encased in quotation symbols.

j. Click the down-pointing arrow next to the *Text Qualifier* list box and click *{none}* at the drop-down list. Access removes all of the quotation symbols from the text data in the preview section.

k. Click Next.

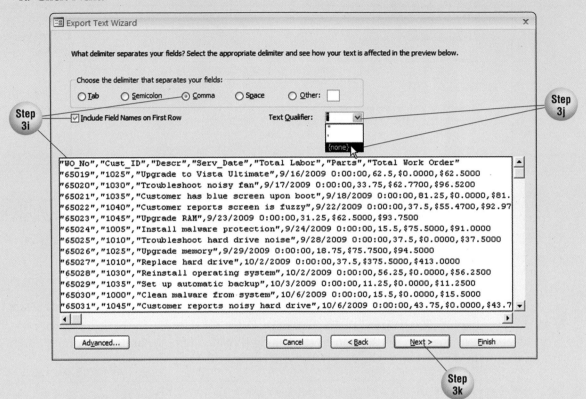

l. At the last Export Text Wizard dialog box, with *[d]:\Access2007L2C8\TotalWorkOrders.txt* (where [d] is the drive for your storage medium) entered in the *Export to File* text box, click Finish.

m. Click the Close button at the Export - Text File dialog box to close the dialog box without saving the export steps.

4. Click the Start button, point to All Programs, point to Accessories, and then click Notepad.

5. At a blank Notepad window, click File and then click Open. Navigate to and then double-click the exported file named *TotalWorkOrders.txt*.

6. Click File and then click Print to print the exported text file.

7. Exit Notepad.

Saving Export Specifications

QUICK STEPS

Save Export Specifications
1. At last Export - Text File dialog box, click *Save export steps*.
2. If necessary, edit name in *Save as* text box.
3. Type description in *Description* text box.
4. Click Save Export button.

Saved Exports

Access allows you to save export steps similar to how you learned to save import specifications for an import routine that you are likely to repeat. The last step in the Export - Text File dialog box displays a *Save export steps* check box. Click the check box to expand the dialog box options to display the *Save as* and *Description* text boxes. Type a unique name to assign to the export routine and a brief description that describes the steps. Click the Save Export button to complete the export operation and store the specifications for later use.

Project 2b Exporting a Query as a Text File and Saving Export Steps

1. With the **RSRComputerServ8.accdb** database open, export the TotalLabor query as a text file using Tab as the delimiter character by completing the following steps:
   a. Select the query named TotalLabor in the navigation pane.
   b. Click the Export to text file button in the Export group.
   c. With *[d]:\Access2007L2C8\TotalLabor.txt* (where [d] is the drive for your storage medium) entered in the *File name* text box, click OK.
   d. Complete the steps in the Export Text Wizard as follows:
      1) Click Next at the first dialog box with *Delimited* selected.
      2) Click *Tab* as the delimiter character, click the *Include Field Names on First Row* check box, change the *Text Qualifier* to *{none}*, and then click Next.
      3) Click Finish.

e. Click the *Save export steps* check box at the Export - Text File dialog box.

f. Click in the *Description* text box and type **TotalLabor query for RSR Computer Service work orders as a text file.**

g. Click the Save Export button.

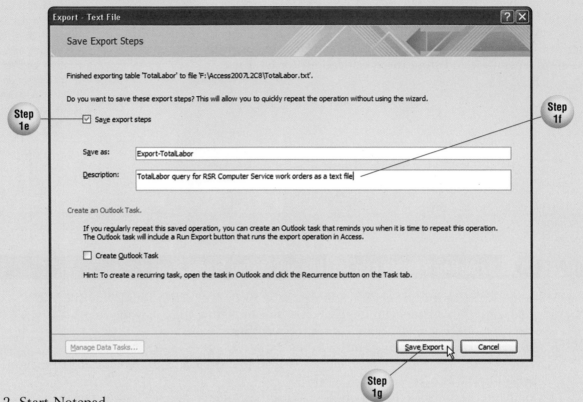

Step 1e

Step 1f

Step 1g

2. Start Notepad.

3. At a blank Notepad window, open the exported file named *TotalLabor.txt*.

4. Print the exported text file and then exit Notepad.

Repeating a Saved Export Process

Saved Exports

Once an export routine has been saved, you can repeat the export process by opening the Manage Data Tasks dialog box with the Saved Exports tab selected shown in Figure 8.9 by clicking the Saved Exports button in the Export group in the External Data tab. Click the desired export name and click the Run button to instruct Access to repeat the export operation.

Figure 8.9 Manage Data Tasks Dialog Box with Saved Exports Tab Selected

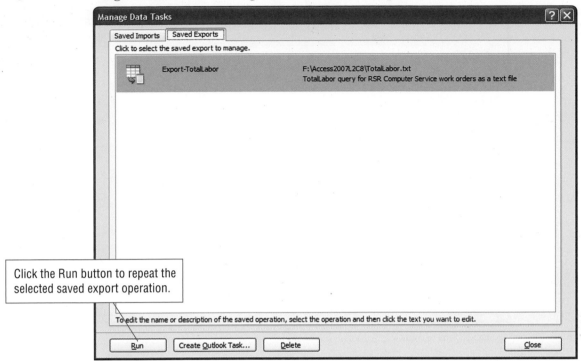

Click the Run button to repeat the selected saved export operation.

 **Publish a Database Object**

You will publish a report as an XPS file.

Publishing Database Objects as PDF or XPS Files

An add-in application for the Microsoft Office 2007 suite is available for download that allows you to publish Access 2007 objects as a PDF or XPS file. When the add-in application has been downloaded, the Export group in the External Data tab contains a button labeled PDF or XPS. Click the object in the navigation pane that you wish to export and then click the PDF or XPS button to open the Publish as PDF or XPS dialog box shown in Figure 8.10.

QUICK STEPS

Publish Object as PDF or XPS
1. Select object in navigation pane.
2. Click External Data tab.
3. Click PDF or XPS button.
4. If necessary, navigate to desired drive and/or folder.
5. If necessary, change file name.
6. If necessary, change *Save as type* to *XPS* or *PDF*.
7. Click Publish button.
8. Click Close button.

PDF or XPS

Figure 8.10 Publish as PDF or XPS Dialog Box

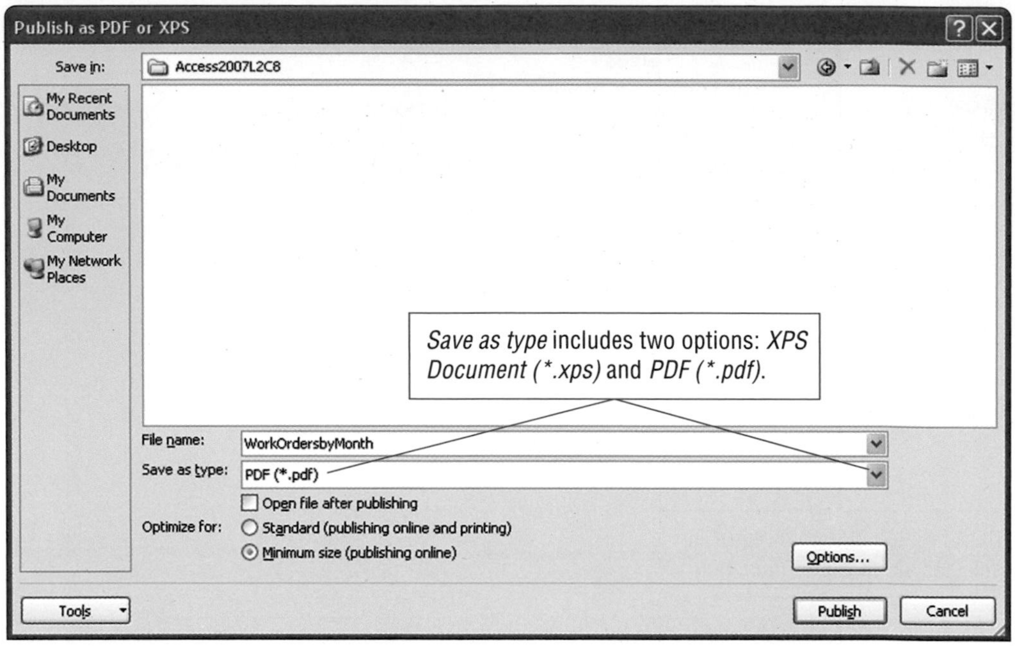

XPS stands for *XML Paper Specification* which is a fixed-layout format with all formatting preserved so that when the file is shared electronically and viewed or printed, the recipients of the file see the format as it appeared in Access and cannot easily change the data. The *Save as type* option also includes *PDF*. PDF stands for *Portable Document Format* which is also a fixed-layout format with all formatting preserved for file sharing purposes.

Once you have selected the required file format, navigate to the desired drive and/or folder in which the file should be stored and change the file name if necessary. Click the Publish button when finished to create the file.

Finding the PDF or XPS Add-in for Download

In order to publish an object in PDF or XPS format, you have to first download the free add-in from the Microsoft Web site. If the Export group in the External Data tab does not contain the PDF or XPS button, click the Office button, point to Save As, and then click *Find add-ins for other file formats* as shown in Figure 8.11.

Figure 8.11 *Find add-ins for other file formats* Option in Office Button Drop-
down List

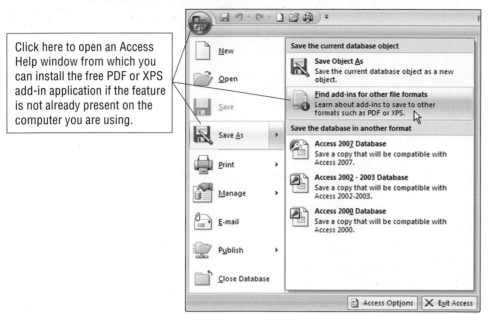

Click here to open an Access Help window from which you can install the free PDF or XPS add-in application if the feature is not already present on the computer you are using.

This causes an Access Help window to open with the topic *Enable support for other file formats, such as PDF or XPS* displayed. In the *What do you want to do?* section, click the <u>Install and use the Save as PDF or XPS add-in from Microsoft</u> hyperlink. At the next Help topic, click the <u>Microsoft Save as PDF or XPS Add-in for 2007 Microsoft Office programs</u> hyperlink. This link connects you to the page with the add-in application at the Microsoft Download Center. You will be required to first click the Continue button to validate that you have a valid copy of Microsoft Office 2007 installed on the computer you are using. If you do not have the Office Genuine Advantage software installed, you will be prompted to install the program that checks your system for valid Microsoft software. Follow the prompts to install the software in order to proceed to the next step.

Once your copy of Microsoft Office 2007 has been validated as genuine, the Continue button changes to the Download button. Click the Download button to run the application that installs the PDF or XPS application. Follow the prompts to install the add-in. A message displays when the installation is completed. Click OK, close Internet Explorer, and then close the Access Help window.

Once installed, the PDF or XPS button appears in the Export group in the External Data tab and also on the Office button Save As drop-down list.

Note: You may need to install the PDF and XPS add-in application before completing this project. If you are using a computer in a school computer lab, check with your instructor before installing software.

1. With the **RSRComputerServ8.accdb** database open, export the WorkOrdersbyMonth report as an XPS file by completing the following steps:

   a. Select the WorkOrdersbyMonth report in the Navigation pane.

   b. Click the PDF or XPS button 🖼 in the Export group.

   c. If necessary, navigate to the Access2007L2C8 folder at the Publish as PDF or XPS dialog box.

   d. With *WorkOrdersbyMonth* entered in the *File name* text box, publish the report as an XPS file by completing the following steps:

      1) If necessary, click the *Save as type* list arrow and then click *XPS Document (*.xps)*.

      2) If necessary, click the *Open file after publishing* check box to clear the check mark.

      3) Click the Publish button.

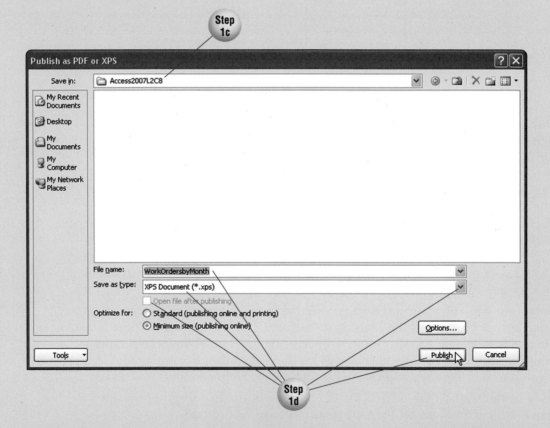

   e. Click the Close button at the Export - XPS dialog box to close the dialog box without saving the export steps.

2. Close the **RSRComputerServ8.accdb** database.

Viewing an XPS Document

Similar to PDF files that require the Adobe Reader program in which to view documents, you need a viewer in order to read an XPS document. The viewer is provided by Microsoft and is included with Windows Vista; however, to view an XPS document using Windows XP, you may need to download the viewer application. If you try to open an XPS document by double-clicking the file in a file list and are presented with a Windows dialog box in which a message displays that Windows cannot open the file, click the Cancel button to close the dialog box and then go to the Microsoft Web site. Search for the viewer by typing *XPS Document Viewer* in the search box. Click the <u>View and Generate XPS</u> hyperlink. At the View and Generate XPS page, you can choose to download the Microsoft XPS Essentials Pack which includes a stand-alone XPS viewer application or the Microsoft .NET Framework 3.0 application which includes XPS viewing and generating capability. Since Microsoft Office 2007 includes the ability to publish as XPS, consider the XPS Essentials Pack if you simply want to view XPS files that you generate from Office.

Select, download and install the appropriate software in order to open, view, and/or print a file with the *.xps* extension. The WorkOrdersbyMonth.xps document created in Project 3 is shown in the stand-alone XPS viewer program in Figure 8.12.

Figure 8.12 WorkOrdersbyMonth.xps Opened Using XPS Viewer in Microsoft XPS Essentials Pack

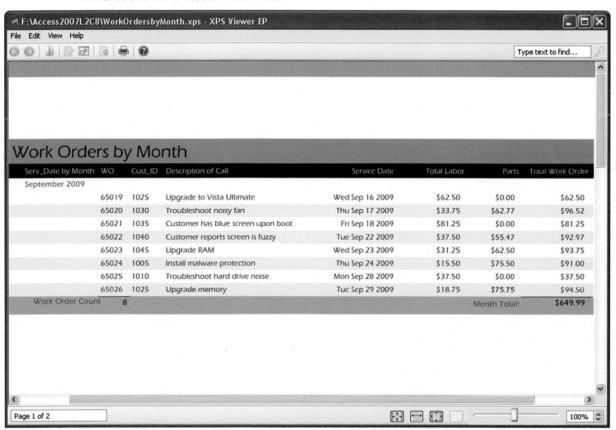

The .NET Framework 3.0 application opens XPS documents in an Internet Explorer window. The WorkOrdersbyMonth.xps document created in Project 3 is shown in an Internet Explorer window in Figure 8.13.

Figure 8.13 WorkOrdersbyMonth.xps Opened in Internet Explorer

In this chapter you have learned to import data from another Microsoft program and to import and export using a text file format to exchange data between Access and other non-Microsoft programs. To distribute Access data with formatting preserved in a non-editable format, publish an object as a PDF or XPS file.

CHAPTER summary

- An object in another Access database can be imported into the active database using the Import Access database button in the Import group of the External Data tab.

- At the Get External Data - Access Database dialog box, select the source database location and file name.

- At the Import Objects dialog box, select the objects you wish to copy into the current database and click OK.

- If the source object is a table, you can choose to import or link the source table.

- In a linked table, the data is not copied into the active database but resides only in the source database.

- You can edit source data in a linked table in either the source or destination database.

- Use an import routine if the source data is not likely to require changes or updates.

- Link to source data that requires frequent changes to reduce the potential for data entry or missed update errors.

- You may also decide to link to a source table that is shared among several different databases within an organization.

- Access stores the full path to the source database when a table is linked. If you move the location of the source database the links will need to be refreshed.

- Open the Linked Table Manager dialog box by clicking the Linked Table Manager button in the Database Tools group in the Database Tools tab to refresh links.

- A text file is often used to exchange data between dissimilar programs because a text file is recognized by nearly all applications.

- Import a text file into an Access database by clicking the Import text file button in the Import group of the External Data tab.

- When a text file is selected for import, Access launches the Text Import Wizard which guides you through the steps to import the text into a table.

- If an import operation is often repeated, consider saving the import steps so that you can run the import routine without having to walk through each step.

- Save import steps at the last Get External Data dialog box.

- Open the Manage Data Tasks dialog box to run a saved import by clicking the Saved Imports button in the Import group of the External Data tab.

- Export Access data in a text file format using the Export Text Wizard by clicking the Export to text button in the Export group of the External Data tab.

- Within the Export Text Wizard you are prompted to choose the text format, delimiter character, field names, text qualifier symbols, and export path and file name.

- You can save export steps at the last Export - Text File dialog box in order to repeat an export operation.

- Click the Saved Exports button in the Export group of the External Data tab to run a saved export routine.

- Access includes a feature that allows you to save an object in XPS or PDF format in order to distribute Access data with formatting preserved in a non-editable format.
- In order to publish an object in XPS or PDF format, you need to have an add-in installed.
- Access provides an option from the Office button Save As drop-down list to connect to the download page if the add-in application is not installed on the computer you are using.
- Publish an object by selecting the object name in the navigation pane and then clicking the PDF or XPS button in the Export group in the External Data tab.
- To view a document exported in XPS format you need a viewer that is available from Microsoft.

COMMANDS review

FEATURE	RIBBON TAB, GROUP	BUTTON	OFFICE BUTTON DROP-DOWN LIST
Export data as Text file	External Data, Export	Text File	
Import or link data from Access database	External Data, Import		
Import data from text file	External Data, Import	Text File	
Linked Table Manager	Database Tools, Database Tools		
Save object as XPS file	External Data, Export		Save As
Saved exports	External Data, Export		
Saved imports	External Data, Import		

CONCEPTS check

Test Your Knowledge

Completion: In the space provided at the right, indicate the correct term, command, or number.

1. Click this button at the Import Objects dialog box to choose whether or not relationships between tables will be imported.

   _____

2. Click this button in the Import group in the External Data tab to link to a table in another Access database.

   _____

3. Data that is not likely to be changed should be brought into the active database from another database using this method.

   _____

4. Data that is updated frequently should be brought into the active database from another database using this method.

   _____

5. If the location of a source database has moved, open this dialog box to refresh the link to the source table.

   _____

6. This type of file format is used to exchange data between programs for which an application-specific file format converter is not available.

   _____

7. A file in which each field is separated by a comma has this file extension.

   _____

8. Click this check box at the last Get External Data dialog box to store the steps used in the import process in order to repeat the import routine at a future date.

   _____

9. The Export Text Wizard is launched from this button in the Export group in the External Data tab.

   _____

10. XPS is a document format that stands for this type of document specification.

    _____

SKILLS check

Demonstrate Your Proficiency

Assessment

1 IMPORT AND LINK OBJECTS FROM ANOTHER ACCESS DATABASE

1. Open the database named **VantageStock8.accdb** and enable content.
2. Using **VantageVideos8.accdb** as the data source, integrate the following objects into the active database.
   a. Import the form named WebProducts.
   b. Link to the tables named WebProducts, WebOrders, and WebOrderDetails.
3. Display the Relationships window and create a relationship between the WebProducts and WebProductsCost tables using the field named *WebProdID*. Save and close the Relationships window.
4. Modify the WebProducts form as follows:
   a. Open the form in Layout view.
   b. Delete the *Retail Value* label and text box control objects.
   c. Display the Field List pane and show all tables in the pane. Expand the field list for the WebProductsCost table.
   d. Add the field named *CostPrice* below the *Selling Price* field in the form.
   e. Move, resize, and format the field as necessary so that the cost price displays similarly to the selling price.
   f. Modify the form title to *INVENTORY STOCK AND PRICING*.
   g. If necessary, move the clip art image to the right to avoid overlap.
5. Save the revised form, print the form for the first record only, and then close the form.
6. Open the WebProdCostsWithSupp query in Design view and modify the query as follows:
   a. Add the WebProducts table to the query.
   b. Add the *SellPrice* field to the query design grid, placing the field between the *Product* and *CostPrice* columns.
   c. Add a calculated column at the right of the *CostPrice* column that subtracts the cost price from the selling price. Display the column heading *Gross Profit*.
7. Save the revised query and then run the query.
8. Print the query in landscape orientation and then close the query.

Assessment

2   IMPORT A TEXT FILE

1. With the **VantageStock8.accdb** database open, append records from a text file as follows:
   - The data source file is named ***WebProducts.csv***.
   - Append a copy of the records to the end of the existing WebProductsCost table.
   - Save the import steps. You determine an appropriate description for the import routine.
2. Open the WebProductsCost table and print the table datasheet.
3. Close the datasheet.
4. Close the **VantageStock8.accdb** database.

Assessment

3   EXPORT AND PUBLISH ACCESS DATA

1. Open the **VantageVideos8.accdb** database and enable content.
2. Export the query named CustWebOrders to a text file as follows:
   - Include the field names and remove the quotation symbols.
   - Save the export steps. You determine an appropriate description for the export routine.
3. Open Notepad, open the CustWebOrders.txt file, and then print the document.
4. Exit Notepad.
5. Publish the WebSalesWithTotalByDate report as a PDF document named TotalWebSales.pdf.
6. Open the TotalWebSales.pdf document in Adobe Reader and print the document.
7. Exit Adobe Reader.
8. Close the **VantageVideos8.accdb** database.

CASE study
Apply Your Skills

Part 1

You are ready to finish your work as an intern at Deering Sales. As one of your last assignments, the office manager has asked you to integrate the sales database with the human resources database. Open the database named **DeeringHR8.accdb** and enable content. Import the following queries as tables from the database named **DeeringSales8.accdb**: SalesByRep and SalesRepWithQuotas. ***Hint: At the Import Objects dialog box, click the Options button in order to instruct Access to convert the query to a table upon import.***

After importing, modify the tables as follows:

- Add an Autonumber field to the beginning of the SalesByRep table with the field name *SalesID* and assign the field the primary key.
- Make *RepID* the primary key field in the SalesRepWithQuotas table.

Create a one-to-many relationship between the Reps_HireDateComm table (one table) and the SalesByRep table (many table). Create a one-to-one relationship between the Reps_HireDateComm table and the SalesRepWithQuotas table.

Create a query to calculate the commission owed on each sale using the Reps_HireDateComm and SalesByRep tables. Name the query SalesCommissions. You determine appropriate fields to include in the query results datasheet and the required calculation. Add a total to the bottom of the calculated column to show the total commissions owing in the query results datasheet and then print the datasheet.

Create a report based on the SalesCommissions query that is grouped by the sales representative last name. Include a subtotal in each group to show the total commission owed to each sales representative, as well as a grand total at the end of the report. Save the report using the default name and print the report.

Part 2

The sales manager would like the SalesByRep data exported from the database to use in a custom software package that accepts comma separated data files. Create the text file for the manager including field names and quotations symbols as text qualifiers. Save the export steps since the manager has advised this data exchange file will be required often. Print the text file for your records.

The CEO has requested an electronic copy of the SalesCommissions report you created in Part 1. The CEO is not well versed in Access and has asked that you send the report with the formatting as displayed in Access but in a file that can be opened on her laptop that does not have Microsoft Office software. Publish the report using the default name and e-mail the report to your professor as an e-mail attachment using an appropriate subject line and message.

Part 3

You want to find out if Access and Outlook can integrate to collect data using e-mail messages and automatically update tables when replies are received. You decide to research this topic using Access Help. Use the search phrase *collect data using e-mail* to locate a related Help topic. Locate and read an article that describes when to use data collection and the steps that should be completed before starting to ensure a successful data collection process. Compose a memo in your own words addressed to your instructor using Microsoft Word that provides the following information.

- Describe two scenarios in which data collection using Access and Outlook would be appropriate.
- What is the name of the wizard that assists you with completing and sending the data entry form as an e-mail message?
- What software is needed by the recipients of the e-mail message in order to view the form?
- Which field data types cannot be updated using this feature?

Save the memo in Word and name it **Access2007_L2_C8_CS_P3-Memo.docx**. Print the memo and then exit Word.

Advanced Reports, Access Tools, and Customizing Access

ASSESSING proficiency

In this unit you have learned to design and create reports with grouping, sorting, totals, and subreports; to use Access tools to analyze tables and improve database efficiency; to automate a database using macros and a switchboard; to configure startup options and customize the database and navigation pane; and to integrate Access data with other programs.

Note: Before beginning unit assessments, copy to your storage medium the Access2007L2U2 subfolder from the Access2007L2 folder on the CD that accompanies this textbook and then make Access2007L2U2 the active folder.

Assessment 1 Import Data from Text Files and Create Reports for a Property Management Database

1. Open **BenchmarkPropMgtU2.accdb** from the Access2007L2U2 folder on your storage medium and enable content. In this unit you will continue working with the residential property management database started in Unit 1. The database design and objects have been modified since Unit 1 based on feedback from the property manager and the office staff.

2. Import data into tables from two text files as follows. Save each set of import specifications for future use. You determine an appropriate description for each set of import steps.
   a. Append the data in the text file named *TenantsU2.csv* to the Tenants table.
   b. Append the data in the text file named *LeasesU2.csv* to the Leases table.

3. Design and create reports as follows:
   a. A report based on the LeasesByBldg query with all fields included except the building code field. Group the records by the building name and sort by Unit No within each group. Name the report BuildingsAndLeases. Include the current date and page numbering in the page footer. Add your name as the report designer in the report footer. Insert an appropriate clip art image in the report header. You determine the remaining layout and formatting elements including a descriptive report title.
   b. A report based on the RentalIncome query with all fields included except the building code field. Group the records by the building name and sort by Unit No within each group. Name the report IncomeByBuilding. Sum the rent and annual rent columns and count the unit numbers. Show the statistics in the group footer and as grand totals at the end of the report. Include appropriate labels to describe the statistics and format

the values to a suitable numeric format if necessary. Add your name as the report designer in the report footer. Insert an appropriate clip art image in the report header. You determine the remaining layout and formatting elements including a descriptive report title.

4. Print the BuildingAndLeases and IncomeByBuilding reports.

Assessment 2 Use Access Tools to Improve the Property Management Database Design

1. With the **BenchmarkPropMgtU2.accdb** database open, use the Table Analyzer Wizard to analyze the design of the Tenants table. Let the wizard decide the fields for each table. Accept the proposed split of fields into two tables and name each of the new tables appropriately. Assign primary keys as required to each table and allow Access to create a query using the original table name.

2. Use the Performance Analyzer feature to analyze all objects in the database. In the *Analysis Results* list, use the Optimize button to fix each *Suggestion* item (displays with a green question mark).

3. Use the Database Splitter to split the database into two files in order to create a back-end database. Accept the default file name at the Create Back-end Database dialog box.

4. Close the **BenchmarkPropMgtU2.accdb** database.

5. Open the **BenchmarkPropMgtU2_be.accdb** database and enable content.

6. Use the Database Documenter feature to generate a table definition report for the Leases table with the following options: *Include for Table* set to *Properties* and *Relationships*, *Include for Fields* set to *Names, Data Types, and Sizes* and *Include for Indexes* set to *Nothing*. Print and then close the report.

7. Close the **BenchmarkPropMgtU2_be.accdb** database.

Assessment 3 Automate the Property Management Database with Macros and Command Buttons

1. Open the **BenchmarkPropMgtU2.accdb** database and enable content.

2. Create the following macros. You determine appropriate comment text to document each action. Run each macro to make sure the macro works properly, print each macro's definition, and then close the macro.
   a. A macro named Q_LeasesByTenant that opens the LeasesByTenant query in Datasheet view and Edit mode.
   b. A macro named Q_LeaseTerms that opens the LeaseTermsAndDeposits query in Datasheet view and Edit mode.
   c. A macro named R_Bldgs_Leases that opens the BuildingsAndLeases report in report view.
   d. A macro named R_Income that opens the IncomeByBuilding report in report view.

3. Open the BldgsAndMgrs form in Design view.

4. Create two command buttons in the Detail section below the Site Manager tab control object as follows. You determine appropriate text to display on the face of each button.
   a. A button at the left that runs the R_Bldgs_Leases macro.
   b. A button at the right that runs the R_Income macro.

5. Test each button to make sure the macros display the correct report and use Print Screen to make a screen capture of the BldgsAndMgrs form with the buttons displayed. Print the screen capture by pasting the image into a blank Word document. Exit Word without saving.

6. Make sure all objects are closed.

Assessment 4 Create a Switchboard for the Property Management Database

1. With the **BenchmarkPropMgtU2.accdb** database open, create a switchboard form using Switchboard Manager. The switchboard will have three pages as shown below. You determine appropriate descriptive text to display next to each command button. Edit each page name to the titles shown below.

> *Page 1 – Main Menu*
> - Go to the Queries Menu.
> - Go to the Forms and Reports Menu.
> - Exit the database.

> *Page 2 – Queries Menu*
> - Run the Q_LeasesByTenant macro.
> - Run the Q_LeaseTerms macro.
> - Go to the Forms and Reports Menu.
> - Go to the Main Menu.

> *Page 3 – Forms and Reports Menu*
> - Open the BldgsAndMgrs form in edit mode.
> - Open the TenantsAndLeases form in edit mode.
> - Open the BuildingsAndLeases report.
> - Open the IncomeByBuilding report.
> - Go to the Queries Menu.
> - Go to the Main Menu.

2. Test each menu item to make sure each command button opens the correct query, form, report, or switchboard page.
3. Use Print Screen to capture an image of each switchboard page. Print each switchboard page image by pasting the image to a blank Word document. Close each document without saving and exit Word.

Assessment 5 Configure Startup and Security Options for the Property Management Database

1. With the **BenchmarkPropMgtU2.accdb** database open, configure the following startup options:
   a. Set the switchboard form as the startup display form.
   b. Create an application title for the database. You determine an appropriate title.
   c. Hide the navigation pane.
2. Close the **BenchmarkPropMgtU2.accdb** database and then reopen the database in exclusive mode with content enabled.
3. Assign the password BpmU$2 to the database file.
4. Make an ACCDE file from the database saving the copy in the same folder and using the same file name.
5. Close the **BenchmarkPropMgtU2.accdb** database.
6. Open the **BenchmarkPropMgtU2.accde** database using the password.

Assessment 6 Decrypt the ACCDE Copy of the Property Management Database

1. Close the **BenchmarkPropMgtU2.accde** database.
2. Reopen the database in exclusive mode using the password.
3. Permanently decrypt the database by removing the password.
4. Change the startup option to display the navigation pane.
5. Customize the navigation pane to hide all of the table and macro objects.
6. Close the **BenchmarkPropMgtU2.accde** database.

Assessment 7 Export and Publish Data from the Property Management Database

1. Open the **BenchmarkPropMgtU2.accde** database.
2. Export the LeaseTermsAndDeposits query as a text file. Include the field names in the first row and remove the quotation symbols. Do not save the export steps.
3. Open Notepad, open the LeaseTermsAndDeposits.txt file, and then print the document.
4. Exit Notepad.
5. Publish the IncomeByBuilding report as a PDF document named **BenchmarkRentInc.pdf**. Do not save the export steps. *Note: If the PDF add-in is not installed on the computer you are using, export the report as a Word rtf document*.
6. Open the BenchmarkRentInc.pdf document in Adobe Reader and print the report. *Note: Open the report in Word and print if you exported in rtf format at Step 5*.
7. Exit Adobe Reader (or Word).
8. Exit Access.

WRITING activities

The following activities give you the opportunity to practice your writing skills along with demonstrating an understanding of some of the important Access features you have mastered in this unit. Use correct grammar, appropriate word choices, and clear sentence constructions when required.

Activity 1 Create a New Database for Renovation Contracts by Importing Data

You work for a sole proprietor home renovation contractor. The contractor has an old computer in his basement that he has been using to keep invoice records for renovation contracts. The computer is from the Windows 98 operating system era and the software program the contractor used is no longer being sold or updated. The contractor was able to copy data from the old system in a tab-delimited text file named **DavisRenos.txt**. Create a new Access database named **DavisRenos.accdb** and import the data from the old system into a new table. Modify the table design after importing to change the *Amount* field to Currency. Design and create a form based on the table to be used for entering new records. Design and create a report to print the records including a total of the invoice amount column. The proprietor is not familiar with Access and would like you to create a user-friendly menu that can be used to add new records using the form you designed and view the report.

Create the menu using switchboard manager and configure startup options so that the menu is the only object displayed in the work area when the database is opened. Test your menu to make sure each button functions correctly. Using Microsoft Word, compose a quick reference instruction page for the proprietor that instructs him on how to open the database, add a new record, view and print the report, and exit the database. Save the Word document and name it **Access2007L2_U2_Act01.docx**. Print the document.

Activity 2 Design and Publish a Report for a Painting Franchise

You are helping a friend who has started a student painting franchise for a summer job. Your friend has asked for your help designing a database to store job information and revenue earned from the jobs over the summer. Create a new database named **StudentPainters.accdb**. Design and create tables to store the records for painting contract jobs that include the date the job is completed, the invoice number, the homeowner name, address, and telephone number, and the contract price. Enter at least 10 records into the tables. Design a report to print the records in ascending order by date completed. Include statistics at the bottom of the report that provide your friend with the maximum, minimum, average, and total of the contract price field. Include appropriate titles and other report elements. Add your name in the footer as the report designer. Publish and print the report as a PDF document named **PaintingContracts.pdf**. *Note: If the PDF add-in is not installed on the computer you are using, export and print the report as a Word rtf document.*

Buying a Home

Within the next few years you plan on buying a home. While you save money for this investment, you decide to maintain a database of the homes offered for sale within the area you are interested in buying. Design and create tables and relationships in a new database named **Homes4Sale.accdb**. Include fields to store data that would be of interest to you such as: the address, asking price, style of home (condominium, ranch, two stories, semi-detached, etc.), number of bedrooms, number of bathrooms, type of heating/cooling system, property taxes, basement, and garage. Design and create a form to be used to enter the information into the tables. Research on the Internet at least 5 listings within the area that you wish to live and use the form to enter records for each listing. Design and create a report that groups the records by style of home. Calculate the average list price at the end of each group and at the end of the report. Include appropriate titles and other report elements. Add your name in the footer as the report designer. Publish and print the report as a PDF document named **AvgHousePrices.pdf**. *Note: If the PDF add-in is not installed on the computer you are using, export and print the report as a Word rtf document.*

Meals on Wheels Database

You are a volunteer working in the office of your local Meals on Wheels community organization. Meals on Wheels delivers nutritious, affordable meals to citizens in need of the service such as seniors, convalescents, or people with disabilities. The organization requires volunteers using their own vehicle to drive to the meal depot, pick up meals, and deliver them to clients' homes. The volunteer coordinator has expressed an interest in using an Access database to better organize and plan volunteer delivery routes. Create a new database named **MealsOnWheels.accdb**. Design and create tables and relationships to store the following information. Remember to apply best practices in database design to minimize data redundancy and validate data whenever possible to ensure accuracy.

- Client name, address, telephone, gender, age, reason for requiring meals (senior, convalescent, or disability), meals required (breakfast, lunch, dinner), date service started, and estimated length of service required.

- Volunteer name, address, telephone, gender, age, date started, availability by day and by meal (breakfast, lunch, dinner), and receipt of police check clearance.

- Incorporate in your design an assignment for both the client and the volunteer to the quadrant of the city or town in which he or she is located. The volunteer coordinator divides the city or town by north, south, east, and west and tries to match drivers with clients in the same quadrant.

- Any other information you think would be important to the volunteer coordinator for this service.

Design and create forms to be used to enter the information into the tables and then use the forms to enter at least 8 client records and 5 volunteer records. Make sure you enter records for both clients and volunteers in all four quadrants and for all three meals (breakfast, lunch, dinner).

Design and create queries to extract records of clients and volunteers within the same quadrant. Include in the query results datasheet the information you think would be useful to the volunteer coordinator to set up route schedules. Design and create reports based on the queries. Print the reports.

Create a one-page switchboard for the database to be used as a main menu to provide access to the forms, queries, and reports. Configure startup options to display an application title, the switchboard form, and hide the Navigation pane when the database is opened. Close the database and then reopen it. Use Print Screen to capture an image of the Access window. Print the image from Word and then exit Word without saving.

Dollar symbol ($): custom numeric format creation and, 18

Double quotation symbols (""): for entering zero-length strings, 14, 31

Download button, 293

Drag and drop method: macro creation and, 237, 263

Drawing: horizontal and vertical lines in forms, 142

E

Edit button, 264

Editing
attached files, 30
charts, 190, 194
existing switchboard forms, 249–250
macros, 238, 263
main switchboard pages, 247–249
relationship options, 43
relationships, 46–47, 66
source data in linked tables, 297
switchboards, 263
text file in Notepad, 280
text in label control objects, 167

Edit Relationships button, 46

Edit Relationships dialog box, 42, 43, 44, 46, 47, 64, 79

Edit Switchboard Item dialog box, 245, 247

Edit Switchboard Page dialog box, 247, 248, 264

Encryption
of databases, 257, 264, 265
of databases with a password, 258
defined, 257

Encrypt with Password button, 257, 258

Ending date: creating a query to prompt for, 78

Enter Parameter Value dialog boxes, 76, 77, 98

Entity(ies), 9, 41

Entity-relationship diagram, 64

Equals sign (=): formulas beginning with, 125, 142

Error checking options
changing, 264
configuring, 255
customizing, 256
types of, 256

Excel worksheets, 8

Exclamation mark (!): as format code for text or memo fields, 16

Exclusive mode
database decryption and, 258
databases opened in, 257, 264

Exclusive use, 250

Exit Application command, 247

Exponential notation, 18

Export group, 286, 290

Exporting
Access data in text file format, 286, 297
queries as text files, 286–288
queries as text files and saving export steps, 289–290

Export process: repeating, 290

Export specifications: saving, 289

Export steps: saving, 289–290

Export - Text File dialog box, 287, 289
last, saving export steps in, 297

Export Text Wizard, 286
choosing formats and characters within, 297
dialog boxes, 287, 288

External Data tab, 271, 272, 275, 285, 286, 290, 297

F

Field length: field size property used for restriction of, 11

Field List pane, 106, 141, 164, 193

Field names: abbreviations for, 10

Field properties
modification of, to add captions and disallow blank values in fields, 14–15
restricting data entry and data display with, 13–14

Fields, 31
adding existing, 143, 195
adding to forms, 109, 110–111, 141
adding to reports, 162, 164, 165
aliases added to, 99
aliases created for, 89–90
changing tab order of, 116–117, 143
creation of, and allowance for multiple values, 57
criteria, 76
designing for new databases, 8–9
disallowing zero-length strings in, 13–14
dragging from Field List pane to Detail section of report, 193
field properties defined for, 13
grouping records in reports and, 177
modifying field properties to add captions and disallow blank values in, 14–15
in query design grid, 76
requiring data in, 13
ungrouping, 131–132, 144
viewing and updating in multiple tables, 124

Field size: changing, 7

Field size property
changing, 31
restricting field length with, 11

Field values: placement of, in query results datasheets, 99

File format converter, 286

File New Database dialog box, 203

File Open dialog box, 272, 274, 281

Files: attaching to records, 28–30

Fill/Back Color button, 183

Filter by Form feature, 74

Filter By Form window, 98

Filter criteria, 98

Filter Name argument: restricting records displayed in reports with, 233

Filters: saving as queries, 74–75, 98

Find button, 138, 142

contacts database created with, 203–204
databases created with use of, 202–203, 224
Text: changing display of, in tab at top of a page
   within tab control objects, 141
Text Box button, 125, 142
Text box control objects, 106, 112, 143
Text data fields: zero-length strings entered into, 14
Text data type, 11
Text fields
   creating custom format for, 16–17
   default width setting for, 11
   format codes for, 16
Text files
   exporting data as, 298
   importing, 297
   importing Access data in, 286
   importing data from, 298
   importing data to Access from, 280
   queries exported as, 286–288
Text Import Wizard: launching, 297
Themes: AutoFormat options aligned with, 167
Third normal form, 62, 63, 65
Title button, 107, 108, 141, 143, 163
Title feature, 195
Titles
   adding, 108–109
   adding to reports, 162, 163–164
   changing, for active databases, 264
   creating, 107
Tools group, 106
Total labor: creating a query and calculation of, 86
Totals option box: in Group, Sort, and Total pane,
   181
Trust all content from this publisher, 260
Trust Center, 260
Trust Center dialog box, 260, 262
Trust Center options: viewing and/or modifying, 264
Trust Center settings
   exploring, 261–262
   viewing for Access, 260
Trust Center Settings button, 264
Trusted Locations list, 260
Trusted publishers, 260

U

Unassociated label and control: checking for, 256
Unbound control objects, 107, 125, 141
Underline formatting: applying to controls, 113
Underscore characters (_): as separators in field
   names, 10
Ungroup button, 127, 132
Ungrouping fields, 131–132, 144
Unset Database Password dialog box, 258, 259
Update button, 91, 96
Update errors: missed, reducing potential for, 297
Update query, 92, 99
   changing labor rates with use of, 95, 96–97
   modifying records with use of, 96

Up One Level button, 279
Uppercase format code: for text or memo fields, 16
Use control wizards, 144
Use Control Wizards button, 119, 120, 142, 168,
   169, 240, 263

V

Validation Rule field, 24–25
Validation Text field, 24–25
.Value: field values placement in query results
   datasheets and, 88, 99
Values: creating field to lookup, in another table,
   52–55
Variance function: numeric fields and, 181
Vertical lines: drawing in forms, 142
Vertical spacing: adjusting between controls, 127, 143
Viewer: for reading XPS documents, 295, 298
Visual Basic for Application (VBA) code, 259

W

Where Condition argument: restricting records
   displayed in reports with, 233
Wildcard character (*): locating records without
   specifying entire field value and, 138, 142
Windows Vista: viewer included with, 295
Windows XP: viewing XPS document with, 295
Wizards, 201
Work orders
   customers and, 40
   sample of, 8, 9
WorkOrdersbyMonth.xp
   opening in Internet Explorer, 296
   opening with XPS viewer in Microsoft's XPS
      Essentials Pack, 295

X

XML Paper Specification files. *See* XPS files
XPS add-in: finding for download, 292–293, 298
XPS button, 294
XPS document: viewing, 295–296, 298
XPS files
   database objects published as, 291–293
   publishing reports as, 294
   saving objects as, 298

Y

Yes/No data type, 11
Yes/No field, 13

Z

Zero (0) format code: for numeric fields, 18
Zero-length strings: disallowance of, in a field, 13–14,
   31
ZIP code entries, 13
ZIP codes: input masks for, 22
ZIP field, 15
Zoom: Size Mode property changed to, 131, 142, 174

Access 2007 Feature	Ribbon Tab, Group	Button, Option	Keyboard Shortcut
Access Help window		⊚	F1
Add existing fields in a form	Form Design Tools Design, Tools		
Add existing fields in a report	Report Design Tools Design, Tools		
Add field	Table Tools Design, Tools	Insert Rows	
Add record	Home, Records	New	Ctrl + Shift + +
Add Total row to query design	Query Tools Design, Show/Hide	Σ	
Advanced Filter Options	Home, Sort & Filter	Advanced ▾	
Align multiple controls at same position	Form Design Tools Arrange, Control Alignment	Left Right	
Append query	Query Tools Design, Query Type		
AutoFormat	Report Design Tools Arrange, AutoFormat		
Back up database		, Manage, Back Up Database	
Change tab order of fields	Form Design Tools Arrange, Control Layout	Tab Order	
Clipboard task pane	Home, Clipboard		
Close database		, Close Database	
Compact and repair database		, Manage, Compact and Repair Database	
Conditional Formatting dialog box	Report Layout Tools Format, Font		
Create ACCDE file	Database Tools, Database Tools		
Create command button	Form Design Tools Design, Controls		
Create datasheet form	Create, Forms	More Forms ▾	
Create macro	Create, Other		
Create query in Design view	Create, Other		
Create table in Design view	Create, Table		
Crosstab Query Wizard	Create, Other	, Crosstab Query Wizard	
Customize Access options		, Access Options	
Datasheet view	Home, Views	, Datasheet View OR	
Date and Time	Report Design Tools Design, Controls	Date and Time	
Delete field	Table Tools Design, Tools	Delete Rows	
Delete query	Query Tools Design, Query Type		
Delete record	Home, Records	X Delete ▾	
Design view	Home, Views	, Design View OR	
Documenter	Database Tools, Analyze	Database Documenter	
Edit relationships	Relationship Tools Design, Tools		
Encrypt database	Database Tools, Database Tools	Encrypt with Password	
Export data as Text file	External Data, Export	Text File	
Export object	External Data, Export	Word OR	
Field List window	Report Layout Tools Format, Controls		
Filter	Home, Sort & Filter		
Filter by form	Home, Sort & Filter	Advanced ▾, Filter By Form	
Filter by selection	Home, Sort & Filter	Selection ▾	
Find and Replace	Home, Find	/ Replace	Ctrl + F, Ctrl + H
Find Duplicates Query Wizard	Create, Other	, Find Duplicates Query Wizard	
Find Unmatched Query Wizard	Create, Other	, Find Unmatched Query Wizard	
Form	Create, Forms		
Form view	Form Design Tools Design, Views		
Form Wizard	Create, Forms	More Forms ▾, Form Wizard	
Group & Sort	Report Design Tools Design, Grouping & Totals OR Report Layout Tools Format, Grouping & Totals	Group & Sort OR	
Group selected controls	Form Design Tools Arrange, Control Layout		
Image	Form Design Tools Design, Controls		
Import data from text file	External Data, Import	Text File	
Import Excel data	External Data, Import		
Import or link data from Access database	External Data, Import		
Indexes	Table Tools Design, Show/Hide		
Insert a chart	Report Design Tools Design, Controls		
Insert page in tab control	Form Design Tools Design, Controls		
Insert Subdatasheet dialog box	Home, Records	, Subdatasheet, Subdatasheet	
Label control object	Form Design Tools Design, Controls	Aa	

Access 2007 Feature	Ribbon Tab, Group	Button, Option	Keyboard Shortcut
Labels Wizard	Create, Reports	Labels	
Layout view	Home, Views		
Line	Form Design Tools Design, Controls		
Linked Table Manager	Database Tools, Database Tools		
Logo	Form Design Tools Design, Controls		
Make table query	Query Tools Design, Query Type		
Margins	Print Preview, Page Layout		
Merge Access data with Word	External Data, Export	, Merge it with Microsoft Office Word	
Multiple Items form	Create, Forms		
New Query dialog box	Create, Other		
Object Dependencies task pane	Database Tools, Show/Hide	Object Dependencies	
Open dialog box		, Open	Ctrl + O
Page numbering	Report Design Tools Design, Controls		
Page Setup dialog box	Print Preview, Page Layout		
Paste Table As	Home, Clipboard		Ctrl + V
Performance Analyzer	Database Tools, Analyze	Analyze Performance	
PivotChart	Home, Views	, PivotChart View	
PivotTable form	Create, Forms	More Forms ▾, PivotTable	
PivotTable view	Home, Views	, PivotTable View	
Primary key	Table Tools Design, Tools		
Print orientation	Print Preview, Page Layout		
Print Preview		, Print, Print Preview	
Print relationships report	Relationship Tools Design, Tools	Relationship Report	
Property Sheet	Report (or Form) Design Tools Design, Tools		F4
Query design window	Create, Other		
Relationships window	Database Tools, Show/Hide		
Remove filter	Home, Sort & Filter	, Clear filter from xxx OR Advanced ▾, Clear All Filters	
Report	Create, Reports		
Report Design	Create, Reports		
Report view	Home, Views		
Report Wizard	Create, Reports	Report Wizard	
Run macro	Macro Tools Design, Tools		
Run query	Query Tools Design, Results		
Save as 2000 Database		, Save As, Access 2000 Database	
Save as 2002 - 2003 database		, Save As, Access 2002 - 2003 Database	
Save As dialog box		, Save As	
Save database		, Save	Ctrl + S
Show or print table		, Print OR	
Show Table in a query	Query Tools Design, Query Setup		
Show Table dialog box	Relationship Tools Design, Relationships		
Simple Query Wizard	Create, Other	, Simple Query Wizard	
Sort, ascending or descending	Home, Sort & Filter	OR	
Spelling checker	Home, Records	Spelling	F7
Split database	Database Tools, Move Data		
Split Form	Create, Forms		
Subform	Form Design Tools Design, Controls		
Subreport	Report Design Tools Design, Controls		
Switch to Datasheet view from Design view	Table Tools Design, Views		
Switch to Design view from Datasheet view	Home, Views		
Switchboard Manager	Database Tools, Database Tools	Switchboard Manager	
Table Analyzer Wizard	Database Tools, Analyze	Analyze Table	
Table templates	Create, Tables		
Title in a form	Form Design Tools Design, Controls	Title	
Title in a report	Report Design Tools Design, Controls		
Ungroup selected controls	Form Design Tools Arrange, Control Layout		
Update query	Query Tools Design, Query Type		
Use control wizards	Form (or Report) Design Tools Design, Controls		